R [illegible]fat

The Theology of a Missionary

Bruce Ritchie

Handsel Press

Haddington 2025

Luviri Press

Mzuzu 2025

British Library Cataloguing in Publication Data:
a catalogue record for this publication
is available from the British Library

ISBN 978-1-917841-04-7

Handsel Press, 35 Dunbar Rd, Haddington EH41 3PJ, Scotland

ISBN 978-99960-86-55-7

Luviri Press, P.O. Box 130, Zomba, Malawi

Printed by Short Run Press, Exeter

Cover Design by West Port Print, St Andrews, Scotland

Dr Steven Paas (Veenendaal, Utrecht, Netherlands)

'I am delighted to recommend this original study of one of the outstanding figures in mission history, Robert Moffat of Scotland. Dealing with Christian witness among the Namaqua, Tswana, and Ndebele peoples of southern Africa, Dr Ritchie's book is a well-written and scholarly presentation of a missionary's thinking. Ritchie's challenging account of Moffat's Christ-centred theology and faith can help to equip and encourage present missionaries, especially (African) Christians who are called to re-introduce the light of Jesus to those secularised countries from where missionaries were once sent.'

Prof. Mark W. Elliott, FRSE (Professor of Biblical and Historical Theology, UHI and Professorial Fellow, Wycliffe College, University of Toronto)

'This is an impressive book, which is methodologically ground-breaking and refreshing in its execution. It is a systematic theology done via church history of a very lived and living sort, based on primary research of the first order. Dr Ritchie digs deep into the mind of the 19th Century missionary, Robert Moffat of Kuruman. After an enlightening section on Moffat's preparation for his life's work, the book examines Moffat's thinking on 'The Nature and Knowledge of God', 'The Power and Providence of God', 'The Commonality of All Humanity', 'The Centrality of Jesus Christ', plus sections on church, mission and 'civilisation' as understood by one of the classical Protestant missionaries. This book gives us much more than facts and figures: it offers a perception of what was going on in the hearts and minds of the missionaries, based on thorough archival research. I am delighted to recommend it.'

Prof. Emma Wild-Wood: Professor of African Religions and World Christianity, Edinburgh University; Co-editor, *Studies in World Christianity*; Series editor 'Religion in Transforming Africa'.

'In lucid prose, Ritchie examines the spiritual motivation of one of Southern Africa's most prominent missionaries. Recent mission histories rarely delve into the intellectual commitments that compelled Europeans to overseas evangelism. Ritchie's thorough research provides a comprehensive biography of Moffat that places his theology - its formation in Scotland and its testing among the Tswana - at the centre of the narrative. For southern Africans who wish to know more about a man who is still widely respected, and for Scots whose collective memory of Moffat has largely disappeared, this is a valuable and insightful book.'

For

Grace, Elizabeth and Alison

Contents

Acknowledgements

THIS BOOK ORIGINATED as a doctoral thesis for the University of Malawi, and I am delighted to acknowledge the help, encouragement, and support of Professor Klaus Fiedler who, at every stage, gave his time unsparingly as supervisor. His insights, suggestions and accessibility for discussions and exchange of views contributed immeasurably. Principal Saidi Chiphangwi and fellow members of staff at Zomba Theological College (now Zomba Theological University) were also extremely encouraging throughout the time I was engaged in this work. Kind enquiries were supplemented by suggestions from their own fields, and by references to yet more books and sources!

Without the interest and encouragement from my wife Grace, and our two daughters, Elizabeth and Alison, it would have been far more difficult to fulfil this project. I thank them for their support, especially Grace, who read the whole text and made numerous helpful suggestions. These few words are inadequate to express my appreciation, but this book is dedicated to them.

I am also indebted to John Riddell who, many years ago, brought me to Christian Faith, and without whom the journey taken over the intervening decades would never have begun.

Bruce Ritchie, Inverness, 2025

Front Cover Images: Robert Moffat of Kuruman (1842) by William Scott, by kind permission of the National Portrait Gallery, London; Mary Smith (Mary Moffat), artist unknown, by kind permission of the Scottish National Portrait Gallery, Edinburgh.

Abbreviations and Contractions

AAK	*Apprenticeship at Kuruman,* Schapera (ed.)
ATR	African Traditional Religion
BFBS	British and Foreign Bible Society
BFBSEC	British and Foreign Bible Society Inwards Correspondence
BNR	*Botswana Notes and Records*
BOT	Banner of Truth
CT	Cape Town
CULBSA	Cambridge University Library, Bible Society Archives
CUP	Cambridge University Press
DLFL	*David Livingstone: Family Letters*
DLSAP	*David Livingstone: South African Papers, 1849-1853*
DNB	*Dictionary of National Biography*
DSCHT	*The Dictionary of Scottish Church History and Theology*
Edin	Edinburgh
EUNCL	Edinburgh University, New College Library
KCRB	*Kuruman Church Record Book*
FES	*Fasti Ecclesiae Scoticanae,* Scott (ed.)
FHRC	Falkirk Historical Research Centre
JSAS	*Journal of Southern African Studies*
JSM	John Smith Moffat
Lives	*The Lives of Robert and Mary Moffat, John Smith Moffat*
LMC	*Livingstone's Missionary Correspondence: 1841-1856*
Ldn	London
MJ1	*The Matabele Journals of Robert Moffat, Volume 1. Wallis (ed.)*
MJ2	*The Matabele Journals of Robert Moffat, Volume 2. Wallis (ed.)*
MLSSA	*Missionary Labours and Scenes in Southern Africa*
MM	*The Matabele Mission: 1858-1878*
NAS	The National Archives of Scotland, Edinburgh
NLS	The National Library of Scotland, Edinburgh
NLSA	The National Library of South Africa, Cape Town
OUP	Oxford University Press
RM	Robert Moffat
RUM	Robert Unwin Moffat
SBET	*Scottish Bulletin of Evangelical Theology*
SJT	*Scottish Journal of Theology*
SPCK	Society for the Propagation of Christian Knowledge
SPGH	Society for Propagating the Gospel at Home
SOAS	School of Oriental and African Studies, London

Introduction

THIS IS A STUDY OF THE missionary theology of Robert Moffat (1795-1883). Its genesis lay in reading Moffat's book, *Missionary Labours and Scenes in Southern Africa,*[1] especially chapter 17, in which Moffat offered a theological analysis of the problem of 'the knowledge of God' amongst people who had not yet heard the Christian Gospel. Moffat was an artisan, more skilled with his hands than in writing theological monographs. Yet, through his calling he was a theologian, and if not shaped by college study he was shaped by the piety and traditions of his upbringing. The once revered status of the classical missionaries has been eroded in recent times. David Livingstone has suffered from this trend and so has Moffat. Views on Moffat range from high admiration to disregard. Du Plessis described Moffat as, 'undeniably the greatest missionary which that Society [LMS] sent to South Africa—the greatest in natural ability, in patient devotion to duty, and in deep, transparent piety.'[2] But Moffat's countryman, Andrew Ross, concluded that Moffat's influence in the general history of South Africa 'cannot be estimated as anything more than marginal.'[3] From a median position, De Gruchy has called for a reassessment of Moffat's positive contributions.[4] Our book, whilst recognising critiques made by critics, attempts to expound Moffat in terms of his own values, beliefs, and theology.

There has been little examination of the theology which missionaries took to the mission-field. There are studies on the strengths and weaknesses of their missionary methods; their place in the political, social and religious history of the areas where they served; and their appreciation, or lack of appreciation, of the nuances of indigenous culture and belief. All of these have, of course, a theological dimension. Yet there has been a paucity of

---

1 RM, *Missionary Labours and Scenes in Southern Africa,* (Ldn: John Snow, 1842).

2 J. Du Plessis, *A History of Christian Missions in South Africa,* (Ldn: Longmans, Green, 1911), 154. Cf. Lye & Murray, *Transformations on the Highveld: The Tswana and Southern Soto,* (Totowa: Barnes & Noble, 1980), 65.

3 A.C. Ross, *John Philip 1775-1851: Missions, Race and Politics in South Africa,* (Aberdeen University Press, 1986). Gabriel M. Setiloane, *The Image of God among the Sotho-Tswana,* (Rotterdam: Balkema, 1976), 89, included Moffat in a list of missionaries whose attitude toward the indigenous people he considered insulting. Anthony Sillery, *Sechele,* (Ldn: OUP, 1954), 118ff, also viewed Moffat negatively.

4 Steve de Gruchy, 'The Alleged Political Conservatism of Robert Moffat', in: John De Gruchy (ed.), *The LMS in Southern Africa: Historical Essays in Celebration of the Bicentenary of the LMS in Southern Africa, 1799-1999,* (CT: David Philip, 1999), 17-36.

research into the very thing which motivated men and women to commit themselves to such arduous undertakings, namely their personal faith. But, just as mission can only be properly evaluated if the mind-set of the indigenous peoples is taken seriously, so also the mind-set of the missionary must be understood. With Moffat, this involves a serious consideration of his Scottish religious and social roots. He came from a specific culture, with a specific religious background, and with specific beliefs. The Scotland into which Moffat was born was a melting-pot of Enlightenment, Revivalism, and Presbyterianism. Moffat never studied these issues formally, but he experienced their influence in the Church and society around him. An osmosis of ideas and values took place. These factors—subconscious but influential in their latent power—were part of the man who arrived in southern Africa in early 1817. Generalisations are insufficient to do justice to the complex labyrinth of convictions which a man such as Moffat carried with him. The very lack of an extended formal theological training meant that more than one tradition existed in his mind. We try to untangle these strands and show why Moffat had his particular approach and message.

We want to understand the mind and faith of this remarkable pioneer. It is partly because Moffat was raw and untrained that the subject has appeal. Intriguingly, he made an immense impact despite his almost total lack of preparation for the task; he forged the establishment of Christianity in a large area of southern Africa. But what was the message he carried? Why did he think as he did? What was the system of belief he strove to communicate? What was it in his teaching which, despite all the drawbacks of his presuppositions and methods, found a response in the indigenous population? Any missionary's 'effectiveness' would, of course, be due to a variety of factors: personal presence, political power, economic advantage, the attractions of trade, etc. Yet, once these factors are allowed for, what was the religious system which a missionary such as Moffat sought to communicate? And if conversions took place at all for religious reasons, rather than for only personal, political or economic ones, that message must have had a persuasive power in itself. What was it?

A Variety of Methods

Our fundamental question is: what was the nature of the theology which Moffat brought to Africa? Answering this will involve some anthropology, missiology and church history, though our core perspective is theological. There has been little examination of the doctrinal systems which the classical missionaries operated with. Certainly, with Moffat this is virgin territory. There have also been few serious works on Moffat himself, and what has been already written is mainly from a non-theological point of view. But five writers who have touched on Moffat's thought are Wallis, Schapera, Smith, Willoughby, and Northcott.

1. The Anthropology Approach. Following the 1941 discovery of a body of Moffat papers in an ironbound pine-chest at Quagga's Kerk, Cape Province, South Africa, two major collections of Moffat's writings were published. First, in 1945 J.P.R. Wallis edited and published two volumes of Moffat's letters and journals relating to his five visits to Moselekatse, the Ndebele king (1829, 1835, 1854, 1857, 1859-60).[5] Wallis very briefly discussed aspects of Moffat's thinking, but from an anthropological standpoint rather than from that of systematic theology.[6] Second, another collection was published in 1951 by Isaac Schapera. Schapera's 1951 book, *Apprenticeship at Kuruman*, is an edited selection of Moffat's letters up to 1828; and Schapera critically discussed the merits and demerits of Moffat's awareness of indigenous culture, again from an anthropological perspective.[7] Schapera had a keen interest in Moffat and Livingstone, publishing large selections of their correspondence.

2. The Inculturation Approach. The missionaries Edwin William Smith and W.C. Willoughby followed in the footsteps of Moffat but with different approaches. Smith produced publications on mission, language, translation and culture, plus several missionary biographies, including one on Moffat.[8] Smith is regarded as a pioneer of inculturation,[9] and in his book on Moffat he

---

5 Wallis (ed.), *The Matabele Journals of Robert Moffat*, 1829-1860, Vols 1 & 2, (Ldn: Chatto & Windus, 1945). Wallis' account of the 1941 discovery is in: MJ1, ix. Cf. Baxter & Burke, Guide to the Historical Manuscripts in the National Archives of Rhodesia, (Salisbury: National Archives of Rhodesia, 1970), viii. Before the discovery of Quagga's Kerk chest, only a few pages of Moffat's 1835 Journal were in existence, and found in: Percival Kirby, Robert Moffat's Visit to Mzilikazi in 1835, (Bantu Studies, Monograph No. 1: Witwatersrand University Press, 1940).

6 Wallis, MJ1, x.

7 Schapera, *Apprenticeship at Kuruman: Being the Journal and Letters of Robert and Mary Moffat, 1820-1828,* (Ldn, Chatto & Windus, 1951), xi-xxix. Schapera was the author of several relevant studies. Cf. Schapera: *Ethnographical Survey of Africa, Southern Africa, Part III: The Tswana,* (Ldn: International African Institute, 1953), (abbr. *The Tswana*); Schapera, *A Handbook of Tswana Law and Custom,* (Ldn: OUP, 2nd edn, 1955); and Schapera (ed.), *The Bantu Speaking Tribes of South Africa,* (CT: Maskew Miller, 1937). Schapera and Wallis both criticised Moffat for a lack of interest in indigenous culture, but they were too severe. The SOAS archives contain notebooks in which Moffat has detailed observations on local culture. David Hammond-Tooke, quoted extensively from Moffat's observations on Tswana burial rites: Hammond-Tooke, *The Roots of Black South Africa, An Introduction to the Traditional Culture of the Black People of South Africa,* (Johannesburg: Jonathan Ball, 1993), 155.

8 Smith, *Robert Moffat, One of God's Gardeners,* (Ldn: SCM, 1925).

9 Smith became famous as a missionary/anthropologist with linguistic talents. Born in South Africa in 1876, Smith believed that the form in which Christianity is expressed in any culture

discussed Moffat's weaknesses in appreciating the indigenous concept of God and other issues.[10] Willoughby, in his book on Bantu religion,[11] also engaged in a severe critique of Moffat's thinking,[12] and expounded the Bantu worldview in a positive light. Willoughby believed that the response of 'the human spirit to the Eternal Spirit'[13] was a universal experience, and hence there was a significant measure of universal validity in all religious experiences. From an inculturationist viewpoint Willoughby saw Moffat as the, 'exemplification of the truth that if an able and zealous missionary is not trained in Comparative Religion and Social Anthropology, he may labour long among African tribesmen without being able to discern those indigenous religious ideas that lie ready to his hand and would help him immensely in his work.'[14] Gabriel Setiloane, a Tswana theologian, has also commented on Moffat's perceived inability to understand Tswana culture, especially in relation to the concept of God. This is examined in the appropriate chapter.

3. The History Approach. Apart from E.W. Smith's biography, there are only two other major historical accounts of Moffat's life.[15] After Moffat's death in 1883, his son, John Smith Moffat, published a biography of his parents.[16] Despite its age, and despite the hagiographical tendency of a son writing about his parents, this work has lasting value with well researched information, an economy of style, and significant quotations from Moffat's

---

should be appropriate to that culture. He opposed the assumption that traditional customs were necessarily wrong. In his Hartley Lecture, *The Golden Stool* (1926), he promoted radical Africanisation of Christianity, suggesting that African baptismal names, dances, drama, indigenous music, and the Christianisation of initiation and marriage ceremonies would help Christianity to be more rooted in African experience. He argued that if Christianity was identified with Western imperialism, it was likely to be rejected when the empires fell. His first principle was: 'Christ, not western civilisation.' Though Smith wanted to reduce the influence of missionaries, he respected the work of his predecessors and wrote biographies of several, including Moffat, which are notable for placing their subjects in their social and historical contexts. Cf. *International Bulletin of Missionary Research,* Vol. 25/3, 126-130.

10 Smith, *Robert Moffat: One of God's Gardeners,* 96-114.

11 W.C. Willoughby, *The Soul of the Bantu,* (Ldn: SCM, 1928). Willoughby was a long-time missionary among the BaMangwato, whom Moffat encountered in his early years in Africa (*MJ1,* 161). He wrote about Bantu beliefs in a positive light, hence his sub-title was, 'A Sympathetic study of the magico-religious practices and beliefs of the Bantu Tribes of Africa'.

12 Willoughby, *The Soul of the Bantu,* 299ff.

13 Ibid, xi.

14 Ibid, 299. Willoughby appreciated that, 'these sciences had not come into their own till Moffat's work was well-nigh done.'

15 There are many minor biographies on Moffat, but with no fresh material. William Walters, *Life and Labours of Robert Moffat, D.D.* (Ldn: Walter Scott, 1882); J.C. Western-Holt, *Robert Moffat,* (Ldn: Oliphants, 1954), for children. D. J. Deane, *Robert Moffat, the Missionary Hero of Kuruman,* (Ldn: Pickering & Inglis), has some original material.

16 JSM, *The Lives of Robert and Mary Moffat,* (New York: Armstrong & Son, 1888).

letters and journals. It also alludes to an autobiographical *Memoir* of Moffat's life which, unfortunately, seems not to be extant. Then, in 1961 Cecil Northcott published a biography of Moffat, which originated as his PhD thesis.[17] As well as giving a historical perspective, Northcott also discussed Moffat's thinking, especially around the influence of William Roby of Manchester on his theology.[18] Northcott also made comments on Moffat's understanding of indigenous culture. But his main concern was historical and political, rather than theological. Also to be mentioned is the Comaroffs' historico-political critique of LMS missionaries.[19] Coming from a Marxist perspective, the Comaroffs fire volley after volley at the missionary enterprise. An entire thesis could be devoted to their opinions: we pick up their arguments at salient points.

Invaluable as these studies are from the important perspectives of anthropology, inculturation, and history, they do not expound the core theology which lay behind Moffat's work. Our book differs by having the doctrines of his faith as its primary concern. Schapera's profound insights are immensely important, but Moffat was not an anthropologist. Moffat's evaluation of indigenous culture and beliefs was always the evaluation of a missionary from a particular background. As a missionary, Moffat came to Africa with a strong message, a robust theological system, and a deep piety. His interpretation of what he observed sprang from these. With different roots, evaluation and interpretation, he may have been quite different.

Until he was overshadowed by his illustrious son-in-law, David Livingstone, Moffat was feted as the pre-eminent missionary to Africa of the Victorian era. Even after Livingstone's personality began to dominate the public mind, Moffat was still viewed as the Grand Old Man of the missionary movement and treated with respect and admiration. Two audiences with Queen Victoria (1872 and 1876), a doctorate from Edinburgh University (1872), the Freedom of the City of London (1877), and a host of other honours accompanied him into retirement.[20] Yet, despite his contemporary status, relatively little work has concentrated on him, with the state of research on missions in South Africa hampered by an understandable concentration on the scandal of apartheid.

---

17 Northcott, *Robert Moffat: Pioneer in Africa,* (Ldn: Lutterworth, 1961).

18 Ibid, 23f.

19 Jean & John Comaroff, *Of Revelation and Revolution: Christianity, Colonialism, and Consciousness in South Africa, Vol. 1,* (Chicago: University of Chicago Press, 1991).

20 A report of Edinburgh University conferring Moffat's DD, is in *The Scotsman,* (20.4.1872).

For his entire career of 53 years, Moffat was a missionary of the London Missionary Society (LMS), with the standard reference works on the LMS still those by Lovett and by Ellis.[21] Goodall & Orchard, in a 1949 report commission by the Congregational Union of England and Wales, dealt with some of the later history of the LMS, albeit with reference back to its foundational principles.[22] As already noted, Andrew Ross provided an interpretation of the wider southern African role of the LMS, in his book on Moffat's LMS superintendent, John Philip. The story of Congregationalism in South Africa—inextricably bound up with that of the LMS—is covered by Briggs & Wing, in their historical survey.[23] Also of interest are a collection of essays celebrating 200 years of the LMS in South Africa, edited by John de Gruchy.[24] For more bibliographical details of the LMS in South Africa the reader should consult Margaret J. Cowie's, *The London Missionary Society in South Africa: A Bibliography compiled by Margaret J. Cowie.*[25] The work done by Schapera in bringing to publication numerous collections of David Livingstone's letters, annotated by Schapera's detailed notes and comments must not be overlooked,[26] since neither Moffat, nor the LMS in southern Africa, can be studied without studying Livingstone.

Ihe late nineteenth and early twentieth centuries saw a flood of small biographies featuring Moffat, alongside other missionary heroes and heroines of the time. These works, often written for children or young people, mostly relied on Moffat's own *Missionary Labours*, or on John Smith Moffat's *Lives,* with no extra original material. The already mentioned 1925 work by Smith, and Northcott's 1961 book are the only weighty additions. In 1974 Mora Dickson wrote a biography, not on Robert Moffat but on his wife Mary, which provided a feminine perspective on the Kuruman enterprise.[27]

---

[21] Richard Lovett, *History of the LMS: 1795-1895,* (Ldn: 1899), and William Ellis, *History of the London Missionary Society,* (Ldn: 1844). Lovett's book is complemented by Norman Goodall's, *History of the London Missionary Society: 1895-1945,* (Ldn: 1954).

[22] Goodall, N. & Orchard, R. K, *Church and Mission: A Discussion of the Relation of the London Missionary Society to the Congregational Union,* (Ldn: LMS, 1949).

[23] Briggs & Wing, *The Harvest and the Hope: The Story of Congregationalism in Southern Africa,* (Johannesburg: UCCSA, 1970).

[24] John De Gruchy (ed.), *The London Missionary Society in Southern Africa: Historical Essays in Celebration of the Bicentenary of the LMS in Southern Africa, 1799-1999,* (CT: Philip, 1999).

[25] Margaret J. Cowie, *The London Missionary Society in South Africa: A Bibliography compiled by Margaret J. Cowie* (CT: University of CT Libraries, 1969).

[26] (i) Schapera, (ed.): *David Livingstone, Family Letters: 1841-1856, Vols. 1,2,* (Ldn: Chatto & Windus, 1959). (ii) Schapera, (ed.): *Livingstone's Missionary Correspondence, 1841-1856,* (Ldn: Chatto & Windus, 1961). (iii) Schapera, (ed.): *David Livingstone South African Papers: 1849-1853,* (CT: Van Riebeck Society, 2nd Series No. 5, 1974). (Abbr: *DLFL, LMC,* and *DLSAP*).

[27] Mora Dickson, *Beloved Partner: Mary Moffat of Kuruman,* (Ldn: Gollancz, 1974).

Dickson not only researched the known library and archival sources but gained access to personal letters still possessed by the family. The other serious secondary sources dealing with Moffat are the extended introductions written by Schapera and Wallis in their respective collections of Moffat's letters and journals. Apart from these sources, Moffat is usually referred to only in passing by writers whose focus is elsewhere and whose information is dependent on one of the writers mentioned above.

Karel Schoeman has brought together important local documents from before the Kuruman era.[28] Most research into the mission at Kuruman has focused on the work of translation and printing. In 1987, the Kuruman Moffat Mission Trust published F.R. Bradlow's *Printing for Africa,* which is entirely concerned with the publishing work at Kuruman.[29] Two articles by Alistair Sandilands, in 1971 and 1972 respectively, also concentrated on the work of translation carried out at Kuruman, bringing to light new material.[30] But on research into the *systematic theology* of missionaries (as distinct from the theology of mission) there is very little. There is none on the theology of Robert Moffat. Consequently, the literature dealing with our specific area of enquiry is limited. In 1984 Stuart Piggin published his book, *Making Evangelical Missionaries: 1789-1858,* in which he discussed some of the theological training given to that generation of missionaries.[31] Klaus Fiedler has published work on some of the theological principles operative amongst classical missionaries, focusing especially on their eschatology.[32] Brian Stanley's book, *Christian Missions and the Enlightenment*, touches on several

---

28 Schoeman, *The Mission at Griquatown: 1801-1821,* (Griquatown: GTV, 1997). See also: Karel Schoeman: *A Thorn Bush that Grows in the Path: The Missionary Career of Ann Hamilton, 1815-1823,* (CT: NLSA, 1995: SA Library General Series No. 23). Ann Hamilton was estranged from Robert Hamilton, who was Moffat's Kuruman colleague for many years.

29 F.R. Bradlow, *Printing for Africa,* (Kuruman: Kuruman Moffat Mission Trust, 1987).

30 Alistair Sandilands: 'Historical Background of the Tswana 'Centenary' New Testament', *Botswana Notes and Records, Vol. 3,* 1-5, (Gaborone: 1971); and Sandilands: 'The Ancestor of Tswana Grammars', *Botswana Notes and Records, Vol. 4,* 101-106, (Gaborone: 1972). These articles were prompted by work on a new translation of the SeTswana Bible.

31 Stuart Piggin, *Making Evangelical Missionaries: 1789-1858,* (Sutton: Courtnay, 1984).

32 Klaus Fiedler, *The Story of Faith Missions: From Hudson Taylor to Present Day Africa),* (Oxford: Regnum Books, 1994), especially 272-291. Cf. Fiedler, 'Shifts in Eschatology—Shifts in Missiology' in: Jochen Ebner (ed.), *Hope does not Disappoint,* (Bonn: VKW, Bangalore, 2001). Philip Capp also wrote on the relationship between eschatology and mission, cf. Capp: 'Eschatology: It's Relevance to Mission from an Evangelical perspective', *Missionalia,* Vol. 15, No. 3, Nov. 1987, 110-117.

philosophical and theological issues;[33] and from an Indian context, rather than an African one, Ian Maxwell's PhD thesis addressed similar concerns.[34]

A Variety of Challenges

Our aim is to give an account of Moffat's theology, based on an examination of his writings, both published and unpublished. What we shall see is that Moffat's missionary theology was a moderate Calvinism which had been profoundly influenced by the values of early-nineteenth-century Scottish culture, enriched by the Evangelical Revival, and occasionally modified by the situation he encountered in southern Africa.[35] Our aim is to understand Moffat from within his own mind-set. Any person should, as far as possible, be assessed from within that person's self-understanding; only then can there be accurate appreciation of what that person did well or poorly. In addition, Moffat was not an academic scholar in the formal sense.[36] That must be borne in mind when engaging in an academic analysis of his thinking.

Of critical importance is what Moffat took to Africa in terms of his understanding of God, and his understanding of humanity. Assuming the equality of all humanity before God, was of central importance for everyone called into missionary activity. Of similar importance was belief in an eschatological hope of an imminent and blessed reign of Christ upon the

---

[33] Stanley (ed.), *Christian Missions and the Enlightenment,* (Grand Rapids: Eerdmans, 2001).

[34] Ian Maxwell, *Alexander Duff and the Theological and Philosophical Background to the General Assembly's Mission in Calcutta to 1840,* (1995, PhD, University of Edinburgh).

[35] 'Moderate Calvinism' has the typical Calvinist emphases on the honour, holiness, and sovereignty of God, but less on extreme election which characterises 'hyper-Calvinism'.

[36] JSM, *Lives,* 23: 'Whatever gifts may have been bestowed upon Robert Moffat to fit him for his work as a missionary, it certainly could not be said that they came in the form of collegiate opportunities.' Yet, when Moffat translated the Bible into SeTswana language he put a complete tongue into written form for virtually the first time! As Sandilands pointed out in his 1972 article, 'The Ancestor of Tswana Grammar' 101ff, it was Isaac Hughes who wrote the very first Tswana grammar between 1828 and 1858, but Moffat's part was a major intellectual achievement, translating, where possible, from Hebrew and Greek. RM, *To Henry Knolleke, BFBS,* 5.3.1861, (CULBSA/BFBSEC/Inwards/2/80), gives a detailed account of Moffat's methods. Beeching, *An Open Path: Christian Missionaries, 1515-1914,* (Ldn: Hutchison, 1979) 216ff, scorned Moffat's translation, but a first translation always has errors. For the rest of his life Moffat was revising his work, forming a translation committee at Kuruman. His BFBS correspondence, now in the UBS archives in Cambridge University, is illuminating. His translation work shows a prodigious talent, like that shown by other Scots from humble rural backgrounds such as the linguists William Murray and John Leyden. 'Moffat's study of the phonetic aspects of Bantu language a century ago adumbrated the phonetic and tonetic approach of modern University linguists.' (Sandilands, 106). In Moffat's *Journals* spaces occur where he left out a word or a name, hoping for a better one later, (e.g. *MJ2,* 132, 192). Moffat was not always exact, but he had a feel for scholarly standards.

earth, of which reign the missionary enterprise was understood to have a privileged preparatory role. Important also was the ethical monotheism of the Judaeo-Christian tradition, affecting not only the nature of Moffat's message, but his perception of indigenous religion. Moffat never wrote a formal theology, apart from chapter seventeen of *Missionary Labours*. His doctrine cannot be read directly and must be reconstructed indirectly. His theology was forged in a busy missionary life, and expressed in actions, attitudes, conversations, reactions, letters, speeches, and sermons. This off-the-cuff aspect of his theologising gives his thinking both ruggedness and integrity. His thoughts never became polished doctrine and were never separated from real life. For Moffat and his missionary colleagues, issues were not resolved through interchanging papers at academic colloquia. Issues were dealt with under the pressure of day-to-day preaching, teaching, discipling, disciplining and working out the faith as best they could, in relation to the situation on the ground.

1. The Single-Source Problem. A missionary theology is forged in the inter-relationship of the missionary and those to whom he takes his message. Unfortunately, there are no written records from the African side. It may be argued that, since our aim is to understand Moffat's inner mind and theological convictions, this is not an absolute hurdle. Nevertheless, insofar as Moffat's theology presupposes personal thoughts concerning indigenous attitudes, then the lack of a voice from the African viewpoint is regrettable. In Moffat's *Missionary Labours,* and elsewhere, he frequently 'quoted' the views of Africans whom he debated with. But these 'quotations' are his own recollection of what they said, and his own version of what they meant. His personal theological beliefs were stated in relation to what he understood the Tswana or Ndebele beliefs to be on sin, death, or God. For example, the theological conversations which he had with the Ndebele king, Moselekatse, occupy a significant portion of Wallis' two volumes, *The Matabele Journals of Robert Moffat*, but there is no way of checking whether the reports given by Moffat of these conversations were accurate. Neither can we check the accuracy of Moffat's *interpretation* of what he remembered Moselekatse having said. We acknowledge this difficulty. However, there are mitigations to this single-source problem.

To begin with, anthropological studies can provide balance.[37] And yet twentieth and twenty-first century Tswana or Ndebele society is not the

---

[37] Cf. Schapera, *The Tswana*; *A Handbook of Tswana Law and Custom*; Schapera, *The Bantu Speaking Tribes of South Africa*; Brown, *Among the Bantu Nomads,* (New York: Negro Universities Press, 1926, 1969); Lye & Murray, *Transformations on the Highveld: The Tswana*

same as that of the nineteenth century. Nor can it be assumed that societies which have now lived within a Christian environment for two centuries, have an oral tradition which exactly preserves original beliefs.[38] Another mitigation is that other non-African journals and books, contemporary with Moffat, mention his work, and offer critiques.[39] Though these do not give an indigenous African perspective, they provide some corrective input.

Moffat lived amongst Africans for over fifty years. By and large he won their confidence. It was not only a convert such as Africaner who admired Moffat, but also a determined non-convert such as Moselekatse, who held him in high esteem. Given the respect gained and maintained over a long period, it seems reasonable to conclude that Moffat did have a perceptive if imperfect understanding of indigenous culture. And if, from time to time, Moffat misinterpreted the African dimension, then part of his own *self-understanding* was precisely a result of that misinterpretation. Our primary aim is not to see whether Moffat was one hundred percent accurate: our task is to comprehend his theology, and to try and grasp what exactly it was in his message which made an effect on the people of Kuruman and beyond.

Ideally, it would benefit to access Tswana 'folk-memory' concerning Moffat, or to access writings from the descendants of the men and women who met him and who, through the family line, passed on their memories, reflections, and opinion of him and his work. There seems to be a warmth attached to his name, but this cannot answer specific questions on the relationship between Moffat and his contemporary Tswana.[40] Nevertheless

---

and Southern Soto); Pauw, *Religion in a Tswana Chiefdom,* (Ldn: OUP, 1960); Smith (ed.), *The Bushmen of Southern Africa: A Foraging Society in Transition,* (Claremont: David Philip, 2000); Smith, (ed.), *African Ideas of God,* (Ldn, Edinburgh House Press, 2nd. Ed. 1961); Werner, *Myths and Legends of the Bantu,* (Ldn, Harrap, 1933); Volz, *Chief of a Heathen Town: Kgosi Sechele and the Arrival of Christianity among the Tswana,* (African Studies Program, University of Wisconsin-Madison, 2001); Willoughby, *The Soul of the Bantu,* 1928); Hammond-Tooke, *The Roots of Black South Africa*; plus other articles from *Botswana Notes and Records*.

38 This is something which Alice Werner, *Myths and Legends of the Bantu,* frequently commented upon as she sought to arrive at the 'original' version of a story.

39 Some of Livingstone's letters gave a severe critique of his father-in-law's observations and conclusions, with Livingstone holding a more positive view of African beliefs and culture than Moffat. Reference may also be made to the correspondence of fellow missionaries at Kuruman, now lodged in the LMS archives at the SOAS. Other contemporary publications include: John Philip, *Researches in South Africa (1828),* (Reprint: New York, Negro Universities Press, 1969); and John Campbell, *The Life of Africaner: A Namaqua Chief of South Africa,* (Ldn: Religious Tract Society, c. 1830).

40 Two main factors affect accessing 'folk-memory'. First, the length of time between Moffat leaving southern Africa in 1870 and the present day. Second, the lack of a continuous indigenous community at Kuruman. During the nineteenth century, there were several movements away from Kuruman and, whilst these helped to spread Tswana Christianity, they

it seems that Moffat is perceived as having made a positive contribution towards the life of the people.

2. The European-Perspective Problem. Moffat was European, hence the single-source problem, discussed above, is compounded by the fact that that specific single-source operated from a different and non-indigenous cultural and philosophical perspective. Gabriel Setiloane writes: 'No study of a culture is adequate which fails to catch the *inwardness* of that culture.'[41] A major complaint about the early Christian missionaries to southern Africa is that they failed to 'catch the inwardness' and were unaware of the need to inculturate the message which they brought. Karel Schoeman, in the introduction to his anthology of early documents concerning the LMS mission at Griqua Town, pointed out that, in his anthology, all the quoted writers had been born in Europe and formed by the North European Enlightenment, and in consequence their judgment concerning indigenous society was largely negative with a built-in bias.[42]

What Setiloane and Schoeman say is important, and we accept the broad implications. Yet they do not paint a complete picture. Just as the mind, heart, soul and culture of an indigenous people must be properly understood, so must also the mind-set of the individual missionary. Evangelism involves two parties: speaker and hearer. Both need to be analysed. Moffat was a Scotsman in Africa, and his religion, faith and piety were moulded in his native land. There were other influences, but Moffat was essentially representative of working-class Scottish faith, culture and world-view. This was what he brought to Africa, and his contribution cannot be understood and appreciated without an examination of what was deeply rooted in his mind, heart and soul. After these matters are analysed, then of course it is important to raise questions. Did he appreciate African culture and spirituality appropriately? Did he adapt and apply his faith fittingly to this new context? Did he make any effort in this direction? Was he prepared to learn from, and be enriched by, the lifestyle and spirituality of the people amongst whom he worked for so many years? Was he able to reflect on his presuppositions and distinguish them from the essentials of Christian faith?

---

resulted in a broken tradition at Kuruman itself. Then, under the Apartheid system, the South African Government used the Bantu Education Act, and the Group Areas Act, to designate the mission station as a 'White Area': not only was the mixed Kuruman community broken up, but mixed education at the Mission School and mixed worship in the Kuruman Church ceased. Apart from the church, the buildings fell into ruin. The new post-1980 community, has few direct connections with what existed beforehand.

41 Lye & Murray, *Transformations,* 15f.

42 Schoeman, *The Mission at Griquatown: 1801-1821,* 22.

These are relevant questions. Yet, it is vital to first uncover Moffat's faith in his own terms and from his own context and culture. That supplies the datum essential for any other analysis. Moreover, we must not assume that the broad terms 'Western' or 'European' are sufficient to identify his thinking, as if all missionaries had a homogeneous mind-set. Such terms are blunt instruments of analysis, as much as the term 'African'. We need to reveal the individual strands which made up the complex fabric of the theology which Moffat brought with him.

Moffat was always a 'front-line' missionary. He rarely had the opportunity to stand back from his work and place it in a wider context. Above all else, he ardently believed that the way of Christ was the way for all men and women. Central to his aims and goals as a missionary was his desire to *change* the beliefs and mind-set of those whom he encountered. A desire to change implicitly carries with it a tendency to dismiss existing beliefs, with blind-spots in relation to positive qualities in the existing culture. In all these things Moffat was not guiltless. If he erred, he did so through having a burning desire to share the message of the Gospel with fellow men and women created by God and possessing immortal souls.

John Philip, the LMS official superintendent in Southern Africa, is sometimes viewed as the well-rounded missionary, with an inclusive overview of the political and social dimension of the missionary task, in contrast to Moffat's limited pietistic outlook. However, Philip was never a missionary in the pure sense. He never had the care of native converts. He never had to deal with day-to-day issues at the sharp end of creating, nurturing and discipling a new-born believing community which Moffat had to deal with all the time. The worker at the 'coal-face' may lack some of the broader philosophy of his superintendent; but he engages with the task in a totally different way. But did Moffat have a broader philosophy than simple pietism? Did he seriously address social and political concerns?

The Principal Sources

Moffat's published works are available for purchase or in libraries. His unpublished works are scattered among various collections in both Africa and Britain.[43] Much of the unpublished material is in the form of letters written to correspondents. Many items are brief notes. Though few letters

[43] The Billy Graham Archives, Wheaton Bible College, USA, hold an 1871 letter by Moffat to Bergne of the BFBS, concerning the slow proceedings of Bergne's committee and Moffat's expenses while working on his translation of the Old Testament.

deal directly with theological matters, there are indirect allusions to religious issues scattered through Moffat's epistolatory corpus. Before any of Moffat's works in English were published, he printed several Catechisms, Hymn Books, Scripture portions etc., in SeTswana.[44] Apart from these, Moffat's published writings are in three groups.

1. Direct Publications: In 1840 the LMS published Moffat's Sermon: 'Africa, or Gospel Light shining in the midst of heathen darkness. A Sermon on Isaiah 9:2 preached before the Directors of the London Missionary Society'.[45] In 1842, the publishers John Snow issued Moffat's *Missionary Labours and Scenes in Southern Africa*, which had great success until eclipsed by Livingstone's *Missionary Travels* a decade later. In 1863, Moffat wrote an account of his life's work for children entitled, *Adventures of a Missionary; or Rivers of Waters in Dry Places, an Account of the Introduction of Christianity into South Africa*.[46] This was written in the third person and is little referred to. Moffat also contributed to publications such as the *Missionary Magazine*.

2. Anthologies of Letters, Journals, and Speeches: There are three main collections. In 1843, John Campbell collected and edited several speeches Moffat made before he left for Africa at the end of his furlough.[47] Campbell reconstructed these speeches from Moffat's own notes and from those of some hearers. Moffat read and approved the text before he sailed for Africa, and so it may be regarded as primary Moffat material. In 1945 J.P.R. Wallis edited a double set of Moffat's letters and journals, written during Moffat's five journeys to the Ndebele king, Moselekatse. These were published under the title, *The Matabele Journals of Robert Moffat (Vols. 1 & 2).* Wallis worked with three editions of Moffat's *Journal,* and Wallis' published edition represented what he believed to be Moffat's earliest completed version.[48] In 1951 Isaac Schapera edited and published his collection of Robert and Mary

---

[44] A full list of these publications can be found in Bradlow, *Printing for Africa*. Another list of items printed at Kuruman, nearly all of which were by Moffat, is in Sandilands, 'The Ancestor of Tswana Grammars', *Botswana Notes and Records, Vol. 4, 1972,* 101-106.

[45] RM, *'Africa: or Gospel Light shining in the Midst of Heathen Darkness. A Sermon on Isaiah 9:2 preached before the Directors of the LMS,* (Anniversary Sermon for the LMS, 13.5.1840, (Ldn: Snow, 1940), hereafter abbreviated to: RM, *Africa.*

[46] RM, *Adventures of a Missionary; or Rivers of Waters in Dry Places; an Account of the introduction of Christianity into South Africa and of Mr. Moffat's Missionary Travels and Labours,* (1863, New York, 1869; reprint. Miami: Mnemosyne, 1969).

[47] Campbell (ed.), *The Farewell Services of Robert Moffat in Edinburgh, Manchester and London*, (Ldn: Snow, 1843), hereafter abbreviated to: *Farewell Services.*

[48] Wallis' decision to publish Moffat's 'first' edition was commendable, but he left out sections of 'evangelical comment' (*MJ1,* 1) which appeared in later editions. Wallis was more interested in Moffat's deeds, than in Moffat's evangelical attitude.

Moffat's early letters and journals, as *Apprenticeship at Kuruman,* covering the period until 1828. Schapera used manuscripts which were available in the National Archives of Zimbabwe, plus microfilm copies of supplementary material in the LMS archives at the SOAS in London.

3. Hymns: Less well known, but important in understanding Moffat's piety, are the hymns which he translated from English, or composed as original SeTswana hymns. The first hymns he translated were published along with his SeTswana version of *Brown's Catechism.*[49] This small collection was added to as the years passed. The modern United Congregational Church of South Africa SeTswana hymnal, *Dihela,*[50] still has one-third of its hymns attributed to Moffat.

- - -

Moffat's unpublished primary material is distributed widely, of which the following contain nearly all the known extant material.

1. *The Kuruman Moffat Mission Library.* The Library of the Kuruman Mission Station in South Africa has, in its archives, the *Kuruman Church Record Book*, covering the years 1825 to 1880. The book was purchased around 1852, with entries from before that date added from older documents. Most entries until 1870 are in Moffat's own handwriting. Moffat was ostensibly only the secretary, recording the decisions of the Kuruman Church Meeting, but he was such a dominant figure that the decisions (and appended comments) reflect his own views. The Kuruman Moffat Mission Library also has an original copy of Cecil Northcott's PhD thesis.

2. *The National Library of South Africa, Cape Town.* The Grey Collection, within the National Library of South Africa in Cape Town, has original copies of some Moffat letters. It also holds a rare, printed version of Moffat's translation into SeTswana of *Brown's Catechism*. The library also has a set of the SeTswana newspaper published at Kuruman during the 1850s.[51]

3. *The School of Oriental and African Studies, London.* The School of Oriental and African Studies (SOAS), University of London, is the official home

---

[49] The version we consulted was, *Buka ea Pocho ea Tuto le Poluko tsa Yesu Kereste,* (1831, 2nd edn). This was Moffat's translation of *Brown's Catechism* into SeTswana (Grey Collection copy, NLSA, CT, ref: Grey/9/c/3/8). For an English version, see: William Brown, *Christian Instructions for Children from Three to Seven years of age, Containing: A Catechism; Passages of Scripture; Hymns,* (2nd Ed. Edin: James Robertson, 1820).

[50] UCCSA, *Dihela,* (CT: UCCSA).

[51] Cf. William Ashton (ed.), *Mokaeri oa Becuana, le Muleri oa Mahuki,* (Kuruman: 1857, and running to 20 editions until 1859). All editions are in the NLSA, CT, [Grey/10/c/22/4]. All printed by William Ashton, Kuruman.

for the archives of the Council for World Mission (CWM), formerly the London Missionary Society.[52] The SOAS has an almost complete collection of manuscript letters from LMS missionaries in the field which were sent to the various secretaries of the LMS, with replies. These are collected in boxes, one for each year, making it easy not only to access a specific missionary's writings, but to read his colleagues' letters on a particular issue. The SOAS also has a large quantity of Moffat's personal letters mainly, but not all, written after his retirement to a variety of individuals.

The SOAS has two sets of lectures copied out by Moffat in 1817, as he waited for permission to travel beyond the boundaries of Cape Colony. One is a 460-page copy of William Roby's *Theological Lectures,*[53] which Moffat heard in Manchester in 1816. The other is a 70-page copy of David Bogue's *Missionary Lectures.*[54] Moffat did not attend lectures by Bogue, but copied the notes of his fellow missionary James Kitchingham, who had been a student at Bogue's seminary in Gosport.[55]

The SOAS also contains fragments of Moffat's *Journal,* including a hitherto thought lost portion of the *Journal* from 2nd January 1860 onwards.[56] Most of the *Journal* was published by Wallis in *The Matabele Journals of Robert Moffat.* Wallis remarked that no trace of journal or letter to Mary Moffat, later than 2 January 1860, had come to light.[57] This puzzled Wallis. But in March 2004 we found more of the *Journal* in the SOAS archives. Curiously, on a previous visit, in January 2004, the lost *Journal* was not in the box where we found it in March. The same was true of other material which cropped up on our second visit. Other material may lie deep in the SOAS vaults.[58]

---

52 The LMS started in 1795 as *The Missionary Society,* before becoming *The London Missionary Society.* In 1966 it became *The Congregational Council for World Mission.* From 1977 it has been known as *The Council for World Mission.* A guide to CWM collections is published in leaflet form as, *SOAS Library: Guide to the Council for World Mission Collections.*

53 Roby, *Theological Lectures,* (SOAS/CWM, Home Odds Box 25).

54 Bogue, *Missionary Lectures by David Bogue: Tutor, Missionary Seminary Gosport,* as transcribed by Robert Moffat (1817), (SOAS/CWM Home Odds Box 25).

55 James Kitchingham (1791-1848) was from Manchester. He was ordained at Surrey Chapel London, on 30.9.1816 as LMS missionary no. 167. He sailed to Africa on 31.10.1816, and died at Port Elizabeth in 25.6.1848, (LMS, *Annotated Register of LMS Missionaries: 1796-1923,* 43).

56 RM, *Occasional Journal: 1860-1862, 1868,* (SOAS/CWM/Africa/Moffat/Pers/Box 4).

57 Wallis (ed.), *MJ2,* 166, footnote 1.

58 The rediscovered *Journal* does not cover the whole remaining period of Moffat's fifth visit to Moselekatse. It commences on 1.4.1860 and continues until he reached home on 21.8.1860. Some entries are brief, since Moffat was involved, from dawn to dusk, in building houses for the new Ndebele Mission for which Moselekatse had just given final permission in mid-December 1859. Moffat was 64 years of age, and the manual labour left him exhausted

Additionally, the SOAS has the manuscript of a sermon which Moffat apparently wrote on board ship en route to Africa in 1816. There are also a collection of sermon notes, said to be Moffat's but with ambiguous provenance, and so we have not drawn on these for our work.[59] On single pieces of paper, or inserted into notebooks, can also be found observations on Tswana customs, language and proverbs, plus reflections on life in Africa (all original manuscripts). Importantly, the SOAS also has a complete collection of the published LMS Annual Reports including reports from each mission station, covering all the years Moffat was in South Africa.

4. *Cambridge University Library.* Cambridge University Library is the repository for the archives of the United Bible Society, formerly the British and Foreign Bible Society. It has a few manuscript letters by Moffat to Secretaries of the Society, mainly on translation issues. In addition, the Bible Society Register for incoming correspondence contains several of Moffat's letters copied into the register by the Secretary.

5. *Edinburgh University, New College Library.* This library, in the School of Divinity, holds several manuscript letters by Moffat, nearly all written after his retirement from South Africa in 1870. These are mainly in the James Cunningham and William Dickson collections. The New College collection includes the *Lord's Prayer* in SeTswana in Moffat's hand, as well as the verse of a SeTswana hymn, also in his hand.

6. *The National Library of Scotland.* The NLS (Edinburgh) has a collection of autograph Moffat material, plus photocopies of material held elsewhere. These are not in a file exclusively dedicated to Moffat but are mainly in the Library's extensive collection of documents relating to David Livingstone.[60] The NLS also holds contemporary publications, often first editions, providing primary sources for the intellectual, spiritual and social life of Scotland during Moffat's formative years.

7. *The National Archives of Scotland.* The NAS (Edinburgh) is the repository for all Scottish ecclesiastical and legal documents. These include Kirk Session records, Baptismal Registers and sundry other material. Kirk

---

when evening came, which was traditionally his writing hour. Yet, it would be unusual for him to write nothing from 2nd January to 31st March. There may be pages still to be found.

[59] The handwriting for the notes is varied. Though Moffat's handwriting altered, depending on haste and writing materials, there is sufficient doubt for us to be hesitant in citing them as genuine Moffat. Occasionally the handwriting is similar to that of Roger Price, who became Moffat's son-in-law. The note accompanying this collection simply states, 'Sermon notes, *believed to be* from Robert Moffat.'

[60] NLS, Manuscripts Division, (MSS 10701-10780, 10997, passim).

Session records for churches with which Moffat or his parents were associated are particularly useful: these include Ormiston, Tranent, Musselburgh, Haddington, Larbert, Bothkennar, Falkirk, Polmont and Inverkeithing. It appears that no material from the hand of Robert Moffat himself is lodged in the National Archives of Scotland, though there is a legal agreement involving himself, his father, and Inverkeithing Burgh Council.[61]

8. *Falkirk Historical Research Centre.* The Moffat family lived in the village of Carronshore, beside the River Forth, for the first eleven years of the nineteenth century. Falkirk Historical Research Centre has microfilm copies of all local Baptismal Registers, recording the birth and baptisms of Robert Moffat's younger siblings. The same material is available in the Archive section of Falkirk Public Library. These centres also have a considerable amount of material relating to local history, including the works of local historian James Love, who published several short monographs featuring Robert Moffat.[62]

9. *Haddington Library Archives.* Ten miles from the village of Ormiston where Moffat was born, Haddington Library Archives has original and microfilm copies of the Baptismal Registers of several local parishes, including a microfilm copy of those for Ormiston.[63] The Archives also hold a file on Moffat, containing contemporary newspaper reports, mainly concerning visits to Ormiston by Robert Moffat after his retirement, speeches made by him in London, and obituaries. Most are from the newspapers, *Haddingtonshire Courier* and *Haddingtonshire Chronicle.* These provide material of only indirect interest, though there are allusions to Moffat's critical opinion of British Government policy in southern Africa.

10. *The Zimbabwean National Archives.* Papers found in 1941 at Quagga's Kerk, Cape Province, South Africa, were transferred to the Archives of Southern Rhodesia, now the National Archives of Zimbabwe. This newly

---

61 *Contract between the Burgh of Inverkeithing and Robert Moffat Senior and Robert Moffat Junior*, (undated and incomplete), (NAS/B34/15/53), concerning a water channel near the family home: Two date stamps are attached: 19.9.1843 and 9.4.1844. Moffat returned to Africa before 1844, but he was regarded as the main heir of family effects.

62 James Love, *The Schools and Schoolmasters of Falkirk*, (Falkirk: Falkirk Herald Office, 1898); Love, *Local Antiquarian Notes and Queries, Vol. I*, (Falkirk: Johnstone & Co., 1908); and Love, *Local Antiquarian Notes and Queries, Vol. IV*, (Falkirk: Johnstone & Co., 1928). Falkirk Historical Research Centre holds a collection of Love's field notes, albeit not yet catalogued.

63 Northcott indicated that the Ormiston Baptismal Registers were held in the NAS. Northcott researched in the late 1950s; but in 2003 the NAS did not hold the relevant documents. The Haddington material—photocopies of Moffat and his mother's baptismal records—confirms that Northcott's information was correct, but where he accessed his sources is uncertain. No one at Haddington knew where the originals now are.

discovered material included the original copies of many of the letters and other material quoted in John Smith Moffat's *The Lives of Robert and Mary Moffat.* The find also provided material enabling Wallis to publish Moffat's journals of his five visits to Moselekatse, as well as being the definitive source for Schapera's edited collection of the Moffats' early correspondence and journals, which were published as *Apprenticeship at Kuruman.* There were already copies of some of this material in the archives of the LMS, but there was also much—especially from Moffat's earliest years—which was unique and previously unknown. Baxter and Burke, in their comprehensive *Guide to the Historical Manuscripts in the National Archives of Rhodesia,* not only list the important documents in the available material, but give extracts and summaries, though they do not give an exhaustive listing.[64]

11. *The British Library.* The British Library has no original Moffat material but holds books which Moffat referred to in his own writings, and which helped to mould—or provide a framework for—his thinking. For example, the British Library is the only known holder of John Ellis' work, *The Knowledge of Divine Things from Revelation not from Reason or Nature,*[65] which is cited extensively in Moffat's *Missionary Labours.* It also holds a miscellaneous selection of Moffatiana, such as programmes for nineteenth-century missionary meetings which focused on Moffat and his work.[66]

Orthography

We have used modern spellings in most of the main text, whilst keeping Moffat's original orthography in direct quotations.[67] Thus in the main text 'Bechuana' becomes 'Tswana', 'Sechuana' becomes 'SeTswana', and 'Matabele' becomes 'Ndebele', etc. However, we have retained Moffat's spelling 'Moselekatse' for the Ndebele chief, since modern renderings lack unanimity, though 'Mzilikazi' is the most common. Schapera gives a helpful list of Tswana names as used by Robert and Mary Moffat, along with the twentieth-century equivalents.[68] Moffat's spelling of African names is

---

[64] The Quagga's Kerk material is in the Zimbabwean National Archives (Boxes MO5 and MO6). We were unable to visit the Zimbabwean Archives, and we rely upon the extensive extracts quoted by John Smith Moffat, Schapera, Wallis, Baxter and Burke.

[65] John Ellis, *The Knowledge of Divine Things from Revelation not from Reason or Nature*, (3rd ed., London: William Baynes, 1811).

[66] Cf. Cherry, *Pleasant Evenings with Reading and Song: Book no. 2: Incidents in the Life of Robert Moffat, the Apostle of Africa,* (Ldn: Sunday School Union, Weekes & Co., c. 1882).

[67] The same could be argued of Moffat's early nineteenth-century spelling in which the so-called American 'z' in place of an 's' (e.g. evangelize) was standard in Britain at the time.

[68] *AAK,* 293ff.

inconsistent, but in direct quotes we have retained his variants, apart from a few occasions when it seemed obvious he simply made a spelling mistake. We used Matumo's *SeTswana-English-SeTswana Dictionary* as a reference for current Tswana orthography.[69] Alterations were made even within Moffat's lifetime. The Bible translation committee which Moffat established at Kuruman made several changes in 1864, and by 1870 an orthography controversy was raging.[70] Moffat's correspondence with the BFBS during, and just before, 1870 reveals the extent of the orthographical disagreement between Kuruman and the nearby Hanoverian Lutheran Missionaries. What Moffat wanted was one translation, and with an agreed orthography, in order to avoid confusion. Several terms used by Moffat and his contemporaries are now considered offensive. Thus, apart from when directly quoting contemporary sources, we have used *San* instead of 'Bushman', *Khoikhoi* instead of 'Hottentot', and *Xhosa* instead of 'Kafir'. We have retained terms such as 'tribe' and 'native', using them alongside 'people', 'group' and 'indigenous'.

Might our study be too sympathetic? That is a danger. Yet, Schapera, Wallis, Smith, Willoughby and Northcott all admired Moffat, and, perhaps for that reason, their honest criticisms carried force. Though sympathy with the subject does run the risk of minimising negative aspects, it can also motivate the enquirer to accurately expound the positive aspects of the subject's thinking. It is this desire—to gain a proper understanding of Moffat's faith—which is our aim.

---

69 Z.I. Matumo, *SeTswana English SeTswana Dictionary,* (Gaborone: Macmillan, 1993).

70 The correspondence on this issue, between Moffat and the British and Foreign Bible Society, is in the UBS archives at Cambridge University Library. Cf. Sandilands, 'The Ancestor of Tswana Grammars', *Botswana Notes and Records,* Vol. 4, 1972, 102.

Time Line

1795: Robert Moffat born at Ormiston, East Lothian, Scotland on 21.12.1795.[71] Mary Smith, (his future wife) born on 24.5.1795 in England. After a few years the Moffat family move to Carronshore on the Firth of Forth near Falkirk. His mother (Ann Gardiner) takes the family to the Rev. Robert Caldwell's Congregational Church in Falkirk.

1809: Becomes an apprentice gardener under John Robertson at Parkhill, near Polmont, and attends the Rev. Patrick MacFarlan's Church of Scotland congregation in Polmont.

1812: After completing his apprenticeship, Moffat obtains a post with Lord Moray, Donibristle, Fife, near his parents' new home at Inverkeithing. The family attend the Rev. Ebenezer Brown's secessionist Burgher Church.

1813: Moves to England to be under-gardener for Mr Leigh of High Leigh, Cheshire. He comes under Methodist influence through the Okey family.

1815: Meets William Roby, minister of Grosvenor Street Independent Church in Manchester, and explores the possibility of a call to the mission field under the LMS. The LMS rejects his first application. In order to be nearer Roby for instruction he changes to the employment of James Smith at Dukinfield, near Manchester, and meets Smith's daughter Mary.

1816: Appointed LMS missionary and ordained at Surrey Chapel London on 30th September 1816. He sails to South Africa on 18 October 1816, on the *Alacrity,* arriving at Cape Town on 13.1.1817.

1817: Starts missionary career, and attends the 1817 unofficial missionary 'Synod'. On 22.9.1817 he gains permission from the Cape Governor to cross the frontier of the Colony. He is sent by the LMS to Africaner's kraal in Namaqualand to relieve Johan Ebner.

1819: Takes Africaner to Cape Town. Robert marries Mary Smith on 27.12.1819 in St. George's Church, Cape Town.

1820: Robert and Mary accompany the deputation of John Campbell on his visit to the Interior. Sent by LMS to work with Mothibi's BaThlaping at Lattakoo along the Kuruman River, and settled at New Lattakoo on 27.5.1819. The Cape authority resists the appointment and so the LMS send the Moffats to solve problems at the Griqua Town station (about 100 miles from New Lattakoo).

1821: 17.5.1821: the Moffats return to New Lattakoo on permission coming from Cape Town. They settle down to long-term work with Mothibi's BaThlaping.

---

[71] This is the date in the Ormiston Parish records. Wallis, *MJ2,* 275 has 12.12.1795.

1823: The Kuruman (Seoding) site is 'purchased' from Mothibi's BaThlaping, and the mission moves to the new site in 1824, after the agreement is ratified, with the mission station being laid out in 1825. Mantatee invasions take place in 1823 with the battle of Dithakong.

1826: Moffat's SeTswana translation of *Brown's Catechism* with *Lord's Prayer* and *Scripture Selections* is printed in London.

1827: Moffat lives from March to June with the BaRolong in Tswaing village in order to develop his language skills.

1829: The Kuruman Awakening occurs. Moffat completes his translation of Luke's Gospel: Moffat's first visit to Moselekatse and the Ndebele who were based near present-day Pretoria (Tshwane) takes place.

1830: Visit to Cape Town to publish the SeTswana version of Luke's Gospel and elementary educational books in SeTswana, and returns to Kuruman in 1831 with a printing press.

1835: Moffat's second visit to Moselekatse and the Ndebele takes place, along with Dr Andrew Smith. 1836 sees a short-lived attempt by American (ABCFM) missionaries to settle and work among the Ndebele.

1837: The Boer 'Great Trek' into land beyond the boundaries of the Colony and outside British rule intensifies.

1838: The great Church at Kuruman is completed and opened.

1839: Moffat is unable to print the SeTswana New Testament in Cape Town, and is advised to sail to London to have it done. The Moffat family arrive in London in 1839, and stay in Britain until 1843. During that time Moffat is heavily engaged in visiting, deputation, and in writing *Missionary Labours and Scenes in Southern Africa.* Moffat meets the young David Livingstone in 1840 and assures Livingstone that he would 'do for Africa'. Livingstone goes to Africa as an LMS missionary and arrives at Kuruman in 1841.

1843: The Moffats arrive back in Kuruman on 13.12.1843.

1845: Mary Moffat (daughter) marries Livingstone at Kuruman on 9.1.1845.[72]

1852: The Sand River Convention takes place, at which the British Colonial authority effectively gives the Boer settlers autonomy beyond the Vaal River and excuses them from the obligations of British law with respect to the indigenous peoples. Under the terms of the Convention the indigenous peoples are denied arms and ammunition.

1853: Missionary conference takes place to discuss the implications of the Sand River Convention and the way it is being implemented by the Boers. Moffat travels to Bloemfontein to argue the missionary viewpoint on

---

72 Wallis, *MJ2,* 276, has 2.1.1845. Our date, 9 January, is taken directly from the *KCRB.*

behalf of the indigenous population. Unfortunately, the Sand River Convention is upheld.

1854: The Bloemfontein Agreement is passed, with the British Government giving more autonomy to the Boers. Moffat's third visit to Moselekatse and the Ndebele, who had moved to present-day southern Zimbabwe, takes place.

1857: Moffat completes the SeTswana version of the whole Bible. Moffat's has his fourth visit to Moselekatse and the Ndebele, with the aim of preparing for an LMS mission station to be founded among them.

1859: Moffat's fifth visit to Moselekatse and the Ndebele occurs. Moffat helps to establish the LMS mission station at Inyati, under the leadership of his son John Smith Moffat, and returns to Kuruman in 1860.

1860: Moffat hears news of the Makololo disaster. The LMS mission to the Makololo at Linyati was intended to be a sister mission to the mission to the Ndebele at Inyati.

1862: Mary Livingstone (daughter) dies at Chipunga on the Zambezi. Robert (son) also dies suddenly.

1870: The Moffats leave Kuruman and return to England on health grounds. Mary Moffat dies on 19.1.1871.

1872: Receives the degree of Doctor of Divinity *honoris causa* from the University of Edinburgh, and has his first audience with Queen Victoria.

1874: Identifies Livingstone's remains and attends Livingstone's funeral in Westminster Abbey.

1876: Has second audience with Queen Victoria.

1877: Visits Paris to speak at missionary meeting. Freedom of the City of London.

1883: 8.8.1883:[73] dies at Leigh, Kent. Buried in Norwood cemetery beside Mary.

---

[73] There is debate over the date of Moffat's death. The *Dictionary of National Biography,* 13/547 has 8.8.1883. *Encyclopedia Britannica* (15th Ed), 8/221 gives it as 9.8.1883. Wallis, *MJ2,* 276 has Thurs. 9th August. JSM, *Lives of Robert and Mary Moffat,* states that his father died on Thursday August 10, 1883. But Thursday was August 9. Did JSM remember the day of the week or the date with more accuracy? Was he wrong with both? The *Scotsman* obituary has: 'Dr Robert Moffat, the Nestor of African missionaries, died at half-past seven o'clock on Wednesday night at Leigh in Kent.' (*Scotsman,* 11.8.1883).

PREPARATION

Chapter 1
The Parental Home

ROBERT MOFFAT WAS BORN on 21 December 1795 in the village of Ormiston, East Lothian, Scotland, to Robert Moffat (Snr) and Ann Moffat (née Gardiner). He was their third son, after Alexander (1790) and William (1792), and was followed by Richard (1799), Helen (1803), Ann (1805) and James (1808).[1] Robert Moffat (Snr) was a ploughman in the neighbouring parish of Pencaitland, becoming a Customs Official at Portsoy in the North-East of Scotland in 1797. He then transferred to Carronshore and later to Inverkeithing, on the south and north shores respectively of the River Forth, retiring in 1847.

Ormiston was a planned village, set out to exhibit John Cockburn's philosophy of social improvement and progress. There had been an ancient hamlet at Ormiston, but the new village was laid out around 1740 by Cockburn, with a coal mine opened near-by in 1743. A new Ormiston House was built in 1745-49 but, due to financial problems, Cockburn had to sell the estate. Soon afterwards he started a brewery, which gave work for the local population. Enlightenment concepts of progress and improvement were big factors in the social thinking of the middle and later eighteenth century, both on a community and an individual level. This was characteristic of the environment which Robert Moffat (Snr) and Ann Gardiner grew up in. A belief in the values of progress and improvement—almost as spiritual virtues in their own right—was one of the underlying principles which the young Moffat would take to southern Africa. The drive which missionaries had to 'improve' and 'civilise' the life of the indigenous African, has to be understood in the context of an enormous movement towards self-

---

1 Robert was the third son, but, by the time of his father's death in 1847, he was principal heir. This was why the Quagga's Kerk Chest contained many family papers. The eldest son, Alexander, died in 1825. We assume that William, the second brother, died before 1847. After Alexander's death, Robert's fraternal correspondence was carried on with younger brother Richard. The Moffats followed Scottish practices in naming their children. The first son (Alexander) named after the paternal grandfather (Alexander Moffat); the second son (William) named after the maternal grandfather (William Gardiner). Robert and Mary Moffat continued the tradition, with their first son named Robert, after Robert Moffat (Snr), and their second son named James, after James Smith, father to Mary (Smith).

improvement, as a sign of godliness, which helped to transform Scotland during the eighteenth century.

Ann Gardiner

Ann Gardiner's family had lived for several generations in the Ormiston area.[2] She was born in 1767, in the gardener's cottage at Ormiston Hall to William Gardiner and Helen Johnston. Her father was head gardener at Ormiston Hall, the residence of Lord Hopetoun. In later life, Moffat credited his mother for having impressed and moulded his early ideas concerning religion. Writing to her in 1847, after hearing of his father's death, he stated: 'Wherever I am, I never forget how much I owe to your prayers. The first dawn of reflection respecting my soul commenced with hearing you pray.'[3] Her grandson, John Smith Moffat, testified to her spiritual passion, commenting that she 'united a sternness of religious belief, bordering on gloomy vindictiveness, with one of the tenderest and most loving hearts that ever beat'.[4]

Ann taught her children the importance of family roots, where they came from, and the community of which her people had been part for many years.[5] In a letter, later cited in the *Haddingtonshire Courier*, Moffat had written: 'Well do I remember during my boy-days my mother, during one of her visits to Ormiston, taking me to the spot and pointing with her hand to the spot, adding, "There, my dear laddie, is the very spot where you were born."'[6] She was an intense person. Intense about her faith, the scriptures, her family, her roots, and her children. With that passion, seasoned by maternal affection, she fostered a due seriousness about the things of God. She also trained her offspring domestically, sons as well as daughters. John Smith Moffat gave a glimpse of the interior of the Moffat cottage during his father's childhood years:

> The lads were gathered by the fireside, and while their mother taught them [not without remonstrance] to knit and sew, she would read aloud, in such missionary publications as were then to be had, the story of the dauntless

---

2 In Scottish Law a woman never loses her maiden name. Ann Gardiner was legally known as Gardiner or Moffat. 'Gardiner' was the spelling on her baptismal record.

3 RM, *To his Mother,* 11.9.1847 (JSM, *Lives,* 259).

4 JSM, *Lives,* 4.

5 In August 1872, after retiral from Africa, Moffat spent a Sunday at Ormiston and preached there. His grandparents were buried in the Ormiston graveyard. In the grounds of Ormiston Hall, the cottage still stood in which his mother had been born; but the cottage in which he himself had been born was not standing, (*Haddingtonshire Courier*, 23.8.1872).

6 RM, *Letter,* cited by *Haddingtonshire Courier,* 24.4.1885.

pioneers of the gospel; and more especially of the work of the Moravians in Greenland and in the East Indies.[7]

Though irksome at the time, Robert Moffat blessed her insistence when, in later life, he had to fend for himself. Years later, reflecting on the difficulties involved in ordinary living whilst based in the remote tribal villages of Namaqualand, Moffat wrote: 'My dear old mother, to keep us out of mischief in the long winter evenings, taught me both to sew and knit; and when I would tell her I intended being a man, she would reply, "Lad, ye dinna ken whar your lot will be cast". She was right, for I have often had occasion to use the needle since.'[8] She was firm, strict, and practical, and Moffat expressed deep affection for her on many occasions. In 1871, on receipt of some literature, he wrote to his friend William Dickson of the Free Church:

> How grateful do I feel to you for not only directing my attention to the *Nursery Songs* but supplying me with a copy and also a *Children's Record* ... they bring back 'auld lang syne' and the soft sweet tones of a mother's love. Well do I remember when I would not take my porridge because I could not get milk with it. Ma used to rag 'Just go to the school as you are and there is one lesson you are sure to learn before your return, that 'hunger is good kitchen'. This was right for so I found it.[9]

Ann Gardiner died in 1854, and Robert Moffat heard of her death around the time he returned from his epic third journey to Moselekatse: 'She died as she had lived, a godly consistent woman, and was called to the Heavenly City, at the age of eighty-four.'[10]

Ann Gardiner: Her Spiritual Independency

Robert Moffat (Snr) and Ann Gardiner contributed two distinct Church traditions to their family. James Love, the Falkirk historian, cited Moffat telling a Newcastle audience in 1843: 'My father was a Churchman, but my mother was an out-and-out Independent, and went to Falkirk every Sabbath, even through snow in the middle of winter, and took me to hear a Mr Caldwell.'[11] The epithet 'Churchman', which Moffat applied to his father, referred to a person who was a member of the established Church of

---

7 JSM, *Lives,* 4. JSM may have intended to write 'West Indies', as the Moravian mission was strongest in the West Indies, and there was hardly any in the 'East Indies'.

8 RM, *MLSSA,* 148.

9 RM, *To William Dickson,* 10.12.1871, (UENCL/WD9/3/1).

10 Deane, *Robert Moffat,* 144. According to Ormiston Baptismal Records, she was born in 1767, making her 86 or 87 when she died, not 84.

11 Love, *Local Antiquarian Notes and Queries, Vol. IV,* (Falkirk: Johnstone & Co., 1928), 29f. In Newcastle, Moffat met up with the aged Rev. Caldwell after a gap of 30 years. JSM, *Lives,* 3, also noted this dual spiritual heritage.

Scotland. But what did 'Independent' mean in relation to his mother? What was her spiritual heritage? Within an eighteenth-century Scottish context, the term 'Independent' was a fluid term, applicable to several denominations, but essentially meant 'being independent of the established church'. Ann's feisty character and independence of will regarding her personal spiritual legacy is underlined in her choice of church.

Moffat's parents were married in Ormiston Parish Church, and it appears that all of their children were baptised as infants in the Church of Scotland. The names of Alexander, William and Robert are in the Baptismal Register of Ormiston Parish Church; Richard's name in that of Larbert Parish Church; and Helen, Ann and James at Bothkennar Parish Church.[12] Each was recorded in the appropriate Church of Scotland Baptismal Register of the parish in which the family was residing at the time. However, the inclusion of a name in a Church of Scotland Baptismal Register is not conclusive proof that the baptism took place under the auspices of the Church of Scotland. Prior to the process of civil registration being established in Scotland in 1855, certificates of baptism and marriage were the sole legal proof that such events had ever taken place; therefore, some parish registers of the Church of Scotland were used to record baptisms and marriages which took place in Secession or other Churches. Helpfully, most entries specify the particular church to which the couple or parents belonged, but sometimes the only clue to the denomination lies in the name of the minister who celebrated the marriage or baptism.[13] Unfortunately, the recording of data was not uniform, and minister's names were not always documented.

For example, the baptismal records for Ormiston and Larbert do not include the officiating minister's name; but for the baptisms of Helen, Ann and James, the Bothkennar Register explicitly names the Rev. Mr Caw, the local Church of Scotland minister, as the officiating clergyman.[14] It is this unambiguous mention of the Rev. Mr Caw which proves that the act of

---

12 We used three sources for the baptismal records. (i) A photocopy extract of Robert's baptism in the *Baptismal Records of Ormiston Parish Church* was viewed at Haddington Library Archives, East Lothian, Scotland. (ii) Richard's entry was viewed on a microfilm copy of the *Baptismal Records of Larbert Parish Church*, at Falkirk Public Library (FPL, Microfilm, OPR/473/2). (iii) Helen, Ann and James' records were viewed on a microfilm copy of the *Baptismal Records of Bothkennar Parish Church,* at the Falkirk Historical Research Centre (FHRC, Microfilm, Box 546, Section 473). The baptismal records for Moffat's two elder siblings were not viewed, but there is no reason to doubt they were baptised in Ormiston Parish Church.

13 Baptie, *Registers of the Secession Churches in Scotland,* (Aberdeen: Scottish Association of Family History Societies, 2000), 1.

14 *Bothkennar Parish Church Baptismal Records*, (FHRC/OPR/473/2).

baptism for Helen, Ann and James took place in the Parish Church, rather than the Parish Church Baptismal Register simply being the place to record baptisms occurring elsewhere.

Why is this significant? It is noteworthy because, by the time the latter three baptisms took place, Ann Gardiner was already attending Mr Caldwell's independent Congregational ministry in Bank Street, Falkirk, five miles from the family home.[15] This detail reveals the spiritual life of the Moffat home. Robert (Snr) was a Church of Scotland man, and it appears that, in deference to his position as head of the family, all the children were baptised in the established Church even though his wife preferred to worship elsewhere. She took the children to her preferred congregation. She wanted a clearly evangelical ministry to have the greatest influence in their lives, and the Bank Street Congregational Church was a product of the Evangelical Revival which swept Britain in the later eighteenth century. Thus, the Calvinism which characterised Scottish family life, was complemented by a revivalist tradition, imported into the family by their mother.

The established Church of Scotland of the late eighteenth and early nineteenth centuries had a mixture of Moderates and Evangelicals. The Moderates had ascendancy from about 1760 to 1820, during which period a person such as Ann Gardiner, with a strong evangelical piety, might doubt whether a local Church of Scotland minister would preach a 'true Bible believing Gospel'. It was felt that the evangelical message was found more frequently from preachers in the Seceders or old Dissenter tradition, or from the pulpits of the new Congregationalist and Baptist congregations. Such preachers, characterised as 'feeling' preachers, were favoured by men and women with an evangelical piety, who disliked ministers whom they regarded as 'moralising' or 'rationalising' pulpit-men of the Moderate school. Ann Gardiner wanted to ensure that her children would not be affected by insipid churchmen and took her family to hear Mr Caldwell, the independent Congregational minister.

The Moffat family had moved to Carronshore, in the parish of Bothkennar, around 1800, having spent a brief period in nearby Larbert. It was then that Ann Gardiner started attending Caldwell's Church in Falkirk. But was her 'Independency' a new thing? Or had she always been so? If she had been Church of Scotland in Ormiston she would most likely have been happily Church of Scotland at Carronshore. So, was her 'Independency' a long-standing feature of her spiritual life? If so, what form had it taken in the years

---

[15] Caldwell was sent to Falkirk by the new Scottish Congregational Church in 1802. He was ordained in 1803 when the church building was completed.

before she married, given that Scottish Congregationalism did not come into existence until 1799? We cannot be one hundred percent certain which denomination Ann Gardiner was affiliated to before her marriage, but a likely possibility is that the Gardiners were of the Burgher persuasion.[16] It is that hypothesis, examined in the next few pages, which appears to fit best.

Ann's father was head-gardener at Ormiston Hall, the residence of Lord Hopetoun. She spent her childhood and youth around the gardener's house near the entrance to Ormiston Hall private grounds, and less than 40 yards from the nearby Parish Church.[17] The family, having a house from Lord Hopetoun and being in the employment of Lord Hopetoun, would be expected, though not compelled, to attend the local Parish Church of which Lord Hopetoun was the patron.[18] Yet it is possible that the Gardiner family observed the expected formalities in regard to the local Parish Church (especially for Baptisms and Marriages) but had deeper, more heart-felt, associations with a different brand of religious expression. There were many reasons why working-class families tended towards Secessionist, Independent, or other Dissenting congregations: one factor was that this was one of the few areas of life in which they could assert independence of mind and action from those to whom they were dependent on, and subservient to, in daily life.

Dissent was considerable. The 1765 General Assembly of the Church of Scotland had noted with concern that there were 120 meeting-houses in the country with 100,000 persons in attendance who once had been members of the Established Church. Brown pointed out that 'large numbers of the rural lower orders left the Established Church in the 1760s and 1770s, as a result of often violent patronage issues which rent parishes asunder. They formed congregations of the Secession Church or, less often, the Relief Church which came into being in 1761.'[19] By the 1820s, about 32 percent of the population

---

16 Or was she always Church of Scotland? She was, after all, married in the Parish Church, despite Burgher ministers being allowed to conduct weddings. Alternatively, she may have been married in Ormiston Kirk because her family were Lord Hopetoun's tenants.

17 W.Y. Whitehead, *History of Ormiston,* (Haddington: Croal, 1937), 58: confirmed by observation 12.2.2004. Cf. Annie Lyell, *Ye see it a': the Ormiston Story,* (Haddington: East Lothian Council, 2001).

18 For 200 years the Patronage issue caused divisions in Scottish church life. Presbyterianism emphasised the right of congregations to choose and call their own ministers: the Patronage system invested that authority in the local Patron, usually the landowner. The British Parliament reimposed patronage in the Church of Scotland in 1712.

19 Brown, *The Social History of Religion in Scotland since 1730,* 29ff. The 1820s are 40 years after the time Ann Gardiner was a young lass growing up at Ormiston. But Brown's figures point to an ever-growing tradition of working-class dissent, from the mid-eighteenth century until well into the nineteenth.

of the Scottish Lowlands (including Ormiston and East Lothian) were Presbyterian dissenters. In the *Second Statistical Account for Scotland* (1845), the entry for Ormiston noted: 'Some of the servants in families connected with the Establishment belong to Dissenting congregations and vice versa.'[20] Though the *Second Statistical Account* was later than our period, and reflected a post-1843 Disruption situation,[21] it described what had been common for many years: that a considerable percentage of the working-class asserted a spirit of independence in their religious life.

If the Gardiner family, like many of their peers, were associated with a church other than the Parish Church, what were their options? There was no Congregational Church near Ormiston until 1804 when a congregation was formed in nearby Haddington.[22] But that was after Ann Gardiner had left the area. She left either in 1797 to accompany her husband to Portsoy, or in 1799 when the family moved to Larbert and then to Carronshore. 1799 is the latest possible date she was permanently resident in Ormiston. Thus, apart from the Church of Scotland, her spiritual background had to be either a Praying Society or one of the many Secession Churches which emerged in the eighteenth century. Our favoured option is that she had links with a Secessionist Burgher Church, possibly in the nearby town of Tranent, though the evidence is inconclusive.[23]

Or had she been part of a 'Praying Society'? Praying Societies were scattered throughout Scotland, flourishing in the late eighteenth century.[24] There were three main types at that time.[25] (i) *Society Folk.* The 'Society Folk' belonged to the Cameronian sect which stood outside the established Kirk, but there is no evidence of Cameronians in East Lothian. (ii) *Covenanting*

---

[20] *Second Statistical Account for Scotland, 1845,* Vol. 2, 148.

[21] At the 1843 Disruption in the Church of Scotland almost one third of the ministers of the Church of Scotland left their charges and formed the Free Church of Scotland.

[22] *The History of Congregationalism in Scotland from 1798-1848,* Section 6.1, (Unpublished Ms., National Library of Scotland, (ABS.8.88.8).

[23] During the eighteenth century, Presbyterianism in Scotland had several splits, creating a range of Presbyterian Churches. The initial movement took place in 1733, usually called the First Secession: these congregations formed into the Associate Presbytery—known from 1744 as the Associate Synod—outside the established Church. The new Church grew quickly as it already had the nucleus of congregations in the *Praying Societies.* During the 1740s, the Associate Synod itself split into Burghers and anti-Burghers. Other groups emerged from the Presbyterian 'pot'. The Tranent Secessionist congregation, that of John Brown in Haddington, and that of Ebenezer Brown in Inverkeithing, were all Burgher congregations. Burleigh, *Church History of Scotland,* (Ldn: OUP, 1960), gives a chart tracing the various Presbyterian factions.

[24] Henderson, G.D, *The Church of Scotland,* (Edin: Church of Scotland, 1939), 119.

[25] Methodism did not make large inroads into Scotland. There were few Methodist Praying Societies or informal meetings such as Moffat later found at High Leigh in England.

Legacy. Many Praying Societies came into being as a legacy of Covenanting times. These were attended by folk who still formally adhered to the established Church, but supplemented its services with communal devotions. These were para-church groups, with individuals attached to both the Praying Society and the Kirk. Attendees were usually of the 'humbler classes of society.'[26] (iii) *Denominational Out-Station.* One reason why Praying Societies were popular was the distance to the nearest full congregation of a preferred denomination. Though many were prepared to walk considerable distances to the church of their choice on a Sunday, some could not, and held cottage meetings which had a tacit connection with that congregation elsewhere. After a time, some of these cottage meetings were raised into congregations of full status within their preferred denomination.

Though some cottage meetings were linked to the established Church of Scotland, many of the Praying Societies, even in the first half of the eighteenth century, provided fertile soil for the growth of Secessionist Churches.[27] From 1740 onwards, the Associate (Burgher) Presbytery capitalised on the situation since, in many districts throughout Scotland, there were groups discontented with the spiritual food that was being provided for them by the parish minister. 'The Associate Presbytery undertook to supply the needs of these groups as far as possible. Students were trained for the ministry and settled where there was a demand. Some of the new churches had to serve a large area, and people walked long distances to the services. In some places Praying Societies had to be left to carry on as best they could for a time. Lay elders found an opportunity of giving special service, and in the new church acquired a position of larger influence than had been assigned to them in the Church of Scotland. Congregations which wished to have an ordained minister had to make suitable provision for his maintenance.'[28]

Ann Gardiner: Her Burgher Roots?

Data for late eighteenth-century Ormiston and its environs shows that Praying Societies existed in two adjacent towns. One was Musselburgh, eight miles distant; the other was Tranent, three miles away. In Musselburgh the

---

26 MacKie, *A History of Scotland,* 300.

27 Members of Praying Societies had an empathy with the Secessionist movement. Through the course of the eighteenth century, many Praying Societies were absorbed into the Associate Presbytery (Synod). They had a *Theological Empathy,* being evangelical, with no trace of moderatism. They also had an *Ecclesiastical Empathy,* with a desire to exclude the secular authority from having any say in the governance of the Church.

28 Henderson, *The Church of Scotland,* 107.

Praying Society had, by the latter years of the eighteenth century, become a Burgher Congregation in its own right.[29] The Tranent Praying Society had also been elevated into a full congregation of the Burgher Church, and it is that congregation which, in our opinion, may have been the Gardiner's spiritual home. There were in fact three Burgher congregations within range of Ormiston village. They were at: Musselburgh (eight miles), Haddington (ten miles), and Tranent (three miles). There was also an Anti-Burgher congregation in Haddington. Apart from these, there were no other denominations in the area, apart from the established Church of Scotland.[30] It is unlikely that the Secessionist church in Musselburgh was the spiritual home of the Gardiner family, given that the route to Musselburgh passed through Tranent, which was five miles closer. Moreover, Musselburgh was a fishing-town on the Forth, and fishing communities generally did not mix with rural communities. This was not an absolute rule, but it strengthens the intuition that Musselburgh would not have been the Sabbath destination for Ann's family.[31]

Haddington Burgher Church is a serious contender, and there are weighty arguments in its favour. Firstly, it was the county and market town for the area, and traveling to it was a familiar journey. Secondly, the minister of the Burgher Church in Haddington had been the redoubtable Dr John Brown, a man renowned throughout Scotland for his godliness and scholarship. Sitting at the feet of such a ministry is something which Ann's parents may have valued, and they may have remained part of the congregation even after Brown's death in 1787. Thirdly, there is evidence that some people did go to Haddington each Sunday from the villages of Pencaitland and Ormiston.[32] That does not prove that the Gardiners did so, and though distance would not deter a pious family in search of spiritual food, there was a Burgher Church much closer, in Tranent, along a flat and easy road.

The Burgher Church of Tranent came into being in 1770, and there is evidence that some people from Ormiston attended it. A note in the Tranent

---

29 MacKelvie, *Annals and Statistics of the United Presbyterian Church,* (Edin: Oliphant, 1873), 216.

30 Apart from the Burgher and Anti-Burgher traditions, the main Secessionist church in Scotland was the Relief Church. There is no record of a Relief congregation local to Ormiston.

31 Sinclair's *First Statistical Account for Scotland, 1790,* mentioned no place of Christian worship in Ormiston apart from the Parish Church. Admittedly, the entries for the *First Statistical Account* were nearly all written by perish ministers, who sometimes ignored the existence of competing denominations. However, no evidence is extant of an alternative worship meeting.

32 Small, *History of the Congregations of the United Presbyterian Church from 1733-1900,* (Edin: D.M. Small, 1904), 517.

Burgher Kirk Session minute of 1 November 1779, concerning new elders, points out that two elders ought to be from Tranent, and one elder each from Prestonpans, Seton Mack-Merry, and Ormiston.[33] A subsequent minute reveals that no elder was appointed from Ormiston, though there were new ones from the other locations.[34] Though no elders were ordained from Ormiston, the desire to have one in the village indicates that Ormiston folk were attending the congregation.[35]

Additional circumstantial evidence for the Burgher hypothesis lies in the fact that, when the Moffat family moved from Carronshore across the River Forth to Inverkeithing in 1811, the congregation they attended there was the Burgher congregation of the Rev. Ebenezer Brown. He was the son of the famous Dr John Brown of Haddington. Ebenezer's brother, William, was the author of a popular instructional booklet, *Brown's Catechism*, which Robert Moffat took to South Africa.[36] It was the first theological document translated by Moffat into SeTswana, and which he committed to memory before setting out on an evangelism tour of several villages in 1827.[37]

If the Gardiners had been 'Burghers' why did Ann not attend the Burgher Congregation in Falkirk, whose minister from 1794 to 1834 was the Rev. Henry Belfrage? Belfrage was a man of evangelical and missionary persuasion, and was one of the early Directors of the LMS.[38] Why did she not sit under his ministry? What appears to have happened is that she had developed a 'cottage-meeting' attachment to a Congregational presence near where she lived, and when the Congregationalists built a church in Falkirk it was natural for her to go there. Robert Caldwell came to Falkirk in 1802 and was ordained in 1803. But her link to Congregationalism may have already begun before that date.[39] When the Moffats arrived in Carronshore, there was already, in the parish, an informal gathering of Haldane[40]

---

33 Brough, *Two links in a Chain: Wishart St Andrews Church Tranent,* (Tranent: 1977), 14. Also, *Tranent Associate Congregation Session Minutes* 1777-1819, (NAS/CH3/560/1).

34 *Tranent Associate Congregation Session Minutes* 1777-1819, (NAS/CH3/560/1).

35 The attachment which the Moffat family (including Ann Gardiner) later made with the Burgher Church under the ministry of the Rev. Ebenezer Erskine in Inverkeithing makes it unlikely she was ever an Anti-Burgher. Anti-Burghers were less zealous about Foreign Missions, for which she had a clear passion.

36 Brown, *Christian Instructions for Children from Three to Seven years of age, Containing: a Catechism; Passages of Scripture; Hymns,* (2nd edn, Edin: James Robertson, 1820).

37 RM, *To Mary Moffat,* 25.4.1827, (*AAK,* 264).

38 LMS, *Transactions,* Vol. 1, 1795-1802, (2nd ed: London, LMS, 1804).

39 During the years 1799 to 1803 (apart from part of 1799, when they lived briefly in Larbert) the family was domiciled at Carronshore in the Parish of Bothkennar.

40 The Haldane connection is examined in Ch. 2.

Congregationalists. It was this gathering which became one of the seeds for the soon-to-be established Congregational Church in Falkirk. Congregationalism attracted several people of Burgher persuasion, who found the type of ministry to their liking.[41] Our supposition is that, initially, Ann Gardiner attended the local Bothkennar Parish Church along with her husband, but also contacted this new and exciting group. When the Congregational Church was established in Falkirk, the natural thing was for her to attend it. There was never any need to go to Mr Belfrage's Church. It was not that she looked around in Falkirk for a spirituality akin to her own. Rather, she found it in her neighbourhood and followed it when it constituted itself in Falkirk. The informal evangelical meeting of Haldane Congregationalists near Carronshore, so congenial to Burgher piety, may have been her bridge to involvement with Bank Street Congregational Church.

If Ann Gardiner had Burgher roots, what would these imply? To begin with, if Burgher convictions were conveyed to her offspring, that may explain why Moffat was unwilling—initially at least—to become involved in Church-State or Mission-State relationships in southern Africa. Secessionism in general, and Burgher Congregations in particular, strove to separate church life from the influence of the Civil Magistrate or Secular Authority. Many other factors would play their part in Moffat's attitudes, and these will be examined in due course, but this is a relevant consideration.[42]

Another Burgher emphasis was Foreign Mission. During the eighteenth century, the established Church of Scotland was unenthusiastic about foreign mission. The Anti-Burghers accepted the concept but were unwilling to collaborate with other groups. In contrast, foreign mission in cooperation

---

[41] Kirk, *Annals of Erskine,* (Falkirk: Erskine Church, 1987), 22f: 'In 1801 there seems to have been a flourishing group of Independents at Grangemouth, which some members of the Associate Congregation were in the habit of attending'. Cf. Anon, *The History of Congregationalism in Scotland from 1798-1848*, section 17, 8. We also note that the entry for Bothkennar in Sinclair's *Statistical Account for Scotland, Vol. 17* 293, (publ. 1790s) stated that, in the late-eighteenth century, quite a number had 'removed from Carronshore to Grangemouth' (a short distance away). The *Statistical Account* also stated: 'The people in general attend the established Church; of those who do not there are about 9 Burghers, an equal number who are connected with the Relief congregation in Falkirk; 8 anti-Burghers, 2 Cameronians, and 2 Episcopalians.' (294). It may have been Burghers who found the Independent meeting congenial.

[42] Northcott's assertion that the Moffats were pious in the manner of 'United Presbyterians who combined their Calvinism with a lively evangelical interest in foreign parts which Ann Moffat imparted to her brood' is wrong' (*Robert Moffat: Pioneer in Africa*, 17). The UP Church did not exist until 1847. Northcott's error was copied by Comaroff, *Of Revelation and Revolution, Vol. 1,* 82.

with other Christian organisations was congenial to the Burgher ethos.[43] Burgher spirituality also emphasised the importance of spiritual rebirth and conversion. Church of Scotland ministries varied as to their emphasis on the new-birth, whereas all Burgher ministries held a consistent doctrine. It was noted by the contemporary writer Thomas Carlyle that, 'a man who awoke to the belief that he actually had a soul to be saved or lost was apt to be found among the dissenting people.'[44] Soul-concern was core to evangelical piety. At the same time, though it may seem that Burgher spirituality would have had a positive response to the Evangelical Awakening, Burgher leadership had been cool towards both Wesley and Whitefield.[45] Nevertheless, the piety of the Evangelical Revival found its way into Burgher cottages, as it found its way into families belonging to many denominations. Signs of that piety can be discerned in the hymns which Ann Gardiner loved.

Ann Gardiner: Her Hymns and their Piety

The established Church of Scotland discouraged hymns, even for family worship. Only the Psalms of David, in metrical form, were regarded as fitting for worship, though, by the end of the eighteenth century, paraphrases were gradually coming into use in Church of Scotland parishes, with hymns still taboo. For Ann Gardiner, however, hymns were immensely important, and she had several favourites which her son remembered. Fortunately, both the Burgher and the Congregationalist traditions were more positive about hymns than was the Church of Scotland. At the same time, it should be noted that in the original Secession churches there were no hymns as part of Sabbath public worship, though they were accepted as an appropriate means of worship within the home.[46] Conversely, the Congregational Church in Falkirk was full-square in the Revivalist tradition, fully employing its rich evangelical hymnody in congregational worship.

---

43 This is illustrated by the publication by William Brown of his three-volume work, *History of the Propagation of Christianity among the Heathen since the Reformation,* (Edin: Blackwood, 1854). This was one of the first histories of Foreign Missions. William Brown was the son of the Burgher Professor, John Brown of Haddington. He was also author of *Brown's Catechism*. He became Secretary to the Scottish Missionary Society after his own hopes of Foreign Mission work came to nought.

44 Cited by Henderson, *The Church of Scotland,* 108.

45 MacKie, *A History of Scotland,* 302. When Whitefield, as an Anglican Calvinist, came to Scotland in 1741, he intended to co-operate with the Secessionist Associate Presbytery, but was rejected. Instead, he worked with Church of Scotland evangelical ministers.

46 Scott, *Annals and Statistics of the Original Secession Church,* (Edin: Elliot, 1886), 20. In traditional Burgher Church worship on the Sabbath a psalm was given out with a preface on its meaning. Then there was a lecture, plus an exposition of Scripture.

It was Isaac Watts, the English Independent, who took decisive steps towards the foundation of an English hymnody. English Presbyterians, such as Richard Baxter, advocated the use of hymns alongside metrical psalms, as early as the end of the seventeenth century. On the other hand, Scottish Presbyterians were reluctant to embrace 'non-Scriptural worship songs.' But ripples came from the Great Awakening in the United States, arousing congregations to the need for a warmer language of praise. English Presbyterian worship made its own contribution, with George Whitefield playing a leading part in the Evangelical Revival and introducing many of Isaac Watts' hymns at his meetings. Then the Wesleyan hymns from the Methodist movement also became increasingly popular as the eighteenth century proceeded.

Scottish Presbyterians were less open to hymns than their English counterparts, but, though Methodism never took root in Scotland as it did in England, hymns did percolate into the religious culture, finding acceptance amongst ordinary church members. The Relief Church in 1792 was the very first Presbyterian denomination to officially publish a hymn book,[47] but it was pre-eminently the Congregationalist and Baptist Churches which promoted their use. The words of popular hymns were also printed in 'Gospel' magazines, which were widely read by those with a leaning towards an evangelical piety. Significantly, not all 'evangelical' hymns of the period were 'evangelistic': there was a strong seam of highly moralistic hymns. When Moffat translated the Burgher William Brown's *Catechism* into SeTswana, he also translated the small group of heavily moralistic hymns which Brown had appended to his *Catechism,* many composed by Isaac Watts.

During the latter part of the eighteenth century, the influence of the Evangelical Revival fanned an increasing popularity of hymns in Scotland as well as in England, with many Christian men and women developing a deep love for such items of praise. If she had been a member of a Burgher congregation, then the youthful Ann Gardiner would have been exposed to hymns, albeit on the periphery of Church life. At Falkirk Congregational Church, however, the adult Ann Gardiner experienced directly a wide range of contemporary hymns, with their evangelical piety and revivalist theology. Moffat often mentioned two hymns in particular which his mother loved, both of which came from the stable of warm, evangelical, revivalist piety.

When, as a young, single missionary, Moffat was alone at Africaner's kraal

---

[47] Forrester & Murray, *Studies in the History of Worship in Scotland,* (Edin: Clark, 1984), 89.

in 1818,[48] he sought solace from loneliness by playing the violin. 'More than once, I took my violin, (once belonging to Christian Albrecht) and, reclining upon one of the huge masses, have, in the stillness of the evening, played and sung the well-known hymn, a favourite with my mother, *'Awake my soul in joyful lays, To sing the great Redeemer's praise'*.'[49] The hymn had been written by Samuel Medley, and there are several versions of the first verse. Two of the most common are:

Awake, my soul to joyful lays, And sing thy great Redeemer's praise; He justly claims a song from me; His loving kindness, oh, how free!	Awake, each saint, in joyful lays, To sing the great Redeemer's praise; He justly claims a song from thee, His loving-kindness, oh how free!

There were other favourites. The day before Moffat died in 1883, he asked that his mother's favourite hymn, *'Hail, Sovereign Light'*, be read to him.[50] This was the hymn *'Hail, Sovereign Love'*, composed by Jehoida Brewer, and based on Psalm 119:114.[51] Brewer had close associations with the early LMS, preaching a sermon at one of the first LMS annual meetings on 10 May 1798. The words of the hymn were first published in *Gospel Magazine,* October 1776, and the best-known form of the first verse is:

Hail, sovereign love that first began
The scheme to rescue fallen man;
Hail matchless free eternal grace,
That gave my soul a hiding place.

There is an indication that this hymn had a direct influence on Robert Moffat, especially its later lines: *'Enwrapped in thick Egyptian night, And fond of darkness more than light, Madly I ran the sinful race, Secure without a hiding place'.* In the *Matabele Journals*, Moffat wrote of Moselekatse being in an *'Egyptian'* darkness: 'Oh, it makes one melancholy to see a nation living in the bright sunshine of a tropical climate, surrounded by hills and dales all

---

48 Jager Africaner was an infamous Namaqua Chief. Before his conversion his raids were feared by European settlers. He heard the Gospel through the LMS and was converted through Johann Ebner c.1812, well before Moffat's arrival. Moffat's contribution was to mentor him over two years, resulting in a permanent change in Africaner's beliefs and character. The culmination of this process came when the transformed Africaner went with Moffat to Cape Town to meet the Cape Governor who had put a price of £100 on his head (Moffat's initial salary was only £40 per year). Africaner died in 1823. After his conversion he was the jewel in the crown of LMS missionary work in southern Africa. Cf. John Campbell, *The Life of Africaner: A Namaqua Chief of South Africa,* (Ldn: Religious Tract Society, c. 1830).

49 RM, *MLSSA,* 108.

50 Deane, *Robert Moffat,* 178.

51 Jehoida Brewer (Sylvestris) was born in 1752. He died in 1817.

clothed in nature's loveliest green, in mental darkness, *black as an Egyptian night*.'[52]

Both hymns came from the evangelical revivalist tradition. Ann Gardiner accessed these hymns, and many others, either at Ormiston through popular publications such as the *Gospel Magazine,* or at Falkirk through the worship life of Bank Street congregation. Other hymns, which early Scottish hymn writers, such as Ralph Erskine, were producing, were more lugubrious. These resembled poems rather than lively spirited worship songs, though they were also widely circulated and loved in their time.[53]

ANN GARDINER: HER INTEREST IN MISSIONS

Another influence which Ann Gardiner introduced to her children came when she read to them stories featuring Moravian missionaries: 'She would read aloud, in such missionary publications as were then to be had, the story of the dauntless pioneers of the gospel; and more especially of the work of the Moravians in Greenland and in the East Indies.'[54] Years later, Moffat testified how these accounts gave him strength during the barren years in southern Africa. In 1822 he wrote to George Burder at the LMS in London:

> You will see from the preceding journal what our situation is. The prospect is neither calculated to encourage or cheer, but we labour in hope. The power of God exhibited in Greenland and the South Seas stimulates us to persevere. Though the vision be for an appointed time, at the end it shall speak and not lie; though it tarry, it will surely come, it will not tarry.[55]

When, as a young man of twenty, he read a notice advertising a missionary meeting in Manchester, he recalled tales his mother had read to him about the Moravian missionaries in Greenland and Labrador. These, in conjunction with the missionary meeting advertisement, excited in him a desire to be a missionary.[56] In the second chapter of his *Missionary Labours and Scenes in Southern Africa*, Moffat reminded his readers that, 'the small Moravian church of Herrnhut sent forth her missionaries more than a century ago, to

---

52 RM, *Journal,* 15.12.1859, (*MJ2,* 247).

53 Ralph Erskine (1685-1752) was a hymn-writer, noted for his *Gospel Sonnets.* Younger brother of Ebenezer Erskine, he corresponded with Wesley and Whitefield. His *Gospel Sonnets,* first published as *Gospel Canticles, or Spiritual Songs, 1720,* was reprinted several times. Erskine was noted for playing the violin, unusual for a minister in his day.

54 JSM, *Lives,* 4.

55 RM, *To Burder, LMS,* 5.8.1822, (*AAK,* 52).

56 Cf. Moffat's *Memoir* (JSM, *Lives,* 16ff). The Congregational Church in Falkirk, with strong connections to the missionary movement, would also foster an interest in Foreign Missions.

the fur-clad inhabitants of Greenland.'[57] Moffat was not drawing on facts learned as an adult, but on stories absorbed as a boy.

Which specific publications may have been read by Ann Gardiner to her children? She may have accessed articles in the *Gospel Magazine,* or she may have had a book. Of the few books available at the time, a strong candidate would be the 1774 publication, *A Brief Account of the Mission established among the Esquimaux Indians on the coast of Labrador by the Church of the Brethren or Unitas Fratrum.*[58] This was a slim volume, only 33 small pages, and priced at a modest six-pence.[59] Its date, size and price put it within the reach of the Moffat family. Children's books as such were virtually unknown at that time, but this work was written in non-technical language, and in a style that a pious mother could read easily to her family. There is no proof that this was the volume which Moffat alluded to in later life, but the number of books on the subject was limited, and there is little doubt that the story it told, the incidents it highlighted, and the approach it took, formed the core substance of any other book or article on the subject. What was its focus?

Firstly, it had a clear core message: 'The word of the cross, and of the great atoning sacrifices, has been, at every opportunity, yea without cessation, preached by us unto the Esquimaux.'[60] Secondly, it gave high profile to the work of peacemaking between Esquimaux tribes, carried out by the Moravian mission.[61] Thirdly, it gave an extended account of the death of an Esquimaux named Annouke, who was one of the first converts, and who, on his deathbed was reported to have spoken of departing to be with the Saviour in very pious terms.[62] Accounts of converts dying a Christian death with peace and serenity were regarded as important testimonies in marking the progress of the gospel. Fourthly, the theme of 'civilisation' was featured: 'Though by these means, the outward situation of these poor

---

57 RM, *MLSSA,* 19.

58 *A Brief Account of the Mission established among the Esquimaux Indians on the coast of Labrador* (Ldn: The Brethren's Society for the Furtherance of the Gospel, 1774, printed by Lewis, 1 Paternoster Row); we consulted a microfilm copy at the NLS (microfilm, 3.39.728). This slender book drew from the diary of Johann Schneider who, with his wife and others, was one of the original Moravian missionaries to that area. Other contemporary publications, such as Schneider's *Diary* and Crantz' *History of Greenland,* are too ponderous to be read to children. If Ann Gardiner read to her children from articles in publications such as the *Gospel Magazine,* the stories would come from a similar source, and contain similar material.

59 Six-pence was half a shilling. In 1815, as an apprentice gardener, Moffat received 15 shillings a week. His father, as a Customs Officer, could afford a six-penny booklet.

60 Anon, *A Brief Account,* 13.

61 Ibid, 15f.

62 Ibid, 20ff.

savages may be greatly improved and rendered more human, yet it is certainly of incomparably greater importance, that they may be brought to Jesus Christ by the preaching of the gospel; that they may be sanctified by true faith in Him and thereby with greater certainty be civilised and made moral human creatures.'[63] Later LMS missionaries believed that evangelism brought civilisation, which in turn brought a higher morality. Thus, in this small book, along with the thrill of an adventurous narrative, the themes of preaching, piety, peacemaking, and moral transformation on a communal and individual level were central. Similar themes became presuppositions for Moffat in his own missionary life. They were present and prominent in all missionary literature of the time and became core values in Moffat's ministry at Kuruman.

Ann Gardiner: Her Love of Scripture

Ann Gardiner sought to instill into the hearts and minds of her children knowledge of, and reverence for, the Bible. One of the most quoted incidents between Moffat and his mother occurred when he left Scotland in 1813, to begin work as a gardener in England. Moffat described the scene in the Bible Society magazine *Gleanings for the Young,*[64] movingly relating how his mother tearfully implored him to do one special thing for her. He was loath to agree until he knew what it was. However, the emotion which his mother displayed made him assent unconditionally. She then told him her request:

> 'I only ask you whether you will read a chapter in the Bible every morning and another every evening?' I interrupted by saying: 'Mother, you know I read my Bible.' 'I know you do, but you do not read it regularly, or as a duty you owe God, its author'. And she added: 'Now I shall return home with a happy heart, inasmuch as you have promised to read the Scriptures daily. O Robert, my son, read much in the New Testament. Read much in the Gospels—the blessed Gospels: then you cannot well go astray. If you pray, the Lord Himself will teach you.'

Though it can be tempting to read too much significance into this incident, there are points in Moffat's account which reflect his later attitude to the Bible.[65] For example, from that date, and for every day of his life, Moffat had a regime of morning and evening prayers, which included reading Scripture. This consistent religious exercise became an unintended but valuable tool in mission, underlining to those around him the importance which he placed in

---

63 Ibid, 30.

64 Cf. JSM, *Lives,* 7ff. It was often alluded to by Moffat in his speeches.

65 Even if Moffat did not reproduce the exact words of the conversation, how he *chose* to report the incident gives insight into his thinking.

the written Word of God. Wherever he was: at Kuruman, travelling, or in a village, he loyally observed this exercise which originated as a filial promise.

Moffat recorded his mother as saying that such discipline was part of a 'duty you owe God'. In Moffat's account, the emphasis on the duty he owed God came before the benefits he would personally receive. For Robert Moffat, religion was first and foremost humanity's right *duty* to God; that was more important than any beneficial results which religion might impart. The glory of God came first. The blessing to humanity came second. Moffat's theology was a God-centred theology rather than a human-centred one. Men and women 'owed' God faith, obedience, repentance. In his preaching Moffat would emphasise that it was the duty of humanity to obey, love and worship God. As a 'preacher of righteousness'—never describing himself as an evangelist—he stressed that humanity begins to fulfill this calling to righteousness when the right obedience of faith is rendered to God.

In Moffat's account, his mother said: 'If you pray the Lord himself will teach you'. By quoting these words Moffat drew attention to a central tenet of his own understanding of the relationship between Scripture and the Christian. Moffat stressed that, for any person, despite lack of education and formal training, if a person humbly and prayerfully sought God as they read his Word, then understanding would be given to them. In southern Africa, especially with Chief Africaner,[66] Moffat noted how converts seemed to be given a miraculous capacity from God to drink in his Word and grasp its meaning at an astonishing level for people who were reading it for the first time. This convinced him that all that people needed in order for them to be converted was an ability to read and the Bible placed into their hands.[67] But did this reduce Moffat's drive to establish a formal training centre for Native Teachers? Did he think that if converts were taught to read and write, then putting the translated Word into their hands was enough? These questions are considered in our later chapters on indigenisation.

The over-riding concern of his mother was the centrality of the Bible. The sheer obviousness of this fact should not be overlooked. Whether Moffat truly reproduced the actual words of his mother, or whether his memory of her expressions was coloured by later emphases in his own theology, is not important. What is clear is that he highlighted the centrality of Scripture in her faith and in his faith. As a experienced missionary, he stressed that it was

---

66 RM, *MLSSA,* 109. Moffat and Livingstone noted the same with Chief Sechele.

67 RM, *To Jowett,* 8.4.1841, (CULBSA/Jowett/1841/2/28). Moffat emphasised the importance of placing translated Bibles into people's hands even more strongly in: RM, *To Bergne,* 22.5.1867, (CULBSA/BFBSEC/Inwards/5/198).

through the Bible that the Spirit of God operated, and that if the Bible taught such and such a thing then it was true. The Bible was the Word of God. Therefore, it was the immediate primary focus of faith.

Robert Moffat (Snr)

Robert Moffat (Snr) was born in 1768 to Alexander Moffat and his wife, Grizel Nicol, in the Parish of Pencaitland, East Lothian. Among the Quagga's Kerk *'Moffat Papers',* discovered in 1941, was a testimonial of residence, dated 19 December 1787, which stated that Robert Moffat (Snr) resided at Ormiston and was fit to be admitted unto any Christian society where 'Providence may order his lot.'[68] Robert (Snr) had started working life as a ploughman, but on 9 January 1797 was appointed by the Salt Commissioners to be an officer of the Salt Duty at Portsoy, Banffshire.[69] He stayed there until 1799, when the Salt Duty was merged with Excise, at which point he moved south to the River Forth which was a busy trading waterway. From 1799 until 1811 his duties as Coastal Warden were on the southern shores of the Firth of Forth. From 1811 until 1847, he held a similar post at Inverkeithing on the northern shore.[70]

A man appointed as a Customs Officer needed strength of character and an independent mind. Communities did not always approve of the government restrictions on 'free trade', especially concerning popular items such as wine, brandy, gin, spirits or salt. A Customs Officer, as custodian of the law, had to live with unpopularity. He required a strong sense of duty and correctness. On land, he could, in theory, call on local militia to assist him, but most of the public welcomed cheaper goods and cooperation was not readily given. Thus, Customs Officer Robert Moffat (Snr) had employment which did not attract popularity and which needed rectitude and moral fibre.

Robert Moffat (Snr) had each of his family baptised in the Church of Scotland, though his views seem to have had a latitudinarian aspect to them. The evidence for this lies in a letter he wrote to his son when the younger Robert was only sixteen. He encouraged young Robert to join the church at Polmont, near where he was currently employed:

---

68 Baxter & Burke (ed.), *Guide to the Historical Manuscripts of Rhodesia,* 324.

69 Ibid, 324. Smith, *The Scottish Smuggler,* (Edin: Birlinn, 2003), 34f: 'Salt was extremely important to the Scottish economy, as it was an essential preservative for the fishing industry and for meat, which was preserved in brine. ... Salt was an easy target for taxation, being such an essential commodity ... The collection of 'salt duties' occupied a large part of the customs officers' working hours in most outports.'

70 'Moffat Cottage' is a private house in Inverkeithing, and is noted as the place where David Livingstone once stayed on a visit to the grandparents of his wife, Mary Moffat (Jnr).

> I shall only say that it is certainly incumbent on every person when they become of age to join themselves to some Christian church or other. You must necessarily be the best judge yourself.[71]

The phrase 'some Christian church or other' indicates that the father was not insisting that it be the established Church of Scotland that his son should join. Any Christian church would do. Understandably, he could not insist on young Robert joining the established Kirk, since his feisty, spirited wife, both by example and by nurture, had made a strong statement for independence of choice in spiritual matters. It also appears that, by the time Robert Moffat (Snr) went to live in Inverkeithing in 1811, his allegiance to the Kirk was weakening. In Inverkeithing he no longer attended the Church of Scotland but went to Ebenezer Brown's Associate Burgher Church along with his wife and the rest of the family. Evidence that Robert Moffat (Snr) may not have been a member of the Inverkeithing Church of Scotland lies in its membership lists: he is not named in any of the Communion Roll lists for Inverkeithing Church of Scotland, though he lived until 1847.[72]

There is other evidence that young Robert Moffat, after he started work as a gardener at Donibristle, near Inverkeithing, was closely allied with Ebenezer Brown's ministry. Before he left for Africa in 1816, he spoke with the Rev. Dr Waugh in London during his examination by the LMS Directors. Dr Waugh said to him: 'Are you not one of Ebbie Brune's lads?' To which, Moffat replied: 'I had heard him frequently and knew him well.'[73] In an 1835 letter to his brother Richard, Moffat asked to be remembered to the Rev. E. Brown.[74] Additionally, on deputation in 1842, Moffat spoke at a missionary meeting in what had been Brown's church.[75] It appears that the Rev. Ebenezer Brown had become minister for the whole Moffat family. Though Brown's influence on young Robert was not as lengthy as that of the Rev. Robert Caldwell in Falkirk, the choice of ministry indicates the kind of piety

---

71 Moffat (Snr), *To RM*, 22.6.1812, (Baxter & Burke, *Guide,* 325).

72 Cf. *Communion Roll of Inverkeithing Church of Scotland: 1844-1856,* (NAS/CH2/195/44). There is no corresponding extant list of members for Inverkeithing Associate Burgher Church for the period in question; but if Robert Moffat (Snr) did join it, then he was never an elder. Cf. *Session Minutes of Inverkeithing Associate Burgher Church* from 1820 onwards, (NAS/CH3/452/3).

73 RM, *To his Parents,* 23.9.1816 (JSM, *Lives,* 26).

74 RM, *To Richard Moffat,* 12.6.1835, (*MJ1,* 138).

75 *The Scotsman,* 2.11.1842: 'On the evening of Monday last, the friends of this indefatigable missionary assembled in the Secession Church of Inverkeithing and presented him with a gold watch and chain'. The *Scotsman* noted that the meeting was crowded, with the Rev. J.D. Fleming in the chair and Moffat giving a blessing at the end. The Rev. Fleming had been ordained as colleague to Ebenezer Brown on 15.12.1835 and succeeded him after his death on 28.3.1836. Cf. MacKelvie, *Annals and Statistics of the United Presbyterian Church,* 182.

now favoured by the whole Moffat household: clearly evangelical and non-conformist—in the Scottish sense—being a Secessionist piety rather than that of the established Parish church. It would, of course, still be Calvinist, since all Scottish denominations saw themselves as part of a Calvinist heritage.

The only extant documentary evidence concerning Robert Moffat (Snr)'s view on theological matters comes in correspondence he had with his son after young Robert moved to England in 1813 to work as a gardener at High Leigh, Manchester. When Robert had a conversion experience through Methodist influence whilst at High Leigh, he informed his parents what had happened. His father replied with a letter which included both thankfulness to God and cautionary advice to his son. He focused on two matters: the conversion experience itself, and Robert's association with the Methodists.

On conversion, his father was pleased that Robert had 'got sight of the evil nature of sin', but he urged his son not to be 'high-minded, but to fear'.[76] What was meant by 'high-minded'? The letter indicates that Robert (Snr) had in mind spiritual ecstasies, such as being 'brought up into the third heaven' and seeing things which were not 'lawful to utter'. His concern was about the danger of spiritual pride through his son having had a special religious experience. The father reminded Robert that intense spiritual experiences brought intense temptation, citing the Apostle Peter who, 'although he made more pretensions of love to the Saviour than any of the disciples, yet how soon was he tempted of the adversary of souls to deny his great Lord and Master'.[77] Robert (Snr) stressed that it was more important to 'fear God' than to claim exceptional spirituality. Obedience in discipleship was paramount. This raises intriguing questions. Did Robert (Snr) understand conversion as being a change in his son's status before God from 'death' to 'life'? Did he understand it in terms of 'being saved' as understood in evangelical piety? Or did he regard its importance primarily in bringing home to his son a deep sense of sin and unworthiness before God, resulting in profound moral change? The extracts from his letter, as preserved in John S. Moffat's *Lives,* suggest that the central aspect, as far as Robert (Snr) was concerned, was a profound sense of sin and unworthiness. In this respect, Robert (Snr) had focussed on a major emphasis of Scottish Calvinist spirituality.

On Robert's association with the Methodists, his father urged him to exercise caution:

---

76 Moffat (Snr), *To RM,* (JSM, *Lives,* 14).

77 Ibid, 15.

> You seem to be much attached to the Methodists. I verily believe they are a set of men who have done much good. But at the same time, I do not altogether go in with some of their tenets; and, as there are different sects of these preachers, some of which are said not to be very sound in the faith, it would take one to examine well for themselves, and to follow them no further than they follow the Word of God.[78]

Robert's mother may have been more enthusiastic about the Methodist connection, insofar as she had worshipped contentedly in the Congregationalist tradition at Falkirk. However, her possible Burgher background might have tempered this.[79] Nevertheless, Robert (Snr) appears to have belonged to the old school of Scottish Presbyterianism which frowned at Methodism. This is most likely what he had in mind when he wrote: 'I do not altogether go in with some of their tenets.' John S. Moffat—without directly citing the letters in question—recorded that young Robert replied to his father's letter, stoutly defending his friends. JSM added that there was evidently a severe struggle in his mind 'between the Calvinistic faith of his fathers in which he had been brought up, and the teachings to which he was now listening'.[80] Was young Robert experiencing a tension in his own mind? Or was he struggling with the awkward situation of having to defend his new principles to his father? John Smith Moffat, with unique access to family 'table-talk', may have represented something which was shared with him: that, at the time of young Robert's conversion, there had been a theological struggle in his thinking. Northcott caught the situation well: 'In the year of Waterloo he expounded to Inverkeithing the differences between Wesley and Whitefield in pious phraseology.'[81]

Robert Moffat's father was a cautious man. In every circumstance he advised prudence and carefulness. Thus when, at the close of 1815, Robert diffidently wrote home to his parents to tell them he was ceasing work at High Leigh and taking up new employment near Manchester, his father immediately sensed that Robert had wider plans. In his letter, Robert confessed to his parents that his new wages should be fifteen shillings per week, but that 'mine will be only twelve or thirteen, on account that I will only work five days in a week'. The reason for this—not yet confided to his parents—was that he no longer worked on Saturdays, to have time to be taught by William Roby with a view to missionary service. But his father read

---

78 Ibid, 15.

79 John Brown of Haddington, father to Ebenezer Brown of Inverkeithing, set out Burgher reservations concerning Methodism. Cf. John Brown, *An Historical Account of the Rise and Progress of the Secession,* (Edin: Guthrie & Tait, 1819), 60f.

80 JSM, *Lives,* 15.

81 Northcott, *Robert Moffat,* 21.

between the lines. He cautioned his son to think over the whole issue carefully and soberly:

> You have left us to conjecture how you are to employ yourself on the sixth day. But if my opinion be rightly founded, I presume that you mean to endeavour to fit yourself for another line of life; but I would have you duly to consider the importance of such an undertaking, and to weigh well what our Saviour says to the builder in the Scriptures, and to first sit down and count the cost, and to see whether you have sufficient to finish or not ... We think that you might both live usefully to your neighbours and profitably to yourself without engaging in a line of that kind; neither do we think that your health would altogether agree with such an undertaking, as I verily believe that you will find a close application to study as hard an undertaking as anything you have hitherto engaged in.[82]

This response was characteristic of Robert (Snr). His son would exemplify the same characteristics of 'dour common-sense'. The father wedded spirituality to careful wisdom, not to flights of fancy.

When, in May of the following year, Robert told his parents his full plans, they loyally supported him, though fearful they might never see him again. In this, and in a youthful incident of going off to sea, they had the view that he was free to make his own decisions so long as he thought things through properly. When the time came for departure for Africa, Robert (Snr) bid 'his son God speed, declaring that whatever may be his own feelings and those of Robert's mother, they dare not oppose his design, lest haply in so doing they should be found fighting against God.'[83] His influence on his son may not have been as fiery and passionate as that of Robert's mother, but there was conviction in his religion. Carefulness, caution, and a sense of the vital importance of obedience to God came from his Calvinist heritage, along with strong moral character. Robert Moffat (Snr) retired from his position as Coastal Warden in 1847, fifty years after entering the service. He died a few months later.

---

82 Moffat (Snr), *To RM*, (JSM, *Lives,* 21).

83 JSM, *Lives,* 22.

Chapter 2
School, Catechism and Church

EVER SINCE THE REFORMATION and Knox's call for a national system of education, Scotland had, in theory, placed a high value on universal schooling. However, despite good intentions and a series of Acts of the Scottish and Union Parliaments, the situation at the beginning of the eighteenth century was poor.[1] Various Acts placed responsibility with local heritors[2] to make things happen, but the laws were widely ignored. Fortunately, matters improved during the century. In the Lowlands, if not in the Highlands, there were opportunities for large sections of the community. Basic instruction became available to the lowest and poorest; as well as to the highest and richest. Herman has cited well-documented evidence that, by 1750, seventy-five percent of Scottish Lowland children could read, compared with only fifty-three percent of those in England.[3] A major motivating factor in the Scottish context was the desire to read the 'Word': Scotland saw itself as the Land of the Book.

SCHOOL

Until the 1872 Education Act, most Scottish schools, whether Parish Schools or Burgh Schools, were closely linked to the local Kirk Session of the established Church and were under the supervision of the local Presbytery.

---

1 Graham, *Social Life of Scotland in the Eighteenth Century,* 417. The 1627 *Commissioner's Report on the State of Parishes* testified that most parishes were without a school, schoolmaster, or any means of maintaining one. A 1633 Act attempted to remedy this, as did one in 1643, another in 1696, and yet another in 1748. In 1802 the Schoolmasters' Act was passed, which gave clear parameters for the salaries of schoolmasters, along with security of income. As a consequence, this gave the scholars security of education.

2 'Heritors' were local landowners who financed local public projects, such as the building and maintenance of churches and schools. The heritor system applied mostly in rural parishes. In towns and cities, the role was carried out by 'burgesses.' Parish schools were inspected by the Presbytery; Burgh schools by the Town Council. A candidate to be a schoolmaster for a parish school had to pass a rigid examination, mainly in theology, before the Presbytery. A candidate for a similar post in a Burgh school had to pass an examination in Latin, English, arithmetic, poetry, and the ability to sing a psalm, before an investigating committee consisting of the Minister and some Council representatives (Graham, *Social Life, 434*).

3 Herman, *The Scottish Enlightenment,* (Ldn: Fourth Estate, Harper Collins, 2001), 19f.

The Church of Scotland enjoined a duty of inspection on Presbyteries: 'the General Assembly of the Church of Scotland, sensible that the invaluable blessings of a religious life, and the happiness and permanent security of every well-regulated government are chiefly founded in the early education of every class of the community, have widely appointed a Presbyterial visitation and examination, yearly, of all the schools in Scotland.'[4]

Church influence meant that Calvinist factors were strong in the education of children. Moffat's school years were when the family lived around Carronshore, in the Presbytery of Linlithgow, with that Presbytery on record as being particularly assiduous in supervising schools. For example, at the close of the year 1799, the Presbytery of Linlithgow summoned all the public and private teachers within their bounds, 'in order to examine them as to their general qualifications for the duties of their office and to ascertain if they had neglected to take the Oath of Allegiance'.[5] The curriculum, within the Falkirk area where Moffat went to school, included: 'Principles of the Christian Religion, the Assembly's Catechism and Proofs, repeating the Scriptures, as well as English and Arithmetic.'[6] The Catechism was usually the *Shorter Catechism*, though, in 1799, one schoolmaster, a Mr Dunlop, taught *Brown's Catechism.*[7] Catechical Instruction was central in eighteenth-century Scottish education. In his study, *Education in Stirlingshire from the Reformation to the Act of 1872,* Andrew Bain commented on the 1728 regulations, which required children to learn the Catechism by heart, and to have a knowledge of the principles of Christianity, with one hour per week to be spent by the teacher on hearing the repetition of the Catechism and on proposing explanatory questions, 'for their inner ease and growth in

---

4 Sinclair, *The First Statistical Account of Scotland, 1791-1799, Vol.19,* 438. Even schools not under the direct governance of a Kirk Session were inspected, supervised and authorised by the Presbytery. There were a few independent 'adventure' schools, mainly in the major towns and cities, plus a few for poor families in parts of the country. Population growth necessitated more schools; every 'adventure school' saved the expense of a public one.

5 Love, *Schools and Schoolmasters,* 67f. Cf. Graham, *Social Life,* 35, who referred to the scruples of Jacobites in taking the oath of allegiance to a Hanoverian King. The zeal of the Presbytery of Linlithgow in the supervision of educational standards was not temporary: 'In 1809 we find the Presbytery of Linlithgow objecting to the mode in which one schoolmaster of Falkirk, a Mr. Young, examined his pupils' (Love, 75). According to the report, Mr Young lost his temper in dramatic fashion.

6 Love, *Schools and Schoolmasters*, 68.

7 Ibid, 68. William Brown was born in 1784, and his catechism was not written until around 1812. Thus, the *Brown's Catechism* which Mr Dunlop taught would have been an edition of John Brown of Haddington's work, *An Help for the Ignorant,* (1758), which tried to explain the *Shorter Catechism* more clearly.

Christian knowledge.'[8]

As the eighteenth century progressed, education widened from the strict syllabus of Bible, Catechism, Writing and Arithmetic, which had been the sum total at its start.[9] Nevertheless, the importance of teaching the principles of the Christian Faith—especially the doctrines of the Catechism—remained constant. The published version of the *Shorter Catechism,* which was made available to school-children, included not only religious knowledge, but was typically printed with the following aids to education and spirituality in one slim booklet:

The Shorter Catechism

Multiplication Tables

The Lord's Prayer

The Apostle's Creed

A Grace for before a meal and a Grace for after a meal

List of Roman Numerals

A shorter and easier Catechism for Children inside the rear cover

A Morning Hymn and an Evening Hymn

An ABC of the letters of the Alphabet

This one volume was a primer for general education, with each child exposed to the religious and spiritual tradition represented by the *Shorter Catechism*, or one of a similar nature. Thus, each child learned Reading, Writing and Arithmetic from a theological textbook. All education was regarded as Christian education. Whatever draw-backs there may have been in the Scottish system in terms of curriculum or quality, one thing was clear and served as a foundational principle: education was the door to holiness and progress, since education brought the ability to absorb the principles of the Word of God. Education, godliness, and the social good went together. The entry for the Parish of Dunning, in Sinclair's *First Statistical Account of* Scotland, typical of the times, stated that the surest and firmest part of the 'foundation of private and public happiness is laid in an early education', in which 'the principles of the Christian religion, the teaching of which is the most prominent feature of education in parochial schools, are so deeply rooted in the soul, that they become the means of preserving thousands

---

8 Bain, *Education in Stirlingshire from the Reformation to the Act of 1872*, (Ldn: University of London Press, 1964), 128.

9 Ibid, 117.

from infidelity, and a life of immorality and wretchedness.'[10] Moffat took this view to Africa and made it central in his work at Kuruman.

Moffat's introduction to formal education was through Mr William (Wully) Mitchell, the Bothkennar parish schoolmaster, with *The Shorter Catechism* his first instruction book.[11] At school, his 'progress was but slow, his hands often being made to suffer for the dullness of his brains'.[12] John Smith Moffat recorded that, after learning the alphabet A,B,C of the title page, his father, as with all his fellow pupils, had to start learning the questions and answers of the *Catechism:* 'I went plump into the first question: What is the chief end of man? I tugged away at this till I got to the Amen'.[13]

Mitchell was a strong disciplinarian. Speaking in London, in 1873, Moffat stated that he left school as a consequence of the severity of the master, who, though his left side was paralyzed, had 'awful power in his right'.[14] The 'awful power' referred to punishment in Scottish schools which, until late in the twentieth century, was given by the teacher hitting the outstretched hand of the pupil with a length of thick leather, the 'strap' or 'taws'. This stifling environment was not for Moffat. On his doorstep was the Firth of Forth, full of great sailing vessels: at the mouth of the Firth was the open sea. Books were abandoned and at the age of ten the young Moffat 'ran off to sea'. His parents displayed a remarkably tolerant understanding of their son's behaviour and regularised this escapade. With their consent, Robert made several voyages in the coasting trade on the vessel of a friend of the family. After his adventurous appetites were satisfied—for the time being—he left the sea 'to the no small joy of my parents'.[15]

At the age of about eleven Robert accompanied his older brother, Alexander, to William Paton's school at Falkirk. This school was mainly for writing and bookkeeping, but senior pupils were given the opportunity to learn astronomy and geography after school hours.[16] Alexander was such a pupil, and Robert waited for him in the large classroom where the lessons were given. Robert later recalled that he listened to these lessons attentively.

---

10 Sinclair, *The First Statistical Account for Scotland, 1791-1799, Vol. 19,* 438. This extract typifies educational theory in Presbyterian Scotland. Christian education was the justification for all education.

11 RM, *Letter* (undated), (JSM, *Lives,* 2).

12 Deane, *Robert Moffat,* 21.

13 RM, *Letter* (undated), (JSM, *Lives,* 2).

14 *The Haddingtonshire Courier,* 28.3.1873.

15 RM, *Letter* (undated), (JSM, *Lives,* 3).

16 Ibid.

'What I could not understand my brother explained on our way home'. He absorbed an elementary awareness of astronomy and geography. Attendance at Paton's school continued for six months. Moffat wrote that it was 'the last I ever attended'.

Paton's School had a good reputation, with Paton mentioned, along with others, as having been examined by the Presbytery of Linlithgow in 1799. As part of the inspection, he had to produce a certificate as evidence that he had taken the Oath of Allegiance to the King which was imposed on all schoolteachers. He satisfied the Presbytery, unlike an anti-Burgher named Barclay who declined taking the Oath.[17] Many years later Paton was remembered by the older generation in the Falkirk area, as a celebrated 'teacher of writing' who had been active from 1793 if not earlier.[18]

After leaving school, Moffat started work as an apprentice gardener. He attended occasional evening classes and studied Latin and mensuration. He also picked up some knowledge of blacksmithing,[19] and learned to play the violin. These were useful skills in Africa. Once, at Africaner's village, it was necessary to repair a wagon, and Moffat needed a forge with bellows. He made a set from two goat-skins and a circular piece of board, and used a blue granite stone as an anvil. Rudimentary tongs and hammer helped complete the task.[20] Moffat's *Journals* have several other references to blacksmithing in remote places, with bellows manufactured from whatever was available.

Moffat was an inquisitive learner. John Smith Moffat wrote that his father 'had a craving, which clung to him through life, to learn something of whatever he came in contact with, and many of the accomplishments of which he thus gained a smattering proved of unlooked-for value to him afterwards.'[21] This intellectual curiosity made him maximise his natural abilities. Most cultures have examples of men and women, born in poor conditions, and recipients of broken formal education, who, in later life, display significant ability. Moffat was such. He gained passable proficiency in Dutch, SeTswana, Greek and Hebrew, as well as in numerous practical skills. Within the strong-willed and rebellious boy lay an able mind.

---

17 Love, *Schools and Schoolmasters,* 68. Anti-Burghers were more extreme in rejecting anything that savoured of alliance with the State. The Independency views of Ann Gardiner did not stretch to insisting that her children be only educated by someone who would reject the Oath of Allegiance. Thus, if she was Secessionist, she was not anti-Burgher.

18 Ibid, 68f.

19 RM, *MLSSA,* 116f.

20 Deane, *Robert Moffat,* 23.

21 JSM, *Lives,* 5.

CATECHISM

Catechical Instruction was central in eighteenth and nineteenth-century Scottish schools, with the *raison d'etre* behind Scottish education being the conviction that reading was important because a person who could read would have access to Bible and Catechism. Emphasis on catechical instruction in Scotland came with the Reformation.[22] A 1581 Catechism by John Craig was the first Scottish Catechism to have widespread use in the Kirk. This was supplemented by *A Form of Examination before Communion* (1592) which was given the full authority of the Kirk at the 1592 General Assembly.[23] The Assembly ruled that this short catechism should be purchased by congregations, read in families, and taught in schools. It remained in use until it was displaced by the Westminster Assembly's *Shorter Catechism* of 1647.[24]

The *Shorter Catechism* eventually gained domination in the Scottish Kirk, but it did not have an immediate monopoly. Several Catechisms were used for Christian instruction in both church and school. That a schoolmaster, such as Dunlop of Linlithgow Presbytery, chose to use *Brown's Catechism* instead of the *Shorter Catechism* was not unusual. Even where the *Shorter Catechism* was drilled into the pupils at school, at home it might be supplemented by a parent's favourite choice. For the generation of Moffat's parents, as well as his own generation, several Catechisms were in regular use in cottage-piety.

The Westminster *Shorter Catechism* was not Moffat's first choice in mission work, despite knowing it well, having been taught it at school by William Mitchell. Eventually, in 1835, he translated it into SeTswana. Writing in his *Journal,* on his second visit to the Ndebele chief, Moselekatse, he stated: 'I shall now commence translating the *Assembly's Catechism*, to be done at intervals, being a work I can do at intervals, which is not the case with Scripture, which requires me to refer to many books. The former is a human composition, and admits of some latitude being taken.'[25] Moffat's translation was completed in three weeks. On 9 July 1835, he wrote: 'Tonight

---

22 Lachman, 'Catechisms: Scots and English', (*DSCHT,* 142f).

23 T.F. Torrance, *The School of Faith,* (Ldn: James Clarke, 1959), 97ff & 243ff. The full title of the 1581 work was, *A Short Sum of the Whole Catechism wherein the Question is put and answered in few words for the greater Ease of the Common People and Children.1581.* The 1592 publication was known as *A Form of Examination before Communion,* or, more simply, *Craig's Short Catechism.* John Craig was a Dominican theologian who converted through reading Calvin's *Institutes* in Italy. He returned to Scotland in 1561. From 1579 to 1594 he was chaplain to the King, and minister of the Church of the Palace of Holyroodhouse in Edinburgh.

24 Graham, *Social Life,* 438, records usage in the eighteenth century.

25 RM, *To Mary Moffat,* 17.6.1835, (*MJ1,* 84).

I have completed a kind of translation of the *Assembly's Catechism*. It has been with sufficient difficulty, for though I lead a wretched idle kind of life, yet I meet with innumerable hindrances to study and straightforward writing.'[26] There is no doubt that Moffat held the *Shorter Catechism* in high regard. Yet, though the Westminster Fathers believed that the *Shorter Catechism* was a text suitable for the young and those of less intellectual ability, it was often judged too difficult for both home-field and the mission-field. In Moffat's view, *Brown's Catechism* was simpler, though from the 1840s onward the *Shorter Catechism* was also used at Kuruman.

In place of the *Shorter Catechism*, David Bogue and William Roby—both intimately involved with the LMS and influential on Moffat—recommended John Willison's works. Willison had been a minister in Dundee and was the author of several influential evangelical devotional publications. His *Mother's Catechism* (c.1700) *was* well used in Scotland, England and farther afield. Its full title was: *A Mother's Catechism: being a Preparatory Help for the Young and Ignorant to their easier Understanding the Assembly's Shorter Catechism.* As the longer title reveals, it was designed to be a simple introduction to the *Shorter Catechism,* since that was proving difficult for the young. Though Willison wrote his simpler catechism with the intention that it should be a bridge to the *Shorter Catechism,* many preferred to remain with Willison's version. Bogue, the official LMS tutor at Gosport Seminary, recommended *Willison's Catechism* as eminently suitable for the mission field.[27] Roby also recommended Willison's works to the students whom he prepared for mission.[28]

Following the example of the Westminster Assembly, authors of catechisms often published two versions: a longer work, and a shorter, simpler composition, with David Bogue recommending that missionaries should follow this practice.[29] Dr John Brown of Haddington's two popular catechisms, published in the mid-eighteenth century, were affectionately known as *'Big Broon'* and *'Little Broon'*.[30] The author saw them as simply explications of the *Assembly's Catechism,* though this modest claim does not

---

26 RM, *Journal,* 9.7.1835, (*MJ1,* 106).

27 Cf. Moffat's 1817 copy of, Bogue *Miss. Lect.* 8, 'On Catechising'. Moffat followed Bogue's general advice closely but used *Brown's Catechism*. Bogue also recommended Isaac Watts' Children's Catechism. Cf. Roby, *Miss. Lect.* 9, 'On Writing and Publishing Books'.

28 Cf. Roby, *Theol. Lect.* 76, 'The Lord's Supper', where Roby recommended Willison, *On the Sacraments.* Also, *Lect.* 80, 'Family Religion'. Roby recommended Willison, *On the Sabbath*.

29 Bogue, *Miss. Lect.* 8, 'On Catechising'.

30 The editions which we consulted were: John Brown, *Two Short Catechisms, mutually connected,* (edited by Ebenezer Brown, Paisley: S&A Young, 1811: NLS Microfilm copy Mf.13(4[8]).

do justice to the radical restructuring of the catechical questions under John Brown's pen, or to his creative theological approach. In *'Big Broon',* Brown started with the Trinity, relating it to salvation: *'Q1. Who made you? God: Q2. Who redeems you? Christ: Q3. Who sanctifies you? The Holy Spirit.'* And in his Christological sections Brown used the *Triplex Munus* of Christ as Prophet, Priest, and King, as his basic framework. John Brown explained that the Redeemer had this three-fold office in order to 'cure my three-fold misery' of Ignorance, Guilt and Bondage'. Christ as Prophet educated through Word and Spirit (to take away Ignorance). Christ as Priest obeyed God's law and died for me (to take away Guilt). Christ as King delivered me from the power of sin and Satan (to take away Bondage). As an aside, our observation is that if John Brown's third way of understanding the atonement—with its *Christus Victor* paradigm—had been used more in the African context, then evangelism might have been greatly aided. John Brown's Catechisms had a beauty in both form and content, and were popular in Scotland and abroad. Yet that beauty came with a sophistication which made his catechisms still difficult for the mission field. To present the doctrine of the Trinity in the first three questions and answers is perhaps good dogmatics, but difficult evangelism.[31] It was his son, William Brown, who radically simplified his father's works.

BROWN'S CATECHISM

William Brown, John Brown's son, composed a catechism which was to prove supremely suitable for the young. And it was the son's composition which, in the nineteenth century, became popularly known as *Brown's Catechism,*[32] a title which his father's work had held previously. The son's version was simpler, and of a different structure to his father's. For example, the first three questions and answers of William Brown's work are: *Q1. Who made*

[31] Willison's popular *Mother's Catechism* did just that. Its opening was similar to John Brown's Catechism: 'Who made you? God. Who is it that redeems you? Christ. Who is it that sanctifies you? The Holy Ghost. Of what are you made? Of dust. What doth that teach you? To be humble and mindful of death.'

[32] The copy of (William) *Brown's Catechism* we accessed was the 1820 2nd edn in the British Library: William Brown, *Christian Instructions for Children from Three to Seven years of age, Containing: a Catechism; Passages of Scripture; Hymns,* (2nd Ed. Edin: James Robertson, 1820). There is also a copy in EUNCL, published by William Oliphant of Edinburgh, but has no date. Copies are extremely rare, and there is no copy in the NLS, or at the Kuruman Moffat Mission Library. An 1831 second edition of Moffat's SeTswana translation of *Brown's Catechism* was consulted in the Grey Collection, NLSA, Cape Town (Grey/9/c/3/8), and has the title: *Buka ea Pocho ea Tuto le Poluko tsa Yesu Kereste.* Moffat's SeTswana *Brown's Catechism* followed the English one almost question for question, occasionally omitting a difficult question, and sometimes inserting an extra one.

the sun, the moon, and the stars? It was God: Q2. Who made the sea, the trees, and the beasts? It was God: Q3. Who made you? It was God.'[33] If these wonderfully simple statements are compared with the opening questions and answers of John Brown's, then the suitability of William's version for pioneer mission amongst hitherto unreached peoples becomes self-evident.

Composing an easily understood Catechism might be expected of a man such as William Brown, who had a passion for foreign mission. As early as 1814, when thirty-one years of age, he wrote and published one of the first major works on Foreign Mission, entitled, *History of the Propagation of Christianity among the Heathen since the Reformation,* and he trained as a Doctor of Medicine to prepare himself for the mission-field. This aspiration was not realised, though he was ordained with the intention of going to China. When service abroad came to nothing, he became Secretary to the Scottish Missionary Society. It was *Brown's Catechism* of 1812, which Moffat took to Africa and which was the first theological document ever translated into SeTswana. In 1822 Moffat wrote to Burder of the LMS:

> I have translated Dr William Brown's Catechism in his '*Christian Instructions*'. The catechism being originally intended for children, I have made a few alterations and additions. It is the most suitable I ever met with, is used, and well understood.[34]

Brown's Catechism was central in Moffat's early missionary work. He translated it in 1822 at the outset of his missionary career, while he was still learning SeTswana. It was not until 1835, 13 years later, that he translated the *Assembly's Catechism*. Smith commented that he had a copy of Moffat's SeTswana Catechism on his desk as he wrote his biography of Moffat. Smith did not say that the translation was of *Brown's Catechism,* but his description leaves little doubt. He stated that before him, as he wrote, lay 'a little volume of thirty-five pages, containing a Catechism, in the form of one hundred and thirty-six questions and answers, and some portions of Scripture which—except perhaps for a primer or two—was the first book published in the Chuana language.'[35] In the 1823 Report to the 29th LMS Annual Meeting, Moffat's achievement was highlighted:

---

33 Brown, *Christian Instructions for Children from Three to Seven years of age, Containing: a Catechism; Passages of Scripture; Hymns,* Q&R: 1-3. These simple questions and answers were replicated in Moffat's SeTswana translation.

34 RM, *To Burder, LMS,* 5.8.1822, (*AAK,* 53).

35 Smith, *Robert Moffat: One of God's Gardeners,* 168. Smith gave details of the publication, recording that the title page read: 'Bechuana Catechism, with translation of the third chapter of the Gospel by John, the Lord's Prayer, and other passages of Scripture, etc. in that language, by Mr. Robert Moffat, Missionary at Lattakoo: Printed for the LMS by J. Dennett, Leather Lane,

> Mr. Moffat has attempted a translation into Boschuana of the Catechism contained in Dr W. Brown's *'Christian Instructions'*, with the requisite adaptation to adults, it having been originally intended exclusively for children. This Catechism is in use and is well understood by the Boschuanas. Mr. Moffat has also attempted several smaller translations, for the use of the people, among which is one of the Lord's Prayer.[36]

The first edition was printed in London in 1826.[37] Moffat revised his translation in 1828. At that time, he added translations of passages of Scripture which had been printed in English versions of *Brown's Catechism,* following the Questions and Answers.[38] For many years, this was the 'Kuruman Catechism' and was frequently reissued. The LMS 1833 Annual Report stated: 'Mr. Moffat printed an enlarged edition of 500 copies of *Brown's Catechism* and *Christian Instructions*, Scripture Lessons for Schools on the British System and a number of hymns.'[39] Even a cursory examination of *Brown's Catechism* quickly reveals why his was preferred to the *Shorter Catechism.*[40] The questions and answers are brief, clear, and unmistakably direct.

Catechical instruction, both in methodology and content, was influential in Moffat's own spiritual formation. And David Bogue, in his *Missionary Lectures,* which were diligently transcribed by Moffat in 1817, also gave a prominent place to catechising. Bogue recommended that both the teacher

---

Holborn, 1826.' Smith's details correspond with those of the 1831 SeTswana version in the Grey Collection. The second edition of the English version of *Brown's Catechism* had Scripture verses after the Questions and Answers, but John 3 was not included. Presumably, if such an important passage of Scripture had been in the 1st edn, it would not have been omitted from the 2nd edn. Introducing John 3 into the SeTswana version may have been Moffat's decision, underlining the doctrine of regeneration through spiritual rebirth.

36 LMS: *Report to the 29th Annual Meeting, 1823*, 103.

37 Moffat (tr.), *Buka ea Pocho ea Tuto le Poluko tsa Yesu Kereste,* (Ldn: LMS, 1926). On 15.3.1827, the LMS Directors wrote to Moffat: 'By this opportunity we shall send out a case, addressed to the care of the Rev. Mr. Miles, containing the Bechuana Spelling-book and Catechism, 1000 copies of each, with strong covers adapted to the use of young children' (*AAK,* footnote 29, 272).

38 RM, *To Richard Moffat,* 30.12.1828, (*AAK,* 290).

39 LMS: *Report to the 39th Annual Meeting, 1833*, 92.

40 In 1822 the *Heidelberg Catechism* was circulating in the Cape Colony in a Dutch version. Moffat did not refer to the *Heidelberg Catechism* but would know of it. He may have judged it too difficult for new converts. On the translation of the *Heidelberg Catechism* into English and its authorisation for use in the Colony see, *Letter from the Cape Governor to the Political Commissioner,* 7.7.1825, in: Hofmeyr, Millard, Froneman (eds), *History of the Church in South Africa: A Document and Source Book,* (Pretoria: UNISA, 1991), 87.

and the pupil should learn a simple Catechism by heart, and listed the following benefits:[41]

1. The heathen receive into their minds the knowledge of Christianity.[42]
2. Their prejudices against Christianity will be sensibly overcome.
3. Many falsehoods and superstitions are banished from their minds.
4. They are prepared for effective hearing of the preaching of the word.
5. Conscience is made more susceptible of useful impressions of Providence.
6. Those who are catechised can convey many useful ideas to other heathen.
7. Catechising will be often found to be the means of conversion.

But to what extent did Robert Moffat apply Bogue's principles in his usage of *Brown's Catechism?* Firstly, he memorised it. Whilst living in the villages in 1827, on concentrated language study, Robert wrote to Mary at Kuruman: 'The difference of dialect made me at first think that I had lost what I knew on the road, but by daily intercourse I became the more familiar with the sounds and phrases which I may hear every hour. I committed the whole of the Catechism, etc., to memory, which also became better stored with a variety of words, by which I find that I am able to reason with and address them in a way pretty well understood'.[43]

Secondly, he based evangelism on it. Moffat used the *Catechism* as the basis for discussion, with his preaching and evangelism invariably along the lines of the *Catechism's* teaching, vocabulary and phraseology. As early as 1825 he wrote: 'We visit the Bechuanas regularly, and every Sabbath a catechetical meeting is held in their language.'[44] Thirdly, he encouraged Africans to read it. In February 1828, he noted: 'There are already four Bechuanas who are reading Mr Brown's *Catechism* in their own language, and in a short time I trust to be enabled to put a number more into that class.'[45]

Fourthly, he encouraged converts to memorise it. Later in 1828, Mary Moffat wrote to her father with encouraging news: 'The attendance on public worship is very good. A chapel must soon be built, Mr Hughe's dwelling house being much too small. The singing goes on charmingly, and to hear many of them repeat the catechism [Brown's], with copious extracts from

---

41 Bogue, *Miss. Lect.* 8, 'On Catechising'.

42 At the start of the nineteenth century the word heathen' was used to refer to people unenlightened by the Christian revelation. Respected figures in European history, such as Plato and Pythagoras, were also termed 'heathen', cf. Roby, *Theol. Lect.* 10.

43 RM, *To Mary Moffat,* 25.4.1827, (*AAK,* 264).

44 RM, *Journal,* 30.5.1825, (*AAK,* 191).

45 RM, *To Richard Moffat,* 15.2.1828, (*AAK,* 281).

scripture, is very gratifying. The fixed and serious attention of some of them to the preacher induces us to hope that the Spirit is at work in their hearts.'[46] This letter came just before the 1829 spiritual 'Awakening' at Kuruman.

Some statements in Brown's *Catechism* may have caused bewilderment among the Tswana as they tried to make sense of the missionary teaching. Moffat was not always aware of this bafflement, since listening was normally marked by great politeness, though he occasionally mentioned laughter when he stressed a particular point.[47] In an African context, laughter is not necessary a sign of ridicule. It can signify incredulity. Both the ridiculous and the incredulous give rise to laughter, and laughter in response to some of Moffat's teaching may have been occasioned by the strangeness of his teaching in relation to traditional beliefs. Sometimes *Brown's Catechism* would challenge traditional beliefs. Sometimes it would appear to homologate established ideas. These are illustrated by the following examples.

Question 12 asked: 'Does God always see you?'[48] The *Catechism's* answer was: 'Yes: he sees me wherever I am, both by night and by day'. But there was a strong Tswana belief that the night made a person 'invisible' to 'God'. Clegg, in a study on Tswana cosmology, concluded: 'The sun is the eye (or the lantern) of God, who, realising that his people cannot be expected to work all the time, chooses not to watch them all the time. Because God is not watching during the night, it is at this time that evil or corrupt deeds are done.'[49] The teaching of *Brown's Catechism* on the omniscience of God would provoke interesting reflection.

In contrast, where *Brown's Catechism* apparently dovetailed with traditional beliefs came in Question 6, 'Where does He dwell?' Answer, 'In heaven'; and in Question 7, 'Where is heaven?' Answer, 'It is far away, beyond the sun, the moon, and the stars.' The Tswana accepted that the supreme being lived 'far away', in fact so far away that he had little direct dealings with men and women. The spirits of the ancestors were the immediate supernatural forces to reckon with. Thus, what *Brown's*

---

[46] Mary Moffat, *To James Smith*, 30.12.1828, (*AAK,* 292). Cf. LMS, *Report to the 35th Annual Meeting, 1829*, 81f: 'The missionaries are encouraged by observing the unremitting attendance of the people on the preaching of the word. Every Sabbath, before the forenoon service, Mr. Moffat catechises the children and the adults and reads to them a chapter from one of the Gospels.'

[47] Cf. RM, *Journal,* 25.5.1823, (*AAK,* 82) and, *Journal,* 6.5.1827, (*AAK,* 251).

[48] Qu. 12 in the original English version, and Qu. 12 in the SeTswana version (Grey Collection).

[49] Clegg, 'Some Aspects of Tswana Cosmology', *Botswana Notes & Records,* Vol. 18, (Gaborone, 1986), 34.

Catechism stated on this point would not cause surprise.[50] Eventually, the Tswana would realise that their view of the 'remoteness' of God was not totally shared by Christian theology. Nevertheless, the uncomplicated form of *Brown's Catechism*—with simple statements, such as Jesus 'went about doing good'[51]—made it an easy document to relate to and understand. Other parts might be more disturbing for the hearers.

Brown's Catechism was designated as Catechism suitable for children from 3 to 7 years of age. At the same time, it was unsparing in its evangelical challenge. Its spiritual demands were the same as those which had confronted Moffat as a child in Scotland, and which later moulded his missionary theology. Consider the following:

Q34. Do you ever do anything perfectly good?
R34. No; there is sin in everything I do.

Q35. Is God angry with you when you do what is evil?
R35. Yes, very angry.

Q36. What does God do to children who are bad?
R36. He sends them to hell when they die.

Q37. What kind of place is hell?
R37. It is a place that burns with fire and brimstone.

Q38. Do you deserve to be sent to hell?
R38. Yes: for I am often very bad.

These are followed by other Christian truths:

Q39. Where do good children go when they die?
R39. To heaven.

Q40. What kind of place is heaven?
R40. A very happy place.

Q41. Is it as a reward for being good children that they go to heaven when they die?
R41. No: we can never deserve heaven for any good things we do; if we ever go there it must be through the love[52] of Jesus Christ.[53]

---

[50] Qu. 6 & 7 in the SeTswana version correspond with Qu. 6 & 7 in the English version.

[51] Qu. 49 in the English version: Qu. 47 in the SeTswana version.

[52] The English text has a footnote stating, 'Or merits'.

[53] Qu. 34 to 41 in the English version are replicated in the SeTswana version (also Qu. 34 to 41), apart from Answer 41 in the SeTswana version which has a simpler response along the lines of: 'It is Jesus who helps you get to heaven rather than to the fire'.

This latter series of Questions and Responses gave a platform for extended teaching on who Jesus is, why the cross is necessary, the nature of true faith and salvation:

Q71. What must you do, that Jesus Christ may take you to heaven?
R71. I must believe in him.

Q72. What is it to believe in Jesus Christ?
R72. It is to credit what the Bible says about Christ as Saviour, and to trust in him to save me.

Q73. Will you ever believe in Jesus Christ of yourself?
R73. No: never.

Q74. Why will you never believe in Jesus Christ of yourself?
R74. Because I am so bad.

Q75. Who then can make you believe in Jesus Christ?
R75. God only.

Q76. Should you ask God to make you believe in Jesus Christ, and to give you the other good things you need?
R76. Yes.[54]

As well as conveying a challenging evangelicalism, *Brown's Catechism* was the conduit of basic Calvinist principles including: total depravity (Q&R:34), the inability of sinful humanity to respond to grace apart from an enabling given by God Himself (Q&R:75,76), and an emphasis on moral living (Q&R:89-103). But Moffat did not introduce a stricter doctrine to Africa than had nurtured himself and his siblings. From childhood they had been taught that the eternal destiny of a man or woman, boy or girl, is settled by their response to Jesus Christ.

Throughout his many years of missionary service, Moffat saw himself as a 'dying man' appealing to other 'dying men'.[55] Brown's *Catechism* fostered this urgency, teaching that even children must be made aware of the awful consequences of not being in Christ: *'May you die very soon? Yes: though I am well today, I may be dead before tomorrow'* (Q&R: 113). It was not seen as mercy to spare solemn truths. In his translation Moffat adapted the wording so that it referred directly to adults rather than children, but the teaching was unaltered. Moffat's upbringing fostered in him a responsibility to share the whole gospel—awful warnings as well as joyful blessings—as a central feature of his message.

---

[54] Qu. 71 to 76 (English version) correspond closely to Qu. 72 to 77 (SeTswana version).
[55] RM, *To Mullens, LMS,* 15.1.1868, (SOAS/CWM SA Reports Box 1).

CHURCH

Ann Gardiner enjoyed the ministry of the Rev. Robert Caldwell of Bank Street Congregational Church in Falkirk. And for her son, 'all his life through, Mr Caldwell's earnest teachings left recollections never to be effaced'.[56] When Moffat met Caldwell at Newcastle in 1843, almost thirty years after he had sat under his ministry, he expressed deep appreciation of the role Caldwell had played in his early life.[57] Caldwell himself had been a direct product of the Haldane Revival.

The last decade of the eighteenth century, and the first decade of the nineteenth, had seen a new phenomenon in Scottish Church life. Until then, Scottish church life since the Reformation had been almost totally the preserve of Presbyterianism and Episcopalianism, with a rash of various sects and secessions. But in the 1790s, the brothers Robert Haldane and James Haldane—wealthy men who were deeply committed to evangelical mission at home and abroad—became the progenitors of what is known as the Haldane Revival.[58] They had both been affected by evangelical movements, and both went through a conversion experience. Subsequently, Robert Haldane heard of Christian work in Bengal in India and, along with William Innes, David Bogue, and Greville Ewing,[59] wanted to go there as a missionary. But travel permits, under the control of the East India Company—traditionally hostile to missions—were denied and their plans were unrealised. Nevertheless the attempt created a great friendship between the four men.

Robert Haldane's brother, James, had been influenced by John Campbell of Edinburgh.[60] John Campbell was in the Church of Scotland until the tension between the increasing attraction of an independent evangelical church and

---

56 JSM, *Lives,* 3

57 Love, *Local Antiquarian Notes and Queries, Vol. IV,* 30.

58 Cf. Alexander Haldane, *The Lives of Robert and James Haldane,* (3rd edn, 1853, reprinted: Edin: BOT, 1990).

59 Greville Ewing (1767- 1841) trained for the ministry of the Church of Scotland. He became editor of the *Missionary Magazine* in 1796. One of his reasons for leaving the Church of Scotland was its refusal at the 1796 General Assembly to become institutionally involved in Foreign Mission. David Bogue and Greville Ewing were brothers-in-law.

60 Two John Campbells impinged on Moffat's life. John Campbell (1766-1840), mentioned here, promoted Sunday Schools, established societies for 'fallen women', and was concerned about slavery. He became a Congregational minister, helped found the *British and Foreign Bible Society* and was a director of the LMS. He visited South Africa on behalf of the LMS in 1812-1814, and in 1819-1821, writing a book after each visit. Dr John Campbell (1794-1867) was a Congregational Minister who founded *The British Banner* newspaper in 1848. He edited a selection of Moffat's lectures and sermons, delivered during Moffat's 1839 to 1843 visit to Britain, *The Farewell Services of Robert Moffat in Edinburgh, Manchester and London.*

the fading charms of a non-missionary minded Kirk, proved an unequal struggle. In 1797, whilst still in the established Kirk, Campbell had formed a Society, independent of clerical superintendence, for the establishment of Sunday Schools in destitute locations. James Haldane embraced the concept and within six months had 34 such schools in operation near Edinburgh. His brother Robert joined the project. Frustrated in his hopes of mission in India, Robert now saw an opportunity for evangelical mission at home and was prepared to give considerable finance for this work.

Robert and James Haldane established the *Society for Propagating the Gospel at Home* (*SPGH*). Initially, they tried to work within the structures of the established Church, simply training lay-people to go and preach the evangelical message in different parts of Scotland. They expected that lay-preachers would be welcomed by parish ministers, with converts absorbed into the local church.[61] Haldane preaching tours of several parts of rural Scotland took place, taking the revivalist evangelical message into remote corners.[62] It was a clear policy of the *SPGH* that the itinerants were not allowed to preach for money.

However, though the *SPGH* intended to aid the whole church in Scotland, the disapproval of non-sympathetic ministers resulted in its preachers being excluded from Presbyterian pulpits. The Church of Scotland General Assembly of 1799 sent out a 'Pastoral Letter' warning against itinerant and independent evangelists. In the previous year, the Anti-Burghers had forbidden their members from hearing them. Similarly, the Relief Church declared against lay-preaching.[63] These developments, on top of the Church of Scotland's refusal at the 1796 General Assembly to sponsor Foreign Missions, plus the general antipathy of the powerful Moderate party, persuaded the Haldanes to work outside the Kirk.

Rejected by the mainstream Churches, the *SPGH* established 'Tabernacle' preaching stations, initially in Edinburgh, Glasgow, and Dundee. On 29 November 1798, Greville Ewing preached his last sermon as a member of the Church of Scotland and resigned from being minister at Lady Glenorchy's Chapel.[64] He threw in his lot with the Haldanes and the emerging

---

61 Alexander Haldane, *The Lives of Robert and James Haldane,* 193.

62 Cf. James Haldane, *Journal of a Tour through the Northern Counties of Scotland and the Orkney Islands in Autumn 1797: undertaken with a view to promote the knowledge of the Gospel of Jesus Christ,* (Edin: Ritchie, on behalf of SPGH, 1798). Other tours took place.

63 Henderson, *The Church of Scotland,* 120.

64 Lady Glenorchy was widowed in 1771. She came under evangelical influence and committed herself to encouraging like-minded persons. She built a chapel in Edinburgh, which was within the Church of Scotland, and which was dedicated to evangelical causes. She

Congregationalist denomination. It was but a small step before the preaching stations became independent Churches. A new denomination was formed with a Congregational polity, and with a theological emphasis straight from the Evangelical Revivalist tradition. Ordination was 'validated' by the congregation; and in 1799 James Haldane—hitherto a layman—became the minister of the Edinburgh Tabernacle with its 310 members.[65] Greville Ewing became minister of the Glasgow Tabernacle.

In 1798, even before his final separation from the Church of Scotland, Robert Haldane had sent ten students to David Bogue's Seminary in Gosport, England, to be trained for *SPGH* work. He then established a Scottish theological College to train ministers. In its early years, Haldane's College had a peripatetic existence between Dundee, Edinburgh and Glasgow.

By 1808, both Robert and James Haldane were convinced that immersion was the proper mode of baptism, and they left the Tabernacle Churches—now called the Scottish Congregationalist Church—and became Baptists. Greville Ewing took over the leadership of the paedo-baptist Scottish Congregationalist Church. Some Congregational Churches, which the Haldanes founded, were divided by them leaving, but, after a short period of readjustment, congregations settled down and continued their work.[66]

The Haldanes brought something new and exciting to Scottish Church life and attracted many of an evangelical piety including Ann Gardiner. Her son, Robert, was to share that admiration for the Haldanes. In July 1854, as he waited to approach Moselekatse's headquarters after his long ox-wagon journey from Kuruman to Matabeleland, he wrote:

> I was much interested in reading a review of the lives of the Haldanes. What nobles they were in the Kingdom of Christ! How few have been so highly favoured, and all brought about [by], or through the instrumentality of a praying mother! How truly it has been said that woman holds in her bosom the destinies of empires! This of course applies to such as have the control of the education, as well as the earliest influences of a mother's voice and a mother's love.[67]

---

founded other chapels at Carlisle, Matlock and Strathfillan, and left large sums in her will to the SPCK. She had a role similar to that of Lady Huntingdon in England.

65 James Haldane was ordained in the new Scottish Congregational Church on 3.2.1799. His ordination was 'validated' by 'approbation of the gathered congregation' after 'answering four searching questions satisfactorily' (Alexander Haldane, *Lives,* 238).

66 After the Haldanes adopted Baptist principles, the Bank Street Congregation in Falkirk split into Congregationalists and Baptists. See: R. Polland, *'I will build my Church': A History of Falkirk Baptist Church,* (Edin: Polland, 1999), 5f.

67 RM, *Journal,* 16.7.1854, (*MJ1,* 221).

Moffat's early religious background was thus tied to radical events within Scottish spirituality. And specifically, through Robert Caldwell, Patrick MacFarlan and Ebenezer Brown, he was exposed to three major strands of churchmanship: Robert Caldwell for Independency and Congregationalism; Patrick MacFarlan for the established Kirk; Ebenezer Brown for the Secessionist tradition. In England, Moffat also met with Methodism and Anglicanism, as well as the English form of Independency.

The Rev. Robert Caldwell, minister of Falkirk Congregational Church from 1802 until 1813, was a direct product of the Haldane movement.[68] At an early age, he had moved to Edinburgh with his parents, who attended the ministry of the Rev. Dr James Peddie of Bristo Street Associate Synod (Burgher) Church. At 14 years of age, Caldwell became an apprentice mason, following this trade until he was over 20. In 1793 he began to attend a Sabbath evening School, conducted by a John Clark. Then, just as James Haldane's life was changed by meeting John Campbell, so was Caldwell's. Campbell established fellowship prayer-meetings which Caldwell attended, and in 1795 when Campbell opened another Sabbath evening school, Caldwell became one of its teachers.[69] After 1799 Caldwell left Peddie's ministry and joined the first Scottish Congregational Church formed in Edinburgh under James Haldane. Peddie had wanted Caldwell to study for the ministry of the Secession Church, but, even when attending Peddie's ministry, Caldwell had been drawn to Congregational principles. In January 1800 he began at the Haldane

---

[68] See: R. Kinniburgh, *Fathers of Independency in Scotland: or, Biographical Sketches of Early Scottish Congregational Ministers, 1798-1851,* (Edin: Fullarton, 1851); W.D. McNaughton, *The Scottish Congregational Ministry: 1794-1993,* (Glasgow: Congregational Union of Scotland, 1993); and James Love, *Local Antiquarian Notes and Queries,* Vol. I, 88ff. Robert Caldwell (1777-1850) first became a member of the Secession Church, and then joined the Circus Congregational Church, Little King Street, Edinburgh. After studying at Robert Haldane's Theological Seminary, he was appointed preacher at Falkirk in the spring of 1802-1803. Subsequently he became minister of: Bank Street Congregational Church Falkirk. 1803-1813; Wick 1813-1832; and Howden on the Tyne Independent Church, Newcastle, 1834-1842.

[69] Kinniburgh, *Fathers of Independency in Scotland: or, Biographical Sketches of Early Scottish Congregational Ministers, 1798-1851*, 445f. These prayer-meetings drew Christians from various denominations, and included mutual visitation for encouragement, upbuilding and 'kind fraternal interest'. They were 'churches' in all but name, and purported to have more of a New Testament form of meeting and worship than the existing Kirks. They were strict about admission to the Lord's Table, a strictness approved by 'earnest believers' (446).

Theological Seminary, first under William Innes, and then Greville Ewing who had strong views on ministerial training.[70] The main subjects were:[71]

The Depravity of Human Nature

The Innate Corruption of Humanity

The Scheme of Mercy through a Mediator

The Necessity, Sufficiency and Efficacy of Christ' death on Calvary

Justification by Faith

The Connection between Faith and Works

The Necessity and Nature of Regeneration

Brotherly Love

Active and Diffuse Benevolence

The Necessity of Cultivating Universal Holiness.

If Caldwell's preaching reflected the emphases of his training, then the Bank Street Congregation in Falkirk was grounded in principles of Calvinism seasoned by revivalism.[72] The last subject in the list, 'holiness', emphasised purity of life.[73] This emphasis was a major factor in the nineteenth-century missionary movement: a missionary could not be used by God unless he lived a holy life. Of interest also is the emphasis on 'benevolence', referred to in the penultimate article. 'Benevolence' as a positive human trait, was brought to the fore in Scottish philosophy by Francis Hutcheson, Professor at Glasgow University in the eighteenth century.[74] Hutcheson reacted against Calvinistic pessimism regarding human nature, and rejected the view that morality—even within corrupt humanity—was primarily based on selfish interest. He

---

70 Greville Ewing, *A Memorial on Education for the Ministry of the Gospel,* (Glasgow: Lang, 1808). Ewing argued for a seven-year training period (10ff.), including: the liberal arts, English Grammar, Latin, Greek, Hebrew, as well as comprehensive biblical and theological study: 'Those who go through this scheme will not be trained in habits of idleness.' As an early ministerial student, Caldwell experienced a 'fast-track' programme.

71 *The History of Congregationalism in Scotland from 1798-1848,* 20.

72 The Haldanes were not Arminians. When, James Haldane's erstwhile partner of his Independent days, Ralph Wardlaw, appeared to swerve from the Reformed view of the atonement, Haldane struck a thoroughly Calvinist note in a short work. !n 1841 it was members of Wardlaw's Chapel who encouraged Moffat to publish an account of his missionary labours. See: RM, *To Walter Inglis,* 31.12.1842, (NLS/MS/10997/207). Robert Haldane's *Commentary on Romans,* is still in print.

73 'Holiness', as in 'The Holiness Movement', would later refer more to an 'enabling power' that comes from a dedicated life than to 'purity' as such. Originally, 'holiness' simply equated with 'moral purity before God' as an end in itself: in sympathy with this emphasis Moffat designated missionaries as 'preachers of righteousness'. Cf. RM, *Journal,* 11.7.1824, (*AAK,* 123f) and RM, *MLSSA,* 270.

74 Herman, *The Scottish Enlightenment,* 53-71; and Keay & Keay, 'Francis Hutcheson', *Collins Encyclopaedia of Scotland,* (Ldn: HarperCollins, 1994), 531.

argued that an intuition of virtue, like the intuition of beauty, is universal and basic to moral decisions, and that 'sympathy' is a more powerful factor than 'self-love'.

This more positive understanding of human behaviour found a response in religious circles towards the end of the eighteenth century, with admirers including Thomas Jefferson of the American founding fathers. Hutcheson's philosophy offered hope for the future and a celebration of the potential of humanity, in contrast to the dark doom of traditional Presbyterian theology. There could be optimism. There could be changes for the better. And it was optimism which influenced the world-view of many early missionaries who, without losing other Calvinist principles, believed a better future would be ushered in with the millennial reign of Christ.

Caldwell's studies continued until the spring of 1802 when he was invited to become Congregationalist pastor in Falkirk.[75] Falkirk had previously enjoyed the occasional ministrations of agents of the *SPGH*, but local Christians wanted a more regular arrangement. On 22 November 1803, Caldwell was ordained and inducted to the charge, with James Haldane, Ralph Wardlaw, and Greville Ewing officiating. It was to his ministry that Ann Gardiner took her family. But what did the young Moffat absorb under Caldwell?

A huge contrast with the established Kirk at Bothkennar was the use of hymns in worship, as opposed to the exclusive use of metrical psalms. That by itself opened Moffat up to a different expression of spirituality, with his mother's favourites no doubt learned and sung within the context of the revivalist tradition celebrated in Bank Street. Another contrast was the place given to the congregation in decisions. The Bank Street Congregation was strong on the role of the whole Congregation exercising authority. This contrasted with the Presbyterian principle of only elders doing so. At Kuruman, Moffat applied clear Congregationalist principles in his ecclesiology. The LMS as an institution also had a Congregationalist flavour. Importantly, the Bank Street congregation represented an ecclesiastical polity of total independence from the state or any secular authority. This can account for some of Moffat's differences with John Philip—the LMS superintendent in southern Africa—who was moulded by a Church of Scotland polity, though Philip later joined the Congregationalist Church.[76]

---

[75] As noted in Ch. 1, there was a flourishing group of Independents at Grangemouth.

[76] John Philip, whilst initially in opposition to the Colonial Authority, had the end view of allying the secular authority to help implement his policies. For Moffat, the secular authority was not to be engaged with, so long as it did not obstruct the work of the mission. Philip saw

Evaluating the permanent effect of childhood or youth influences is an inexact science. But these factors do contrast what Moffat would have experienced if his spiritual upbringing had been totally within the established Church of Scotland. After leaving Falkirk in 1813, Caldwell had fruitful ministries in Wick and Newcastle-upon Tyne.[77] He retired in 1842 and was reunited with Moffat in 1843.

From 1809 until 1812 Moffat was an apprentice gardener at Parkhill, Polmont, near Falkirk, under a Mr John Robertson, who was described as 'a hard man, though withal a just one'.[78] The Church of Scotland minister of Polmont was the Rev. Patrick MacFarlan. In a letter, written late in life, Moffat stated that he had sat under MacFarlan's ministry. This allusion occurs in an 1873 note, written to William Dickson after a nostalgic visit to Scotland: 'Of course, I went to Polmont and stood on the spot (now walls only)[79] where I was wont to listen to the Rev. Mcfarline who afterwards went to Glasgow.'[80]

This is a clear reference to Patrick MacFarlan.[81] MacFarlan was the minister whom Robert Moffat (Snr) had in mind when, in an 1812 letter, he urged his son to join the church at Polmont.[82] Though there is no proof that Robert did join the congregation formally, we do know that, in accordance with his father's wishes, he made a call on the minister, which was greatly appreciated by his father: 'We were very happy to hear that you had called on the Minister and to learn that he had given you so many good counsels.'[83]

Why did Moffat attend the established Kirk at Polmont, since Caldwell was still minister in Falkirk? Admittedly, Falkirk was five or six miles from

---

the secular authority as a force to be used; Moffat saw it as a force of which to be independent. In that respect Philip had a Presbyterian paradigm though he was a Congregationalist, whereas Moffat represented the traditional Independent Congregationalist concept.

77 McNaughton, *Early Congregational Independency in the Highlands and Islands and the North-East of Scotland,* (Tiree: Trustees of Ruaig Congregational Church, 2003), 232ff.

78 JSM, *Lives,* 4.

79 The Old Parish Church of Polmont was built in 1731-32. This was used during Patrick MacFarlan's ministry, and in which Moffat worshipped. By the mid-nineteenth century a new church was built. Cf. Thain, *The New Parish Church of Polmont, 1845,* (Polmont: 1995).

80 RM, *To William Dickson,* 29.11.1873, (EUNCL WD9/3/6).

81 Biographies of Moffat by JSM, Northcott and Smith, have no reference to MacFarlan. The clue comes from the William Dickson letter of 1873. That Moffat went to see the ruins of MacFarlan's old Kirk indicates that his ministry had been an important one. 'Where I was wont to listen' conveys the sense of regularly sitting under his ministry.

82 Moffat (Snr), *To RM*, 22.6.1812, (Baxter & Burke, *Guide,* 325).

83 Ibid.

Moffat's place of work, but little more than the distance from Carronshore to Falkirk, which his mother, along with her children, had taken in her stride for several years. A split in the Bank Street Congregation, occasioned by the Haldanes becoming Baptists, may have been a factor. Or perhaps it was a positive choice which young Robert made, having heard of MacFarlan's qualities. Or perhaps it was simply an instance of a young man asserting some independence. Whatever the reason, Moffat's connection with MacFarlan was from his fifteenth to his seventeenth years of age, an impressionable time for a maturing mind.

The Polmont minister was a young man—only 29 when he came to Polmont—but his stature was proven in the years that lay ahead. He became one of very few ministers who would be both Moderator of the General Assembly of the Church of Scotland (1834) and, after the Disruption of 1843, Moderator of the General Assembly of the Free Church of Scotland (1845). Significantly, at the time of the Disruption MacFarlan was minister of the West Church Greenock, which was the wealthiest congregation in the Church of Scotland, and enjoying the richest living of any incumbent.[84] Yet he was prepared to align himself with the dissenters at the 1843 General Assembly, knowing that it would mean expulsion from his charge, and loss of comforts and privileges, as proved to be the case.[85] MacFarlan was also sought after as a speaker at events connected with the Evangelical cause in Scotland, with his calibre evident from an early age.[86] Moffat, in his mid-teens, and at a vital stage of his own intellectual formation, was sitting under the ministry of this outstanding minister who himself was in his early thirties. The established Kirk, into which Robert Moffat (Snr) insisted his children were baptised, had at last, in the person of Patrick MacFarlan and his ministry, supplied a meaningful influence on the youthful Robert Moffat.

---

[84] Brown, *Annals of the Disruption,* Edin: MacNiven & Wallace, 1884), 176, noted that, as early as 1839 MacFarlan had declared: 'It has pleased God, in His providence, to fill me, as far as stipend is concerned, a fuller cup than has fallen to any of my brethren; but this I say ... I would rather cast that cup to the ground than I would taste it again, embittered as it would be, if I were to yield by the consciousness of having deserted what I believe to be my duty to God and my duty to the Church.'

[85] Brown, *Annals of the Disruption,* 1.

[86] In 1826 MacFarlan preached on, '*The Influence of the Holy Spirit essential to the success of the Gospel*'. In 1834 he published a pamphlet advocating the popular election of ministers and critical of the patronage system. In 1834 he was examined before the Committee of the House of Commons on the Patronage Question. These identify MacFarlan as a leader in the evangelical wing of the established Church of Scotland. However, his 1827 argument that the Glasgow Bible Society should be allowed to circulate the Apocrypha along with the canonical Scriptures, was frowned on by several of his evangelical colleagues.

What did Polmont give Moffat? MacFarlan's evangelical Presbyterian teaching and theological stance would be important, but the Presbyterian framework of discipline at Polmont would also make an impression. Though Moffat would see discipline applied in every congregation with which he was associated, the overwhelming concern of the *Polmont Old Parish Church Kirk Session Minutes: 1810-1834*[87]—indeed the *only* recorded concern—was the enforcement of discipline within the congregation. Church discipline was a high-profile activity in early-nineteenth-century church life. Though hearings were conducted within the privacy of the Kirk Session, the consequences of sentence, repentance and admonition were enacted publicly. The major role of discipline in Church life had a formative influence on Moffat's ecclesiology.

In every denomination in the eighteenth and early nineteenth centuries, discipline was central. Kirk Session records for Polmont Old Parish Church, during the years Moffat attended MacFarlan's ministry, are exclusively concerned with matters of discipline, especially in relation to pregnancies outside marriage. Yet, in the Polmont records there is not the variety of offences such as we find in the later Kuruman records where, under Moffat's leadership, faults such as disloyalty, gossip, and backbiting were treated with as much seriousness as sins of a sexual nature.[88] The purpose of discipline was quaintly referred to in the *Polmont Old Parish Church Kirk Session Minutes*, as being a process in which a penitent 'seeks discipline' in order to be helped. Thus, on 28 February 1813, we read of a lady '*wishing to be admitted to discipline* and to be again restored to the privileges of the church: having been seriously admonished and rebuked she was desired to appear again before the Session on this day three weeks.'[89] This illustrates the theory behind church discipline: a person *sought* the discipline of the church in order to restore their walk with God. The Kirk Session saw discipline as a 'means of grace' not a punishment. Whether penitents saw it that way is dubious. But ministers and elders comforted themselves with the thought that what they meted out was part of the merciful work of the Gospel in a sinner's life.

---

87 *Polmont Old Parish Church Kirk Session Minutes*: 1810-1834, (FHRC/CH2/1134/3).

88 Cf. *Kuruman Church Record Book: 1825-1880,* (Kuruman Moffat Mission Library, Box A3: KCRB-A3) passim. In the Polmont records there is no variety of *punishments* such as found in the Kuruman records. In Polmont, the formula was simply admonishment and rebuke before readmittance to full fellowship. If there were levels of suspension and excommunication, then these were not recorded. At Kuruman there were degrees including Suspension; Separation; Being Cut Off; Excommunication. Moffat did not copy the Presbyterian disciplinary system in every detail. We discuss this more fully in Ch. 25, on Moffat's ecclesiology.

89 *Polmont Kirk Session Minutes*: 1810-1834, 28.2.1813, (FHRC/CH2/1134/3).

We can also detect theological emphases, which resonate in Moffat's later work, in an address which MacFarlan gave in 1826 to the *Society in Scotland for Propagating Christian Knowledge* on the work of the Holy Spirit in mission gives insight into the mind-set of those who held to evangelical Presbyterian principles in the missionary activity. His title was: '*The Influence of the Holy Spirit essential to the success of the Gospel'.* Other Presbyterians held to these same principles, and they illustrate a Presbyterian approach to evangelical action. MacFarlan took as his text, Zechariah 4:6: *'Not by might, nor by power; but by my Spirit, saith the Lord of Hosts'.*[90] The Gospel only progressed by the work of the Holy Spirit:

> The conversion of sinners, or the building up of the church, would be effected – not by the might of political influence and authority – not by the coercive measures nor the temptations of an earthly kind, which the folly or wisdom of men might suggest – not even by the fascinations of human eloquence, nor even by the miracles which in former ages accompanied the preaching of the gospel, but by the Spirit of the Lord enlightening the minds of men in the knowledge of the truth, convincing them of sin, and inclining them to turn unto God through the only Saviour, and to become his willing and obedient people.[91]

MacFarlan deplored the interference of the State in Christianising heathen nations, pointing to:

> Those wretched nations which in the dark ages were compelled at the point of the sword to make profession of Christianity, have been denominated Christians as if they were on an equality with those among whom the gospel has been preached in purity and received in faith ... mere professors of Christianity have been regarded as constituting the Church of Christ.[92]

Spiritual work could not be done by a secular authority. The result would be a bastard Christianity, creating mere lip-profession. Worst of all, it would not produce a *deep-rooted* moral change of heart and character. MacFarlan thus emphasised what was to be a principle in Moffat's missionary convictions, namely: 'the terrors or the enticements of men in power have created many professors of Christianity; but have not made one Christian: they have left men, as to the essential ingredients of their character the same persons as before.'[93] As MacFarlan pointed out, the real conversion of sinners is the

---

90 MacFarlan, *The Influence of the Holy Spirit essential to the Success of the Gospel: A Sermon preached before the Society in Scotland for Propagating Christian Knowledge,* (Edin: SSPCK, Waugh & Innes, 1826), 5.

91 Ibid, 14. His criticisms were primarily directed at Roman Catholic missionary methods. Cf. his address to the 1845 Free Church Assembly.

92 Ibid, 15.

93 Ibid, 16.

work of the Spirit, and so 'there is no nation, and no individual, to whom the Gospel may not be preached with success'.[94] This was an argument which cut across the old argument of the Moderates, that some races were incapable of receiving the Gospel.[95]

Throughout his missionary career Moffat put these points into practice. For example, he was extremely reluctant to involve the State government in the work of mission, beyond what was necessary in terms of permission and protection. Moffat sought to keep the Mission separate from political interference or 'help' as much as possible. Also, for Moffat the real signs of true conversion lay in moral change and transformation of character and life. At Kuruman, many dozens each year professed Christian faith and sought full church membership: but only a few were admitted, and evidence of change of life was crucial. Moral transformation was decisive. On MacFarlan's other point, Moffat was also convinced that the Gospel was for any race anywhere.

Another of MacFarlan's emphases was questioning over-excitement. He pointed out that 'a mental excitement may be produced which may be mistaken for real piety, but if not accompanied by the light and energy of the Holy Spirit will fade away'.[96] He preferred solemn sorrow over sin, rather than ecstatic and emotional experiences. This would be reflected in Moffat's thinking. In 1829, when the Kuruman Awakening began to be accompanied by emotional phenomena, Moffat was concerned. Similarly, Moffat downplayed the role of visions and dreams in favour of what he regarded as a more clear-headed way of coming to know God. For Moffat, knowledge of God was through the Word, not through a dubious foundation of ecstatic visions.

MacFarlan's emphases, as laid out in his 1826 address, were not unique. They echoed many Presbyterian pulpits, and reveal important missionary principles from a Presbyterian, Reformed, and Calvinist perspective. MacFarlan's conclusion was: 'We have no reason to hope for success, unless the means which we employ for the conversion of sinners be agreeable to

---

94 Ibid, 45.

95 By the time MacFarlan gave this address, the attitude of the Kirk towards Foreign Mission had changed. In 1824 and 1825 the Kirk's General Assembly made decisive moves towards a policy of active involvement in the work of Foreign Missions.

96 Ibid, 17. MacFarlan may have had in mind problems Jonathan Edwards met during the Great Awakening. Edwards had to defend spiritual excitements against cynics on the one hand, and against over-enthusiasts on the other. Cf. Campbell, Iain D, 'Jonathan Edwards' *Religious Affections* as a Paradigm for Evangelical Spirituality', *SBET,* Vol. 21, No. 2, 2003.

the word of God.'[97] Such uncomplicated principles were also lodged deep in the foundations of Moffat's theology.

Moffat's last minister before he left Scotland for England was the Rev. Ebenezer Brown of the Burgher Congregation in Inverkeithing. At the end of 1812, Moffat's apprenticeship at Parkhill expired and he obtained a post at Donibristle, seat of the Earl of Moray near Aberdour, a few miles from the new family home.[98] A former Donibristle gardener, Peter Greig, had already made his mark in the missionary world. In 1796 Greig had been the very first missionary appointed by the newly formed Edinburgh Missionary Society.[99] Donibristle House was only two miles from Inverkeithing, and it was easy for the young and energetic Moffat to walk to his parents' house. The Earl of Moray had a private Anglican chapel, but Moffat rarely attended Anglican worship. Though there was a Presbyterian Church at nearby Dalgety Bay, his preference was to be with his parents for the Sabbath services. Moreover, the possibility of hearing Ebenezer Brown was a great attraction, as were home comforts and home cooking. As John Smith Moffat noted: 'for a twelve-month he had the opportunity of frequent intercourse with his own family circle only a few miles away.'[100]

Ebenezer Brown was a son to the great Dr John Brown of Haddington, and older brother to the Rev. William Brown. Ebenezer wrote explanatory notes on his father's Catechisms *'Big Broon'* and *'Little Broon',* with his notes, coupled with the Catechisms, re-published regularly in the nineteenth century. Ebenezer, along with virtually all Secessionist and Evangelical ministers, had a passionate seriousness about the things of God, and about the urgent need of sinners to find salvation.[101] The type of ministry which Brown conducted on a Sunday was described by Alexander Haldane, who cited a Mr Brougham and a Mr Denam, who heard Brown preach in 1823. As usual, he spoke from the psalm which was to be sung, and then lectured and then preached. The subject of the lecture was Acts 16:20-34. Though the service was long 'they did not tire'. His exposition was on the providence of God. They commented that this sermon was more useful to them than many of Edward Irving's famous orations![102] Brown's subject for that day, 'The

---

97 Ibid, 48.

98 JSM, *Lives,* 5.

99 Simpson, *Dalgety Bay: Heritage and Hidden History,* (Dunfermline: Dalgety Bay & Hillend Community Council, 1999), 71.

100 JSM, *Lives,* 5.

101 Cf. Ross, *From Scenes Like These,* (Edin: Birlinn, 2000), 64.

102 Haldane, *The Lives of Robert and James Haldane,* 590. Edward Irving (1792-1834) established a congregation in London and edged towards a new Pentecostalism. The Haldanes

Christian's trust in the Providential Care of God, no matter what happens', was a repeated theme in evangelical preaching. Sermons on resignation and faith in divine providence—despite adverse circumstances and suffering—were major topics of pastoral preaching. Moffat drew deeply on such convictions when faced with tragedy in Africa.

Ebenezer Brown's morning service consisted of an expository lecture,[103] followed by a sermon in more general terms.[104] These two types of address were adapted by Moffat for Kuruman. Thus, in 1868, John Smith Moffat wrote of a typical Sabbath: '[The] custom in the regular way is to give New Testament reading in the morning, a topical sermon in the afternoon, and Old Testament exposition in the evening.'[105] The pattern of Lecture (exposition) complemented by Sermon was a standard model, providing the foundation of the evangelical teaching ministry in the mission field.[106] All ministry, including evangelism, was viewed as ministry of the Word, which provided not only the truth of God but the power of God. It was the avenue to life and light.[107] The power of the Spirit was accessed by ministering the Word of God, and yet Moffat would come to learn that preaching by itself was inadequate. In evangelistic settings he had to supplement preaching with discussion. David Bogue was already aware of that need.[108]

---

were anti-Irving: cf. James Haldane, *Answer to Mr. Henry Drummond's defence of the heretical doctrine promulgated by Mr. Irving, respecting the person and atonement of the Lord Jesus Christ,* (Edin: 1830). Irving's Christology was suspected of undermining the sinlessness of Christ. Moffat, in: RM, *To Mary Moffat,* 19.5.1835, (*MJ1,* 50), wrote of the 'many tongued' Mr. Irving.

103 Scotland followed Calvin's Geneva where an exposition of Scripture in a form similar to the later 'lecture' concept, had been a central feature. The forenoon service consisted of a prayer; a lecture on a passage of Scripture, commented on verse by verse; a prayer followed by a Sermon; a prayer; a psalm sung, and the benediction said. The same order was followed in the afternoon, without the lecture.'

104 This replicated his father's pattern at Haddington, where the Morning Service included a lecture and sermon; the Afternoon Service a second sermon; the Evening Service an 'exercise'.

105 JSM, *To the LMS Directors,* 12.10.1868, (Deane, *Robert Moffat,* 165).

106 Bogue distinguished between 'an exposition of the scriptures' and 'a proper sermon'. Both should be used (Bogue, *Miss. Lect.* 4, 'On Preaching (2)').

107 Moffat was later concerned that Anglicans & Lutherans relied on liturgy rather than the Word in evangelism. Cf. RM, *To Tidman, LMS,* 3.11.1851, (SOAS/CWM/SA/Box 26/1/A): 'It is very difficult for the missionary to make the untutored savage understand that there are some sections of that Church which we seek to establish which are not so particular if they only get their children baptised, their youth confirmed, and take the Lord's Supper.'

108 Bogue, *Missionary Lecture,* Lect. 6, 'On Reasoning about Religion with the Heathen'. Bogue, *Lect*. 7, 'On Conversation', advised similarly. Cf. RM, *Journal,* 6.5.1827, (*AAK,* 251).

Chapter 3

Conversion, Calling, Commissioning

THE MINISTRIES WHICH MOFFAT sat under in Scotland were all evangelical and Calvinist, with revivalist influences experienced both in the family home and in the Falkirk Bank Street congregation. At the end of 1813, having completed his apprenticeship as a gardener, Moffat moved to High Leigh, Cheshire, in England, where he was to be engaged as an under-gardener. A new chapter of his spiritual life would now open. He reached High Leigh on 26 December 1813. Though his work kept him busy, he managed to devote some time to reading. Mrs Leigh noticed this, and lent him books and encouraged him to pursue his studies.[1] Soon there began a series of spiritual encounters which eventually resulted in deep personal changes, affecting both his faith and his future.

AVERSION TO ANGLICANISM

Mrs Leigh was an Anglican, and after Moffat came under Methodist influence she tried to persuade him to find his spiritual home in the Church of England: the Leighs did not approve of Methodism. However, Moffat had already formed negative views about the Anglican Church. In a letter to his parents, written a month after arriving at High Leigh, he wrote about Mrs Leigh wanting him to attend the Anglican chapel since, 'there was no difference betwixt the Church of Scotland and England.' He told her there was in fact a great deal of difference, and he 'explained a little of the rules in Scotland.'[2]

Moffat conceded that the Anglican singing was very fine, but that was about all. He told his parents: 'I can assure you any person may be a minister in the C of E if they can read well; I think a good deal of their singing but nothing else'. Nevertheless, in later life Moffat became acquainted with the Church of England Prayer Book. In 1857, at Moselekatse's kraal, he wrote about the Ndebele reluctance to modernise their blacksmithing skills, saying that it reminded him 'of a sentence in the English prayer book: "As it was in the beginning is now and ever shall be."'[3] As time passed Moffat became aware that within Anglicanism there were at least two schools, the

---

1 JSM, *Lives,* 11.

2 RM, *To his Parents,* 25.1.1814, (Baxter & Burke, *Guide,* 325).

3 RM, *Journal,* 30.10.1857, (*MJ2,* 108).

Evangelical wing and the High Church circle. The polarisation of these two groups increased as the nineteenth century progressed. Moffat was concerned that much of the support which Livingstone generated in Oxford and Cambridge through his 1857 lectures came from the Oxford Movement within the High Church sector. In a letter to his son, John Smith Moffat, Moffat expressed doubts about the worth of High Anglican missionaries assisting Livingstone's work:

> It appears that [Livingstone] is anticipating the arrival of the constellation of clerical worthies from the universities with great pleasure. He is of course not aware that they are belonging to the school of Dr Pusey, and the Evangelicals of the Church of England are boldly sounding the alarm at such a popish party going to eastern Africa.[4]

Moffat believed that Anglicanism focused on Christianisation, rather than on a person's individual surrender to the moral and spiritual challenge of the Word of God. In his view, the Anglican approach did not make 'heart-converts'. In 1851 he wrote to Arthur Tidman of the LMS:

> It is very difficult for the missionary to make the untutored savage understand that there are some sections of that Church which we seek to establish which are not so particular if they only get their children baptised, their youth confirmed, and take the Lord's Supper.[5]

Moffat's view of Anglican theology was not helped by the baptismal regeneration controversies which took place in the Anglican community in Cape Town.[6] Around 1848, there was an intense baptismal regeneration debate in southern Africa. When Bishop Gray arrived in February 1848, he wrote back to England, that the Baptismal Regeneration controversy was

---

4 RM, *To JSM,* 27.11.1860, (Baxter & Burke, *Guide,* 316). Pusey was part of the Oxford Movement which promoted High Church principles. Moffat was suspicious of High Churchmanship, though Pusey reputedly stated, 'I love the Evangelicals, because they love our Lord.'

5 RM, *To Tidman, LMS,* 3.11.1851, (SOAS/CWM/SA/Box 26/1/A).

6 Anglican Missions did not penetrate the Kuruman area, but Hanoverian Lutheran Missions did, and Moffat had similar reservations regarding their theology. In 1860 he wrote to John Smith Moffat at Inyati: 'Did I inform you in my last that the Hanoverian missionaries whom we know are now living on their own resources as they—I think most justly—will not submit to the superintendent sent out to Port Natal (Durban) with almost unbounded powers. ... I should not wonder at their offering themselves to our Society, but some of their tenets, especially baptismal regeneration, would be in the way.' See: RM, *To JSM,* 1.9.1860, in: Wallis, (ed.): *The Matabele Mission: 1858-1878,* (Ldn: Chatto & Windus, 1945), 114, fn. 2, hereafter abbreviated to *MM.*

raging, and that the pulpit of the Cape Town cathedral had been used for proclaiming pamphlets against that doctrine of the Church.[7]

Moffat's unease with Anglicanism may have had social roots as much as theological ones. There was a class difference as well as a theological one between LMS missionaries and their Anglican counterparts. Most Scottish missionaries in Africa, such as Robert Moffat, David Livingstone, Mary Slessor, Robert Laws, etc., had working-class roots, and came from dissenting traditions which were closely allied with working-class people.[8] Though the fathers of Moffat, Livingstone and Laws had taken steps away from purely manual labour, they had a working-class pedigree. In contrast, Anglican missionaries came almost exclusively from the Universities of Oxford and Cambridge and, in the main, represented the privileged sectors of society, with a different approach in their relationships with people. Moffat knew that, in Scotland, the Episcopalian (Anglican) community was mainly composed of rich landowners, such as the Earl of Moray for whom he had worked at Donibristle.

Despite these differences, when Moffat retired he was held in such high esteem that, on St Andrew's Day 1875, at the request of Dean Stanley, he was invited to lecture in Westminster Abbey on African missions. Many years earlier, the Leighs' disappointment that this upright young man did not want

---

[7] Hofmeyr, etc. (ed.), *History of the Church in South Africa: A Document and Source Book,* (Pretoria: UNISA, 1991), 91. Bishop Gray did not belong to the evangelical camp. In the same letter Gray stated: 'As to our Church here, the only two clergy belong to a little evangelical alliance; one holds prayer-meetings in school, the other officiates in a school at Green Point, turnabout with dissenters.' Du Plessis quoted Andrew Murray: 'I [Andrew Murray] tried to probe him [Bishop Gray] on Puseyism, but he says there is no such thing in the Colony, only different shades of opinion. 'The jealousy of the Dissenters and the ignorance of others is the cause of all the outcry''. See: Du Plessis: *The Life of Andrew Murray of South Africa,* (Ldn: Marshall Brothers, 1919), 113.

[8] Cf. Chukwudi A Njoku, 'The missionary factor in African Christianity: 1884-1914', Kalu, Ogbu U (ed.): *African Christianity: An African Story,* (Pretoria: University of Pretoria, 2005), 218-255. Cf. Comaroff, *Revelation and Revolution, Vol. 1,* 80ff. Njoku and the Comaroffs argued that such people had very little status in Britain, and were in search of fame and status, (Njoku: 230), with missionary activity giving the chance to become important, which would never have occurred at home, and that their lowly background affected their zealous piety, with an emphasis on heaven and hell. This is a superficial argument. First, it was inevitable that working-class people would comprise the majority of the missionary community since, in Britain the ratio of the aristocracy to the working classes was less than 1 to several thousands. Second, the Evangelical Revival had been mostly among working classes. Third, the LMS specifically recruited artisan working men, since people used to refined living might not survive in frontier situations. Fourth, young men from wealthy families already had careers marked out for them.

to share their Anglican faith never damaged Moffat's position with them. In any case, very soon the whole course of his life was to change.

Methodism and Conversion

Moffat was brought up in a pious Christian home and appears to have always accepted the faith of his parents as his own. However, whilst at High Leigh, he came to a 'conversion' or 'spiritual awakening' experience through Methodist influences. Not long after arrival, Moffat had his first encounter with Methodism. Devout neighbours took him to the home of the Okeys at Northwood, where he began to attend services and class meetings.[9] The Wesleyan Methodists had been in the High Leigh area for some time, and the passionate appeal of evangelists at these meetings found a response in the young Scotsman. This resulted in a profound experience. At the Okeys he met and heard the Rev. Joseph Beaumont, who was a significant Methodist preacher. In a letter written to a Wesleyan minister in 1877 Moffat wrote:

> I discovered ... that the Wesleyans came on certain Sabbaths to a farmhouse some miles from the place of my abode. When it was possible for me to leave, I went thither, and occasionally heard Mr. Beaumont or a local preacher.[10] From curiosity I once went to Warrington to see a love-feast. I had comparatively little intercourse with the Wesleyans, but the more I knew of them the more I admired them for their Gospel simplicity, love and zeal. From this early acquaintance I have always felt an attachment; and have had the honour and the privilege of much delightful intercourse with the missionaries of that society since the days of Barnabas Shaw.[11]

Moffat described his spiritual experience under Methodism as conversion. He was convinced that, without the spiritual change which it accomplished, he was unregenerate and on the way to eternal loss in hell.[12] He wrote of his experience in a unpublished personal *Memoir,* now only extant as extracts quoted by John Smith Moffat in his *Lives.* After this experience, the nineteen-year-old threw himself into the work of the Methodist meetings and made

---

9 Dolan, *The Northwood Story,* (Manchester: Dolan, 1983), 20.

10 Cf. Joseph Beaumont (Jnr): *The Life of the Rev. Joseph Beaumont, M.D.,* (Ldn: Hamilton, Adams & Co., 1856). Beaumont was a renowned preacher despite having a speech defect (41). He was a friend of Adam Clarke the bible commentator (43); and was based in the Warrington circuit (35ff.). Beaumont's theology was typically postmillennial. See: Beaumont, 'Sermon IV: The Coming of the Kingdom of God', *Choice and Select Sermons by the Rev. Dr Beaumont,* (Ldn: Partridge, 1859) 46-67. For Beaumont's thoughts on the Millennium see: *Sermon XXIV,* (347-359); and *Sermon XIX,* (268-286).

11 RM, *To a Wesleyan Minister,* 7.1.1877, (Marrat, *Robert Moffat,* 4). Barnabas Shaw was a Wesleyan missionary who went to South Africa around the same time as Moffat.

12 RM, *Memoir,* (JSM, *Lives,* 13).

his first attempt at preaching. He was not an official preacher—his name was not on the Circuit Plan as a preacher at Sunday services—but, as Dolan has suggested, he probably preached in the form of a testimony or in giving a brief message of exhortation.[13]

Robert and Mary Moffat had affection and respect for Methodism and Methodist missionaries.[14] In 1830 they sent their school-age children to the Wesleyan school at Salem, near Grahamstown, South Africa. They were very attracted by the religious dimension of the school. Mary wrote to Miss Lees of Manchester: 'The strict attention paid to the religious instruction of the children compensates for the want of some advantages.'[15]

Yet, if encounter with the Methodists brought warm friendship into Moffat's life, it also brought crisis. Following the promise to his mother to read part of the Bible every day, especially the Gospels, he found that his readings made him feel uneasy concerning his relationship to Jesus Christ. He then began to read more in the Epistles, especially in the Epistle to the Romans. This brought a profound sense of sin and of unworthiness before God: 'I fell on my knees, and felt as if my sins, like a great mountain, were tumbling down upon me, and that there was but a step between me and the place of woe.'[16] Moffat alternated between hope and despair. He first attempted to deal with this conviction of sin through a reform of his own life 'by forsaking foolish and worldly company, vain thoughts, and wicked imaginations'. Still no peace came. Confusion deepened. Then a dawning:

> One evening, while poring over the Epistle to the Romans, I could not help wondering over a number of passages which I had read many times before. They appeared altogether different. I exclaimed with a heart nearly broken: 'Can it be possibly that I have never understood what I have been reading?' turning from one passage to another: each sending a renovation of light into my darkened soul. The Book of God, the precious, undying Bible, seemed to be laid open, and I saw at once what God had done for the sinner, and what was required of the sinner to obtain the divine favour and the assurance of eternal life. I felt that, being justified by faith, I had peace with God through the Lord Jesus Christ, and that He was made unto me wisdom and righteousness and sanctification and redemption.[17]

In his *Memoir,* Moffat concluded this account of his conversion by quoting a hymn he was to refer to on many occasions, *'Oh to grace how great a debtor,*

---

13 *Warrington Methodist Plan, 1814-1815,* (Dolan, *The Northwood Story,* 20).

14 JSM, *Lives,* 165. The Moffat house at Kuruman still has their statuette of John Wesley.

15 Mary Moffat, *To Miss Lees,* 15.9.1830, (JSM, *Lives,* 168).

16 RM, *Memoir,* (JSM, *Lives,* 13).

17 RM, *Memoir,* (JSM, *Lives,* 13f).

Daily I'm constrained to be'.[18] Like many of the hymns which he treasured, it was from the Evangelical Revival tradition. Its theology reflected his conversion experience. It expressed a realisation that all man has is sin, but what God gives is grace sufficient to bring mercy and new birth. Moffat testified at a Methodist meeting that he thought he could now see the chains which had bound him, and that his 'fetters of guilt were now rent in twain.'[19] But what was it which changed him from being simply a good-living, pious young man, to being a 'converted soul'? According to Moffat's own account, there was:

1. Awareness of, and sorrow over, the depth of his personal sinfulness.
2. Realising that God in Christ did everything needed for his salvation.
3. Being justified by faith he had peace with God through Christ.
4. Entering a living relationship with God in Christ.

All these points are standard evangelicalism. Even allowing for Moffat writing his *Memoir* according to a accepted style, he clearly expressed the conviction that there had been something missing in his spiritual life until that point. Before High Leigh, Moffat would have assented intellectually to each of these points. But what had formerly been an assent in the mind seems to have become a reality in his heart and soul. In his *Memoir*, when reflecting on his troubled state before conversion took place, Moffat wrote that the question which troubled him was: 'What think ye of Christ?'[20] And in 1843, on furlough in Britain, he spoke of this phase in his spiritual life:

> In obedience to that promise [to his mother concerning daily Bible reading] I read the Word of God and God poured out His Spirit from on high. My dark heart was enlightened. I saw the Saviour, that Saviour that died for me; and from that day to the present, I have lived upon the faith of the Gospel.[21]

Moffat pointed to personal knowledge of the Saviour, rather than to abstract knowledge of Christian principles. This was the understanding of conversion in the Great Awakening and in the Evangelical Revival. When 'the affections of the heart' were touched by Christ, and when there was created a love for, and faith in, Christ alone, then regeneration was deemed to have taken place.

---

18 Written by Robert Robinson (1735-1790). The common first line is, *'Come Thou Fount of every blessing'*. First published in 1758, it appeared in Robinson's, *A Collection of Hymns used by the Church of Christ in Angel Alley,* 1759. Robinson was a Methodist minister, who later moved to the Baptist church and pastored in Cambridge. He wrote several hymns, as well as some theology. His later spiritual life was difficult.

19 RM, *To his Parents,* 23.11.1814, (MO 5/1/1 Zimbabwe National Archives), (Gann, *A History of Southern Rhodesia,* (Ldn: Chatto & Windus, 1965), 41).

20 RM, *Memoir,* (JSM, *Lives,* 12).

21 RM, *Walworth Address,* (*Farewell Services,* 62).

Common to both Jonathan Edwards—who was prominent in the American Great Awakening—and his Scottish counterparts was a conviction that true piety must be distinguished from its counterfeit. For Edwards and his Scottish contemporaries, the primacy of the heart in religion was fundamental. This made for authentic spirituality.[22] For Edwards, and for revivalist theology in general, true religion largely consisted in 'holy affections', and that religion was not 'primarily an affair of the intellect but of the heart'.[23] Yet the head, or mind, was of course important, and Edwards gave two crucially important roles for the mind. Firstly, the mind received the propositional truth of the gospel. Secondly, the mind measured experiences against that truth. Any spirituality which failed to engage the mind, failed to engage the whole person. Yet the 'beauty of Christ' touching the 'affections of the heart' was a vital anchor.[24]

Jonathan Edwards' theology was the engine behind much of the revivalist tradition. Through his own conversion experience, Moffat touched the core of that tradition when his own heart was moved and transformed by affection for Jesus Christ. The pietistic hymns, so beloved by his mother, were now immensely meaningful and beloved for himself.

Moffat's dramatic account of his conviction and conversion, is written in a manner typical of many testimonies connected with revivalism. His narrative has clear similarities to John Wesley's account of his conversion in 1738, and whose awakening helped launch the Evangelical Revival of the eighteenth century. Moffat's references to struggling with the meaning of the Epistle to the Romans, plus his eventual discovery of 'justification by faith alone', are also reminiscent of Martin Luther's experience. Luther longed to understand Paul's Epistle to the Romans, eventually realising that it was God who made the sinner righteous, and that the sinner was justified simply by faith in surrender to Christ. Such parallels may not have been accidental. Yet, even if Moffat borrowed images and expressions from the experiences of men such as Luther and Wesley to help express his own spiritual journey, he did so in order to try and describe his personal experience.

There is a further point, which is important in relation to Moffat's later criteria of assessing whether a person had truly become a Christian. Moffat accepted his own need for a conversion experience despite a pious upbringing, regular church attendance, knowledge of the Bible, and a

---

22 Iain D. Campbell: 'Jonathan Edwards' *Religious Affections* as a Paradigm for Evangelical Spirituality', (*SBET,* 21/2, 167f).

23 Cited by Campbell, 'Jonathan Edwards' *Religious Affections*', 173.

24 Campbell: 'Jonathan Edwards' *Religious Affections*', 185.

relatively moral upright life. In later life, he would look for more than mere outward profession, church attendance, or head-knowledge of the Bible as evidence that a person had truly become a Christian.[25] His own spiritual journey meant that he had stringent criteria for deciding whether a person was truly converted. Alongside moral transformation, church attendance, and bible knowledge, had the 'affections of the heart' been moved by Jesus Christ?

THE MISSIONARY CALLING

A journey to Warrington changed Moffat's life.[26] One summer evening he needed to travel there, about six miles away. As he entered the town, he noticed a placard advertising a missionary meeting. The Rev. William Roby of Manchester was to preside. Moffat had never seen such a notice before. As he read the placard, 'the stories told by his mother of the Moravian missions in Greenland and Labrador, which had been forgotten for years, came vividly to mind.'[27] At that moment the possibility of a new purpose to his life came to him: the possibility of being a missionary. The meeting had in fact already taken place; but a short time later, when he again visited Manchester, to attend a Wesleyan Conference, he found William Roby's house, and requested an interview. 'He received me with great kindness, listened to my simple tale, took me by the hand, and told me to be of good courage.' The result was that Roby promised to write to the Directors of the LMS.

After waiting a few weeks, Moffat received a summons from Roby. In preparation for possible missionary service, he wanted Moffat to study under him, and so he found new employment for the young man in a nursery garden belonging to a Mr James Smith at Dukinfield, near Manchester, much nearer Roby's base. Meanwhile Roby had heard from the LMS Directors. They could not accept Moffat since they had had so many applications and had 'to

---

[25] When Hugh Miller, the stonemason who helped build the Kuruman church, died suddenly in 1834 Mary Moffat wrote: 'There is great obscurity on his eternal state. He possessed much knowledge on religious subjects; he loved the cause and people of God, but never decided. He was the child of pious parents, who died when he was very young, and his reverence for sacred things was great. His Bible was found in his bed, and his driver testifies that he read much in it'. See: Mary Moffat, *To her Father,* 20.8.1834, (JSM, *Lives,* 182f). The Moffats looked for a 'decision' for Christ as evidence of rebirth. Millen's religious traits were not seen as sufficient.

[26] Details are given in Moffat's *Memoir,* (JSM, *Lives,* 16ff).

[27] RM, *To Mary Moffat*, 12.11.1859, (from Moselekatse's kraal), (*MJ2,* 218): 'I well remember that from the first moment that my thoughts were turned to the state of the heathen, everything of a missionary character within my reach was greedily devoured, and even now I long to read the sufferings and successes of missionaries of bygone days.'

select those who possess the most promising acquirements.'[28] But Roby was convinced that Moffat had potential, and he was prepared to spend time on him. It was then, in the autumn of 1815, that Moffat wrote to his parents explaining that he was changing employer and that he would only work five days a week with his new employer. This was to give time for study on Saturdays, though he did not yet tell his parents his full plans. Eventually, he confessed that missionary service was in his mind. His new employer, James Smith, owned Dukinfield, which was closer to Manchester and to Roby than High Leigh. The Smiths provided Robert with more than just employment. In due course their daughter Mary became his wife.

Smith was a Scotsman, originally from Dunkeld in Perthshire.[29] John Smith Moffat wrote that Smith grew up deeply imbued with the Covenanter spirit, with every mountain and glen reminding him of his persecuted forefathers.[30] The Smiths were a devout couple, whose house was a welcome meeting-place for many, and they were vitally interested in Christian missions both at home and abroad. Their daughter, Mary, had been educated at the Moravian school near Fairfield. She was a young woman of exactly Robert's age, with a pious reputation, and an interest in the missionary cause.[31]

In 1879, when well into his eighty-fourth year, Moffat was approached by a young lady named Emma Pitman who wanted to write about Mary Moffat in an article entitled 'Heroines of the Mission Field.'[32] After several reminders from Emma, Moffat wrote a short synopsis about his wife. He stated that nearly the whole of the latter part of her education was completed at the Moravian school at Fairfield near Manchester: a 'providence of God' for which 'she never ceased to feel lively gratitude.'[33] Mora Dickson, a later biographer of Mary, pointed out that Moravians stressed order, discipline, the simplicity of the Gospel, a church life based on a deeply spiritual and emotional Christian fellowship, the centrality of loving Jesus, a delight in singing, and the belief that it was not lawful to bear arms.[34] Mary's

---

28 Roby, *To RM,* 27.11.1815, (JSM, *Lives,* 19).

29 The marriage certificate between James Smith and Mary Grey of York, 18.4.1792, gives Smith's address as 'Bowden, Cheshire'. He may have had links with the village of Bowden, near Melrose (Baxter & Burke, *Guide,* 324). Before going to England, he was called James Dow.

30 JSM, *Lives,* 295.

31 Mary's parents resisted Robert and Mary's marriage. They feared that their daughter would succumb to disease in Africa. Moffat set off alone in 1816. Three years later Mary followed him. In December 1819 they married in St. George's Church in Cape Town. Their 50-year marriage ended when Mary died in 1871, months after they returned to England.

32 The correspondence started on 16.1.1879, continuing until 18.11.1880.

33 RM, *To Emma Pitman,* 9.12.1879, (SOAS/CWM/Africa/Moffat/Pers/4).

34 Dickson, *Beloved Partner*, 14f.

schooldays were happy. She never forgot the Moravians, and they aroused in her an interest in missionary work overseas. Years later, she wrote to her father, reminding him of the time he had taken her to the first missionary meeting held in their area: 'My mind was powerfully affected. I was very young and had not the slightest prospect of joining the missionary band, but I thought the cause was worth a thousand lives.'[35]

Robert also had an affectionate regard for the Moravians. Before he left for Africa, indirect Moravian influence had touched his life in several ways. He first heard of them through the stories his mother told about the exploits of their missionaries, a memory rekindled when he saw the missionary poster near Manchester. The Moravians were one of the very first Protestant groups to take foreign mission seriously. In the late eighteenth century, whilst the national Church in Scotland debated whether it should be involved in foreign mission or not, the Moravians had been doing so for years.[36] The Moravians became involved in southern Africa when, in 1737, Georg Schmidt was sent there from Herrnhut, Germany. Schmidt came with the approval of the Dutch East India Company, and he established a station at Genadendal (Valley of Grace) in the Cape Province, patterned on the Herrnhut model.[37] Moffat visited Genadendal almost a century later, feeling a 'holy envy' at what Schmidt had accomplished.[38] But Schmidt had differences with the Dutch Church in southern Africa, and that brought problems.

Jan van Riebeck had brought Christianity to southern Africa in 1652 in the first permanent colony of the Dutch East India Company.[39] Unfortunately, the Boer descendants of these pious Dutchmen saw nothing inconsistent in their profession of Christianity and their possession of slaves, creating a poisoned legacy for the centuries to come. The Dutch clergy did not welcome Schmidt. They resented him infringing on their territory, and they did not like the progress he was making with the Khoikhoi. Worse, he was starting to baptise them. The Dutch clergy believed they alone had the authority to administer sacraments. But Schmidt refused to hand over his converts to them for the

---

35 Dickson, *Beloved Partner,* 18

36 The Moravian missionary track record is impressive. Cf. 'Moravian Brethren', in J.D. Douglas (ed.) *The New International Dictionary of the Christian Church,* (Exeter: Paternoster, 1978), 676. At one point, the Moravians had one missionary for every 60 communicant members, whereas, even in the hey-day of Protestant missions, the proportion in other Protestant churches was one missionary for every 5,000 communicant members.

37 Hofmeyr (ed.), *History of the Church in South Africa: A Document and Source Book,* 75ff.

38 RM, *MLSSA,* 20.

39 Moorhouse, *The Missionaries,* (Ldn: Eyre Methuen, 1973), 33.

baptismal rite. Consequently, they laid charges against him in Amsterdam, and the Moravian returned to Europe in 1744, heartbroken.[40]

Remarkably, when Moravians were allowed to return in 1792, they found Schmidt's first missionary congregation still alive. Moffat cited one old lady, Vehettge Tikhuie, baptised by Schmidt and given the name Magdalena, who remembered her former teacher, though she was now 80 years of age. She also produced a New Testament, bearing the marks of constant use, which he had presented to her.[41] What Schmidt had done was not only to preach, but to found a school. Though he had been removed, he had left the Bible among a partially literate people. Moffat saw that the new Moravian mission was able to build on the foundation of residual faith and goodwill established by Schmidt half a century previously, and 'through divine help, the Moravian Missions have prospered, and spread their branches'.[42]

Aspects of Schmidt's approach were echoed by Moffat, whose missiology also centred on teaching people to read and in giving them the Bible. The case of Magdalena reinforced Moffat's conviction that, if the Bible were supplied, and if a work was done obediently with a real love for the people amongst whom that work took place, then God would inevitably, in time, add blessing. The piety which Moffat took to Africa overlapped with swathes of Moravian piety. Mary's faith—nurtured by Moravians—so coincided with Robert's, that they were of one mind in the work they did for 50 years.

The Moravian Brethren had a spirituality characterised by 'holiness', in the original sense of the term. This meant 'purity of life before God'. It was the importance of 'purity of life' which characterised Moffat's faith. Yet, Moravian 'holiness' and the Presbyterian 'morality' of Moffat's Scottish roots were not identical. Moravian holiness, and that of the Evangelical Revival, had a warmth about it, which a legalistic Presbyterian morality could lack. One was motivated by a 'love of Jesus'; the other by a 'fear of the Law'. But the two streams intermingled in Robert Moffat. In 1857, when Moffat thought he had come across Moravian missionaries, he was overjoyed![43] That they turned out to be Hanoverian Lutherans was a disappointment, since he had an aversion to Lutheran 'popish' symbols. Nevertheless, he established a good working relationship with them.

---

40 Ibid, 34.

41 RM, *MLSSA,* 21. –Cf J.A. Millard, "Tikhuie, Vehettge Magdalena,"(DACB).

42 RM, *MLSSA,* 22.

43 RM, *Journal,* 22.8.1857, (*MJ2,* 38). It is difficult to evaluate Moffat's knowledge of Lutheranism. He had heard of the sixteenth-century Melanchthon, noting the similarity of a MaShona to an image of Melanchthon. See: RM, *Journal,* 1.9.1854, (*MJ1,* 285).

The Missionary Commissioning

Moffat was accepted by the LMS on his second application. He was ordained after interview and, since his current church membership was with Roby's Manchester congregation, he was ordained as a Congregationalist minister. During his days in London before leaving for Africa he made a visit to the LMS Museum, and his reflections on what he saw reveal what he expected to find in the mission field. In a letter to his parents, he described the visit:

> I spent some time in viewing the Museum, which contains a great number of curiosities from China, Africa, the South Seas, and the West Indies. I am unable to describe the sensations of my mind when gazing on the objects of Pagan worship! Alas! How fallen are my fellow-creatures, bowing down to forms enough to frighten a Roman soldier, enough to shake the hardest heart. [I must] be devoted to no other employment but to preach Christ to these degraded, despised, yet beloved mortals.[44]

From these remarks and from his later writings, it is evident that when Moffat arrived in Africa he expected to find what he saw in the museum, especially as he had read in the Bible of the Apostles encountering religious systems in which idols and images played a major part. In later years, he expressed surprise that, where he worked, such images were difficult to find. Moffat expected to find recognizable religious artifacts and practices, against which background he could present the Gospel message. The actual situation was to be different from what he anticipated, and this would affect his whole interpretation of indigenous beliefs.

He then paid a hurried visit to his parents in Scotland, not knowing if he would ever see them again. On 13 September 1816, he bade farewell to Roby, whose kindness had meant so much. The valedictory service was held at Surrey Chapel London on 30 September. Then, on 18 October, and along with eight other missionaries, he left Gravesend on the *Alacrity,* arriving at Cape Town on 13 January 1817. Moffat and four others were for Africa. The remainder were to sail to the South Seas. Originally, Moffat had also been earmarked for the South Seas, but this decision was altered shortly before the party left England.

The Shipboard Sermon

In December 1816, on board ship, and nearing southern Africa, Moffat preached a sermon on *Matthew 24:44*: *'Therefore you also must be ready; for the Son of man is coming at an hour you did not expect.'* His sermon shows

---

[44] RM, *To his Parents,* Sept. 1816, (Deane, *Robert Moffat,* 30f).

what was filling his mind at that time.[45] The young, raw, eager missionary expounded his theology to his fellow travellers. In later years, he often alluded to Richard Baxter's striking phrase: 'Preach as never sure to preach again, as a dying man to dying men'.[46] And, in his shipboard sermon, Moffat articulated that sense of urgency about the eternal destiny of his audience. Moffat divided the text into Exhortation and Argument. The Exhortation was: 'Be ye also ready.' The Argument was: 'For at such an hour as ye think not, the Son of Man cometh.' Towards the end of the sermon Moffat quoted directly from Baxter: 'Can a man' says the worthy Mr. Baxter, 'who is condemned to die tomorrow forget his doom? No, he dreads the event.'

Moffat's theme was 'Being Ready', and of how the human heart could be made ready for this coming of the Son of man. 'Being ready' was to 'have the heart renewed by divine grace'. Without grace, no turning to God was possible since 'man's heart in a state of nature is at war with heaven.' 'Being ready' also involved knowledge of our true nature. Moffat rejected the romanticist idea of a primitive innocence, and that 'ignorance is the mother of devotion'. Instead, he declared that 'the scriptures of truth assure us that "the people perish for lack of knowledge"'. He stressed: 'We must naturally infer that if all mankind are in a state of spiritual blindness, they must be made sensible of it before they be led to embrace a better system. [The] sinner who is ignorant of his own evil and depraved heart, thinks he has no need of such a Saviour. He walks in his own imagination'.

'Being ready' included knowledge of God. In a philosophical section of his sermon, and directly inspired by the teaching he had received from Roby, Moffat proclaimed that God is the One who says: 'I have being in myself, and consequently I give being to all.' Quoting Roby, almost word for word, Moffat stated that 'God is infinite in all his perfections.'[47] He explained in his sermon

---

45 RM, *Sermon on Matthew 24:44,* Dec. 1816, (SOAS/CWM/Africa/Moffat /Personal/Box 4). The provenance of a separate collection of sermon notes 'believed to be' Moffat's in the SOAS collection is uncertain, but this 1816 sermon is genuinely Moffat's.

46 E.g. 'The large attendance on Sabbath services and the riveted attention to the preaching of the Gospel are to *'the dying man speaking to dying men'* encouraging. I often look at the fixed and earnest interest manifested by so many countenances and wonder I do not hear the cry 'what must I do to be saved?' I am often deeply humbled when I see so little fruit and ... the necessity of only looking to, and praying for, the Spirit's gracious and soul reviving influences'. See: RM, *To Mullens, LMS,* 15.1.1868, (SOAS/CWM SA Reports Box 1).

47 Cf. Roby, *Theol. Lect.* 8, 'The Names and the Nature or Spirituality of God': 'His perfections are infinite and, consequently, He can never be fully comprehended by any created mind.' 'He is possessed of underived being in himself, and is the only cause of being to others.' Northcott stated that Moffat copied out Roby's *Lectures* after he disembarked. However, it seems that on board ship Moffat was already transcribing and had come to Lecture 8, and possibly Lecture 12, 'The Knowledge, or Omniscience, of God'.

that 'a knowledge of Jehovah is essential, since it is by contemplating his admirable perfections that we discover our own deformity. The sinner cannot apprehend Christ until assisted by the Holy Spirit to discover his own righteousness to be as filthy rags'. For Moffat, it was knowledge of the holy purity of God which truly revealed the intensity of human sin.

He further emphasised that 'being ready' involved not only knowledge of ourselves and of God, but of Jesus Christ: 'He is the ambassador of heaven, sent to declare the will of God to men and is, thence, called: the messenger of the covenant, the faithful and true witness.' Any true knowledge of Jesus Christ had to include knowledge of atonement through the sacrifice of Christ: 'His divine nature was the altar; his soul and body was the burnt sacrifice. These he resigned: the one to deadly wounds; the other to inexpressible anguish.' But where could this knowledge come from? Moffat was clear: 'Such knowledge is only derived from the Bible, and if accompanied with the Holy Spirit it is calculated to make us wise unto salvation.'

What would prove that a person had been seized and convicted by God, and was now ready for the coming of the Son of Man? Moffat set out criteria which remained with him all his life: the evidence would be moral change and transformation of character and life. Such a person would have, 'a sincere love of God', 'an aversion to sin', and 'a thirst after holiness.' The true Christian would be 'obediential to the commandments of God'. Men and women of faith would be like the 'wise virgins', 'living in the habitual exercise of faith and holiness'. The term 'habitual' was central. Any change had to be lasting. In passing, we note that, in the mission field, these would be exacting standards to expect in new converts from societies with no Christian tradition. Yet Moffat would be uncompromising in his expectations. His justification for having such high requirements came from his conviction that real change came as a work of God, not man, and therefore the same fruit of a new lifestyle should be evident in any work of God in any place or culture.

The theme of 'urgency' was returned to when Moffat alluded to another of his favourite and enduring motifs: men and women being possessed of 'immortal souls'. He asked, perhaps with the ship's crew in mind: 'Are we sensible that we have—treasured in our breasts—an immortal soul that will exist through all eternity?' Are we aware that: 'We must be either happy or miserable through all eternity according to the life which we have lived here?' This was the message proclaimed by the LMS recruit as he prepared to disembark, on the threshold of a fifty-four-year missionary career.

Chapter 4
The Tutelage of William Roby

William Roby had links with the evangelical movement in Scotland, through the Haldanes.[1] He had accompanied James Haldane on an mission tour in 1799, and had been invited by Robert Haldane to take up a post in Scotland.[2] When he met Moffat, he quickly assessed the spiritual pedigree of the young man who came to his house, and the brief, but intense, theological education, which Moffat received from Roby was the only substantial training he had for the mission field. The sum of it is found in a 470-page copy of Roby's *Theological Lectures,* transcribed in 1817 by Moffat's own hand, and which is now in the archives of the *School of Oriental and African Studies*. Echoes of what Moffat learned from the lectures occur throughout this book, as we discuss Moffat's missionary theology. So, what was Roby's theological outlook? What was the tenor of his churchmanship?

Roby was an English 'Independent' which, in the English context, was identical with Congregationalism. The essence of Congregationalism is that any specific church or congregation has autonomy in its decision making. No congregation is answerable to any external ecclesiastical authority. Though there were regional Associations, these were loose, voluntary affairs which could not interfere in the internal matters of a congregation. They were for mutual encouragement, and not to exercise authority over congregations. By the late eighteenth century, English Independency was flourishing, and many Scots who migrated into England saw it as a congenial spiritual home. At that time, the so-called Presbyterian churches in England had an Arian, or Unitarian, Christology. In contrast, the Independent Churches seemed Calvinist, evangelical and more acceptable.

Roby's parents were Church of England, and Roby retained a high regard for the Church of England's official theological basis, *The Thirty-Nine Articles.* He regularly challenged Anglican clergy on whether they really believed the *Articles* to which they had subscribed. He also published several books, but

---

1 For William Roby (1766-1830), see: Gordon Robinson, *William Roby and the Revival of Independency in the North,* (Ldn: Independent Press, 1954). For Roby's theology, see his *Defence of Calvinism,* (Ldn: Williams & Smith, 1810); also, his *Theological Lectures,* (SOAS/CWM, Home Odds Box 25).

2 Robinson, *William Roby,* 112ff.

it is his unpublished *Theological Lectures* which give his theological system. Our aim, in this chapter, is not to summarise all of Roby's theology, but to highlight two important areas which interacted with Moffat's missionary outlook. Other aspects are picked up at appropriate stages. The issues presently considered are Roby's doctrines of election and revelation.

William Roby and the Doctrine of Election

Roby was a Calvinist. He himself stated that Calvinists 'are distinguished from other bodies of Christians especially by their professed belief of those doctrines which relate to the decrees of God.'[3] For Roby, these doctrines gave Calvinism its specific identity.[4] Thus, for him, the cardinal doctrines of Calvinism were: Personal Election and Reprobation, Particular Redemption, the Speciality and Efficacy of Divine Grace in the Conversion of Sinners, and the certain Perseverance of the Saints. He set out his Calvinism in his book, *A Defence of Calvinism,* in which he sought to refute the charge of a Mr S that the doctrine of 'particular atonement' in Calvinism involved the damnation of infants, that it only allowed a small number of people to be saved, and that it envisaged multitudes of unhappy wretches imploring divine mercy in vain.[5] Calvinism was familiar to Moffat from his Scottish roots, long before he was taught it by Roby. But did he absorb Roby's version into his thinking?

'Particular Atonement' is the same as 'Limited Atonement', which teaches that Christ did not die for the sins of everyone but only for the sins of the elect. It is also sometimes called 'Effective Atonement' since a consequence of the doctrine is that the death of Christ makes effective, and not just possible, the salvation of those for whom he died. On this basis, Roby argued that Calvinism offered *more* hope, not *less,* concerning salvation. He claimed that Calvinism exhibited *more* of the grace and love of God, not *less,* since particular atonement made salvation *certain* for some, whereas Mr S only saw salvation as *possible* for many. Roby insisted that a *certain* salvation for *some* exhibited a God of greater love, than a salvation which was only *uncertain* for an *undefined number.*[6]

---

3 Roby, *A Defence of Calvinism: or, Strictures on a recent publication entitled 'St. Paul against Calvin',* 15. Roby's protagonist was Mr Edward Smyth.

4 Roby, *A Defence of Calvinism,* 16, taught that the Calvinist doctrine of the divine was the only stable position between a Stoic notion of a fatalism independent of God, and the notion that all events happen by chance.

5 Ibid, 7

6 Ibid, 84.

Mr S also charged Calvinists with teaching that some children who died in infancy and so never had opportunity to respond to the Gospel, had already been damned by the eternal decree of God. In response, Roby declared that though Calvinists maintained that, while mankind in general deserved to perish on account of original sin, it was no part of their system that any perished on this account alone:

> The body of Calvinists are inclined to draw a favourable conclusion regarding children dying in infancy. They do not, however, suppose that children are saved on account of their harmlessness or innocence but only through the merit of the Redeemer's sacrifice.[7]

Then Roby turned the argument:

> According to Mr. S., God has not decreed to save any one of our race [except] on certain conditions to be performed by themselves. What then must be the state of children dying in infancy? We cannot suppose that they have repented, believed or performed, personally, any condition whatever. Infant damnation follows much more naturally from the system which Mr. S. has adopted than from that of his opponents.[8]

Roby argued that a predestinarian Calvinist system at least allowed for some children being saved—through its doctrine of election—whereas an Arminian system, which required human response, resulted in all children who were too young to respond in faith remaining unsaved.

How did Moffat, as a protégé of Roby, apply this? Moffat made very few allusions to the doctrines of election and predestination, but what is significant is how he reacted to the death in infancy of his own children. In the Kuruman cemetery there are graves of three Moffat children who died long before they could ever know, understand, or respond to the Gospel.

Baby Robert (1825).[9] The inscription on his head stone, set into the wall of the old school-room, reads: 'Here lies the body of Robert the son of Rbt and Mary Moffat; Obt. Aug 21st, 1825, aged 5 days. *Ba ba rubitseng mogo Jesus Morimo. O tla ba lere nia*. 1 Thess 4:14.' This inscription is the oldest known example of written SeTswana, and the Scripture text, chosen by the Moffats for their baby son, expressed a strong positive hope: *'For since we believe that Jesus died and rose again, even so, through Jesus, God will bring with him those who have died.'*

---

7 Ibid, 8.

8 Ibid, 84f.

9 This 'Robert' died in infancy. A subsequent son, born in 1827, was also given the name 'Robert'. Similar renaming took place after Elizabeth died in 1832, with a subsequent child, born in 1839, given the same name.

Baby Elizabeth (1832). 'Here lies the body of Elizabeth, the daughter of Robert and Mary Moffat, who died of small pox, January 1832 aged 10 months, Luke 18:16'. The text chosen for baby Elizabeth was: *'Let the little children come to me, and do not stop them; for it is to such as these that the kingdom of God belongs.'*

Baby Unwin Moffat (1859), grandson to Robert and Mary. 'Unwin, infant son of John Smith and Emily Moffat, who died at Kuruman 15 April 1859 aged four months; Luke 10:20 *'Rejoice because your name is written in heaven'.*

Only the most hair-splitting analysis could conclude that such inscriptions do not imply that these infants are in heaven. The whole thrust of the hope, engraved in stone, points to confidence concerning their eternal destiny. These gravestone inscriptions are written theology as much as any letter, journal, or book. What they say was clearly affected by emotions of loss and grief, but it is precisely because the authors were so affected that the real theology of the heart is revealed. What does a man or woman *really* believe? Ask them when faced with death and the answer is given.

Moffat did not believe in the automatic damnation of children who die in infancy. Neither did Roby, though we cannot see how Roby's doctrine of election and particular atonement can support the positive hope concerning the eternal destiny of *specific* children, which hope the Moffats expressed on the gravestones. Roby's doctrine of election may make salvation *certain* for some, but which ones? How can there be any confidence that *these particular* children were among that number?[10] Writing in 1826, Moffat offered more indications of his belief that infants who died went to heaven:

> Fegeland's child was committed to the dust about noon. Happy babe, though early called to taste the fruits of the fall [death]. You are now beyond the reach of woe, destined forever to escape the storms and dangers of human life. I would not for ten thousand worlds resume my course. Oh! How enviable is the state of those who have finished their course, and entered the heavenly mansions, where there is fullness of joy.[11]

---

10 David Livingstone also expressed confidence in the salvation of his dead infant daughter. In an 1850 letter to his parents, he wrote: 'Have just returned from burying our youngest child. Never conceived before how fast a little stranger can twine round the affections. She was just six weeks old when called away to see the King in his beauty. I have not the smallest doubt but that she is saved by one whom she could not know. She is home now.' See: Livingstone, *To Mr and Mrs N. Livingston,* 18.9.1850, (*DLFL, Vol. 2,* 103). See also: Livingstone, *To Mr and Mrs N Livingston,* 4.12.1850, (*DLFL, Vol. 2,* 116). Kuruman missionaries assumed salvation for children who died before knowing anything about the Gospel. There is no evidence that this extended to children of non-Christian families.

11 RM, *Journal,* 26.3.1826, (*AAK,* 214).

Moffat envisaged the dead child entering the full glory of heaven. Moffat was not saying that 'innocent' babes go to nothingness: he was stating that they receive a full salvation. This confidence is inconsistent with full-blown Calvinism, indicating that Moffat's Calvinism was a moderate version, at least in respect of the doctrines of election and atonement.

Roby also disagreed with Mr S's accusation that Calvinism taught that only a few were chosen to be saved,[12] quoting the Calvinist hymn-writer Augustus Montague Toplady: 'What a very small portion, comparatively, of the human species falls under the decrees of preterition and non-redemption'.[13] As a counterblast to Mr S, Roby pointed out that every clergyman of the Church of England had agreed to the *Thirty-Nine Articles*, article 12, and, if Mr S was criticising a Calvinist theology of predestination, then he was by-passing the implications of his own *Thirty-Nine Articles*.[14] In Roby's view, the Calvinism of the *Thirty-Nine Articles* was the same as that of the *Westminster Confession,* of which Mr S. was so critical.

Yet, there is at least one point at which the Calvinism of Roby differed from that of the Westminster Assembly. Roby was infralapsarian in his thinking rather than supralapsarian, teaching that election to salvation occurred *after* Adam's fall, whereas the Westminster Divines taught that election occurred *before* the creation of the world.[15] Roby taught that God elected to salvation and simply left the rest to the consequences of their sin. Hence, for Roby, God's election was an expression of grace, with damnation *our* choice, not God's.[16] Roby did not push the doctrine of election into a supralapsarian position as had the Westminster Assembly.

---

12 Roby, *A Defence of Calvinism,* 8.

13 Toplady, *Works, Vol. 6,* 89, quoted by Roby, *A Defence of Calvinism,* 9. Roby was keen to present Calvinist doctrines as mild, though, if pressed, he adhered to the full 'TULIP' doctrines which characterised the Calvinist framework: T (total depravity); U (unconditional election); L (limited atonement); I (irresistible grace); P (perseverance of the saints). Roby's acceptance of 'total depravity' is in his *Theol. Lect,* 'Appendix on Prayer' (447).

14 Roby, *A Defence of Calvinism,* 10.

15 *The Westminster Confession of Faith,* Ch. 3. Roby, *A Defence of Calvinism,* 16, was anxious to argue that Calvinists were misrepresented if they were accused of teaching that God predestinated persons to damnation without any regard to sin.

16 Roby, *A Defence of Calvinism,* 16, taught that God elected 'a great multitude which no man can number out of all nations to make a display of his unmerited mercy and of his righteous vengeance leaving the rest to the fatal consequences of their depravity and guilt.' Sin is the only cause why any are doomed to destruction. Sin alone leads to destruction Grace alone leads to salvation. These operate under the sovereignty of God's will (16). Roby stressed that a general proclamation of the gospel to all, but 'the beneficial results of Christ's sacrifice were not left uncertain or indeterminate; that it was not designed for the actual redemption of every individual of mankind, but only of those who were chosen in him for salvation.' (17).

In relation to this, Moffat believed that Van der Kemp, the first LMS missionary to southern Africa, and founder of Bethelsdorp, had an extreme doctrine of predestination, which had resulted in immorality among converts. Moffat's opinion was that Van der Kemp's particular brand of Calvinism created problems. He wrote in *Missionary Labours*: '[Van der Kemp's] ultra notions on the subject of predestination left a leaven in some of the African churches, which it required the labour of many years to remove.'[17] What Moffat had in mind was a moral irresponsibility arising from Van der Kemp's doctrines, as he understood them:

> [Bethelsdorp] has been the seat of missionaries, but equally the seat of crime. All who have now fallen into gross sin (adultery) either were at Bethelsdorp or had previously lived there. The founder himself of that once renowned station had a character far from being unblameable; neither did his doctrines tend to a holy life. To us who are acquainted with his character, it is painful to see his name placed among the worthies in their public eulogiums. More of the evil (I conceive) is to be traced to the system and doctrines introduced, than the temptations around, for the sin has been perpetrated where there were the most missionaries.[18]

It is difficult to know whether Van der Kemp taught predestination in the way which Moffat implies. Moffat may have been over-sensitive to the possibility of a predestinarian theology undermining moral restraint in converts, because of the Scottish context from which he came. There was a strand of late eighteenth and early-nineteenth-century Scottish thinking which explored the extreme effects which an extreme doctrine of predestination might have on moral responsibility. In Scotland, Robert Burns in his satirical poem *Holy Willie's Prayer*, and James Hogg in his later work, *The Private Memoirs and Confessions of a Justified Sinner,* both examined the question: 'If God's predestination is absolute, and if every event is preordained, can there be any fault in any action for a saved person?' Moffat jumped to the conclusion, possibly erroneously, that Bethelsdorp converts did not strive for a holy way of life because Van der Kemp taught absolute predestination.

---

17 RM, *MLSSA,* 42. Enklaar, *De Levensgeschiedenis van Johannes Theodorus Van Der Kemp* (Wageningen: Veenman en Zonen N V, 1972), 80ff, argued that Van der Kemp's views on predestination were less harsh than reputed. Enklaar held that Van der Kemp's evangelical piety meant that his faith was warmer than his formal theology. Van der Kemp's, *De Theodicee van Paulos,* set out his theological reflections concerning the righteousness and justice of God in the light of Paul's Letter to the Romans. His fatalistic thinking on theodicy, evil, God's will etc., was moulded by the tragic loss of his daughter and first wife (Cf. *AAK,* footnote 42, 68). We are indebted to Dr Steven Paas, Zomba Theological College, for translating from the Dutch.

18 RM, *To Alexander Moffat,* Jan. 1823, (*AAK,* 68f). In public Moffat praised Van der Kemp; in private letters he often condemned him.

For Roby, preaching and proclamation were the *means* which God, in his sovereignty, had appointed to 'excite persons to an earnest concern for their souls, to faith in the Lord Jesus Christ for salvation, and to the diligent discharge of their Christian duty'. He insisted that such preaching and proclamation were also the means by which these things were 'made effectual by the Holy Spirit.'[19] The 'futility' of some being unable to respond—since God had already elected those who would be saved—was not discussed. Yet, for Roby, as a major figure in the LMS, this issue was important. Was the missionary task pointless if God's decrees were already fixed? Or, if men and women appeared to 'respond', was that response in vain if they were not among the elect?

These theological questions have been asked on many occasions and in many contexts, but how did Roby deal with them? His primary response centred on obedience. The Church was called to obey, even if it did not fully understand, and obedience included the great commission to evangelise which Jesus gave to the Church. But is evangelism genuine if election has already determined the number and identity of the saved? Roby did not deal with this, apart from stressing that, without divine grace, 'no man has any proper inclination or *ability* to turn unto God.' He added that converting grace 'is not communicated to persons in general, but only to the elect in particular'.[20] For Roby, the question of an 'ability to turn to God' did not need to be defended. All was under God's sovereignty. None deserved mercy anyway. We should be grateful that God elected any at all.

For Roby and his contemporaries, the purpose of evangelism was firstly *theocentric* and only secondly *anthropocentric*. The primary purpose of preaching and proclamation was to honour and glorify God. Preaching and proclamation could not alter the number of the elect; but they did make known God's grace and God's glory over all the earth. In making these things known, God was honoured. Preaching and proclamation were tools which uncovered a treasure hitherto hidden; namely, the richness of God's mercy to some. On the human side, preaching and proclamation were relevant as

---

19 Roby, *A Defence of Calvinism,* 27.

20 Ibid, 18. Roby referred to Article 17 of the *Thirty-Nine Articles.* For a Calvinist there was no 'moral' problem in God determining who would be saved. No one deserved mercy; and for God to grant salvation to *any* was an enormous act of grace. God had no need to pardon any sinner; therefore, those who were not elected could have no complaint. Whilst this was 'logically coherent' it made grace arbitrary. It also seemed to clash with the thrust of the New Testament which appears to present a God who yearns for the salvation of the world and whose desire is that none should perish. There is a nominalism at the heart of Calvinism: the Gospel comes from the contingent *will* of God, and not from the ontological *nature* of God.

the means by which the elect were brought into the light and were enabled to know God, and thus to worship and rejoice in Him.

Much twenty-first-century evangelism assumes that a response is only meaningful if it is 'free' from the side of the human respondent. In contrast, traditional Calvinist theology of evangelism had the focus on God. In Calvinist theology, the purpose of proclamation was to exalt God among the nations. Proclamation centred on the majesty of God, as being sovereign in deciding to save any out of an undeserving humanity. Which individuals were able to receive that grace was secondary. God's honour was satisfied by making his purposes known. God would decide who were to be the recipients.

Roby also applied the doctrine of election to the Christian life, since the people of God were 'destined for good works'. Mr S had argued that Calvinism set aside the necessity of faith and holiness, but Roby countered:

> Genuine Calvinism, whilst it renounces the idea of faith and holiness being the meritorious causes of salvation, does not suppose that persons, possessed of reasoning powers, may be saved without them. [Calvinism] teaches us that persons give no proper evidence of their being in a state of salvation, but by a credible profession of faith and holiness; and that the sincerity and truth of this profession are not fully confirmed except by final perseverance therein.[21]

This general defence was supplemented by a more robust argument, in which Roby tied together God's *election* of a person and the *holiness of life* which that person, in virtue of their election, would necessarily exhibit. Someone who was decreed to salvation was also decreed to holiness and a God-fearing life.[22] Therefore, a person deliberately being ungodly was unlikely to have been elected. Roby taught that 'divine grace produces a disposition in persons by which they yield voluntary obedience to their heavenly Father.'[23] Holiness of life was established by God's election. Its formation in an elect person was as inevitable as their salvation, since the same divine election established both.

This principle—that holiness of life was inevitable since it did not come by human endeavour but by divine decree—lay behind the expectation that true converts would manifest a radical transformation of life and manners, moving from sinful ways to righteous living. This was certainly Moffat's view. He had high requirements, rooted in high expectations. Within a Calvinist framework, 'faith' without 'holiness' was a contradiction. Not because of an

21 Ibid, 22.
22 Ibid, 29.
23 Ibid, 31.

imperative laid upon men and women, which they might struggle to fulfil, but because holiness issued from the same decree which brought salvation.

A person's background, history, and culture were irrelevant. Anyone elected by God to salvation would also be elected to good works, whatever their background, history, or culture. The same manner of life should occur in Africa, as in Scotland, England or any other part of the world. What God ordained in Scotland and England, he would ordain in Africa. What the Holy Spirit created in Scotland and England, he would create in Africa. The fruit of holiness would be the same everywhere, since it was the result of election. Thus, it was inevitable that a missionary, such as Moffat, expected to see 'Scottish' Christian lifestyle in Africa, because that lifestyle was not in fact 'Scottish' but was something ordained by God for everyone. Because the character and decrees of God were invariant to time or place, then the same fruit *must* be expected; if not, then the nature of God altered according to circumstances, and that was theologically unacceptable. Roby taught that true conversion and regeneration meant that: 'the soul becomes anxious to enjoy the favour and to be employed in the service of God.'[24] For Roby, the true marks of regeneration and conversion were seen in a desire to please God and serve God. These were the signs to be looked for when assessing a person's profession of faith.

Roby was a Calvinist Evangelical, for whom the object of all religion was the glory of God.[25] Yet he was more moderate than some Calvinists, especially in refusing to push Calvinism into a supralapsarian, double-decree, position. Piggin argued that was because Roby was influenced by the moderate type of Calvinism favoured by Edward Williams, one of the LMS founders in 1795, and who delivered the charges to the very first LMS missionaries in 1796.[26] Piggin's summary of Williams' theological position shows strong similarities with Roby's theology. In Piggin's view, Williams attempted to bridge the gap between the popular preaching of the day, which was the product of the Evangelical Revival—and which invited all to receive the mercy of a loving God—and the popular conception of Calvinist theology with the harsh God who predestinates some to damnation; Williams was concerned to remove serious theological hindrances to the Evangelical Awakening of the period.[27] Thus Williams, and Roby after him, had a moderate Calvinism in which every man's damnation was of himself,

---

[24] Ibid, 18.

[25] Roby, *Theol. Lect.* 2, 'Religion', emphasises that the purpose of human existence is: 'To aim at the advancement of His glory, as the highest end of our lives'.

[26] Piggin, *Making Evangelical Missionaries: 1789-1858,* 81ff.

[27] Ibid, 81ff.

and every man's salvation was all of God. Christ's death was a surety only for the elect, but yet Christ paid the price sufficient for all men.[28] This was a theology of the best of both worlds. For Roby, Calvinism exalted the majesty and the sovereignty of God, and challenged men and women to live lives of holiness and obedience.

When we consider Moffat's position, there is no indication that he took on board all of Roby's doctrines, such as Particular Atonement. On this, we disagree with Northcott, who argued that Moffat was so profoundly influenced by Roby, that he totally embraced Roby's doctrines of election. Northcott averred that for Moffat, the 'sovereignty of God' as it appeared in Roby's formal Calvinism, conditioned Moffat's approach to native peoples, since it was God's sovereignty which determined 'whether any should be redeemed' and the 'persons who should be redeemed'.[29] We would disagree. Although Moffat had a strong sense of God's sovereignty in all things, there is nowhere, in all his writings, any indication that he accepted the doctrine of particular election. In fact, Moffat explicitly stated his belief that Christ had died for everyone, even those who would perish. For example, in 1878 he wrote of how solemn it was to 'think of the stream of human beings rushing on to the vast eternity, and still more so to think of the multitude moving along without a thought of their future destiny'. He stated his concern:

> Our hearts sink within us at the thought of the *untold myriads perishing for whom Christ died.* How the reflection wakens our inmost emotions to exclaim. 'Oh, to grace how great a debtor!' and 'Why was I made to hear His voice?'[30]

For Moffat, there were some 'for whom Christ died', who yet were perishing. That was *not* a doctrine of particular or limited atonement. Several other Independents, including the theologian Ralph Wardlaw, thought similarly.

---

28 Ibid, 83. Bebbington, *Holiness in Nineteenth Century England,* (Carlisle: Paternoster, 2000), 32f, argued that a major factor in moderating Westminster Calvinism in the eighteenth century was the influence of Jonathan Edwards. Bebbington argued that Edwards' position became the template for evangelical piety until 1900. In high-Calvinism, the human contribution is almost non-existent. Edwards modified this, arguing that the lost bore responsibility, and that the sinner was responsible for his own fate. Bebbington further argued that 'moderate' Calvinism lay behind the missionary societies of the 1790s, including the Baptist Missionary Society, the LMS, and the CMS. In this way an 'evangelical Calvinism' emerged.

29 Northcott, *Robert Moffat,* 23.

30 RM, *To Mrs Goulty,* 23.3.1878, (JSM, *Lives,* 400). 'Why was I made to hear His voice', is Moffat's rendering of Isaac Watt's hymn, 'Why was I made to hear Thy voice, and enter while there's room; when thousands make a wretched choice, and rather starve than come?' For Moffat, this expressed bewilderment that so many, for whom Christ died, chose to reject him.

William Roby and the Concept of Revelation

One of Roby's major publications, directly pertinent to Moffat's theology, was his, *Lectures on the Principal Evidences and the Several Dispensations on Revealed Religion, Familiarly Addressed to Young Persons,* first published in 1818. Moffat quoted from it in his 1842 *Missionary Labours.* Though Moffat left Britain before these lectures were printed, the thinking behind them had been taught to students like Moffat before the published version was issued.

For Roby, the idea of God was not innate. Nor could it be obtained by intuition. It required divine revelation.[31] Roby's premise was that there was no 'natural' knowledge of God whatsoever. All knowledge of God was by 'special revelation'.[32] He opposed the eighteenth-century tendency to promote natural religion as the basis for theology. Several eighteenth-century thinkers had questioned whether special revelation could ever be a proper basis for religion: it seemed that religious 'fair play', in the form of a common religious experience available to all humanity in any time or at any place, could only be achieved if knowledge of God were independent of a specific historical revelation which, by its very nature, was not universally accessible. For such thinkers, a knowledge of God which depended on a specific revelation to a specific people in a specific place at a specific time did not have universal validity, and made God arbitrary in His blessings. They strove to build theology on a foundation of reason and nature, as entities which were available to anyone anywhere. Within this approach 'special revelation' could only have value if it confirmed a natural knowledge of God which was already available and knowable from reason and nature. This view assumed five pillars of innate religious knowledge, common to all religions:[33]

1. That there is a God.
2. That He ought to be worshipped.
3. That virtue is the chief element in this worship.
4. That repentance for sin is a duty.
5. That there is another life of rewards and punishments.

---

[31] Cf. Roby, *Theol. Lect.* 1, 'The Existence or Being of God': 'The idea of God is not innate; It is not obtained by mere intuition; It was originally communicated by Divine revelation; It is *confirmed* by various rational inferences'.

[32] Roby, in his *Theological Lectures,* and in his book, *Lectures on the Principal Evidences and the several dispensations on Revealed Religion,* drew heavily on the eighteenth-century writer John Ellis, especially his, *The Knowledge of Divine Things.* Ellis' arguments were also used by Moffat in *Missionary Labours.* These arguments are examined in our following chapters.

[33] H. Cuncliffe-Jones, *Christian Theology since 1600,* (Ldn: Duckworth, 1970), 39.

Mainstream evangelical theology was not totally hostile to this rationalistic natural theology. Evangelical theology taught that there was a measure of a natural knowledge of God's existence and of his character. That was why all were without excuse before God, even if no special revelation through Scripture or by proclamation had been given. Traces of this can be found in the *Westminster Confession*.[34] William Paley, in his *Evidences of Christianity* (1794) and his *Natural Theology* (1802) also argued that natural theology could give knowledge, not only of God's existence, but of God's qualities and character.[35] Thus, in the early nineteenth century, it was not unusual for evangelical theology to include some natural theology. That was the position which the young Robert Moffat assumed: that all men and women, everywhere, would have some natural knowledge of God.

Roby taught differently. As such, he was unusual in rejecting the validity of natural theology as being, in any sense, a basis for the knowledge of God. Contrary to nearly all of his contemporaries, Roby did not assume that all humanity everywhere would have an awareness of the supreme being. But the young Moffat, however much he respected his teacher, did not adopt Roby's position, at least not to begin with. Thus, despite being instructed in Roby's view, Moffat initially held the older evangelical position of a complementary relationship between revelation and natural theology. It was much later that he felt compelled to re-examine Roby's teaching on this subject, because of what he thought he encountered in Africa. But in 1816 when he set off for Africa, Moffat fully expected that, wherever he went, he would uncover a universal awareness of a supreme being, which would be a vital starting-point for evangelism and conversion.[36]

*

William Roby's tuition was important for Moffat. Whilst at Dukinfield, he saw him once or twice a week for instruction. Then, when Moffat was accepted by the LMS, he moved to Manchester for more intensive study under Roby. Though it was only for a few months, it was Moffat's only formal training for fifty-four years of missionary work. In total, Roby prepared about ten LMS missionaries. From 1803 until 1808, he had a formal Training College, preparing itinerant preachers as well as LMS candidates.[37] By the time Moffat

---

34 *Westminster Confession of Faith,* Ch. 1.

35 Paley never viewed natural theology as marginalising revealed theology. However, eighteenth-century rationalism employed natural theology for that very purpose, viewing a religion built solely on special revelation as inadequate and unjust.

36 RM, *MLSSA,* 121, where Moffat admitted to having initially disagreed with Roby.

37 Piggin, *Making Evangelical Missionaries: 1789-1858,* 100. Roby encouraged the members of his church to be evangelists, though he was uncomfortable with the term. He believed that

arrived, the course included the grammatical construction of English, sermon composition, logic, Church history, geography, use of globes, principles of natural and moral philosophy, Greek, Hebrew, plus Roby's eighty *Theological Lectures,* which each student copied out for himself.[38] Roby had already published several works which would be available to Moffat.[39]

Moffat conceded that Roby had immense influence on him. In 1870, in the vestry of Grosvenor Street Congregational Church, Manchester, looking back to the birth of his missionary calling, Moffat recorded that he met there with Roby 'nearly every Sabbath evening about 53 years ago.'[40] Roby's impact was seminal. Moffat stated in 1843 that a 'remarkable providence brought me under the eyes and under the care and under the tuition of the late venerable William Roby. That was the man that nurtured my youthful mind; that was the man that established my view; that was the man that pointed me to the heathen world.'[41]

When Moffat left for Africa in October 1816, he had known Roby for only two years, though three months of that time had involved intensive full-time theological training. Direct tuition, on a one-to-one basis, imparted an enormous amount of information. Roby had much to give, and Moffat absorbed Roby's teaching like a sponge soaking up water.[42] Their discussions would touch deep areas of faith. As far as Moffat was concerned, Roby was a theological giant. Northcott felt that Moffat found in Roby's system three guiding principles for practical affairs: Acceptance, Duty, Obedience. Moffat adhered to these through his long life.[43]

---

the office of 'evangelist' was restricted to the primitive Church, (Roby, *Theol. Lect.* 77, 'Church Fellowship'). Bogue, *Miss. Lect.* 2, 'Employment of a Missionary', was of the same opinion.

38 Dickson, *Beloved Partner,* 17f.

39 See: Robinson, *William Roby (1766-1830),* 165-171 for a list of Roby's publications. Those published before 1816, and which Moffat had access to before he left for Africa, included: *The Dangerous Tendency of Socinianism (1791; The First Principle of Christianity; or a Catechism for Children (1798; Civil Magistracy defended (1798); An Apology for Christian Missions to the Heathen (1801); On the Ministerial Example of Christ (1803); An Answer to a Layman's 'Few Plain Reasons for Adhering to the Doctrines of the Church of England' (1809); Scripture Instructions, Containing Questions Relating to the Principal Doctrines of Revealed Religion (1809); A Defence of Calvinism (1810); The Glory of the Latter Days (1814).*

40 RM, *Note,* 23.9.1870, (SOAS/CWM/Africa/Moffat/Pers/4).

41 RM, *Walworth Address,* 1843, (*Farewell Services,* 63). Robert and Mary Moffat called their fostered African daughter 'Sarah Roby' after William Roby's wife. At the modern Kuruman Moffat Mission one of the rooms is named the 'Sarah Roby Room'.

42 Roby-like concepts used by Moffat in his 1816 'Shipboard Sermon' confirm this.

43 Northcott, *Robert Moffat,* 23.

The Nature and Knowledge of God

Chapter 5
The Concept of God`

ONE OF THE MOST controversial parts of Moffat's thinking was his view that some of the indigenous peoples whom he met—though not all—had no concept of God or of a supreme being. In this he has been severely criticised, not least by Willoughby, Smith, Schapera and Setiloane.[1] But why did he come to that conclusion? This is puzzling, not least because in 1816, on the eve of departing for Africa, he had written to his parents: 'I long to be engaged in the blessed work of saying to the heathen, "Behold your God!"'[2] Yet, he later stated that some of the peoples had no such concept. Moffat was not alone in his opinion. Van der Kemp[3] and Schmelen[4] thought similarly, though Campbell,[5] Shaw,[6] and Livingstone[7] did not.

---

1 Willoughby, *The Soul of the Bantu,* 299ff; Smith, *Robert Moffat: One of God's Gardeners,* 101ff; Schapera, *Apprenticeship at Kuruman*, Introduction; and Setiloane, *The Image of God among the Sotho-Tswana,* 76ff.

2 RM, *To his Parents,* 1816 (JSM, *Lives,* 24).

3 For Van der Kemp on the Xhosa, see: RM, *MLSSA,* 257.

4 For Johann Heinrich Schmelen, LMS missionary to the Namaqua, see: RM, *MLSSA,* 123f.

5 Cf. RM, *To Alexander Moffat,* 25.2.1822, (*AAK,* 57).

6 Moffat's soul-mate, the Wesleyan Barnabas Shaw, in *Memorials of South Africa,* (Ldn: Mason, 1840), was more circumspect. Shaw made distinctions between groups: [The Namaqua] 'Respecting every truth of what has been called Natural Religion, they are totally in the dark; not generally having any idea even of a supreme being.' (Shaw, *Memorials*, 45). ... [The San]: No kind of religious worship whatever has been observed to prevail amongst them.' (55). ... [The Xhosa]: Of a Divine Being, (whom they call Uhlanga or Supreme) they have some indistinct notion; as likewise of the immortality of the soul: but as to a state of future rewards and punishments, they are altogether in ignorance.' (62) ... [The Tswana]: The Bechuanas believe in the existence of a good and a bad Being, superior to themselves; yet have nothing relative to the soul or a future state and have not the most distant idea of any religious worship. Superstitions and practices of the most ridiculous character are extremely prevalent.' (65)'. Shaw did not work directly with the Tswana, but with the Namaqua. Moffat probably read Shaw's book before he wrote *Missionary Labours* in 1842.

7 Livingstone, *To Charles Livingstone,* 16.3.1847, (*DLFL,* Vol. 1, 192): 'Your question regarding the complete annihilation of the idea of a supreme being in the Bechuana mind is rather difficult of solution. We come after missionaries have been in the country 30 years. *Morimo* or God or Chief is at every man's mouth. Intelligent natives say their forefathers spoke of God in the same way. A man escapes from an elephant or lion. He instantly exclaims, 'How good God is to me! What a heart God has to me!' A person is sick or dies: the exclamation then is, 'God has no heart', i.e. He is not kind.' Schapera suggested that Charles' question may have been prompted by Moffat's statement in *MLSSA,* 243. In 1847 Livingstone did not yet give unequivocal endorsement for Tswana theism, and he was aware of the difficulties of

Our aim is to understand what drove Moffat to his position. To his credit, Moffat tried to ascertain what the concept of God actually was amongst the Tswana and other groups. He tried to make allowance for the influence of Christian teaching on indigenous ideas.[8] And he also tried to use insights from the likes of Schmelen, Kay, Pringle, and Sparrman who observed indigenous beliefs.[9] In comparison with modern methods for investigating indigenous religious phenomena, his available techniques were poor; but within his parameters he did attempt to be objective. For example, he corrected some statements made in John Campbell's book, *The Life of Africaner*, in which Campbell claimed that some Namaqua had no names and could not count beyond five. Moffat emphasised the need to live with people before coming to conclusions:

> I have dwelt much with the Namaqua, as well as among the people referred to, but I never knew a man who had not a name; and I have sat and been taught by many infant lips to count more than ten, even when no missionary had laboured among them. It is, however, but just to remark, that it must be to a resident, not a *swallow* visitor that we must look for correct information on subjects abstract in their nature.[10]

In this chapter, our task is to give an account of Moffat's understanding of the indigenous concept of God, and to evaluate some of his conclusions. This is a delicate task for various reasons, not the least of which is that in the twenty-first century we cannot return to the exact situation which Moffat faced in the nineteenth. Modern studies on indigenous peoples come after two hundred years of exposure to Christian teaching. Traditions, myths,

---

extracting traditional beliefs from missionary influenced statements. However, by 1851, he had changed his mind. See: Livingstone, *Article for The British Quarterly Review, (xiv),* 1851, (DLSAP, 100f): 'The testimony of intelligent natives is invariably that there was a knowledge [before the missionaries came] of a supreme being who made all things'. Livingstone's article was titled 'Moffat's Mistake'. An offended and hurt Moffat then wrote to Tidman of the LMS. See: RM, *To Tidman, LMS,* July 1852, (SOAS/CWM/SA/Box27/1/A): 'How he came to write as he has done about what is called 'Moffat's Mistake' I cannot conceive, for all that I ever heard from his lips went to establish all I have ever written on the subject'.

8 After asking someone if his traditions had a story concerning the Flood, Moffat concluded that the person had been influenced by Christian teaching. Further investigation confirmed that Christian influence had been a factor, (RM, *MLSSA,* 126).

9 Moffat cited Kay and Pringle in *Africa,* 53f, and in *MLSSA,* 258ff. 'Kay' is probably the Rev. Stephen Kay, a Wesleyan missionary, who met Moffat in 1821. In 1833 Kay published *Travels and Researches in Caffaria*. 'Pringle' is a reference to Thomas RM, *African Sketches: Narrative of a residence in South Africa,* (Ldn: Moxon, 1834). RM, *MLSSA,* 259, also cited Dr Sparrman, a reference to Anders Sparrman, *A Voyage to the Cape of Good Hope,* (1786). Sparrman sailed with Captain James Cook, recording ethnographical issues.

10 RM, *MLSSA,* 125.

legends, and beliefs have all been modified, and identifying pre-Christian strands is difficult.[11]

Another factor is that primary information from the period is limited. Written sources are overwhelmingly from non-indigenous communities, and oral tradition is subject to the problem of Christian influence noted above.[12] Archaeological data, relating to religious customs, rituals and beliefs, is in meagre supply. Thus, despite being aware of the inbuilt problems of having to deal with written material from only non-indigenous writers, we are still heavily dependent upon them. Understandably, African scholars question the insights, reasoning, and evaluation of non-indigenous writers. This is understandable, since cultural differences can make a newcomer obstinately blind to what may be significant to a person from a different background. The whole field is full of sensitive issues, especially if it is felt that conclusions are linked to racial stereotypes. Polarisation rapidly occurs. Positions taken are seen as being symbolic of prejudices involving ethnicity, culture and politics. Conclusions are viewed as indicating deeper underlying attitudes concerning race.[13]

There can also be the suspicion that if the concept of a supreme deity is absent, then this may be seized on by some as evidence that those who lack the concept are intellectually inferior. A highly sensitive presupposition is

---

11 Livingstone conceded this. See: Livingstone, *To Charles Livingstone,* 16.3.1847, (*DLFL,* Vol. 1, 192). But by 1851, Livingstone was aware of oral traditions which he believed pre-dated Christian influence, and which pointed to a clear Tswana notion of God Cf. Livingstone, *Article for The British Quarterly Review, (xiv), 1851,* (*DLSAP,* 101f).

12 E.W. Smith, 'The Idea of God among South African Tribes', *African Ideas of God,* 78-133, suggested evidence for a concept of God among the Tswana, pre-dating missionary influence. He cited an evening prayer of the BaRolong; an ancient hymn sung as morning broke; the memory of a priest-doctor concerning his aged grandmother praying *'Modimo, mme'* ('O God my mother'); and a traditional tale of a very old woman who also prayed *Modimo we, mme'* (Dear God, my mother). Though these examples may pre-date Christian activity, did Smith prove so? Were the ladies describing God as mother, or were they describing their departed mothers as *Modimo*? In Smith's subsection, 'The Bantu of the Central Region: The Sotho-Tswana Tribes' (116-122), he gave an excellent analysis of the issue, but was less convinced of Tswana theism than when he criticised Moffat in, *Robert Moffat: One of God's Gardeners.*

13 Moffat's reluctant conclusions have to be disentangled from the racist presuppositions of some Afrikaner anthropologists such as W.W.M. Eiselen. Eiselen was involved with Henrik Verwoerd's apartheid philosophy, and argued that Africans had no indigenous religion. The term *godsdiens* (religion), Eiselen insisted, should be reserved only for what he called 'an elevated culture'. Lacking such a culture Africans might have *geloofsvorme* (patterns of belief) but no *godsdiens.* Willoughby, *Race Problems in the New Africa,* (Oxford: Clarendon Press, 1923), felt it necessary to affirm that indigenous tribes had a clear notion of a supreme being. By the early 1920s, the issue was already politicised and used to argue that indigenous peoples were inferior. Willoughby wanted to refute this.

created, which holds that 'to believe that a tribe or race has no concept of the deity is to believe that it has inferior intellectual and spiritual capability'. This is not a logically necessary conclusion, but it can become an emotional one. Significantly, Moffat did not make this inference. For example, in discussing the San, he wrote: 'Though shrewd in their minds and active in their dispositions, they have neither name nor knowledge of a Divine Being.'[14]

Some theologians work from a pan-African perspective, promoting a homogenous view of African ideas, assuming an 'African' way of thinking or an 'African' concept of God. Local variations may be acknowledged but are seen as minimal: the homogeneity of a pan-African world-view is dominant. However, this has the disadvantage of attributing a prevailing concept in one tribe or place to other tribes or places. With Moffat, it is important to evaluate his understanding of specific peoples in specific places, and not to view his conclusions as a comment on all Africa.

Aware of these caveats, we endeavour to engage with the issue. At the centre of the discussion is the question: what was Moffat's definition of the terms 'God' and 'religion'?' Moffat interacted with several indigenous groups, but especially with the Tswana and the Ndebele. Consequently, we focus on the understanding of the concept of God which Moffat thought he found or did not find in these two specific peoples. The two groups also contrast one another, which may have had a bearing on the way they expressed their beliefs. The Tswana were mainly a peaceful people, under non-dominant leaders. The Ndebele were a warrior nation, under a despotic 'god-like' chief, Moselekatse, who had absolute and ruthless authority.

Moffat's Concept of God

What was Moffat's conceptual framework? Could he recognise the idea of God in another culture? Did he define God in such a way that an African concept was necessarily excluded? Did he look for an exact reflection of his prior understanding in the beliefs and practices of Africa? Moffat's ability to

---

14 RM, *Africa,* 19. For Moffat, it was the *loss of knowledge* concerning a supreme being which caused the problem, not *lack of intellectual ability*. Insufficient intellectual capability being the cause presupposes an evolutionary approach to human intellect and spiritual awareness, in which humanity evolves towards higher intellect and spirituality. Moffat did not work with an evolutionary model. He believed in a 'regression' of humanity, not its 'progression'. Groups may *lose* knowledge of God; they do not *evolve* toward it. Such groups are fully human, with equal intellectual capacity. They have simply 'lost' something of immense importance. Moffat did not assume that humanity added religious awareness as it developed intellectually. He assumed that all people had had that knowledge, but, for some, it had been lost.

recognise the concept of a supreme being in another culture was certainly affected by his presuppositions concerning the nature of deity. William Roby had commenced his *Theological Lectures* with the statement:

> Theology is a discourse on the existence, the attributes, the purposes, of God. By the term *God* we mean that self-existent Being who is the cause and the governor of all other beings, of whom, and through whom, and to whom are all things. The existence of this supreme being is the first principle in theology and the foundation of all religions.[15]

Moffat homologated Roby's teaching that God is a self-existent being who is the cause and governor of all other beings. In his 1816 *Shipboard Sermon,* and echoing Roby, Moffat said: '[God is the one who says] 'I have *being* in myself, and consequently I give *being* to all.'[16] For Roby, the clear fundamental attributes of God as supreme being were self-existence, being the cause of all other beings, and being the governor of all other beings. Moffat's own views were either remarkably coincidental to Roby's or directly derived. Thus, taking Moffat's writings as a whole—particular examples are cited later—Moffat's core vision of deity involved seeing deity as a self-existent creator and lord,[17] plus the associated concepts of otherness and personhood. In Moffat's mind, these were essential for any entity to be given the dignity of deity. Creatorhood and lordship were explicit for Moffat. Implicit were the concepts of otherness and personhood.

1. God as Creator. In Moffat's conversations with Africans, he frequently asked if they had the idea of a creator. The question was most often posed when trying to find out whether they had a concept of God at all. Moffat found it inconceivable that there could be a notion of a supreme being

---

15 Roby, *Theol. Lect.* 1, 'Existence or Being of God'. Roby added: 'It is by the attributes of self-existence and independence that God is eminently distinguished from all other beings.' Cf. Roby, *Theol. Lect.* 9, 'Attributes of God'.

16 RM, *Shipboard Sermon, 1816.* RM, *MLSSA,* 262, also alluded to eternity of existence, as appropriate for any proper deity.

17 Reference to these two factors which, for Moffat, accompanied any adequate concept of deity, is illustrated in two of Moffat's furlough speeches. (i) RM, *Walworth Address,* 1843, (*Farewell Services*, 72), '[Formerly] the idea of a being that made the world, or governed the world, never floated in [Tswana] minds.' (ii) RM, *Barbican Sermon,* 22.1.1843, (*Farewell Services,* 116), '[The Tswana] had no idea of a Divine Being. They laughed us to scorn because we told them that God had made the stars and the sun and the moon and man; and that it was God that made the winds to blow, the rains to descend, and the grass to grow. They supposed that it was in the power of man to do these things, and they considered us as intruders of their ancient code of laws. They trusted in man for rain, instead of trusting in the living God; and, when it rained at a time they did not like it, they would curse God. They would not believe that there was a God; they told us that it was all nonsense. They used to say, 'Your fables are very good, but ours are just as good.'' In both extracts, Moffat focused on the need to recognise a creator and governor, for there to be a proper concept of deity.

without that supreme being also being creator. But this may have introduced an immediate difficulty, since Werner has suggested that, in Tswana culture, the High God was not always connected with creation, and that the earth was often assumed to have existed before all things.[18] Human beings and animals were sometimes spoken of as made by the High God, but sometimes as if they had originated independently.[19] This cosmology would immediately, and possibly unknowingly, create problems for Moffat's mode of enquiry.

2. God as Other. God as creator also involved the concept of 'otherness' or 'distinctness', though not necessarily 'remoteness'. In Moffat's theological tradition, true deity was not to be confused with the creation, even if, in God's providential care, he may be immanent to it. In Moffat's Reformed tradition, the otherness, distinctness and transcendence of God, was expressed by the concept of God as spirit; and, in the early nineteenth century, every Scottish schoolchild knew by heart the *Shorter Catechism* definition of God: *'What is God? God is a Spirit, infinite, eternal, and unchangeable in his being, wisdom, power, holiness, justice, goodness and truth.'*[20] God as spirit made God different from anything created.[21] And if any entity were to be regarded as belonging to the genus of 'deity' then the idea of 'otherness', as indicated by the term 'spirit', must apply. However, 'spirit' was not intended to point to a class of *spirits,* of which God was the pre-eminent: Moffat never tried to express the concept of deity as an extension of a general concept of 'spirits'. He never tried to explain God as the 'Great Spirit', and he never tried to make a connection between the 'spirits' and God as 'Spirit'.[22] Rather, he tried to define the concept of deity in terms of a

---

18 There are general Bantu creation myths, but their use among the Tswana is undecided. Schapera, *The Tswana,* 59, felt that the Tswana 'High God' was also creator. Eugene Casalis, who worked among the BaSuto Tswana from 1833 onwards, thought that they had 'entirely lost the idea of a creator', cf. Casalis, *The BaSutos,* (Ldn: Nisbet, 1861), 238ff, and cited by Smith, 'The Idea of God among South African Tribes', 119f. Casalis was a French Reformed Church missionary and arrived in southern Africa in 1833. He resumed the work of earlier French missionaries among the BaSuto, whose paramount chief was Moshesh.

19 Werner, *Myths and Legends of the Bantu,* 20f. Aidan Southall, 'Tswana Religion', (*The Encyclopedia of Religion*, Vol. 15, 75-77), stated that *Morimo,* the Tswana 'High God' was seen as creator. Southall did not deal with the issue of identifying pre-Christian Tswana concepts.

20 *The Shorter Catechism,* Qu. 4.

21 Moffat's faith identified God with absolute goodness, but he would have accepted the idea of an 'evil' deity as evidence of the concept of a supreme being.

22 There is a possible exception to this rule. In 1823 Moffat met a group of impoverished Tswana, and wrote: 'They are ignorant in the very extreme and seem to know nothing whatever of the God of all spirits'. See: RM, *Journal,* 22.5.1823, (*AAK,* 80). This is the only occurrence of the phrase 'God of all spirits.' Using this phrase does not mean that Moffat thought of God being the ultimate spirit within a genus of 'spirits'. Moffat meant that God was

transcendent being who was the governing subject of creation, providence and judgment.

3. God as Lord. As well as asking if his listeners had a notion of a creator, Moffat repeatedly enquired if they had the idea of a 'governor' of all things. 'Governor' was Moffat's way of referring to God's lordship and providential guidance. For Moffat it was inconceivable for any entity to have the title God if that entity were not respected, loved, feared, obeyed, and accountable to as lord and judge. A God without that role and status would be no god at all. The essential lordship inherent in deity also underpinned God's role as judge. It was of the essence of deity that such deity was a personal being to whom human beings were morally accountable. If no such relationship existed, then, from Moffat's perspective, there was no God or a supreme being.

4. God as Person. God as lord had the related concept of personhood. The notion of deity within the Judaeo-Christian tradition included this. A God who was lord and judge must have personhood, otherwise he could not decide, will, command, or enter into meaningful relationship with His creatures.[23] In Moffat's mind, true deity could not be an impersonal force. He could never identify deity with magic, since magical 'forces' do not have a personal mind able to exercise discriminative volition. Deity had to have a quality of existence which enabled will, decision, conscious relationship, knowing, and doing, all in a manner appropriate for a personal being. Even the Tswana theologian Setiloane questioned whether the term *Morimo* (sometimes spelled *Modimo*)—which early Tswana interpreters suggested to the missionaries as an equivalent for God—had the notion of personal being.[24]

What we see is that it was difficult for Moffat to recognise a concept as deity, God, or supreme being, which did not have such basic characteristics. These were essential for any deity, not just a Christian notion of deity. Significantly, Moffat never recorded that he asked the abstract question: 'Do you have a concept of an Absolute, Infinite, or Great Spirit?' In practice he

---

over all spirits, just as He was over all humanity. Livingstone wrote that the Boers believed that the Khoikhoi knew 'little of the Great Spirit', see: Livingstone, *The South African Boers and Slavery,* (c. 1853), (*DLSAP,* 72).

23 Some of Smith's examples indicate that in pre-Christian Tswana piety the worshipper did enter a 'personal relationship' with *Modimo* (God). But in some cases, *Modimo* may have been used of an ancestral spirit not a 'deity'.

24 Setiloane, *The Image of God among the Sotho-Tswana*, 77: '*Modimo* cannot be described by epithets in the personal class. It is to say that, while humanity is a sufficient analogy for the understanding of 'badimo' it is wholly inadequate in the case of *Modimo*. ... Whether or not 'He' is a pronoun suitable to the Christian God, it is proposed to denote *Modimo* as IT.' This creates difficulties for Willoughby and Smith, who, rejecting Moffat's conclusions, claimed that traditional Tswana religion had a clear notion of *Modimo* as personal being.

asked: 'Are you aware of a Creator and Governor of the Universe before whom you will stand in judgment?'[25] This was the point of contact which Moffat tried to find in evangelism. At the Athenian Areopagus (Acts 17:24ff.), Paul focused on God as creator and God as lord of the Universe. This shaped Moffat's own approach.

Moffat looked for awareness of a Being who had made all things and who was lord over all things. For him, God's otherness and personhood were the inevitable consequences of creatorhood and lordship. He arrived in Africa believing that such a notion of God would be universal, even if complicated and distorted by polytheism or local interpretations. Moffat would have accepted polytheism as knowledge of the concept of deity. Given his premises, Moffat eventually concluded that he encountered an absence of both monotheism and polytheism in some peoples. This startled him.

Moffat's Concept of Religion

What was Moffat's understanding of 'religion', given that he so forcefully stated that the Tswana had none?[26] In his 1840 LMS *Sermon*, preached in London, he remarked: 'When the Missionaries commenced their labours among the Bechuanas did they find among them anything like idolatry, religion, or religious awe? No, they found a nation of infidels! They laughed at the notion of "one mightier than man".'[27] In *Missionary Labours*, Moffat expanded on this, alluding to the types of practices he expected to find among indigenous peoples if they had a religion:

> The situation of the missionary among the Bechuanas is peculiar, differing, with slight exception, from any other among any nation on the face of the earth. He has no idolatry to arrest his progress, and his (the missionary's) mind is not overwhelmed with the horrors which are to be found in countries where idols and idol temples are resorted to be millions of devotees... He meets with no sacred streams, nor hears of voluntary victims to propitiate the anger of imaginary deities. He seeks in vain to find an altar, or a single emblem of heathen worship. No fragments remain of former days, as mementos to

---

[25] RM, *Journal,* 25.5.1823, & 27.5.1827, (*AAK,* 82, 257). God's distinction from the created universe was central to Moffat's conception of God as Lord.

[26] Cf. RM, *Journal,* 26.7.1824, (*AAK,* 129): 'I entered into conversation on the subject or subjects of my address. They have no religion of their own, and of course not tenacious of any tenets. It is verily the case with them as our Redeemer declares, for every thought and action of their lives concentrates in, 'What shall we eat, and what shall we drink, and wherewith shall we be clothed?' The missionary must have patience and, in a religious point of view, consider them as children, nor wonder though they require to be taught the A. B. C a thousand times over.' Schapera was scathing: 'This statement is, of course, completely erroneous.' (fn. 33).

[27] RM, *Africa,* 19.

> the present generation, that their ancestors ever loved, served, or reverenced a being greater than man. A profound silence reigns on this awful [serious] subject.[28]

Moffat believed that the presence of religion amongst a people would be shown by the presence of 'idols and temples, sacred streams, sacrificial victims, and altars and emblems of heathen worship'. This was what missionaries to other countries, especially India, had found. When Moffat did not find these among the Tswana, he found it difficult to see how they had a real religion.[29] He was aware of Tswana practices which he described as 'superstition' or 'magic', but he was unable to discern a sense of the sacred, though he was cognisant of a fear of spiritual powers which were linked with superstitions and magic. But was Moffat's definition too narrow? Could religion be defined in a way which included 'superstition' and 'magic'?

Moffat knew that spiritual forces were taken seriously by the Tswana, especially forces mediated through magicians, sorcerers, diviners, witches and rain-makers. But he made a distinction between 'religion' and what he categorised as superstition or magic. Religion had to do with a deity to whom humanity was morally accountable, whereas superstition had to do with practices which sought to bring 'luck' or 'knowledge'. What lay at the heart of recognizable religion for Moffat, was moral accountability. This came not only from his immediate Presbyterian roots, but from the pervasive ethical monotheism of the Judaeo-Christian tradition. Roby had taught that religion was the *moral* response evoked in humanity by an awareness of God as

---

28 RM, *MLSSA,* 243. See also: RM, *Africa,* 16: '[In Africa] No temples, no altars, no sacred groves there; no shasters, no Koran, no holy relics there; not one solitary idol there; neither 'the likeness of anything in the heavens above or in the earth beneath' to represent a sacred being; no idea in the minds of the multitude that there is anything greater or more powerful than mortal man ... there is not the shadow of an idol god, nor the slightest belief remaining that there is a Creator, Preserver, or Governor of all things.' Note Moffat's emphasis on the necessity of believing in a *creator* or *governor* in order to have a notion of deity. The phrase 'Creator, Preserver, or Governor' was used by Roby, *Theol. Lect.* 2, 'On Religion'.

29 Setiloane, *The Image of God among the Sotho-Tswana,* 105, wrote: 'The missionaries then concluded that the people did not have any religion.' But Setiloane was too sweeping. Moffat came to this conclusion, but not all did. Later missionaries had more sensitivity to indigenous religion. Livingstone saw that 'sacredness' in African culture was different from 'sacredness' in European culture. Cf. David & Charles Livingstone, *Narrative of an Expedition to the Zambezi and its Tributaries: and of the discovery of the Lakes Shirwa and Nyassa, 1858-1864,* (Consulted edition: London: Duckworth, 2001), 390ff. Livingstone's comments were written after observing tribes in the Nkhotakhota region of Malawi rather than at Kuruman. Livingstone's ability to recognise religion in a different form is impressive. His account of indigenous religion in the Nkhotakhota region is positive and affirmative.

creator, preserver, and governor.[30] This definition, focusing on the moral dimension, did not, for Moffat, fit with a religion in which he deemed that 'low' moral behaviour emanated from 'vague' senses of superstition or numinosity. Moffat's concentration on the ethical nature of the living God created, in his mind, a sharp differentiation with traditional practices which he viewed, somewhat harshly, as not promoting morality.

Since Moffat's day, the term 'religion' has gained a wider definition. It is now more common to view religion in broad terms, as the expression in a culture of a human response to the numinous. Within this context, religion is viewed as simply the expression in belief, ritual, and ceremony, of the *feelings* which arise within a person when exposed to the numinous, whatever form that takes. Appreciation of music, or human love, may be viewed as religious events. Religion is thus understood as dealing with the effects of mystical forces on the human psyche. Within this understanding 'magic' can be grouped with 'conventional religion', the main difference being that magic is usually an impersonal and mechanical affair.

This, more recent, emphasis on the *subjective* religious consciousness was quite different from Moffat's evangelical faith. For Moffat, religion involved a moral and spiritual response to the deity. For Moffat, even false religion involved worship of a personal divine being. But magic, divination, sorcery, or the manipulation of impersonal forces did not fall within his definition. Fear of, and reverence to, the ancestral spirits, with resultant effect on lifestyle, could possibly come under this definition—apart from the fact that the ancestors originated as created beings, hence could never be true deities with self-existence. What is clear is that any discussion on the question of whether Moffat was correct or incorrect in stating that the Tswana had no

---

30 The word 'religion' comes from the Latin *religio*: a restraining rule or code of behaviour in response to the supernatural. This classical sense, with its emphasis on moral accountability to deity, was what Roby taught. Cf. Roby, *Theol. Lect.* 2, 'On Religion': 'Having discussed the Being of God we proceed to religion, as the natural consequence. In attending to this subject, we may consider; *1. The Nature of Religion:* Religion, according to the proper signification of the term, denotes the active consciousness of moral obligation [and] *2. The Basis or Foundation of Religion*: It is established on the firmest ground: *It is founded in the very being of God.* Admitting the existence of God, religion or moral obligation, must, as a natural consequence, exist in one form or another. ... *Religion is founded on the very nature of conscience*: (Romans 2:14, 15). This faculty is essential to the nature of man and impels him to acknowledge the existence and equity of moral obligation.' See also, Roby, *Theol. Lect.* 8, 'The Names and the Nature or Spirituality of God'.

religion, depends enormously on whether the debate accepts or rejects Moffat's definitions.[31]

Moffat had no training in comparative religion or social anthropology. Willoughby, one of Moffat's strongest critics, acknowledged that Moffat was handicapped by this difficulty.[32] However, there were forms of non-Christian religion of which he did have a slight knowledge, but which were perhaps different from African forms of religious expression. For example, as a serious Bible reader, Moffat encountered references to pagan gods in its pages. The Scriptures also mentioned idols, used in the cult of these pagan deities, and referenced temples and holy places. General European culture also knew of the polytheistic pantheons of Greece and Rome, and the setting of the New Testament within the Greco-Roman world meant that any Bible-man had a passing familiarity with classical mythology. As mentioned earlier, Moffat knew about non-Christian religions, represented by items displayed in the LMS museum, which Moffat visited in 1816:

> I spent some time in viewing the museum, which contains a great number of curiosities from China, Africa, the South Seas, and the West Indies. It would be foolish for me to give you a description. Suffice it to say that the sight is truly awful [dreadful], the appearance of the wild beasts is very terrific, but I am unable to describe the sensations of my mind when gazing on the objects of Pagan worship! Alas! How fallen are my fellow-creatures, bowing down to forms enough to frighten a Roman soldier, enough to shake the hardest heart. Oh, that I had a thousand lives, and a thousand bodies! All of them should be devoted to no other employment but to preach Christ to these degraded, despised, yet beloved mortals.[33]

---

31 Northcott, *Robert Moffat,* 73 (also, 74, 75): 'But as for religion, was there any? Moffat, with preconceived ideas of the evidence to look for, concluded that there was none; and, in the Christian meaning of religion, he was probably right, but at the same time profoundly wrong. ... It was a gloomy outlook for the young Moffat as he tried to find religious links, even wordless ones, which might faintly coincide with his own theology.'

32 Willoughby's approach to indigenous spirituality was summed up in his book, *On the Relation of a Heathen Man to God,* where he taught that God revealed himself to every culture in a way appropriate to that culture. It was in Willoughby's major work, *The Soul of the Bantu* (299f.) that he discussed Moffat at length: '[Moffat's work is an] exemplification of the truth that if an able and zealous missionary is not trained in Comparative Religion and Social Anthropology, he may labour long among African tribesmen without being able to discern those indigenous religious ideas that lie ready to his hand and would help him immensely in his work'. Willoughby acknowledged that such sciences had not come into their own 'till Moffat's work was well-nigh done'.

33 RM, *To his Parents,* 1816 (JSM, *Lives,* 26). Cf. *Farewell Services,* 134ff. Willoughby, *The Soul of the Bantu,* (296ff), accepted that the use of images was minimal south of the Zambezi. Even Livingstone admitted that, south of the Zambezi, there was a less detectable concept of deity and religion, cf. Monk (ed.), *Livingstone's Cambridge Lectures,* (Cambridge: Bell, 1858), 16f. Livingstone said this even though he recognised worship existing without a need for physical

Moffat thought he did not find similar objects in southern Africa. This puzzled him. Yet the absence of idols was, in one sense, a positive mark in favour of the Tswana for Moffat. The Tswana did not make carved idols, and Moffat approved their scorn of people who did. In Edinburgh, in 1842, Moffat cited the Tswana attitude to idols as a mark of intelligence, referring to an encounter with a Motswana with whom he had discussed tribes who worshipped man-made objects. The Motswana said to Moffat: 'After this, never call Bechuanas foolish or ignorant. I take that piece of wood, and cut it and carve it, but what would my people think of me, were I to worship it as my God? They would throw me over a precipice, that I might die the death of a madman.' Moffat commented to his Edinburgh audience that these sentiments proved that the Tswana were not 'inferior' in their reasoning.[34]

However, despite vigorously defending the intellectual ability of the Tswana, their lack of idol worship denied Moffat a starting-point for his 'Paul in Athens' approach. He expressed his frustration in *Missionary Labours,* writing that a people such as the 'Bechuanas, who had never had the slightest idea of idols, or of idol service, could have no notion whatever of the object of missionaries beyond that of secular interests'.[35] Setiloane commented that the Hindu Temples and the Marias of Polynesia had accustomed the LMS missionaries to the idea that pagan worship must necessarily show an altar and a visible god.[36] In not seeing these among the Tswana, Moffat had a limited view of their spirituality.

---

artifacts. Cf. D & C Livingstone, *Narrative of an Expedition to the Zambezi and its Tributaries,* 390ff.

34 RM, *Edinburgh Speech,* 3.11.1842, (*Farewell Services,* 17). This sentiment was repeated in Moffat's *Walworth Address* a few months later: 'Though they were ignorant [of God] yet they had no idol worship ... they looked upon idol worship as a very personification of madness itself.' (*Farewell Services,* 72).

35 RM, *MLSSA,* 236.

36 Setiloane, *The Image of God among the Sotho-Tswana,* 104.

Chapter 6
Moffat and Tswana Theism

THE TSWANA ARE A homogeneous group, with individual Tswana sub-groups having similar culture, customs, religion, language and social structure. The greatest differences are between the Western and Eastern sub-groups. Since Moffat was almost exclusively involved with the Western sub-group peoples, the BaThlaping, BaRolong, BaHurutse, and BaKwena, differences between these two major subgroups do not affect our study. Our task in this chapter is to examine extracts in which Moffat stated that the Tswana lacked a concept of God.

Moffat did *not* say that no African tribes had a concept of the divine—something of which he is sometimes accused. He was aware that the Namaqua and the Xhosa had words for God, though, in each case, he inferred that the gods in question were not pre-existent divine beings, but warrior heroes from history. Moffat knew of *Tsuikuap* (*Utiko*) among the Namaqua, and of *Uhlanga* (*Thlanga*) among the Xhosa; and, in his LMS sermon, *Africa,* he considered both groups in extended detail.[1] Moffat followed Kay and Pringle in assuming that such gods were deified chiefs or heroes.

Moffat's ability to express himself in striking fashion was well illustrated in *Missionary Labours* when he wrote that Satan, 'has employed his agency, with fatal success, in erasing every vestige of religious impression from the minds of the Bechuana [Tswana], Hottentots [Khoikhoi], and Bushmen [San]; leaving them without a single ray to guide them from the dark and dread futurity, or a single link to unite them with the skies.'[2] This statement was crafted to make a dramatic impact on the home readership, and there is little doubt that Moffat believed his own rhetoric. His elaborate theory of the 'Lost knowledge of God'—dealt with in a later chapter—would be unnecessary had he only been engaging in hyperbole. And it was not only in *Missionary Labours* that Moffat expressed such statements. His *Letters* and *Journal* contained similar sentiments.

---

1 RM, *Africa,* 18-53.

2 RM, *MLSSA,* 244. Cf. RM, *Africa,* 14: 'You may ask, are there tribes or nations on the face of this earth who are so degraded as to have lost all traces of a Divine Being, and among whom there is no tradition, no *manes* of the dead, no spirit in the winds? Yes, such there are, and I shall now exhibit them to your view.'

For example, in 1823, whilst on a journey to Makaba of the BaNgwaketse, Moffat tried to locate a concept of God, both among the Tswana with whom he was travelling, and among those whom he met on the way. In his questions, he linked the concept of God with that of creatorhood:

> I enquired ... at the eldest one of the poor Bechuanas if he knew who made all things. He replied: 'No'. I enquired if he knew anything about God. '*Kee ueetsee leena haila',*[3] said he: 'I know the name (Moreemo) only.' I asked if it never occurred to his mind to enquire who it was who made the thunder roar, the lightning flash and rain descend, and grass to grow. He gave a significant laugh, and asked if people were to think on such things.[4]

In 1824, on an expedition to the north, Moffat spent time with Makaba:

> In the course of the forenoon, I went up to the town, accompanied by two of the principal men in our company. I introduced the subject of religion, by asking if the Wankets [BaNgwaketse] possessed any knowledge of God. Makabe very emphatically answered by asking: 'How can we know? No man ever taught us.'[5]

Makaba's response may have been strategic. Makaba wanted missionaries to live in his village, because he saw them as bringing prestige, protection, and trade. And even if Makaba did reply in the terms recorded by Moffat, then his words, with an apparently innocent request for 'teachers', may have been a ploy to further his ambitions. On the other hand, if Makaba's reply were naively genuine, then it indicates why Moffat came to the conclusions he did. Importantly, though Moffat was aware of the revered position which Makaba held in the eyes of his people,[6] Moffat never stated that Makaba's people regarded Makaba as a god, in contrast to the Ndebele attitude to Moselekatse. Though Makaba was a powerful ruler, he had not been 'deified' as the Ndebele king had been, in Moffat's perception.

In 1827, Moffat spent several months in a BaRolong village in order to improve language skills. Whilst there, he wrote that he had had several conversations with different individuals, but that he,

> found it a hard thing to instill knowledge into their dark and benighted understandings. However, they do learn a few truths, for I find on asking them sometimes what their own views exclusively are of Creation, Providence, etc., they generally take care to abide by what they have heard from me, and scruple not to declare a downright falsehood, that these ideas are original or what they have always believed. They seem generally to think that what they

---

3 Schapera favoured: *ke itse leina hela,* 'I know the name only' (*AAK,* 82: fn. 20).

4 RM, *Journal,* 25.5.1823, (*AAK,* 82).

5 RM, *Journal,* 8.8.1824, (*AAK,* 141). Moffat called the BaNgwaketse, 'Wankets'.

6 RM, *To James & Mary Smith,* 21.9.1824, (*AAK,* 159).

> call *Morimo* is wise, and they habitually call anything notable by that name – a horse which is swift is *Morimo*, a man who is cunning at work *Morimo*. At the same time, they will tell you he lives in the depths of the earth.[7]

What we see is that Moffat again concentrated on creation and providence. But he also realised that Morimo was a complicated concept. Morimo was multifaceted. Morimo was not limited to an individual personal being, yet it bridged the gap between the material and the immaterial. What Moffat discovered was that, for the BaRolong, Morimo was a complex concept, associated with whatever was powerful or outstanding in daily life. In some ways it simply expressed the superlative. Thus, Morimo did not have the clear 'otherness' of individual personal deity which Moffat looked for. What he was finding was that the term Morimo—used by missionaries for many years as a straight equivalent for 'God'—was more nuanced than originally envisaged. But could it also carry Moffat's idea of deity? And if it simply meant the 'ultimate', did any SeTswana term carry Moffat's notion of a deity?

The Problem of 'Morimo'

Moffat regularly used the term Morimo *for* God.[8] In this he followed the practice of the first missionaries to the Tswana who, when they asked Tswana interpreters for a word to denote 'God', were given Morimo.[9] Moffat's use of the term dated from his earliest contact with the Tswana, and he later inscribed it on the tombstone of his infant son Robert.[10] Morimo was the word which Moffat ever after used for 'God', both in his SeTswana Catechism and in his Bible translations. But if, as Moffat insisted, the Tswana had no concept of a supreme being, then why was Morimo readily available? Or was there, as Setiloane has implied, a misunderstanding from the beginning?[11]

Moffat understood Morimo as an equivalent for God, despite later being aware that the Tswana had a broader understanding of Morimo than

---

7 RM, *Journal,* 27.5.1827, (*AAK,* 257). Cf. Smith, 'The Idea of God among South African Tribes', 117, who suggested that the word construction behind *Modimo* might imply it meant: 'that which pervades what you see and gives it its ability'. Smith referred to Willoughby, *Race Relations in the New Africa,* (Oxford: Clarendon Press, 1923), 77.

8 *Morimo* is also *Molimo.* In modern SeTswana the word is *Modimo.*

9 RM, *MLSSA,* 262, 267.

10 'Here lies the body of Robert, the son of Robert and Mary Moffat: Ob. August 21st, 1825, aged 5 days. *Ba ba rubitseng mogo Jesus, Morimo o tla ba lerenia* (Those who fall asleep in Jesus will be brought back by God)'. 1 Thess. 4:14.

11 Setiloane, *The Image of God among the Sotho-Tswana,* 78.

originally assumed. Was it because Moffat realised that the Tswana applied Morimo to many things, that he had difficulty in allowing that the Tswana had a proper notion of deity? Perhaps. And yet, despite learning that Morimo was used in non-deistic contexts, he continued using it, taking the view that, whatever Morimo originally meant, it had now, through the teaching and preaching of the missionaries, been clothed with a new meaning, that of referring to the God of the Bible. There is a progression in Moffat's understanding of Morimo, which took him to the verge of grasping the indigenous concept, but which he failed to seize. There was a conceptual framework he could not absorb. He uncovered clues, but could not make connections. In the following sections we trace his changing understanding of the term.

In his early writings, Moffat used Morimo confidently, as the direct equivalent of the word 'God'. In these documents, there is no trace of Moffat employing a circumlocution. For example, in 1821 Moffat wrote: 'I pointed to a small stream within a few feet of where we stood, and asked if it was not the power of God which made that stream to issue from the rock, as well as cover the heaven with clouds.'[12] In this extract, Moffat used 'God' without difficulty. If, at that time, Moffat thought the Tswana had no concept of God, how could he expect to be understood? If no specific word was reserved for deity, why was he not forced to create a new word, or use an alternative?[13]

We can also ask why Moffat never listed the word 'God' as presenting difficulty in translation. By 1822 Moffat realised that SeTswana might be more awkward to master than he first envisaged. In his *Journal*, he noted difficulties connected with sound, grammar, and vocabulary.[14] Significantly, he did not mention the word 'God' as creating difficulties. Thus, though Moffat wrote that 'Kingdoms, crowns, thrones and sceptres' were 'unknown here', he did not include 'God' in the catalogue. Argument from silence is

---

12 RM, *Journal,* 19.8.1821, (*AAK,* 24). Cf. *Journal,* 12.8.1821, (*AAK,* 22) & *Journal,* 14.10.1821, (*AAK,* 28). When Mary Moffat wrote to her parents in 1820, she gave no indication that people around Griqua Town had any difficulty with the concept of God. See: Mary Moffat, *To her Parents,* 8.4.1820, (JSM, *Lives,* 84).

13 Cf. Bogue, *Miss. Lect.* 4, 'On Preaching (2): 'When a missionary finds the heathen using words to express their false ideas in religion should he make use of the same word to denote the true God?' Moffat either considered that *Morimo* came within the allowance permitted by Bogue, or he thought it to be non-deistic. The former is most likely.

14 Cf. RM, *Journal,* 6.2.1822, (*AAK,* 44): 'The more I become acquainted with the language, the greater difficulties rise in view: the great want of small words, chiefly of the conjunctive, the great length of some, the aspirate guttural in others, and particularly the immense difficulty of translating theological ideas. Kingdoms, crowns, thrones and sceptres are unknown here.'

rarely conclusive, yet raises important issues. If Moffat had real difficulty in explaining the supreme being, then it is reasonable to assume that problems with such a critical word would have been highlighted.

Another early record in Moffat's *Journal* questions Moffat's later rejection of a concept of God among the Tswana. This is in his account of conversations with a rain-maker, in which he recorded that the rainmaker spoke of 'God':

> I remarked that I wished to prove from his knowledge whether he was indeed a rainmaker, for I had seen no signs of it yet. He said that my God dwelt in the south; that their God dwelt in the north. He proved this by referring to their corn being so different to ours. I assured him that all what the Bootchuanas cultivated was to be found in the south, and he looked rather stupid when I informed him that my native country was in the north, that my God ruled over all the earth. ... I pointed out to him ... he had been guilty of telling lies, that he took the honour on him which belongs to God alone.[15]

The accuracy of Moffat's record of the conversation is not relevant. What is important is that, in Moffat's self-understanding, and in his own account of the conversation, the concept of 'God' occurs and requires no explanation. This was in 1821, during Moffat's early period in Africa. He had not yet probed the indigenous meaning of *Morimo*.

However, as the years passed, Moffat slowly came to realise that Morimo might not be expressing what he, and other missionaries, originally thought it did. By 1822 he began to move towards this position, making the following entry in his *Journal*: '[I enquired of a chief] where he thought that God dwelt. He answered that some Bootchuanas think he lives in the earth; others (who may have heard something of the Christian religion) suppose him to be in heaven; and others again know nothing about the thing which is called 'Moreemo'.'[16] This extract has several important points:

1. Moffat was aware of a Tswana myth that Morimo lived in the earth.
2. Moffat was aware that Christian teaching could modify the myth.
3. Moffat was beginning to develop the belief, later to be axiomatic for him, that some groups had no knowledge of Morimo whatever.

It was the latter of these which shaped Moffat's future analysis of Tswana thinking. Yet, at the time, it was the first axiom—that Morimo lived in the earth—which created doubts in Moffat's mind as to whether Morimo should be thought of as a deity. If Morimo were a 'thing' that lived underground—where the dead went—was such a 'thing' a god? Moffat also became

---

15 RM, *Journal,* 15.10.1821, (*AAK,* 29).

16 RM, *Journal,* 24.3.1822, (*AAK,* 49).

convinced that, in Tswana thought, Morimo not only lived underground but originally referred to a malevolent entity.[17] Moffat mentioned this aspect of Tswana mythology more than once. For example, in his 1840 LMS *Sermon,* he stated:

> All that they knew on this subject was what they had heard from people in the north; viz., that this Morimo was a thing that lived in a hole under a hill, and being wise and cunning, sometimes came out and did malicious deeds, in killing cattle and inflicting diseases. But so little reverence had they for this foreign deity, if such it might be called, that I have heard them frequently say, 'We wish we could get hold of this Morimo, and we would transfix it with our spears.'[18]

The disrespectful attitude towards this spiteful entity was returned to later in Moffat's speech: 'This Morimo, known to few, was only kept in remembrance by sorcerers and rain-makers and sometimes used as a bugbear.'[19] These statements show that, although the first missionaries had asked for a word equivalent to 'the high or Heavenly One', the Tswana interpreters had reinterpreted the question as being about *a supernatural entity who had power over them*: hence, though Morimo lived 'underground' and not in the heavens, they offered Morimo. But in Moffat's evolving understanding of the indigenous concept of Morimo, did that match up to a supreme being? The following passage from 1822 would indicate perhaps not:

> As for Moreemo (God), they [the Tswana] suppose he lives in the earth [and] is a malicious being taking delight in the injury of man. Sometimes they threaten to kill him if they could get him. A chief expressed himself to that effect a few days ago.[20]

If Morimo were a thing which they could 'kill' if they could get him, then this was a different type of deity from what Moffat allowed to be 'God'. Could

---

17 We write 'entity' rather than 'spirit' or 'being'. Tswana scholars, such as Setiloane, point out that *Morimo* was an impersonal 'It'. Smith agreed with Setiloane; cf. Smith, *African Ideas of God,* 118. Smith made no comment on the implication: that if a missionary views personal being as essential to the nature of deity, then it is difficult to see *Morimo* as God.

18 RM, *Africa,* 20. Cf. *Journal,* 24.3.1822, (*AAK,* 49), & RM, *To Alexander Moffat,* 25.2.1822, (*AAK,* 55). See also, RM, *To James & Mary Smith,* 20.8.1822, (*AAK,* 63).

19 RM, *Africa,* 20f. Northcott commented: '[Moffat] recognised the word *Modimo* or *Morimo* as suggesting a name for God, the supreme being; but to him, 'this *Morimo* served the purpose of a bugbear, by which the rain-maker might constrain the chiefs to yield to his suggestions when he wished for a slaughter-ox without which he pretended he could not make rain'. Moffat, with his Christian intuitions, could not discover anything of the character of *Morimo* except that he was cunning or malicious, and failed to see in him a personality capable of doing good, or endowed with the possibility of doing so. He was forced to the conclusion that the hearts of the Bechuana 'are darkened' and that they are 'spiritually buried, and without knowledge, life, or light' (*Robert Moffat,* 74). Cf. Southall, 'Tswana Religion', 76.

20 RM, *To Alexander Moffat,* 25.2.1822, (*AAK,* 55).

deity be killed? Could Moffat ever see such a 'thing' as being a 'supreme being', or even belonging to a pantheon of gods? Could Morimo, as Moffat now thought Morimo was understood in the indigenous sense, ever have the dignity, stature, power, immortality, and 'god-ness' that Moffat would require before seeing it as a 'god', even a 'false god'?

It was after Moffat started asking probing questions about what the Tswana actually believed about Morimo, that he reassessed matters. His questioning arose because he did not get the answers he expected when he discussed religious concepts in his evangelism, especially ideas about a creator and governor of all things. We can imagine him, after such discussions, going home and saying to Mary, 'The more I find out about the idea of Morimo which the Tswana have, the less can I see it as being an idea about God!' It is easy to see how he would conclude that, if Morimo were the ultimate Tswana being, then it fell far short of what should be in a concept of deity, even a mythological one.

That Morimo was viewed as a 'thing' which lived underground shocked Moffat. He did not know that, in some southern African tribes, 'deity' was linked with the earth rather than the sky. Additionally, apart from the 'underground' nature of Morimo, Moffat was also discovering that Morimo was an entity attributable to many things. Morimo was, in some sense, a transferable, multi-dimensional entity, applicable to any being which had power, skill, cunning, swiftness, strength or ability. Though Moffat did discover some clues to this meaning of Morimo, and though he began to realise that Morimo was not a conventional type of individual personal deity, he was unable to grasp its deeper nature. But what were some of these clues?

In 1822 Moffat encountered a young man called Tsousan who came from some distance away: 'On enquiry I found that the name Moreemo was known and applied to the more cunning among them, but nothing beyond was known.'[21] Here Morimo was applied to a clever human being. As previously quoted, in 1827 Moffat wrote: 'They seem generally to think that what they call Morimo is wise, and they habitually call anything notable by that name—a horse which is swift is Morimo, a man who is cunning at work Morimo. At the same time, they will tell you he lives in the depths of the earth.'[22] Moffat noted two things: a Morimo concept, and a Morimo myth of an underground being. Moffat understood the myth better than the concept.

---

21 RM, *Journal,* 26.4.1822, (*AAK,* 50).

22 RM, *Journal,* 27.5.1827, (*AAK,* 257). Cf. *Morimo* as a 'cave-dweller' (*MLSSA,* 261ff).

Then in 1854 Moffat recorded: 'Anything with them is Morimo who can do a thing cleverly, whether that thing be good or bad.'[23] The idea that Morimo included the manifestation of things unusual or powerful emerged in another 1854 incident, when some Tswana were intrigued by Moffat's oxen-pulled wagon: 'Most of the people here never saw a wagon before, and their remarks respecting it are extremely ludicrous. "It is", they say, "god" [Morimo]; and the wheels are gods and this and that is god. When the question is put, what "god" is, and where he dwells, they are bewildered. I had a long tug with them on the subject, but oh, they are ignorant!'[24] Moffat would have been aghast had he met the Sotho poet who spoke of his favourite cow as 'Modimo of the dewy nose'![25]

What Moffat described in these extracts was an indigenous notion of Morimo, and he was doing so in a way which actually corresponds closely with how some modern scholarship understands the original notion. Southall, following Setiloane, wrote: 'Modimo is believed to be the source and root of all existence', and that Modimo is, 'intangible and all-pervasive, irreparably part of human experience but not directly sensed.'[26] In this understanding, Modimo is not an individual personal deity, but is the 'ground-of-being' behind everything, manifesting itself most clearly in things which are strong, powerful, cunning, unusual, novel, and wise.[27] For the Tswana, it is even possible to say, *'motho ke Modimo'* (man is Modimo), which also implies that prayers to Modimo may not always be prayers to a 'deity'. They may be prayers to an ancestor who is seen as Modimo.

The Meaning of 'Morimo'

Moffat listened carefully to the Tswana when they spoke of Modimo. His difficulty was in making a shift in his own mind, enabling him to bridge a conceptual gap. He failed in this, but his perceptive listening should be noted. He did become aware of the indefinite, transferable, numinous' quality of *Morimo.* But he could not make sense of it because, in looking for a notion

---

23 RM, *Journal,* 2.7.1854, (*MJ1,* 206).

24 RM, *Journal,* 10.7.1854, (*MJ1,* 213).

25 Smith, *African Ideas of God,* 119.

26 Southall, 'Tswana Religion', 75.

27 Modimo can even be identified with a human being. Cf. Southall, 'Tswana Religion', 75: 'It is a basic premise of Tswana thought that a representative is identical with the person being represented, or that a symbol is that which it symbolizes. Hence the Tswana say *'Motho ke Modimo'* (Man is *Modimo*), something that implies a far greater degree of interaction than the English "there is something of the divine in every man"'. It is no surprise that Moselekatse was called Morimo*,* which Moffat, with his simple notion of Morimo as individual deity, saw as blasphemy.

of a supreme being, he was searching for an individual personal divine being which *Morimo* both was and was not. Given these considerations, we can identify five stages in Moffat's reflection on this topic:

1. The early Moffat followed his predecessors in accepting Morimo as an adequate word for 'God'.
2. Around 1822 Moffat began to ask searching questions about the actual nature of Morimo.
3. Moffat developed serious reservations as to whether the indigenous understanding of Morimo really expressed any adequate idea of deity in terms he understood, in which deity had individual personal being.
4. Moffat collected evidence of the multi-faceted indigenous notion of Morimo but was unable to make sense of these clues.
5. Moffat concluded that, if Morimo were indeed the ultimate expression of Tswana belief in a 'superior entity', then, because that entity did not represent ultimate, individual, personal deity, the Tswana must have no concept of a supreme being.

It was because Morimo was already in widespread use, as the SeTswana equivalent for God, that Moffat continued to use the term in his preaching and translating. No other SeTswana word filled the gap. But if Moffat had been able to interpret the clues which he uncovered when searching for the indigenous notion of Morimo, then he would have evaded many of the negative verdicts poured upon him. Yet that would have required advanced skills in modern anthropology. Even if he had gained a more sympathetic view of the full indigenous idea of Morimo, would he ever have described it as a supreme being? Probably not. For Moffat, deity had to have an individual personal quality. A 'ground-of-being' behind all things, even if sometimes manifested as a personal agent, would not constitute deity for him.

Despite accepting Morimo as the SeTswana word for God, and despite it eventually becoming clothed with biblical meaning, were the first Tswana interpreters wise in using it? Certainly Morimo, as understood in the full indigenous sense, left no room for another god, such as a 'High God'. This was because, if Morimo were indeed the 'ground-of-being' behind all things then it was itself the 'High God', though not to be visualised as an individual personal deity. It is unsurprising that no other word, and no other god with a different name, was supplied by the interpreters. Morimo encompassed everything 'spiritual'.[28] It was the ultimate concept available.

Use of the word Morimo for the Christian God predated Moffat. The early missionaries used Tswana interpreters, who were able to translate from Dutch to SeTswana and vice versa, Dutch being the trade language which several Tswana could speak. Moffat stated that the specific concept for which the first missionaries had tried to find a SeTswana equivalent was 'the high or heavenly One'.[29] They wanted to identify a 'transcendent being'. If, in fact, there was no 'heavenly One' or 'sky deity', in SeTswana mythology, but only a being who lived underground, then the Tswana interpreters appear to have grasped that what the missionaries wanted was an ultimate supernatural entity. So, the interpreters simply relocated the primary place of residence. Morimo was 'high' in the sense of the 'ultimate'.

Setiloane has sharply criticised Moffat's inability to grasp the concept of Modimo.[30] Yet Setiloane was aware that Modimo—as a malevolent entity which lived underground—pointed in the wrong direction for his own intentions, namely a desire to prove that the pre-Christian Sotho-Tswana had a clear concept of a transcendent entity. Because of this, Setiloane minimised the myth of the underground entity and maximised the more sophisticated notion of a multi-dimensional 'ground-of-being' behind the cosmos.[31] Setiloane strongly insisted that Modimo was never an entity with individual personal being—as personal being would be understood by Europeans. In this way Setiloane distanced Modimo from the 'evil thing' which Moffat claimed had been described to him by the Tswana.

Moffat felt that the people to whom he spoke had both concrete and abstract notions in mind: Modimo was both a *thing* that lived underground, *and* it also had a wider, more numinous, quality as anything wise, cunning, or powerful. Moffat, with his presupposition that Modimo should have individual personhood, could make sense of the former (though he despised the idea), but not the latter. As already noted, Setiloane tried to move the meaning of Modimo totally to the abstract concept of the 'ground-of-being

---

28 Setiloane, *The Image of God among the Sotho-Tswana,* 78: 'The fact is that there was much more to *Modimo* than the missionaries dreamed of, rather than the much less which they came to think'.

29 RM, *Africa,* 20.

30 Setiloane, *The Image of God among the Sotho-Tswana,* 76ff. Setiloane's thesis was weakened by not fully proving that he was expounding a pre-Christian notion of God.

31 Which 'image' of *Modimo* was uppermost in the minds of the Tswana whom Moffat met? *Modimo* the myth? *Modimo* the concept? Did they differentiate?

for the cosmos'. In order to make his point, Setiloane utilised an elaborate etymology lying behind Modimo.[32]

Firstly, Setiloane argued that Modimo, in its traditional sense, had no personal quality at all, but represented the 'numinous'.[33] He further suggested that, in using Modimo for God, Moffat incorrectly[34] thought that *Modimo* was the singular for *Badimo* which are the ancestral spirits, and hence thought of Modimo as being similar to the ancestral spirits though much greater.[35] In this way Modimo could be conventionally understood as an entity with individual personal being. That was not, however, how Moffat derived the word. Moffat took Modimo from the indigenous Tswana interpreters. It was the Tswana who supplied it.

Secondly, Setiloane argued that, when Moffat first wrestled with the etymology of Modimo, it was at a stage when Moffat still thought that Modimo pointed to a conventional notion of a supreme heavenly being, and when Moffat, by his own admission, was still persuaded that he 'could discover innate ideas of a Divine Being in the most untutored savage'.[36] Setiloane claimed that Moffat also tried to derive *Modimo* from *godlimo* (above/high) and *legodimo'* (heaven/sky), approximating to 'He who is in the

---

32 Smith, 'The Idea of God among South African Tribes', 116ff, had a lengthy discussion of the etymology behind *Morimo.* Smith and Setiloane had points of difference and similarity in their analyses.

33 Setiloane, *The Image of God among the Sotho-Tswana,* 76f, pointed out that Moffat himself came to this conclusion, quoting *MLSSA,* 262.

34 Setiloane, *The Image of God among the Sotho-Tswana,* 106. Southall interpreted Setiloane differently: 'The fact that *badimo* is the plural form of *Modimo,* an honorific term used to express awe and reverence toward elders as well as toward the supreme being, indicates that the differences between *Modimo*, the ancestors, and human beings, is one of degree rather than kind' (Southall, 'Tswana Religion', 75-77). We hold that Setiloane did *not* link *badimo* and *Modimo* in this way. Lye and Murray pointed out that *badimo* and *Modimo* belong to different noun classes. Lye and Murray offered support for Setiloane's description of *Modimo* as the ground-of-being for the cosmos, and cut across any forced connection between *Modimo* and *Badimo:* 'The Sotho-Tswana traditionally recognised a supreme being, *Modimo*, a remote though persuasive spiritual force. *Modimo* is closely associated with natural phenomena. ... It evokes a sense of awe. It represents the ultimate source of man's well-being, but is not directly involved in the affairs of the living. Its influence is mediated through the ancestors, *badimo,* and the Sotho-Tswana direct their ritual activities towards the *badimo* rather than to *Modimo.* The words share the same root –dimo, although its basic meaning is controversial. Significantly they belong to different noun classes.' (*Transformations,* 123).

35 Moffat wrote that *barimo* 'is never used in this form' i.e. as the plural of *Modimo.* Moffat interpreted *badimo* as non-personal, and 'a state or disease, or what superstition would style bewitched' (RM, *MLSSA,* 261).

36 RM, *MLSSA,* 265.

sky'.[37] Setiloane pointed out that, apart from the etymological impossibility of there being a form *Mogorimo,*[38] Moffat betrayed himself by assuming that the 'divine being' lives in 'heaven above'. However, we again emphasise that Moffat did not coin the word. He used what had been supplied by the indigenous peoples.

Thirdly, Setiloane argued—and this was the heart of his hypothesis—that, though by derivation *godimo* means 'above' and *legodimo* means 'sky', for an indigenous Motswana the primary reference of both is to numinosity. It is not that Modimo is 'he who is in the sky' but that *legodimo* (sky) is a primary manifestation of Modimo, where Modimo is the ground-of-being behind all phenomena, especially any strange, powerful or feared phenomena. Setiloane concluded: 'Whatever may be the arguments for supposing that *bomodimo* [divinity][39]—and its analogues in other societies—represents a primeval force later personalised in *Modimo*, it has to be insisted that *all oral evidence* presents *Modimo* as *motlhodi,*[40] 'source', of *bomodimo* and of the whole cosmos. It was a name wholly unsuitable, in this sense, for the Christian God.'[41] Setiloane insisted that *Modimo* was linked to *Motlhodi* and backed this up by citing 'all' oral evidence. Unfortunately, he provided no supporting evidence for this important claim, which was the crucial link in his argument.

Setiloane offered a sophisticated semantic analysis. Paradoxically, he revealed how diligently Moffat had tried to discover, through SeTswana

---

37 Setiloane, *The Image of God among the Sotho-Tswana,* 76f. What Moffat actually wrote was: '*Mo* is a personal prefix, and *rimo* is from *gorimo,* 'above'. From the same root *legorimo,* 'heaven', and its plural *magorimo* are derived.' (*MLSSA,* 260). Casalis similarly suggested that *Modimo* came from *mo-holimo,* meaning, 'He who is in the sky', see: Casalis, *The BaSutos*, 248. Smith and Setiloane both reject this theory.

38 But Moffat did *not* argue that there was a word *Mogorimo.* Setiloane's second point, that Moffat originally assumed that the divine being was in heaven 'above', is valid.

39 Matumo, *Setswana-English-Setswana Dictionary,* 505, states that *Bomodimo* means 'Divinity' (or 'the divinely' or 'of the divine'). Also, 'Bo', as part of its many meanings, can, as a prefix, signify abstract qualities (Matumo, 16). Matumo also states that *Modimo* has no plural (247). Matumo defined *Modimo* simply as 'God', which is clearly a Christian influenced meaning. In stating that *Modimo* has no plural, Matumo was specifically referring to *Modimo* (a class 1 noun) with a capital 'M'. But Matumo also listed *modimo* (a class 3 noun) as the singular of *medimo,* meaning 'a demi-god'. In distinguishing between *Modimo* and *modimo,* Matumo was building his definitions on contemporary language usage. Smith, 'The Idea of God among South African Tribes', 118, pointed out that *medimo* included: (i) the dead in their collective capacity, and (ii) the demi-gods. Among the *medimo* are 'godlings' associated with initiation ceremonies and to whom oaths are taken. But many of these may be 'deifications of ancient heroes'.

40 *Motlhodi:* 'The eye of a fountain' (Matumo, *Dictionary,* 273).

41 Setiloane, *The Image of God among the Sotho-Tswana,* 78.

linguistics, a notion of deity which he could recognise. Moffat listened more carefully to the Tswana than did some who came after him, and who made a quick but superficial identification between Morimo and a supreme being. Setiloane's thesis was that *Modimo* originally referred to an abstract notion of numinosity as the 'fountain' or 'source' of being, rather than to a conventional individual personalised entity. Moffat did sense something of that. He did realise that Modimo was different from his own notions of deity, but he could not take his thinking further. That was why he viewed some indigenous descriptions of Modimo as nonsensical.

We need caution when assessing Setiloane's hypothesis. Despite his strong credentials as a native SeTswana speaker, it is difficult to know if Setiloane—and Southall following him—had enough evidence to come to the conclusions he did. Was Setiloane deliberately trying to find alternative ideas of 'being' in indigenous thought from those of Western thought? Did he want to prove that indigenous notions contrasted with 'individualistic' concepts of personal being in the Western mind? Did he bring that agenda to his analyses? Yet Moffat had already provided enough clues to show that Modimo was a concept beyond that of individual personal being. Moreover, as Moffat had pointed out—a century before Setiloane—subsequent identification of Modimo with God made it almost impossible to discover pre-Christian Tswana thinking about Modimo.[42] We can only raise questions. Setiloane used linguistic analysis as a tool to get behind the opaque curtain of Christian influences. Whether he succeeded is difficult to ascertain.

However, if Setiloane and Southall are correct, and if Modimo should not be thought of in terms of individual personal divine being, then this raises enormous questions affecting Moffat's first critics. For example, Willoughby claimed that Modimo, understood in terms of a supreme being in the conventional sense, was present in Tswana thought. But can Willoughby and Setiloane both be correct? Willoughby, entering the field in the late nineteenth century, claimed to find a concept of Modimo which was agreeable to notions of deity as understood in a European sense. On that basis, he found Moffat's rejection of traditional Tswana theism perplexing—even though he was vaguely aware of the 'transferable' quality of Modimo:

> The word *Modimo* was used of any ancestral spirit, and if you ask one of these people what *Modimo* he is speaking to in his prayer he will tell you the name of someone long dead. If you ask him who made the world, he will reply: *Modimo*. And if you ask him the name of this *Modimo* who made the world he will tell you that it is just the Great *Modimo* ... but the people never thought

---

42 RM, *MLSSA,* 262.

of praying to the Great Spirit direct; they pray to the spirits of their ancestors who have gone forward into the town of the Great Chief of the spirit world.[43]

Willoughby wrote of the 'Great Spirit'.[44] If this were an expression which he used in discussions, then it may explain why he received more positive answers to his questions than Moffat did. Moffat looked for specific notions of a creator and governor, not simply an extension of the spirit concept.

Whatever answer is given to these difficult questions, missionary influence would forever afterwards link Modimo irrevocably with the idea of a personal supreme deity. Setiloane's analysis is helpful, but he left questions unanswered. He demythologised and minimised the 'in-the-ground' myth in order to promote a more elevated concept of Morimo as a pervasive spiritual principle. He felt that behind the myth lay a complex abstract notion. But did his etymological analysis really take him that far? Importantly, did the ordinary Tswana of Moffat's day think in terms of the myth or of the abstract concept? If the *former* then Moffat correctly perceived what they believed.

All of this may simply prove that our western mind-set cannot grasp what may be obvious within an African world-view. Nevertheless, as far as the correctness or incorrectness of Moffat's conclusions are concerned, we offer the verdict of 'undecided'. So much depends on the definition of terms. If we accept Moffat's definitions then his conclusions are justified. Moreover, though Setiloane and Moffat differ, neither of their positions supports commentators who view Morimo as a conventional 'High God'.

Marginalisation and Tswana Theism

Even among scholars who are inclined to view Morimo as a 'High God', there is acknowledgement that, for traditional Bantu in general, this concept, when existing, was marginalised.[45] Werner stated that the core of Bantu religion was the cult of the dead, and that belief in a High God was vague—in some tribes almost forgotten—but that everywhere, among Bantu-speaking peoples, the spirits of the departed were recognised, honoured, and

---

43 Willoughby, *Race Problems in the New Africa*, 64ff, (Northcott, *Robert Moffat,* 74).

44 Smith, *Robert Moffat,* 101-13, expressed *Modimo* in terms of the 'Great Spirit', arguing that in Tswana thought *Modimo* was defined as 'the one greatest Spirit, the supreme being' (111). Yet Smith, a critic of Moffat, admitted: 'This belief in a supreme being does not constitute a religion which has a real effective influence over daily conduct. *Modimo* is a remote and rather otiose being. The everyday religious faith of the Bechuana centres in, firstly, their charms (i.e. amulets and talismans) and, secondly, the ancestral spirits' (110f.).

45 Cf. Alice Werner, *Myths and Legends of the Bantu,* 20f.

propitiated.[46] Schapera came to a similar conclusion, with especial mention of the Tswana:

> In pre-Christian times, so far as can be gathered, the Tswana believed in a High God named Modimo, who was regarded as the creator of all things and the moulder of destiny. He was vaguely associated with the phenomena of the weather, and punished innovations or departure from established usage by sending wind, hail, or heat, and withholding the rain; and death, if not attributable to sorcery, was spoken of as an 'act of God'.
>
> He was, however, considered too remote from the world of man to be directly approached in prayer, although at times the ancestral spirits might be implored to intercede with him. There were also many myths about Dingwe, a cannibalistic ogre against whom children were especially protected by charms, and about ... demi-gods associated with caves and engraved footprints on rocky outcrops ... offerings of meat, corn, and beer were occasionally made to them, together with prayers for rain, fertility of crops, and success in war, but on the whole they seem to have been of minor importance.[47]

Schapera chose his words carefully. He wrote: 'as far as can be gathered'. He knew that interpretation of pre-Christian beliefs is difficult, but yet was confident enough to propose that Modimo was considered to be far too distant from humanity to be approached directly.[48] Schapera's view was that Modimo was present in traditional religious thought, but was detached, due to the dignity of his deity.[49] Southall suggested that Modimo was marginalised because Modimo was too 'dangerous' to be encountered

---

[46] Alice Werner, *Myths and Legends of the Bantu,* 81.

[47] Schapera, *The Tswana,* 59. Cf. Hammond-Tooke, *Roots,* 149f: 'The concept of a supreme being, or High God, was not highly developed in traditional thought. All Southern Bantu believed in such a god, but he was a vague, distant figure, taking little interest in his creatures. ... This comparative absence of myths is puzzling, and contrasts with the rich mythology of the San.'

[48] *AAK,* xxi. Schapera, in his co-written article (with Eiselen) 'Religious Beliefs and Practices' in, *The Bantu Speaking Tribes of South Africa,* (CT: Maskew Miller, 1937), 247, agreed that the concept of 'God' was so marginalised among the Tswana as to be almost irrelevant. Schapera held that, in the ritual life of the Bantu, there was a well-defined belief in certain supernatural beings: 'Foremost among these are the spirits of dead ancestors, round whom there has developed an elaborate system of worship. The people also believe in a supreme being, closely associated with the sky, and in lesser deities of various kinds; but these do not enter nearly as intimately into their daily life.' Eiselen's later association with apartheid philosophy undermined the acceptability of this article. Setiloane rejected a 'sky god'.

[49] Cf. Brown, *Among the Bantu Nomads,* 114f: 'From their earliest years children are taught that the word *Modimo,* in so far as it refers to the creator, is a great taboo, the mere mention of which in the ears of the people would cause death to the profane one'. The taboo did not apply to chiefs, doctors, mourners, or those on whom sorrow had fallen, or who are lost. The name *Modimo* could be invoked in non-verbal ways including specific hand gestures. Yet in 1847 Livingstone claimed the name *Modimo* was everywhere.

directly.[50] Whether the reason be 'respect' or 'danger', the effect is the same. Even Moffat's great critic, Smith, when summarising general Bantu religion admitted that the supreme being was pushed so far to the circumference of thought that often his very name was forgotten.[51]

The picture is further confused by the importance of 'totems'. Each Tswana group has a species of animal as its object of honour, veneration, avoidance or praise.[52] And each totem has, attached to its cult, a myth telling how each group acquired its totem.[53] If a totem is dishonoured inadvertently, purification must take place. It is also considered polite to address or greet a person by the name of his totem. Brown has pointed out that, whilst totems were not 'worshipped', they were 'venerated', even 'feared' as if they were gods, with the primary relationship between the Tswana and the totem being that of 'fear'.[54] Thus, the 'High God' (if existing) was not only marginalised by respect, danger, or the ancestral spirits, but by attention given to the totems. In contrast, Moffat brought with him the biblical notion of the 'Living God', in which God directly interacted with humanity here and now. The difference between the 'Living God' and a marginalised concept was immense.

T. Cullen Young, in his essay, 'The Idea of God in Northern Nyasaland' offered a helpful insight, though he wrote about a different region of Africa (Malawi) and a different Bantu people (the Ngoni).[55] He argued that the non-African has to discover what are the frontier lines of the area within which the spirits of the ancestors are dominant: only then can he or she map out the remaining area, where something other than ancestral presence and power operates, and where direct reference to a Power behind the ancestors may be looked for. Young concluded that it was there that the idea of God

---

50 Southall, 'Tswana Religion', 76, suggested: 'A person cannot come into direct contact with *Modimo* and remain unchanged'.

51 Smith, 'The Idea of God among South African Tribes', 133. Smith attributed this to wars, disturbance and displacement, causing people to lose faith in their old gods and instead venerating ancestral heroes or turning to superstition. But he also argued that deep inside people there remained 'the decayed remnant of a clearer monotheistic faith' (133), enabling people to respond to the idea of the Christian God. Ultimately, he was not far from Moffat.

52 Schapera, *The Tswana,* 35.

53 Brown, *Among the Bantu Nomads,* 27, 'One thing stands out very clearly and that is that in no case is the tribal name necessarily that of the totem. ... but a tribe, or especially a clan within a tribe, may bear two names, that of the ancestral chief and that of the totem'.

54 Brown, *Among the Bantu Nomads,* 36f.

55 T. Cullen Young, 'The Idea of God in Northern Nyasaland', in: Smith (ed.) *African Ideas of God,* 38ff. John Mbiti, *African Religions and Philosophy,* (Oxford: Heinemann, 2nd Ed, 1990), has a chapter, 'The Nature of God', in which he draws a sophisticated picture of the African concept of a supreme being. The absorption of Islamic ideas of God into traditional African religious thought, in East and Central Africa, also consideration.

may be found. To a certain extent, Young ended up with a 'deity of the gaps': whatever cannot be explained by reference to ancestral power may be explicable by positing a higher Power. Importantly, he homologated Setiloane's point, that, whereas in the Judaeo-Christian tradition ultimate spirituality is located in ultimate personhood, in Tswana (African) thought, ultimate spirituality is a power encompassing everything as the ground-of-being for the universe, the world, life and humanity.

There is the lingering thought that the ancestral spirits were not seen as channels *through whom* to approach the supreme being, but were the final end and goal of religious devotion. Ralph Tanner, who tried to disentangle original African beliefs concerning ancestral spirits from later Christian influences, conceded that, though in *theory* ancestral spirits were intermediaries to the supreme being, in actual *practice* the supreme being dropped almost totally out of view.[56] Severe marginalisation created non-existence in all but name.

---

56 Ralph E.S. Tanner, *Transition in African Beliefs,* (New York: Maryknoll, 1967).

Chapter 7
Moffat and Ndebele Theism

MOFFAT'S FIVE JOURNEYS TO the Ndebele—1829, 1835, 1854, 1857 and 1859-60—are recorded in his *Journals* and *Letters*, with his conclusions concerning Ndebele theism emerging out of lengthy conversations with Moselekatse, the Ndebele chief. Moselekatse had been one of Chaka's under-leaders, but following an incident around 1822 he and 300 warriors fled from Chaka's wrath.[1] He then built up a formidable fighting force, using it to dominate tribes over a wide area. His feared, ruthless, despotic tyranny became a byword. It was this warrior, with his awesome reputation, whom Moffat first met in 1829, and with whom he struck up an extraordinary relationship. By 1829, Chaka had been murdered by his brother Dingaan, and so Moselekatse, for the time being, felt secure within his extensive territories.[2]

Why did the relationship between Moffat and Moselekatse develop as it did? One factor may have been Moffat's fearlessness. Moselekatse was surrounded by fawning sycophants who lived in terror of their master. Moffat was different, and his style, the things he talked about, plus his direct honesty and presence, had their effect.

THE 1829 CONVERSATIONS

In 1829 some traders journeyed to the interior to shoot elephants and to barter.[3] Moselekatse received them peacefully, and when they left he sent two of his under-chiefs with them in order to obtain better knowledge of his white neighbours.[4] Moselekatse was aware of the existence of Kuruman, though it was 400 miles distant, and was anxious to learn more. The two chiefs arrived at Kuruman with a small retinue of attendants and observed

---

1 The larger group of Zimbabwean Ndebele trace their origins to the Khumalo clan who left the region of KwaZulu-Natal under the leadership of Moselekatse in 1822. The subsequent history of the Khumalo was one of conquest and absorption, first among the Sotho of the middle Vaal and then among the Tswana of the Marico valley (Cf. D.D. Phiri, *From Nguni to Ngoni: A History of the Ngoni exodus from Zululand and Swaziland to Malawi, Tanzania and Zambia,* (Limbe: Popular Publications, 1982), 11-53).

2 Moffat, *Journal,* 3.8.1835, (*MJ1,* 128), recorded Moselekatse as saying: 'The only enemy he feared was Dingaan'. Under Boer pressure, Moselekatse relocated far north in 1838.

3 RM, *MLSSA,* 510.

4 RM, *MLSSA,* 511.

the life of the station. Public worship in the chapel fascinated them. Moffat commented: 'They listened to the hymns, and to the address, part of which only they understood, and were much surprised when they heard that the hymns were not war songs.'[5]

When the time came for the chiefs to return to Moselekatse, Moffat knew they would be traveling through unfriendly territory. If anything happened to them, then Moselekatse's retribution could be dire.[6] Moffat resolved to accompany them as far as Mosega, which was on the boundary of Ndebele territory, some 300 miles from Kuruman. After seeing the chiefs through the most dangerous section, Moffat realised he could not return to Kuruman without meeting Moselekatse himself. Good manners made this a necessity. He could not risk the envoys reporting to Moselekatse that he had been invited to meet him but declined. As they travelled, they saw evidence of Ndebele power. Formerly populous towns had been reduced by Moselekatse's warriors to heaps of stones, mingled with human skulls. Eventually, Moffat arrived at Moselekatse's kraal, 100 miles east of Mosega, on the slopes of the Magaliesberg, near where Pretoria was later established.

Moffat's judgment was correct. Not only was it necessary to protect the envoys out of fear of negative consequences, but Moselekatse regarded care given to his envoys as care given to himself. Moffat and his group were welcomed by 'a thousand warriors', who surrounded the Kuruman party, pounding and stamping the ground with their feet as they roared a war-song. Then Moselekatse appeared. Moffat wrote:

> I told him that I was a teacher from God, who was the creator of all things and the governor among the nations, and in visiting him I had also in view the time when his people also might receive messengers from God, to tell them of another and a better world beyond the grave.[7]

Moffat referred to three cardinal aspects of Christian belief. These remained central in his presentations to Moselekatse over many years:

1. God is the creator of all things.
2. God is the governor among the nations.
3. There is another and better world beyond the grave.

The first two underlined that Moffat's God was the God of all. He was not simply a tribal god. Nor was he limited to a particular place. Nor was he a deity in a pantheon of other deities. God was the Creator of *all* things, and

---

5 Deane, *Robert Moffat*, 106.

6 RM, *MLSSA*, 513. Cf. RM, *Journal*, 1829, (*MJ1*, 6f).

7 RM, *Journal*, 1829, (*MJ1*, 15).

God was the governor among *all* the nations. Thus, the concept of God which Moffat presented to Moselekatse was Moffat's consistent definition of deity: the Being who 'made all things' and who 'ruled all things'.[8] Moffat continued:

> I next explained to him the nature and extent of divine government, a particular and retributive providence even among those like the Matabele, who knew not God.[9]

At this juncture the phrase 'who knew not God' simply meant that Moffat was concerned that the Ndebele did not know the *true* God, rather than that they had *no idea* of God. This spills into the next extract:

> When I told [Moselekatse] that death was only a separation between the soul and the body, he remarked that the soul could not be seen. To which I replied that a pain could not be seen but felt, neither was the wind seen but everybody knew wind and believed in wind. On hearing this he remarked that I must have been born in ancient times. He added that all he knew about the first people was that they ate cow dung until they got other food. On enquiring what was meant by the name *Morimo,* he said that he supposed that it was the name of God.[10]

Moselekatse's Ndebele had defeated Tswana tribes, such as the BaHurutse and BaKwena, and had taken over much of their territory. It is not surprising that Moselekatse knew the word Morimo*,* nor is it surprising that Morimo had found its way into SiNdebele. Moselekatse's reply, in which, according to Moffat, Moselekatse supposed that the SeTswana term Morimo was the name of God is significant. Recording Moselekatse's reply in this way points to Moffat assuming that Moselekatse's Ndebele had a concept of deity.

Moffat then found that the Ndebele had their own term *'Setutu'*. Moselekatse explained that, in his language, the name Setutu would be used. When Moffat probed further about this god Setutu*,* he recorded that Moselekatse 'could tell me nothing respecting his nature or works'. Moffat then pushed Moselekatse even harder for more information about Setutu, or Morimo, or 'God', but the only detailed material which Moselekatse gave to Moffat related to the ancestors, not to Setutu:

---

8 Bogue, *Miss. Lect.* 6, 'Reasoning about Religion with the Heathen', advised: 'But the chief source of satisfactory answers may be found in the analogy of natural and revealed religion, since difficulties similar to them in revealed religion are found in nature, especially in the creation and government of the world'. Moffat's presentation of Christianity to Moselekatse followed Bogue's advice to the letter. Moffat tried to make a point of contact through focusing on the 'creation and government' of the world.

9 RM, *Journal,* 1829, (*MJ1,* 15).

10 RM, *Journal,* 1829, (*MJ1,* 16).

> He appeared to have some shadows of ideas respecting an influence possessed by separated spirits, especially those of great men. He stated that he prayed to Molimo, but from what he said, it appeared that he prayed or spoke to the late Machobane, his father.[11]

Moffat encountered a way of thinking in which God, the ancestors, the living, and the dead, were bound together, and in which personal identities were intertwined, transferred and combined.[12] At this point, Moselekatse made a declaration which was to define his relationship with Moffat for the rest of his life. He said that, 'as his father was dead, Molimo had raised or, more literally, made for him another father in myself, and in future he would call me Machobane.'[13] Henceforth Moselekatse called him either 'Moffat', 'Ra-Mary' (father of Mary), or 'Machobane'.[14]

What Moffat met was a nominal belief in a supreme being, but a supreme being which had minimal influence or direct involvement in the lives of men and women. Little was said about Setutu. The important forces by far were the ancestors. Theoretically, Moselekatse ascribed to a belief in 'God' or the 'supreme being', but, in practice, Setutu had a very minor place in day-to-day religious life. As with the Tswana, the concept of God was marginalised. At the same time, Moselekatse's response, in his very first conversation with Moffat, that Morimo must be God, should not be overlooked. He presented a conscious awareness of a 'God' concept.

The 1835 Conversations

Moffat and Moselekatse's conversations in 1835 were along similar lines. It was on this visit that Moffat came to his considered opinion that, for the ordinary Ndebele man or woman, Moselekatse took the place of God:

> [He] is the God or Morimo to thousands, and thousands tremble at his nod; but he may yet be made to tremble before Him whose place he arrogantly, though ignorantly, claims in the hearts of his subjects.'[15] ... All seem to adore Moselekatse as if he were a god.[16]

---

11 RM, *Journal,* 1829, (*MJ1,* 16). A human ancestral spirit could be called *Morimo.*

12 This corresponds with the idea of *Morimo* in Tswana thought having multiple definitions.

13 RM, *Journal,* 1829, (*MJ1,* 16). Machobane was the name of Moselekatse's father. Machobane was murdered by Chaka around 1819.

14 E.g. RM, *Journal,* 1829, (*MJ1,* 31). In 1835, Moselekatse used 'Machobane' in addressing Moffat: '(Moselekatse) then began expatiating on the joy he felt on again sitting in his old place with his old friend, calling me *Machobane,* his father,' cf. RM, *Journal,* 10.6.1835, (*MJ1,* 75, 79). 'Ra-Mary' referred to Moffat's daughter, not his wife.

15 RM, *Journal,* 10.7.1835, (*MJ1,* 109).

16 RM, *To Richard Moffat,* 12.6.1835, (*MJ1,* 137).

Moffat was keen to discuss theological matters more deeply, and on 25 June 1835 he wrote in his *Journal*: 'I talked a little while with him on the knowledge they had of a supreme being, enquiring where the first men had come from and where they were made. He replied that they came from the North.'[17] This conversation was interrupted by pressing business which Moselekatse had to attend to. But the fact that Moffat had again engaged him in a discussion about a supreme being indicates Moffat's great interest in this area. Moffat wanted to establish a point of contact through the general concept of a supreme being. It was against Moffat's interests to overlook that idea in the Ndebele mind if it were there. A few days later, he noted:

> I was told that (Moselekatse) was going to pray to God, i.e. *Morimo*, or, as they pronounce it, *Molimo*. Moselekatse kept walking about like a public speaker ... He appeared to talk with great spirit, but, from what I heard, the substance of what he said was vain boasting instead of prayer, an abundance of adulation to those he esteemed, and I found I came in for an ample share. ... 'Moffat is saved by God. God is good to him. My companion, who is as Machobane, is come. God must preserve him [so] that he may return home in safety.'[18]

Moffat interpreted Moselekatse's prayer as Moselekatse speaking to himself, and he was appalled that 'prayer' should contain so much self-adulation—though this was a cultural routine. Yet, even in Moffat's heavily filtered account, we can discern Moselekatse referring to 'God'. A parallel concentration by Moselekatse on his own honour is not to be unexpected. But what is surprising is that, in *Missionary Labours*, Moffat did not concede that the Ndebele might be an exception to the general non-theism which he claimed to find in southern Africa.

The 1854 Conversations

In 1854 there were initial difficulties in communication, owing to the timidity of a new interpreter who was terrified to say anything that might displease Moselekatse.[19] Eventually, the visit yielded a rich harvest of theological interaction. Intriguingly, in Moffat's comprehensive record of the 1854 conversations, there is little reference to the Ndebele being unaware of the

---

17 RM, *Journal,* 26.6.1835, (*MJ1,* 91).

18 RM, *Journal,* 30.6.1835, (*MJ1,* 96). Moselekatse was following the conventional broad use of *Morimo.* Smith pointed out that even among the Tswana the word *Molimo* was also applied to highly venerated persons, see: Smith, 'The Idea of God among South African Tribes', 118. He added: 'Well-beloved missionaries may be spoken to, or of, in the same way'.

19 RM, *Journal,* 30.7.1854 & 2.8.1854, (*MJ1,* 246f & 250).

supreme being.[20] If Moffat's record is at all reliable, then discussion concerning God and the ways of God took place with a clear perception of what was being referred to. In 1829 and 1835 there had been some hints in Moffat's record that he feared the Ndebele had the same functional absence of a concept of the supreme being as he thought was true of the Tswana. In 1854, such hints were less. Perhaps he now differentiated between Tswana theism and Ndebele theism. Or perhaps Moselekatse had learned Moffat's way of thinking. Or perhaps Moselekatse's mind was no longer virgin territory: two encounters with Moffat, plus a brief meeting with some American missionaries,[21] had introduced him to Christian concepts.

What Moffat was convinced of, was that, in the piety of the ordinary Ndebele, Moselekatse was the one significant, absolute personage and power to whom they related and to whom they gave total homage.[22] Moffat often mused on the absolute position of the chief, and on the slow process which real conversions must take in such circumstances:

> What a change must be affected before these people can be brought to the obedience of faith! Moselekatse is the god they adore.[23] Nothing is lovely but that which he loves, and nothing is law but that which proceeds from his lips.[24]

He later added:

> It requires caution to have to do with a tyrant who receives from his people the honours which are due to Jehovah alone, and who is looked to by them

---

[20] One exception may be Moffat writing that Moselekatse and the Ndebele shared the 'destiny of the nations that forgot God'. See: RM, *Journal,* 14.8.1854, (*MJ1,* 260).

[21] In 1836 a group from the *American Board of Commissioners for Foreign Mission* went to work among Moselekatse's Ndebele. This was discontinued in 1837 after Boer raids.

[22] Moffat, *Journal,* 24.6.1854, (*MJ1,* 233), wrote with disgust on Moselekatse being given religious devotion: '[If a person comes close to Moselekatse] He must give him one or more of his titles, which are as follows, *Molimo* (god), *Konyama* (lion), *'Ntlou enkholu* (great Elephant), *Enkhosi ea pakate* (king within).' Moffat's discomfort with praise given to Moselekatse in a manner which, in Moffat's view, should only be given to Jehovah, is discussed by Vail and White, 'The Development of Forms: Ndebele Royal Praises', in: Leroy Vail & Landeg White, *Power and the Praise Poem: Southern African Voices in History,* (Charlottesville: University Press of Virginia, 1991), 84-111. The Tswana also composed praise poems for chiefs, but it seems that what was rendered to Moselekatse was of a far more intense type. On praise songs for Tswana chiefs see: Schapera (ed.), *Praise Poems of Tswana chiefs,* (Oxford: 1965).

[23] When Moffat met Moselekatse in 1854, he found him crippled. The LMS transcript of Moffat's record, states: 'Though we had been among the Matabele for nearly two weeks [still traveling to Moselekatse's headquarters] no one whispered one word of what must have been well known. Probably it would have been deemed presumptuous for vulgar lips to talk of one afflicted whom they revered as God.' RM, *Journal,* 22.7.1854, (*MJ1,* 229).

[24] RM, *Journal,* 16.7.1854, (*MJ1,* 221). Accepting an external, higher divine law, to which even a chief must be subject, required a radical change of worldview for all.

> as the only God that exists, in the heavens above or in the earth beneath. Tell one of his subjects that the last rain that fell was not the production of Moselekatse's power and he will look on you as a madman who has outraged the bounds of common sense.[25]

Moffat only had access to the 'public face' of the Ndebele. He had no way of finding out what religious thoughts they had in their private minds. He had no way of knowing if this constant, absolute adulation of Moselekatse was simply for their own protection and security, and if there were a parallel piety reserved for a 'real' deity. It should also be noted that it was only on the 1859-60 visit that Moffat was with the Ndebele during December and January, the time of year when their religious ceremonies were concentrated.

It was on this third visit that Moffat persuaded Moselekatse to allow him to preach openly to his people, an opportunity he had waited for since 1829. When permission was granted, Moffat's theme in his first sermon, on 27 September 1854, was: '*The happiness of the people whose God was Jehovah*.'[26] Moffat focused on the greatness of God, the sin of humanity, and the subsequent obligations of humanity before God. After emphasising these points, Moffat turned to the 'blessings'. God's glory came first. Human blessing came second. Significantly, Moffat spoke of 'Jehovah' and not just 'God'. The name 'Jehovah' served to distinguish God from other possible gods. Bogue had noted that Baptist missions sometimes used Jehovah for that reason.[27] Thus, Moffat was not preaching about any deity, but about the biblical Jehovah, and using the specific name 'Jehovah' emphasised this. At the same time, using 'Jehovah' was not an absolute rule for Moffat.

For a whole week, Moffat preached daily to large gatherings. And in Moffat's record of that week, there is no reference to having to explain the idea of God. He appears to have taken for granted that the people would understand the concept.

Why had Moselekatse been unwilling to allow Moffat to preach to his people? Was it a fear of white influence over the Ndebele? Was it to protect Ndebele traditions? Moffat's view was that Moselekatse feared losing his absolute power if devotion and obedience were given by his people to God

---

25 RM, *Journal*, 20.9.1854, (*MJ1*, 309).

26 RM, *Journal*, 27.9.1854, (*MJ1*, 315).

27 Bogue, *Miss. Lect.* 4, 'Preaching (2)'. *UJehova* was used by early Wesleyan missionaries to the Zulu; and *Jehova* was used by Newton Adams of the American Board of Commissioners for Foreign Missions as he worked among the Zulu. Later missionaries did not always follow this, seeking (with difficulty) an appropriate Zulu word. See: Smith, 'The Idea of God among South African Tribes', 103f.

as a higher authority.[28] Moselekatse's reluctance to allow Moffat to teach had been unequivocal. Moffat wrote: 'Moselekatse is just as afraid of religious instruction as a condemned criminal [of] the gallows. If any of his people happen to be sitting at our fire when we commence worship, they start up and quickly walk off.'[29] He frequently linked Moselekatse's unwillingness to hear the Gospel, or to allow his people to hear the Gospel, with protection of his power, which, for Moselekatse, was a central principle:

> He knows that man's universal depravity and God's universal power, if proclaimed to him and his people, would denude him of all his pretensions and power in their eyes. In their judgment he rules all above and all below in this quarter: the heavens are his and all their treasures of rain and all those phenomena. He, and he only, gives rain, and he, and he only, receives those praises and those honours which belong alone to Jehovah. *I am not done with him yet.*[30]

This was Moffat's interpretation. Thus, Moffat identified two fundamental no-go areas for Moselekatse. Firstly, no one must think Moselekatse imperfect in any way: therefore, Moselekatse was unwilling to accept the Christian doctrine of sin, since to do so would be to lose his majesty. Secondly, no one must think of a being superior to Moselekatse: since absolute monarchy can have no rivals, in heaven or on earth. His favourite method of avoiding instruction was to agree with Moffat, and affirm that he already loved God and God's Word. Moffat wrote: 'On one occasion, when pressing him rather close, he remarked, "God's word is good and I know you are beloved of God and I love his word too—it is good"'. I asked him how he

---

[28] Moselekatse came from the Chaka generation of absolute despots who sought total power, and who protected that power ruthlessly. Phiri argues that this type of chieftainship was untraditional, (D.D. Phiri, *From Nguni to Ngoni,* 11f).

[29] RM, *Journal,* 8.9.1854, (*MJ1,* 293).

[30] RM, *Journal,* 10.9.1854, (*MJ1,* 297f), (our italics). Despite Moffat's statement: 'I am not done with him yet', he wrote in a resigned way about Moselekatse and focused on the future: '[I told Moselekatse] I only desired two things, 1st, that he hear me tell him about God and the life to come, of which I had yet much to say, and 2nd, that he, and his children after him, be kind to teachers of whose character he now knew something, that they were men who would do him and his people good and not evil, who will speak the truth and not lie.' See: RM, *Journal,* 11.9.1854, (*MJ1,* 299). At this point Moffat was looking to the labours of others in the future. He did not know that Moselekatse would soon grant permission to preach. Moffat's summary highlights that he wanted to speak of 'God' and 'the life to come'. Everything revolved around these doctrines. Moffat's refusal to trade, or personally profit from his encounters with the Ndebele, was, in his mind, crucial to establishing a reputation for integrity. Moffat mentions that he, 'wished [Moselekatse] fully to understand, what I had so often told him, that I am not come for ivory. I have brought nothing for barter, and if I return to the Kuruman without a single tusk, I shall return thankful that I had seen him and thankful for the kindness he had shown me.' Establishing integrity was vital for mission.

could love that which he did not know. He persisted that he knew it and loved it: then followed his winding up of that subject by *exit!*'[31]

THE 1857 CONVERSATIONS

On the fourth visit to Moselekatse, in 1857, there were few theological conversations. This was because in 1857 Moffat had the sharply focused goal of preparing the way for the establishment of an LMS station among the Ndebele. All negotiations were concentrated on that aim, and general discussion was reduced. Nevertheless, Moffat again used the term 'God' in his conversations without any need for explanation. Moffat also noted that he did not hear the term Modimo applied to Moselekatse as much as in the past, and had his own reason why:

> I went in to Moselekatse this afternoon. He had about eleven of his *lintunas* or chief men sitting in a circle before him, responding to every word he uttered, no matter how silly, with the usual adulatory epithets. I do not hear the word Molimo as usual. He may have forbidden its use. Knowing how painful it is for me to hear it.[32]

THE 1859/60 CONVERSATIONS

During the extended 1859-60 visit, when the LMS mission station was set up, Moffat recorded only a few matters of theological interest. He again emphasised that absolute chieftainship still filled the horizon of the people's thinking. It dominated to such an extent that, in Moffat's view, the Ndebele understood sin primarily as an offence against the chief rather than being an offence against deity: 'They have no knowledge that they can sin or do any wrong against anyone greater than Moselekatse.'[33] Moselekatse, in Moffat's understanding, had become the supreme being and, to a certain extent, he had even displaced the ancestors or the community as the person whom one was fearful of sinning against. Three extracts from Moffat's writings are of particular relevance. Firstly, in a letter written to Holloway Helmore, who was on the sister Makololo mission, Moffat wrote:

> The peculiarity of Government is a fearful barrier. There is no god the Matabele fear or love—if love it may be called—but Moselekatse; but nothing

31 RM, *Journal,* 12.9.1854, (*MJ1,* 303) (Moffat's italics).

32 RM, *Journal,* 13.11.1857, (*MJ2,* 115).

33 RM, *Journal,* 15.12.1859, (*MJ2,* 247).

> is too great for [God's] omnipotence. We must look heavenward for the fulfillment of the gracious promises of Him who has sent His servants hither.[34]

Secondly, there was a 'blessing' which Moffat received from some Ndebele women. Moffat noted that they cried to him as he travelled:

> 'Peace be with you. May *Molimo* go with you and bring you safe to Moselekatse. May no evil hinder your progress. May you have rain and travel happy. We are happy to see you all.' - Blarney in part! This mode of salutation not often heard here: could not but make a favourable impression.[35]

The Ndebele women commended Moffat to the care of Molimo. This was an extraordinary action if the Ndebele had no concept of God, unless they were simply saying what they knew Moffat would appreciate. But that seems unlikely. Moffat appreciated the 'blessing' despite his scepticism.

Thirdly, during the long days of waiting for Moselekatse to grant the party a site for a mission station, Moffat wrote:

> There is no reason given why oxen are not sent or why the subject of our removal [to a permanent location] is dropped. We only hear that there is a gathering of people, and a feast to be held in honour of their gods – *manes* of the dead? – that great quantities of beer are ordered to be made or prepared, while the *Machaha* [young warriors] are to come in from all quarters.[36]

Moffat explicitly used the phrase 'their gods'. As far as he understood things, the 'gods' were the spirits of the ancestors and, in Moffat's eyes, not 'gods' at all. Nevertheless, he stated that *for the Ndebele* these spirits were 'gods'. Moffat gave no other clue as to how he understood 'their gods', apart from a link with the ancestral spirits.

When Moffat left Moselekatse in June 1860 his personal contact with the Ndebele was at an end after thirty-one years. Over that period his discussions with Moselekatse had been lengthy and deep. Moffat pushed his questions and demanded answers. He stayed with the Ndebele and engaged in these conversations for months at a stretch. Admittedly, Moffat worked through an interpreter. Admittedly, he came with his own 'mind-set'. Admittedly, he only had deep discussions with one individual. Yet, notwithstanding these caveats, it is difficult to spend so much time in intense conversation without

---

34 RM, *To Holloway Helmore,* 22.21860, (SOAS/CWM/Africa/Personal Box 1/22). Moffat argued that despotic chieftainship made it difficult for men and women to see God as Governor of all.

35 RM, *To Mary Moffat,* 17.8.1859, (*MJ2,* 180).

36 RM, *Journal,* 3.12.1859, (*MJRM- 2,* 236). On Moffat's previous visits to the Ndebele, he returned home before November. On the 1859/60 longer visit, he was with the Ndebele through December and January, the time of year when important Ndebele religious rituals took place. Moffat encountered these for the first time.

absorbing something of what a person truly believes. The same can, and must, be said of Moffat's extended conversations with the Tswana. Moffat may not always have come to correct conclusions, but he came to them after lengthy, probing, consistent questioning. We may disagree with Moffat, but what we cannot do is to aver that he made judgments after fleeting, hasty, or superficial encounters.

Moselekatse called Moffat 'Machobane', which had been the name of Moselekatse's now-deceased father. Moselekatse was serious about this. But what did he mean? Did he put Moffat in place of his father? Was Moffat now his father in person? Was the spirit of Machobane in Moffat speaking through Moffat?[37] Had *Morimo* or *Setutu* created a new father for him in Moffat?[38] Was Moselekatse simply giving respect? Was he saying that he would regard Moffat's wisdom as he regarded his father's wisdom? The answer is difficult to determine, but it seems that, for Moselekatse, Moffat had truly taken the identity of Machobane. Consequently, in a very real sense, the original Moffat was 'dead'. Thus, when Moffat left for Kuruman, at the end of his 1835 second visit to the chief, Moselekatse said to him: 'When you return home and the people salute you, tell them that you are not Moffat; that Moffat has been murdered by Moselekatse and his Machaha.'[39] Moffat existed no more, but Machobane existed.

The definition of what Moselekatse meant proved elusive all through their relationship. But what was clear was that Machobane, whether as an ancestral spirit, or as Moffat, or as both at the same time, was a more vital figure in Moselekatse's spiritual awareness than the supreme being, Setutu or Modimo, in whom he had only a thin theoretical belief. 'God' did 'exist' somewhere in Moselekatse's theology, but he occupied no active place in Moselekatse's life. Moselekatse's notional recognition that there was a 'God' became non-theism in practice. It was this functional non-theism which struck Moffat so sharply. Technically, it was not a-theism, but a spirituality in which God was unnecessary because of the powerful presence of the ancestors, especially the major ancestor in Moselekatse's lineage, his own father Machobane.

---

37 Some entries in Moffat's *Journals* might mean that Moselekatse viewed Moffat as having the 'spirit' of Machobane. Cf. RM, *Journal,* 10.6.1835, (*MJ1,* 76): 'He answered … "My men fear to tell me some things. You are Machobane, who feared nothing; you will tell the truth"'.

38 Cf. 'Machobane' in Moselekatse's prayer, in: RM, *Journal,* 30.6.1835, (*MJ1,* 96).

39 RM, *Journal,* 5.8.1835, (*MJ1,* 130). *Machaha:* warriors.

Theism and Absolute Chieftainship

Functional non-theism was unsurprising in a society in which total power lay with the chief, and in which, as Moffat noted, his subjects were 'taught to view him as supreme'.[40] Moselekatse was an absolute despot after the Chaka model, in a way undreamt of by the Tswana Kgosi who depended on continued tribal approval in order to exercise their authority. The absolutism of Moselekatse's chieftainship is seminal to this discussion. True supremacy has no rivals, or it is not a true supremacy. Moreover, if a chief has real, total and absolute power, then that power can only be power if somehow it is also carried beyond death. A power limited to this life only, is not absolute power. It is not a power to be in real fear of, since the simple expedient of death destroys it. There can be no real sharing of absolute power, and so God is pushed to the periphery. God is theoretically acknowledged, but, in practice, he is absent. Within such a society and culture, the chief *de facto* becomes Modimo. This was Moffat's conclusion: 'Moselekatse is the God or Morimo to thousands';[41] 'All seem to adore Moselekatse as if he were a god.'[42]

In the Old Testament, Jehovah is described as jealous of his honour and unwilling to share his glory with another.[43] What Moffat saw in Moselekatse was a chief whose glory could likewise not be shared with another, even the gods. Thus, Moselekatse became God, with other 'gods' so reduced in their stature, importance and relevance that they were 'no gods'. The chief was the operative deity within the day-to-day life of his people. In Moselekatse this went beyond the Tswana principle of *Modimo* being manifested in some persons of outstanding ability, cunning or power. Moffat wrote:

> The first instance of any of his subjects listening to other laws than his own, or acknowledging other powers beyond those of a man who hears himself called heaven, god, the sun a thousand and one times every day, would only require the lifting of a finger, and he would never be seen more.[44]

At the same time, the Moffats, father and son, observed that this absolute monarch participated in religious ceremonies. In 1859, John Smith Moffat

---

40 RM, *Journal,* 26.6.1835, (*MJ1,* 92). Phiri, *From Nguni to Ngoni,* 11f, argued that despotism and paramount chieftainship were unknown among the Nguni (including Ndebele and Zulu) until the nineteenth century.

41 RM, *Journal,* 10.7.1835, (*MJ1,* 109). This could be seen as simply an example of the Tswana concept of *Morimo* being associated with whatever is powerful or outstanding. Moffat had never met this expression of direct identification among the Tswana he knew.

42 RM, *To Richard Moffat,* 12.6.1835, (*MJ1,* 137).

43 Cf. Isaiah 42:8.

44 RM, *Journal,* 6.8.1854, (*MJ1,* 256).

wrote that Moselekatse used to remain in entire seclusion for some days, in a hut built and set apart for the purpose:

> It was supposed that during this period of seclusion the chief was in private conference with the spirit of his departed father Machobane. Evidently we have here a survival of some kind of ancestor worship, of which there are traces among the Bantu tribes. There was also some connection between this and the eating of the first fruits which were becoming available at this time of year, though the general harvest was not until later.[45]

Moffat was also aware of Moselekatse taking part in religious exercises. He recorded that, in the late 1830s, Moselekatse had sent envoys to try and find where he was, and whether he was still alive, since rumours of Moffat's death had reached him. Though the envoys did not meet Moffat, Moselekatse eventually learned that he was alive, prompting a ceremony:

> After having this information corroborated by succeeding enquiries he slaughtered a great number of oxen to the *manes* of the dead, hoping that the separated spirit of his father, Machobane, might answer his enquiries as to where I was and [the] hope of seeing me once more.[46]

There is no mention of a 'god' in Moffat's account of the ceremony, only of the ancestors. Moselekatse did not himself tell Moffat about this ritual: Moffat learned about it from 'one of his chief warriors'. The *manes* of the dead were the spirits of the dead; and connection with Machobane either lay in Moselekatse's belief that there was a link between Moffat and the spirit of Machobane, or simply in Machobane being the most important ancestral spirit to whom Moselekatse would appeal. But Moffat refused to categorise an ancestral spirit as a 'god'. This has to be kept in mind when evaluating his statements. For Moffat, an ancestral spirit was the spirit of a creature, and hence could not be self-existent. Nor could an ancestral spirit be the creator or governor of all.

Whatever was in Moselekatse's mind, the ceremonies he participated in showed that Moselekatse did appeal to spiritual forces beyond himself. In a letter to Tidman of the LMS, Moffat gave further details on Ndebele beliefs:

> I talked to some Matabele who were present and put a few questions in reference to God, government, immortality,[47] etc. ... They said that the Matabele believed that there was a town underground where Machobane, the father of Moselekatse, lived and where there were Matabele cattle, etc. The speaker, being one of the more intelligent, was asked if *all* went thither.

---

45 RUM, *JSM,* 87.

46 RM, *Journal,* 8.10.1854, (*MJ1,* 327).

47 Three topics: God, Government, Immortality. These were the same topics which Moffat discussed with Moselekatse in 1829 on their first meeting (*MJ1,* 15).

> This he could not tell. I then enquired if there was another place for those who did not go thither. This also he could not answer. When I enquired if those in that nether region had taken their bones and their flesh with them, he seemed at a loss, and then answered he thought not. ... What is the custom of their forefathers and the law of the chief, they take for granted. Moselekatse occasionally offers a sacrifice, or a killing of cattle, to the *manes* of his departed father, and pretends to ascertain coming events, or obtain information on points on which he is at a loss, by intercourse with the dead. This gives him no little influence over the minds of his people.[48]

Moffat made it his business to find out about indigenous beliefs. But he was not an anthropologist, and he elicited information through aggressive rather than sympathetic questioning. Moreover, he had the specific purpose of *refuting* 'erroneous' ideas which did not accord with his Christian faith. Nevertheless, he *did* enquire. Decisively, he asked his questions before Christian concepts had irrevocably permeated the culture.

What Moffat discovered was very little reference to God, but an overwhelming concentration on the departed ancestors,[49] with the primary location for the ancestors being in the 'earth', not in the 'heavens'. It was mostly in his conversations with the Ndebele that Moffat referred to the ancestors. He mentioned them rarely in relation to the Tswana. Questions about Modimo dominated his conversations with the Tswana.

Marginalisation and Ndebele Theism

With the Tswana, Moffat was convinced they had no concept of a supreme being. In contrast, his account of the Ndebele supplied evidence that Moffat reckoned they were aware of a deity, though such a deity was non-functional in the life of the tribe since, in his opinion, Moselekatse had become 'god' to his people. The praise-songs in honour of a chief in Ndebele culture were always going to appear to Moffat as expressing sentiments which he would reserve for God alone.

If we assume that the original Ndebele shared similar religious concepts with other Nguni, such as the Zulu and the Swazi, then, in the absence of clear information on pre-Christian Ndebele religion, reference to Zulu theism may be helpful.[50] Traditional Zulu thought had the entity *uMvelinqangi*, also

---

48 RM, *To Tidman, LMS,* 10.5.1855, (*MJ1,* 370f).

49 Eleanor Preston-Whyte, 'Zulu Religion', *The Encyclopedia of Religion,* Vol. 15, 593, quoting Eileen Jensen Krige: 'The real vital religion of the Zulus is their ancestor worship'. See also: E.J. Krige, *The Social System of the Zulus,* (Pietermaritzburg: 1936), 280f.

50 In Smith (ed.), *African Ideas of God,* the Ndebele are not dealt with, though the Shona, whom Moselekatse's Ndebele displaced in southern Zimbabwe, are. In *The Encyclopedia of*

known as *uNkulunkulu,* which was sometimes referred to as a supreme being. Preston-Whyte stated that *uMvelinqangi* was the 'first-comer' who emerged from a reed-bed, followed by human beings, animals and nature as a whole.[51] *UMvelinqangi* was the first, and hence the most important, of all beings. But it is difficult to see *uMvelinqangi* as a 'creator' in the Christian sense.[52] Preston-Whyte also added that there is little evidence that *uMvelinqangi* was worshipped directly, but that ideas about him probably served as explanatory constructs for the natural order. *UMvelinqangi's* alternative designation, *uNkulunkulu*, literally meant 'the old, old one' and it was this term which some missionaries among the Zulu used for 'God'. Whether or not they should have is still debated.

Distinct from *uMvelinqangi* was *iNkosi yeZulu*, the 'lord of the sky and the personification of heaven' who was associated with thunder and lightning which were greatly feared.[53] But if, among the Zulu, a 'supreme being'—whether *uMvelinqangi* or *uNkulunkulu*—was a relatively clear concept, then it seems it was less so with Moselekatse's Ndebele. Moselekatse's style of authoritarian chieftainship may have contributed to this.

The Zulu insisted that they did not hear of God first from white men. Werner cited a Zulu source: 'The Lord of whom we hear through you we have already heard of before you came. But he is not like the *uNkulunkulu* who, we say, made all things. But the former we call a king, for, we say, he is above; *uNkulunkulu* is beneath'.[54] Lobengula, Moselekatse's Ndebele successor, is reported to have spoken to the missionaries in similar vein: that the Ndebele knew of God before the missionaries came. Clues gleaned from Moffat's

---

Religion, the Ndebele and Shona are dealt with in the same article, but the emphasis is on the Shona. For Zulu thought, see: Smith, 'The Idea of God among South African Tribes', 102-110; and Preston-Whyte, 'Zulu Religion', 591-595.

51 Preston-Whyte: 'Zulu Religion', 592.

52 Smith had a long discussion on whether, in Zulu religion, *uNkulunkulu* and *uMvelinqangi* are gods, deified men, or simply first beings. He suggested that two concepts may be merged: (i) the first man; and (ii) the creator. Yet he conceded that they are meant to be the same (Smith, 'The Idea of God among South African Tribes', 103-107). *UNkulunkulu* was certainly viewed as the progenitor of humanity and hence the most revered figure. Is a progenitor the same as 'God'? Moffat would demand eternal existence as an attribute of deity (*MLSSA,* 262).

53 Alice Werner, *Myths and Legends of the Bantu,* 50. It is possible that *Setutu,* of whom Moselekatse spoke, was this god who was distinct from *Unkulunkulu*. If so, then *Setutu* was the 'sky-god', whereas *Unkulunkulu* was the god underground. The fact that the dead went 'underground' gave *Unkulunkulu* great importance. Smith, 'The Idea of God among South African Tribes', 108, suggested that *Inkosi epezulu* was the Lord over *Unkulunkulu.* With so many fluid concepts, it is no surprise that missionaries struggled to find the best word which could carry their message about God.

54 Alice Werner, *Myths and Legends of the Bantu,* 50.

many conversations with Moselekatse agree with that observation, though Moffat himself never penetrated to an adequate appreciation of Ndebele theism. Moselekatse dwarfed everything for Moffat.

*

When Moffat made unequivocal statements in his LMS *Sermon* and in his *Missionary Labours* concerning the lack of a concept of a supreme being among the tribes whom he encountered, he over-simplified a very complex situation. It is also true that Moffat sometimes embellished matters when moving them from his *Journal* into *Missionary Labours.* This was probably for the sake of impact, and Moffat certainly succeeded in that aim. Unfortunately, it also resulted in scholars being sceptical about his interest in, and knowledge of, indigenous beliefs. This is to be regretted, since Moffat did in fact discuss such matters with a determined tenacity, albeit from the viewpoint of a missionary. Moreover, though he was unable to fully grasp the deeper notion of *Modimo* which existed in the Tswana thought-world, Moffat did uncover clues which pointed in that direction. Moffat's achievement was to remove a simplistic identification between Modimo and a European/Judaeo-Christian concept of a supreme being, which his predecessors and successors hastily assumed. It would be later generations which would reposition each concept in its proper place.

Chapter 8
The Theory of the Lost Knowledge of God

RIGHTLY OR WRONGLY, Moffat concluded that in southern Africa he met some peoples who had no concept of God or a supreme being. For Moffat, this introduced a practical problem in relation to evangelism, and also created a philosophical problem in relation to the knowledge of God. This was because he came from a theological culture which assumed that all of humanity, in every corner of the earth, had a natural knowledge of God through general revelation.[1] Accordingly, he expected that any people, anywhere on earth, would have a sense of the being of God. That 'sense' might be misinformed, twisted, broken or limited, but it would be there. However, what Moffat thought he encountered were peoples with no such understanding. This took him by surprise and, as we shall see, led him to suppose that natural religion and general revelation were, by themselves, insufficient to create awareness of the supreme being. What Moffat felt himself forced to conclude was that all knowledge of God depended upon special revelation, and on the content of that revelation being transmitted from one generation to the next.

Moffat devised a theory of the 'Lost Knowledge of God'.[2] In this theory humanity—including all races—had an initial, perfect, and primal knowledge of God. This initial perfect primal knowledge was then lost by some peoples in the transmission of their traditions. He felt that this theory could explain the phenomenon before him and also be true to important Bible passages. What he found was that he had to change his ideas concerning the knowledge of God in the light of what he experienced. This involved a total revolution in his thinking. It was an unexpected revolution, reversing widely accepted interpretations of Scripture. Critically, it altered his whole understanding of general revelation. Moffat had to rethink from first principles.

---

1 Cf. RM, *Africa,* 17: 'I am aware that some do not take this view of the subject; for I have often read and heard that the idea of a supreme being under some character or name exists in every nation; and that every human mind, in whatever land or clime, retained some notions of the necessity of an atonement.'

2 Cf. Setiloane, *The Image of God among the Sotho-Tswana*, 105: 'But the missionaries really did not believe that they were confronted with a Tabula Rasa in matters of religion. They rather seem to have thought that the Sotho-Tswana had had a religion, but that it had died out.'

In this chapter, the validity of Moffat's conclusion that some tribes had no concept of a supreme being is not under discussion. That has already been discussed. What we now examine is the knock-on effect which this conviction had on Moffat's general theological understanding, especially his theory of the 'Lost Knowledge of God'.

It is important to underline that, in Moffat's mind, there was no thought that there was a lack of knowledge of God because some races had deficient intellectual capacity. For Moffat, the knowledge of God had been *lost.* It was not that a particular human group had been unable to *formulate* it or *produce* it. The knowledge of God had been *lost* in a breakdown of handing on that knowledge from one generation to the next. Moffat vigorously disagreed with phrenologists and others who argued that so-called primitive races lacked intellectual capacity for sophisticated spiritual ideas.

Moffat's Initial Expectations

Arriving in Africa in 1817, the young Moffat assumed that, as a missionary, he had come to add a 'saving' knowledge of God to an already existing 'natural' knowledge of God. He envisaged countless thousands who already had an awareness of the reality of God: what he had to do was to add the Gospel message to this foundation. He fully expected to find a concept of the supreme being. He assumed that this concept would have a clear, central and important place in the life and thought of the peoples whom he would meet. He expected this, and indeed almost depended upon it, for his rudimentary missiological principles to work. He did not come with a preconceived notion that people would not know about God. The reverse was the case.

Writing in 1842 and looking back on twenty-five years of service, Moffat revealed that he had expected to operate with a 'Paul in Athens' type of missiology. Just as Paul took the Athenian 'Altar to the Unknown God' as his starting-point and then tried to lead his audience to Christ, so Moffat expected to move his hearers from a natural awareness of the supreme being to Christian Faith. But when he thought he perceived a lack of a concept of God, he realised that this made his chosen mode of evangelism irrelevant:

> The missionary could make no appeals to legends, or to altars, or to an unknown God, or to ideas kindred to those he wished to impart. His was not the work of turning the stream backward to its ancient course. Their religious system, like those streams in the wilderness which lose themselves in the sand, had entirely disappeared ... I have often wished to find something, by which I could lay hold on the minds of the natives—an altar to an unknown

> God, the faith of their ancestors, the immortality of the soul, or any religious association—but nothing of this kind ever floated in their minds.[3]

Moffat wanted to find the idea of the supreme being in Namaqua, Tswana and Ndebele culture. He believed that in it lay the natural starting-point for mission. His surprise at the lack of the concept—as he interpreted what he observed—testified to the unexpectedness of the situation he found himself in. Moffat stated that his preconception of all peoples everywhere having a 'natural' knowledge concerning basic spiritual truths was challenged by what he encountered. He then examined the effects of this on knowledge of God:

> Their ignorance, though to a calm reasoner on the subject, not to be wondered at, was distressing in the extreme, and perfectly confounding to my preconceived notions about innate and intuitive ideas, and what some call natural light.[4]

Moffat had believed that certain truths about God, such as his existence and power, were self-evident to all peoples anywhere because of a 'natural light' available to all humanity. This is what he meant by the phrase 'innate and intuitive ideas'. Elsewhere he expressed himself more directly:

> I am aware that the popular opinion is that 'man is a religious creature', that 'wherever (man) is to be found, there also are to be traced the impressions and even convictions of the existence of a God'.[5] It is also commonly believed, that wherever man is found scattered over the widespread surfaces of earth's domain, the knowledge of a 'vicarious offering'[6] or sacrifice, by way of atonement, has retained its seat in the human mind.
>
> Such were my own views when I left my native land; and, entertaining such views, I persuaded myself, or rather tried to persuade myself, that I could discover rays of natural light, innate ideas of a Divine Being, in the most untutored savage; - that I could never be at any loss to make appeals to something analogous to our own faith in the religious notions even of those among whom not a vestige of temple, altar, image, idol, or shrine was to be found.[7]

---

3 RM, *MLSSA,* 244f. This passage is frequently quoted as an example of Moffat's inability to recognise indigenous spirituality.

4 RM, *MLSSA,* 121.

5 Calvin quoted Cicero in support of his belief that all humanity has an awareness of the supreme being (Calvin, *Institutes,* I, iii, 3). Cf. Watson, *A Body of Divinity: Sermons upon the Westminster Assembly's Catechism,* (Ldn: BOT edn, 1958), 29.

6 Some eighteenth-century natural theology held that the light of nature was able to convey not simply a sense of the existence and power of God, but even some of his attributes. Paley extended his 'watchmaker' argument in this direction (Cooper, *Paley's Watchmaker,* 201ff). Others argued that even the atonement was knowable through natural theology. This seems to be what Moffat was alluding to.

7 RM, *MLSSA,* 265f.

He was reluctant to abandon these assumptions: 'I was determined not to be driven from the sentiments entertained by a vast majority of the respected advocates of religion in my own native land of light'.[8] Moffat was stubborn. His convictions were difficult to displace. But he had to accept a paradigm shift in his thinking. His original belief that there was a cluster of 'innate and intuitive ideas' concerning God available to all humanity—and that these were the basis for a common knowledge of the supreme being—had to be changed to the notion of the 'Lost Knowledge of God'.

The subsequent development of Moffat's theory of the 'Lost Knowledge of God' closely parallels the growth of his conviction that he met tribes with no concept of God, or of a supreme being, though his analysis was not expressed until the 1840s. Thus, Moffat had no reference to a 'Lost Knowledge of God' in his very earliest letters or *Journal*. The first traces occur in the later 1820s. In 1827, Moffat wrote of a village woman, that she was really of the number 'that forgot God.'[9] It is true that in *Missionary Labours,* he wrote of the Namaqua, whom he met in his earliest years in Africa, as having lost the knowledge of God. However, these were retrospective reflections. It is also noteworthy that, in the accounts of his visits to Moselekatse in 1829 and 1835, Moffat did not refer to a 'lost knowledge' though he did think that Moselekatse and the Ndebele had little awareness of a supreme being. Theological reflection on the problem came mainly during his time in Britain from 1839 to 1843.

During his furlough in Britain, Moffat put his theory on paper. In May 1840 he delivered a lecture-sermon on Isaiah 9:2 to the LMS, entitled *'Africa: or Gospel Light shining in the midst of Heathen Darkness'.* In this keynote speech, Moffat discussed at length his perception that the tribes which he worked with lacked a concept of a supreme being. Though he did not fully elaborate his theory of the 'Lost Knowledge of God', he did hint at it, referring to, 'Degrees of Satanic delusion which have arisen since Noah and his family left the ark'.[10] Moffat also stated in his speech that, for some races, 'every traditionary account of what was, or who is, in relation to God, having

---

8 RM, *MLSSA,* 121.

9 RM, *Journal,* 21.4.1827, (*AAK,* 247f). The incident was in a village where Moffat was for language study: 'This afternoon, sitting on my fore chest, I entered into conversation with a young widow, who seemed more sprightly than wise. My first question was, what would become of her after death? She stared at me with the utmost astonishment, as if she had said, 'Shall I die?' repeating my question, assuring her that death would spare neither of us, she at last answered, that she knew not. I gave her a plain scriptural answer, namely that she should go to hell if she died in her present state. I added that the wicked would be turned into hell, etc., etc., and pointed out that she was really of the number that forgot God.'

10 RM, *Africa,* 14.

become extinct, they bear ample testimony that it is not in nature alone to lead to nature's God.'[11] Moffat referred to 'traditionary' accounts, and to the insufficiency of nature 'to lead to nature's God'. He would enlarge on both of these in *Missionary Labours.* Thus, by 1840 Moffat could speak of, 'Nations without the light of Divine Revelation.'[12]

By the time Moffat published *Missionary Labours* in 1842, he had given his theory of the 'Lost Knowledge of God' extensive analysis, and he devoted a considerable section of his book to the concept. The standard edition of *Missionary Labours* has 620 pages, with twenty-seven of these (256 to 283) containing a detailed theological discussion on the issue. The 'Lost Knowledge of God' is the only theological matter which Moffat ever analysed in a systematic fashion, and his extended discussion in *Missionary Labours* is his main presentation. It was during the latter part of 1840 through 1841 that Moffat did the reading which lay behind his thoughts in *Missionary Labours.*

Moffat's letters and *Journals*, written after his return to Africa in 1843, contain only a few references to what had now become his settled opinion on the matter, though in 1854 he wrote of Moselekatse and the Ndebele as sharing the 'destiny of the nations that *forgot* God'.[13] However, in his later writings, he did not dwell on this theory, even though he often repeated his perception of people having no concept of the Supreme Being.

The Concept of Revelation

Key to Moffat's theology was his axiom that all humanity had an original perfect knowledge of God, which humanity now no longer has. With many peoples, that original perfect knowledge had diminished, but was still extant. Unexpectedly, for a few peoples it had totally vanished. It was this total lostness which Moffat referred to when he wrote, as earlier quoted: 'Their religious system, like those streams in the wilderness which lose themselves in the sand, had entirely disappeared.'[14] Knowledge of the supreme being was not something which humanity, through its intellectual ability, had attained. It was something which had been 'given' but then 'lost'. Thus, knowledge of the supreme being did not depend on intellectual ability, but upon faithfulness in handing on the tradition.

---

11 RM, *Africa,* 16.

12 RM, *Africa,* 45.

13 RM, *Journal,* 14.8.1854, (*MJ1,* 260).

14 RM, *MLSSA,* 244f.

This was the reverse of some later nineteenth and twentieth-century thought which presupposed an evolutionary development in each area of human life and experience, including the religious consciousness. This held that, as part of the general ascent of man, there was an 'ascent of the religious consciousness', with it growing from 'less' to 'more'.[15] With Moffat, the opposite held. With Moffat, the 'fall' of humanity into sin resulted in a diminishment from 'more' to 'less'.[16] In extreme situations, this decrease had resulted in the knowledge of God becoming functionally zero. Moffat wrote of the converted Namaqua chief, Africaner, considering nature, saying:

> 'Are these the productions of some great Being? How is it that His name and character have been lost among the Namaqua, and the knowledge of Him confined to so few? Has that knowledge only lately come to the world? How is it that He does not address mankind in oral language?'[17]

From Africaner's perspective—as interpreted by Moffat—such knowledge had 'only lately come to the world'. From Moffat's perspective, it had been revealed to all at the beginning of humanity, but had been lost.

1. The Given Knowledge of God. Moffat taught that, in the early epochs of human existence, God imparted direct knowledge of himself to humanity. This special revelation took place on two main occasions. Firstly, there was a universal knowledge of God at creation, during the days of Adam. Secondly, there was a universal knowledge of God after the flood, during the days of Noah. At these times everyone on earth (countable on the fingers of two hands) had a special and adequate knowledge of God. At creation Adam and Eve had a perfect primal knowledge of God. And with the renewal of the earth after the Noahic flood, Noah and his family also had a perfect primal knowledge of God. During these two periods the knowledge of God was universal.[18] Thereafter, all knowledge of God was dependent upon that specific knowledge being properly handed on to each subsequent generation.

---

15 Moffat did not think that because a people had no knowledge of a supreme being then that people had not evolved in intellectual ability. That was not his position.

16 It is with this understanding that Moffat uses the phrase 'the poor degraded African' in *MLSSA,* 227. In this context the word 'degraded' described the Fall and its consequences. Moffat had the anthropology of a pre-Darwinian age. He did not think in terms of people being where they were because they had not progressed to a certain state; but that they were where they were because they fell from humanity's original station. Moffat thought in terms of degradation from a higher state rather than of evolution from a lower one.

17 RM, *MLSSA,* 183.

18 RM, *MLSSA,* 270.

In Moffat's mind, the whole world in every age, had been populated by the descendants of Noah. Therefore, knowledge of God for all peoples came from that Noahic source. But everything depended on the faithfulness of each generation passing on that knowledge to the next generation. Thus, for Moffat, what humanity sometimes interpreted as a knowledge of God gained through nature (natural religion) or innate ideas (intuitive knowledge), was actually a knowledge which had been handed down from an original direct special revelation. Even the religious consciousness of humanity—that subconscious awareness in the human mind of the divine being, which was sometimes attributed to innate ideas—had its roots in an original historical God-given revelation.

2. The Sole Knowledge of God. For Moffat, all knowledge of God was through 'special revelation'.[19] There was no other source. He developed this thesis extensively, concluding that a person could only see God in nature if that person's mind had already been partially illumined by revelation through Scripture or Christian teaching. In remarking on how the converted chief, Africaner, became aware of the Creator God in a totally new way, Moffat commented:

> His mind had received an impetus, not from the light of nature, bright as her pages **appears** to one even partially illumined by the voice of revelation, but from what he had heard from the missionary.[20]

In Moffat's theology, humanity saw God by the 'light of nature' *if and only if* humanity had already received the light of revelation. Moffat put aside any possibility of there being a purely innate knowledge of God in the mind of Africaner. Africaner's awareness of the Creator God was by revelation, not by innate ideas, or by reading the book of nature alone. Special revelation was the sole source of knowledge of God. Any culture, at any time, in any place, which had a concept of God or of the supreme being, had drawn that knowledge from the original revelation imparted to Adam or Noah:

> All the knowledge of divine things existing in every nation, from the refined Greeks down a thousand gradations, through the numberless shades of polytheism to the rude barbarian, is to be traced to Divine Revelation, whether written or traditional, and not to innate or intuitive ideas.[21]

---

19 Revelation, not unaided reason, was the rule and standard of religion. Roby placed this at the heart of his system. Cf. Roby, *Theol. Lect.* 1, 'The Existence or Being of God'; also *Lect.* 3, 'The Proper Rule or Standard of Religion'.

20 RM, *MLSSA,* 183. The missionary who first influenced Africaner was Christian Albrecht.

21 RM, *MLSSA,* 270.

Moffat was writing about *all* human knowledge of God. He was not just saying that a Christian understanding of God required special revelation, but claimed that even a vague concept of the divine being required a God-given special revelation. This raises questions as to how he understood biblical texts such as Romans 1:20, and we examine his exegesis later in this chapter.

The knowledge of God, originally given to humanity, was in a process of being 'lost'. It was not in a process of being 'gained'. There are some hints of this approach in early Reformed thinking. Calvin wrote in terms of the knowledge of God being constantly renewed and occasionally enlarged by God.[22] This concept of 'replenishment' enabled Calvin to hold on to the idea that all peoples everywhere still had a concept of the Deity despite the Fall, though such knowledge required to be 'renewed'. But Moffat felt he had to abandon the idea that *all peoples* still had a concept of the Deity. He was prepared to live with a theology which contemplated a total loss of the knowledge of God among some races, something Calvin was reluctant to do.

But if the knowledge of God was conveyed from one generation to the next, why was it seemingly absent among the Tswana? In Moffat's analysis, the void was created by human beings not efficiently conveying the primal knowledge to subsequent generations. Once the 'tradition' was broken, contemplation of nature by itself could not recover it. For some reason, the Tswana had not received the 'tradition' of the knowledge of God, and the evidence of nature alone was insufficient for them to recreate the notion of the reality of the supreme being. That was how Moffat saw the matter.

Elsewhere, Moffat wrote that the power of nature revealed the 'awfulness' of God,[23] but in no way did he use that as a basis for a knowledge of God. The responsibility for 'handing on' was a human responsibility. If that tradition failed, then the fault and guilt lay with humanity. But why might such knowledge be transmitted imperfectly? One reason was Satan:

---

22 Calvin, *Institutes,* I, iii, 1. The context of *Institutes* Book 1, chapter 3, is a discussion on the 'knowledge of God naturally implanted in the human mind'. It seems clear that Calvin directed all his remarks in this section to that 'natural knowledge'. See also: 'All men of sound judgment will therefore hold, that a sense of Deity is indelibly engraven on the human heart. And that this belief is naturally engendered in all, and thoroughly fixed as it were in our very bones, is strikingly attested by the contumacy of the wicked.' (*Institutes,* I, iii, 3). The conviction that humanity has always had a universal knowledge of God was fundamental to Calvin: 'As no man is found, however barbarous and even savage he may be, who is not touched by some idea of religion, it is clear that we are all created in order that we may know the majesty of our Creator.' (Calvin, *Instruction in Faith, 1537,* 17).

23 RM, *Journal,* 21.11.1857, (*MJ2,* 122).

> [Satan] has employed his agency, with fatal success, in erasing every vestige of religious impression from the minds of the Bechuana, Hottentots, and Bushmen; leaving them without a single ray to guide them from the dark and dread futurity, or a single link to unite them with the skies.[24]

Moffat added: 'God originally imparted the knowledge of His own being to man; and that *tradition* has circulated the report through the nations of the earth, which has undergone, by satanic influence on the minds of fallen creatures, all those modifications presented to us in the pantheon, or in the minds of the savages.'[25] Satan had influenced Europeans who developed a pantheon of gods, as much as he had influenced the Tswana who forgot God.

What about the eighteenth-century emphasis on natural religion, and its reaction against revealed religion? What about the Enlightenment tradition which exalted the 'primitive' who was unspoiled by the faults of 'civilisation'? What about the view held by some that the untouched tribes of Africa might reveal humanity in its natural state as the 'noble savage' with a true natural religion? Moffat was fiercely critical of all such ideas. When he was with Moselekatse in 1854, his sentiments on the impoverished nature of 'natural religion' were reinforced by the degradation and cruelty which he saw around him: 'Let the advocates of natural religion and haters of Christianity come here and try the reverse, and they will soon be suicides, as many of Moselekatse's subjects become, because their chains are chains of darkness clinched by the tyrant hand of war'.[26] Moffat rejected the romanticist notion that primitive tribes might represent the original virtues of humanity. In a similar way he discounted any idea that their primitive simplicity meant they had a pure, unsullied, knowledge of their creator.

MOFFAT'S BIBLICAL ARGUMENTS

How did Moffat substantiate his position? Was it from Scripture? Was it on philosophical grounds? Moffat certainly sought support from Scripture for his change in his thinking, aware that he was departing from the mainstream, in which general revelation was seen as preparing the way for revealed religion. In Moffat's system, special revelation became the one and the only source of knowledge of God, and he was confident there was a Scriptural basis for his argument:

> This view of the subject we shall find, on more minute inquiry, in perfect accordance with the declarations contained in the inspired volume. For, 'it is

24 RM, *MLSSA,* 244.
25 RM, *MLSSA,* 271.
26 RM, *Journal,* 30.7.1854, (*MJ1,* 248). He expressed similar sentiments in *MLSSA,* 272.

He that teacheth man knowledge. I am the Lord that maketh all things, that stretcheth forth the heavens alone, that spreadeth abroad the heavens by myself.' These are the revelations of the great 'I AM', and without such a revelation the world by wisdom could never have found out God.[27]

The two major passages in Scripture normally appealed to for a universal revelation of God through nature are Psalm 19 and Romans 1:20. Moffat nowhere gave a dedicated analysis of these passages but combined them in his overall argument. Quite often he conflated his theological exegesis, and he could move without warning from one to the other. For clarity, we separate his treatment of these two sections of Scripture.

1. Psalm 19. Reformed thought usually interpreted Psalm 19:1-4 to mean that the created order witnessed to God in such a way that the existence of God could be known by the light of nature alone.[28] But Moffat wrote:

> That the stupendous earth and heavens, the endless variety of order and change, and the dazzling beauty and grandeur of everything touched by the finger of Jehovah, do testify with a voice,[29] loud as the thunder's roar, clear as the noontide beam, there can be no question; but surely not by uttering speech to a *previously uninformed mind*, and conveying the *primary idea of the existence of God.* This, in my humble opinion, is not what the Apostle intended to convey [in Romans 1:20], but simply that God *originally imparted the knowledge of His own being to man, and that tradition has circulated the report through the nations of the earth*, which has undergone, by satanic influence on the minds of fallen creatures, all those modifications presented to us in the pantheon, or in the minds of the savages.[30]

In this extract Moffat made several important points:

1. The natural world does speak of the reality of God.[31]

---

27 RM, *MLSSA,* 270.

28 E.g. (i) Calvin, *Commentary on the Psalms (19:1)*: 'Scripture, indeed, makes known to us the time and manner of the creation*; but the heavens themselves, although God should say nothing on the subject*, proclaim loudly and distinctly enough that they have been fashioned by his hands: and this of itself abundantly suffices to bear testimony to men of his glory.' (ii) *Westminster Confession of Faith,* I,1 has *Psalm 19* as one of its 'proof texts' under-girding its statement: 'Although the light of nature, and the works of creation and providence, do so far manifest the goodness, wisdom and power of God, as to leave man inexcusable.' Calvin goes as far as to say that the heavens themselves, 'although God should say nothing on the subject', bring the knowledge of the Deity to humanity. What Calvin emphasised was the efficacy of a natural revelation without a special revelation. *The Westminster Confession* combined a purely 'natural light' with evidences of God through his actions in providence etc.

29 Moffat was reflecting on 1:20, but he also had Psalm 19:1-2 in mind.

30 RM, *MLSSA*, 271, (our italics).

31 Even Roby, whose view Moffat eventually came to accept, and who rejected the concept of innate ideas of God implanted within the human mind, taught that the natural world gave

2. But this 'speech' cannot be heard by a 'previously uninformed mind'.
3. The natural world, by itself, cannot give a 'primary idea of the existence of God'.
4. The 'primary idea of the existence of God' came from a direct special revelation from God given at the origin of humanity.
5. Humanity normally conveys this given knowledge of God from generation to generation (the process of tradition).
6. Satanic influences have corrupted this given knowledge of God in its conveyance, with humanity now having many incorrect notions of the supernatural.

Moffat was convinced that for the human mind to have knowledge of the Deity through the contemplation of nature, the mind required previous light from a special revelation. He was confident that this understanding fitted in with the meaning of Psalm 19.

2. Romans 1. Concerning Romans 1:20, 'For since the creation of the world God's invisible qualities, his eternal power and divine nature, have been clearly seen, being understood from what has been made, so that men are without excuse,' Moffat wrote:

> The Scriptures, so far from teaching us that we may infer the being of God from the works of creation, assert that our knowledge of the visible universe, as the production of God's creative power, is derived, not from the deductions of reason, but from a belief of the divine testimony revealing the fact: 'Through faith we understand that the worlds were made by the word of God, so that things which are seen were not made of things which do appear.' (Hebrews 11:3). Such as advocate the dignity of human reason may spin a fine theory, but let them go to the hut, or the den of the sunburnt African, and ask if any system has been spun by these children of nature.[32]

Moffat's main statements concerning Romans 1:20 were:

1. God can only be seen 'in nature' if a man or woman brings prior faith to that looking.
2. Faith in God cannot come 'ex nihilo' simply by encounter with nature.
3. Prior faith in God is required in order for us to recognise the signs in nature of the One in whom we already believe.

But what about Paul's words: '[God's power and divine nature] have been clearly seen, being understood *from what has been made'*? In an interesting footnote,[33] Moffat quoted John Ellis who gave a useful interpretation of the

---

ample evidence, by both its existence and evident design, that there is an almighty creator (Roby, *Theol. Lect.* 1, 'Existence or Being of God').

32 RM, *MLSSA,* 272.

33 RM, *MLSSA,* 271.

word 'made'—as in 'what has been made'—in Romans 1:20.[34] What Ellis argued was that the term translated 'made' (Greek: *poiemasi*) might also mean 'things which are *done'*, and thus could refer to revelatory *acts* of God, and to things which God has *done* in history. As quoted by Moffat, Ellis paraphrased Paul:

> The works of God, or things which He had *done*, not only of creation, but of providence, in the deluge, in the wonderful preservation of the church, and destruction of his enemies, in his many appearances, miracles, and interpositions with mankind, which, through all ages, had been related to them, and were a sensible demonstration of omniscience, omnipotence, invisibility, and immateriality, *even his eternal power and godhead,* which alone could effect such wonderful things.[35]

Building on Ellis' understanding of *poiemasi,* Moffat's exegesis of Romans 1:20 had two main principles:

1. At the creation of the world the knowledge of God was universal.
2. Afterwards, the knowledge of God was in the things He had 'done'.

Thus, Romans 1:20 was not pointing to a knowledge of God which subsisted in the static existence of the things He had 'made', but a knowledge of God through the dynamic activity of God in Providence and History.[36] But is there mileage in Ellis' analysis? Does modern scholarship support it? Herbert Braun, in G Kittel's *Theological Dictionary of the New Testament,* offers a highly detailed discussion of the use of the verb *poiein* (to make).[37] Braun agrees that in the Septuagint *poiein* can refer to both (i) Yahweh creating heaven and earth, and (ii) Yahweh's actions in history. However, when Braun considers Romans 1:20, he understands *poiemata* to refer to the works of creation, though he does not discuss *poiemata* in Romans 1:20 in a context of having to choose between the alternatives (i) and (ii). Braun is more concerned to make a link between Pauline thought and the Stoic understanding of God being known through his works. If he had been asked the specific question 'Is it possible that Paul might have in mind the alternative Septuagint usage of *poiein* in terms of God's actions in history?' we are unsure as to how Braun might have answered. Ellis' exegesis was creative and original, but we cannot determine its ultimate validity.

Where does this leave Moffat? Granted that his theological interpretation of Romans 1:20 was not totally dependent on Ellis' scholarship, it is still the

---

[34] John Ellis, *The Knowledge of Divine Things,* (Ldn: William Baynes, 1811).
[35] RM, *MLSSA,* 271.
[36] Cf. Karl Barth, *A Shorter Commentary on Romans,* (Ldn: SCM, 1959), 26-29.
[37] Cf. Kittel, *Theological Dictionary of the New Testament, Vol. 6,* 458-484.

case that if Ellis was on solid ground, then Moffat's position would also be solid. Nevertheless, even without Ellis, Moffat's exegesis was not without foundation.

We should not underestimate the enormous departure from traditional theology which Moffat felt necessary to make. A universal knowledge of God through natural religion was an assumed truth. It was presumed that, though knowledge of God gained purely through natural religion may well be incomplete and insufficient for salvation, such knowledge would exist in every corner of the world, in every tribe and race. Such was the general interpretation of Romans 1:20. Moffat turned this upside down. In his view, theory did not correspond to reality, and so the theory had to change.

Moffat was driven to conclude that all knowledge of God was only by special divine revelation. Nature in itself was mute and dumb. It was only a prior faith that could recognise the hand of the Creator in His creation. That prior faith might be a weak, diluted, error-strewn notion of divinity, but so long as it was there then the Maker of all things could be sensed. But if this prior existing faith, however emaciated, were truly absent, then humanity was unable to know of God simply through the voice of nature.

MOFFAT'S PHILOSOPHICAL ARGUMENTS

Having shown how his theological understanding of Romans 1:20 was based in real life missionary experiences, Moffat attempted to establish a wider, philosophical basis. He argued that all philosophical notions of God ultimately rely upon Revelation:

> Philosophers and poets find no difficulty in following nature to nature's God, when they have revelation to lead the way, but let them point out to us nations who have found the Almighty without other aids than their own resources. It is to this that Tertullian refers, when he asks them, 'Which of your poets, which of your sophisters, have not drank from the fountains of the prophets?' And thus, as Dr Ellis expresses it, 'their noblest flights took wing from the gospel.[38]

Moffat argued that contemplation of nature, by itself and in itself, may lead to great thoughts about nature, but not to great thoughts about God: 'Many heathen philosophers, who possessed advantages vastly superior to any of Africa's sons, instead of inferring from works of creation the existence of a

---

38 RM, *MLSSA,* 272. The quote from Tertullian was taken from his *Apology,* 47. He wanted to establish chronological priority for the Scriptures over the writings of the classical philosophers, relating them as 'source' and 'offspring'. He stated that without the source of scripture the philosophers' minds would be arid.

supreme being, generally maintained that the *matter*, and some even that the *form* of the world itself, was eternal, and others again substituted parts of the visible universe for God Himself.'[39] Because nature can be incorrectly interpreted, contemplation of it does not necessarily lead to the proper goal. Moffat pointed out that natural religion could just as easily lead a person to Atheism as to Theism: 'Even no less a person than the learned philosopher Dr Clarke,[40] the defender of natural religion, admits that "of the philosophers themselves, who should have corrected some of the errors of the vulgar, some argued themselves out of the belief of the very being of God."'[41] If natural religion, or natural theology, had the potential to lead some towards atheism, then how could it be argued that natural religion inevitably led to a true universal awareness of the supreme being?

On a deeper level, Moffat cited Jonathan Edwards' argument that 'matter' cannot prove 'spirit'. Contemplation of nature (matter) could never arrive at the necessary existence of God (spirit). Moffat quoted an extended passage from Edward's *Miscellaneous Observations,* including:

> Man, left to himself, would be apt to reason: 'If the cause and the effects are similar and conformable, matter must have a material cause, there being nothing more impossible for us to conceive than how matter should be produced by spirit, or anything else but matter.'[42]

Moffat accepted Edwards' argument that the necessary conformity and similarity of cause and effect meant that contemplation of the nature of existence here and now could only lead to a first cause which is 'both good and evil, wise and foolish, or else there must be two first causes, an evil and irrational, as well as a good and a wise principle.'[43] Moffat's conclusion was frank:

> It appears evident then, from what has been written, that all the relics of theology to be found in heathen lands, are only the remaining fragments which have been handed down by a vitiated and defective tradition.[44]

---

39 RM, *MLSSA,* 272f.

40 Samuel Clarke and William Paley emphasised the proofs of natural religion, especially the 'Watchmaker' argument. Bishop Butler (*Analogy of Religion,* London, 1736) maintained that natural and revealed religion were so far one that the truths of natural theology provided a basis for the characteristic truths of the Christian faith, such as miracles, the incarnation, and redemption.

41 RM, *MLSSA,* 273.

42 Ibid.

43 Several sermons by Edwards related to the issues. E.g. *A Thorough Knowledge of Divine Truth; A Divine and Supernatural Light;* and *Christian Knowledge.*

44 RM, *MLSSA,* 274.

It was unambiguous. Humanity left to itself had no ability to 'discover God'. But humanity did have the potential to 'forget God'. If there were any widespread knowledge of God, then it was as traces of a primal knowledge, handed down from the beginnings of creation. But if that primal knowledge had not been conveyed properly in human tradition, then the light could be totally extinguished, and contemplation of nature in itself was unable to revive, or create *ex nihilo*, an awareness of a spiritual supreme being.

The Available Theology

Moffat came from early nineteenth-century Scotland. He carried the theology of that time, in which Man was understood as a 'religious creature' with inbuilt religious instincts. These inbuilt religious instincts would express themselves as an awareness of the Deity. Protestant theology had traditionally been comfortable with a basis of natural religion, to which was added revealed religion through Scripture. Revealed religion contained those truths which a man or woman could receive only as a result of deliberate divine revelation, such as the Trinity, the Incarnation, the Cross, and the Resurrection. Natural religion contained truths about God which a person could 'read' from nature itself: truths such as God's existence, certain of the divine attributes, the fact of sin and, possibly, the need for atonement.

Moffat's tradition assumed that a natural knowledge of God through general revelation was present amongst all peoples everywhere. The task of the missionary was defined within this assumption. The role of the Christian was to be the messenger of God, used by God to transform this universal general awareness of the supreme being to a specific faith centred on Jesus Christ. This formed the background to Moffat's original theology. He was taken by surprise by what he thought he encountered in Africa.

John Calvin laid the foundations for Reformed theology. In his *Commentary on Romans,* Calvin wrote that knowledge of God, through the evidence of His works in creation, was available to God's creatures 'everywhere'.[45] That knowledge was of God's 'eternal power and divinity'. It lacked matters which can only be known through a special revelation in Christ or Scripture, nevertheless it was a clear awareness of a supreme being. Calvin repeated his thesis in the *Institutes* where he stated that the human mind is naturally imbued with the knowledge of God,[46] that the knowledge

---

45 Calvin, *Commentary on Romans,* 1:20.

46 Calvin, *Institutes,* I, iii, 1: 'Since, then, there never has been, from the very first, any quarter of the globe, any city, any household even, without religion, this amounts to a tacit confession, that a sense of Deity is inscribed on every heart. Nay, even idolatry is ample evidence of this

of God is displayed in the fabric and constant government of the Universe, and that, though the pure knowledge of God has been corrupted, all humanity everywhere is aware of the supreme being.[47]

Calvin did consider the possibility that some tribe 'farthest removed from civilisation' might have no knowledge of God, but rejected it, citing Cicero in support.[48] Humankind has an innate knowledge of God imbued by the Creator. It was this universal innate knowledge of God which rendered all of humanity responsible to God and which left no-one guiltless before God. Humanity had an 'intuitive' knowledge of God and his Law, thus was morally accountable. This was central to Calvin's interpretation of the Gospel, laying the foundations of thought for those coming after him:

> That there exists in the human minds and indeed by natural instinct, some sense of Deity, we hold to be beyond dispute, since God himself, to prevent any man from pretending ignorance, has endued all men with some idea of his Godhead, the memory of which he constantly renews and occasionally enlarges, that all to a man being aware that there is a God, and that he is their Maker, may be condemned by their own conscience when they neither worship him nor consecrate their lives to his service.[49]

Moffat came to question the ideas of 'natural instinct' or 'innate knowledge', and from two perspectives. On the one hand, from his experience. On the other hand, from being a defender of revealed religion against the supporters of natural religion. Eighteenth-century enthusiasts for natural religion liked the concept of 'innate ideas'. Moffat did not.

In the seventeenth century, the Assembly of Divines at Westminster—through its *Confession of Faith* and its *Larger* and *Shorter Catechisms*—had codified Reformed theology, and in the process set the spiritual background

---

fact. For we know how reluctant man is to lower himself, in order to set other creatures above him. Therefore, when he chooses to worship wood and stone rather than be thought to have no God, it is evident how very strong this impression of a Deity must be; since it is more difficult to obliterate it from the mind of man, than to break down the feelings of his nature,--these certainly being broken down, when, in opposition to his natural haughtiness, he spontaneously humbles himself before the meanest object as an act of reverence to God.' See also: *Institutes,* I, v, 1f.

[47] Calvin, *Institutes,* I, iii, 3: 'A sense of Deity is indelibly engraven on the human heart. ... This belief is naturally engendered in all, and thoroughly fixed as it were in our very bones.' Cf. *Institutes,* I, iv, 1f.

[48] Calvin, *Institutes,* I, iii, 1: 'As a heathen tells us, there is no nation so barbarous, no race so brutish, as not to be imbued with the conviction that there is a God. ... There never has been, from the very first, any quarter of the globe, any city, any household even, without religion, this amounts to a tacit confession that a sense of Deity is inscribed on every heart.'

[49] Calvin, *Institutes,* I, iii, 1.

for Scotland.[50] For Westminster, all of humanity had a natural, if not a saving, knowledge of God.[51] Echoing Calvin, the *Confession* stated: 'The light of nature showeth that there is a God, who hath lordship and sovereignty over all.'[52] The *Larger Catechism* reinforced this: 'The very light of nature in man, and the works of God, declare plainly that there is a God; but His word and Spirit only do sufficiently and effectually reveal Him unto men for their salvation.'[53] The phrase 'the light of nature *in man*' hinted at a degree of 'innate knowledge', however small: an assumption which Moffat would discard. Mainstream Scottish theology thus assumed a natural knowledge of God for all humanity. This was the classical Protestant understanding of Romans 1:20. It made humanity without excuse before a holy God.

With this tradition behind him it is no surprise that Moffat went to Africa expecting to find a universal awareness of a supreme being. When, in his view, he did not find this, he sought for an explanation, and found it in John Ellis and William Roby, even though Roby's teaching on this issue had initially been rejected by Moffat. Roby had himself drawn on Ellis, with Ellis' works regularly cited in Roby's *Theological Lectures.* Ellis had been Anglican vicar of St Catherine's Church in Dublin. In 1743 he wrote his treatise *The Knowledge of Divine Things from Revelation, not from Reason or Nature,* in response to John Locke who, in his *Essay on the Human Understanding*, had argued that knowledge of God was attainable by ideas of reflection. Against Locke, Ellis asserted that the knowledge of divine things was only from revelation, not from reason or nature. Ellis felt driven to this because some eighteenth-century philosophy was using natural theology and general revelation to oppose the validity of special revelation through Scripture.

Hitherto Protestant theology had seen general and special revelation as complementary, but eighteenth-century deism and rationalism opposed one to the other. Ellis felt that if he could eliminate the possibility of a natural knowledge of God anterior to revelation, then the contemporary attack on special revelation would be undermined. As we have seen, Ellis needed to reinterpret the word 'made' in Romans 1:20 in a way which was more helpful to his position. Ellis developed his argument in detail, eventually stating:

---

50 Cf. *The Westminster Confession of Faith,* I, 1. The Scripture references were: Romans 2:14f; 1:19f, Psalm 19:1-3; and Romans 1:32 with 2:1.

51 The Westminster Divines understood this to mean that all humanity *had* knowledge of God. General revelation did not simply create the *possibility* of such knowledge, but actualised it amongst all humanity everywhere, with attendant moral responsibility.

52 *The Westminster Confession of Faith,* XXI, 1.

53 *The Larger Catechism,* Qu. 2.

> Now, it is never denied, that the world once knew the true God, and no other; him the righteous Noah preached to his sons, and they to their posterity; but these great truths were, after the dispersion, soon defaced and obliterated. The nations, as David says Psalm 9:17 'forgot God'; forgot him who they had once known, and his true nature and essence, as if they had never been declared to them.[54]

Ellis wrote of humanity 'losing' the knowledge of God. He did not explicitly say that in some nations it might be obliterated altogether, but pointed clearly in that direction. He also rejected the deistic and rationalist position that worship given to sun, moon or stars, or worship given in a polytheistic setting, should be regarded, in some sense, as valid worship given to God or a supreme being.[55] Ellis also complained that legitimate attempts to show how Christian beliefs corresponded to truths in nature had been twisted by deists and rationalists to show that special revelation was unnecessary for either doctrine or morality.[56]

Ellis argued that knowledge of God could, at the most, only be through innate ideas, reason, or revelation.[57] But for Ellis, it was revelation which alone gave real knowledge of God. In particular he argued that John Locke's emphasis on reason and reflection was contradicted by Locke's own axiom that 'there is nothing in the mind that is not first in the senses'.[58] It was the deism and rationalism of the eighteenth century which forced Ellis into breaking with the traditional use of natural theology as a starting-point. This brought a theology which Roby, and later Moffat, found congenial.

William Roby's Position

William Roby taught that there may be some people who had entirely lost the knowledge of God. He did not accept that there was a universal 'natural light' about God. Aware of the implications of eighteenth-century rationalism, Roby based his whole theology on special revelation. Moffat admitted that, before coming to Africa, he had disagreed with his revered teacher, and he described the classic Reformed position as 'sentiments, which I preferred even to those of the late venerable Roby, of Manchester, at whose feet I sat for a short season'.[59] The trainee missionary stuck with

---

54 Ellis, *On Divine Things,* 266f.

55 Ibid, xixff.

56 Ibid, xxiif.

57 Ibid, 2f.

58 Ibid, 133f.

59 RM, *MLSSA,* 121. Livingstone, *British Quarterly Review, xiv (*1851*)*, (*DLSAP,* 100), wrongly suggested that Moffat blindly followed Roby: 'Mr. Moffat honestly believed that he found

the traditional view of Romans 1, even though, on the very first page of his *Theological Lectures,* Roby had stated:

> *Evidences attesting the existence or being of God:* In entering upon this part of our subject, it may not be amiss to suggest some introductory remarks, which, though they are not admitted by Divines in general, appear to be founded on truth: (1) The idea of God is not innate; (2) It is not obtained by mere intuition; (3) It was originally communicated by divine revelation; (4) It is confirmed by various rational inferences: hence the use of argumentation in treating on the subject. There are numerous principles, or evidences, from which we must necessarily infer the existence of God.[60]

This was Roby's dramatic opening gambit. He knew that his view was 'not admitted by Divines in general', yet his rejection of an 'innate' or 'intuitive' knowledge of God was absolute. But the young Moffat stubbornly believed that there *must* be a universal knowledge of the supreme being (however vitiated by paganism), and that there *must,* in some sense, be an 'innate' knowledge of God. It was only after several years that he changed his mind.

Moffat's resistance to this aspect of Roby's teaching must be taken into account when evaluating his rejection of theism among the Tswana. The young Moffat was convinced he would find theism. That he thought he did not find such it, indicates strong forces to the contrary. Though the seeds for Moffat's later view were in Roby's first lecture, Moffat chose to think otherwise. It was his African experience which changed his thinking to that of Roby's. Roby had added:

> Some nations indeed have lost all traditionary notice of a Deity; but these are few. They just serve to show that the knowledge of the being of God is neither innate nor discoverable by the mere light of nature.[61]

Here we see Moffat's later concept of 'The Lost Knowledge of God' clearly set out. Roby, like the later Moffat, taught that knowledge of God was

---

them [Tswana] destitute of the idea of God, of a future state, and the proper conception of sin; ... Mr. M. gives us the key to this, in quoting the Rev. W. Roby's interpretation of the passage in 'Roman' which, in all probability swayed his judgment.' The quotation which Livingstone alluded to was from Roby's *Lectures on the Principal Evidences and the several dispensations of Revealed Religion,* (1818), and appears in Moffat's *Missionary Labours,* 275. By the time Moffat wrote *Missionary Labours* he accepted Roby's theology, but when he first went to Africa he did not. He resisted Roby on this issue for many years.

60 Roby, *Theol. Lect.* 1, 'The Existence or Being of God'. Cf. Roby's *Lectures on the Principal Evidences and the several dispensations of Revealed Religion,* (1818). In the bibliography attached to the end of his first lecture Roby included Ellis' *The Knowledge of Divine Things,* which Moffat quoted from liberally when constructing his theology of the lost knowledge of God. Amongst other works, Roby included two by Jonathon Edwards: *Reformed Theology,* and *Miscellaneous Observations.* Moffat also quoted Edwards' *Miscellaneous Observations.*

61 Roby, *Theol. Lect.* 1, 'Existence or Being of God'.

originally given to all, but that 'some nations' lost the 'traditionary notice' of a Deity. Absence of this had nothing to do with the intellectual or spiritual capacity of races. Absence was because the tradition had been broken.

Whereas Augustine emphasised that deep within the human heart there was a yearning for God, Roby believed that deep within the heart there was unbelief, and that humanity risked falling back into this unbelief if not prevented by the direct action of God himself. Roby wrote: 'Let us pray that we may be preserved from atheistical thoughts. So deeply is atheism rooted in our hearts, that we have need of more than argumentation. We have need of divine influence itself, to produce in us a practical acknowledgement of God.'[62] Innate atheism, rather than innate knowledge of God, was Roby's default position. Yet, wherever the knowledge of God had been lost or corrupted, the process could be arrested through revelation to humanity through the words of the Bible:

> In the earliest ages, men arose, professing to be divinely instructed and commissioned to make known the will of God to their fellowmen. Their professions were accompanied with such satisfactory evidences as to convince those unto whom they were immediately sent, that they were really sent of God. These revelations were professedly received from God, in various ways: as by visions, voices, dreams, suggestions, etc. Being published, they became the sole and authoritative standard of religion among those by whom they were received.
>
> We have reason to believe that these either in their pure, or in their corrupted state, are the source whence all notions of religion have originated. *During the first ages of the world, these revelations in consequence of the longevity of man, were safely conveyed to posterity by traditions.* For various reasons, however, they have, since the time of Moses, been committed to writing.[63]

There were several theological and philosophical forces operating in Roby's time, which influenced his theological approach. His reaction against the eighteenth-century's search for natural religion was a factor. The eighteenth-century intellectual emphasis was on natural religion, in which the religious consciousness of humanity was understood as being built on general rational principles available to all humanity, everywhere, and at all times. It was argued that religion should not be built on what was regarded as a slender and unjust basis of a particular revelation at a particular time to a particular people. 'Fairness' demanded that the concept of revealed religion with its inevitable particularity should be diminished. This was the criticism which Gotthold Lessing made against any religion which was built upon a particular

---

62 Ibid.

63 Roby, *Theol. Lect.* 5, 'Character and Authenticity of the Scriptures', (our italics).

historical revelation. For Lessing the 'historical' must give way to the 'ideal', and the 'particular' must give way to the 'general', otherwise there would be a lack of justice, since all humanity would not be in the same position concerning the ability to know God: the accidental truths of history could not be the basis for the eternal truths of reason. Lessing sought to build religion upon natural revelation, and, for religion to be built upon natural revelation, the knowledge of God must come through the physical senses.

But that was what David Hume and Emmanuel Kant specifically criticised. They insisted that God, who is spiritual, cannot be known through the physical senses. Therefore, knowledge of God through natural theology was in fact impossible. Hume's conclusion was that any knowledge of God was *a priori* impossible. Kant agreed, but conceded that God, as a supremely moral being, might be known through the moral 'impulse' or 'imperative' which exists within humanity. Where Hume and Kant did agree with Lessing was that no noble religion could be built upon contingent 'chance' historical events. True religion, if it exists, *must* be built upon something general.

William Roby rejected all of this in its entirety. The basis for his faith was the particular revelation of God in Jesus Christ, attested in Holy Scripture. Roby defended revealed religion against natural religion, and he welcomed any argument which helped to undermine natural religion. Yet he knew the consequences of his position, fully aware that this created the possibility that there may be peoples somewhere who did not know God at all.

Dreams and Visions

For Moffat, reliable knowledge of God came through the written Word of God in the Bible. Knowledge of God from nature was not only insufficient in content, but may be totally missing unless a spark had already been lit in the mind from revelation. But might revelation come through dreams or visions? Moffat was suspicious of these, and he tended to associate such phenomena with non-Christian pagan experiences. Moffat believed that 'converts' who focused on 'dreams and visions' usually showed little evidence of changed lives, whereas converts who built their faith upon the Word were more likely to display moral transformation. For example, in 1822 Moffat referred to the converted Khoikhoi from Bethelsdorp who had come to New Lattakoo to help start the work. Moffat attributed their 'shallow faith' to their liking for dreams and visions:

> It is impossible to do without three or more men from the Colony; and yet there are evils which we have deeply felt of having such here. For instance, that part of the Hottentots who came here at first, or when the station was

> founded, have all excepting one disgraced the cause. Adultery, fornication, and incest have been the reigning crimes of the baptised Hottentots at Lattakoo. Their conduct has successively wounded our souls, but indeed little else could be expected from a religion founded on feelings and frames, visions and dreams.[64]

Moffat was sceptical.[65] He preferred a solid, substantial reliance on the Bible: 'I admit, with many others, that dreams may be of three classes, human, satanic and divine—those of the latter case being very rare—I have ever found it necessary to discourage, rather than to countenance a regard to them among the heathen'.[66] There were several reasons why he distrusted dreams and visions:[67]

1. Not all dreams came from God. Some were natural (human). Others may have come from Satan.
2. New converts, just beginning to understand the Christian Faith, were prone to giving a superstitious interpretation to dreams.
3. Dreams, and the discussion of dreams, were, by their nature, of absorbing interest. As such they had a high 'gossip' value and detracted from spending time 'in learning to read the law and the testimony'.
4. The discussion of dreams and visions made those who did not have them really desire them, and this brought the danger of relapsing into old ways of thinking.

Though in Tswana culture dreams were regarded as a medium through which the ancestral spirits communicated with the dreamer,[68] there is little evidence that Moffat's antipathy was because of the association between dreams and the *badimo* in Tswana ritual practice and belief. Moffat's desire was to direct converts to the Word. The solid meat for the Christian was found in God's Word. Dreams and visions were insubstantial 'base coin',

---

64 RM, *To James & Mary Smith,* 20.8.1822, (*AAK,* 64). Cf. Enklaar: *Life and Work of Dr J. Th. Van Der Kemp, 1847-1811,* 128.

65 Yet, leading up to his own conversion, one significant event was 'waking in a state of horror from a terrific dream' which brought to him a deep sense of sin (JSM, *Lives,* 13).

66 RM, *MLSSA,* 184. Roby, *Theol. Lect.* 5,'The Character and Authenticity of the Scriptures', appeared to homologate 'Dreams' in some contexts. However, what Roby had in mind were 'vision, voices and dreams' experienced by biblical writers. He did not accept current phenomena as being of divine origin. He also stated: 'Many are imposed upon by revelations, professedly divine, which on examination will not bear the test.' (*Theol. Lect.* 6, 'Divine Inspiration of the Scriptures'). Roby may have had the Koran in mind (*Theol. Lect.* 5).

67 RM, *MLSSA,* 184f.

68 Lye & Murray, *Transformations,* 124. Cf. Alice Werner, *Myths and Legends of the Bantu,* 81: 'The ghosts can communicate with the living through dreams, through signs and omens, and through the medium of diviners or prophets.'

which did not lead to a deep knowledge of God and of the Christian life. Even when dreams were apparently 'Christianised' dreams they were no substitute for the Word of God.[69] Moffat was not impressed by claimed religious experiences. He was only impressed if claimed knowledge of God brought a deep moral transformation of life.

Moffat allowed one exception. That came with Africaner. Moffat conceded that Africaner had a dream which was deeply significant and helpful in his discipleship. Before the dream, his 'judgment appeared to be wavering' and 'he was about to dismiss for ever from his thoughts the graver subjects of revelation, death and immortality'. After this dream he 'never afterwards forsook' the Christian way.[70] In Africaner's dream, he was trapped on a mountain path with a 'furnace of fire and smoke mingled with lighting' on his left. The only escape was to ascend the mountain by a narrow path. However, the heat was so great from the mountain itself, as well as from the 'burning pit beneath' that he felt he could not go on. Then he saw, 'upwards beyond the burning gulf', a person standing on a green mount, 'on whom the sun appeared to shine with peculiar brilliancy'. This figure beckoned him to advance, which he did through the terrible heat until he reached the stranger and 'when about to address the stranger, he awoke'.[71]

After considered reflection Africaner interpreted the path as 'the narrow road leading from destruction to safety, from hell to heaven'; and he interpreted the stranger to be the Saviour. Moffat recorded that, when Africaner described the dream and his journey from the burning path to the Saviour, Africaner would add with tears in his eyes, 'Thank God, I have passed'.[72] The spiritual and moral effect which the dream had on Africaner, plus the fact that it was in harmony with the message Moffat taught, meant that Moffat viewed it positively. Important for Moffat was whether a claimed experience or revelation produced solid Christian morality. Africaner's dream had given to him a sense of fear and trembling before God. That was what Moffat looked for. One of Moffat's own dreams as a young man, as he wrestled with his soul during the process of his conversion, had impressed on him a similar experience of dread before God.[73]

---

69 Moffat cited various dreams with a 'Christian' orientation: some had seen an angel behind a bush; some had seen the Saviour and could tell his form; some had heard a voice from heaven; some had 'travelled' to Jerusalem; some had ascended to the third heaven and returned the same night (*MLSSA,* 184f).

70 RM, *MLSSA,* 184.

71 RM, *MLSSA,* 185f.

72 RM, *MLSSA,* 186.

73 JSM, *Lives,* 13.

The Power and Providence of God

Chapter 9
God and Creation

FOR ROBERT MOFFAT, any adequate notion of deity involved the concepts of creation and providence. A true God had to be pre-existent, eternal, and the creator of all things. Moffat arrived in Africa in 1817, forty-two years before Charles Darwin published *The Origin of Species*, and fifty-four years before Darwin's *The Descent of Man.* Yet in 1817, though the theory of evolution had not yet been formulated with its troubling implications concerning the interpretation of Genesis and the status of humanity, there was awareness that geological investigations raised serious questions about the age of the earth. Speculations that the earth's origins went beyond a strict six-day model had spread much further than academic circles. Though Moffat was from a conservative theological background, and though he was deeply respectful of biblical truth as traditionally interpreted, he was not only aware of some of the issues involved but had a progressive outlook. He felt free to enjoy the discoveries of science, whereas some who came after him lived with a tension between science and faith.[1]

THEOLOGY AND SCIENCE

Perusal of Moffat's writings reveals a vibrant interest in nature. This appears to have been well known since, in an 1868 letter to Dr Mullens of the LMS, Moffat mentioned that an unidentified person had sent him journals on science.[2] Other members of the family inherited this fascination. His interest in geology was shared by his younger son, Robert Moffat , who was a keen amateur scientist and geologist, publishing two papers through the *Royal Geographical Society.*[3] Also, whilst preparing to set off to establish the pioneer mission among the Ndebele, John Smith Moffat and his wife Emily Unwin read Wiseman's lectures on the relationship between science and

1 T.M. Thomas (1828-1884), who arrived in Africa in 1858 to help establish the Ndebele Mission in 1859, was troubled by Darwinism. Darwin rocked the intellectual world with his publications. Cf. Thomas, *Eleven Years in Central South Africa, (1872),* 16, and: 'Often as I have surveyed these [baboons], the very caricatures of humanity, have I thought upon the recent speculations respecting the origin of our race'(109).

2 Cf. RM, *To Mullens, LMS,* 18.6.1868, (SOAS/CMW/SA./Box 35/1/A).

3 Cf. Robert Moffat (Jnr), 'Journey from Colesberg to Steinkopf in 1854-5', *The Journal of the Royal Geographical Society*, (1858, Vol. 28), 153-173.

revealed religion.[4] Moffat, the gardener-missionary, fostered an infectious interest in the glories of God's creation.

As a small boy, attending William Paton's school in Falkirk, Moffat listened to the teaching given to older pupils on geography and astronomy. When these topics crop up in his writings, he never indulges in an extended theological analysis, yet his entries serve as a snapshot of ideas in the Christian mind during the first part of the nineteenth century.

1. Extra-terrestrial Life. Moffat speculated that sentient life might exist elsewhere in the Universe. In 1843 in Walworth, he said: 'Farewell is a word that I think belongs to this world only. It is not in heaven; I do not think it is in Jupiter or Saturn; though I think there are inhabitants there, and in Venus, and in all the rest of the planetary system, yet I do not think that there is any farewell in these orbs.'[5] If Moffat envisaged inhabitants on some planets for whom there was no 'farewell' then, in his mind, such inhabitants not only existed, but must have been untouched by sin and death. We would love to know more of Moffat's thoughts on this issue, but this tantalising fragment is all we have. Moffat's thinking on this, as on general geological theory, largely coincided with that of the Scottish minister Thomas Dick, whose writings proved helpful to David Livingstone. In his book, *Harmony of the Discoveries of Modern Science with Revealed Religion (1842),* Dick, like Moffat, was prepared to accept the existence of sentient beings on other planets: that was how he explained the biblical phrase 'host of heavens.'[6] Significantly, and in relation to other issues which we discuss below, Dick drew on Herschel's work in adducing that astronomy pointed to vast periods of time which had elapsed since the first 'creation out of nothing.'[7]

2. The Copernican Theory. In 1854 Moffat tried to explain the Copernican theory of the Universe and the spherical shape of the earth to Moselekatse. Moffat recorded that he had been, 'trying tonight to make him understand that the world moved, not the sun; that the earth was a globe and not a plain; that people could go round it; and that were he to pierce a hole through the centre to the other side, he would find people there the same as here'.[8] Why

---

[4] Emily Moffat, *To J.S. Unwin*, 27.8.1858, (*MM,* 27). Cf. Cardinal Nicholas Patrick Stephen Wiseman, *Lectures on Science and Revealed Religion delivered in Rome,* (Ldn: 1836). Though Wiseman (1802-1865) was Roman Catholic, his lectures on science and religion were read by Protestants.

[5] RM, *Walworth Address,* 1843, (*Farewell Services,* 88), (our italics).

[6] Thomas Dick, *Harmony of the Discoveries of Modern Science with Revealed Religion,* (Edin: Dalrymple, 1842), 23.

[7] Dick, *Harmony of the Discoveries of Modern Science with Revealed Religion,* 27.

[8] RM, *Journal,* 3.8.1854, (*MJ1,* 251).

did Moffat teach this to Moselekatse? Was it simply to impart information? Or was he trying to persuade Moselekatse that his world-view and knowledge were inadequate, with the inference that Moselekatse needed to admit that his understanding of other things—spiritual as well as physical—might be defective? The context, in his *Journal,* indicates that Moffat wanted to impress Moselekatse with 'superior knowledge':

> We tried to describe to him the speed with which wagons travelled in England, and ships on the sea, but they were far above his conception. He admitted the superior wisdom of the white man. I told him what I have told him again and again, we owe our wisdom to the knowledge of books, and that it was through books we obtained the true and best knowledge, the knowledge of the only living and true God. He however, turned the subject.[9]

Moffat hoped that this would prompt the chief to greater humility, perhaps helping him to also bow to the spiritual teaching which Moffat brought.

3. The Heavens declare the Glory of God. Despite Moffat's theory of the 'Lost Knowledge of God', he retained a conviction that the wonders of nature could help a person sense the reality and power of God. That could never, by itself, be an adequate foundation for faith, but it could serve as a complement to knowledge of God through divine revelation. Moffat was persuaded in his own mind that if those whom he evangelised were more aware of the wonders of nature, then they would find it easier to grasp the concept of a supreme being who is made all things. Thus, in Edinburgh in 1842, he spoke of the use to which he had put a generous monetary gift of £50 from the Marquis of Bath:

> Before I received this liberal donation I had often thought, had I but a good telescope to point the natives to the starry heavens and the wonderful works of creation which they cannot gaze on with their naked eyes; and again had I a powerful microscope to let them see the infinite number of minutiae which are hid from unassisted vision.[10]

A telescope may well have produced remarkable reactions among his Tswana since, as Alice Werner points out, the Bantu generally regarded the sky as a

---

9 Ibid.

10 RM, *Edinburgh Address,* 3.11.1842, (*Farewell Services,* 20f). Moffat noted unusual phenomena such as eclipses. Cf. RM, *To Burder, LMS,* 20.12.1824, (SOAS/CWM/SA/Box9/2/F): 'Today (20.12.1824) we had the pleasure of seeing an eclipse. Morning: commenced at 10h, 45m; Gradual obscuration: 12h, 25m; Afternoon, end of the eclipse: 3h, 5m. From the observations we shall be enabled to ascertain the Longitude with considerable accuracy. About 5/6 of the sun's upper disk was eclipsed.'

solid vault which joined the earth at the horizon.[11] Alas, we have no record of the effect the telescope had on the Kuruman populace.

THEOLOGY AND GEOLOGY

An interest in rock formations recurs frequently in Moffat's travel *Journal.* In 1835, on his second journey to the Ndebele, his interest in the landscape was stimulated by the presence of Dr Andrew Smith of the South African Central Expedition. This was a British Government sponsored expedition, with geographical, geological, and other aims. Moselekatse gave the expedition freedom to travel anywhere within his realm. Moffat described Smith as a 'military doctor, an Edinburgh man, and indefatigable in his researches'[12] whose task was to shed light on the geography, zoology, geology and natural history of the area. Detailed descriptions of geological features were regularly written into Moffat's *Journal,* especially on the long journeys to the Ndebele, when he made numerous notes on the natural phenomena observed *en route.*[13]

As the years passed, Moffat's library at Kuruman acquired several works on geology. On the 1854 journey to Moselekatse, when Moffat mused over the few books which Mary 'allowed' him to take on that expedition,[14] he commented, 'I regret I did not bring a book on geology with me'.[15] In the same letter to Mary,[16] he included an excellent paragraph on earthquakes

---

11 Alice Werner, *Myths and Legends of the Bantu*, 61.

12 RM, *To Richard Moffat,* 12.6.1835, (*MJ1,* 137).

13 Cf. RM, *MLSSA,* 67, 119 etc., plus numerous references to geology in Moffat's *Journals,* many of which are written with evident love of the beauty of the geological features. Of note are the following entries in *MJ1:* 'Substratum of coarse granite' 199, 1854; 'Today I have not met with any granite' 200, 1854; 'Query; which end was uppermost when the layers were horizontally formed?' 202, 1854; cf. 215ff; 226 (very full descriptions); also, excellent writing concerning basalt on 283; see also 284; plus references to limestone, chalk, granite, 289, 1854; and more references to basalt and quartz, 303f, and 344, 1854. There are also several geological references in *MJ2* (e.g. 51, 65, 73, 211, 233f).

14 Before departing on the 1854 journey to Moselekatse, Moffat had exhausted himself with translating the Old Testament into SeTswana. At times Mary had to lock him out of his study. Consequently, when he set off on the 1854 journey, she tried to minimise the number of books he took. This jaded and tired man was revived by the adventure, and not only read everything he had brought, but wrote some of the most extended and interesting portions of all his *Journal* entries. The journey became an almost 'carefree' expedition, though, as was always the case with Moffat, there was 'work for the Kingdom' to be done all along the way, as well as with the Ndebele at journey's end.

15 RM, *Journal,* 10.6.1854, (*MJ1,* 173).

16 Robert was not totally obedient to wife Mary! When at Moselekatse's camp he confessed! Cf. RM, *To Mary Moffat,* 27.7.1854, (*MJ1,* 241f): 'I sat most of the day reading and correcting a few slight typographical errors [in the proofs of the SeTswana Bible] and altering some of

and local geology, stressing that these things happened outside 'the memory of man'.[17] On the same 1854 journey, Moffat made reference, not only to the appearance of the rocks, but to the great forces which must have caused these geological features:

> Terrible convulsions must have once reigned when these mountains (to all appearance from volcanic force) were raised about the surrounding plains. ... These mountains appear to be the result of volcanic force. They have an extremely black appearance, and large fissures and rents, descending the face of the mountains, seem wholly filled with loose broken stones to a great depth ... I think I heard Livingstone state that when he visited the top of the range, on which the Bamanguato then lived, there were what appeared to him the remains of craters of old volcanoes.[18]

Even after Moffat left Africa he maintained an interest in the progress of the geological survey carried out by officers from Cape Colony.[19] During his retirement in England, he exchanged letters with the geologist and mineralogist Professor Tennant, of King's College, Cambridge.[20]

The theological significance of Moffat's fascination with geology lies in the implications it had for his interpretation of Genesis 1. The *Shorter Catechism* stated that the works of creation were completed in six days, as did *Brown's Catechism,* as did William Roby.[21] Moffat had not attended any avant-garde institutions of higher learning in which he inculcated liberal opinions, yet we find him musing on the fact that the stones and the wonderful rock formations which he passed on his journeying, had been there for thousands

---

the words for the sake of uniformity in the translation. This is an interesting subject to me at all seasons, and though I promised to you not to study, this is a pleasing work which does not require close application, and my mind must be employed'. He teased Mary that she had not allowed him to take his Hebrew lexicon on the journey: 'This is your fault, though I dare say you will not admit it to be one, but expect from me a vote of thanks for doing so'.

17 RM, *Journal,* 10.6.1854, (*MJ1,* 175 & 197).

18 RM, *Journal,* 7.11.1854, (*MJ1,* 339).

19 JSM, *Lives,* 370.

20 Professor Tennant, 15 years younger than Moffat, was Professor of Mineralogy and Geology at Kings, Cambridge, from 1848 to 1881. Cf. RM, *To Professor Tennant,* 13.1.1880 & 23.3.1880; and one undated, (SOAS/CWM/Africa/Moffat/Pers/4).

21 Cf. *Shorter Catechism,* Q&A9; *Westminster Confession of Faith* Chapter 4, 1; and *Larger Catechism,* Q&A15. *Brown's Catechism,* Q&R18, mentioned the six days: this was repeated in the SeTswana translation. Cf. *Brown's Catechism,* Q&A22. Roby, *Theol. Lect.* 35, 'Creation', also stressed six literal days: 'The Mosaic account of the creation dates it between five and six thousand years ago [Roby followed Usher's dating] ... every part of creation was instantaneously produced at the time ... the whole was completed by six days.' Roby did not adopt Chalmer's 'gap theory' or anything similar. Chalmer's theory (see below) held that biblical exegesis allowed indefinite time elapsing between God calling the Universe into existence, and the specific 6 days referred to in Genesis 1.

of years *before* the creation of Adam.[22] Moffat envisaged the earth as having existed for much longer than the five days allowed in a strict six-day understanding of Genesis 1. In 1854, he wrote:

> The top [of Kanye hill] appears large, covered with blocks of coarse granite, which form also the basis of the hill. On the sides, as well as on the surface of the plateau, there are large masses of conglomerate, which by volcanic force have been forced up through the granite, containing innumerable pebbles and round stones of all sizes in a black concrete or fused basalt, like immense plum puddings made for the giants of olden times. My companions stared when I told them that the myriads of round stones (few agates) had been rolled about and rolled by the ocean waves *a thousand years before Adam was formed of the dust of the earth*.[23]

Moffat's estimate of how long the earth existed before humanity came on the scene was millions of years out on any modern reckoning. However, from a theological perspective, it is Moffat's blithe acceptance of a non-six-day interpretation which is intriguing. Moffat held an interpretation of Genesis 1 in which a long era of time had elapsed before the creation of Adam. A strict six-day creationist reading of Genesis 1 only allowed for five periods of 24 hours each between the creation of the earth, and the appearance of Adam. Moffat allowed for much more. There is no hint that Moffat felt his faith threatened by geology. He celebrated the knowledge which geology gave him. He saw it as a branch of science which revealed more of the glory of God. Human geologists were making known the wonderful works of the divine Geologist: 'What wonderful changes this globe of ours has undergone. Perhaps these things will be revealed by the Geologist in heaven. They are God's works sought out by all who have pleasure therein'.[24]

There is no trace in Moffat of the unease felt by David Livingstone when faced with some of the results of modern science. By the time Livingstone

---

22 When Archbishop James Usher (1581-1656) dated the creation of the earth as occurring in 4004 BC, he envisaged Adam being created six days after the Universe was brought into being. Unlike Usher, Moffat allowed for extended time before the creation of Adam. Moffat reckoned that it was about 2000 BC when Noah lived (RM, *Africa,* 13).

23 RM, *Journal,* 1.6.1854, (*MJ1,* 150), (our italics). This passage from Moffat's *Journal,* is similar to a passage in Dick's writings: 'There is likewise a species of rock distinguished by geologists by the title of volcanic and basaltic rocks, which owe their origin to volcanic fire, and are sometimes forced up to the surface of the earth in a melted state by the action of subterraneous heat. The principal volcanic rocks are basalt, lava, and greenstone.' (Dick, *The Discoveries of Modern Geology not Inconsistent with Revelation,* 14). It is possible that Moffat, as well as Livingstone, had read him.

24 RM, *Journal,* 1.6.1854, (*MJ1,* 150), quoting Psalm 111:2, which was later adopted by James Clerk Maxwell as the text for the Cavendish Laboratory in Cambridge.

came to Africa, he had reconciled his faith with his science,[25] but during his youth he had struggled to do so. In the David Livingstone Centre at Blantyre, Scotland, there is a display of books which helped him and his father come to terms with science and religion. The Blantyre Works Library provided many of the works they read. Pre-eminent among them, were Thomas Dick's books, including his *Philosophy of the Future State,* and his *Philosophy of Religion.*[26]

1. Thomas Dick. What contemporary theories lay behind Moffat's understanding of Genesis? There were various strands of thinking on this topic. Thomas Dick, for example, championed a theory which, in a pre-Darwinian context, helped to reconcile biblical faith with geological discoveries. Dick posited a positive relation between theology and science, holding that the scientific enterprise was a necessary consequence of Christian faith: 'As [theology] has God for its object, it must include a knowledge of the universe He has formed.'[27] Like Moffat, Dick presented geology and astronomy as aids to faith, not as obstacles,[28] citing famous scientists such as Newton and Boyle who were also theists.[29]

Dick was particularly upbeat regarding recent geological findings, interpreting them as supportive of the Mosaic record: 'We have reason to believe, that as Geologists proceed in their researches and investigations, still more sensible proofs of the authenticity of Revelation will be brought to light.'[30] And Dick allowed for the earth existing for a lengthy period of time before the crucial six-day period of Genesis 1 commenced, writing: 'Moses nowhere affirms that the materials or substance of our world, were created or brought from nothing into existence, at the time when his history commences.'[31] Dick envisaged the materials of the earth as having existed

---

25 When Livingstone left the LMS and conducted his further missionary explorations in Africa under the auspices of the Royal Geographic Society, the young geologist Richard Thornton was assigned to be part of his expedition. In Livingstone's view Thornton was lazy and dismissed him. Whatever lay behind Livingstone's attitude to Thornton, he was not dismissed because Livingstone felt threatened by his geology. Cf. E.C. Tabler (ed.), *The Zambezi Papers of Richard Thornton: Geologist to Livingstone's Zambezi Expedition. Vol. 1, 1858-1860,* (Ldn: Chatto & Windus, 1963).

26 Dick, *The Christian Philosopher: The Connection of Science and Philosophy with Religion,* (Edin: Black, 1823/42); Dick, *Philosophy of a Future State* (Glasgow: Collins, 1828).

27 Ibid, 155.

28 Ibid, 212-230.

29 Ibid, 425ff.

30 Ibid, 213.

31 Ibid, 222. Dick stated that the phrase: 'In the beginning God created the heaven and the earth', was a preface to the six days but covered an enormous era of time. For Dick, the

for perhaps even a million years before Adam appeared.[32] He believed his theory to be further strengthened by the fact that the oldest rocks had no trace of human fossils, proving that, 'man was created at a period later than the great changes and convulsions which destroyed so many millions and millions of animal beings'[33]

2. Thomas Chalmers. Dick published his books from the 1820s to the 1840s, and in them he paralleled some of the ideas set out by Thomas Chalmers, who had had lectured on his theory of creation as early as 1804, and had published on the subject by 1814. Chalmers was one of the most famous leaders of Scottish Church life in the whole nineteenth century. He started as a minister of the Church of Scotland, but became the great figure of the 1843 Disruption, leading one third of the Kirk's ministers out of the Established Church to create the Free Church of Scotland. At the beginning of the century, as well as being a parish minister in Fife, Chalmers lectured in Natural Philosophy at the University of St Andrews, and became one of the first Scots to interpret Genesis in the light of geology.[34]

During the winter of 1803-04, Chalmers presented a series of lectures at St Andrews, in which he outlined a reconciliation between Genesis and the developing science of geology. He stated: 'The writings of Moses do not fix the antiquity of the globe. If they fix anything at all, it is only the antiquity of the species.'[35] Chalmers contended that scripture allowed for an indefinite gap of time between the first and second verses of Genesis 1. This, in turn, allowed for a lengthy passage of time in which geological formations could occur before the traditional six-day creation. In Chalmer's view, the six-day creation represented a restoration of the whole earth after aeons of

---

purpose of Genesis 1:1 was to underline that GOD is the cause of existence, and that the Universe is not self-existent. Cf. Dick, *The Discoveries of Modern Geology,* 21,22.

32 Dick, *The Christian Philosopher,* 223.

33 Dick, *The Discoveries of Modern Geology,* 15.

34 See: C. G. M'Crie, *The Confessions of the Church of Scotland: their Evolution in History,* (Edin: MacNiven & Wallace, 1907), 149-151. James Hutton (1726-97), one of the outstanding Enlightenment Scots in the natural sciences, had been instrumental in establishing that geology pointed to the earth having a great age. Many of his works were published in the 1790s, especially his *Theory of the Earth, (1795).* John Playfair, professor of mathematics at the University of Edinburgh, published *Illustrations of the Huttonian Theory* in 1802. Thus Chalmers was responding to the most advanced scientific opinion. Cf. Broadie (ed.), *The Scottish Enlightenment: An Anthology,* (Edin: Canongate, 1997), 800f; and Daiches (ed.), *The Scottish Enlightenment, 1730-1790: A Hotbed of Genius,* (Edin: Saltire Society, 1996), 116-136.

35 Chalmers, *Memoirs, Vol. 1,* 80f. Quoted by Hugh Miller, *The Testimony of the Rocks,* (Edin: Constable, 1857) *(1857),* 115.

destructive forces working on the primeval materials of creation.[36] Ten years later, reviewing Cuvier's *Essay on the Theory of the Earth,*[37] Chalmers refined his harmonisation of geology with Genesis. In his modified interpretation, the first verses of Genesis 1 referred to three distinct stages:

> Genesis 1:1: the primary creation of the heavens and the earth. This formed no part of the six days' work.
>
> Genesis 1:2a *'The earth was without form and void; and darkness was upon the face of the deep'.* This described the state of things *subsequent* to the primary creation but *prior* to the creative work of the first 'day'. In Chalmers' view ancient geological features came from rocks which belonged to this unspecified extension of time before God's special activity in creating life-forms started; rocks could have existed for thousands of years before humanity, and before the 'six day' period of special creative activity took place.[38]
>
> Genesis 1:2b *'And the Spirit of God moved upon the face of the waters'.* This was the start of special divine creative activity directed towards the earth itself. This was the commencement of the six days.

Chalmers saw no difficulty in regarding the 'days'—after this special creative action started—as natural days, and he was anxious to retain the traditional interpretation of 'day' as having twenty-four-hours. Whatever weaknesses from an exegetical, theological, or scientific point of view, exist in Chalmers' theory, he did provide an interpretation which allowed for rocks on earth

---

36 Lynch, Introduction, ix, to: Thomas Chalmers, *The Evidence and Authority of the Christian Revelation* (1817), (Reprint: Lynch (ed.): Bristol: Thoemmes, 2002).

37 In 1814, Chalmers produced 'his more elaborate scheme of reconciliation between the Divine and the Geologic Records' (Miller, *The Testimony of the Rocks,* 117). In his 1814 review of Cuvier's *Theory of the Earth,* Chalmers argued: 'Between the first act of creation, which evoked out of the previous nothing the *matter* of the heavens and earth, and the first act of the First Day's work recorded in Genesis, periods of vast duration may have intervened' Thus Chalmers still accepted that the 'days' of Genesis were 24-hour days, but that a great expanse of time had existed before these specific 'days' occurred. Thus the 'successive creations of the geologist could all find ample room in the period preceding that creation to which man belongs' (Miller, *The Testimony of the Rocks,* 118). Chalmers' theory neatly accommodated the geology of the early nineteenth century which demanded space, within a Christian theology of creation, for long geological eras. What it did not do was to make allowance for the time needed for the evolution of species. That was a debate many years in the future. Moffat's observations and comments are in line with Chalmers' theories.

38 Miller initially accepted Chalmers' 'gap theory' and his 6 days of 24 hours, but later felt he had to abandon it. In *The Testimony of the Rocks,* Miller equated the biblical 'day' with an indefinite portion of time.

thousands of years before Adam. The theory proved popular, and Moffat's observations were in line with Chalmers' 'gap theory' as it became known.[39]

As the century proceeded, Chalmers' model began to fall apart. The main works on geology at the time were Charles Lyell's *Principles of Geology (1834)* and John Phillips' two books, his *Treatise on Geology (1837)* and his *Guide to Geology (1834, 1853)* which ran to five volumes.[40] The main problem centred on the existence of fossils in rocks. If fossil-bearing *rocks* existed 'thousands' of years before Adam, then the organisms which produced the fossils also existed long before Adam. This created two problems. Firstly, the Genesis narrative appeared to indicate that all *life forms* were created *within* the six-day period, *but* rock-fossils came from long before that. Secondly, fossils come from living things which had died: but according to orthodox theology death only entered the world with Adam. As the theologian Ralph Wardlaw stated: 'It was sin that introduced mortality.'[41] No traditional theologian argued that death (even death of non-humans) existed before Adam: death entered the creation through the sin of Adam, whether that death came to plant, animal, or human life. How could these two phenomena—life forms before the six-day period, and pre-Adamic death—be accounted for?[42]

3. John Pye Smith. Chalmers' creaking reconciliation between Geology and Scripture was adjusted by Dr Pye Smith in the 1830s, 'to suit the more

---

[39] Chalmers gave a clear account of his 'Gap Theory' in, *The Evidence and Authority of the Christian Revelation,* 204ff, and in his *Natural Theology* where he wrote: 'Between the initial act and the details of Genesis the world for ought we know might have been the theatre of many revolutions, the trace of which geology may still investigate. ... The detailed history of creation in the first chapter of Genesis begins at the middle of the second verse.' (Chalmers, *On Natural Theology, Vol. I,* (Glasgow: Collins, 1835) 25). Chalmers was determined to retain the 6 days as 24-hour days. His 'gap theory' received explicit support from geologists such as William Buckland and William Conybeare, before being modified by John Pye Smith in 1839.

[40] Sir Charles Lyell (1797-1875) was a Scottish geologist who built on the foundations laid by James Hutton. Lyell argued for *uniformitarianism,* or the idea that geological changes occurred by slow, gradual changes. This was in opposition to the view that geological changes had been sudden and cataclysmic (*catastrophism*) which could give the earth a relatively young age. Lyell's ideas required the earth to be of a great age. Lyell's *Principles of Geology* was read by Moffat, who quoted directly from it in *MLSSA,* 332.

[41] Ralph Wardlaw, *Systematic Theology, Vol. 3,* (Edin: A&C Black, 1857), 643.

[42] The debate on the possibility of pre-Adamic death was alluded to in an 1848 exchange between the Edinburgh phrenologist George Combe and the Rev. C.J. Kennedy of Paisley, Scotland. Cf. Combe: *Answer by George Combe to the Attack on 'The Constitution of Man' contained in 'Nature and Revelation Harmonious: A Defence of Scripture Truths assailed in Mr. George Combe's work on the Constitution of Man etc., by the Rev. C.J. Kennedy, Paisley.'* (Edin: MacLachlan, Stewart & Co., 1848), 7.

advanced state of geological science at the time'.[43] Pye Smith knew that more account had to be taken of fossils in the geological record. He saw that these implied that plants, which produced these fossils, had flourished during part of the long geological period which Chalmers allowed for, but which Chalmers had always kept separate from, and prior to, the creation of life alluded to in the six days of Genesis 1. Pye Smith realised that fossils meant that biological life forms could not be kept separate from the extended geological era of Chalmer's 'gap'. But was Pye Smith's adjustment of Chalmers' theory simply cosmetic? It would seem not. Pye Smith's theory obliterated an essential part of Chalmers' system, namely the integrity of the six twenty-four-hour days of 'creation'. In traditional theology—the faith which Chalmers and Pye Smith both sought to retain—the biblical six-day period was the period within which *all* life forms had their beginning; but Pye Smith's theory necessitated that some life forms pre-dated that period.

4. Hugh Miller. Noted author, amateur geologist and theologian from Cromarty in the far north of Scotland, Hugh Miller made alternative suggestions. He also puzzled over matching the Mosaic account of creation with geology, and it used to be thought that depression, caused by difficulty in harmonising his geology and his biblical faith, drove him to suicide in 1856, though that conjecture is now largely abandoned, with the cause being a brain tumour. Miller acknowledged the problem which Pye Smith had sought to solve:

> We know further that not a few of the shells which now live on our coasts, and several of even the wild animals which continue to survive amid our tracts of hill and forest, were in existence many ages ere the human age began. Instead of dating their beginning only a single natural day, or at most two natural days, in advance of man, they must have preceded him by many thousands of years.[44]

Miller formulated a different answer, moving away from literal exegesis. He believed that harmonisation could be achieved by interpreting Genesis as a visionary account, not a literal one.[45] The 'days' of Genesis 1 were 'apparent days' in which the Mosaic author had a series of visions concerning the creation of the world. In 1854, Miller gave a London lecture under the title, *The Two Records, Mosaic and Geological.* He followed this up with his book, *The Testimony of the Rocks,* which included the earlier lecture, and in which

---

43 Miller, *The Testimony of the Rocks,* 119. In retirement Moffat corresponded with a Mrs Pye-Smith Sheffield. Cf. RM, *To Mrs Pye-Smith,* May 1883, (SOAS/CWM/SA/Moffat /Pers/4).

44 Miller, *The Testimony of the Rocks,* 122.

45 Nineteenth-century Scottish harmonisers of science and theology never sought to avoid the dilemma by questioning the reliability of science. They had an implicit faith in it.

he published a sequel, entitled *The Mosaic Vision of Creation.* In these, he unfolded his 'prophetic-vision' theory of the six days, acknowledging his debt to the seventeenth-century poet John Milton who had had similar thoughts.

For Miller, the revelatory visions were optical, not auditory: the arrival and departure of each revelatory vision *seemed* to the Mosaic author as a morning and an evening, marked by an increase and decrease of light, marking morning dawn and evening twilight. In Miller's theory, each 'day' stood for the period during which the divinely enlightened imagination of the prophet was active. The 'days' were the measures of the *apparent* time during which the successive scenes were exhibited.[46] Miller's theory enabled the 'days' of Genesis 1 to be interpreted in elastic fashion, and solved the problem of requiring a vast space of time for pre-Adamic life-forms to leave fossils in the rocks. But what was not dealt with was pre-Adamic death. Miller provided a strong solution for one part of the problem, but not for the other.

What can we conclude concerning Moffat and geological theories? What is clear is that, contrary to what is often assumed, Christians of the early nineteenth century were not bound to the idea of a young Earth. Moreover, until Darwin, the debate on 'Geology and Scripture' was not as highly charged as it became, when it was then linked to debate concerning evolution and the nature of humanity. Nevertheless, it was still a bold move in 1804 for Thomas Chalmers to accept current geological theory and to mould his interpretation of Scripture around the findings of the physical sciences. But that illustrated the confident relationship between science and theology which existed in the first half of the nineteenth century. Dick's dictum was widely accepted: 'There must be harmony between the common author of the Universe and Scripture.'[47]

Chalmer's solution carried weight and conviction for many years, and Moffat appears to have understood Genesis 1 within a Chalmers/Dick framework. Moffat's outlook clearly reflected a theological climate which, in the first half of the nineteenth century, was more accommodating of various views than in the post-Darwinian years would be, when debate polarised opinion and hardened attitudes.[48] Moffat never mentioned fossils.

---

[46] M'Crie, *The Confessions of the Church of Scotland,* 151-153.

[47] Dick, *The Discoveries of Modern Geology,* 6.

[48] Kenneth Hylson-Smith, *Evangelicals in the Church of England: 1734-1984,* (Edin: T&T Clark, 1988), 137, pointed out that, within the English context, 'J.B. Sumner and the *Christian Observer* [newspaper] were illustrative of an enlightened Evangelical interest in all things scientific' (137). Hylson-Smith also stressed that some evangelicals in the 1820s and 1830s 'cautiously accepted the theory of such geologists as Baron de Couvier, that the world had

THEOLOGY AND ENVIRONMENT

In some of Moffat's background influencers, there are traces of what might be termed a 'green theology'. For example, he had an instinctive aversion to the gratuitous killing of game animals, and *Brown's Catechism,* Qu. 103, had asked: 'Is it sinful to hurt the birds and beasts?' Response 103: 'Yes'. Similarly, Roby taught: 'There are Religious Duties which we owe to our fellow creatures. We owe humanity even to brutes.'[49] Roby also wrote about not abusing the world: 'We should pray that, whilst we are continued in life, we may enjoy the comforts of life, such as: health, food, raiment, the blessings of God on our worldly employments; contentment with our lot and grace to use the world and not to abuse it.'[50]

This teaching struck a sympathetic chord with Moffat. He viewed the mass killing of game animals for sport as an abuse of God's world. Moffat did shoot game to feed his company,[51] but beyond that, he was sickened by the slaughter perpetrated by some game hunters. In his *Journal,* he displayed a growing concern for conservation. In 1854, after describing how 'sportsmen' indulged in overkill, Moffat expressed with passionate indignation the fear that such habits would exterminate some species:

> English hunters and amateur sportsmen accelerate the work of extermination. They often shoot down these beautiful animals, whether they need them or not, and often in places where there is not an inhabitant and [where they] are soon devoured by the eagles and birds of prey. The Nimrods then get eloquent at the evening bivouac in their descriptions of how they leveled this one with one ball, and how he had a near chance of losing a fine bull or a cow but at last made him bite the earth; and then with a crow – for

---

been created by a long series of geological revolutions extending many thousands of years into pre-history', but that, 'a decided change took place with the various scientific, historical and theological developments of the 1860s'.

49 Roby, *Theol. Lect.* 2, 'Religion', (our italics). Few Reformed catechisms, apart from *Brown's Catechism,* mention the harm which human beings may inflict on other species. *Brown's Catechism* made the issue blunt and clear, perhaps because it was child-centred.

50 Roby, *Theol. Lect.* 'Appendix on Prayer'.

51 J.M. Mackenzie, 'The Hunting Ethos in Central Africa up to 1914' in: David Anderson and Richard Grove (eds): *Conservation in Africa: People, Politics, and Practice,* (Cambridge: CUP, 1987), 42, gives a misleading picture of missionary interaction with hunters. Mackenzie states: 'While in India the soldier and the big game hunter were often synonymous, in Africa the missionaries and explorers were also hunters. Robert Moffat and David Livingstone hunted with famous hunters like Gordon-Cumming, Oswell, and Murray.' Though Moffat and Livingstone met, and sometimes gave accommodation to, hunters, they had little to do with slaughter in the name of sport.

> such are like game-cocks – number how many they have bagged, or rather, destroyed, as if they were beasts of prey instead of lovely antelopes.[52]

Moffat saw beauty in wildlife. He frequently used the terms 'lovely' or 'beautiful' in relation to animals, appreciating the variety of God's creation:

> It has always grieved me to see game shot and left to be devoured by beasts of prey; and such is the bewitching spirit of hunting that these lovely animals that inhabit and adorn the otherwise uninhabitable wilderness – and it needs adorning! – are mercilessly shot down to add to the number of the hunter's trophies.[53]

In 1857, he expressed his low estimation of hunters, and was surprised to find a hunter who was also intelligent! '[I am gratified] to meet an Englishman at such a distance from home, especially if he possesses a little intelligence and general knowledge, so as to lift him above the low level of Nimrodism, a spirit which never raises but degrades.'[54] By 1871 the Kuruman missionary John Mackenzie noted, 'The game has been long since killed or driven to a distance.'[55]

Moffat and Cultivation

Botany and horticulture attracted the youthful Moffat, with gardening proving more congenial than the sea-going life to which he had been temporarily attracted.[56] Through his family, he had an interaction with both the Agricultural and Industrial Revolutions which together had transformed Scotland from the middle of the eighteenth century onwards.[57] His

---

[52] RM, *Journal,* 12.6.1854, (*MJ1,* 182). By the 1870s the problem was acute. T.M. Thomas, *Eleven Years in Central South Africa,* noted that animals were scarcer through over hunting.
[53] RM, *Journal,* 14.6.1854, (*MJ1,* 184).
[54] RM, *Journal,* 3.11.1857, (*MJ2,* 111). Moffat's use of 'degrade' is interesting. He was prepared to use the term concerning his own countrymen. It was used of any person who did not fulfill the purpose that God originally gave to humanity.
[55] Mackenzie: *Ten Years North of the Orange River: A Story of Everyday Life and Work among the South African Tribes from 1859-1869,* (Edin: Edmonston Douglas, 1871), 70.
[56] Moffat, cited in *The Haddingtonshire Courier,* 26.3.1915. Cf. Moffat's remarks on his visit to the village of Ormiston as recorded in *The Haddingtonshire Chronicle,* 23.8.1872.
[57] Cf. John Cockburn, *Letters of John Cockburn of Ormiston to his Gardener: 1727-1744,* (Edin: Scottish History Society, 1904). 'Improving Cockburn,' as he was sometimes known, lived most the year in London, but kept in touch with his head gardener through regular correspondence in which he gave detailed instructions for the garden at Ormiston House. Moffat paralleled Cockburn's long-range 'gardening by correspondence' in a string of letters sent back to Kuruman, whilst on his major expeditions, with detailed instructions for the Kuruman garden (Cf. *MJ1,* 214; *MJ2,* 7, 15, 20, etc.). Moffat's grandfather, William Gardiner, became head gardener after Cockburn had to give up Ormiston House in 1848. The progressive methods which Cockburn established were retained by the new owner, the Earl of Hopetoun. The Comaroffs, somewhat harshly, label Cockburn as a 'capitalist' (*Revelation and Revolution,* 80).

grandfather, William Gardiner, experienced a sea-change in horticultural practices. And his father, in pursuing a career as a Customs Officer, took his family to near Carronshore in the shadow of the great Carron Ironworks, at the heart of the Industrial Revolution in Scotland. Agricultural and horticultural practices needed to change if Scotland were ever to feed its people. Through the centuries Scotland had regular times of famine and starvation. Four times in the 1690s the harvests failed, and hunger became rife. The situation continued late into the eighteenth century. The Law Lord, Henry Cockburn, recorded in his *Memoirs* that, because of famine, in March 1795, about 11,000 persons in Edinburgh—an eighth of the population of the city—were fed by charity.[58] Moffat was a gardener of the new school. He was progressive, and the idea that man should not interfere with 'God's natural methods', was alien to him. He inherited a philosophy of horticulture in which the *wisdom* of the past was retained, but in which the *traditions* of the past were expendable.

At Kuruman, Moffat's 'green' theology accepted that the earth was usable by humanity. The earth was not sacrosanct, but was to be husbanded with care. Traditional practices could be overcome, changed, or set aside. In 1829, he commented on Kuruman converts leaving their old traditions, and imitating the missionaries in leading out water to their gardens. They were raising crops, and not only of their native grain, pumpkins, kidney-beans, and water-melons, but also of vegetables, such as the missionaries had introduced. These included maize, wheat, barley, peas, potatoes, carrots, and onions, as well as planting fruit trees.[59]

However, in an African context there were sociological implications which impinged upon Moffat's emphasis on horticulture. These involved: gender, community, and civilisation. Concerning gender, Moffat was aware that in Tswana society cultivation was viewed as women's work: 'The women who are the cultivators pick the ground to about 4 inches or more, they sometimes unite and finish gardens by turns, but without reward or something in the shape of food. It is considered below the dignity of a man to dig or cultivate the ground. He hunts and goes to war.'[60] The same was true of the Ndebele, though Moselekatse, through his slaves, had developed agriculture to the extent of growing vast acres of grain. In 1854, on Moffat's

---

The term 'capitalist' implies an exploitative relationship between employer and employee. Unless all businessmen are to be so termed, it is difficult to see Cockburn in that light.

58 Cockburn, Henry, *Memorials of his Time:1779-1830,* (Edin: Foulis, 1910 edn), 65f.

59 Deane, *Robert Moffat,* 110f.

60 RM, *Bechuana Customs,* (SOAS/CWM/Africa/Moffat/Personal/Box 4). Schapera, (*AAK,* fn. 32, 187), noted that indigenous beliefs made some hesitate about developing agriculture.

first visit to Moselekatse's new location, in present-day southern Zimbabwe, he expressed admiration of Moselekatse's agriculture.[61]

Moffat was convinced that, if people concentrated on cultivation, there would be an effect on the nature of community. In the 1853 LMS Annual Report, Moffat was quoted as declaring:

> 'The grounds on or near the station are being more generally brought under cultivation ... From among localities less favoured than the Kuruman for purposes of irrigation, numbers have begun to work the fountains, and lead out the water. This, as a matter of course, *has a tendency to separate communities* which reside at places where gardens depend entirely on rain, but the results are favourable.'[62]

Moffat bound together two concepts: 'progress' and 'settled horticulture'. Yet an emphasis on horticulture proved complex. It involved not only the separation of communities—as families drifted to different water sources, as indicated in the quoted extract—but also presupposed a permanence of location for a tribe or clan. The Tswana were used to being semi-nomadic, in the sense of moving to a new nearby-location every few years, as the ground became less fertile. Moffat's vision for the future did not fully dovetail with this semi-nomadic lifestyle. The main BaThlaping tribe under Mothibi moved to a different location in the latter half of the 1820s and, though good relationships continued with them, that part of the BaThlaping tribe was not directly involved in the Kuruman spiritual Awakening of 1829. What remained at Kuruman was a varied population with no resident leader. These were the people amongst whom Moffat did his most dramatic work of evangelism. Yet that circumstance, of no strong local leader, may have helped conversions becoming possible in the way they did at the time.

As far as Moffat was concerned, civilisation had to be rooted in a community which was settled rather than nomadic, and which cultivated the soil rather than being dependent upon hunting. In 1825, discussing the move of the mission station from New Lattakoo to Kuruman with its abundant water supply, Moffat stated: 'By continuing at the old station [New Lattakoo] a complete barrier was ever in our way of being useful in point of civilisation, *which must originate and depend on the culture of the ground*.'[63] Was this simply a passionate gardener seeing human civilisation from the exclusive perspective of his own enthusiasm? Not so. There was a theory of civilisation, promulgated in Scotland during the eighteenth century by Lord Kames, which

---

61 RM, *Journal*, 10.7.1854, (*MJ1*, 214).

62 LMS, *Report to the 59th Annual Meeting, 1853*, 65, (our italics).

63 RM, *Journal*, 30.5.1825, (*AAK*, 188), (our italics).

was specifically based on the concept of settled agricultural communities. This Kamesian socio-economic theory of civilisation is discussed in our later chapter, 'The Process of Civilisation'.

Moffat and Climate

Moffat made generalised, and sometimes erroneous, assumptions as to why the land was in such a poor state in much of southern Africa. He was convinced that irresponsible, widespread cutting of large acacias by Africans had caused desiccation, and he believed that the whole landscape was in need of redemption.[64] Moffat thus saw the landscape suffering from the sin of humanity. This was both in a general sense, in bearing a curse following the sin of Adam; and also in a specific sense, of suffering from irresponsible indigenous practices.

Richard Grove, in his trenchant analysis of Moffat's methods, has posited that it was widespread climate change rather than indigenous practices was crucial. Grove pointed out that Moffat's blame of Africans for the barren state of the landscape was later expounded by John Croumbie Brown,[65] and exploited by the Colonial State authority to justify their criticisms of the indigenous population.[66] Against this culture of blame, Grove argued that the land was barren, not because of indigenous practices, but because of droughts, such as the well-documented ones of 1821-23,[67] 1854-57, and 1862-63, which affected the region. Grove also pointed out that even the Cape Dutch admitted that some European agricultural methods—such as forest clearing, and harmful intensive cultivation of semi-arid land—were responsible for deterioration in soils and pastures.

The early-nineteenth-century traveler, Lichtenstein, had already criticised European land-use methods as being far less suitable than indigenous practices for the semi-arid Cape.[68] Kuruman was outwith the area described

---

64 Nancy J. Jacobs, *Environment, Power and Injustice: A South African History,* (Cambridge: CUP, 2003), 98. Jacobs referred to: Richard H. Grove, 'Scottish Missionaries in Southern Africa', *JSAS,* 15 (1989), 165-172.

65 Richard H. Grove: *Ecology, Climate and Empire: Colonialism, and Global Environmental History, 1400-1940,* (Cambridge: The White Horse Press, 1997), 99, cited John Croumbie Brown's irrigation proposals for South Africa, in: *Reports of the Colonial Botanists* for 1863, 1865, 1866; and *Water Supply of South Africa, and facilities for storing it,* (Edin: 1877), 196-647. Croumbie Brown arrived in South Africa as a missionary with the LMS in 1844. He later taught Botany at Aberdeen University between 1853 and 1862.

66 Grove: *Ecology, Climate and Empire,* 87.

67 Moffat's own *Letters* and *Journal* in *AAK,* testify to the drought of 1821-23.

68 Grove: *Ecology, Climate and Empire,* 89.

by Lichtenstein, and the bounteous permanent water-supply of the Kuruman fountain meant that, at Kuruman itself, Moffat did not directly contribute toward impoverishing the land. Nevertheless, Grove criticised Moffat's theological approach to the issue of native land-use in southern Africa, pointing out that Moffat tended to deride indigenous knowledge and land-use, seeing the barren land as bearing the heavy curse of, 'Man's first disobedience, and the fruit of that forbidden tree, whose mortal taste brought death into the world and all our woe.'[69] In Grove's opinion, this quotation from Milton's *Paradise Lost* was revealing. Moffat equated the presence of drought with a state of original sin and with the expulsion of Adam and Eve from the Garden of Eden. Grove saw this as the guiding metaphor to Moffat's discourse, feeding the preconceptions of other contemporary observers. It set the scene, in Moffat's writings, for a view of drought in terms of morality.[70] For example, Grove cited a confrontation between Moffat and a rain-maker, recorded in detail in *Missionary Labours,*[71] and which, in Grove's opinion, illustrated two very different approaches to the environment. Moffat himself noted that the rain-maker blamed drought on the incursion of the Europeans and their alien religion,[72] whereas, for Moffat, it had been caused by the condition of sin.[73]

Moffat knew that Tswana oral tradition recalled times of bountiful water supply when rivers were larger and fuller.[74] He attributed the cessation of this 'pluvial golden age' to the destructive activities of the Tswana, rather than to the arrival of Europeans and of Christianity.[75] In contrast, the Tswana blamed the coming of Europeans for the barren landscape, though Moffat tried to convince them that it occurred before the missionaries arrived.[76] Grove suggested that Moffat may have been influenced by Humboldt's *Personal Narrative of Travels to Equinoctial Regions of the New Continent: 1799-1844,* in which Humboldt argued that aridity was the consequence of irresponsible deforestation.[77] Grove also proposed that Moffat wielded

---

69 Ibid, 89. Grove referred to RM, *MLSSA,* 66.

70 Ibid, 90f.

71 Ibid, 91. Grove cited RM, *MLSSA,* 327f. This 'confrontation' is recorded at length in *AAK.*

72 Grove cited: RM, *To Alexander Moffat,* 25.2.1822, (Baxter & Burke, *Guide,* 327).

73 Grove: *Ecology, Climate and Empire,* 92. What Moffat had in mind was the 'sin' of wrong practices, rather than a generic sinfulness which brought a Divine 'curse' on the area.

74 RM, *MLSSA,* 329.

75 Grove: *Ecology, Climate and Empire,* 93.

76 RM, *MLSSA,* 329f.

77 Grove, *Climate and Empire,* 97. Grove referred to Alexander von Humboldt's, *Personal Narrative of Travels to Equinoctial Regions of the New Continent: 1799-1804,* 6 Vols, (Ldn: 1819). Grove argued (94) that Moffat appeared to have read Humboldt on desiccation.

Lyell's *Principles of Geology* to argue that irresponsible felling of trees was responsible for the bleak landscape.[78]

Was Moffat, and Europeans like him, ignorant of wider long-term climatic changes? Did this make them attribute aridity exclusively to the sins of the local people?[79] Did this view give colonial authorities a spurious justification for viewing the indigenous population as unable to manage the land themselves? Did it buttress an argument for European paternalism? Possibly. Yet it is difficult to see how Grove could totally exonerate the indigenous population from bearing some responsibility for the state of the landscape.

Where Moffat was based in the early 1820s (the period analysed by Grove) there had not been large-scale European style farming, as noted by Lichtenstein nearer the Cape, with its adverse side effects. There is little doubt that, in the Cape area, some European methods, suitable to wet northern Europe, contributed toward environmental damage in the much dryer South Africa. But the Griqua Town and Kuruman areas were frontier territory, still under indigenous control, yet Moffat saw a barren landscape there as soon as he arrived. Grove also implied that the Tswana blamed the farming *methods* of European missionaries, but it was not only such *methods.* Though the Tswana at times connected drought with the new agricultural techniques, they also believed that drought came because the missionaries brought an alien *spirituality* which offended the ancestral spirits.

Grove had multiple criticisms of Moffat. He accused Moffat of blaming the Tswana, and using blame as an ideological weapon in persuading them that European ideas and religion were superior in every way. He insisted that Moffat's ignorance of climatic changes meant that the Tswana, in his eyes, were entirely culpable for the state of the land. He accused Moffat of spreading the notion that the state of the land was due to sin, especially Tswana sin. He argued that Moffat saw the Cape and Africa as being the site of a Garden of Eden or Promised Land, spoiled by Africans and requiring spiritual and environmental redemption through an intervention which only

---

78 Ibid, 97. Grove stated that Moffat used Lyell even though, in Grove's opinion, Lyell's teaching on geological timescale was 'completely irreconcilable with Genesis'. Grove was unaware of the various ways of interpreting Genesis 1 current in the pre-Darwinian environment. Grove (98) stated that Lyell's vast geological timescale was something which Moffat 'would not, in fact, admit to'. Grove assumed that this was the case for Moffat, though giving no evidence. As we have seen, the situation was more complex.

79 Ibid, 99. Moffat was not averse to discrediting indigenous culture by referring to 'superior' European science and technology, as a way of gaining respect for his ideas. E.g. Moffat's conversation with Moselekatse: *Journal,* 3.8.1854, (*MJ1,* 251).

he and the evangelical message could bring.[80] Though Grove quoted a passage from *Missionary Labours* which stated that transformation of the barren land could be aided by encouraging people to grow indigenous species of timber, Grove insisted that Moffat did little to put this into practice beyond 'some minor attempts at irrigation development'.[81] Grove's claims do carry some weight, exposing generalisations which were applied to the indigenous population. Indigenous tree felling and bush burning had certainly had an effect on the environment, but what Grove rightly emphasised was that indigenous practices were not the *only* cause of environmental problems.

*

Moffat was a gardener, expecting good fruit in due season. As a gardener he knew that preparation, sowing, tending, cutting off bad growth, waiting, and more waiting, were part of the process. A gardener was supremely confident in a right outcome if he did the right thing, at the right place, at the right time. Yet the gardener knew and accepted that, even having done the right thing, he had to exercise patience. The fruit would come from the hand of God. But he would have to be patient. A gardener became accustomed to waiting, expectation, and fruition. It was a process experienced many times. He had trained himself to accept the inexorable processes of nature. It was no use railing against natural forces. He had to work in harmony with them. Yet, he was not a man of passivity, but a man of active labour. Though great forces of nature produce the result, he was also involved.

The juxtaposition of divine sovereignty and human activity is not an insuperable problem for a gardener. Since the providence of God has been proven repeatedly in the natural world, why should he not trust in a similar providence in the spiritual world? A gardener has confidence in the process, and is implicitly a man of trust and faith. The factors he deals with are tried and tested. In the Kuruman Mission cemetery, a grave stone has the words: 'I sow in good soil what I know to be good seed.' That was the Kuruman philosophy of the Kingdom.

---

80 Grove, *Climate and Empire,* 100.

81 RM, *MLSSA,* 332.

Chapter 10
The Theology of Providence

ENLIGHTENMENT AND REASON dominated European intellectual thought in the eighteenth century. There was a reaction against revealed religion, due, among other reasons, to the influence of the Newtonian/Cartesian scientific way of thinking in which events were explained purely as products of identifiable cause and effect within nature, rather than as the result of supernatural agency. This milieu discouraged the notion of God being directly involved in daily life and, in its extreme form, it brought a radical disjunction between God and the world, eliminating the concept of Divine response to prayer, and fostering scepticism about miracles.

Intellectual trends take several generations to permeate the thinking of society and so, whilst philosophical deism gained a foothold in some quarters of the church, there still existed alongside it a tradition which maintained belief in a dynamic interaction between God and humanity. Within that tradition, prayer was of great importance, not just as personal inner spiritual reflection, but as intercession, trusting that God actively intervenes in response to entreaties. There was also confidence in the providence of God, with providence including all activities in which God upheld, protected, guided and provided for his people.

Deism did have the concept of a *general provision,* in which, at the start of creation, God initially provided all that was necessary for humanity, and then left humanity with the responsibility of using such resources. But the evangelical understanding of providence went much further, seeing God providing in response to specific prayer, and interacting with his people throughout life. Moffat was in the evangelical camp. For Moffat, providence was not a marginalised or theoretical concept, but an axiom at the heart of daily living, and an essential premise of faith. That this presupposition was shared within his family is demonstrated by John Smith Moffat who wrote in his *Lives*: 'The Lord of missions knows the end from the beginning, and is working all things according to one harmonious plan. No more impressive lesson is taught in this book than the lesson of faith in a Divine purpose.'[1]

---

1 JSM, *Lives,* ii

The nineteenth-century missionary had faith presuppositions. He or she enjoyed the fruits of intellectual and social development arising out of the Enlightenment whilst also living in a personal Age of Faith. For a missionary, the rightness of what God did, or permitted, was unquestioned. This was a vital conviction for the missionary calling, since a missionary—often isolated for years at a stretch—needed to have total trust in the providential care of the God whom he or she served. In deism, God stood back from daily events. The evangelical missionary required a different theology. It was a doctrine of providence which enabled him or her to set out on hazardous enterprises. But what happened when missions, initiated on a basis of trust, came to nothing or even ended in tragedy? As we shall see, when the perplexities of life intruded upon faith, a man like Moffat took refuge in sentiments similar to Job's: 'Though he slay me, yet will I hope in Him' (Job 13:15). This chapter examines how Moffat understood and applied his faith in the providence of God, and how that impinged upon his understanding of God. But first, there are preliminary issues to consider.

1. Emotion. At its simplest level providence has to do with God caring for his people, and the primary assessment as to whether a person has in fact been cared for is made on an emotional basis. When tragedy strikes, an explanation which is logically and technically 'correct' may, from an emotional perspective, be considered irrelevant if what occurred did not correspond to faith expectations. The question becomes: 'Has my faith been violated?' Emotional impact is at the centre of a doctrine of providence. This factor is especially strong in the case of evangelical believers, whose faith in God is rooted in the 'affections of the heart', rather than in philosophical thoughts concerning a supreme being. Though a theocentric faith sought to minimise the notion that providence was primarily for 'my convenience' or 'my comfort', there would be few believers who did not harbour the conviction that providence meant that Divine benevolence would make 'my life' better. The impact which events have on our emotions affect the feeling as to whether God has really cared 'for me'.

2. Narrative. That being so, we shall need to consider Moffat's response to events, rather than simply analyse his reflections upon theory. How did Moffat *feel* when he experienced specific tragedies? How did he reconcile unwelcome occurrences with his theology? For example, simply to state that on the Makololo missionary expedition nine persons died, may convey a little of the sense of loss which hearing such news induced. But to read Isabella Price's *Journal,*[2] as she daily recorded her hopes, her excitement, the birth of

---

[2] Maud Isabella Slater, *Isabella Price: Pioneer,* (Ldn: Livingstone Press, 1931).

her child, her simple trust in God to look after everyone, and then to consider the terrible outcome, results in approaching the matter from a deeper level. Context and narrative become all-important. Events are intruders which can violate the faith of the believing heart. It is the *feeling* that trust has been violated which raises the sharpest questions. We must try to appreciate how Moffat *felt* when tragedy struck: only then can we begin to value the questions posed and the answers offered. Narrative and story are essential.

3. Testability. Providence is a doctrine which impinges empirically on life experiences. As such, it is testable, albeit by criteria rooted in the emotions. In Moffat's time, providence was one of the few doctrines which were testable in daily life. Doctrines such as the Trinity, salvation, eternal life, were non-testable within the here and now: their proof lay in the future, after death. But providence—evaluated from the perspective of benefits experienced, or prayer answered—was testable in the present. Has God cared for me? Has he provided for me? Has he guided me? Verdicts would come from ordinary people in ordinary life, and the validity of a doctrine of providence rested on theological theory corresponding to lived reality.

The 19th Century Theological Context

Moffat had a straightforward trust in the kindly providence of God. In order to explore his mind on this matter, we need to understand how providence was understood in evangelical thought, and how the Reformed tradition had developed in relation to this doctrine. The seventeenth-century Puritan, Thomas Watson, saw providence as the ordering of all issues and events 'after the counsel of [God's] will to his own glory.'[3] Watson is a vivid example of the Reformed emphasis, in which the purpose of providence was the same as the purpose of everything: namely, to glorify God. Reformed theology is profoundly theocentric, not anthropocentric. The comfort of humanity is not its primary concern, as it might be in a modern exposition. For the Puritans, providence may be benevolent toward humanity, but human comfort is not primary. Rather, providence was God's day-to-day providing for his people *in order* to work all things for his glory. But the ultimate goal was God's glory, not man's comfort. In order to attain that goal, providence may have a dark side as well as a light one.[4] Eighteenth-century evangelical theology grew

3 Thomas Watson, *A Body of Divinity,* 84.

4 Watson, *A Body of Divinity,* 87. Watson provides a good example of Puritan theology: 'The providences of God are chequer-work, they are intermingled. In the life to come there shall be no more mixture; in hell there will be nothing but bitter; in heaven nothing but sweet; but in this life the providences of God are *mixed.*' Also, Watson, *The Lord's Prayer*: 'A good

from Puritan roots, and the theologians of the Great Awakening echoed Puritan doctrine. Jonathan Edwards was described as being, 'unbending in his commitment to the doctrine of providence, the natural extension of God's creative power through time.'[5]

Thomas Vargish, in his book, *The Providential Aesthetic in Victorian Fiction,*[6] has argued that the strong concept of providence in the first half of the nineteenth century in Britain was moulded by the influences of the Great Awakening and Evangelical Revival. Vargish linked the rise of the Victorian emphasis on providence to a movement in theology away from *rationalism* (associated with deism and a distant God) to *feeling* (associated with Evangelicalism and an immanent God). But what lay behind this movement? Vargish mentioned Romanticism, but he mainly pointed to late eighteenth-century and early nineteenth-century evangelicalism with its intense preoccupation with a 'right state of heart'.[7] What he identified was the exact tradition which lay behind Moffat and like-minded evangelicals.

This tradition also stressed that all which God does provide, will, in the end, be shown to be good. At the same time, it did not view providence in terms of Leibniz's supposition that this is the 'Best of all possible Worlds'.[8] Philosophical theology toyed with Leibniz's hypothesis. But evangelical theology, with its strong biblical roots, was consistent in its stance that this is a fallen, imperfect world, and not the 'Best of all possible Worlds'. Instead, the evangelical theologian focused on Paul's statement: 'Everything works together for Good to those who love God.' (Romans 8:28). This was the text to which many turned when dealing with providence. It was a text immensely important to Moffat.[9]

Christian, when under any disastrous providence, should lie quietly at God's feet, and say, 'Thy will be done.'

5 S.J. Stein (ed.), *Jonathan Edwards: Apocalyptic Writings,* (New Haven & London: Yale Univ. Press, 1977), 5. The argument that if there is supernatural activity in the act of *creation* then there must (not merely 'may') also be *ongoing* supernatural activity as acts of *providence,* was embedded in evangelical theology.

6 Thomas Vargish, *The Providential Aesthetic in Victorian Fiction,* (Charlottesville: Univ. Press of Virginia, 1985).

7 Vargish: *The Providential Aesthetic in Victorian Fiction*, 21.

8 G.W. Leibniz (1646-1716), philosopher and mathematician. His contention, heavily influenced by his mathematics, that the universe is the harmonious result of the divine plan and is in fact 'the best of all possible worlds' was satirised by Voltaire in *Candide* (1759).

9 After the Mantatee crisis of 1823, the missionaries at New Lattakoo retreated to Griqua Town for a period. A depressed Moffat, *Journal,* 7.7.1823, (*AAK,* 99), wrote: 'Extreme fatigue, of both body and mind, caused our hands to hang down and our spirits to sink. It is, nevertheless, sweet to reflect that the cause is the Lord's, it cannot fail. He who bore our

What Vargish revealed was the way in which society as a whole accepted a concept of providence. Though Vargish was not a theologian, his perceptions regarding the thinking of society as reflected in its fiction, are illuminating. In nineteenth-century literature, even fictional events were interpreted within a providential framework. Vargish contended that, among the concerns which were important to book-readers, the action of God's will and purpose in the world was central. He argued that most English novelists, before George Eliot,[10] assumed the existence of a providential order to the cosmos and found evidence for such an intention at work in it.[11] This providential world-view was not only used to explain events and coincidences, but underpinned convictions concerning an overall meaning to existence, and an over-arching moral intention in the universe. Vargish also argued that loss of belief in providence went hand in hand with loss in the belief that the universe is purposive.[12]

In many of Vargish's examples from fiction, the 'hand of providence' intervened through 'fortuitous coincidences', with coincidence seen as a guidance of providence for a person's destiny. Though a doctrine of providence could incorporate this, the theological doctrine went beyond coincidence to an emphasis on God's involvement in every detail of life. In literature, the agent of providence was the 'hand of fate', conveying the sense of an impersonal agent at work. In evangelical theology, the agent was the Lord, fostering personal involvement, hope and expectation.

William Roby: The Intellectual Approach

For a believer, the declaration: 'God cares for me' was made in the light of two things. Firstly, what Scripture taught concerning the nature of God (intellectual). Secondly, what happened in real life (experiential). This created two related theologies: one of the mind, and one of the heart. These are illustrated in two leading missionary-minded scholars, William Roby and Ralph Wardlaw, both of whom were highly respected by Moffat. Roby stated that the clear indications of a superintending providence in the world are a

---

infirmities saith, 'Lo, I am with you'. This, with many other precious promises, revives our wounded souls, and assures us that all these troubles shall work together for good'.

10 George Eliot (Mary Anne Evans) was influenced by D.F. Strauss' *Life of Jesus,* and by Feuerbach's *Essence of Christianity,* both of which she helped translate into English, losing belief in Christianity as a divinely revealed religion.

11 Vargish, *The Providential Aesthetic in Victorian Fiction,* 1.

12 Ibid, 3-5.

loud testimony to the being of God, with providence seen in various particulars such as:[13]

1. In preserving the several orders of creatures.
2. In its various acts respecting individuals.
3. In the due proportion of useful and noxious plants and animals.
4. In the due proportion of different sexes.
5. In the continuance and subservience of different climates and seasons.
6. In the judgments which are sometimes executed upon the ungodly in which there appears a remarkable coincidence between their sins and their punishments.
7. In the remarkable deliverances of the righteous.

Roby came close to adopting Leibniz's formula of the 'Best of all possible Worlds', ignoring the disharmony in nature caused by sin. He even went so far as to say that 'disorder' in the world may only be 'apparent'.[14] This trace of an unintended triumph of idealism over realism in his theology perhaps arose from Roby placing his remarks on providence within the context of proofs for the existence of God. Such a context minimised the 'dark' or 'shadow' side of life, apart from misfortune befalling people as a righteous punishment. This was all very well when considering hardships which came to evil persons, but was not satisfactory when trying to explain tragedy affecting good, gentle, pious, God-fearing men and women.

Roby's approach may partly explain why, when moments of tragedy came, a missionary such as Moffat had no *theological* response to give, other than simply to record the facts. Roby's *Lectures* epitomise a strong Calvinist theology. For Roby, the primary purpose of providence was the glory of God.[15] Everything else was subordinated to that end. It is true that providence as benevolence was also mentioned by Roby in terms of 'the welfare and final blessedness of believers individually', and he also wrote of

---

[13] Roby, *Theol. Lect.* 1, 'The Existence or Being of God'. Roby was aware that not everyone saw providential harmony in the universe, and he noted that atheists repudiated the idea of a benevolent providence: 'In opposition to the being of God, [atheists] urge: (i) The existence of useless and noxious creatures; (ii) The existence of moral evil; (iii) The prosperity of the wicked and the afflictions of the righteous, (iv) The craft of politicians who keep up the idea of God, to serve their own designs.' Roby dismissed these points as trivial.

[14] Roby, *Theol. Lect.* 38, 'On Providence'.

[15] Cf. Roby, *Theol. Lect.* 38, 'On Providence': 'The ends [purpose] of Divine providence [are] (i) that God may be glorified; (ii) that Christ may be honoured in his people and upon his enemies; (iii) the good of the Church; (iv) the *welfare* and *final blessedness* of believers individually; (v) the fulfillment of God's designs in the conversion of sinners ... (vi) to execute vengeance on the wicked.' (196). In the same lecture, Roby rejected deism: 'Some allow a general, but deny a particular, providence. ... This is contrary to Scripture.'

God's creatures needing God's constant care. But benevolence to individuals was secondary to the Divine honour.

Ralph Wardlaw: The Emotional Dimension

Nineteenth-century evangelical theology had many treatises, similar to Roby's, which gave comprehensive doctrinal explanations of providence. However, we need to look behind formal presentations to understand the religion of the heart when faced with tension between trust in God and the events of life. We need an evangelical theologian who spoke on providence whilst personally affected by tragedy, and in which he spoke from his grief, rather than repeating theological mantras, possibly in denial of his true emotions. An example is a sermon preached by Ralph Wardlaw in 1812.[16] Wardlaw was deeply involved in the LMS. He was from an evangelical Scottish Congregationalist background. He was admired by Moffat.[17] And Wardlaw gave an evangelical theologian's understanding of providence as it related to personal heartache, when he lost his brother John during the Napoleonic Wars at the battle of Salamanca on 22 July 1812.

There were many nineteenth-century sermons on providence and disaster, with calamities ranging from cholera arriving in a community, to famine in Ireland, to a flood sweeping villagers to their death. In almost every instance the cause of disaster was seen as sin in the nation or community. But Wardlaw's sermon made no recourse to this argument. It is precisely because he excluded this, that his presentation is intriguing. If sin was not a reason, why did tragedy strike? Wardlaw took as the text for his sermon Matthew 10:29f: 'Are not two sparrows sold for a farthing? And one of them shall not fall on the ground without your Father. But the very hairs of your head are all numbered. Fear ye not, therefore, ye are of more value than many sparrows.'

The short title of Wardlaw's sermon was: *The Doctrine of a Particular Providence.* The word 'Particular' is critical. Contemporary theology divided the doctrine of providence under two headings. Firstly, General Providence, which referred to God's overall purposes of creation, salvation, etc. Secondly,

---

16 Ralph Wardlaw, *The Doctrine of a Particular Providence. A Sermon preached in Albion Street Chapel, Glasgow, on Lord's Day August 23rd, 1812, on Occasion of the Death of the Author's Brother, Captain John Wardlaw, who fell in the Battle of Salamanca on the 22nd of the Preceding Month*, (NLS). The sermon conveyed both Wardlaw's theology and his feelings. There is no separate section on the doctrine of providence in Wardlaw's *Systematic Theology.*

17 RM, *To Mary Moffat*, 22.8.1857, (*MJ2*, 39): 'I have finished Wardlaw's *Memoirs.* What a man! How little and ugly one looks beside such a giant.'

Particular Providence, which referred to God's fatherly involvement in specific events of daily life. It was the doctrine of *particular* providence which had the potential for heart-searching. In his sermon, Wardlaw withheld reference to his personal sorrow until two-thirds through it. Then he stated: 'As certainly as the disease is sent by providence so certainly is the ball that pierces the heart of a son, or a brother, and lays him low in the land of strangers, guided to its fatal destination, amidst the din, and smoke, and confusion of the battle, by the eye of the omniscient God'.[18] Then, though grieving for his brother even as he delivered his sermon, Wardlaw set out a lucid argument:

1. Providence must affect every detail of life. Wardlaw stated that a superintending providence cannot be questioned by any who is convinced that there is a God, and that the Universe owes its existence to his creative power. Furthermore, any providence worthy of the name must not be *general* only, but *particular,* including all events in all circumstances. He argued that this was a fixed principle in the Scriptures: 'If [God] exercises no immediate superintendence over the affairs of his creatures, our praises and our prayers are the vain offerings of ignorance and folly.'[19]

2. The nature of God as the 'Lord' demands the doctrine. Wardlaw further argued that, in the Scriptures, Jehovah is consistently presented as 'Governor among the nations', with 'Governor'[20] referring to God's providential care of creation, as much as to God giving the Law. Moreover, 'Governor' implies that all history, if properly interpreted, must be seen as a series of planned actions by God: 'I entertain no doubt that we only want an inspired history of the last twenty years to show us these same principles in uniform and uninterrupted exercise, to keep before our view a constantly presiding Deity by whom everything is adjusted and directed to its end.' [21] If God were not Lord of all circumstances, then he was not Lord of any.

3. Reason, not just Scripture, demands the doctrine. Wardlaw argued that the doctrine of particular providence fitted in with the conclusions of

---

18 Wardlaw, *The Doctrine of a Particular Providence,* 21.

19 Ibid, 25, 27.

20 God as 'Governor' was a title frequently used in the Westminster and Puritan tradition. Roby, *Theol. Lect.* 38, 'On Providence', stated that the providence of God included both the preservation of all things, and the government of all things.

21 Wardlaw, *The Doctrine of a Particular Providence,* 3-5.

'enlightened reason'.[22] 'Whatever it was worthy of God's power to create, it cannot surely be unworthy of that power to *preserve* and *superintend*.'[23]

So far, Wardlaw's argument was along well-trodden paths of evangelical thought from a Calvinist perspective: God is the Lord; all happens under his authority; anything less compromises the divine dignity. However, when Wardlaw came to deal with the tension between providence affecting every detail of life, and the contingency of free human agency, a gap appeared in his reasoning. He admitted this gap. The problem was causality. Wardlaw wrestled with the problem of causality and reached an impasse, admitting that the doctrine of a particular providence had difficulties with, 'the control which this doctrine supposes the Deity to exercise over the volitions of free agents.'[24] Wardlaw asserted two propositions:[25]

1. *Men must be free.* Liberty is necessary to the very idea of their being accountable creatures.
2. *The Divine Being must have some kind of control over the will of these free agents.* Otherwise, the volitions of finite creatures may frustrate the purposes of divine wisdom and the operations of almighty power, which is unthinkable.

Given these propositions, and given Wardlaw's refusal to blame all misfortune on sin, he came to an impasse. Yet he refused to abandon either proposition since each was important to his personal faith. He insisted: 'That *we cannot discover a reconciling principle* between the two propositions which have just been stated, can never be a sufficient reason for questioning the truth either of the one or of the other.'[26] Though deism, with its God not intervening directly in human affairs, offered an exit, Wardlaw dismissed that solution, since his heart-faith was in an imminent, superintending God. He also dismissed any idea that there was an element of randomness or chance in the events of life. 'Speak not of the *fate of war* or the *chance of battle.* It is the language of heathenism. It is the language of atheism'.[27]

---

22 Ibid, 1. Wardlaw did not mean 'Enlightenment reason': he meant reason which had been enlightened by faith and scripture.

23 Ibid, 5.

24 Ibid, 13.

25 Ibid, 14.

26 Ibid, 15, (our italics).

27 Ibid, 20. Wardlaw quoted the line, 'All chance [is] direction which we cannot see', a phrase from Alexander Pope's, *Essay on Man.* The fuller quotation is: 'All Nature is but Art, unknown to thee; All Chance, Direction, which thou canst not see; All Discord, Harmony not understood; All partial Evil, universal Good.' Against any doctrine of chance, Wardlaw was prepared to state that the gunshot which killed his brother was: 'guided to its fatal destination, amidst the

This was strong meat for the congregation of Glasgow's Albion Street Chapel, as they listened to their young minister wrestling with the theological implications of his brother's death. He bared his soul that day. In the end he was simply saying: 'I don't know. I don't fully understand. But I still believe. And I still trust.' As a believer who reflected deeply on his faith, Wardlaw was self-compelled to seek some kind of reconciliation to the paradox of suffering and God's providence. In the end, his solution was to base truth in the *analogy of Scripture* rather than in the *consistency of statements.*

There are three well-established and linked criteria for truth: consistency, correspondence, and pragmatism. *Consistency* usually refers to a logical consistency between statements. *Correspondence* usually refers to a correspondence between a statement and an objective event or entity which is empirically verifiable. *Pragmatism* states that 'truth' is whatever 'works'. If we consider the following cluster of statements: 'God cares', 'God will protect', 'Tragedy strikes', then there is an instant problem with the consistency test. A similar problem occurs if the pragmatic test for truth is applied: God has not protected, therefore the doctrine has not 'worked'. But what about the correspondence test? If faith statements are analogous to something which we already accept as being true, then such faith statements may also be true, even though in our limited wisdom we cannot grasp the principle which connects them.

This was the line which Wardlaw followed, applying the *analogy of Scripture*. Wardlaw regarded Scripture as absolute truth. Therefore, if any life-event corresponded to Scripture truth then it also, *ipso facto,* must be true. He considered Matthew 10:29f, which speaks of God caring for every sparrow, implying a benevolent providence sustaining God's servants, and then cited the sufferings, shipwrecks, beatings, and the imprisonment of the apostles:

> Did these words [Matthew 10:29f] imply that they [Apostles] were never to suffer? Or if they did suffer, that they should, at least, be so protected by Divine providence as never to die in the cause of their master? Subsequent facts show that no such assurance was intended.[28]

---

din, and smoke, and confusion of the battle, by the eye of the omniscient God'. On a similar note, on the way to Moselekatse in 1857, Moffat travelled light though he knew it was a slightly risky strategy. He wrote, *Journal,* 31.8.1857, (*MJ2,* 49): 'We find [it] absolutely necessary to exercise unshaken faith in the Divine promise and Divine government. For, as Dr Cumming justly remarks, 'There are no trifles in the biography of man'. Saith the Scripture, 'Man's goings are of the Lord'. Every little link, no matter how small, makes up the chain of events in human life.' Moffat was not deterministic, but saw God's hand in every detail of life.

[28] Wardlaw, *The Doctrine of a Particular Providence,* 18.

Wardlaw believed that if events in a believer's life had an *analogy* in Scripture, then there was no theological issue. Were events—painful though they may be—consistent with the sacred history recorded in Scripture? He did not appeal to a *philosophical* consistency, but to a *sacred* consistency, even if not yet understood. He wrote: 'My suffering can be consistent with providence because it is analogous to the suffering of the Apostles who, by common consent, were sustained in every way by God'. The Scriptures were the irreducible foundation of faith. If real life experiences were in harmony with the Scriptures, there was no ultimate theological problem, despite pain of heart and perplexity of mind. The Word, as the foundation for evangelical theology, was the yardstick for credibility. This would also lie behind Moffat's reactions in later years. Moffat did not have Wardlaw's theological mind, but his approach was essentially the same.

PROVIDENCE AND BLESSING

Any exposition of Moffat's doctrine of providence needs also to view its application in good times as well as bad. Moffat's writings are full of trust in God providing, and full of thankfulness for instances of blessing. For example, from 1835: '[We had] a load of anxiety which seemed at times more than frail nature could support. But out of all those the Lord hath delivered us, and his name be praised.'[29] Another example is from the 1854 journey to Moselekatse when the cattle wandered off from the encampment but were untouched by lions: 'How much we have to be thankful for, whether in the teeming city or the secret solitude! How condescending is the infinite and eternal Jehovah to guide and guard such helpless sinful worms!'[30]

These positive experiences of providence ministered to core human needs, and fostered feelings of well-being. But what are the essential core-needs of life? Abraham Maslow identified the need to *Survive* as the basic and fundamental human need, closely followed by *Security*, *Belonging*, *Appreciation*, and *Service*.[31] Using this list as a yardstick it is clear that if a believer is to *feel* that God truly cares and provides, then the foundational needs of Survival and Security require to be met.

---

29 RM, *To Richard Moffat,* 12.6.1835, (*MJ1,* 131).

30 RM, *Journal,* 28.6.1854, (*MJ1,* 202, & *MJ2,* 132, & 188).

31 Abraham Maslow (1908-1970). Cf. David Cormack, *Why Did I Do That: Understanding and Mastering Your Motives,* (Ldn: Hodder & Stoughton, 1997), 31f.

Moffat once recorded that it was divine providence which provided antelope meat in the middle of the desert when hunger was intense.[32] On another occasion, in 1854 when Moffat reached Moselekatse, Moffat was in good health, but somehow, within a few days, he was lame from a severe knee infection. But Moffat viewed this sudden and unexpected infirmity as a blessing of providence since Moselekatse was also extremely lame. Moffat wrote: 'I am in the Lord's hands, and I am confident that all will be for the best. It is for *wise reasons* that I should arrive in greatly improved health, with a sturdy body, as nimble perhaps as I was wont to be, *and then the very next day a cripple from an inflamed knee*, without the most imaginable cause, as if to keep Moselekatse company'.[33] For Moffat, divine providence had provided a fellowship of infirmity to deepen the relationship between the two men. He was convinced that everything from God's hands was intended for good outcomes and thus had meaningful purpose.[34]

After deliverance from a lion, Moffat stated: 'We bowed the knee to Him who had mercifully preserved us'.[35] At another time, divine providence was seen as being responsible for Moffat's very experienced wagon-driver inexplicably losing a path he knew well, but thereby avoiding a large group of lions who had gathered at the water pool which the party had been aiming for.[36] Divine providence was also deemed responsible for granting escape from hippopotami. After one such experience Moffat wrote: 'It was with the liveliest gratitude to our heavenly Father that we reviewed the mercies of the day'.[37] He did not take safety for granted: it was a specific blessing of providence.

On another journey, he wrote that it was simply divine protection which ensured that 'no evil befell us during the night'.[38] Again, in 1823, when the fledgling mission was threatened by migrating tribes, Moffat interpreted the deliverance of the station as another striking example of divine providence.[39] The providential protection of God was so strong in Moffat's theology that even Moselekatse began to respect it. Though Moselekatse never converted

---

32 RM, *MLSSA,* 170. For a similar expression of total trust in God's provision see: Mary Moffat, *To her Parents,* 8.4.1820 (JSM, *Lives,* 81).

33 RM, *Journal,* 27.7.1854, (*MJ1,* 241).

34 In Moffat's theology, ill-health may be for a specific positive purpose, or it may be because of a chastisement from the Lord. Mary Moffat also accepted illness as part of God's chastisement (Mary Moffat, *To her Parents,* 9.12.1822, (*AAK,* 65)).

35 RM, *MLSSA,* 161.

36 RM, *MLSSA,* 167.

37 RM, *MLSSA,* 171.

38 RM, *Journal,* 24.6.1854, (*MJ1,* 199).

39 RM, *Journal,* 26.6.1823, (*AAK,* 95, 96).

to Christianity, he had a superstitious respect for the protective power of Moffat's God. When he heard of Boers near at hand he said: 'No man can trust them. They are seeking to kill Moselekatse and Moshete [Moffat], but Moshete's God will not permit them, for he prays; and therefore we shall trust and not now fight with them.'[40]

Though acceptance of the protective power of Moffat's God did not make Moselekatse a believer, one of the factors which made an impression on those who did convert was any experience in which God's intervention was seen as the cause of their protection. If God were seen as the protector of life, or as the supplier of food—both of which are core human needs—then faith came more readily. Moffat gave an account of Nicholas Berends' testimony to the providence of God miraculously protecting him from Titus Africaner's bullet, and of the impression which that made on him.[41] Conviction of supernatural protection often made more impression than conviction of sin, since protection related to survival. When Moffat's God was seen as relevant to these, then the heart was more open to him.

In Moffat's theology, divine providence regulated the course of events so that the right thing happened at the right time, even though that perfect timing might only be seen in hindsight. For example, in 1857 when Moffat was among the Ndebele, he wanted to explore for fountains where a future mission station could be sited. As he prepared the wagons for the survey expedition it rained heavily for several days. Unable to set out, he pondered the immediate future:

> If rains fall heavy and constant, there will be scarcely a possibility of traveling with a wagon. *Doorslag* [boggy ground] will be in every hollow, and, if rains are continuous, even ascents and descents will be attended with difficulty and danger from the nature of the soil of this country north of the Shashane River. But I leave all things with Him, my God and Saviour, who, I firmly hope, has sent me hither for purposes of mercy.[42]

After several frustrating days, Moffat wrote: 'The thunder continues and rains falling heavy [but] I leave all to the care of him who has said, 'Commit your ways to Jehovah and he will direct your paths'.[43] When things did get moving, all went so well that he recorded his thankfulness that he had started

---

40 RM, *Journal,* 26.8.1854, (*MJ1,* 273).

41 RM, *MLSSA,* 81.

42 RM, *Journal,* 21.11.1857, (*MJ2,* 122).

43 RM, *Journal,* 22.11.1857, (*MJ2,* 123). Moffat's trust, despite continued rain, is expressed on page 133: God would do what is best and fitting.

'neither a day earlier or later'.[44] In God's providence, everything was timed for the best outcome at the right time.

Providence and Darkness

Moffat did not restrict 'providence' to outcomes which human beings welcomed. It included whatever God provided. Judgment came from God, so even judgment could be considered providence. In a fully Calvinist theology providence included whatever God decided to do in any situation for the furtherance of his glory. Thus, the provision of punitive judgment as response to sin could also be an act of providence. From a human perspective, providence may appear to have a 'dark' side, but from the divine perspective it was simply the establishing of God's righteousness and goodness in a given situation.

Nevertheless, though it might be easy to accept the 'dark' side of providence when those who suffer are obvious sinners and murderers, what of other circumstances? Ralph Wardlaw affirmed trust in the all-embracing providence of God, despite the grievous loss he had suffered.[45] In the end, he trusted in the nature of God the Father, and he concluded his sermon on providence with a long section on the character of God, especially God's immutable love.[46] But how did Moffat translate this onto the mission-field?

A concept of the 'darkness of God' hovered in the background of evangelical thought.[47] Moffat accepted there was 'darkness' in providence. There was a darkness which God permitted. And there was a darkness which God decreed. Early Protestantism felt no need to defend the character of God from theodicy. God did what he willed, and whatever God willed was right, just, good and perfect. Later Protestantism, aware of rationalist critiques, became conscious of the need to justify that position. A common solution was to make a distinction between God's active will and God's

---

44 RM, *Journal,* 9.12.1857, (*MJ2,* 140. See also 143).

45 Wardlaw, *The Doctrine of a Particular Providence,* 21: 'Take away the firm conviction of this blessed truth and you take away the most soothing balsam of a bleeding heart. Shake the conviction of this truth and you unfix the 'anchor of the soul' and leave the poor frail vessel the sport of contending elements.'

46 Wardlaw, *The Doctrine of a Particular Providence,* 25, 27: 'In joy and sorrow, life and death, his love is still the same.'

47 John Bruce of Forfar (13.1.1814), preached on: *The Moral Discipline of Divine Providence,* (Dundee: Rintoul, 1814). Bruce pointed to Psalm 73:7,8 'In the hand of the Lord there is a cup of *mixture* and he poureth out the same.' Bruce urged his congregation to yield to the inscrutable will of God. his approach was typical of the age.

permissive will. God had no hand in sin, but he might permit it.[48] God might withdraw the influence of his grace, but he was never the cause of evil. Moffat absorbed this theology which, in his mind, enabled prayer, providence and the permissive will of God to go together. Thus, for Moffat, it was valid to pray that God would not *permit* misfortune to overtake a person: 'We only hope that no such evil will be *permitted* to befall us'.[49] But some events may be permitted for reasons human beings could not fathom. God knew more. Thus, belief in providence was not a belief in immunity from evil. It was a trust that all was within God's knowledge; and, because he loved his people, all would eventually work together for good. In a letter to Emma Sapworth, Moffat referred to the Tay Bridge Disaster in Scotland:[50]

> Tay Bridge storms sending to the depths 100s of men and women: The elements would seem as if out of course, but our Heavenly Father knows all and orders and allows all for objects unseen by us but guided by infinite wisdom.[51]

From time to time, difficulties may be permitted specifically in order to remind the forgetful believer of God's normal gracious provision. For example, in 1857 Moffat and his party had such great difficulty finding water that they had to break the Sabbath in order to locate a supply. Having achieved this, the exhausted party held a service of thanksgiving, focusing on Psalm 107: but in the late afternoon the oxen were frightened by the scent of a lion, and, before Moffat realised what was happening, some oxen stampeded in panic. Moffat was shaken and sore, but suffered no serious injury. Looking back on the incident he wrote: 'Perhaps the accident was *permitted* to impress my mind with the divine care that has been exercised over us in our wanderings.'[52]

---

48 Watson, *A Body of Divinity,* 86, considered whether the concept of God 'permitting sin' made God culpable: 'Is it a likely thing that God should make a law against sin, and then have a hand in breaking his own law?', 'Had not sin been permitted, God's justice in punishing sin, and his mercy in pardoning sin, had not been so well known. *The Lord is pleased to permit it, but he has no hand in sin*.' Watson then employed an argument parallel to Augustine's notion that evil is simply an absence of the good: 'God does not infuse evil into men, *he withdraws the influence of his grace*, and then the heart hardens of itself; even as the light being withdrawn, darkness presently follows in the air; but it were absurd to say, that therefore the light darkens the air.' (86).

49 RM, *Journal,* 26.6.1854, (*MJ1,* 201). Livingstone, *To Janet Livingston,* 20.4.1849, (*DLFL,* Vol. 2, 35), expressed the same idea more strongly: 'Satan seems anxious to destroy our mission [Kolobeng], but a chained dog cannot bite unless his master loosens him.'

50 The railway bridge over the River Tay collapsed on 31.12.1879 with 75 deaths.

51 RM, *To Miss Emma Sapworth,* 6.12.1880, (SOAS/CWM/Africa/Moffat/ Pers/4).

52 RM, *Journal,* 7.9.1857, (*MJ2,* 56).

In Moffat's thinking, God did not cause the event but permitted it: and he did so for the purpose of reminding Moffat of all the good things he normally received from God. This theology was totally in accord with the *Confession of Faith* which moulded Scottish piety.[53] But God permitting minor difficulties for educational purposes was one thing. God permitting major catastrophes required deeper reflection.

Sometimes, there was the suggestion that darkness occurred because God positively ordained it. In 1854, journeying through remote bush, Moffat wrote: 'We have just had our evening worship. I often think how comforting the thought is that nothing can happen to us without God's will or permission, and how entirely we are at his disposal. We are never certain when danger is near.'[54] A few days later: 'Hitherto all has gone well, and I feel perfectly resigned to whatever God *appoints*'.[55] In using the word 'appoint', Moffat went beyond the notion of God merely permitting. God may *appoint,* or cause, such circumstances. Moffat also used the word 'appoint' when writing of the death of his infant son Robert.[56]

The subtle movement from God being the *permissive* cause of darkness, to being its *active* cause was also suggested in Moffat's 1821 account concerning a rainmaker whom the Tswana imported at considerable expense. 1821 was a time of prolonged drought, and Moffat was disturbed that the Tswana turned to a rainmaker rather than simply trusting God. Initially, Moffat wrote in terms of God's permissive will: 'Mysterious are the ways of God, that he should *permit* a worm [the rainmaker], a deceiver, to lead a whole nation captive to his will.'[57] Moffat believed that there should be 'trust whether providence is light or *dark'.*[58]

Moffat continued: 'In the evening I preached from Psalm 97:2. I chose this text with a view to exhibit the righteousness and judgment of Jehovah in all his dealings with man, even though a *dark providence* intervenes.'[59] Psalm 97:2, which Moffat preached from, stated: *'Clouds and thick darkness*

---

53 Cf. *Westminster Confession,* Ch. 5: 'Of Providence'.

54 RM, *Journal,* 16.6.1854, (*MJ1,* 185).

55 RM, *Journal,* 18.6.1854, (*MJ1,* 187).

56 RM, *To Kitchingham,* 24.9.1825 (Le Cordeur, *Kitchingham Papers,* 81).

57 RM, *Journal,* 29.11.1821, (*AAK,* 35).

58 RM, *Journal,* 23.8.1821, (*AAK,* 25). Cf. RM, *To Alexander Moffat*, 9.12.1824, (*AAK,* 164): 'For a while our hopes were raised, but dark and intricate are the ways of Providence, for these hopes [of peace among the tribes near the Kuruman] were soon blasted by a civil war, which acquired such a magnitude as to oblige us speedily to abandon the station and retire to [Griqua Town].'

59 RM, *Journal,* 23.8.1821, (*AAK,* 25).

surround him; righteousness and justice are the foundation of his throne.' Moffat was not connecting these 'clouds' with 'rain clouds', but to the notion of a 'darkness' which surrounded God himself. In his sovereign purposes, God might bring the darkness.

Moffat's message was simple: 'Do not look for magic. Simply trust, whatever happens.' This was difficult for his hearers to accept since they were in a desperate situation of drought and possible starvation. Moreover, Moffat refused to promise that his God would provide rain, because God's ways were inscrutable, and a true believer would simply trust. Providence could be dark. The role of the believer was to trust and obey. Moffat was affirming a Calvinist and Puritan interpretation of life under God's direction: accept darkness as part of trustfulness.[60] He was not saying that there was a hidden aspect of God's character hiding behind his love—the *Deus absconditus* of some Reformed thought—he was simply reflecting the theology of his day which accepted the inscrutability of God's will, though convinced of God's ultimate benevolent purposes.

The suggestion that a dark providence had the purpose of training men and women in discipleship was a regular theme. Providence sent difficulties in order to encourage those afflicted to be more devoted to God.[61] Providence *had to* be purposeful, with goodness as its ultimate goal. Providence sending difficulties as 'discipleship training' was in the young Moffat's assertion that it was sometimes 'good to be afflicted'. He wrote to James Kitchingham: 'It gave me considerable pleasure to see by your letter that Mrs Kitchingham had got considerably better. I hope her soul also prospereth: and, like David, saying it was good for her that she was afflicted.'[62] Again, writing in 1821, Moffat gave two examples of God allowing difficulties so as to move his people to greater devotion and zeal:

> Two alarming *providences* [a hurricane damaging the house, and lightning striking near the house] and the heavy affliction of my dear partner[63] have impressed my mind to no small degree. At first it appeared that it was not the will of God that we should remain here, but when I reflected on the existing circumstances ... I was confident that I had not erred in abiding here for a season, but they [the trials and difficulties] were evident calls to *greater*

---

60 This was absorbed into the theology of the Great Awakening. Cf. Jonathan Edwards, *On Religious Affections*: 'It is the duty of God's people to trust in him when in darkness, and though they remain still in darkness.' Romans 8:28 was central to such a theology as the eschatological justification of history.

61 This was the attitude adopted by Isabella Price of the Makololo expedition when her infant daughter Eliza died. Cf. Isabella Price, *Journal,* 9.3.1860, (Slater, *Isabella Price,* 145f).

62 RM, *To Kitchingham,* 8.5.1817, (Le Cordeur, *Kitchingham Papers,* 37).

63 Mary Moffat had a severe illness towards the end of 1820, (JSM, *Lives,* 96).

devotedness and zeal in the missionary work. And I trust that the Lord has granted an increase of grace to that effect, for we both feel willing to devote body and soul, night and day, to [the] service of our Redeemer'.[64]

God allowing 'minor' misfortunes in order to foster deeper discipleship became a regular theme. The idea of training was reinforced by Moffat's use of 'probation' in an 1878 letter.[65] Providence was not necessarily for human comfort, but was to challenge and train the people of God. If the outcome was for the good of a believer, then even difficulties should be considered blessings.

Growth in discipleship required growth of trust. Providence may permit or ordain events which, precisely by being incomprehensible and mysterious, challenged the believer to trust God even in the darkness. True darkness is impossible to understand. It provides no reasons. It clothes itself in mystery. The challenge is to trust even more. As he grew older, Moffat frequently alluded to providence being mysterious. Mystery came when the *meaning* behind events was hidden; and meaning might be *deliberately* hidden in order to make the believer trust even more. In 1874 Moffat wrote to his friend William Dickson, not offering any explanation of God's ways, but acknowledging a mystery in providence, to which the only response was more trust that, in God, there were reasons for what had occurred:

> [I intended to write earlier] little thinking that our heavenly Father had touched you and reduced you to such extreme weakness. Such visitations of a Father's hand are sometimes, to us, unable to scan the Divine purpose, *mysterious*, but our consolation, even under the severest trial is that our dear Saviour [loves] while he sees reason for transferring our affections to his own glorious abode. My heart feels for you while I desire to look up to the upper sanctuary that the compassionate smiles of Him who loves you may sooth, solace and cheer you in your solitary sleepless hours.[66]

Moffat had no easy explanation and no glib solutions.[67] But he would trust. And he would trust despite the darkness. He believed that, in Christ, there were valid, albeit hidden, reasons.

---

64 RM, *To John Melvill,* probably January 1821, (*AAK,* 11).

65 RM, *To Miss Jessie Watt,* 2.3.1878, (SOAS/CWM/Africa/Moffat/ Pers/4).

66 RM, *To William Dickson,* 31.10.1874, (EUNCL/WD9/3/7/Box 2).

67 In his 1867 LMS report, Moffat mentioned the unexpected death of young Mrs Brown who had just arrived in the mission field. Moffat again used the word 'mysterious': 'It was a most painful season to us all, and especially to our deeply affected brother. She had fondly persuaded herself that she had ended her journey and entered the scene of many years labour, but He on whose service she had embarked, thought otherwise. How *mysterious* these things are!' The exclamation mark is in Moffat's own text. Cf. RM, *To Rev. Mullen,* 1.1.1867, (SOAS/CWM/SA/Reports Box 1). Concerning the same incident John Smith Moffat described

Moffat also regarded judgment as part of providence. For example, in 1824, before the outbreak of a civil war among local groups, Moffat unsuccessfully addressed a meeting: 'I expostulated with them on the criminality of their conduct towards God, who had so lately *warned* and awed them with the Mantatee invasion.' Moffat made it clear that the God who had delivered them in the past would not continue to do so since they had not turned to him: 'We pointed out that their indifference toward the Gospel of Christ gave us little reason to hope for that deliverance which had been so singularly displayed on former occasions.'[68] God might warn by permitting misfortune. That misfortune was still an act of providence since it was intended for ultimate good. The mercy of God was not simply for physical protection; it was to give time for repentance. This was touched on in Moffat's 1854 conversations with Moselekatse:

> [Moselekatse] had again been permitted [by God] to rally after the loss of many thousands of the flower of his army [at Mosega], and ... God, who is merciful, in his *providence* had now sent me to warn and beseech him to seek peace with all men; that he and his people had now heard so much from me respecting the will of God and the love of God that he could, from his superior power, make peace with the surrounding tribes on his own terms ... I added that he might wonder that I, a solitary defenceless individual, should take upon me [to] reprove as well as to counsel one whom so many thousands would tremble to offend. I did so because I was a messenger sent from God and that in a very short time he and I must stand at that bar of God's judgment of which I had repeatedly told him. I reminded him again of God's son.[69]

Thus far, God had been patient in his providential mercy, having given a warning at Mosega in 1836. But because warnings were ignored then the following judgment was also providence, though it was now a 'retributive providence'.[70] Moffat also used this phrase in relation to the fate of banditti who had harassed Waterboer's Griqua, with Moffat interpreting events as the execution of divine displeasure:

---

it as an enigma, eschewing any simplistic explanation of events (JSM, *Lives,* 361). The Browns arrived at Kuruman in early 1866. Mrs Brown became ill in April and died in August. John Brown then went to Taung where he worked for many years.

68 RM, *To Alexander Moffat,* 9.12.1824, (*AAK,* 164, 166).

69 RM, *Journal,* 5.10.1854, (*MJ1,* 323). Cf, RM, *Journal,* 5.6.1854, (*MJ1,* 155) where Moffat applied the same doctrine to other tribes.

70 In nineteenth-century evangelicalism, retributive providence was viewed as part of divine strategy in establishing justice upon the earth. David Bogue argued for Christian pacifism on the grounds that nations which pursued a policy of absolute peace, as part of their obedience of faith in the Gospel, would be protected from predatory nations by the retributive providence of a just God. Roby also included God's judgment of the wicked under the heading of providence (Roby, *Theol. Lect.* 38, 'On Providence', 194, 196).

> A *retributive providence* accomplished that which Waterboer had neither men nor means to carry into effect; for he could neither punish the banditti to which his government gave rise, nor defend those who fell a prey to the fearful havoc they made of property and human life. After they had filled their cup, Heaven frowned on them; and those who escaped the war-club and the javelin, disease swept away. ... The bones of the majority lie bleached on many a barren waste, addressing the living in solemn language, "He that taketh the sword shall perish by the sword". The finger of God was so evident that even the Griquas themselves could not help fearing that their former cruelties committed on the Bushmen would not go unpunished.'[71]

When the Boers moved out of the Colony in the 1830s they overwhelmed the Ndebele at Mosega to such an extent that Moselekatse had to retreat far to the north. Moffat had no affection for the Boers, and Moselekatse was his friend, but he saw God's retributive providence at work. For Moffat, God judged the Ndebele for the slaughter they had perpetrated in previous years:

> The evils now coming on the Matabele are only what I expected. Moselekatse has ruled with an iron sceptre, and his warriors have, full often unprovoked, shed the blood of thousands, and thousands more have been driven from affluence to the most abject poverty. I have more than once told him that if he did not change his government and prohibit deliberate destruction of human life, the innocent blood which deluged his country would soon call down vengeance from heaven. It is to us blind creatures, *in the awful mysteries of Providence*, painful to see professing Christians [Boers] becoming the sword of Jehovah[72].

Retributive providence as a synonym for judgment was integral to Moffat's theological understanding. Yet it was still providence.

THE AGENT OF DARKNESS

For Moffat, the sovereign providence of God touched every area of life. No truly accidental events ever occurred. But might secondary causes be involved? In effect, Moffat admitted none. We have already seen that, apart from when God's providence became God's judgment upon warlike peoples, 'sin' was rarely introduced by Moffat as an explanation for events. Moffat did not indulge in introspective searches for secret sins as the causes of divine displeasure. Yet there were other spiritual forces to consider.

Moffat occasionally wrote about battle against Satan, and he accepted the reality of Satan. Nevertheless, he rarely ascribed specific events to satanic agency. Satan had a 'kingdom' or 'realm of influence' which existed

---

71 RM, *MLSSA*, 204.

72 RM, *To Mr Smith, Dukinfield,* 5.4.1838, (JSM, *Lives,* 218).

apart from God's kingdom, and Moffat envisaged Satan having 'influence' with that 'sphere of operations'. But he never allowed Satan being able to intrude upon, or affect the work or purpose of, God or the people of God. For Moffat, Satan was the agent who inspired the religious dances in the villages, but he was never cited as able to interfere with God's servants. Moffat would rather refer to the *mysterious* providence of God, than acknowledge that satanic forces may be to blame for an event.

Nothing competed with the sovereignty of God. There were no other authorities worthy of even a grudging respect. Moffat had no dualism between the power of God and the power of the Devil. This was characteristic of Calvinist theology in general. On the one hand, the powers of evil were acknowledged as real. On the other hand, they were never given the honour of being the determinative force in a specific situation. God alone was sovereign. All things happened within God's plan and providence. God had no rival.

Neither did Moffat try to solve the mystery of misfortune by appealing to influences from the spirit world. Though this could have given him a point of contact with indigenous beliefs, he again would not dilute the sovereignty of God. The Tswana held that each family was under the direct guidance of its own agnatic ancestors, who were interested only in the affairs of their own descendants.[73] And the Tswana accepted that misfortune could be ascribed to an offence against an ancestor.

For the Tswana, 'offence against an ancestor' provided a full explanation of anything that befell a person, with no theological puzzles. The problem of theodicy was eliminated at a stroke! In contrast, Moffat brought a faith which created difficulties where previously there had been none. His theology incorporated an apparent conflict between the character of God and what that same God permitted, or ordained, his people to suffer.[74]

Moffat looked for no explanation for events other than God being responsible for everything. He thought in terms of submitting to the hand of a loving God. And God's purposes would ultimately be understood. God alone guided human destiny. Moffat's mission was to change a whole way of

---

[73] Schapera, *The Tswana,* 59. Alice Werner argued that, among traditional Bantu, it was believed that a man got direction from his father's spirit before starting on any undertaking, either through dreams, a diviner, or omens (*Myths and Legends of the Bantu,* 19).

[74] Absence of rain was easily accounted for by the Tswana. It was the consequence of improper conduct by the tribe or an individual. Moffat's theology was less simple: and, even with the option of appealing to a retributive providence, absence of rain from Moffat's God was not easy to explain.

thinking, and to convey a faith in which the first of the Ten Commandments was established as a fundamental axiom. No other gods were to be acknowledged. No glory was to be given to another. What was adhered to at all costs was that God was the Lord, beside him there was none. It was not that evil spirits did not exist in Moffat's theology. They did. But their 'authority' was never to be recognised. The accusation that this gave God a schizoid character as the author of both good and evil would be met by faith.

In Moffat's evangelical circles, true faith was rooted in the affections of the heart toward Christ. It was the strength of this emotional commitment to Christ which covered the inexplicable and the perplexing. And if this love covered 'a multitude of sins', then it also covered 'a multitude of questions' concerning the providence of God and suffering.

Chapter 11
The Testing of Providence

THE SUPREME TEST OF Moffat's trust in the providential care of God came with the Makololo tragedy of 1860, which Moffat termed 'the fatal Makololo mission'.[1] The Makololo disaster raised questions concerning divine purpose, the efficacy of prayer, and simple trust. It was a mission swathed in prayer, hope and trust, yet almost every member of the missionary group died before even starting any gospel activity.[2] It was not the number of deaths as such which raised questions, but the impact on faith. In missionary activity the believer understood that he or she was invited to place confidence in the providence of God. But did the Makololo outcome also create the feeling that trust had been violated?[3]

Livingstone's visit to Britain in 1856-57 had fired missionary enthusiasm, with a special interest in the Ndebele and Makololo. Livingstone spoke highly of the Makololo and their chief Sekeletu, with whom he had established a good personal relationship. The LMS, inspired by this fresh missionary enthusiasm—and without consulting Moffat—resolved to establish twin missions among the Ndebele and the Makololo, who were about a hundred miles apart. Having decided this policy, the LMS Directors wrote to Moffat in 1857 proposing that he should go for twelve months to Moselekatse, taking two younger men with him, and help plant a mission there.

The LMS letter reached Moffat at Kuruman as he completed translating and printing the Old Testament. He was astonished. Yet, despite being faced with a 600-mile ox-wagon journey in each direction at the age of 61, he made up his mind to go to at once. He felt it vital to make a preparatory visit to gain permission from Moselekatse for the coming of the missionary party.[4]

---

1 RM, *To William Dickson*, 28.5.1875, (EUNCL/WD9/3/9/Box2).

2 The LMS *Annual Report* 1861 (for 1860), devotes eleven pages (9-19) to the tragedy.

3 For sources, see the following. (i) John Mackenzie, *To Tidman, LMS,* 4.12.1860 (SOAS/CWM/32/1/A). (ii) Roger Price*, To Tidman, LMS,* 20.2.1861 SOAS/CWM/32/3/A. (iii) (c) Roger Price, *To Mrs Stuart,* 4.12.1860, (SOAS/CWM, Africa Personal Box 1/28). (iv) Helmore Holloway, *Journal.* (v) Isabella Price, *Journal.* (vi) RM, *To Tidman,* 12.11.1860, (SOAS/CMW/SA./Box 32/1/A). (vii) The LMS *Annual Report 1861.* The best book on the Makololo events is: Stella Kirby, *No Cross Marks the Spot,* (Southend on Sea: Galamena, 2001).

4 After receiving the LMS letter (1857), Moffat immediately went to see Moselekatse. When the mission travelled to Moselekatse in 1859, he accompanied them and stayed into 1860.

Establishing a mission among the Ndebele was dear to Moffat's heart, but he was profoundly uneasy about the LMS' actions.

Moffat was unsparing in aiding the LMS project. At the same time, his deep-rooted concerns about the wisdom of the whole enterprise are on record. In 1858, he wrote to the LMS expressing fundamental doubts on the wisdom of the Ndebele/Makololo enterprise, laying out his fears in his correspondence with Arthur Tidman.[5] Andrew Ross, often a critic of Moffat's missionary style, agreed with Moffat's reservations. Ross pointed out that Tidman and the LMS Directors—against Moffat's advice—allowed the Makololo missionary party to persist in the belief that Livingstone would be waiting for them when they reached Sekeletu's tribe at Linyati: what was worse was that the directors and the missionaries disregarded Moffat's warning and his sensible suggestions to delay until rendezvous was certain, not just possible.[6]

There was an assumption, shared by the LMS and the Makololo mission party, that Livingstone would definitely meet them when they arrived at Linyati.[7] But the erratic Livingstone was not there. He was exploring the Shire River. Moffat's general worries about the whole concept were picked up by Isabella Price, one of the ill-fated members of the Makololo team, when she stayed at Kuruman preparatory to setting out. She wrote to her parents:

> It seems that Mr. Moffat's disposition is of so kind a nature that he cannot bear to say anything that will discourage another, but he has told his colleague Mr. Ashton, that what the Directors could be thinking about to send us up all this way by land, he could not imagine; that it was the most ill-managed piece of business he could possibly conceive of; that if he had known that they intended to send us out when they did, *he would have gone to London and stopped the whole matter,* but it was now too late.[8]

In her letter, Isabella went on to express her own growing unease about the lack of thorough planning, but she placed her confidence in God:

> [Yet] *we believe the Lord our God will be with us, come what may*, and we ought to take courage, when it is promised that 'they who suffer with him

---

5 RM, *To Tidman, LMS,* 20.7.1858, (SOAS/CWM/SA/Box 31/1/B).

6 Ross, *David Livingstone: Mission and Empire,* (Ldn: Hambledon & London, 2002), 157.

7 Cf. Roger Price, *To Tidman, LMS,* 20.2.1861, (SOAS/CWM/32/3/A): 'We all expected to find that Dr Livingstone had either been there, or was there then, and we were greatly disappointed on finding that nothing had been heard of him'. The issue is ably discussed by Kirby, *No Cross Marks the Spot.*

8 Isabella Price, *To her Parents,* 1.2.1859, (Slater, *Isabella Price,* 78).

> shall also reign with him' pray for us that our faith may not fail us even in the darkest hour.[9]

Moffat's worries about the wisdom of the project are clearly on record. Nevertheless, by November 1859, having travelled with the Ndebele mission party, and having absorbed its *esprit de corps,* Moffat threw his hesitations aside and became convinced that God was behind the enterprise.[10] He persuaded himself that perhaps the LMS Directors had been divinely directed.[11] At Inyati, where the Ndebele mission station was built, he further convinced himself that the Makololo Mission, as well as the Ndebele Mission. was in the plan of God, using the word 'providence' when writing to Mary:

> I have always felt rather sanguine about the Makololo mission. It was an unmistakable *providence* which led Livingstone to that people. What could he or any missionary of the LMS have done where the Transvaal Republic have influence? His endeavours to open doors for the introduction of the Gospel to the interior tribes have been signally blessed, so that it may be said that the 'Breaker', human and divine, has got up before the Makololo missionaries. The field is a glorious one. O that I were young again![12]

'Breaker' referred to Micah 2:13*:* 'One who breaks open the way will go up before them; they will break through the gate and go out. Their king will pass through before them, the LORD at their head.' Moffat's use of this dramatic terminology shows how far he had persuaded himself that God was opening up this field. This new confidence, in contrast to his previous reservations, came from the enthusiasm generated by the mission getting underway and arriving among the Ndebele. Moffat had to become enthusiastic. Too many irreversible decisions had been already taken. But late enthusiasm did not cancel the reasons for his original doubts.[13]

---

9 Isabella Price, *To her Parents,* 1.2.1859, (Slater, *Isabella Price,* 83).

10 RM, *To Tidman, LMS,* 5.?.1859, (SOAS/CWM/SA/Box 31/3/B): 'We are comforted with the assurance that God is with us. He has already answered the many prayers which have been offered up for both missions, and has made our way plain before us. We have not met with anything to damp our spirits, nor do I see why anything should be allowed to do so, so long as we feel that we are in the path of duty with the consoling promise of our Lord "Lo I am with you."'

11 RM, *Journal,* 24.11.1859, (*MJ2,* 232).

12 RM, *To Mary Moffat,* 12.11.1859, (*MJ2,* 220).

13 At Inyati responsibility weighed heavily on him. See: RM, *Journal,* 15.12.1859, (*MJ2,* 245), 'It was through my acquaintance with the Matabele that a mission to that people was resolved on, so that, though I never recommended beginning the mission, yet I am indirectly the cause of the brethren coming there.'

The Expedition

The missionary families, who were to be part of the two missions, arrived at Kuruman in early 1859. The Ndebele mission party and the Makololo mission party left in August on different days, reunited briefly in Sechele's village, and then diverged toward their respective destinations. It is the tragic fate of the Makololo mission which concerns us in relation to providence. The extent of the catastrophe is indicated in the following table:

Name	Comments	Outcome	Date
Rev. Holloway Helmore	Leader	Died	22nd April 1860
Mrs Ann Helmore		Died	12th March 1860
Henry Helmore	Child	Died	7th March 1860
Selina Helmore	Child	Died	11th March 1860
Lizzie Helmore	Child	Survived	
Willie Helmore	Child	Survived	
Rev. Roger Price		Survived	
Mrs Isabella Price		Died	5th July 1860
Eliza Price	Child	Died	9th March 1860
Malatsi	Prices' Driver	Died	2nd March 1860
Thabi (Tabe)	Teacher/Driver	Died	7th March 1860[14]
Setloko	Shepherd	Died	April 1860[15]
Conate	Oxen herder	Survived	

The Makololo party was under the leadership of the Rev. Holloway Helmore, who had worked with the LMS in southern Africa since 1839, with the Rev. Roger Price as the other ordained missionary. The Rev. John and Ellen Mackenzie, who were new arrivals to the southern African mission field,

---

[14] Price gives 11.3.1860 for Thabi's death.

[15] Price gives 19.3.1860 for Setloko's death ('that good old man'). The dates are compiled from: Isabella's *Journal*, and Roger's *To Tidman, LMS,* 20.2.1861, (SOAS/CWM/32/3/A). There were five other members of the party, whom we assume to have survived: a son of Thabi (un-named); a second driver with the Helmores (un-named); a first cattle-herd (un-named); a second cattle-herd (un-named); a second native teacher (un-named). There was also a young woman with two children, who acted as a nurse to the Helmore family. She went part of the journey, but not as far as the Makololo.

were also meant to be part of the Makololo Mission, but were spared the dire events because of Ellen's pregnancy. The Mackenzies stayed at Kuruman until Ellen's confinement. After the child was born, the Mackenzies set off to join the others, and on the edge of the Mababe wilderness they met Roger Price and two of the Helmore children, who, along with a few African helpers, were the only survivors of the original party. The Mackenzies escorted them back to Kuruman.

It is not difficult to identify causes for the disaster, but these do not solve the problem of providence since, for a believer, God has power to overcome all ordinary difficulties. Identifiable causes were many: the journey across the desert, often through soft sand, became long and arduous; near the Zambezi the party was repeatedly stricken by disease; arriving unannounced among the Makololo, and with no Livingstone to introduce them, they were unwelcome; extra provisions were denied when their supplies ran low; when they wanted to leave permission was withheld until the survivors handed over nearly all their possessions; It was also rumoured that the Makololo had applied poison, but this was unproven.[16]

The LMS Directors had assumed that if a mission party arrived at a tribe in the company of a known figure they would be welcome. Moffat knew differently. That was why in 1857, two years beforehand, he spent three whole months with Moselekatse preparing the ground for a positive reception for the Ndebele part of the mission. He understood that there was no way a mission could be 'parachuted' into a proud tribe like the Ndebele or the Makololo without a vast amount of preparation. Even so, and despite Moffat's presence with the Ndebele mission when it arrived in 1859, and despite his own son being part of the mission, and despite Moselekatse's great regard for Moffat which had developed over thirty years, it was still touch and go as to whether the Ndebele mission would get off the ground. Chiefs like Moselekatse knew that even if the missionaries were their friends, others may come in their wake who were quite different.

---

[16] Roger Price, *To Tidman, LMS,* 20.2.1861, was convinced that the food had been poisoned: 'Did they die of fever? 'I reply in the negative—Poison!' The LMS and the Cape Governor Sir George Grey thought fever, not poison. Livingstone totally rejected the idea that Sekeletu would have administered poison. Kirby, *No Cross Marks the Spot,* presents the evidence for and against. Price married the second youngest Moffat daughter, Bessie Lees Moffat, in 1861. They returned to the mission field, but not to the Makololo, though they did consider that possibility. Immediately after the disaster Price wrote (*To Tidman)*: 'O that that spirit were in me which was in Christ when he said "Lord, forgive them for they know not what they do."' This was after he heard that Isabella's body had been dug up and her face cut off. His later willingness to return to the Makololo demonstrated that eventually his anger had healed.

Moffat's concern for proper preparation among the Ndebele has to be contrasted with the LMS Directors' naïve assumption that the Makololo would welcome a missionary party without any real preparation whatsoever. The LMS Directors relied totally on Livingstone's optimism and his personal relationship with Sekeletu. Whether Livingstone ever stated that he would be with the Makololo to welcome the missionary party is a matter of debate. The fact is that he was not there. The group walked into a tribe who did not know them, with no personal introduction, and with no preparatory visit to seek approval and permission. Only one member of the Makololo Mission party, Conate, the driver of loose oxen, had previously been with Livingstone to the Makololo.[17] The contrast between the two missions was stark. Moffat, with forty-three years in Africa knew the importance of groundwork and a chief's explicit approval. The LMS Directors totally misread the situation.

A Protective Providence: The Lord is Thy Keeper[18]

Moffat's confidence in the guiding, protecting, and providing hand of God sustained him year after year. He experienced many examples of God's good providence. He also endured times of danger, sadness, and even tragedy, when children died or when plans for the mission took a setback. Through all these experiences there was a humble acceptance of the will of God, and a belief that God never abandoned his work, even if advancement entailed sacrifice or difficulty. But the events of the Makololo tragedy were of a different magnitude. Almost a whole mission was wiped out. In the light of the Makololo events, to what extent could God be described as a Keeper, Protector, and Provider?

In missionary journals there were frequent references to the providential protection of God. Belief in that protection was often rooted in Psalm 121, with its promises of divine shelter.[19] The Psalm was understood to be an

---

17 Isabella Price, *Journal,* (Slater, *Isabella Price,* 97).

18 This sub-title comes from Psalm 121 (AV): '*The Lord is thy keeper*: the Lord is thy shade upon thy right hand. The sun shall not smite thee by day, nor the moon by night. The Lord shall preserve thee from all evil: he shall preserve thy soul. The Lord shall preserve thy going out, and thy coming in, from this time forth, and for evermore.'

19 Psalm 121 was cited frequently by the Moffats. In 1820, on Mary Moffat's first ox-wagon journey into the interior, she sent a letter to her parents telling them about the strange, exciting new country she was seeing. In passing, she wrote: 'The sun has not smitten us by day, nor the moon by night .. Our God has been our sun and our shield, and the shadow of a rock in a weary land. We all enjoy excellent spirits.' Cf. Mary Moffat, *To her Parents,* 1820, (JSM, *Lives,* 75). Psalm 121 was sung at missionary meetings, as missionaries prepared to leave for overseas Cf. *Farewell Services, passim*. It was also an important psalm for Livingstone: cf. Livingstone, *To Mr & Mrs Neil Livingstone,* 13.7.1842, (*DLFL, Vol. 1,* 61): 'Mother need not be

expression of hope—and not a weak or insubstantial hope, but a confident assured hope—and it was the 121st Psalm which had been read together, as a prayer of confidence, by the two missionary groups when they set out from Kuruman. [20] The older Moffats, the younger Moffats, the Sykes, the Thomasses, the Helmores, the Prices, and all their African companions shared the conviction that the God of Psalm 121 would keep, protect and provide. Robert and Mary Moffat took the promises of Scripture seriously.

The journal of Isabella Price, wife to Roger Price, was full of confident trust in God's protective mercy, yet she was to perish, a half-starved emaciated woman, in the Mababe desert on the forlorn attempt to return to Kuruman. It is the contrast and discontinuity between hope—based on a common interpretation of Scripture—with actual events, which brings the doctrine of providence to sharp focus in this episode. Isabella Price's *Journal* conveys the depth of trust which a contemporary evangelical missionary had in God's protection.

Whilst at Kuruman, before proceeding into the interior, Isabella wrote that, though the journey would be difficult, the group would not be alone, 'for we know who has promised to accompany us.' She also wrote, 'we believe the Lord our God will be with us come what may, and we ought to take courage, when it is promised that, "they who suffer with him shall also reign with him"'. She added, 'pray for us that our faith may not fail us even in the darkest hour.' [21] On the journey, when menaced by lions she noted, 'I believe that no evil will befall us.'[22] On the day her baby Eliza died, she wrote:

> *Ah, Providence, how mysteriously art Thou dealing with us!* My own sweet little one has today taken her flight from us. ... [Then a moving account of Eliza's dying and being dressed for burial] ... When I think of her sweet little face beaming with smiles upon me, I feel it is hard to part with one so precious; and yet she is now a little angel, saved from all the evils of life. I do not murmur. *I feel I can say 'Thy will be done',* but my heart bleeds at the

---

afraid on my account. The thought is better still, *the Lord is my keeper night and day.* My times are in his hand.' Similarly, in 1859 Livingstone wrote to John Smith Moffat concerning the latter's commitment to the mission among the Ndebele: Livingstone, *To JSM,* 15.10.1859, (*MM,* 85), 'Don't be anxious as to the future of your family. The blessed Lord is over all, and has all hearts in his hands.'

20 Isabella Price, *Journal,* (Slater, *Isabella Price,* 92).

21 Isabella Price, *Journal,* (Slater, *Isabella Price,* 83, 84).

22 Isabella Price, *Journal,* 20.7.1859, (Slater, *Isabella Price,* 101). Isabella had many other expressions of thankfulness to a gracious providence, e.g. Price, *Journal*, 2.8.1859, (Slater *Isabella Price,* 109): 'We shall lie in bed tonight, almost standing on our feet. Still, we are overwhelmed with joy at the narrow escape we have had, and cannot but feel that 'goodness and mercy do follow' us at every step.'

> parting. *My heart's desire now is that I may become more holy and devoted to the service of my Master.*[23]

These sentiments came from the heart of Victorian evangelical piety. The emphasis was trust whatever happened; but within that trust was perplexity. Isabella's response to grief was a desire to live a more holy life. Perhaps horrible events were intended to make her more devoted, more obedient, and closer to God. In her *Journal* we see Moffat's theology of providence applied *in extremis.* Isabella's desire to live a holier life was not because she felt that sin on her part was the cause of her child's death, but because providence must have had a positive discipleship purpose in permitting such an event. There had to be meaning and purpose in everything God did.

Two days after baby Eliza's death, with five of the group already dead, Isabella recorded: 'That passage of Scripture 'Be still and know that I am God' has much calmed me today.'[24] Three days later, Mrs Helmore had died and her own husband, Roger, was seriously ill: 'I cannot open my heart to Roger, he notices nothing, and seems insensible to everything. Thus I am quite alone and have no one to whom I can unbosom my feelings. But my Heavenly Father is very gracious and lifts upon me the light of his countenance.'[25]

Finally, robbed of virtually everything before being allowed to leave the Makololo, the surviving members set off on the 700-mile journey back to Kuruman, with Isabella perishing on the way. Roger Price buried Isabella in the desert. In the Kuruman cemetery a memorial stone records her death and her baby daughter's death:

> Isabella Price wife of Roger Price, Died on the plain of the Mababe, July 5, 1860, aged 30. Eliza Price, Infant daughter of Roger and Isabella Price, Died at Linyati, March 9, 1860, aged 5 months: They shall hunger no more, Neither thirst any more, Neither shall the sun light on them, nor any heat, for the lamb which is in the midst of the throne shall feed them and shall lead them to living fountains of water, and God shall take away all tears from their eyes.

A Protective Providence: Theological Interpretation

Moffat had to reconcile Isabella's depth of hope and trust, with what had occurred. Her hope and trust was Moffat's hope and trust. Her piety was Moffat's piety. Before leaving for the Makololo, the Prices spent several months with the Moffats at Kuruman. Isabella was a young woman who had an ability to communicate her thoughts, feelings and faith, and there is no

---

23 Isabella Price, *Journal,* 09.03.1860, (Slater, *Isabella Price,* 145f, (our italics)).

24 Isabella Price, *Journal,* 11.3.1860, (Slater, *Isabella Price,* 147).

25 Isabella Price, *Journal,* 14.3.1860, (Slater, *Isabella Price,* 148).

doubt that every aspect of the forthcoming expedition would be discussed at Kuruman during that period. There is also little doubt that Isabella would, at Kuruman, express her utter trust in her 'Keeper', basing that trust on God's Word. That trust was taken to her death. There is explicit evidence that Robert and Mary were deeply impressed by this young woman, with her childlike dependence on her heavenly Father. Late in 1859, Robert wrote to Mary from Moselekatse's village, 'Your admiration of Mrs Price's devotion to the cause is most just. We do most sincerely hope that she has been safely brought through every trouble.'[26]

Given the known faith, piety and character of all involved, there is no doubt that the words of Psalm 121—read together as the parties left Kuruman—expressed sentiments, hopes, and convictions which had been shared and mutually affirmed many times before departure. We do not know if the Moffats read Isabella's *Journal*, which Roger brought back from the Mababe, but they heard the whole story from his lips, and part of that story would be the unchanging continuing trust which Isabella maintained despite catastrophe following upon disaster. Moreover, besides Isabella's death there were the deaths of many others.

The Moffats were aware of the enormous tension between the faith-driven expectations of the missionary families as they set out, and the reality which they learned on Roger Price's return. The Moffats had read Isabella's Christian character in which obedience to, and trust in, her Lord were intense. They were also aware that a young missionary couple, such as Roger and Isabella Price, would pray together every evening, repeatedly committing themselves and the whole enterprise to the fatherly protection of God. How did Moffat reconcile the outcome of events with his faith?

Moffat was with the Ndebele Mission party at Inyati until 18 June 1860, and did not hear of the fate of the Makololo group until November 1860. When he sent a letter to Sir George Grey on 2 October 1860, he still had no idea of the disaster;[27] but by the 12th November he wrote to Tidman of the LMS about the calamity, speaking of being 'plunged into the depth of sorrow' by 'this distressing intelligence.'[28] Moffat wrote especially about Thabi, whom he had known for many years, and about the Helmore who had been co-workers with the Moffats since 1843:[29]

---

26 RM, *To Mary Moffat,* 12.11.1859, (*MJ2,* 220).

27 RM, *To Sir George Grey,* 2.10.1860, (NLS/Ms/10780/mf. 4/3/474).

28 RM, *To Tidman,* 1.11.1860, (SOAS/CMW/SA/Box 32/1/A).

29 Roger Price wrote to the LMS concerning his wife and the others.

> Tabe, who with his son, accompanied him [Rev. Helmore] in his own wagon, was ... an experienced Christian and native teacher. When asked by an individual who met him on the journey, as to what could induce him to visit such a sickly country, his reply was 'Surely I can go where Mr. Helmore goes'. Of course, he expected to return to his family and his people, but his heavenly Master has ordered it otherwise and he has followed his teacher to the Paradise of God. ... Mrs. Moffat and myself were both much struck with [Mr. & Mrs. Helmore's] devotion to the mission they had undertaken and entire resignation to the Divine will. We have enjoyed their interrupted fellowship for seventeen years.
>
> This event has cast a gloom over our spirits and it is impossible not to feel deep concern about the circumstances of the poor little orphans. How mysterious are the [ways] of providence to us, who know only in part and see through a glass darkly. The large amount of expense incurred, the labour and toil involved, valuable instruments cut off and bright prospects enveloped in darkness, are depths of Divine providence which we cannot now fathom, I must only place them to the 'all things' which will work together for good. They, like numberless similar events, will remain mysteries to us till the light of eternity shall be thrown around them when all shall appear harmony and love. What we know not now we shall know hereafter.[30]

This letter expresses Moffat's reaction to the worst tragedy he was ever involved in. Here we see the irreducible axioms of Moffat's doctrine:

1. Providence is *mysterious*.
2. There is a *darkness* which knowledge cannot penetrate.
3. What has happened is still within the *providence* of God.
4. It is mystery because we cannot see the whole picture, and what we do see we see dimly.

Moffat still believed that all things would *work together for good*. In the light of eternity all would appear 'harmony and love', and that some time we would understand why. Moffat was reaffirming trust despite a broken heart and a perplexed mind. These were not the slick, pat conclusions of a theologian who had tied up all loose ends in an over-arching doctrinal schema. These were simply shafts of faith within a sea of confusion. Yet, as such, they were still powerful theological statements.

Moffat never tried to minimise the scale of the Makololo disaster. Nor did he ever attempt to explain it away, even when writing for children in his book *Adventures of a Missionary.* He was honest and realistic. His confidence in the overall wisdom of God meant that he felt no need to spare the details, or give a revisionist reinterpretation of the issue, in order to avert the risk of

[30] RM, *To Tidman,* 12.11.1860, (SOAS/CMW/SA/Box 32/1/A).

children being disillusioned.[31] Moffat did, however, hold onto the eschatological hope of Romans 8:28: that good would come out of evil.[32] Christ *would* reign; his *is* the final triumph.

Faith and Trust

The Makololo tragedy was by no means the only event which brought suffering of mind and soul. What we find in Moffat, as the years passed and as he grew older, is an honesty about his feelings: sometimes struggling with the tension between the mysteriousness of circumstances on the one hand, and obedient resignation to God's will on the other. It was in family situations that the darknesses of life were most keenly felt.

1. Infant mortality. Infant mortality was so common that there was substantial emotional resilience when it occurred. It evoked mourning, but it rarely raised questions concerning divine providence. Robert and Mary Moffat lost three children in infancy. Robert, the first of that name, died at 5 days in 1825. Elizabeth, the first of that name, died 8 months old in 1832. James died aged 6 years in 1839, just after the family boarded ship for the journey back to Britain. When the Moffat's first son died in 1825, Moffat interpreted the event as a correction from God:

> Very lately I have been called to *bear the rod* and Him who hath *appointed* it. My dear partner was delivered of a fine boy, and five days afterwards he was seized with convulsions and died. As a parent you can enter into our feelings, and how difficult it is to be resigned on such an occasion.[33]

For Moffat, the appropriate reaction to dark providence was resignation to God's will, and acceptance that such events were part of divine discipline.

---

31 RM, *Adventures of a Missionary,* 266-288.

32 Cf. RM, *To Tidman,* 12.11.1860. Cf. Moffat *Letter* in, LMS *Annual Report* 1862 (19): 'The hope, which cannot be abandoned by anyone who is at all conversant with the history of missions, that the loss of sacred property and especially the sacrifice of valuable lives in the Makololo Mission will not be in vain. Such events which have so often characterised the introduction of the Gospel among barbarous and semi-barbarous nations, may try the faith of the Christian, but they cannot destroy it. The command, as well as the promise of the presence of the Saviour and the Sovereign of the world, is unalterable. He must reign; and we ought to be thankful for every incident which betokens a change for the better even in the most abandoned.' [This was having heard that Sekeletu of the Makololo felt remorse.] JSM also pointed to good coming out of catastrophe: 'The story of the failure of the Makololo Mission is well known – failure in one sense, but not in the highest, for such episodes leave behind them influences which can never die. For some years nothing was done, but latterly the work has been recommenced [through the Paris Evangelical Missionary Society].' (*Lives,* 333).

33 RM, *To Kitchingham,* 24.9.1825, (Le Cordeur, *Kitchingham Papers,* 81).

2. Family bereavements. In 1862 a different situation occurred, when the Moffats lost two adult children. One was their son Robert , the second of that name. The other was their daughter Mary, David Livingstone's wife.[34] When Moffat wrote about these deaths, he accepted that such sad events were part of 'God's rod', but his emphasis was on the mysteriousness of it all. Yet, within this mystery, he had the conviction that somehow, somewhere, there must be meaning. Moffat's sorrowful acceptance of things was summed up in two phrases he wrote in a long letter to his son-in-law James Vavasseur in London: 'He is the Lord. His will be done' and 'He is too wise to err.'[35]

The mood within the letter was *melancholy* acceptance rather than *affirmative* acceptance, and the pain went deep. Moffat accepted that God did not err, but admitted that God's ways were hard to understand. He desperately wanted to find meaning in what had happened, but found it difficult to do so. Yet, despite sorrow and confusion, he would not disown the hand which held the rod of testing. This tension between faith and sorrow was plainly expressed in the Vavasseur letter:

> You will see that our dear son Robert is no more. His grave had been but just closed when the sorrowful intelligence came that our dear Mary, our first born, had fallen prey to the perfidious fever on the East coast after having joined her husband little more than two months. This was simply stroke upon stroke. Robert's demise was to us all (though often reminded, that in the midst of life we are in death) the least expected. Possessing a strong constitution, in the midst of bustle, with fair prospects, he was with very little warning called hence.
>
> With regard to Mary, we were comparatively prepared to hear of her illness, if not her death. We all wished, if it had been possible, that she had remained at home with her children. Much however may be said on her behalf, compelled as she has been to spend so many years in racking suspense. They are gone. He is the Lord. His will be done. He is too wise to err. While we deeply feel the bereavement we would *kiss the rod* and *own the hand* that holds it.[36]

---

[34] Robert Moffat (1827-1862); Mary Moffat or Livingstone (1821-1862).

[35] RM, *To James Vavasseur,* 4.10.1863, (SOAS/CWM/Africa/Moffat/Pers/4). The extent of his grief was expressed in his annual report to the LMS for 1862: 'This solemn and most afflictive visitation of the Divine will.' (*LMS Annual Report 1863*, 17).

[36] RM, *To James Vavasseur,* 4.10.1863, (SOAS/CWM/Africa/Moffat/Pers/4). In the same letter, Moffat wrote warmly of encouragements at Kuruman and that, 'God is helping us and blessing us, granting tokens of his favour in the additions made to our churches.' Years later, in 1880, Moffat received a photograph of Shupanga, on the Zambezi, where his daughter Mary Livingstone died. The photographed deeply affected him but he wrote in reply: 'Gratitude is a joyous feeling, this I felt towards you [for the gift]' See: RM, *To Professor Tennant,* 23.3.1880, (SOAS/SA/R Moffat/Personal/ Box4).

The word 'mystery' became more frequent as Moffat grew older. Elsewhere he wrote of how mysterious were God's ways.[37] Like Ralph Wardlaw, Moffat never resorted to trying to identify a specific sin for which such an event was the chastening retribution. Having set aside that avenue of explanation, Moffat lived with the inexplicable.

3. Violent tragedy. Four years later, the Moffats were stunned by the violent death of their quiet, unassuming, studious son-in-law, Jean Fredoux of the Paris Evangelical Society. The Moffat's second daughter, Ann, had married Fredoux, who was stationed at Motito, thirty-six miles to the northeast of Kuruman. Early in March 1866, Fredoux started evangelistic work in the BaRolong villages along the margin of the Kalahari Desert. One day he met a trader who had caused problems on a previous visit. Some Africans insisted on the trader going to Kuruman where his conduct could be properly investigated, and they were prepared to take him there by force. The trader resisted and entrenched himself in his wagon with his guns loaded. Fredoux saw that the matter was becoming serious, and went to the wagon to persuade him to cooperate. As Fredoux negotiated, a huge explosion took place. The wagon and its occupant were blown to smithereens, and Fredoux and twelve Africans were killed, with thirty more injured.

In a letter to the Rev. Dr Mullens of the LMS, Moffat wrote of the heavy depression which Ann experienced after the tragedy, and of how Mrs Moffat brought Ann to Kuruman hoping she would stay there: but Ann insisted on returning to Motito.[38] The death of Fredoux, and the emotional problems which beset Ann, affected Moffat as well. He wrote to the Rev. Bergne of the BFBS explaining why his work had slowed:

> The melancholy and tragic death of my son-in-law Mr. Fridaux [Fredoux] … followed by incidents of a rather painful nature deprived me of weeks, I may say months, of valuable time. These events were beyond all human control, and required becoming resigned to the Divine will.[39]

All was in the divine will. For Moffat, the appropriate response was resignation and a resolve to see all circumstances as God's training and

---

37 RM, *Occasional Journal: 1860-1862, 1868,* (SOAS/CWM/SA/Moffat/ Personal/Box4).

38 Ann never recovered from the blow. In 1870 when the Moffats were preparing to leave Kuruman for retirement in England, Moffat asked the LMS Directors for advice, feeling that there was no alternative to taking her with them since she was clearly suffering continued mental stress. See, RM, *To Mullen,* 18.10.1869, (SOAS/CMW/SA/Box 35/2/D): '[Ann] never possessed a strong mind, was in her youth mild and amiable, and was diligent as a school-mistress for many years.'

39 RM, *To Bergne, BFBS,* 18.7.1866, (CULBSA/BFBSEC/Inwards/4/259).

disciplining. But these were events which he had to acknowledge as perplexing.

Moffat had long accepted that, though a Christian may be in the path of divine duty, life may be cut short. Before he left for Africa in 1816, he had written to his parents: 'I have not repented becoming a missionary, and should I die in the march, and never enter the field of battle, all will be well.'[40] From a modern perspective this may seem an alien idea, since measurable achievement has become so important. But for Moffat this was no pious exclamation. It was the expression of a theology in which submission and obedience were of ultimate importance. It was not what a person 'achieved', but what a person 'became' under the hand of God which was of eternal value. God would be satisfied simply with a man or woman being *prepared* to obey and serve as a missionary. This high spirituality lay behind the theology which drove the Moffats.

Because of this, despite the immense pressure which events exerted on his faith, Moffat could hold on to his foundational principles. God was the Lord. All things were from his hand. When good things happened, God was immediately identified as the cause and was praised. When bad things happened, beyond any obvious punitive context, the facts were simply recorded with little theological rationale.[41] He gave thanks for the times of blessing, attributing all good things to God. In times of perplexity he simply recorded the details and alluded to the mystery of providence.

This was vividly illustrated in *Missionary Labours* where Moffat recorded an event from around 1805.[42] Two Griqua men, their mother, their wives and fourteen children were traveling through San country when they were attacked. One man and one girl were killed, and for several days the party struggled on in fear and terror, harried day and night, with the prospect of everyone being butchered. The axle-tree of their wagon broke, and the situation was desperate. Moffat wrote that the party, 'could only lift up their

---

40 RM, *To his Parents,* 23.9.1816 (JSM, *Lives,* 26). Moffat repeated this sentiment when he accompanied the Ndebele Mission in 1859. True to his policy of trustful resignation, he acknowledged that even within God's work there might be an undesired outcome. Cf. RM, *Journal,* 21.12.1859, (*MJ2,* 252): 'We missionaries, the messengers of the Churches in Great Britain, have laid ourselves on the missionary altar, and are gone forth at the divine command to preach the imperishable riches of Christ to perishing heathen. If we fail, or are cut off in the attempt, we only follow the example of the thousands, better than we are, who have gone before us.'

41 The same asymmetry can be seen in Roger Price's writings. Cf. Price, *To Mrs Stuart,* 4.12.1860, (SOAS/CWM/SA/Africa Personal Box 1/28). Tragedy elicited silence. Blessing elicited thankfulness.

42 Cf. RM, *MLSSA,* 219ff.

voices to God in prayer; and at that moment, deliverance the most unexpected was approaching'. The missionary Kok and the explorer Lichtenstein unexpectedly arrived and escorted the Griqua to safety. Of interest, theologically, is how Moffat dealt with the issue of divine protection. Moffat focused on the survivors who were delivered by providence in answer to prayer. Moffat's conviction in that providence was not diluted by any suffering which had also been experienced. Moffat made no attempt to reconcile the problem. He did not work out a theological harmonisation. Perhaps he felt that he did not have to.

For Moffat, the doctrine of providence was not a doctrine of immunity. It involved a trust that God would provide and protect *according to His will.* God alone knew the end from the beginning, the why and the wherefore.[43] God was still the providing God even when he permitted difficulties. God's ways would be justified eschatologically, when all things would be seen to have worked together for good—not that *God* required to be justified.

This approach did not explain why bad things happen to good people. What it did do was to give the believer an attitude in which he or she committed himself or herself to a trust in God whatever might befall here on earth. Moffat started with the presupposition that God was a God of providence. All events were interpreted in the light of that unshakeable truth. The purpose of providence in a believer's life was not protection as such, but the deepening of spiritual life,; and the first fruit of increased spirituality was a spirit of thankfulness whatever the circumstances.

Secularism puts God on trial. God has to justify Himself to the world. His ways require to be vindicated to the doubter. Reasons must be found to exonerate the Almighty from culpability. For Moffat, these were alien premises. God was never on trial. If there were a 'dark providence', then humanity was on trial, not God. Difficulties, even disasters, were a testing of trust and obedience. They were not grounds for questioning God. God was the Lord. Unwelcome responses to prayer were cause for self-examination, not for probing the integrity of the Almighty.

---

43 *The Westminster Confession of Faith* Ch. 5 includes in providence the possibility that God may have a purpose in allowing his children 'for a season' to suffer. This may be, 'to chastise them for their former sins, or to discover unto them the hidden strength of corruption, and deceitfulness of their hearts, that they may be humbled; and to raise them to a more close and constant dependence for their support upon himself.' This view was assumed in both *The Larger* and *Shorter Catechisms,* and widespread in Scotland. The sixteenth-century *Heidelberg Catechism,* Q&A 28, had a similar approach.

Providence is not predestination, though the two have been treated by some theologians as twin aspects of God's irresistible grace.[44] For Moffat and his missionary contemporaries, providence involved the contingency of prayer. Though every outcome was purposed by God, the prayer-life of a believer could affect which outcome came to pass. Prayer was the human activity which brought the full force of benevolent providence to bear on a situation. Thus, in 1828 a possible attack on Kuruman was deflected after prayer.[45] Moffat also cited from the history of the Griqua mission, writing that a threatened attack in 1810, had been 'evidently averted in answer to prayer.'[46] Other examples abound in Moffat's writings.

At the heart of Moffat's theology was resignation to God's will. When tragedy came, obedient resignation was the response. Yet, though this doctrine of quiet resignation was embedded in Moffat's spiritual ancestry, the same doctrine would require a fundamental alteration in Tswana beliefs since these demanded explicit correlation between cause and effect. In Tswana religious tradition, the ancestral spirits had ability to bring trouble to a person who had insulted them. If a convert accepted Moffat's theology of a mysterious darkness of unknowing, then the convert had to give up the philosophy of identifiable cause and effect within Tswana spirituality.

A convert had to learn to simply accept what had happened, without always being able to explain why. Lye and Murray have pointed out that, even in modern times, stories circulate of the way in which Tswana Christians, who resist a diagnosis of ancestral interference, are brought to heel.[47] Moffat's call to simply trust, contrasted tradition in which identifying causes was important in order to put things right with the offended spirit.

*

In 1820 when Moffat learned that permission to live and work among Mothibi's BaThlaping tribe had not been given by the Governor at the Cape, he wrote, 'We were obliged however to submit to the powers that be, and to look to Him who has the hearts of all men in his hand, and to say, "The Lord reigneth."'[48] These words reveal Moffat's faith. God reigns. God's

---

44 Cf. Thomas Watson, *A Body of Divinity,* 86.

45 RM, *To LMS Directors,* 26.8.1828, (*AAK,* 286).

46 RM, *MLSSA,* 196.

47 Lye & Murray, *Transformations,* 124.

48 RM, *To his Parents,* 18.9.1820 (JSM, *Lives,* 86). In his private life, Moffat was not averse to questioning outcomes. E.g. in 1817, Mary wrote from England, saying that after much prayer she had decided that she could not leave her parents and come to Africa to marry him. Moffat refused to accept that this, even after Mary's 'much prayer' was the will of God. He replied, protesting both astonishment and love. Before he was able to send the letter Mary had sent

people live in obedient expectation. God's overall purposes of establishing his glory upon the earth can never be thwarted.[49] This was powerfully expressed at Inyati in 1859, when the future of the Ndebele mission was in the balance:

> I am in the Lord's service, and He will order all things well. After forty years of His goodness to me in the mission field, I have no reason to complain. 'Goodness and mercy have followed me' and when I look back to the past, the solemn eternal past, I am overwhelmed. I see the finger of God pointing during my course through the labyrinth of my life.
>
> While I may wonder where I am, I may also wonder what I am; when I look back on the physical, as well as mental toil through which I have passed. 'O to grace how great a debtor'.[50]

---

him another letter saying everything had changed and she was coming! See: RM, *To Mary Smith,* 25.11.1818 & 16.4.1819, (NLSA/Grey/MSB/349).

49 Conviction that God's purposes would prevail is well-expressed in a letter written at a time of tribal unrest and civil war after the 1823 Mantatee invasions. RM, *To Alexander Moffat,* 9.12.1824, (*AAK,* 169): 'You will be ready to ask, 'Are you not cast down?'; to which I would answer, 'Yes, but not destroyed; troubled on every side, but not distressed; perplexed, but not in despair.' We know that the mighty God of Jacob is our help. The Lord of Hosts is on our side, and however long our hopes soar on the wings of suspense, or rocket in the storm, we are assured of certain success, for strong is the Lord, who judges among the heathen."

50 RM, *Journal,* 2.12.1859, (*MJ2,* 132).

The Commonality of All Humanity

Chapter 12
Equality of Dignity

MOFFAT DID NOT USE the *Imago Dei* as his argument for a God-given universal human dignity. In this respect he reflected his era, though he did speak in terms of the soul resembling God.[1] Employing the *Imago Dei* to express the common dignity and equality of all humanity was a twentieth-century preference. In classical Protestantism the main interpretation of the *Imago Dei,* as typified in the *Shorter Catechism*[2] and in Roby's theology,[3] was that the *Imago Dei* consisted in the rational intelligence of humanity, alongside holiness and morality. As such, it could be argued that whenever Moffat emphasised the rational intelligence of Africans—which he did frequently—he was also affirming that Africans were in the *Imago Dei*. Similarly, when he insisted that converts had a capacity for moral transformation, he was again asserting that Africans were created in the *Imago Dei.*

Even though Moffat did not explicitly use the *Imago Dei* as a paradigm though which to express universal human dignity and equality, these were robustly affirmed in his theology. Proof that all humanity had a commonality was built on Moffat's twin convictions that all had *immortal souls* and that *Christ had died for all,* irrespective of race or colour. In an 1861 letter to a Miss Kent of Colchester in England, he expressed this clearly:

---

1 Cf. RM, *Journal,* 8.8.1824, (*AAK,* 142). 'You were [said Chief Makaba] lately describing the character of God, and from your description of our souls they must resemble God. I answered, in some respects they did resemble.'

2 *Shorter Catechism,* Q&A 10: 'How did God create man? God created man male and female, after his own image, in knowledge, righteousness, and holiness, with dominion over the creatures.' *Brown's Catechism* did not mention the 'image of God.' In the *Heidelberg Catechism, Q&A6,* already circulating in South Africa, the 'rational' aspect of the *Imago Dei* is omitted, and emphasis is placed on the moral: 'Did God then create man evil and perverse like this? No, but God created man good, and according to his own image – that is, in true righteousness and holiness, that he might know God his Creator aright, love him with his heart, and live with him in eternal blessedness, to praise and glorify him.'

3 Roby, *Theol. Lect.* 12, 'The Knowledge or Omniscience of God': 'Scripture informs us that man was originally created in the image of God. Hence, we infer that some of the divine attributes are in certain degrees communicable. These we proceed to consider, beginning with his knowledge ... generally understood in a liberal sense as denoting his Understanding or Intelligence.' Cf. Lect. 37, 'The Creation of Man' where Roby listed: Knowledge and Understanding; Holiness and Righteousness; Dominion, Happiness, Immortality as part of the *Imago Dei.*

> [The Gospel confers] blessings of infinite value on Africa's sable children – her trodden down sons and daughters *who are alike the objects of that love which brought our saviour to suffer and die* ... [We are] activated by Christian principles ... obeying the mandate of *him who tasted death for every man*. ...
>
> [Africa's inhabitants are] driven to the wilds and wastes of dolorous regions, to pass their lives in terror, without a ray of heavenly light to illumine the grave. How distressing it is to dwell on such scenes when *we know that the souls of those sufferers are alike precious to Him* that willeth that all should come to the knowledge of the truth and be saved.[4]

All missionaries implicitly accepted a far-reaching theological proposition which had wide-ranging anthropological implications. This was expressed in simple terms by Moffat in Edinburgh in 1842: 'Jesus died for black Hottentots [Khoikhoi] as well as for white people.'[5]

Moffat illustrated this by referring to an early incident. In 1817, when he made his first journey to the north of Cape Colony, he stayed a night with a Boer farmer. Invited to take evening prayers Moffat asked where the servants were. The farmer's answer indicated that the native servants were not regarded as being on the same level of humanity. The farmer was aghast that Moffat thought that Africans should join the family for evening worship: 'Go to the mountains and preach to the baboons; or, if you like, I'll fetch my *dogs*, and you may preach to them!' Moffat said nothing, but changed his message to the story of the Canaanite woman, and took for his text Matthew 15:27: 'Yet even the *dogs* eat of the crumbs which fall from their masters' table.' After a short time, the farmer told Moffat to stop, called in all his servants to the service, and declared, 'Who hardened your hammer to deal my head such a blow? I'll never object to the preaching of the Gospel to Hottentots again!'[6]

---

4 RM, *To Miss Kent,* 28.8.1861 (NLSA/Grey/MSB/349/1/4) (our italics). Livingstone argued that many Boers, 'believe that the blacks have no souls' (Livingstone, 'The South African Boers and Slavery' (1853): *DLSAP,* 85).

5 RM, *Edinburgh Address,* 3.11.1842, (Campbell (ed.), *Farewell Service,* 24).

6 Moffat loved this story. A dramatic version is in RM, *Edinburgh Address,* 3.11.1842, (*Farewell Services,* 23f). JSM, whilst including it in his *Lives* (33), felt a need to be more diplomatic: 'This must not be taken as an instance representing the universal feeling of a class. Even in those days there were God-fearing and earnest-minded Boers who did their best for their slaves; and now, thanks to the labour of many devoted ministers, there is a true and growing missionary spirit in the Dutch population of South Africa'. JSM frequently took a more moderate position than his father. Livingstone, 'The South African Boers and Slavery': *DLSAP, 1849-1853,* 79), also cited instances of the Boers excluding Africans from worship.

HUMAN ORIGINS: ONE FATHER ADAM

With an anthropology rooted in a conviction that Christ had died on Calvary for the immortal souls of all men and women everywhere in the world, Moffat emphasised that all peoples had a common origin and unity. This position was evident from his earliest days in South Africa. When working among the Namaqua in 1818 he wrote to Burder of the LMS:

> During our stay there I preached frequently, particularly from Paul's address to the Athenians. I also conversed with them on particular points; some replied, if it is so – *that we are all the children or descendants of one father Adam*, how is it that you are white and we nearly black? This I explained.[7]

Moffat's assertion, 'That we are all the children or descendants of one father Adam' was fundamental to his whole thinking. Mary Moffat also used the phrase 'children of Adam' in describing the Tswana at Kuruman.[8] Robert and Mary both believed that Europeans and Africans had a shared humanity. This aspect of Moffat's anthropology also came to the fore in his conversations with Moselekatse, with whom he had several discussions concerning human origins. Moffat and Moselekatse become involved in such talks for two reasons. Firstly, because Moffat had declared that on the last day 'all' shall rise, and this 'all' included everyone from the beginning of time. Secondly, because, in order to give Moselekatse a full explanation of Christian faith, it was necessary not only to expound redemption, but also to explain the fall, and thus touch upon Adamic origins.

In 1829, Moffat recorded that Moselekatse was, 'startled when I informed him that the word of God, which cannot lie, assured us that all mankind, of whatever nation, were made of one blood and derived their origin from one common parent.'[9] Moffat was presenting the monogenetic hypothesis of his

---

[7] RM, *To Burder, LMS,* 20.8.1818 (SOAS/CMW/Africa/Box 7/5/A). Moffat's sentiments were the same as those of his friend, Barnabas Shaw of the Wesleyan Missionary Society. Shaw wrote: 'At our evening's service [the chief] with his people bowed their faces to the ground, and when Jesus was set forth as the Great Shepherd who had black sheep as well as white ... the chief wept aloud and appeared to rejoice as one who had found great spoil.' (Shaw, *Journal,* 3.10.1816, in: Horton Davies, & R.H.W. Shepherd, *South African Missions 1800-1950: An Anthology,* (Ldn: Nelson, 1954), 108).

[8] Mary Moffat, *To her Father,* Oct. 1829 (JSM, *Lives,* 156).

[9] RM, *Journal,* 1829, (*MJ1,* 16f). This is at odds with Ross' statement that with Moffat, 'good was to be done to and for Blacks, but this had nothing to do with brotherhood or equality' (Ross, *John Philip 1775-1851*, 220). The evidence which we present in the rest of this chapter questions Ross' stance. De Gruchy, former director of the Kuruman Moffat Mission, also questions Ross' generalisation (De Gruchy, 'Alleged Political Conservatism of Robert Moffat', 17-36). Even Setiloane, who rarely commends missionaries, stated: 'The evangelical faith which the missionaries had embraced, believed literally in the common source of all man as

time, which stressed a common origin for all humanity. Some, such as Voltaire in France and Lord Kames in Scotland, questioned the monogenetic theory, favouring a polygenetic hypothesis, but they were in a minority.

Moselekatse was not easily convinced that all humanity had a single origin. The San [Bushmen] lived within the bounds of his fiefdom, and he considered them to be 'a mongrel race'.[10] Moselekatse also queried why, if all humanity were of one blood, there were such great differences of physiognomy and skin colour.[11] Moffat gave several explanations, predominantly environmental: 'The physical appearance of man often accorded with their way of living and the nature of the country they inhabited.'[12] Moffat then illustrated his belief—that variations occurred because of differences of lifestyle and environment—by referring to the animals of Moselekatse's kraal. These were clearly the same breed as those owned by poor villagers, but, though the same breed, they were much bigger than those belonging to the poor. Moffat's point was that diversity was not due to different species, but because of the conditions in which they lived.[13]

Moselekatse recognised the force of this logic, but pointed out a possible flaw. He argued that if variations were due to environment rather than to an inherent difference of race, why did the San speak an entirely different language from the other people among whom they lived? Moselekatse was not concerned with *superficial* differences of language between groups: he accepted that many tribal languages were related in some fundamental way. Rather, his argument was based on his observation that the San language with 'clicks' was, in his opinion, totally different from any other language. If, argued Moselekatse, Moffat's contention that environment accounted for differences, then why had this fundamental difference developed despite the San living adjacent to 'normal speaking' tribes? Moffat's response to this perceptive counter-thesis was to argue that perhaps the San 'click' language could still be regarded as a variant on other tribal languages, and that it was

---

Adam, and preached it. They took very seriously the universal application of the work of Jesus Christ for the salvation of men.' (*The Image of God among the Sotho-Tswana,* 117).

10 RM, *Journal,* 1829, (*MJ1,* 17). Moffat conversed with Moselekatse through an interpreter, who translated between SeTswana and SiNdebele, hence there is uncertainty over the precise words which Moselekatse used. If he did use a word equivalent to 'mongrel' it is unlikely he meant that the San were 'non-human' or 'sub-human'.

11 RM, *Journal,* 1829, (*MJ1,* 17).

12 Ibid.

13 That 'conditions' accounted for differences, rather than any innate factor, was crucial for Moffat, especially when he compared European and African society. Cf. *MLSSA,* 282f.

not unique with no connection to other tongues.[14] However, Moselekatse had no desire to accept any theory which related him to the San, however remotely. Nevertheless, he listened politely to Moffat's supposition.[15]

Moffat and Moselekatse's intellectual jousting continued in 1835. On this second visit, theological conversations were delayed for several days until Moselekatse had dealt with some internal issues among the Ndebele. The 1835 relationship was cordial, though the intensity of the 1829 theological conversations was slow to develop. Eventually, seventeen days after reaching Moselekatse's camp, Moffat made the following entry:

> I talked a little while with him on the knowledge they had of a Supreme Being, enquiring where the first men had come from and where they were made. He replied that they came from the north.[16]

This conversation was interrupted by further business which Moselekatse had to attend to: but what is of interest is Moselekatse's belief that the first human beings 'came from the north'. This may be a distant memory of Bantu migrations down East Africa into southern Africa. If so, then this 'memory' partly coincided with Moffat's own theory of human origins, that all of humanity was descended from Noah and his sons.

From a southern African perspective, therefore, the first men did indeed come 'from the north'. Moffat wrote, 'It may not be considered chimerical to suppose that when the sons of Ham entered Africa [from the Middle-East] that the Hottentot progenitors took the lead, and gradually advanced in proportion as they were urged forward by an increasing population in their rear, until they reached the ends of the earth.'[17] Migratory groups rarely have theories concerning the *ultimate* origins of humanity. Instead, myths concerning their *translocation* become the myths of their 'origin.'[18] Even so, faint traces of ideas concerning ultimate origins do crop up from time to time in the wisdom traditions of some groups. For example, with respect to the

---

14 On the uniqueness of click language, see: Trail, 'Linguistic Research among the !xo Bushmen', *Botswana Notes and Records,* Vol. 2, (Gaborone, 1970), 127. Trail stressed that, however much the !xo click speech appeared to be so different from other languages, it 'manifests universal structural features of human language.'

15 RM, *Journal,* 1829, (*MJ1,* 17): 'I said that it appeared evident that they (Bushmen) must have sprung from a source not very distant from the Zulu or Matabele, as they also had many clicks in their language, a peculiarity which characterised the languages of Hottentots, Koranna and Bushmen. [Moselekatse] did not like to admit quite so near a relation to such a people, but admitted that the nations far to the north had no clicks in their language.'

16 RM, *Journal,* 26.6.1835, (*MJ1,* 91).

17 RM, *MLSSA,* 5. This implied that Africans were descendants of Adam, sharing a commonality with Noah, who was descended from Adam.

18 Alice Werner, *Myths and Legends of the Bantu*, 29f.

Ndebele, in the 1829 conversations Moselekatse made a reference to the first humans: '[Moselekatse] added that all he knew about the first people was that they ate cow dung until they got other food'.[19]

Moselekatse was Ndebele. He did not own the 'cave' or 'reed-bed' myth, which figured prominently in Tswana thought. But Moffat heard of the 'cave' story from a separate Tswana source. In his 1840 LMS Sermon, he stated:

> With regard to the origin of man, and the different species of animals, all that the wisest of the wise could say on the subject was, that the animate creation came out of a great cave in the north country, where their footsteps, said they, are still to be seen in the hardened rock.[20]

Lye and Murray have pointed out that, according to their legends, the Sotho and Tswana peoples originated from the 'Cave of Lowe', or from a 'bed of reeds' at Ntsqwana-tsatsi (where-the-sun-rises).[21] Consequently, Sotho and Tswana mothers announce the birth of their child by placing a reed across their doors. Werner, despite intensive research, found very few creation or ultimate origin stories for the southern Bantu, but confirmed the 'reed-bed' story, as did David Hammond-Tooke.[22] It was the 'cave' version which Moffat appears to have known. Werner also cited the Herero theory that their own ancestors came out of a tree called *Omunborombonga*.[23] Significantly, he added that the Tswana did not attempt to account for the origin of the San: the San had been in the country, along with the animals, from time immemorial, before the Tswana came into it.[24]

Apart from his fleeting citation of Moselekatse's theory of human origins, and the Tswana 'cave' myth, Moffat has little reference to indigenous creation myths. As an evangelical missionary, his primary concern was with

---

19 RM, *Journal,* 1829, (*MJ1,* 16).

20 RM, *Africa,* 22. Moffat stated that a Motswana, who claimed to have seen the footprints, offered to take Moffat there: 'Ha, and I shall show you the footsteps of the very first man.'

21 Lye & Murray, *Transformations*, 24.

22 Hammond-Tooke, *Roots,* 150. He added: 'An alternative story referred to the emergence of the first men from a hole in the ground.' Hammond-Tooke also alluded to the 'cave' theory: 'Xhosa told Alberti in 1801 that all people, stock, and all forms of animal life came out of a cavern 'in a land in which the sun rises' and the Tswana ... pointed to certain places where the god's footprints could still be seen on the rocks.'

23 Alice Werner, *Myths and Legends of the Bantu,* 22, 30f. Werner pointed out that Bantu groups frequently failed to distinguish between a non-human creator and the first human ancestor.

24 Alice Werner, *Myths and Legends of the Bantu,* 22. Hammond-Tooke, *Roots,* 150, pointed out that the San, in contrast to the southern Bantu, have a rich mythology. Moffat only had indirect interaction with the San.

a person's eternal destiny after death rather than their origins. His area of interest was in customs associated with death, rather than with birth.[25]

Human Origins: Monogenetic Theory

Anthropological theory has circled around two main theories concerning the origin of humankind, in a debate which continues to the present time:

1. Monogenetic theory. All humankind has a common ancestor. This model is sympathetic to the notion that all humankind not only has the same origin, but shares a common nature, and dignity.
2. Polygenetic theory. Different races of humankind have a distinct origin and ancestry. In this model there is no necessary commonality in the nature and dignity of the different races of humankind.

The influence of the Genesis story of the creation of humankind through one ancestor, Adam, has resulted in the monogenetic theory being dominant in European thought. However, common origin did not automatically mean that all branches of humankind were regarded as having equal dignity. The axiom of equality required further assertions on what it meant to be human, and these are discussed in our following chapters.

When Moffat felt he had to give an intellectual undergirding to his anthropology he turned to James Cowles Prichard, quoting extensively from Prichard in *Missionary Labours.*[26] Though Prichard started publishing in 1813,[27] there are no references to Prichard in any of Moffat's writings before *Missionary Labours* came out in 1842. It seems that Moffat was introduced to Prichard's thinking during his 1839 to 1843 furlough in Britain. Prichard was then in the public spotlight, having published the third volume of his book, *Researches into the Physical History of Mankind*, in 1841. In later years, Moffat had his own copy of Prichard's work at Kuruman, the evidence being an 1848 letter from Livingstone to Moffat, requesting a loan of it.[28]

Moffat found Prichard's theories congenial to his theology. But before describing his theories and Moffat's use of them we note that behind Prichard's thinking was his mentor, Johann Blumenbach, to whom he dedicated his *magnum opus.* Blumenbach was a naturalist, physiologist and

---

25 RM, *Bechuana Customs,* (SOAS/CWM/Afr./Moffat/Personal/Box 4).

26 RM, *MLSSA,* 283f.

27 Prichard, *Researches into the Physical History of Mankind,* (Ldn: J & A Arch, 1813).

28 Livingstone. *To Robert Moffat*, 11.8.1848, (*DLFL, Vol. 1,* 250). There is no reference to Prichard in Moffat's 1840 sermon to the LMS. Moffat's awareness of Prichard may have been aroused with the publication of Prichard's third volume in 1841, one year before *MLSSA*..

anthropologist. He became Professor of Medicine at Göttingen in 1776, where he taught for fifty years. Blumenbach proposed a division of humankind into five groups (originally four), associated with major regions of the world.[29] These groups are still recognised, though modified in modern times. Blumenbach had four axioms:

1. *Monogenicity.* Blumenbach worked with a single-origin (monogenetic) framework, holding to a biblical version of human creation.
2. *Degeneration.* Blumenbach argued that *degeneration*—including 'degeneration' from white to black skin—caused by climate, food, and living habits, accounted for external differences among groups. An axiom of regression was readily accepted in pre-Darwinian thought. After Darwin the paradigm changed from 'regression' to 'progression' (evolution). Though Blumenbach's theories were not new, his reputation made them to be regarded as fundamental principles.
3. *Commonality.* In proposing that external environmental factors were responsible for the state of civilisation of different human groups, Blumenbach insisted that all humanity not only had a common origin, but had a common dignity. He argued against the idea—beginning to penetrate European intellectual circles—that the different varieties of humans were unequal and should be ranked accordingly.
4. *Caucasian Originality.* Blumenbach believed that the original human form was the European white. He selected the term 'Caucasian' for this classification, judging that the women of the Caucasus region in Russia were the most beautiful of all Europeans.

Value judgments about other human groups varied for Blumenbach, insofar as they departed from this ideal.

James Prichard's parents were Quakers, who educated him at home before he went to Scotland to gain his degree in medicine at the University of Edinburgh. He then read for a year at Cambridge before joining the Church of England. After a short time at Oxford, he settled in Bristol as a doctor. In 1813 he published the first edition of his *Researches into the Physical History of Mankind.* The central principle of his book was the primitive unity of humanity. Any divergence from this original unity was a later intrusion through accidental causes which divided humanity into permanent varieties.

---

[29] Caucasian, Mongolian, Ethiopian, American, and Malay.

In 1843, he published his *Natural History of Man,*[30] in which he reiterated his belief in the specific unity of man, pointing out that the same inward and mental nature is to be recognised in all races. He differed from Blumenbach in proposing that Adam had been black, arguing that as Adam's descendants became lighter-skinned they acquired a higher intellect and civilisation. Prichard believed that, given time, all races would become similar to Western Europeans which, in his view, had progressed farther or most rapidly. Blumenbach and Prichard had similar monogenetic frameworks, but there is an interesting variation between them, illustrating that the monogenetic theory, based on the ancestral parentage of Adam, had two possibilities:

1. Regression. Blumenbach contended that humanity had *declined* since Adam, though at differing rates of regress.
2. Progression. Prichard held that humanity had *progressed* from Adam, but at differing rates of development.

In both theories it was the *rate* of either progress or regress which produced variations within humanity. Though Moffat studied Prichard, in his theology he favoured the concept of humanity *regressing*, rather than *progressing*.

One of Prichard's arguments was missiological. The experiences of missionaries, and the ability of Christianity to progress among the Khoikhoi, proved their equality with all other peoples.[31] If the Khoikhoi had been intrinsically intellectually, morally, and spiritually inferior, they would have been unable to respond to the Christian message. This argument was also used against some phrenologist teaching which claimed an inbuilt inability of certain races to respond to 'higher' spiritual truth. As examined in the section on phrenology, in the next chapter, it was also an argument used by Moffat. In the two long quotations from Prichard which Moffat inserted into *Missionary Labours*, he highlighted three of Prichard's emphases:[32]

1. There was no original inferiority between different races.
2. Any differences were because of circumstances, especially the environment in which different races or tribes exist.
3. Differences arose from context, not from intrinsic racial differences or inequalities.

---

[30] James Cowles Prichard, *The Natural History of Man: comprising Inquiries into the Modifying Influence of Physical and Moral Agencies on the Different Tribes of the Human Family,* (Ldn: Bailliere, 1843).

[31] Prichard, *The Natural History of Man,* 520ff.

[32] RM, *MLSSA,* 283f. Moffat quoted from Prichard, *Researches, Vol. ii,* 349f.

In addition to citing Prichard, Moffat provided evidence of his own which supported a positive view of indigenous society. He wrote: 'The civilisation of many African nations is much superior to that of the aborigines of Europe during the ages which preceded the conquest of the Goths and Swedes in the north, and the Romans in the southern parts.'[33] Judged by nineteenth-century views, such a statement was progressive.

Whatever weaknesses existed in the work of early anthropologists such as Blumenbach and Prichard, they held as a central axiom that all humanity had a common origin, and hence all were 'equal'. Blumenbach collected a library of books written by black Africans to demonstrate that they were not inherently intellectually inferior. For both Blumenbach and Prichard, any variations were caused by external factors, and not by any internal issue making one race different from or inherently superior to another. Even if a race were deemed to have a higher 'civilisation' than another, it was because of accidental influences. Moffat embraced this understanding.[34]

Moffat believed that all humanity had a common origin, with variations caused by accidental circumstances and not by inherent differences. As such, if a people were given the same advantages as others, they would 'progress' naturally to the 'higher' civilisation. Accident of birth and environment, not any inherent fault, was what limited humanity. This conviction gave immense motivation to the missionary task of education as well as of evangelisation. Moffat believed that if people were given proper opportunity then they would achieve the same heights.[35] Prichard provided a framework within which Moffat arranged his own thoughts, which he had already arrived at intuitively. But Prichard's anthropological analysis became the intellectual vehicle through which Moffat expressed his insights.

Human Origins: Polygenetic Theory

The field was not uncontested. The theory of *polygenesis*—multiple origins—gathered strength in the latter half of the eighteenth century. Among the European scholars who suggested that the major variants of humankind constituted separate species was Voltaire. He was not a scientific researcher,

---

[33] RM, *MLSSA,* 283.

[34] RM, *Journal,* 28.11.1857, (*MJ2,* 130): 'I told [Moselekatse] that our forefathers were as ignorant and degraded as the Matabele.'

[35] Did this assume that indigenous civilisation was 'lower'? This touches sensitive issues. Suffice it to say that Moffat's anthropological understanding was one in which he affirmed the dignity and abilities of the indigenous population. He believed that, given the same advantages, any people-group would harvest the same benefits.

but he was a vigorous opponent of the Church. Educated by Jesuits, he rebelled against their doctrines, and it was partly because of his opposition to the Church that he rejected monogenesis. Monogenesis was linked with Church dogma that that all humankind was descended from Adam. Against this, Voltaire believed that differences in physical characteristics, as well as differences in the 'state of civilisation' of Africans and Indians, were sufficient evidence to categorise them as a lower species distinct from Europeans.

The full reasons behind Voltaire's attitudes are complex, and it is possible that he also had commercial interests in view. Having invested heavily in commerce and trade, he had an interest in maintaining the colonial system with its slave trade. Whatever drove Voltaire's opinions, he was a highly articulate advocate of the polygenetic theory. Yet, despite Voltaire's considerable influence, monogenetic theory remained dominant, with its linkage to the Bible, at a time when European culture valued biblical notions.

In the Scottish context, Lord Kames advocated separate origins for separate races. Lord Kames, otherwise known as Henry Home, was a Scottish Law Lord who wrote extensively on a variety of topics and who was widely read on both sides of the Atlantic. Along with David Hume, Adam Ferguson, Francis Hutcheson and others, Kames influenced Scottish intellectual thought in the eighteenth century. He was a free-thinker, though, unlike Hume, he was not an agnostic. And, unlike Voltaire, he was not anti-clerical. By modern standards, Kames was both liberal and reactionary. On the one hand, as an issue of principle, he argued that slavery had no place in Scottish Law, ruling that Joseph Knight, an African-born slave sold in Jamaica but brought to Scotland by his master, must be set free. On the other hand, he relished opportunities to send criminals to execution![36]

On anthropological issues, Kames denied that environmental factors were ultimately responsible for variations in biophysical characteristics between different ethnic groups. He insisted that differences in innate behaviour, as well as differences in physical features, were evidence of an inherent intrinsic distinction between species. Kames' *Sketches of the History of Man,*[37] published in 1774, was so well argued that it was looked on, even by some

---

[36] Cf. Herman, *The Scottish Enlightenment,* 90: 'Kames handed out death sentences with a kind of relish that shocked even his fellow judges. Once in a single session he convicted and sentenced two prisoners to be hanged. That evening Kames was in particularly good spirit, boasting to his guests that "he had killed two birds that day". Another time he pronounced the death sentence on an old acquaintance, who had been an opponent at chess: "And that's checkmate, Thomas!" Kames quipped as they led the man away.'

[37] Henry Home (Lord Kames), *Sketches of the History of Man,* (Edin: 1774). The consulted edition was: Henry Home, *Sketches of the History of Man: A New Edition in 3 Vols,* (Edin: Ogle, Alliance & Thomson, 1819). Kames discussed Buffon and Linnaeus.

monogenists, as providing strong arguments for the separation of races. Kames' pronouncements on the inferiority of Africans and Indians carried sway with many, whether they were monogenists or polygenists. At the same time, he was careful in how he expressed himself, since he did not want to challenge the 'Adam' story directly. Nevertheless, his writings favour the idea of there having been multiple creations.

Kames began his book by stating that the question of whether there are different races of men, or whether all men are of one race without any difference but what proceeds from climate or other external cause, was a highly disputed issue.[38] He wrote that: 'There must be different kinds of men, for certain tribes differ visibly from each other no less than the lama and the pacos from the camel or from the sheep.'[39] He argued that if environmental factors accounted for difference then there would be almost an *infinite* number of types, not a modestly *finite.*[40] In his analysis of Linnaeus' classification of primates, he commented: 'A mastiff differs not more from a spaniel than a white man from a negro or a Laplander from a Dane.'[41] Kames then added a long argument against Buffon's hypothesis that climate and environment account for differences of colour, size etc.. He came to the conclusion that differing *species* rather than differing *conditions* must be the reason for different characteristics and temperament:[42]

> In concluding from the foregoing that there are different races [species] of men, I reckon upon strenuous opposition.[43] ... The presumption is that the varieties subsisting at *present* have *always* subsisted; which ought to be held as true, till positive evidence be brought of the contrary.[44]

In his discussion Kames made no reference to Adam or to a common ancestry in Adam: 'Were all men of one species, there never could have existed (without a miracle) different kinds, such as exist at present.'[45] Instead, 'God created many pairs of the human race, differing from each other both externally and internally; that he fitted these pairs for different climates and placed each pair in its proper climate.'[46] Kames was aware that his conclusion sat awkwardly with the Adam story, so he focused on the Babel event as the source of diversities. However, Babel did not really sit well with the overall

38 Home (Kames), *Sketches of the History of Man, Vol. 1,* 3.
39 Ibid, 9.
40 Ibid, 10.
41 Ibid, 11.
42 Ibid, 20ff.
43 Ibid, 27. For Kames, 'race' and 'species' were the same.
44 Ibid, 39.
45 Ibid, 40.
46 Ibid, 41.

thrust of his argument and may have been a 'fig-leaf' to cover his heterodoxy on the Adam story. Elsewhere he mentioned the 'Adam story' simply as a possibility but put no weight behind it.[47]

The Puzzling Issue of the San

Even though Kames had a polygenetic theory, he still championed human equality, showing that it is as wrong to assume a direct relationship between polygenetic theory and inequality, as it is to assume an unswerving relationship between monogenetic theory and egalitarianism. But the mood in Scottish thinking was dominated by Biblical paradigms, and the Scottish Enlightenment was never anti-clerical in the way the French Enlightenment was. In the Scottish Enlightenment, there was never the same blunt clash between faith and intellectual exploration as in France—despite the influence of the genial David Hume. Thus, the monogenetic paradigm survived in robust health into the nineteenth century: for Moffat, it was an undisputed assumption.

How did Moffat exhibit his commitment to the monogenetic theory? In the southern African context the attitude to the San [Bushmen] would be the litmus test.[48] When the Swedish botanist Linnaeus developed a new system for classifying the natural world, his system went as far as excluding the San from *Homo Sapiens.*[49] Given therefore, that a more dismissive attitude existed toward the San than toward any other southern African group, if a theology could affirm that the San were fully human and of the same status as the rest of humanity, then all races would automatically be so. The San

---

47 Ibid, 58: 'Waving the question, whether the human race be the offspring of one pair or of many.' Guinness, *Henry Home, Lord Kames,* (New York: Twayne, 1970), argued that Kames used the Babel story in order to overcome the mono-Adamic origin problem (124).

48 The Bushmen, or San, were viewed as a lower class even before European influence dominated the Cape region. For many generations, the San had been serfs to the Khoikhoi, (Smith (ed.), *The Bushmen of Southern Africa,* 2). The prejudice against the San was sometimes extended by Europeans to the Khoikhoi. Moffat knew that some questioned whether the Khoikhoi in general 'belonged to the human family' (*MLSSA,* 213). Moffat rejected this view.

49 Smith (ed.), *The Bushmen of Southern Africa,* 40. Prichard, *The Natural History of Man,* 513, 515 wrote: 'Writers on the history of mankind seem to be nearly agreed in considering the Bushmen, or Bosjesmen, of South Africa as the most degraded and miserable of all nations, and the lowest in the scale of humanity ... but accurate observers, who cannot be suspected of undue propossession towards opposite sentiments and representations of human nature, have drawn a less unfavourable picture of the moral and intellectual character of the Bushmen. Mr Burchell, who sought and obtained opportunities of conversing with them, and observing their manner of existence, though he found them in the most destitute and miserable state, yet discovered among them traits of kind and social feelings, and all the essential attributes of humanity.'

were the ultimate test-case. If the San were children of a common parent, then all were. If the San were children of God, then all were children of God. In *Missionary Labours* Moffat considered three popular hypotheses for the origin of the Bushmen [San], and rejected all of them:

> Some say they are the progenitors of the nation; others that they are an entirely distinct race; and others, again, that they are Hottentots [Khoikhoi], who have been directly or indirectly plundered of their cattle by the Dutch farmers. That the Bushmen are the people from whom the Hottentot tribes have descended, is irreconcilable with existing facts; that they are a distinct race, is still farther from probability; and that they are plundered Hottentots, is, in my humble opinion, a preposterous notion, resulting from limited information on the subject.[50]

Moffat had no conclusive answer to the question: 'Where did the Bushmen come from?' His preferred thesis was that they were originally village dwelling Khoikhoi who favoured the lonely, isolated nomadic life to that of the town or village, and that their features had been moulded by the environment they inhabited.[51] Moffat was unaware that the San had existed in the region long before Bantu tribes arrived: such ethnological theories were developed after Moffat's time. But what was fixed in his mind was that the San were not a separate race or species. He was convinced that any physical dissimilarity between them and other peoples was due simply to environment and not to any inherent racial differences.

In *Missionary Labours*, Moffat made a powerful statement concerning the San: 'There can be no question that they are children of one common parent with ourselves'.[52] Crystal clear in his thinking was his conviction that San, Khoikhoi, Tswana, Ndebele, and European were part of a common humanity. That was why Moffat viewed with horror the 'kind of policy, once sanctioned by the Cape Colonial government, of extermination [of the San]'.[53] And Moffat was aware that it was not just Europeans—with their prejudices of racial distinction and superiority—who viewed the San with disdain. At the

---

50 RM, *MLSSA,* 7.

51 RM, *MLSSA,* 8f. Moffat repeated this theory in *MLSSA,* 13f: 'Bushmen were originally poor Hottentots, and will in all probability, like their progenitors, in course of time cease to be a distinct people.' Moffat's thesis may have been influenced by Prichard's conjectures. Prichard disagreed with Lichtenstein who, anticipating more modern studies, asserted that the San were unrelated to all other inhabitants of South Africa. Prichard believed that the San were a subdivision of the Khoikhoi, and Moffat appears to have followed this (Prichard, *The Natural History of Man,* 515).

52 RM, *MLSSA,* 59.

53 RM, *MLSSA,* 13.

Kuruman station, Moffat several times had to discipline Tswana church members who joined in raiding parties to destroy San villages.[54]

For Moffat, the San, like all other human beings, were to be approached with the understanding that they were valued members of humanity whom God had created with immortal souls, and whom Christ had come to save. That was why Moffat included the San in his 'brief sketch of the different tribes which have been the objects of missionary labour'.[55] He also cited the work of the Moravian, Georg Schmidt, among the Khoikhoi in the eighteenth century, pointing out that, though some viewed the Khoikhoi as 'outcasts' to 'life eternal', Schmidt had directed them to the 'Lamb of God, who tasted death for them'.[56] Moffat wrote of his rejoicing when San became believers, and when, 'in communion with their fellow Christians' they were able to say, 'Beloved, now we are the sons of God'.[57]

Moffat's use of the phrase 'sons of God' to describe believing San and Khoikhoi is significant. Only human beings, beloved of God and part of Adam's race, could be spoken of as 'sons of God' or as part of the 'human family'.[58] A non-human being, who did not have a soul, and for whom therefore Christ had not come to save, had no place in such a scheme. But San and Khoikhoi did have a place: therefore, their full humanity was a central assumption. Evangelistic activity, in itself, was a strong anthropological statement concerning the status of the San, as men and women with immortal souls. In *Missionary Labours* Moffat devoted almost a complete chapter to the San, highlighting their desire for education.[59] A desire for education indicated a 'rational soul', which was a core attribute of the *Imago Dei* in Moffat's theological tradition.

Moffat had been attacked by San whilst on his early journeys. He had experienced the type of violence which prompted some European travellers to regard them as so barbaric that their humanity was questioned.[60] Moffat

---

54 There were many instances. E.g. LMS, *Report to the 55th Annual Meeting, 1849,* 104; and *Kuruman Church Record Book,* Disciplinary Sessions: 31.12.1837; 11.3.1838; 1839 (date omitted); 14.7.1840; 3.5.1841; 4.9.1841, etc., etc.

55 RM, *MLSSA,* 18.

56 RM, *MLSSA,* 20.

57 RM, *MLSSA,* 213. The term 'now' would, in Moffat's theology, be applied to anyone who had had a conversion experience, and, through adoption in Christ, had become a true child of God. It did not mean that before the 'now' that person was not a human being.

58 RM, *To Tidman, LMS,* 18.6.1858, (SOAS/CWM/SA/Box31/1/A): 'Opening fields for the introduction of the Gospel to large sections of the *human family*.'

59 RM, *MLSSA,* Ch. 4, especially 50.

60 The San retaliated against pastoralists when their hunting grounds and water sources were taken over. Cf. Smith (ed.), *The Bushmen of Southern Africa,* 30.

did not have a rosy-eyed view. Despite this, at no time did he ever consider categorising them as sub-human. Though he referred to their aggressiveness in *Missionary Labours,*[61] he was anxious to explain that they had become so because their whole existence had been threatened:

> Poor Bushman! Thy hand has been against everyone, and everyone's hand against thee. For generations past they have been hunted like partridges in the mountains. Deprived of what nature had made their own, they became desperate, wild, fierce, and indomitable in their habits.[62]

In his 1840 LMS sermon, Moffat made the same point: the San had been driven to violence by the need to respond to what had been done to them: 'I believe the Bushmen in general are only predatory and plunderers, by the *lex talionis* of human nature.'[63] A missionary such as Moffat, with a Calvinist outlook, would be unsurprised by violence. Violence pointed to sin, common to all humanity. Violence did not indicate non-humanity. Violence simply underscored that all humanity was in sin, and proved even more powerfully the need to proclaim the Gospel.

The Troublesome Issue of Variations

Moffat had a clear commitment to the monogenetic hypothesis. But if it were true, why so many differences? For Europeans working in Africa this question was critical. If humanity were one in origin, nature and dignity, why were Africans black and Europeans white? This touched on big issues, and at stake was the whole monogenetic model, with its related assumptions as to the equality of all human beings. A Darwinian world-view, in which adaptation to circumstances was taken for granted, would not have the same difficulty in holding a monogenetic model whilst recognising differences. But in the pre-Darwinian era it was more instinctive to assume that if all humanity were truly one family then all should be similar. Thus, the acceptance by Moffat and others that environmental factors could produce fundamental physiological changes such as skin colour and physique, involved a significant investment of faith that such factors had the ability to effect big mutations.

It was difficult to explain how environmental factors could account for all differences, and Moffat did not, and could not, answer all the questions which arose. Nevertheless, he obstinately held that differences were due to

---

61 RM, *MLSSA,* 53ff.

62 RM, *MLSSA,* 54.

63 RM, *Africa,* 54. Earlier in the sermon (19) he stated, '[The Bushmen] have been compelled to become [piratical] by the cruelty and avarice of those who have taken possession of their lands, their game, and their wild honey.'

external environmental factors and not from any innate or racial features.[64] Moffat was resolute in this. In a remarkable passage—all the more so in being published with a readership from the British general public in mind—Moffat stated directly that if any of the citizens of Britain had to live under the conditions which indigenous Africans had had to live, then they would be at an equivalent stage of civilisation, and *vice versa*:

> In all ages hunger and ignorance have been the great brutalizers of the human race; and, if we look at the large tracts of barren country inhabited by some of the African tribes, it is not surprising that they are what they are—ignorant, filthy, and sometimes very disgusting in their appearance. Degraded as they are, they merit not the epithets which have been heaped upon them, by those who are unmindful that *their* position only has prevented them becoming Hottentots and Bushmen themselves.[65]

The italics for '*their*' are Moffat's own. His readers, in well-to-do 'civilised' Britain, would live in the same way had they not been beneficiaries of an easier environment. It was environment and conditions rather than innate differences which were determinative. This extended to physical features as well as to social ones.

Commonality of origin as children of Adam should automatically imply equality of status. But in the eighteenth and nineteenth centuries the 'curse of Ham' was pressed into service to support deeply-ingrained notions of white superiority, even within a monogenetic model. The 'curse of Ham' was related to the biblical story of Genesis 9:20-27. After the Flood, Noah fell into a drunken stupor, and, whilst he was in this state, his youngest son Ham saw him naked. When Noah awoke, he became aware of what had happened and that Ham had publicised his shame to his brothers, Shem and Japheth. Noah cursed Canaan, Ham's son, and condemned Canaan—and all of Ham's descendants—to the service of Shem and Japheth. All the children of Ham were brought under Noah's curse. In Genesis 10:6 the sons of Ham are listed as Cush, Egypt, Put, and Canaan; and in Psalms 78:51, 105:23, 27 and 106:22 'Ham' is used as a poetical synonym of *Misrayim* (Egypt). Ham was thus regarded by some as the father of the Hamitic peoples.

Early ethnology viewed Egypt as the nation from which Africa was populated, with black Africans known as the 'sons of Ham'. The presumption that black Africans were under the 'curse of Ham' and in subordination to the rest of humanity was then adopted by some Europeans who had an antipathy

---

64 RM, *MLSSA,* 22f; also, 10f.

65 RM, *MLSSA,* 282f.

towards them, or who wished to justify treating them as inferiors.[66]

Moffat regularly referred to Bantu, Khoikhoi and San as 'sons of Ham' or 'sable sons of Ham.'[67] These, and related phrases, occur several times in his writings.[68] He accepted that black Africans were 'children of Ham' as far as ethnological origins were concerned, since that was the view of the time. However, he never linked Hamitic origin with the term 'accursed' though he was aware that others did. For example, he recorded that a sceptical Boer farmer, who could not believe that Africaner's conversion was genuine, had described the Namaqua chief as one of the 'accursed sons of Ham'.[69]

Thomas Morgan Thomas, a young missionary who went with Moffat to the Ndebele in 1859, also referred to the Boer view that Africans were under the Hamitic curse.[70] Moffat was aware of this view, but avoided the epithet. When he did allude to the idea of a Hamitic curse, he stressed that all of humanity was under a curse, not just Africa. In his LMS sermon, he stated:

> We have been told that Africa is under the curse of Omnipotence. Ah! And so were we! It has been said that Africans have not minds capable of understanding and appreciating the blessings of redemption; nor had we till the day dawned, and the day-star arose in our hearts.[71]

Moffat believed that, after the Biblical Flood, the only human beings in the world were Noah and his family, including his three sons: Ham, Shem and Japheth. Africa was then populated by Ham's descendants migrating from the Middle-East down through Africa from north to south. But in Moffat's theory the great migrations did not immediately follow the Flood. That occurred after the events surrounding the Tower of Babel. Thus, in 1854, on seeing a group of about twenty-five men sitting round two large fires and

---

66 This was the case not only in Africa, but in North America where some plantation owners justified slavery by citing the 'curse of Ham', arguing that black Africans should serve all other races. Catastrophic consequences of Hamitic theory are alluded to by Felix Chingota in relation to the Rwandan genocide of 1994, (Felix Chingota, *The Role of the Church in Peace-building,* (Paper for Church Leaders' Workshop held at Boadzulu, 6-11 Dec. 2004).

67 Moffat also used the phrase 'sable daughters', (*Africa,* 44).

68 E.g. RM, *MLSSA,* 50.

69 RM, *MLSSA,* 177.

70 Thomas, *Eleven Years in Central South Africa, (1872)*, 21: 'One thing that surprised and hurt us in connection with these gatherings [for worship in a Boer household] was the absence of coloured people belonging to the place. Many of the Dutch, both in the Colony and beyond it, still believe that the curse pronounced by Noah upon Canaan remains until this day upon his descendants, and treat them accordingly. But this notion is now [1872] becoming less general, and although the coloured people are seldom allowed to enter the Dutch church, still the masters build commodious places of worship for them.' Thomas was no anti-Boer. In the pages preceding this extract Thomas dwelt at length on the hospitality, kindness, piety, and faith of many Boer families he encountered.

71 RM, *Africa,* 33.

talking loudly to each other, Moffat wrote: 'I was reminded of Babel. I sat down, talked to my men about its tower, and how the different quarters of the globe became peopled.'[72]

In Moffat's hypothesis, it was during the Babel dispersal that the descendants of Ham came to Africa. Admittedly, it is uncertain whether Moffat thought of Africa being populated for the first time as a result of this post-Babel migration, or whether a few earlier migrants, such as the San, had already settled there. Yet, even if Moffat allowed for an earlier trickle of migration, the people involved in that earlier 'trickle' were also 'children of Adam' and of the one human stock.

The Commonality of Sin

The supposition of a common descent from Adam had double implications. On the one hand, it was a basis for affirming that all humanity was one. On the other hand, it meant that all humanity shared in the sin of Adam. Moffat rejected the idea, fashionable in Enlightenment circles, that Aboriginal races might well preserve the original innocence of humanity since they had been uncorrupted by the political, social, and religious factors which affected the so-called 'civilised' nations. Moffat's doctrine of sin undercut what, in his mind, was a flawed Enlightenment notion of the 'noble savage'. Traditional Christian anthropology emphasised the sinfulness of all humanity, whereas liberal Enlightenment anthropology celebrated the notion of the 'noble savage' living in a primitive harmony with nature. Thus, there was a major rift between traditional Christian anthropology and liberal Enlightenment anthropology, concerning 'original sin':[73]

1. Traditional Christian Anthropology, moulded by Genesis, taught that all mankind was by nature affected by original sin, and was born as a fallen creature.
2. Liberal Enlightenment Anthropology, rejected the view that man is 'by nature' sinful. It held that sin or evil came to man because of circumstances and culture.[74] Man 'in a state of nature' would have a

---

[72] RM, *Journal,* 26.8.1854, (*MJ1,* 273).

[73] Karl Barth, *Church Dogmatics, IV/1,* (Edin: T&T Clark, 1956), 479, defined the Enlightenment in terms of its understanding of man: 'The theology of the Enlightenment did not begin, as it is often shown to begin, with a criticism of Trinitarian and Christological teaching, or of the miracles of the Bible, or of the biblical picture of the world. ... A natural self-understanding of man was adopted as the norm for Christian thinking.'

[74] E.g., Diderot: 'Nature has not made us evil; it is bad education, bad models, bad legislation that corrupt us', cited in: Peter Gay, *The Enlightenment, An Interpretation: Vol. 2,* (Ldn: Weidenfeld & Nicolson, 1970), 170.

'natural innocence'. He would be the 'noble savage'.

Moffat did not accept this Enlightenment anthropology, and believed he had evidence for his position. For example, after his first meeting with Moselekatse, Moffat reflected on Moselekatse's savage ways:

> Truly the dark places of the earth are full of the habitations of cruelty. *Let such as philosophise on the happiness enjoyed by man in his savage state visit such scenes*, and blush for their own natures, and weep for the ten thousand sighs and ten thousand groans which echo in these gloomy shades, and shudder at the innocent blood shed through the length and breadth of heathen lands; and then tell the world that such are happier in their native sins of robbery, rapine and blood.[75]

Moffat had no room for notions of Aboriginal innocence. All of humanity were children of Adam: therefore, all of humanity were in a state of sin. He viewed all Africans exactly as he would view all Europeans. They were all alike sinners. Calvinism had no philosophical problem with the discovery that some tribes were 'barbaric.' In fact, 'barbarism' confirmed their humanity—as fallen humanity. That was perfectly normal.

Whereas idealism could create disappointed hopes, Calvinist realism straightforwardly confirmed that people everywhere, as common children of Adam, were sinners. Sin was the great equaliser. Men committed evil acts because they were sinners, not because they were racially inferior. The doctrine of sin was a bulwark against racist evaluations. A Calvinist doctrine of humanity as 'humanity in sin' was, for Moffat, a springboard for teaching equality: because Christ has come to save sinners, then all—even the vilest sinners—may become children of God.

Moffat used the doctrine of sin to underpin his argument that all were equal within Ndebele society. They were equal because all were sinners. They were equal because all needed the 'atoning blood of Christ'. This included Moselekatse as well as his subjects. Before God, both chief and subject were equal, a revolutionary concept in Ndebele society:

> [The Ndebele] seem to take it for granted that I have a right to speak what God has commanded to be spoken, and of course listen to language which places kings and beggars on the same level, making all equally guilty before God, and the necessity of all repenting of their sins and turning unto God. This would be awful language to come from the lips of a subject of Moselekatse.[76]

The Calvinist emphasis on the common sinfulness of humanity has sometimes been viewed as a demeaning doctrine for human dignity. Moffat

---

75 RM, *Journal,* 1829, (*MJ1,* 29f), (our italics).

76 RM, *Journal,* 28.11.1857, (*MJ2,* 129).

used it positively, to undercut despotism and to declare that before God all are equal. The equalising consequences of the reformed doctrine of sin should not be underestimated, though it was not easy convincing Africans whom he met that they were sinners. In *Missionary Labours* he recorded that this verdict was stoutly rejected:

> When we attempted to convince them of their state as sinners, they would boldly affirm, with full belief in their inner rectitude, that there was not a sinner in the tribe, referring us to the nations whom they dreaded, or with whom they were at war; especially the despised Bushman.[77]

Setiloane saw this statement as an example of Moffat failing to understand indigenous culture, specifically failing to understand the indigenous idea of sin. Setiloane argued that Moffat and the missionaries could never accept the fact that the Sotho-Tswana had a different understanding of sin. For the Sotho-Tswana, sin could only be wrong-doing of social significance. Consequently, in Setiloane's opinion, the Sotho-Tswana regarded the future judgment of individuals as cruel and unfair, since they did not view themselves as sinful according to their culture.[78] In fact, in a later passage in his *Missionary Labours* Moffat touched on this:

> I made many enquiries to discover if they had any sense of moral evil; it was with great difficulty I could convey to their understanding what I meant to say. They assured me, again and again, that they could not comprehend that there was evil in anything they could do. The term *boleo* (sin) did not convey to them the same meaning it does to us; they applied it to a weapon, or anything else which they thought was not made as they wished. Thus, what we should call an imperfect knife or arrow, they would call a sinful arrow.
>
> But of a sense of sin arising from responsibility, they had no conception; they did not even seem to think that the conduct of those who tyrannised over them was wicked, but merely that it had fallen to their lot to be so treated, or was a thing that happened, like a lion killing a man. When I directed their thoughts to a great Being in the heavens, some looked up with a vacant stare, as if they expected to see something appear.[79]

In African culture 'sin' is viewed as wrongdoing against society rather than as wrongdoing against abstract rules or a remote deity. It is also accepted that sin may be a wrongdoing against the 'living dead' or ancestral spirits; but sin

---

77 RM, *MLSSA,* 254.

78 Setiloane, *The Image of God among the Sotho-Tswana,* 116. It is true that Moffat's writings record people being disturbed by the prospect of a future judgment. However, there is little evidence that it was regarded as cruel or unfair, though an unwelcome surprise. Setiloane assumed that the people to whom Moffat spoke regarded his message as cruel. The evidence does not support that conclusion. Setiloane may have read modern attitudes into the past.

79 *MLSSA,* 383f. Matumo uses *boleo* for sin [*SeTswana-English-SeTswana Dictionary,* 607].

against a remote deity was not considered as serious. However, Moffat was not looking to see how a culture defined sin. He was trying to communicate how, in his opinion, God defined sin. Moreover, despite Setiloane's criticisms, it should be noted that Moffat was eventually able to communicate his ideas, even though indigenous notions always had the potential to reappear since they were part of the cultural background. But at the Kuruman Awakening of 1829 individuals wept over their sins as personal sins against God. Their humanity was part of the commonality of all humanity. It was a humanity under sin and a humanity receiving grace.

Chapter 13
Equality of Intellect

IN MOFFAT'S THEOLOGY all of humanity had a commonality of origin, and a commonality in sin. Critically, all humanity also had a commonality in intellectual capacity, and this conviction found sharp expression in Moffat's comments on phrenology. Phrenology is the pseudo-science of character analysis, based on characteristics of the skull, which was founded in the eighteenth century by the German anatomist, Dr Franz Joseph Gall, and elaborated by Johann Caspar Spurzheim. Gall assumed that specific brain regions are associated with particular parts of the body.[1] More controversially, he also assumed that moral qualities, such as integrity or depravity, were similarly localised and associated with specific bumps and ridges of the skull. Though many contemporary researchers rejected the scientific validity of phrenology, it enjoyed fashionable approval through the nineteenth century and into the twentieth.

PHRENOLOGY AND INTELLIGENCE

Phrenology's more discerning advocates concentrated on the shape of the skull, not simply its size. In the popular mind, however, phrenology implied a correlation between skull size and intelligence. Thus, even a serious writer such as George Calvert declared: 'The broad phrenological doctrine is that a small brain *cannot* manifest a powerful capacious mind.'[2] On this basis, sweeping conclusions were made about the intellectual and moral capacity of various races. Those with small bodies and correspondingly small skull size—such as in southern Africa and Polynesia—were assumed to have an inferior intelligence and moral capability.

In Britain, phrenology reached its zenith during the middle decades of the nineteenth century, prompting a vigorous debate concerning the nature of humanity. It was, of course, a *sine qua non* of the missionary community that all peoples, including aboriginal indigenous peoples, had immortal souls

---

1 George H. Calvert (ed.), *Illustrations of Phrenology,* (Baltimore: Neal, 1832), 11-17.

2 Cf. Calvert (ed.), *Illustrations of Phrenology, 1832,* 29. Calvert tried to 'prove' this by comparing drawings of Raphael's skull with that of a native from New Holland (Australia).

given by God, and were intelligent human beings in the full sense.[3] Without that conviction, the whole missionary enterprise, and the dedication of lives to the conversion of such peoples, lacked sense. Though these assumptions were accepted within the missionary community, wider European society had doubts concerning the intellectual, moral, spiritual and social capacities of some races. Phrenology appeared to give a 'scientific' basis for these doubts. Extreme phrenologists such as George Combe doubted whether some non-European peoples had an adequate religious capacity at all.[4]

George Combe was an Edinburgh Lawyer's Clerk, becoming a Writer to the Signet in 1812.[5] Around 1817, after Moffat had left for Africa, Combe was attracted to Spurzheim's doctrines, and in 1820 became a founder member of the Phrenological Society. In 1824, he published *Elements of Phrenology,* which was strongly criticised in the September 1825 issue of the widely-read journal *Edinburgh Review,* though great crowds came to hear his lectures.[6] But it was Combe's 1829 book, *Essay on the Constitution of Man,* which became his most famous production, with fifty thousand copies sold by 1838, just before Moffat returned for furlough in 1839. Several religiously inclined individuals had resigned from the Phrenological Society because of Combe's *Essay on the Constitution of Man,* and when Moffat returned to Britain the whole phrenology issue was a hot topic, especially in Edinburgh, with strong views on both sides. Combe claimed that phrenology demonstrated there were certain groups who, quite bluntly, did not have the required intellectual or religious capacity to adopt Christianity.[7] He stated that 'the native American savages, and native New Hollanders [aboriginal Australians], cannot, with their present brains, adopt Christianity or civilisation.'[8]

Combe's views caused an outcry in religious circles, especially among the missionary minded. And though not all phrenologists shared Combe's

---

3 Roby taught that the soul was 'a thinking substance subsisting distinctly of itself' (*Theol. Lect.* 37, 'The Creation of Man'). This was in line with Calvinism, which equated the soul with the rational part of human nature. If a person had a soul, then they were also rational persons.

4 The capacity for 'religious reflection' was linked to a person's ability to feel *veneration, wonder* and *awe*. Though phrenologists were often viewed as atheistic, the capacity for 'religious reflection' was still important to them. Cf. David de Giustino, *Conquest of Mind: Phrenology and Victorian Social Thought,* (Ldn: Croom Helm, 1975), 128: 'While the philosophy of Combe and Spurzheim was not explicitly atheistic, it was suspicious by the company it kept.'

5 'Writer to the Signet' in the Scottish legal system denotes a senior lawyer.

6 Cf. *The Scotsman,* 26.3.1825.

7 Quoted in: Gillespie, *Exposure of the Unchristian and Unphilosophical Principles set forth in Mr. Combe's 'Constitution of Man',* (Edin: pamphlet, 1837: NLS, ABS.2.97.33/19), 5.

8 Cf. Gillespie, *Exposure of the Unchristian and Unphilosophical Principles,* 8.

opinions, he represented a significant body of opinion.

In Edinburgh, W.H. Gillespie responded to Combe, publishing his pamphlet, *Exposure of the Unchristian and Unphilosophical principles set forth in Mr. Combe's 'Constitution of Man'* (1837).[9] Though Gillespie did not always represent Combe's thinking accurately, it is his reaction to Combe on innate racial distinctions based on phrenology which is important. Gillespie was a member of Edinburgh's Nicolson Square Methodist Church, and, like Combe, belonged to the city's legal profession. Gillespie's main proposition was theological. He argued that the command of Jesus to evangelise the whole world undermined Combe's basic thesis.[10] Jesus' command was to take the Gospel to all peoples, therefore all must be intellectually, emotionally, and spiritually capable of responding. Moreover, as Gillespie also pointed out, Combe's *a priori* argument could not cancel the reality of conversions having already taken place amongst some of the very peoples whom Combe described as inherently incapable of becoming Christians.

Drawing data from the *Wesleyan Methodist Missionary Society Report* for April and October 1836,[11] Gillespie stated that, 'The facts set forth in these extracts are not reconcilable with phrenology as set out by Mr. Combe'. He continued:

> The dogma that no human being whose skull resembles the common type of the skulls of American Indians, or New Hollanders, can become a Christian is legibly enough written in *The Constitution of Man.* The dogma is sufficiently contrary to Scripture. It opposes the expectations, it mocks the sacrifices, of Christians.[12]

In Gillespie's view, missionary activity had both an *a priori* and an *a posteriori* impact on Combe's version of phrenology. *A priori:* missionaries could not accept Combe's theories since that would mean that their enterprise was doomed before it started, and that Jesus' Great Commission was incapable of fulfillment. *A posteriori:* missionary results indicated that Combe's predictions were untrue since conversions were already taking place amongst peoples whom Combe had declared to be inherently incapable of

---

9 Cf. 'Gillespie, William H', (*DSCHT,* 361). Gillespie wrote a number of apologetic works including a book against the philosopher D.F. Strauss entitled: *The Truth of the Evangelical History (1856).* He also published: *The Theology of Geologists (1859);* also, a defence of the cosmological and ontological arguments entitled, *The Argument, a priori, for the Being and Attributes of the Lord God the Absolute One and the First Cause (1872).*

10 Gillespie, *Exposure of the Unchristian and Unphilosophical Principles,* 11.

11 Ibid, 12ff.

12 Ibid, 17.

receiving Christianity.[13] Gillespie did not reject the whole of phrenology. He simply stated his disagreement with Combe's conclusions concerning certain races being excluded from any possibility of understanding and responding to the Gospel. That was the fundamental point on which Gillespie would not yield: a capacity for meaningful religious response.

Gillespie was prepared to concede some ground. But even if some of phrenology's conclusions were correct, and even if certain skull sizes and shapes may be indicative of lesser intellectual or moral capability, did intellectual and moral ability have to be possessed to an incredibly high level before a person could become a Christian?[14] He argued that any difference of intellectual, moral or spiritual capacity which *may* result from differences in skull capacity could never be so great as to make a race unable to fully know, understand, or respond to the Gospel.

Moffat had a similar approach to that of Gillespie, disagreeing with some of phrenology's conclusions but not with all.[15] Significantly, because of his direct interaction with the San, Khoikhoi, Tswana, and Ndebele, Moffat took a much stronger line than Gillespie regarding intellectual abilities. He argued for full equality of intellectual capacity between races, whereas Gillespie—who had no real experience of other peoples—conceded the possibility that phrenological analysis might point to some of them having lesser abilities. Moffat rejected this, vigorously affirming that Africans had an intellectual power equal to any European.

That was the standard missionary viewpoint. John Philip wrote: 'So far as my observation extends, it appears to me that the natural capacity of the African is nothing inferior to that of the European. At our schools, the children of Hottentots, of Bushmen, of Caffres, and Bechuanas, are in no respect behind the children of European parents.'[16]

---

13 Combe, *A System of Phrenology,* (Edin: John Anderson, 2nd edn, 1825), 474f, had, in fact, accepted that conversions, religious advance and civilisation (to a certain extent) among South Sea islanders had taken place, and he wanted some skulls to examine. However, he also stated that the power of mental manifestation bore a proportion to the size of the cerebral organs, with the Hindu head small and the European large: 'in precise conformity with the different mental characters' (465). Even the 10th edn of one of Combe's works stated: 'All other things being equal, the mental manifestations are vigorous in proportion to its size. ... the larger and more prominent the forehead, the greater will be the intellectual powers', (*Elements of Phrenology,* (Edin: MacLachlan & Stewart, 10th edn, 1873), 16).

14 Gillespie, *Exposure of the Unchristian and Unphilosophical Principles,* 8.

15 RM, *Barbican Sermon,* 22.1.1843, (*Farewell Services,* 110).

16 Philip, *To J.B. Purney,* May 1833: DJ Kotze (ed.), *Letters of the American Missionaries: 1835-1838,* (Cape Town, The Van Riebeeck Society, 1950), 28.

African Intellectual Ability

As a missionary who had committed his life to the evangelisation of other races, and from his actual experiences in the field, Moffat was anxious to dispel the prejudice that indigenous peoples had inadequate intellectual, emotional, spiritual, or social capacities. When he returned to Britain in 1839, the phrenology debate was in full swing, notably in Edinburgh, and it is no surprise that references to phrenology in his writings come from that period. As he stayed longer, especially after visiting Edinburgh in early November 1842, he began to refer more often to issues raised by phrenology.[17] In January 1843, he preached at the Barbican Church, London, stating:

> People [thought Bushmen to be madmen] because wise men and philosophers and phrenologists, who could measure by the inch all the bumps on the head (I am not reflecting on phrenology) had concluded that the Hottentot was only just an animal to fill up a gap between the ourang-outang[18] and the human species.[19]

A few months earlier, on 21 November 1842, at Walworth Church in Manchester, Moffat had been even more forceful:

> Most of you have heard an awful character of the Africans—that they were just the connecting link between the baboons, or the ourang-outang and the human species. People of the greatest gravity imaginable, after a sober enquiry into the subject, after a rigid investigation into all the angles and developments of the skulls of Scotchmen and Irishmen and Englishmen and Africans, and no one knows who else, brought together from the east and the west, from the north and the south, and placed under the judgment of some great phrenologist, have come gravely to the conclusion that while the heads of the rest were heads of men, the head of a Hottentot was not the head of a man, and therefore he got classified in the position in which they in their wisdom placed him, between the ourang-outang and the human species.
>
> The first missionaries, consequently, to the Hottentots, were regarded by such characters as enthusiasts; they were spoken of as fanatics because they went to preach the Gospel to beings, or rather to animals that were supposed

---

17 The first references to phrenology in Moffat's extant writings and speeches are from late 1842. There was no reference to phrenology in his 1842 *Missionary Labours,* mostly written during 1841. After returning to Africa, he made several references.

18 A century before Darwin, Lord Monboddo in Scotland and Jean Jacques Rousseau in France speculated that human beings had descended from primates such as the Orangutan. Under this scheme, even if various races were 'human', different races may be at a different stage of development (evolution) from the primal ancestor. The Monboddo/Rousseau school, in breaking away from the biblical idea that all humanity is essentially the same, allowed the possibility of immense variations of status depending upon different rates of progress. It was probably these speculations which Moffat had heard.

19 RM, *Barbican Sermon,* 22.1.1843, (*Farewell Services,* 110).

> to be incapable of comprehending the great doctrines of divine revelation. But let our Hottentot churches bear testimony.[20]

The relatively small physical stature of the typical Khoikhoi [Hottentot], with correspondingly small skull size, had led some phrenologists to assume that they had lower intelligence, or even a lower place in the order of living creatures. Moffat rejected this on two counts. Firstly, on the basis of his own experience of native intellectual ability. Secondly, that, even if this dubious phrenology were accepted, then the size of some African heads should indicate greater intelligence, not less! These two issues, native intelligence and cranial capacity, were frequently discussed by Moffat.

1. Native Intelligence. In his Edinburgh address of 3 November 1842, mindful of the city being the epicentre of the phrenological debate, Moffat stated:

> Let me assure you, after twenty-three years of experience of Africans, that they can be taught and that they will be taught until that infamous libel that they are incapable of learning, with which they have been branded, shall have been forever wiped away.[21]

Moffat saw clear evidence of intellectual ability, not only in the Tswana eagerness to learn, but in the sophistication of their societal arrangements:

> Go into one of their public parliaments, and there you will see the profoundest order, while orator after orator, or senator—call them if you please—after senator, rises and describes the state of the nation, the different movements that are to be attended to, or plans that are to be devised, or exertions made, in order to save the state or the town.[22]

In *Missionary Labours,* Moffat wrote that, though the Tswana's appearance did little to impress the outsider, they were 'acute reasoners and observers of men and manners'.[23] Moffat's use of the term 'reasoner' to describe the Tswana is significant. In Scottish Presbyterian Calvinism, one of the features which distinguished a human being from other species was ability to 'reason', which ability was regarded as an essential component of the *Imago Dei*.[24] Stating that a people were 'acute reasoners' was recognising them as true human beings with abilities and talents given by God, equal to those of their European counterparts.

---

[20] RM, *Walworth Address,* 21.11.1842, (*Farewell Services,* 70f).

[21] RM, *Edinburgh Address,* 3.11.1842, (*Farewell Services,* 16).

[22] RM, *Walworth Address,* 1843, (*Farewell Services,* 75). Moffat argued that the intellectual and emotional abilities of the Tswana (75ff.) confirmed they were unmistakably human in the same sense as any European.

[23] RM, *MLSSA,* 237.

[24] *The Westminster Confession of Faith,* 4/2. Cf. *Larger Catechism,* Qu. 17.

2. Cranial Capacity. Small dimensions were certainly not the case with the Ndebele, and Moffat exploited that point. He argued that phrenologists, who made disparaging conclusions based on skull size, were contradicting their own logic when it came to the Ndebele. If skull size indicated intelligence, then the average Ndebele must be the equal of the European in brainpower, if not more! Moffat said that Moselekatse's head was far more advanced phrenologically than his own: 'I feel sure phrenologists would pronounce his developments (bumps) to be far superior to mine. They, with shaven head, can be seen to effect.'[25] Some Ndebele had heads of a University don:

> Those who listened to me today are my fellow creatures from the common stock; many, very many, having countenances and heads, one would think, enough to entitle them to the philosopher's or professor's chair.[26]

Moffat's view of African intellectual abilities was quite different, for example, from that of Mauch who, in 1871, was the first European to see the ancient Zimbabwe ruins. These Shona remains predated Moffat and Mauch by several centuries, but Mauch never imagined that they might be the work of black men. He speculated that Hebrew and Phoenician architects during the days of the Queen of Sheba and Solomon must have been responsible for them! In contrast, Moffat believed in the equal abilities of black and white. For Moffat, the Ndebele were not hampered by lack of intelligence. If they were hampered by anything, it was the conservatism of their culture:

> It has always been a mystery to me in human nature that people with capacities and heads that might stand beside our great geniuses cannot of themselves go a handbreadth beyond what was done by their earliest forefathers.[27]

---

25 RM, *Journal,* 16.11.1857, (*MJ2,* 119). By 1856 Combe was aware that some Africans had large cranial capacity: 'The argument that the Negroes are incapable of civilisation and freedom is prematurely urged ... The Negro head presents great varieties of moral and intellectual development, and I have seen several which appeared fully equal to the discharge of the ordinary duties of civilised men.' (Combe: *The Constitution of Man considered in Relation to External Objects*, 272). Even by 1825, Combe had been aware of large skulls: 'The skull of the Negro evidently rises in the scale of development of the moral and intellectual organs.' (*A System of Phrenology,* 468). However, his argument was that the overall *shape* of the African skull, not its size, indicated a deficiency in intelligence and an inability to reflect intellectually: 'One feature is very general in description of the African tribes; they are extremely superstitious. They purchase fetishes, or charms, at a high price, and believe them to be sure preservatives against all the evils of life. This character corresponds with the development which we observe in the Negro skull, for they exhibit much Hope, Veneration, and Wonder, with comparatively little reflecting power.'(470). Though Combe admitted that religious capacity was high, because intellectual capacity was low then religion was manifested as superstition.

26 RM, *Journal,* 11.10.1857, (*MJ2,* 94).

27 RM, *Journal,* 30.10.1857, (*MJ2,* 108).

Moffat wrote these statements after forty years in Africa, and there is nothing in his earlier writings to indicate that he ever thought differently. What he now found was that he could refute the derogatory pseudo-scientific racism of some phrenologists on their own grounds. Moffat was paternalistic, but not racist. He had no doubt regarding the intellectual capacity of indigenous Africans. In his view, it was climate and circumstances which resulted in them not fulfilling their potential, plus the inhibiting factors of culture and tradition. These fostered a reluctance to utilise intellectual curiosity, and were why, in Moffat's judgment, these people did not go 'a handsbreadth beyond what was done by their earliest forefathers.'

Comparisons are odious. Cultural comparisons particularly so. European progress and development in technology and the fine arts did not necessarily mean that European Society had advanced in human dignity over other societies. Moffat, as a man of his time, assumed that it had, and his comments must be understood from that perspective. But Moffat utterly rejected any notion of an innate intellectual superiority of the European.

Chapter 14
Equality of Freedom

PRE-ENLIGHTENMENT PRESBYTERIANISM in Scotland could be as doctrinaire, reactionary, and intolerant, as religion found elsewhere, but—and this is an important aspect of the Scottish context—a spirit of dissent was always near the heart of its Presbyterianism. Scottish Presbyterianism had been born in, and moulded by, dissent when, during the sixteenth and seventeenth centuries, it needed to define its position over against the monarch.[1] Dissent did not always translate into liberalism,[2] but where it did, then basic assumptions of society were challenged. It is therefore not surprising to find that a man such as Moffat, though conservative theologically, had an instinctive abhorrence toward slavery and the misuse of authority.

John Philip and David Livingstone became far more celebrated voices of protest, but Moffat made his own mark. Livingstone's declaration that slavery was 'an open sore' on the face of Africa is well-known. Yet in 1840, before Livingstone had even left Britain for the first time, Moffat had declared, concerning Africa: 'The demon of slavery must be banished from her shores.'[3] As soon as he arrived in Africa in early 1817 he was brought face to face with slavery at the Cape Colony, both in its direct form and in the guise of bonded labour. Later that year, he had to consider aspects of the 'native question' when he became involved in discussions with his LMS colleagues. These discussions had far-reaching consequences for the status of indigenous peoples within the mission itself.

The European presence in southern Africa originated in the sixteenth century with the Dutch East India Company settlement at the Cape, where they established a stop-over port *en route* to India and the east. Until 1795 the European authority at the Cape was Dutch. From 1795 to 1802 the British took control. From 1802 until 1806, under the terms of the Peace of Amiens, the Dutch resumed political power. From 1806 onwards, the principal European authority was British. The original colony was a small settlement,

---

1 Cf. Jurgens Johannes van Wyk, *The Historical Development of the Offices according to the Presbyterian Tradition of Scotland,* (Zomba: Kachere, 2004), 22ff.

2 Livingstone was scathing about Scots who, when abroad, oppressed the indigenous population. Cf. Iain Whyte, 'Scotland's Anti-slavery Battle': Church of Scotland, *Life and Work,* (Edin: June 2005), 6-9.

3 RM, *Africa,* 32.

but as decades passed this increased considerably until, by the time Moffat came in 1817, the Cape Colony under European jurisdiction included most of modern Cape Province.

Over the centuries, many Dutch families became Boers (farmers) and, as they took control of more territory, the indigenous peoples had to either move out of their traditional lands or remain as bonded servants or slaves of the new occupiers. During the nineteenth century, the Boers' insatiable desire for more land, plus frustration with aspects of British rule, resulted in them expanding their area of occupation. Following the passing of Ordinance 50 in 1828, in which indigenous peoples were given a measure of equal rights within the Cape Colony,[4] the Boers redoubled their efforts to secure land elsewhere. From the 1830s onwards, the 'Great Trek' took place which resulted in the establishment of the Free State and the Transvaal Republic.

All these events impinged on missionary activity, and many of Moffat's anthropological views were expressed within that context. That was the setting within which Moffat, as a British citizen, operating under permission granted by the British Governor, forged his contacts with indigenous peoples. Yet, whatever correct or incorrect theories Moffat held concerning the background, origins, and inter-relationships of the indigenous peoples whom he encountered, he worked from the axiom that they shared a common humanity not only among themselves, but also with Europeans. This was in contrast to the Boer attitude in which both direct slavery and bonded-labour were accepted as totally reasonable. At the same time, aspects of the Boer way of thinking had permeated the LMS community.

At the present-day Kuruman mission station, Robert and Mary Moffat's old house has been furnished as closely as possible to how it looked in their time, including some articles which originally belonged to them. On a shelf in the main room is an 1826 book entitled, *Africa Thy Chains Are Broken,*[5] which had two sub-titles: *The Negro's Friend*, and *The Sheffield Anti-Slavery Album*.

---

[4] On 15 July 1828, Ordinance 50 was issued by the Cape Government, which removed all discrimination on the basis of race from the legal system. Six years later, slavery itself was abolished, though a four-year period of so-called 'apprenticeship' followed during which the ex-slaves laboured under more or less the same restrictions as before. John Philip, who campaigned for Ordinance 50, spent the rest of his life fighting against the dilution of both Ordinance 50 and the dilution of the emancipation of slaves.

[5] Samuel Roberts (main author), *The Negro's Friend: the Sheffield Anti-slavery Album (in Prose and Verse),* (Sheffield: Blackwell, 1826).

In later life, Moffat also prized Harriet Beecher Stowe's novel *Uncle Tom's Cabin,*[6] declaring that it brought to life so clearly the horrors of slavery:

> I have read *Uncle Tom:* there was no stopping, bleered een and all [Scots: 'sore eyes not withstanding']. It is a real masterpiece: it is saturated with Divine Love. It is an almost perfect development of the workings of the human mind under the full sway of Divine love or wholly under the power of the Devil. Think only of those scenes having been enacted over and over a thousand times. The horrors of slavery are awful beyond all colouring. Poor afflicted Africa! [7]

These books were read by Moffat after he had been in Africa for some years, but from the moment he arrived in Cape Town in 1817 he had been appalled at the treatment of slaves. In a letter to his parents, he described their pitiful life and the ill-treatment they endured.[8] A few months later, he attended a meeting of LMS missionaries in Cape Town.[9] At this stage he was not yet twenty-two years of age, and he was the junior member of the missionary group, yet, at this 'Synod'—as it designated itself—he had the self-confidence and courage to challenge some accepted practices of mission stations regarding slavery.

THE 1817 MISSIONARY SYNOD

The Synod met in order to discuss various matters. It had not been officially called by the LMS, and its informal nature meant that some LMS workers, such as Moffat's friend James Kitchingham, did not attend despite having been invited. Though unofficial, the meeting dealt with important issues. These included: the relationship with the parent LMS body in London; a disciplinary issue involving the missionary James Read; and the current usefulness of the rules for a mission station which had been composed by the late Dr Van der Kemp some years previously.

The meeting was instigated, chaired and minuted by the Rev. George Thom, a senior LMS missionary, and the rule for debate was that every

---

6 Harriet Beecher Stowe, *Uncle Tom's Cabin, or: Life among the Lowly* (1852). This was one of the many books which Moffat read on his long journey to Moselekatse in 1854. Stowe wrote *Uncle Tom's Cabin* while living in Brunswick, Maine, U.S. It was serialised in an abolitionist paper, the *National Era*, and issued as a book in 1852. Its success was unprecedented, with 500,000 copies sold in the United States alone within five years.

7 RM, *To Mary Moffat,* 31.5.1854, (*MJ1,* 146).

8 RM, *To his Parents,* 27.1.1817, (Baxter & Burke, *Guide,* 326). On slavery in the Cape Colony see: Nigel Worden & Clifton Crais (ed.): *Breaking the Chains: slavery and its Legacy in the Nineteenth-Century Cape Colony,* (Johannesburg: Witwatersrand University Press, 1994)

9 The Minutes for this 'Synod' meeting are in the SOAS archives, (SOAS/CWM/Box 7/2/C).

member, in alphabetical order, gave his view.[10] When the Synod came to consider slavery,[11] the Synod was unanimous in agreeing: 'It is not proper that a slave should be bought or sold by any missionary.' However, there was lack of unanimity on some of the related questions.[12]

The first question concerned Received Slaves: 'What is a missionary to do with slaves whom he receives by marriage, or before or afterwards as a present?' Evans stated: 'I would make no law for that brother to make them free but I would recommend him to so do.' Siedenfaden said: 'I would leave it to the conscience of my wife.' Marquard equivocated: 'I would leave this question to be decided by the directors.' Then Moffat introduced a new direction to the debate when he declared outright: 'A law should be made by our Society declaring them free.' Once Moffat had given the lead Taylor agreed: 'I would recommend them to give them their liberty.' Thom, in the chair, held to the current rule operating in the Cape community, arguing that such a slave should be 'free at 25 years of age, or at his [Thom's] decease if before they arrived at that age.'[13]

The second question concerned Born Slaves: 'If a missionary thinks it his duty to keep the slaves he receives by marriage, or present, or legacy, and they have children born in his house, are such children to be free from their birth or at the age of maturity or not at all?'[14] In so far as Thom's minutes accurately record proceedings, Moffat had more support this time. Evans, Marquard and Moffat all said: 'Free from their birth'. Siedenfaden held to the old rule: 'If they become Christians and could support themselves, I would make them free.' Taylor stated: 'Free at birth or at 25 years of age.' Thom's

---

[10] Thom arrived in 1812 en route to India and was asked by the military authorities to remain at the Cape to work among the soldiers and residents. He had been a member of John Philip's congregation in Aberdeen, Scotland. The dates 1812-1818 are given for Thom's official time of service with the LMS. The LMS verdict on Thom is in Richard Lovett, *History of the London Missionary Society: 1795-1895, Vol 1,* (Ldn: Henry Froude, 1899), 535f: 'Thom was a well-meaning but highly opinionated man, more eager to listen to charges against his brethren than to sift and weigh carefully the evidence upon which the charges were based. .... Thom's zeal outran discretion and ... his very evident sympathy with Cape Town opinion unfitted him for wisely judging the state of affairs at Bethelsdorp and elsewhere.'

[11] It would seem that the Synod treated direct slavery and bonded-labour as equivalents.

[12] 1817 Synod Minutes, 14.8.1817, 12.

[13] Thom's position, spelt out in more detail than the other views, was: 'All adults I would declare free from the day of my marriage and all children free at 25 years of age, the law of maturity of the Colony; or free on the death of myself and wife if we die before they are even that age which I have done. A period of service is necessary to remunerate for the trouble and expense of education of such children.' (1817 Synod Minutes, 14.8.1817, 12).

[14] In the Cape Colony the age of maturity was 25 years.

position is not recorded, but his response to the first question would seem to reveal his overall attitude.

The minutes of the Synod were written by Thom, who did not share Moffat's radical views. Hence, the clear record of Moffat's position in a minute written by someone of an opposing opinion suggests that Moffat made his point robustly. Northcott proposed that one reason why Thom stuck to the conventional policy amongst the European community at the Cape was because he had his eye on who might read the minutes, with implications for his own standing with the Cape Government.[15] This is certainly a possibility. It is also possible that Thom's position was compromised by his appointment as pastor of the local Calvinist Society, especially since the Calvinist Society had its main membership in the military garrison. Originally, Methodists and Calvinists worshipped together in Cape Town, but in 1807 a number of the soldiers formed a Calvinist Society because there had been a disagreement with the Methodists. Thom, who arrived at the Cape in 1812, was asked by the military authorities to work among the soldiers and residents.[16] Thus, though an LMS missionary, he was tightly tied to the colonial establishment.

Even without extra complications in Thom's case, it appears that several LMS missionaries saw no moral problem in retaining people as bonded-labour until they reached a certain age. The justification for this indirect slavery was, in Thom's own words, that 'a period of service was necessary to remunerate for the trouble and expense of the education of such children.'[17] This was anathema to Moffat, who made his position clear.[18] It is clear from

---

[15] Northcott, *Robert Moffat,* 36. The 25-year rule developed from Dutch rules concerning captured San. Cf. Susan Newton-King, 'The Enemy Within', *Breaking the Chains,* 234f: 'The rules governing the apprenticeship of 'Bushman' children were not formally codified during the period of Dutch East India Company rule and they appear to have varied according to the whim of the local authorities (thus between 1786 and 1790 'Bushman' children were usually apprenticed *until* the age of 18 or 25 years, whereas after 1790 they might be apprenticed *for* 25 years), but it was always in a master's interest to give the lowest possible estimate of an apprentice's age.' The captured San were regarded as 'voluntary servants'. In due course the 25-year rule came to be applied to slaves/bonded-labourers from all indigenous communities.

[16] Hofmeyr (ed.), *History of the Church in South Africa,* (Pretoria: UNISA, 1991), 97.

[17] 1817 Synod Minutes, 14.8.1817, 12.

[18] Ross, *John Philip 1775-1851,* mentioned Thom and the 1817 Cape Town 'Synod', but only to attack them for condemning Read, stressing that they backed the Boer attitude. Read was unpopular among the Boers for his liberal views on the native question. Ross grudgingly admitted that the fornication charges had substance (49). Though Ross linked the Boer dislike of Read with the Synod's condemnation of him, there was no link: the Synod dealt with Read on a matter of sexual immorality, not on the issue of the 'native question'. Ross gave no credit to Moffat for standing up for freedom and for ending the complacent acceptance of slavery

the 'Synod' minutes that Moffat made a strong, consistent, and persuasive argument for the LMS missionaries to abolish every vestige of slavery from their households.

Slavery and Bonded-Labour

What may have influenced Moffat's thinking was the situation in his homeland, where bonded-labour had only recently been eliminated. Formal slavery had never been incorporated into Scottish Law as it had been into English Law.[19] However, the principle of bonded-labour, in which children born into coal-mining or salt-panning families had to work for the mine-owner or salt-pan-owner, had existed for centuries, and was regarded with hateful resentment within the **affected** communities of lowland Scotland. One of the areas of Scotland where the bonded-labour system operated longest and most forcefully was East Lothian, the county of origin for Moffat's parents.

The Moffat and Gardiner families lived only a few miles from Port Seton and Prestonpans where coal mining and salt panning were major industries. A subtle distinction between slavery and bonded-labour was not recognised by those of a liberal outlook. Working-class people regarded bonded-labour as slavery in all but name. This view was shared by Henry Cockburn, a major Scottish Law Lord of the nineteenth century, who described the situation unequivocally as 'slavery':

> There are few people who now know that so recently as 1799 there were slaves in this country. Twenty-five years before, that is in 1775, there must have been thousands of them; for this was then the condition of all our Colliers and Salters. They were literally slaves. They could not be killed or directly tortured; but they belonged, like the serfs of an older time, to their respective works, with which they were sold as a part of the gearing ... wives, daughters and sons went on from generation to generation under the system which was the family doom
>
> The first link of their chain was broken in 1775 by the 15th Act of George III, chapter 28; but this last link was broken in June 1799 by the 29th Act of George

---

by some LMS missionaries. Ross, as part of his wider defence of Philip and Read, portrayed Thom, Moffat etc. as reactionary, missing out Moffat's vital intervention.

19 At the union of the Scottish and English Parliaments in 1707, the independence of the Scottish Legal system was retained, and Scotland did not adopt the slavery Law which England passed in 1698. Even after 1707, English Legislation did not automatically become Scottish legislation. Thus, in 1777, Lord Kames and others were able to free Joseph Knight on the principle that slavery was inimical to the principles of Scottish Law. In England slavery was legalised by charters (1631, 1633 and 1672), by an Act of Parliament (1698), and by treaty (1713, 1725, 1745). Cf. Shaw, *The Kingdom of God in Africa,* (Grand Rapids: Baker, 1996), 128.

III, chapter 56 which enacted that from and after that date *all the Colliers in Scotland who were bound Colliers at the passing of the 15th George III, chapter 28, shall be free from their servitude*. This annihilated the relic.[20]

The slave-like situation of fellow working-class families would be well known to the Moffat and Gardiner families, with the full emancipation of such workers as recent as 1799. Amongst those inclined towards church dissent—as was Moffat's mother—there was a natural solidarity with the plight of those unfairly treated by the 'ruling-classes'. Given this background, it is not surprising that, when the slavery and bonded-labour systems existing in the Cape Colony resembled so closely a situation so recently rejected in Scotland, Moffat took the position he did at the 1817 Synod. He spoke up, despite the system being complacently accepted by some LMS missionaries.[21]

Generally, the LMS dissuaded its missionaries from interfering in the political arrangements of the country in which they served. David Bogue taught that missionaries, 'should not, in the remotest degree, intermeddle with the political arrangement of the people.'[22] The phrase, 'political arrangement of the people' can be interpreted in one of two ways. It can refer to indigenous tribal systems. Or it can refer to colonial political government, similar to that existing at the Cape. The title of Bogue's lecture

---

[20] Cockburn, *Memorials of his Time:1779-1830,* 70-72. its appreciation of Burns' philosophy, Robert Moffat's son-in-law David Livingstone quoted these exact words in reference to the idea that Europeans, Americans, slaves in America, and Africans are all brothers. Cf. David Livingstone, *To Mr and Mrs N Livingston and Daughters*, 28.7.1850, (*DLFL, Vol. 2,* 93).

[21] At the Bethelsdorp Community, founded by Van der Kemp, there were differing views on the subject of slavery. Cf. Briggs & Wing, *The Harvest and the Hope,* 19: 'For two years Mrs Smith was the maternal genius of the place, running the knitting school so well that the articles made produced a handsome profit, catechising her pupils as they worked, and using the principles of 'Equality, Fraternity and Liberty' of the French Revolution found fertile soil among the Scottish working classes. The eighteenth-century Scottish poet Robert Burns wrote: 'Then let us pray that come it may, and come it will for a' that, when man and man the world o'er shall brothers be for a' that.' Burns' words were adopted by the USSR Communist Party as expressing communist ideals of international brotherhood. Long before the Politburo expressed her spare time to visit the families settled there, or prepare the women for full church membership. Had she stayed at Bethelsdorp, its story might have been very different. But, like most other Dutch people at the Cape, she owned slaves, and it was this divergence of opinion between her and the other missionaries which led to her leaving, though she remained a friend of the institution to the end of her days.'

[22] Bogue, *Miss. Lect.* 18, 'Conduct and Doctrine of Missionaries respecting Civil Government.' That this was 'official' LMS policy is confirmed by remarks made at the 1823 trial of the LMS missionary John Smith, who was accused of fomenting unrest among plantation slaves in George Town, Demarara. The prosecuting counsel said Smith had been warned by the LMS that, *'he was sent here not for the purpose of attempting any alteration in the temporal condition, or any interference with the political state of the slaves*, but simply and solely for the great end of instructing the negroes in the pure doctrines of our holy religion.' (our italics).

was 'The Conduct and Doctrine of Missionaries respecting Civil Government,' which indicates that Bogue had the latter scenario in mind. In the early part of Moffat's career, this appears to have been how he interpreted Bogue's advice and may account for his unease at Philip's more direct form of political interference. However, the 1817 'Synod' was not considering the policy of the Civil Government or Colonial Authority, nor was it considering indigenous tribal arrangements: it was dealing with internal LMS policy, and the attitude and practice of LMS households. As such, Moffat felt free to take a stand.

The date is important. In 1817 John Philip had not yet come to southern Africa: he arrived in 1819. Philip's liberal and humanitarian views gave the lead for other missionaries to follow, and it was largely due to his indefatigable campaigning that the British Government passed Ordinance 50 of 1828, giving legal status and civil rights to the Khoikhoi. However, it should not be overlooked that, before Philip arrived, Moffat had already challenged views within the LMS. Moffat had the courage to stand firm over against seniors within his own missionary movement.[23] Moffat helped to change complacent attitudes within the LMS, enabling Philip to challenge civil attitudes. If the LMS had not already set its own house in order, Philip's task would have been even more difficult.

Andrew Bank has contended that a blithe acceptance of slavery, or its sanitised version of bonded-labour, within the 'Christian' European community at the Cape, handicapped missionary work. He argued that 'Christianity failed as a tool with which to reshape the perceptions and values of Cape Town slaves, and, increasingly, was eclipsed by Islam as the religion of the urban under-class.'[24] He pointed out that there were only six slave baptisms per annum throughout the Cape Colony between 1810 and 1824. In contrast, Islam could boast well over 1000 urban slave converts by 1831.

---

23 Philip's campaign for political change in the Cape Colony was a departure from LMS policy as taught by Bogue. Philip's resounding success took the LMS into new territory. Technically he may have been acting outside traditional LMS policy and this, along with other issues, made Moffat uneasy with his actions. But Philip was surely right. Moffat was timid in the wider area of political issues. Moffat's stance was also affected by his relationship with Philip which, though it started positively, deteriorated through the 1820s. Some of Robert and Mary Moffat's comments on John Philip were excessively critical, almost abusive. In later years Moffat took a more public stance on political matters. He came to realise that if the welfare of the indigenous peoples was a real concern to him then he had to become involved. He wrote to newspapers. He made personal journeys to try and influence British-Boer talks at Sand River in 1852. He intervened at Bloemfontein in 1854. In 1817 however, the policies being discussed only affected LMS rules, and Moffat felt at ease to argue for change.

24 Bank, 'The Erosion of Urban slavery at the Cape', *Breaking the Chains,* 87.

Slavery and bonded-labour were not only problems within the European community. They also existed within the indigenous population. Schapera has pointed out that among the western Tswana such as the BaRolong, BaNgwaketse, BaKwena, BaNgwata, and BaTawana—all of whom Moffat knew well—there was a system of hereditary serfdom.[25] This was a form of bonded-labour, with slaves, 'semi-slaves', and serfs all designated as *Malata,* and classified below 'lower commoners' (*BaTlhanka)* and 'immigrants' (*BaFaladi*).[26]

Strangely, though Moffat frequently commented on slavery among the Ndebele, he did not allude to hereditary serfdom among the Tswana. Moffat's lack of comment on this issue is uncharacteristic for a man normally so forthright. This may have been because the system of hereditary serfdom was so deeply established, and so widely accepted, that it may have been 'invisible' to Moffat, whereas, among the Ndebele, slavery in the form of human plunder through conquest was transparently obvious. With the Ndebele, their slaves were clearly victims under oppression. With the Tswana, the system of hereditary serfdom around Kuruman was not so clear.

Confronted with the explicit slavery operating among Moselekatse's Ndebele, Moffat made his views clear. In 1857, Moselekatse was astonished to discover that Moffat paid his native servants. Moffat wrote: 'When reference was made to the wages paid to my men, he seemed to wonder. His people are a nation of slaves. Everything animate and inanimate is his, though he could not help adding, "You do well to be kind to your people."'[27]

---

[25] Schapera, *A Handbook of Tswana Law and Custom,* xii.

[26] Cf. K.K Prah: *Notes and Comments on Aspects of Tswana Feudalism in the Pre-Colonial Period,* (National Institute for Research in Development and African Studies Documentation Unit, Working Paper 15. Gaborone, 1977), 13. *Malata* were common among the western Tswana in the late pre-colonial period, performing menial tasks in society. Sometimes they were not too different from the slightly better placed 'lower commoners' (*BaTlhanka*).

[27] RM, *Journal,* 5.12.1857, (*MJ2,* 135).

Chapter 15
Equality of Civil Rights

MOFFAT WAS PROUD OF what he saw as the positive merits of his own culture, though he accepted that these had come through accidental circumstances, and not through any racial or genetic advantage.[1] He vigorously opposed the notion that some indigenous peoples were less than human. That could not be since Christ had come to save them. They were human beings created by God and for God.

At the same time, though the phrase 'children of God' was intended to affirm the commonality of all humanity, there were some who preferred to stress that humanity was adult, not childlike. For them, true maturity came from humanity standing on its own feet, and not because of a dependency relationship with God.[2] But that could never be the missionary view: for the missionary, humanity achieved fulfilment precisely in being in relationship to God, rather than in being free of any reliance on him and trusting simply in itself. This crystallises a vital difference between missionary philosophy and secular philosophy. For the missionary, 'freedom' came through being a child of God. For the secularist, 'freedom' came when all paternalism, divine as well as human, was left behind. But for a man such as Moffat, the term 'child of God' was a glorious designation, and, in viewing all humanity as being of one family, he regarded abuses of the indigenous population as abhorrent.

Equality is not true equality if it is simply an abstract notion. Equality only becomes real when it is a working principle in vital areas of life. Thus, the commitment a missionary such as Moffat made to the concept of equality requires to be evaluated in terms of how he translated his ideas into reality. Moffat's 1817 policy regarding freedom for slaves within the context of LMS

---

1 Moffat's belief in the higher value of European culture led him to write to Tidman of the LMS. Cf. RM, *To Tidman, LMS,* 2.10.1860, (*MJ2,* 270): 'Neither is [Moselekatse] blind to the superior ability and sagacity of the white man. But it will require time to bring his despotic soul to submit to the superior judgment of those whose sole object is the evangelisation of the Matabele.' Moffat did not mean that Europeans were inherently superior, but that they had developed further.

2 Gay, *The Enlightenment, An Interpretation: Vol. 2,* 174: 'The point of Christian anthropology was that man is a son, dependent on God. Whatever the *philosophies* thought of man—innately decent or innately power-hungry, easy or hard to educate to virtue—the point of the Enlightenment's anthropology was that man is an adult, dependent on himself.'

missionary households has already been discussed, as have been his views on phrenology in relation to the vital intellectual, moral, social and spiritual capacity of different ethnic groups. On each occasion, Moffat demonstrated an instinctive feeling for the equality of all humanity. In this chapter we deal with equality from the perspective of pertinent human rights. In passing, we note that the abstract concept of 'human rights' was present in nineteenth-century missionary thinking. John Smith Moffat used the term when writing about German and Swiss missionaries taking up the work in the Transvaal, and 'bravely coping with difficulties incident to a state of society in which their people are not regarded as being entitled to *human or civil rights*.'[3]

THE RIGHT TO LAND

Moffat agreed with Van der Kemp's view that the Khoikhoi were 'the rightful owners of a territory now no longer theirs.'[4] Bad as the situation had been in Van der Kemp's time, by the 1820s the Khoikhoi in the Cape Colony had been deprived of virtually all their land, so that their traditional way of life had become impossible. In formal law the Khoikhoi had few rights, and these few were often forfeited through lack of proper judicial oversight in areas remote from Cape Town. The efforts of John Philip to secure the passing of Ordinance 50 did bear fruit, but too often the law was ignored in isolated areas. Apart from settling at a few missionary institutions, all that the Khoikhoi could do was to become vagrants in their own country, or to enter the service of the farmers, where they became little better than slaves.[5] In his children's book, *Adventures of a Missionary,* Moffat made a strong statement on this issue:

> [The Boers] wished to take [the land] from the Hottentots and keep it for themselves; and as they were stronger than the poor natives, they did not find much difficulty in conquering them. The Dutchmen took possession of as much land as they wished to live on; and, very unjustly, they made the Hottentots build their houses, weed the gardens, and tend the cattle. For all this labour the natives were not paid.[6]

Boer farmers, ever expanding their territory, were responsible for virtually all of the land loss. Boer wealth consisted mainly of large herds of cattle, which demanded extensive grazing in a country notorious for its droughts. This, together with the custom of allotting a new farm to each son in their

---

3 JSM, *Lives,* 271.

4 RM, *MLSSA,* 22f. Moffat went public concerning Khoikhoi land-rights. In later years, he openly criticised British policy when it connived in Boer land-grabbing.

5 Briggs & Wing, *The Harvest and the Hope,* 32.

6 RM, *Adventures of a Missionary,* 11.

large families, meant that they continually required more territory.[7] Lye and Murray have noted that, as the trekkers drifted towards Natal, they often left their grazing stations to newly arriving trekkers who were pouring out of the Colony. Temporary grazing rights were usually granted by chiefs to the Boers, but, 'even though no ownership was implied by the initial grants of grazing rights by the chiefs, the transfer of these rights from Boer to Boer gradually diminished the original understanding and replaced it with an assumption of title to the land.'[8]

John Philip tried to persuade Boer settlers to buy land properly, but his advice was ignored.[9] Yet Philip's efforts highlight an important principle of the LMS: it recognised that the land belonged to the indigenous population. Consequently, the LMS itself only acquired land by agreement with, and purchase from, the local community. The whole concept of land 'ownership' does, of course, presuppose a settled community, which was not always the Tswana pattern, and so the question of who, within tribal culture had authority to sell, is a huge issue. The LMS may sometimes have assumed that a chief had rights similar to a feudal baron,[10] but that assumption may not always have been correct. Livingstone, for example, wrote that, among Tswana and other South African tribes, 'the idea of buying land was quite new.'[11] Nevertheless, the LMS did attempt to work with liberal principles and intentions.

These were the principles which Moffat sought to put into effect at Kuruman. He did not grab land for the mission station, but bought it after agreement. Even in buying it, there was recognition that the land still 'belonged' to the indigenous peoples, though its use was granted to the Mission in perpetuity. The 'purchase' of Kuruman took place over the years 1823 and 1824. In *Missionary Labours* Moffat wrote:

> At our request Mothibi, two or three of his chiefs, with Peclu, his son and heir-apparent, accompanied us to the spot. After examination, it was agreed that about two miles of the valley, from the ford downward, should henceforth be

---

7 Briggs & Wing, *The Harvest and the Hope,* 32.

8 Lye and Murray, *Transformations,* 63.

9 Briggs & Wing, *The Harvest and the Hope,* 37.

10 Moffat saw similarities between African tribal systems and feudalism (*MLSSA,* 390). In Scottish Law, until 2004, the 'feudal superior' received a feu-duty in perpetuity from parties who 'owned' a piece of his land and had a house on that land. The land was still the 'property' of the feudal superior, though 'owned' by others.

11 Livingstone, *Missionary Travels and Researches in South Africa,* (Ldn: 1857), 19.

> the property of the London Missionary Society, and that for the same, remuneration should be given on my return from Cape Town.[12]

When Moffat returned from Cape Town in 1824, the original engagement for the land, on which to establish the new station, was ratified.[13] Mothibi expressed himself as satisfied with the forty pounds of beads offered for the right to use the new site in perpetuity of occupation. But how did that sale relate to the land rights of the indigenous peoples?

1. The procedure showed that Moffat, and the LMS as a body, recognised and accepted the existing 'ownership' of the land by the indigenous peoples. They did not regard it as unclaimed land, but that it belonged to the tribe and their chief Mothibi.
2. The land was purchased with the agreement of the tribe, not simply as a private agreement with the chief. It was not only Mothibi (the chief) and Peclu (his heir apparent) who were involved in the transaction, but also others.[14]
3. Clear limits were recognised as to the boundaries of the area to be occupied by the mission station. When, in 1854, Moselekatse expressed a wish to visit Kuruman, 600 miles away, Moffat emphasised an important point to the Ndebele chief: 'I told him that the Kuruman was a poor place and that the country did not belong to the missionaries but to the natives; that we had only a small spot in which we lived.'[15]

---

12 RM, *MLSSA,* 375f. *Missionary Labours* was written in 1842. Moffat's contemporary account of the 'sale' is in an 1824 letter to Burder of the LMS. Cf. RM, *To Burder, LMS,* 20.1.1824, (SOAS/CWM/SA/Box9/2/A): 'After having effectually diffused into the minds of chiefs and others the advantages which would result from our remaining in the Valley, Mothibi the King, his son Peclu, and others accompanied Brother Hamilton and myself to the spot alluded to when Mothibi stated that he fully understood and approved of our plan, and after very little ceremony ceded to us a suitable portion of the valley which we accepted only on condition that we were allowed to pay. Accordingly, a comparatively small sum (about £5) was agreed.'

13 RM, *MLSSA,* 378. For details of the 'land sale' for Kuruman, see *AAK,* 113.

14 Our visit to Kuruman in 2003 coincided with a meeting of Trustees of the Mission Station. We asked them when it was that the land became the outright 'property' of the LMS/Congregational Church of South Africa. They were unsure, but suggested that ownership was simply 'assumed', until the early days of the Apartheid era when it then became important to formally register land ownership or risk losing it. At that point legal 'ownership' may have been established. Yet, in 1917 the LMS felt it had enough ownership rights for it to sell some of the land to the Kuruman municipality.

15 RM, *Journal,* 26.8.1854, (*MJ1,* 274). Livingstone also recorded that he purchased land from native tribes on behalf of the LMS. Livingstone's point was that he *purchased* land under *voluntary* agreement, in contrast to the Boers who *took* land by *force*. Deane, *Robert Moffat,* 80f, following JSM, stated that in 1824 the Kuruman site became the 'property' of the LMS with remuneration given. Moffat's statement: 'The country did not belong to the missionaries

These points still leave unresolved the question as to whether the land was given outright into full possession of the LMS, or whether Mothibi and the tribe were still the 'feudal superiors' as in the existing land ownership models in Scotland.

Moffat's account of the 'sale' of the land at Kuruman by Mothibi,[16] as recorded in the *Apprenticeship at Kuruman* papers, was heavily criticised by Schapera.[17] Schapera's point was that Moffat failed to understand that the native peoples would never sell land outright. However, there is nothing in Moffat's account which claims that the land was sold outright. What was not taken into account by Schapera was that, in coming from Scotland, Moffat came from a culture in which outright land sale hardly ever occurred. It is reasonable to assume that Moffat brought that understanding to Africa.[18] The concept of a feudal superior in Scottish land law meant that individuals were accustomed to owning a property—even a considerable property—without ever owning the land on which that property was set. In Scotland (until November 2004) land still belonged in perpetuity to the feudal superior, and a feu-duty was paid to him or her.

At Kuruman, the LMS appears to have been given rights for the use of the designated land, but at no point was this understood to mean that the land itself was now theirs. In such a situation, the question of land ownership is,

---

but to the natives', may mean: (i) that the Tswana were still regarded as the permanent 'feudal superior', or (ii) that all the country, apart from the mission, belonged to the Tswana.

16 RM, *To James & Mary Smith,* 1.9.1823, (*AAK,* 110, cf. Schapera's fn. 23. In his monograph *The Tswana,* Schapera wrote that in Tswana culture: '[a man] is free to give away or lend out some of his land, but he cannot claim payment in return: sale and rent of land are both unknown in tribal law.' (21)

17 *AAK,* 110, fn. 23.

18 With the Scottish situation in mind, we can address Jacobs' unease that the land agreement between Mothibi and Moffat had very different meanings for each man. Jacobs, *Environment, Power and Injustice,* 60, wrote: 'For Mothibi the transaction amounted to granting use rights to a subordinate, and Moffat's gift served as tribute rather than payment. Moffat, however, understood that the agreement transferred permanent ownership, a proposition that made no sense to shifting cultivators.' However, in Scottish land-law 'ownership' of a property did not undermine the ongoing rights of the 'superior'. Hence it was perfectly possible for Moffat to understand Mothibi's permission as permission for use in perpetuity, without believing that the BaThlaping had abandoned the notion that the land was still theirs. In 1850, Robert Moffat Jr. surveyed and mapped the mission, and the missionaries obtained the signature of Gasebonwe, Mothibi's son, on the document, though Gasebonwe did not understand the transaction as a transfer of title. By 1858, Gasebonwe challenged the LMS claim on the basis of Tswana tenure customs. 'How the missionaries placated Gasebonwe is not clear, but they retained their hold on the land' (Jacobs, *Environment, Power and Injustice,* 80). Significantly, Gasebonwe's 'claim' was not based on the intrinsic impossibility of a sale, but on his belief that Moffat had not paid enough for it.

to all practical purposes, a dormant issue. It only becomes a problem if the person or organisation to whom these rights of usage have been given then attempts to sell the land or these rights to a third party. They would then be guilty of transgressing tribal culture. This is what the Boer community did, to the consternation and anger of the tribes who had granted to a particular family some land usage rights in good faith. The mistake of the Boers was to assume full ownership of the land itself, and to treat it as something at their disposal. The LMS situation at Kuruman was different.

By 1917 the situation had changed. In that year the Kuruman municipality paid £9,500 to the LMS for most of the LMS Kuruman estate, with the LMS retaining ownership of the church and other buildings on the remaining 17 hectares of land, out of an original area of over 200 hectares.[19] In accepting this payment the LMS was technically assuming total ownership of the land itself. This was almost 100 years after the original transaction, and the original understandings had been forgotten.

THE RIGHT TO BE FREE FROM OPPRESSION

Moffat nailed his colours to the mast at the 1817 Synod with respect to the issue of slavery in LMS mission households. That bold stance makes all the more unfortunate his opposition, during the 1820s, to John Philip's campaign for a legal change in the status of native Africans within the Colony. Reasons for Moffat's antipathy to Philip's crusade, and his reluctance to challenge the Civil Authority during the 1820s, will be examined later. However, after the 1820s Moffat showed that the spirit of 1817 was still alive in his thinking.

In his later years, Moffat was less inhibited to challenging the authority of the State than during the 1820s when he was tightly committed to Bogue's advice not to interfere in political arrangements. That being the case, it is unfortunate that his hostility to Philip's campaign has been seized on as supposedly proving a lack of concern for social issues.[20] Commentators, who either are unaware of his 1817 stance and his later activism, or who choose

---

19 Jacobs, *Environment, Power and Injustice,* 152. Jacobs pointed out that this marked the end of the era of irrigation in the service of evangelisation. It also resulted in black people being denied the water supply after Moffat's dam was destroyed by the municipality. The Apartheid Group Areas Act of 1950 meant that black parishioners were no longer allowed to attend services at the mission, which was to be a white area.

20 , who wrote the 'Moffat' article for the *DSCHT,* sharply criticised Moffat for having a pietism which ignored wider social issues: 'Moffat always opposed John Philip's commitment to justice as a distraction from the true missionary vocation.' (*DSCHT,* 598). But Ross omitted Moffat's intervention at the 1817 Synod, his political involvement after the 1852 *Sand River Convention,* and his campaign for native rights which he sustained to the end of his life.

to ignore these episodes of Moffat's life, are able to depict Moffat as a pietist missionary who lacked a wider vision of human needs.

1. *The Sand River Convention (1852)*

It was Boer advance, and their inexorable trespass on native land—regarded by the Boers as 'empty'—which stirred Moffat to protest. A wave of Boer migrations out of the Colony, across the Orange River and beyond, began during the 1830s, in what is usually termed the Great Trek, though there was no single trek, but a series of treks. This led to the dislocation of many tribal groups. The issue came to a head on 17 January 1852 at the *Sand River Convention* at which the British Government, represented by their agents C.M. Owen and W.S. Hogge, gave the Boers authority over all land north of the Vaal River, and at which the British agreed not to interfere with Boer governance, nor provide guns to native Africans.[21] The Boers of the Transvaal were thus guaranteed freedom to manage their own affairs without let or hindrance.[22] Britain would abstain from encroaching on Boer territory north of the Vaal, so long as the Boers kept out of the country to the south.

What stuck in the throats of missionaries was that the Convention explicitly disassociated the British Government from any responsibility vis-à-vis the indigenous peoples. Both parties, Boer and British, agreed to facilitate mutual trade, extradition of criminals, and free movement across the boundaries. The Transvaalers promised to abstain from slavery, and the British Government assured them of an open gunpowder market and disclaimed 'all alliance whatever and with whomsoever of the coloured nations to the north of the Vaal river.'[23] Moffat was incensed at how his own

---

21 The *Sand River Convention* was signed on 17.1.1852 and ratified at Rustenberg on 16.3.1852. Even in September 1852, the LMS missionary William Ashton still naively believed that final formal ratification in London by Royal Assent could be blocked. See: Ashton, *To Tidman, LMS,* 25.9.1852, (*DLSAP*, 172f): 'The three [LMS mission] stations are ruined [by Boer attacks], and if something is not done to check these lawless beings every other mission among the Bechuanas will share the same fate. *Attention should be called to the treaty and if possible before it is ratified by the Queen [Victoria] a clause inserted, binding them to leave the natives independent and not to molest missionaries in the discharge of their functions.* Edwards and Inglis, and Livingston too, ... should immediately [go] to Bloemfontein and see the Commissioners, for, even as the treaty stands, I think they can shew that the Boers have broken it and demand compensation for their property destroyed', (our italics).

22 For *The Sand River Convention,* see Appendix 4.

23 Walker, *History of South Africa,* 261. In 1856 the region became the Boer Republic of the Transvaal. Northcott described the situation well, cf. *Robert Moffat,* 193: 'There were 5000 families of Europeans in the Transvaal lands scattered in remote loneliness on their farms, ill-equipped to manage the affairs of an infant republic, leave alone the control of large masses of Bantu. *But they knew that the hand of Britain in the form of edicts from the Cape was now*

country, Britain, had betrayed the indigenous peoples.[24] He feared that the end result of the *Sand River Convention* would be that Transvaal Boers would operate outside British law and that any safeguards, poor as they were, would be ignored.[25] He also realised that, for the sake of political expediency, this would be connived at by the British authorities.

The missionary voice was ignored. The British Government simply wanted to get rid of the knotty problem of the Boers by giving them autonomy in areas far away from the Cape Colony. The scenario was repeated in 1854 when the question of Boer autonomy in the Orange River Sovereignty (later the Orange Free State) was dealt with in the *Bloemfontein Agreement.* Before that, and increasingly disturbed by the course of events, Moffat travelled to Bloemfontein in July 1853, on behalf of the missionaries, to argue for the native people. Political machinations meant his pleas came to nought.

2. *The British Banner Letter (1853)*

Moffat had made friendships with many Boer families. Nevertheless, he was only too aware that Boer rule would result, not only in the native peoples losing land, but in them becoming victims in a regime of subservience and servitude. In early 1853, he wrote a letter to the editor of the *British Banner* newspaper on the worsening native situation following the *Sand River Convention*. This hand-written letter ran to thirty-seven large pages. Publication in the *British Banner* was intended by Moffat to influence public opinion in Britain. The section cited below has, as far as we are aware, not

---

removed from their affairs, and that if they chose to fight with the tribes no outside government would interfere,' (our italics).

24 Whilst Moffat despaired, a different emotion prevailed among the Boers: 'There was a shout of joy. Amity was established. The leaders agreed to differ in the future. The *Sand River Convention* was unanimously accepted. Hymns and psalms were sung; old enemies clapped each other on the back.' Cf. Bulpin, *Lost Trails of the Transvaal,* (Somerset West SA: Stephan Phillips, 2002 edition: 1st edn, 1956), 105.

25 Even Bulpin, who is proud of the Boer indomitable spirit, admitted: 'The collapse of authority [in the Transvaal] had allowed one or two opportunist scoundrels to contaminate the name of all their fellows by indulging in commercial kidnapping and trading in African children under the cloak of the apprenticeship system. All it needed to put the whole Transvaal in the wrong was for one trader or missionary to report to the outside world that he had seen an entire wagon-load of woebegone African children being carted about as articles of trade.' (Bulpin, *Lost Trails of the Transvaal,* 143; See also: Northcott, *Robert Moffat,* 195. Letters from Boer participants in the raid on Sechele's BaKwena confirm the carrying off of women and children for distribution among the farmers. Cf. Pieter E. Scholtz, *To A.W.J. Pretorius, Commandant-General,* 12.9.1852, (*DLSAP,* 152f): 'Plenty of women and children were captured and much livestock taken [at Sechele's village].' These letters, plus other evidence, indicate that the kidnapping of women and children was not only carried out by 'opportunistic scoundrels', but by Boer leaders. It was a policy openly practised and openly accepted.

been previously published.[26] The following extended quotation gives a flavour of Moffat's passion concerning the issues, and shows that Moffat was no pietist ignoring the plight of a persecuted people (all italics ours):

> We think it is high time to be out-spoken and to point out existing evils which timely attention to may yet prevent calamities more dire than have ever befallen the Colony of the Cape of Good Hope for we are solemnly warned that 'there is a God that judgeth in the earth'. ...
>
> We have for some time past been observing the aspect of affairs between the Orange and Vaal Rivers ... [we hoped that events] would have induced the colonial Government to attempt something in order to prevent the further destruction of property, liberty and life, and which call loudly for enquiry into the present state of affairs among the Trans Vaal Boers. If it indeed be so that the colonial Government considers it hopeless to attempt to arrest the progress of anarchy, bloodshed and slavery beyond the Vaal River, *we must try what an appeal to the British public will effect*. Let the facts of the case be sounded in the ears of Christian men and women in Britain.
>
> Let the subject be laid before our beloved Queen and we will vouch that from the throne the voice of appeals will be echoed back in tones of sympathy for the oppressed and trodden down tribes of the interior ... Are such men [the Boers] to become the barriers to further researches into the geography and natural history of yet unexplored regions? Is the work of exterminating one tribe after another and to make slaves by wholesale, to be permitted to proceed with impunity under the very nose of our colonial authorities, and that too with the professed sanction of the Queen of England?
>
> Are the thousands and ten-thousands of aborigines to be left to the mercy of those who are the avowed enemies of missionary operations and to every form of instruction calculated in any degree to benefit our fellow men just because they are not white, or rather red men like ourselves? Will the English nation suffer this? ...
>
> ... *[Moffat then has a long section on Boer atrocities and policy]* ...
>
> Let the saints of the Most High weep and pray over the wars of South Africa. Mary Queen of Scots with good reason trembled at the idea that John Knox was making her the subject of his prayers. 'Prayer moves the hand that moves the world.' We know this and therefore do not put our trust in princes. We ask not the sword to be unsheathed to settle disputes and adjust rights between the Boers and the natives.

---

[26] Schapera referred to, and quoted from, another letter of Moffat to the *British Banner,* dated 14.2.1853, (*DLSAP,* 37ff). The section cited dealt mainly with the problem of Livingstone's 'Iron Pot' story, which denied Boer claims that Livingstone supplied the BaKwena with arms and ammunition. Whilst the two dates may have originally been one but altered by a copyist error, in our judgment Moffat may have written two letters to the *British Banner,* one on the 4th and the other on the 14th.

> We feel for the misguided Boers who are bringing down on themselves and on their posterity the curse of omnipotence. There is no time to be lost, and if England hopes to escape the doom which rests on other nations which have distinguished themselves by acts of injustice and oppression, let her go on in her Godlike career of advancing 'peace on earth and good will to men. We confide in your raising your powerful voice on behalf of the much-injured tribes of the interior.[27]

The *Sand River Convention* gave autonomous control of the Transvaal to the Boers. By 1853, the LMS missionaries were not only seeing the fulfillment of their gloomy predictions but were aware that a similar thing was about to happen in the Orange River Sovereignty, even nearer the western LMS heartland. A crisis meeting was held on 12 July 1853 at Likhatlong, Holloway Helmore's LMS station. The meeting was prompted by William Thompson, LMS agent in Cape Town. This was to discuss Boer misrule of the native population following the *Sand River Convention,* and the threat of a similar thing happening in the Orange River Sovereignty. Helmore was appointed secretary of the meeting, with Moffat in the chair. Those present were Moffat, Hughes, Ross, Solomon, Inglis and Helmore (all LMS); Jousse (Paris Evangelical Missionary Society); and Mayforth (Berlin Missionary Society).

3. *The Missionaries 'Memorial' (1853)*

The meeting at Holloway's station drew up a *Memorial,* to be presented to Sir George Russel Clerk, the British Government agent at Bloemfontein. Moffat, Inglis and Solomon were appointed to travel there, to present the *Memorial,* to argue the case for the native population, to protest against Boer misrule, and to argue in favour of the British Government asserting its authority and implementing British law in the areas affected. Moffat's seniority in the missionary community, plus his role as chairman of the meeting, plus being appointed as an envoy to deliver the *Memorial*, leaves no doubt that the *Memorial* was totally in line with Moffat's personal stand, and that the decision to formally lobby the official Government representative, was something he put his weight behind.[28] The missionaries were concerned that the British Government would cede Boer autonomy

---

27 RM, *To the British Banner,* 4.2.1853, (SOAS/CWM/SA/Box 29/1/B).

28 Northcott, *Robert Moffat,* 208: 'Never a conscious politician, Moffat was nevertheless ready to instruct the British Government in what he believed to be its honourable duty.' De Gruchy, conscious of the perception that Moffat stood apart from political issues, expressed the matter more strongly, underlining that neither Moffat nor LMS were silent about the Sand River & Bloemfontein issues. De Gruchy pointed out that even the Comaroffs, without mentioning Moffat, conceded the missionary concern. It was *Moffat* 'who protested in a way that would have made Read and Philip proud.' ('Alleged Political Conservatism of Robert Moffat', 31).

over the whole region north of the Orange River, all the way from the Transvaal to the Atlantic Ocean. Their fears that the Boers would expel every LMS station in that territory were not without foundation.[29] Every mission north of the Orange River (including Kuruman) would be forced to be abandoned. The expulsion of all LMS missionaries from the Transvaal before the end of 1852 had made that clear.[30] And even more important than the survival of the mission stations, was how the indigenous peoples would be treated. The *Memorial,* addressed to Sir George Clerk, set out the issues:

> You have arrived in this country at a most eventful period of its history: a great extent of country north of the Vaal River is in a very disorganised state, and a tone of feeling has been given to the native mind, both within and beyond the Sovereignty, which we cannot look upon without the deepest regret and the greatest apprehension. A very general impression has been made upon the native mind that the white man is combining for the destruction of the black.
>
> The cause of this feeling is principally the events which have recently transpired in the Trans-Vaal country. It cannot be unknown to you that there have lately been much commotion and bloodshed in that quarter. The immigrant farmers have always entertained very low views of the rights and privileges of the aborigines – have ever seized upon every opportunity of showing their superior might and of bringing the natives into subjection; but since the Convention made between Her Majesty's Assistant Commissioners and the immigrant farmers in 1852, their demands and [?] have passed all bounds. Since that Convention several native chiefs have been attacked and five mission stations, four belonging to the London and one to the Wesleyan Society, have been destroyed by the Boers.
>
> We have no hesitation in stating it to be our firm conviction that these attacks have been unprovoked on the part of the natives, and can be traced to no other source than the love of plunder, the lust of power, and the aim of obtaining constrained and unpaid labour on the part of the Boers. Nothing will satisfy them but the entire destruction of native [?], the complete subjection of all the native tribes to the arbitrary authority of the republic. ...

---

[29] The record of the meeting, sent from Helmore to Tidman of the LMS in London, alluded to this: 'The Boer have declared their intention to possess themselves of the whole country north of the Vaal River down to the Atlantic Ocean and Pretorius showed to Mr Inglis a document written by Mr Owen one of her Majesty's Assistant Commissioners sanctioning the claim'. See: Helmore, *To Tidman, LMS,* 12.7.1853, (SOAS/CWM/SA/Box28/1/B). For Owen's hostile attitude see: Northcott, *Robert Moffat,* 209.

[30] The Boer expulsion of Edwards and Inglis from the Transvaal in 1852, meant the end of LMS influence there. The rise of the Dutch Reformed Church in the 1850s gave the Boers a church more congenial to their interests. In 1860 the Berlin Society was allowed to enter the Transvaal followed by the Swiss. These missions avoided the awkward questions raised by LMS missionaries concerning treatment of the indigenous population.

> We have also to lament that notwithstanding the insertion of an article in the Convention between Her Majesty's Assistant Commissioners and the Trans-Vaal Boers, whereby slavery was expressly prohibited, many hundreds if not thousands of the natives are, under various disguises, held in slavery by the Boers.[31] In fact the whole system pursued by them towards the natives under their control is reducing them all to a state of servitude which cannot be distinguished from slavery.
>
> The result of these movements is that a general combination is being formed among the natives in order to resist the encroachment of the Boers, and we have the dark gloomy prospect of a long and bloody war between the black and white races in the Trans-Vaal country.[32]

Unfortunately, the 53-year-old Sir George Clerk, a former Governor of Bombay in British India, saw his task simply in terms of dealing with a tricky administrative issue between the Boers and the British. He was uninterested in justice and human rights. Efficient administration, not moral questions, was his forte. The meeting with Clerk at Bloemfontein was a huge disappointment to Moffat. After he returned to Kuruman, he wrote to Tidman in London:

> We are filled with anxiety as to the final results. Are the thousands and tens of thousands to be exterminated or driven to deserts or pestilential regions, or are they to be permitted to remain in the lands of their forefathers?[33]

In October 1852 Moffat had written to his brother Richard, 'These Boers were never very civilised and, during the lawless life they have been leading for years, they have no manners, become more savage than their swarthy neighbours ... the natives were thought to be bad enough but compared to the Dutch Boers beyond the Vaal they are saints'.[34]

---

[31] Northcott pointed out that, after the *Sand River Convention* of 1852*:* 'The heart of the missionaries' charge against the Boers lay in the apprenticeship or 'in-booking' (*inboeken*) system whereby boys were indentured to a master until the age of 25 and girls until they reached 21 ... apprenticeship smacked of slavery ... Children taken in kraal raids, or received as presents from local chiefs, were registered with the *Landrost* on the payment of a fee ... and a child could be transferred to another master on the payment of a transfer fee ... parents might sell their children ... Even President Pretorius, as late as 1865, managed to purchase 'three little Kaffirs' for 2 white blankets ... [which gave him] 11 years' work out of each of the girls, and 17 out of the boy' (Northcott, *Robert Moffat,* 202). This was slavery!

[32] LMS Missionaries, *Memorial to George Russel Clerk, Her Majesty's Special Commissioner for the Orange River Sovereignty,* 13.7.1853. The version we consulted was the copy sent by Holloway to the LMS, (SOAS/CWM/SA/Box28/1/B).

[33] RM, *To Tidman, LMS,* 8.8.1853, (SOAS/CWM/SA/Box 28/1/B). Cf. RM, *To Tidman, LMS,* 12.11.1853, (SOAS/ CWM/SA/Box28/1/C), in which a discouraged Moffat again expressed real fears about the future of the native people.

[34] RM, *To Richard Moffat,* 18.10.1852, (Northcott, *Robert Moffat,* 211).

4. *The Bloemfontein Agreement (1854)*

Sir George Clerk's orders in 1853, from the British Government, were to 'get the British out of the Orange River Sovereignty'.[35] After he dealt with the missionaries it took him until February 1854 to settle issues relating to the Orange River Sovereignty. Despite his efforts, Clerk was unsuccessful in his ultimate goal of handing over to the Boers *all* the land north of the Orange River, including the Griqua Town and Kuruman areas plus all the land to the Atlantic. The *Bloemfontein Agreement*, also known as the *Orange River Sovereignty*, signed on 2 February 1854 registered the triumph of the feared and disturbing view that 'the colonist must ultimately prevail against the native'. The British Government was tired of troublesome disputes with Boer farmers in the, as yet, unprofitable interior of southern Africa.

Moffat's involvement in the political debate of the early 1850s, the missionaries' *Memorial,* his journey to Bloemfontein and his advocacy there on behalf of native rights, are not well known. Even less known is the perseverance with which afterwards he pursued this issue in his writings. Moffat expressed his theology on the rights of the native tribes not only in his journeys, advocacy, and writing to newspapers, but also in the pressure he tried to exert on others to apply themselves. In the years which followed, and as unrestrained Boer policy increased, Moffat was not silent. In 1858 he wrote to Sir George Grey, Governor at the Cape, bringing to Grey's attention the following quotation from the Boer newspaper *Staat Courant*: 'Unless the natives are brought into subjection or *annihilated* the country must be given up.'[36] A day later, he wrote to Arthur Tidman of the LMS, urging him to use the influence of the *Aborigines Protection Society* to address a worsening situation:

> Why cannot the *Aborigines Protection Society* send out an agent to enquire into the sources of the present unhappy state of affairs which now threaten the extermination of the native tribes? Let him enquire into the Treaty made by Hogge and Owen, the representatives of the British Crown with the Transvaal Boers in which it is guaranteed to them that arms and ammunition they can have or purchase from John Bull to their hearts content while the native tribes who had never once offended are prohibited purchasing a flint, percussion cap, gun, or a single ounce of ammunition. The friends of the *Protection Society* have long known this. What have they done? They may

---

[35] Northcott, *Robert Moffat,* 207.

[36] RM, *To Sir George Grey,* 30.11.1858, (SOAS/CWM/SA/Box 31/1/B).

> have been active, but their efforts have never reached us who ought to feel the most interested.[37]

Moffat's highlighting of the situation in the Transvaal continued in his retirement. In 1883, just weeks before his death, he wrote:

> But at the present time I refer especially to the sufferings of the Bechuana tribes from the Dutch Boers of the Transvaal—a subject which deeply affects me for I see towns burned where I have often preached to attentive [people] the saving doctrines of the Prince of Peace, and an unoffending people shot down in cold blood after they had been robbed of their property. How little is done for native interests.[38]

In the same letter, he expressed hope that the House of Commons might do something. One of the very last letters he wrote was to his friend William Dickson on the same subject: 'I have felt much affected [by] the reported sufferings of the Bechuanas, robbed [by] the Transvaal Boers. Our Prime Minister knows all about it but hitherto has done nothing.'[39]

Moffat trusted naively in 'British justice' and 'British fair-play'. He may have been inexperienced politically, but he did not divorce his missionary work from issues of justice and peace. In the 1850s he was prepared to take the missionary case to the highest echelons of politics and power. Moffat was unsuccessful at Bloemfontein in 1853, but his instincts—deeply rooted in a theological understanding of humanity as having a common origin, equality and dignity—impelled him to make a stand, just as he had in 1817.

If Moffat had openly supported Philip during the 1820s, his reputation would be high, ranking with that of Philip and Livingstone. Nevertheless, the actions which he did take—in 1817, in the 1850s, and afterwards—reveal a man who placed himself in the eye of controversy for his beliefs. Moffat was not a political strategist like Philip. He was not comfortable lobbying in the corridors of power. Moreover, even if he had had the skills of a John Philip, the agreements between the Boers and the British at the Sand River and at Bloemfontein would most likely have been sealed anyway. The Boers wanted freedom within their 'living-space.' The British wanted rid of the problem of Boer discontent. For the politicians on both sides, the indigenous peoples were irrelevant.

---

37 RM, *To Tidman, LMS,* 1.12.1858, (SOAS/CWM/SA/Box 31/1/B) .

38 RM, *To William Dickson,* 13.3.1883, (EUNCL/WD9/3/22a/26/Box2).

39 RM, *To William Dickson,* 19.7.1883, (EUNCL/WD9/3/24/Box2). De Gruchy, 'Alleged Political Conservatism of Robert Moffat', 34, wrote: 'Until the final hours of his life Moffat remained passionately concerned about issues of justice and peace for the black inhabitants of southern Africa.'

THE RIGHT TO BEAR ARMS

The willingness of Moffat to speak out on political issues in the 1850s, in contrast to his reluctance in the 1820s, was matched by his change of mind regarding the rights of indigenous peoples to have firearms. By the 1840s, the northward advance of the Boers was causing devastation among the native tribes. As the Boers advanced, the natives were dispossessed of their lands, and missionaries were expelled from their regions.[40]

It is in this context that Moffat wrote passionately of the iniquity of a law, created by the British authorities in the aftermath of the *Sand River Convention*, forbidding the indigenous peoples to have arms. In an important passage in a letter to Tidman of the LMS, concerning his 1854 visit to Moselekatse, Moffat quoted Moselekatse and recorded his own unease at the restrictions which his own British Government had placed on trade with some native tribes, depriving them not only of the benefits of commerce but also the possibility of owning guns and ammunition to defend themselves against the Boers:

> [Moselekatse] asked, 'Do the English not trade with the Boers who ran away from their Government, and do not the English supply them with guns and ammunition, while they know the Boers use it to destroy the natives, that they may take their country?'
>
> This was a question I felt some reluctance to answer; for it was impossible for me to deny the fact that the English did enter into a treaty to supply those very Boers with arms and ammunition. I was only glad that he appeared not yet to have heard of the law promulgated by our Government – the iniquity of which law the English language would fail to describe, though the consequences it may one day repent – that the native tribes north of the Vaal River be not allowed to purchase a single ounce of ammunition.[41]

The underlining replicates heavy underlining by Moffat himself in the original manuscript. He employed strong, emotional language: 'The iniquity of which law the English language would fail to describe.' This letter was composed several months after Moffat returned to Kuruman. It was not written in the passion of the moment. That he still expressed himself with such emotion, even after a gap of many months from his conversation with Moselekatse, indicates intense feeling on the subject. Moffat was profoundly embarrassed by the policy adopted by the British Government.

---

[40] Deane, *Robert Moffat,* 133.

[41] RM, *To Tidman, LMS,* 10.5.1855, (*MJ1,* 372f). In private correspondence Moffat expressed indignation at such unfair treatment. See: RM, *To one of his Children,* 20.8.1856, (JSM, *Lives,* 316).

On the return journey from Moselekatse in 1854, the same points which had been made by Moselekatse were put to Moffat by Khosilintse at Sechele's camp, even more forcefully:

> We are told that the English love all men. [Yet] they give or sell ammunition, horses and guns to the Boers, who have red teeth, to destroy us, and if we ask to buy powder, we can get none. No, no, no! Black man must have no ammunition: they must serve the white man. Is this their love? The English are not friends to the black man. If I am accusing the English or the Boers falsely, tell me!'[42]

Moffat had been glad at Moselekatse's camp that the Ndebele chief had not pursued the issues. But with Sechele and Khosilintse he had no such reprieve. Moffat knew there was no answer he could give which could defend the injustice of a British position which left the native Africans defenceless against the powerful Boer. No wonder he wrote: 'I was right thankful to depart [the meeting], for though I had had many tough bones to pick in my missionary career, I never was in my life so completely floored.'[43]

Reflecting on Khosilintse's dramatic words, Moffat later wrote to Tidman: 'His eloquence was not that of fine language or modulated voice, *but it was the deep tones of a stricken soul.*'[44] In the same letter, Moffat referred to having reconstructed Khosilintse's speech from 'my penciled memorandum in my note book.'[45] Presumably Moffat made notes in his wagon as soon as the meeting with Khosilintse was over. Khosilintse spoke in SeTswana, and by 1854 Moffat was fluent in the language. Moffat wanted to give a *verbatim* account of Khosilintse's dramatic speech, adding marginal glosses to explain expressions which he put into Khosilintse's mouth.[46]

The whole of Moffat's record, both in style and content, points to Moffat being deeply disturbed by the course of events, and being totally convinced of the unfairness and fundamental injustice of the British policy. The *Orange River Sovereignty* (which became the *Orange Free State* in 1854) was, in Moffat's opinion, following the *Transvaal* in working towards a virtual extermination of the 'aborigines'.[47]

---

42 RM, *Journal*, 22.11.1854, & RM, *To Tidman, LMS*, 10.5.1855, (*MJ1*, 379).

43 Ibid.

44 RM, *To Tidman LMS*, 10.5.1855, (*MJ1*, 381).

45 RM, *To Tidman, LMS*, 10.5.1855, (*MJ1*, 380).

46 When Moffat quoted Khosilintse as saying that the Boers had 'red teeth', Moffat explained the phrase in a marginal note as 'implying great cruelty' (*MJ1*, 379). Marginal notes to explain phrases points to Moffat recording indigenous idioms not known to his readers.

47 RM, *To Tidman, LMS*, 10.5.1855, (*MJ1*, 382).

However much in 1854 Moffat was genuinely grieved at the defencelessness of the indigenous peoples, he had not been so positive about them having arms in 1826, especially close to Kuruman. At that time, he wrote: 'Without referring to the natural bent of the heathen disposition, we have every reason to believe that the ostensible cause of these evils [raids and cattle stealing] among the Batlapees is the introduction of muskets, ammunition, and horses.'[48]

Moffat's two views are not contradictory. They relate to dissimilar cases. The vulnerability of the Kuruman in 1826 was a genuine concern, and the recent devastating 1823 Mantatee raids from the east were still raw in the memory, and possibly recurring. But the situation was reversed in the 1850s. In the 1850s it was the native tribes who were highly vulnerable as Boer advancement increased. Moffat was a pragmatist, rather than an ideologue. He had no objection in principle to bearing arms, so long as possessing arms was for defence and not aggression.[49] Such fine distinction in theory may not remain so in practice, but that was his philosophy.

In 1827, during his extended time in the villages in immersive language study, this attitude meant that Moffat assured Chief Sebegwe that the missionaries would not supply him with arms. Moffat's point was not that Sebegwe and his people should not have arms as such, but that it was not the calling of a missionary to supply them:

> I took an opportunity of informing him [Sebegwe], as well as all that were assembled, that we as missionaries came for the purpose of instructing them about God and their immortal souls, and not to give, or be the means of giving *or procuring for* them,[50] either guns or ammunition.[51]`

Moffat did not want to become involved in the supply of guns and ammunition. His ultimate reason for refusing to be involved in trading firearms did not come from pacifism, but from a concern to separate trade of any kind from missionary work. He lamented missionaries who became too deeply involved with trading, resulting in their motives being suspect, and their concentration on spiritual issues being diluted. Moffat repeatedly stressed that he was not in missionary work for financial gain. It was

---

48 RM, *To Burder, LMS,* 13.11.1826, (*AAK,* 232).

49 See Ch. 19, 'The Peace of Jesus: Idealism'.

50 In Schapera's edition the words *'or procuring for'* are in italics. These were not in Moffat's original draft, but were included in the transcript sent to LMS Directors. The addition may have been to make a specific point to the LMS. Without these words, Moffat's original entry reads: 'missionaries came for the purpose of instructing them about God and their immortal souls, and not to give, or be the means of giving them, either guns or ammunition.' (*AAK,* 237).

51 RM, *Journal,* 25.5.1827, (*AAK,* 256).

important to establish purity of motive: therefore, to emphasise that he was different from speculators, he refused to become involved in trading. On his first visit to Moselekatse he made this point explicitly, emphasising that he lived on support from home in Britain: 'I referred to the chiefs who had been a while at the Kuruman, to assure him that we did not live on our flocks or gardens, but on foreign support, and that he saw we were not traders, as I had so often refused to trade.'[52] When Robert and Mary Moffat's eldest son decided to be a trader rather than a missionary, he had an uphill task to convince his mother that a trader could also be honourable and a Christian![53]

For Moffat, the missionary must be a missionary, *simpliciter.* The missionary was an emissary of the 'Prince of Peace', and aggression was inimical to that task. Nevertheless, as a pragmatist, Moffat accepted that, in self defence, even a Christian people must have the means of protection.[54] Thus, in 1856, he wrote again to Tidman objecting to, 'the English or Colonial Government putting their veto on a single shot of ammunition being sold to the peaceable Bechuana, while those whom they well know, as plunderers and murderers [the Boers], are allowed to procure to any amount they please. [The Bechuanas] do not understand this, and it is beyond our power to explain it without covering our faces with an impenetrable black veil.'[55]

---

52 RM, *Journal,* 1929, (*MJ1,* 27). Moffat's son-in-law, Livingstone, promoted 'Commerce and Christianity' as forces which could result in the emancipation and Christianisation of Central Africa. Moffat was adamant that the missionary should not be involved in an activity which was commonly seen as for personal enrichment, and not the occupation of an honest man. Cf. RM, *Journal,* 26.8.1857, (*MJ2,* 43). Moffat believed that some missionaries lost their sense of vocation when they became involved in trading, though he was pleasantly surprised at the character of some traders with whom he had contact, cf. *Journal,* 1929, (*MJ1,* 44).

53 Dickson, *Beloved Partner,* 204.

54 The Boers contended that Kuruman and Livingstone's station at Kolobeng were ammunition supply centres for the indigenous tribes. Schapera has carefully examined the evidence, concluding that, though Livingstone's evidence cannot always be relied upon, it is difficult to see Kolobeng as a supply point, or to describe Livingstone as a 'gun-runner' (*DLSAP,* 33-45). The evidence against Moffat at Kuruman is miniscule.

55 RM, *To Tidman, LMS,* 28.10.1856, (SOAS/CWM/SA/Box 30/1/A).

Chapter 16
Equality of Personal Rights

BEING A MISSIONARY TO the San, Khoikhoi, Tswana or Ndebele meant that these people were important enough for one's whole life to be devoted to their spiritual good, since Christ had given his life for them at the cross.[1] They were objects of God's love. The missionary's view was quite different from that of trader-explorers such as a Dr Colquhoun who regarded Khoikhoi and San as hopeless cases, with the San being regarded as hardly rational, and incapable of civilisation.[2] Yet, as Moffat pursued his missionary activity, believing in the common humanity and dignity of the peoples whom he encountered, he became convinced that certain social aspects required transformation.

THE RIGHTS OF WOMEN

'O Mary, this is a land of female woe.'[3] One aspect of Moffat's philosophy, consistent through his fifty years in southern Africa, regarded the status of women and children. In coming from nineteenth-century Britain, Moffat did not come from a society in which the rights of women and children were ideal. Unequal property rights, child labour, atrocious factory conditions and more, were all part of British society. Nevertheless, in Africa, in this area of society, Moffat displayed an instinctive opposition to unfairness.

In 1815, John Campbell wrote that Tswana women, 'Do not appear under any restraint in the presence of men but are free and cheerful.'[4] Campbell was a traveller, passing quickly from place to place before reporting back to the LMS on the state of their mission stations. In contrast, Moffat lived

---

1 RM, *To Miss Kent*, 28.8.1861, (NLSA/GREY/MSB/349/1/4): '[Missionary work is] conferring blessings of infinite value on Africa's sable children – *her trodden down sons and daughters who are alike the objects of that love which brought our saviour to suffer and die*' (our italics).

2 Cf. Philip, *Researches in South Africa (1828)*, xi.

3 RM, *To Mary Moffat*, 6.10.1857, (*MJ2*, 88). One of Moselekatse's daughters had gone missing, after being suspected of having had an illicit sexual relationship. A few days later, some bones were found with a knife lying near. It was thought that these were her bones, that she had committed suicide, and that her dead body had been devoured by wolves. Later it was discovered that these were the bones of a different person. Some young women were driven to suicide from the fear of cruel punishment after sexual indiscretion. Moselekatse's daughter was still alive. After Moffat arrived, his presence ensured that at least two of the chief's daughters who had committed indiscretions were spared death.

4 Campbell, *Travels in South Africa: At the request of the Missionary Society*, 274.

among the people, and his perceptions were different. In 1822 he wrote of how, in Clogho's village, it seemed that women were spoken of in the same way as cattle, 'supposing them an inferior sort of animal'.[5] In 1827, he was witness to the severe beating of wives by husbands.[6]

In 1854, when he preached to Sekhomi's people, Moffat had to insist that women, as well as men, should be given the opportunity to hear the gospel. On that occasion, he recorded in his *Journal* that when the people were called, 'It was objected [to] that the women should come into the khotla or that part of the fold where the men always meet, but Sekhomi overruled it by telling them that it was my wish, as the word of God was for all.'[7] Moffat asserted that women, as much as men, had both a right and a need to hear the Gospel.[8]

In 1857, he recorded with great sadness the suicide level among Ndebele women, attributing this to the way they were treated. Significantly, he was prepared to critique British society on the same issue, putting the suicide problem in England in the same league as that among the Ndebele: 'I heard today, while conversing with one of [Moselekatse's] people in reference to the condition of females, that suicides were frequent. Who can wonder? Human nature is the same whether under a tyrant's rule, or in England, *infamous for suicides*.'[9]

The significance of Moffat's *Journal* entries is that he was moved to action because of the unfair way women were treated. Many observers would have been unhappy with what they saw, but for Moffat it was not only important enough to record but was also important enough to try to change. He insisted on change where change was within his influence, such as ensuring that women were allowed into the 'men only' area to hear the gospel preached. He was convinced that polygamy contributed towards the demeaning of women. His opinion was that a herd of wives became regarded as a herd of cattle, rather than one wife being cherished and valued.[10] Moffat's repeated

---

5 RM, *Journal,* 19.3.1822, (*AAK,* 47).

6 RM, *Journal,* 22.4.1827, (*AAK,* 249).

7 RM, *Journal,* 6.11.1854, (*MJ1,* 337).

8 RM, *Journal,* 22.11.1857, (*MJ2,* 123): 'They, as well as the men (*lintunas, mantota* and *machaha*) sat and listened to the great truths of death, judgment and eternity.'

9 RM, *Journal,* 5.10.1857, (*MJ2,* 84).

10 There were some safeguards for women in traditional Tswana law, but in practice it was difficult for a woman to avail herself of such provisions. Schapera, *A Handbook of Tswana Law and Custom,* 28, observed, '(Tswana) women are on the whole regarded as socially inferior to men, and in Tswana law are always treated as minors. ... Women take no public part in the government of the Tribe, and all the political offices are kept exclusively in the hands of the men.' Schapera also points out a few of the 'safeguards': 'In tribal law the main grounds for

description of his own wife Mary as his 'beloved partner'[11] was neither convention nor hyperbole. He meant it. Roby had taught:

> The part of Adam's body from which that of Eve's was formed was probably intended for our instruction. She was not formed of the upper part of man; nor of the lower part; but of one of his ribs. Might not this signify that she was not to usurp dominion over the man; nor to be treated by him as an inferior; but to be held as a companion near his side—to have a place in his affections, near his heart—to be guarded and cherished under the arm of his protection and care (1 Corinthians 11:8,9; Ephesians 5:28,29).[12]

That was Moffat's outlook also. To a man was given leadership and responsibility, but these should result in care and protection, not in abuse or exploitation. Livingstone had similar views. Writing from Kuruman in 1841, having observed local conditions, Livingstone stated:

> In this country the women are in abject slavery, and have to build the houses, plant the corn, etc., etc., and when mere children are bartered for; their consent is never asked, and the men don't care how many wives they have, the more wives the more corn etc. he gets into his possession by their means. And the hard work they have to do soon making them look old, they are then thrown off. Forced to subsist on different kind of wild roots, they are frequently, when ill especially, unable to return home at night and are devoured by the wolves, or they perish from hunger in the endeavour to get food. Do you ever pray for your sisters who perish by wolves?[13]

Setiloane, who was concerned about defending traditional practices wherever possible, disagreed with Moffat's reading of the situation. He argued that the missionaries misunderstood the positive aspects of the role of women in Tswana society: 'So affronted were [the missionaries] by this apparent cruelty of Sotho-Tswana men to their women folk (another instance of lack of culture and civilisation) that the missionaries were never able to concede the other side of the picture—how traditional practices and custom still secured the women a place, even of some power.'[14] Who gives

---

divorce are a husband's sorcery, cruelty, or non-support, and a wife's sorcery, barrenness, desertion, or failure to perform her domestic duties. Adultery, a valid ground in civil law, is seldom treated as such in the tribal courts, unless often repeated: usually the husband merely claims compensation from his wife's lover, whereas if he himself is the offender she has no legal remedy. A divorced woman returns to her parental home, and can then be married again', (Schapera, *The Tswana,* 42). Schapera also noted that, in a polygamous household, each wife has her own compound, fields, cattle and domestic utensils, which after her death were inherited by her own children' (40).

[11] 'Beloved partner' was a term frequently used by missionaries to describe their wives. Missionary societies were slow to recognise female missionaries in their own right.

[12] Roby, *Theol. Lect.* 37, 'The Creation of Man'.

[13] Livingstone, *To Janet Livingston (Sister),* 8.12.1841, (*DLFL,* Vol. 1, 40).

[14] Setiloane, *The Image of God among the Sotho-Tswana,* 99ff.

the proper picture: Moffat or Setiloane? On the one hand, Moffat and Livingstone viewed the situation through their own cultural lenses. On the other hand, Setiloane looked at the situation as it was 100 years later, not as Tswana society operated on the ground in the mid-nineteenth century.

What effects did Moffat's applied theology have? An important aspect was that Moffat applied church discipline equally to men and women. Men were disciplined for ill-treating their wives, as much as women were disciplined for marital 'faults'.[15] Also, one of the effects of conversion in the lifestyle of people at Kuruman was that some men purchased wagons and used oxen for labour which formerly had been performed by women.[16]

This type of change was cited by Moffat in his lectures in Britain. At Moffat's 1842 Edinburgh meeting, the Rev. W. Alexander said, in summarising Moffat's work: 'We have seen women raised from the degrading position of a drudge to man's exaction, and a slave to man's passions, to her proper place as the gentle companion and sweet helper of man's earthly pilgrimage.'[17] In some indigenous groups there was an understandable suspicion among men to a message which was likely to deprive them of the services of their (many) wives, who built their houses, gathered firewood for their fires, tilled their fields, and reared their families. This unease created a barrier to evangelism.

Despite the many difficulties encountered in creating new attitudes, Moffat was optimistic about the social changes which might take place among the BaThlaping, especially when Peclu, chief Mothibi's converted son and heir apparent, would eventually take power: 'When Peclu has the reins of government into his own hands, he may be induced to make alterations in some of the inconsistencies of their system, which tend to check the increase of knowledge and improvement, and keep the weaker sex in a state of comparative slavery.'[18] Unfortunately, these hopes were dashed when Peclu died young.[19] Moffat saw change of society as starting with transformation of the family. But he also realised that change in customs in tribal society

---

15 E.g. *KCRB:* A woman separated from Church fellowship for taking a married man (5.11.1837); A man separated for taking a married woman (31.12.1837), and other examples.

16 Deane, *Robert Moffat,* 119.

17 W.L. Alexander, *Address,* 3.11.1842, (*Farewell Services,* 8).

18 RM, *To Burder LMS,* 8.5.1824, (*AAK,* 115).

19 Peclu, son of Mothibi, heir to the chieftainship of the BaThlaping, died suddenly in 1825. Cf. RM, *Journal,* 30.3.1825, (*AAK,* 180), 'We ourselves were inclined to hope that on his assuming the regal powers a favourable change would likely succeed, but the Judge of all the earth has otherwise determined.'

must carry the authority of the chief. That was a major reason why he had invested so much time in Peclu's spiritual development.[20]

In 1879, when Emma Pitman contacted Moffat concerning an article about Mrs Moffat which she was writing, he replied with enthusiasm and, significantly, referred to Paul's chapter on Christian women: 'I read last night Paul's last chapter to the Romans. Could I help thinking of your noble purpose?'[21] The Moffats lived and worked in an era where the wife of a missionary was not accounted a missionary herself. That change, and the concept of a woman being called to be a missionary in her own right, only came later.[22] Moffat, as was the custom of the time, described the wives of missionaries as 'partners in labour.'[23]

The Rights of Children

The plight of young children was concerning. In a moving passage, Moffat recorded how he and Mary found and adopted a child who was going to be buried alive and left to die:

> We have also two Bushman children, a brother and a sister, the latter about five or six years of age, the former about three, both orphans, which I procured on my return from a journey to Griqua Town. The boy was just on the point of being thrown into the grave of his father, when humanity stepped forward and rescued him from the jaws of so unnatural a death.[24]

---

20 The authority of the chief was rarely, by itself, sufficient to make a tribe change established custom. An absolute despot such as Moselekatse might have that ability, but few others. When Sechele of the BaKwena adopted a Christian manner of life, his people strongly resisted. The authority of a chief was not absolute, unless the individual were a Chaka or a Moselekatse. A chief's authority rested on the consent of the tribe. The obedience of a tribe towards any individual chief was great, but not total. Moffat noted this in his *Journal.* Cf. RM, *Journal,* 6.6.1854, (*MJ1,* 161f): 'I began by stating that if the chiefs of this country were like those in some countries, he had only to cancel the unnatural and unscriptural custom with one word, and his subjects would say 'Amen'. But the case was otherwise; that I knew the real position of the Bechuana chiefs as well as most men did, and I knew that *the chiefs feared their subjects more than they did their chiefs.*' (Our italics).

21 RM, *To Emma Pitman,* 16.1.1879, (SOAS/CWM/Africa/Moffat/Pers/4).

22 All LMS missionaries were male until Maria Newell in 1827. John Owen Whitehouse, *A Register of Missionaries and Deputations from 1796 to 1877,* (Ldn: Yates & Alexander, 1877), gives a 'Register of Female Missionaries from 1827-1876', including Maria Newell. She died in 1831 in Bangkok. The next female LMS missionary, E.M.H. Sturrock (Peelton, South Africa) was not appointed until 1864. Thereafter, female missionaries were more frequent. Maria Newell is also listed as missionary 270a, in the *Annotated Register of LMS Missionaries: 1796-1923.*

23 RM, *MLSSA,* 166.

24 RM, *To Alexander Moffat,* 25.2.1822, (*AAK,* 59f). This incident is featured in JSM *Lives,* 106. JSM wrote that it was the dead *mother* who was going to be buried, and that both the boy

A few years later, a similar incident occurred: 'Some months ago an inhuman mother buried her female child alive, when about one month old; which was removed by Mrs Moffat after being a night and a day in that appalling situation.[25] She has been adopted, and baptised Sarah Roby. She is doing well.'[26] The child was named after the wife of William Roby, and one of the rooms at the present-day Kuruman Moffat Mission is 'The Sarah Roby Room.' However, though little Sarah was 'adopted', cared for, and generally treated as part of the family, she did not appear in the official family name lists.[27] Thus 'adopted' should read as 'fostered'. An edition of *Brown's Catechism,* belonging to Sarah Roby inscribed with her name, and dated 1836, is in the Grey Collection of the South African National Library in Cape Town.[28]

Male European missionaries marrying African women—an option which Moffat himself entertained—and missionary families taking African children into their homes where they were brought up alongside the missionary's own children, were relatively common during the first half of the nineteenth century.[29] These became rarer in the century's second half, probably because of a hardening racial polarisation.

As well as referring to children being abandoned or interred with a dead parent, Moffat noted children being offered for sale for the price of an ox or a sheep or beads: 'This morning two elderly persons came and presented their children for sale. I believe an ox, or a sheep was expected for one, and a handful of beads for the other. I began to point out how unnatural such

---

and girl were to be thrown into her grave. The boy (named 'Dicky' by the Moffats) and the girl (Ann) were part of the Moffat household for many years.

25 Moffat added a note, 'embedded in stones and during the night it rained heavy'.

26 RM, *To Burder, LMS,* 20.5.1826, (SOAS/CWM/SA/Box10/1/C).

27 See the 1836 statistical return to the LMS, (SOAS/CWM/SA/Box15). An 1842 painting of Moffat, now in the National Scottish Portrait Gallery, Edinburgh, includes the African children Sarah Roby and John Mokoteri (fostered), both of whom are described as Moffat's adopted children.

28 See: Grey/9/c/3/a: *Second Edition of Bechuana Catechism*: inscribed 'Sarah Roby, 1836'. In this 2nd edn, the Q&A are not numbered, unlike the 1st edn. The revision was prepared by Moffat and Edwards. There is no solid information on the adult Sarah Roby.

29 The LMS missionaries Van der Kemp and James Read both married African women. Moffat mentioned the possibility in his 25.11.1818 reply to Mary's letter of 27.8.1817, though he did not want to, because he still hoped that Mary would be able to be his bride. Mary had stated that she might never be able to come to Africa since her parents needed her. Robert preferred to hope, and, because of that hope, he did not want an African bride, indeed was not sure if so marrying was wise. Nevertheless, he accepted that the possibility of marrying an African bride was a serious option. Cf. RM, *To Mary Smith,* 25.11.1818, (Grey/MSB/349): 'I can only remark that I have seen and learned much during my stay in Africa. I have seen native wives and Cape ones too, and my thoughts at present are that I could not easily brook the idea of taking a native, but, rather that, than fall into sin.'

conduct was, and the evil consequences which would accrue from such traffic.'[30] According to Moffat, some Boer kidnapped native children by force to become their slaves. Moffat referred at length to this, and to the grief of their bereft parents, in his *Journal*:

> There are many hearts among them [Africans] mourning over their captive children. One man, like some others, retained only one of four [after a Boer raid]. How we should feel if John, Bessie, and Jeanny were slaves among Algiers! The Boers are not a whit better.[31]

This extract followed Moffat recording that an African had told him that none of the children had been able to make their escape from slavery: that they had seen some of their children in Viljoen's house and other Boer houses at Mosega, but they dared not speak to them! Moffat had a profound anger towards the Boer for such inhumanity, especially because the Boers were understood to be Christians by the indigenous Africans. Moffat despaired over them, despite having friends in the Boer community, whose kindness he had experienced on many occasions.

In Moffat's view the Boers were a terrible example of white people who professed to be Christian. In *Missionary Labours* he crystalised his view concerning the difference between the British and the Boers in words he put into the mouth of Africaner addressing some missionaries: 'As you are sent by the English, I welcome you to the country; for though I hate the Dutch, my former oppressors, I love the English: for I have always heard that they are the friends of the poor black man'.[32] *Missionary Labours* was written in 1842 with a British readership in mind. After 1852 Moffat might not have written so confidently in praise of British attitudes.

In another passage, he cited Africaner as wondering whether the Boers really followed the same God as the missionaries: '(Africaner) became the more bewildered, especially when he thought of the spirit of the Gospel message 'good-will to man'. He often wondered whether the book he saw some of the farmers use said anything on the subject; and then he would conclude, that if they worshipped any such being, he must be one of a very different character from that God of love to whom the missionaries directed

---

30 RM, *Journal,* 30.7.1824, (*AAK,* 131). The same event was referred to in *MLSSA,* 389f.

31 RM, *Journal,* 5.6.1854, (*MJ1,* 155). Moffat was aware of child-kidnapping in the African community. One of his great achievements with Moselekatse was to persuade him to release Troey and Macheng, who had been kidnapped by the Ndebele in the 1830s and kept prisoner until 1854 and 1857 respectively. Moffat wrote a moving account of Troey's liberation after his intercession with Moselekatse (*MJ1,* 269f, 321ff). Details on Macheng are in *MJ2*, 115, 135ff, and 140ff. For more details and subsequent history, see 155ff.

32 RM, *MLSSA,* 72.

the attention of the Namaquas'.[33] Moffat compared Moselekatse's tyranny with that of the Boers, writing of the 'nature and extent of the oppressions of the Transvaalian government', convinced that 'history would bring appalling cruelties to light, but there is a day which *will* declare it'.[34] He added: 'What an idea these natives must form of the character of the white man, always aggressive, always unjust, always cruel.'

Moffat even called the Boers *Christian tyrants.* When he passed the site of an 1836 battle between the Ndebele and the Boers with their allies, he commented: 'There lie the bones bleached in the valley, but which will in the end rise in judgment against their *Christian tyrants* who compelled them to go and assist them in their expedition of rapine and murder'.[35]

The Right to Marry

When discussing the interaction between missionary teaching and African culture vis-à-vis marriage, attention frequently focuses on polygamy versus monogamy. Polygamy was certainly a critical matter, but there was another deep-seated issue which occurred in certain groups. That of enforced celibacy. Nineteenth-century British society largely accepted the principle of marriage between a man and a woman through free agreement and consent of both parties. African indigenous society, by and large, did not have the same approach. There was therefore a clash of cultures between: marriage by individual consent, marriage by community consent, marriage by parental consent, and marriage by consent only of the chief,[36] In 1824 Moffat also noted that infant betrothal was common among the BaThlaping.[37]

Moffat's views on marriage within an African context were not primarily focused on individuals having freedom of choice. We have found no instance of him trying to introduce notions of 'love choice' in opposition to native practices. What he was more concerned with was the basic issue of young men and women having the right to marry someone—anyone! This problem was acute among the Ndebele, over whom Moselekatse had absolute control concerning the marriage affairs of his people.[38] None of the young men could

---

33 RM, *MLSSA,* 183f, cf. 239.

34 RM, *Journal,* 10.7.1854, (*MJ1,* 213).

35 RM, *Journal,* 19.7.1854, (*MJ1,* 225).

36 Sometimes there was a combination of practices. Schapera, *The Tswana,* 41, pointed out that in Tswana tradition a man's first wife was generally selected for him by his parents; any others he chose himself.

37 RM, *To Alexander Moffat,* 6.6.1824, (*AAK,* 118).

38 T.M. Thomas pointed out that, among the Ndebele, all children were regarded as Moselekatse's. '[A man] said '[My daughter] is not mine, but the king's; she is only mine by

marry without his consent. Occasionally he might withhold permission for any marriages to take place, resulting in his young men and women burning with frustration. Traditionally, the chief would give permission for marriage after a young man made his first kill of an enemy of the chief.[39] Or sometimes he would grant marriage permission to a whole regiment of *machaha* at once as the reward for some unusual feat of arms.[40] However, since he restricted his warriors' activities when Moffat was present, and because, during the 1850s, the Ndebele engaged in only limited aggressive warfare, the young men had few opportunities to qualify for marriage rights.

Giving or withholding permission to marry was one of the ways in which Moselekatse maintained despotic authority. On his 1854 visit, Moffat several times referred to the many daughters of Moselekatse who were condemned to perpetual virginity and not allowed to wed. This was in addition to the bleak future faced by some of Moselekatse's Ndebele warriors, who similarly were not allowed to marry.

In a letter to Tidman, Moffat mentioned that several of Moselekatse's young warriors came to him. They asked Moffat to intercede with their chief and obtain permission for them to marry and to have families.[41] Moffat's intercession did produce a change, and Northcott was of the opinion that the change was a much greater achievement than Moffat realised.[42] The potential for social transformation by the Ndebele adopting different marriage customs was seen as crucial by Moffat:

> During all my interviews with [Moselekatse] I have never failed to endeavour to recommend a reform in the social condition of his people. Thousands of both sexes live and die without being permitted to marry. This system as a

---

birth, for we are all the king's, and therefore cannot say that our children are ours, or that we are our own', (*Eleven Years in Central South Africa,* 63).

39 When Moselekatse fled from Chaka in 1822 the 300 who went with him were nearly all young male warriors: women and children left behind. They had to gain wives by conquest. Hence the tradition of a warrior only being given a woman after making a kill.

40 L.H. Gann, *A History of Southern Rhodesia: Early Days to 1934,* (Ldn: Chatto & Windus, 1965), 30. Machaha were Moselekatse's warriors.

41 RM, *To Tidman LMS,* 10.5.1855, (*MJ1,* 376), In this letter Moffat referred to 8.10.1854, when the young men asked him to intercede. This was not mentioned in his contemporary *Journal* record for that date (326ff.). In his daily *Journal* record Moffat was preoccupied with the position of the captive Troey: or he may have mistaken 8 October for 28 October when writing officially to Tidman, six months later. See: RM, *Journal,* 28.10.1854, (*MJ1,* 332f).

42 Northcott, *Robert Moffat,* 238f. Thomas, *Eleven Years in Central South Africa,* 260, reckoned that half of Ndebele males never wed. For those who did, it was common for them to be older. Whilst 50% may be high, Thomas' comments show a significant social problem.

> matter of course gives rise to a great deal of discontent and desertion, besides being the source of much wickedness.[43]

Moffat believed that if young men and women had greater freedom for marriage, then some of the causes behind tribal warfare would be eroded.

This hope extended to his views on polygamy. His mentor, William Roby, taught that God's original union of only one male with one female was a 'loud testimony against the abominable sin of whoredom, adultery, polygamy and divorce.'[44] Moffat's objection to the practice of polygamy was primarily rooted in his interpretation of Scripture, but he went deeper than Roby, and added sociological reasons as to why he saw polygamy as not only contrary to God's law, but injurious to a community as a whole. Whilst with the Ndebele in 1857, Moffat observed that the chief's many wives had few children. He concluded that polygamy was no remedy for increasing a nation:

> There were no less than ten of this town's wives [wives of Moselekatse in this particular village] sitting in a space something less than a forehouse, none of them young, yet only one of these ten had had two children. Polygamy is not the way to replenish the earth or increase a nation. Even Rehoboam, who had seventy-eight wives and concubines, had only eighty-eight sons and daughters, one child and a fraction to each wife. The Matabele are kept up and increased by taking boys and girls from the conquered tribes.[45]

Moffat believed that when the groups around Kuruman became increasingly monogamous under Christian influence, the overall population increased. He stated, in his 1840 LMS *Sermon*: 'Polygamy and oppression are arrested in their progress, and population is increasing.'[46] On these grounds alone Moffat believed that abandoning polygamy led to a healthier self-sustaining society.

---

43 RM, *To Tidman LMS,* 2.10.1860, (*MJ2,* 270, 171).

44 Roby, *Theol. Lect.* 37, 'The Creation of Man'. Missionary insistence on male converts putting away all wives except one is a complex issue. Livingstone, *To RM,* 8.7.1850, (*DLFL,* Vol. 2, 84), also followed the LMS line: 'Jesus put it as from the beginning, one man to one wife.' Setiloane argued that polygamy allowed men and women to have second partners without disgracing existing partners by rejecting them. He cited a situation which occurred because of Moffat's strictness: 'According to Sotho-Tswana law and custom this man's action [of putting away his second wife] was a very shameful insult to the woman's family. [Also] a few years before the occurrence [of a convert woman running away with a man from his wife] this man and woman would have been able to live together, without shame, she as his second wife, and the harmony of the polygamous household would have been preserved.' (*The Image of God among the Sotho-Tswana* , 102f.). Setiloane quoted the missionary John Cameron: 'I am in doubt whether it be the wisest plan and most likely to secure the happiest results, to force a polygamist on embracing Christianity to put away all his supernumerary wives.'

45 RM, *Journal,* 22.10.1857, (*MJ2,* 102).

46 RM, *Africa,* 43.

Moffat was aware that in any society the number of males and females are roughly equal—to within a few percentage points at most—hence if each male has even only two wives, there is a huge deficit in the number of available females. This meant that raiding neighbouring tribes in order to procure more females became common. Hence, for Moffat, polygamy led to either to kidnapping or to denial of marriage rights.

As stated earlier, Moselekatse tried to limit Ndebele raids when Moffat was with them, but sometimes the young warriors could not be restrained, as in 1859: 'Moselekatse is also said to be annoyed with his *machaha* to the south having lately forcibly taken away children from the Makalaka, some of whom were killed in the fray. It is their system of rearing warriors, and it is possible he may be vexed at it taking place while we are here.'[47]

Moffat also observed that just as young men and women who were refused permission to marry burned with frustration, so did neglected wives of a polygamous chief, sometimes with tragic consequences, as in 1857, at Moselekatse's kraal:

> Lately one of the king's concubines had been detected in illicit intercourse with another man. She was before the gate of the fold in which my wagon now stands. A council was held. Moselekatse was not present. She pleaded guilty, adding that she had no idea that she, a woman, was intended to live with the mere name of wife or concubine, that she had acted according to her own impulse as a woman, and did not see wherein she had erred; that she knew she would be killed and that she preferred death rather than live with the mere name of wife. She was taken to the forest by the hangman, for there seems to be something like another Calcraft[48] here, and hung by the neck, and her guilty paramour speared. I am laying up these facts for they are not solitary, to preach a sermon at some fitting occasion to his majesty. Of course, touching his wives is like touching the apple of his eye, but events of a similar character may be referred to without giving offence.[49]

Moffat saw social reform as an essential part of mission. His Calvinist roots stressed that in all Christian work the glory of God came first. Hence the

---

47 RM, *Journal,* 3.12.1859, (*MJ2,* 237).

48 'Calcraft' was an English hangman.

49 RM, *Journal,* 5.10.1857, (*MJ2,* 84f). Moffat returned to the topic in 1859: 'Those [wives] who are with his majesty enjoy his presence; but his many wives at the many distant towns pine in disgust, and this accounts for delinquencies, which if caught, end in death, or escaping with paramours to the Bamanguato or beyond the Limpopo. Sometime since an instance occurred; the men escaped but the women (his wives, whom probably he never knew) were captured and butchered. Such a government needs the axe putting to its root. I have told Moselekatse before, and may have occasion to tell him again, that his kingdom, with laws regnant, respecting the celibacy of his—or the great majority of his—subjects, cannot stand.' See: RM, *Journal,* 1.11.1859, (*MJ2,* 209).

primary purpose of evangelism was to glorify God by establishing the values of God's kingdom of righteousness throughout the earth. The salvation of souls, though of immense importance, was a human benefit and therefore secondary to the primary purpose of establishing the reign of God everywhere. Societies were not only to be saved, but they were also to be transformed. Gospel proclamation which omitted the call to a new way of life for society as a whole did not make sense to Moffat. In applying his vision of transformation, Moffat thought out why some customs should change. They must change because, in his opinion, they did not correspond to God's will; but they must also change because they restricted, frustrated, and degraded the people. He appreciated that change involved 'putting an axe to the root', with a radical and total transformation.

Moffat did not envisage any compromise between Christ's authority and chieftainship authority. Two kings, and two authorities, could not co-exist. Either there was the reign of Moselekatse or there was the reign of Christ. Similarly, Moffat did not simply identify polygamy simply with a voracious male sexual appetite. He saw polygamy as connected with issues of power and authority, rather than with lust. The transformation of the relationship of men to women, and of the nature of the home and family life, were, in Moffat's eyes, key to establishing a Christian society.

Moffat had a complex task in applying what he believed to be God's biblical plan for society. He was aware that, even if marriages became monogamous, the quandary of whom a person may marry remained. In 1854, on his way to see Moselekatse, Moffat stopped at Sechele's village. One matter he had to discuss with Sechele was the possibility of Sechele's daughter, Ope, becoming the wife of her uncle Khosilintse. Moffat deemed this marriage unsuitable. But was it within the degrees of prohibited consanguinity in Leviticus?[50] Moffat called the possible marriage 'a dirty sin in the eyes of God'[51] But was this because Moffat considered the man to be too old, and marrying an extremely young woman would be an unjust imposition on the girl?

Though Tswana custom concerning consanguinity did not exactly match Levitical law,[52] the differences were minimal. And in general, Moffat seems

---

50 What Leviticus 18:12f focuses on (from a male perspective) is possible marriage of a man with his father's sister or his mother's sister, and forbids both. The situation of a woman marrying her father's brother or her mother's brother is not directly considered.

51 RM, *Journal,* 6.6.1854, (*MJ1,* 162).

52 Schapera, *The Tswana,* 41, pointed out that in Tswana society a man may not normally marry such close relatives as his sister, parent's sister, or sibling's child, but some tribes (e.g. BaNgwaketse and BaRolong) formerly permitted marriage with an agnatic half-sister, and that

to have allowed what Scripture did not forbid. He also strove to separate biblical precept from European conventions. Thus, for example, in 1872 he could not understand why parts of the Free Church sought to extend consanguineous prohibitions beyond scriptural rule: 'I cannot help wondering at my countrymen being in general opposed to marriage with a wife's sister. I never heard a reason worth calling a reason for that view of the subject.'[53]

The Right to Education

At the heart of the missionary emphasis on education was evangelism. It was believed that if men and women learned to read the Bible then they would become Christians more easily. Kuruman's remote and isolated location meant that there were few other incentives in education. Religious instruction was the clear focus.[54] Bogue stressed that through education 'the influence of the pagan hierarchy will be hereby greatly diminished and perhaps destroyed',[55] and Moffat observed that one fear behind Moselekatse's resistance toward schools was the perception that his authority, and the traditional structures of his society, would be undermined by people learning to read and write.

Moffat valued education, and the right of both male and female to have access to it. Co-educational philosophy was assumed at Kuruman. In 1848, the number of children attending the mission schools at Kuruman and its surrounding villages came to around 470.[56] In 1852 Moffat reported that 45 boys and 80 girls were enrolled at the primary school which the mission had

---

some other tribes still allow it with a brother's daughter, whilst not with a sister's. All Tswana, on the other hand, encourage marriage with first cousins.

53 RM, *To William Dickson,* 17.6.1872, (EUNCL WD9/3/4A). There was discussion at the Free Church General Assembly, in May 1872, on the propriety of a man marrying his deceased wife's sister. Leviticus 18:18 appeared not to forbid it, so long as the first wife had died. In 1854, Moffat had a discussion with Sechele on consanguinity. Cf. RM, *Journal,* 8.6.1854, (*MJ1,* 166): '[Sechele] then took up the New Testament. We then turned to the case of a man having his father's wife, and the point he wished particularly explained was his being handed over to Satan, (1 Corinthians 5:1f.) which his own case made him view as a rather serious matter.'

54 The LMS 1885 *Annual Report*: 'There are no self-interests at work in Bechwanaland—such as have influenced Cape Colony, and much more India—to make education valued by the people. To the Christian education is associated with means of grace; to others it is only an accomplishment, regarded by most heathen as useless, or perhaps prejudicial. The consequence is that education in Bechwanaland is very partial and very elementary. If a man or woman can read the Bible, their aspirations in this direction are satisfied.' (Cited in: Lovett, *History of the London Missionary Society: 1795-1895,* Vol. 1, 633).

55 Bogue, *Miss. Lect.* 10, 'Of Setting up Schools'.

56 LMS, *Annual Report,* 1849.

established, with an average of 90 pupils attending on any one day.[57] These were full-time schools, requiring the skills of native teachers as well those of missionary families. Day education was an important duty for Kuruman native teachers in addition to preaching and catechising responsibilities.

Wing has pointed out that the school at Kuruman, started by Moffat in the 1820s, was the mother of all the educational work of the LMS among the BaTswana, and that there was still a mixed, co-educational, multi-racial LMS primary school on the station at Kuruman until 1956, when the apartheid Bantu Education Act enforced closure.[58] The LMS emphasis on education for all was a powerful statement of its belief that all races had equal intellectual ability, and that both male and female had the right of access to schooling.

In due course, Moffat could report: 'Our day, Sabbath, and infant schools, as also our printing-presses, are at work, to supply the increasing needs of a reading population'.[59] Yet several times he also had to record that Christian education was not always popular. Sechele's people especially, after they expressed disapproval of their chief's conversion, put up strong objections and resistance to any Christian education.[60]

At the same time, it may have been Moffat's emphasis on education primarily as a tool to enable a person to read the Scriptures which resulted in Kuruman not reaching the heights of Lovedale under James Stewart in South Africa.[61] There were, admittedly, other reasons, with sparse population and de-population in the Kuruman area among them, but one factor appears to be that Moffat was not driven by the goal of education for its own sake, as was Stewart. Yet, in Moffat's system, education went further than simply learning to read and write, important though that was. Moffat

---

57 Cf. *Kuruman Church Record Book,* for 1852.

58 Joseph Wing, 'Water from the Rock', in: B. Thorogood (ed.), *Gales of Change, Responding to a Shifting Missionary Context: The Story of the LMS, 1945-1977,* (Geneva: WCC, 1994), 31.

59 RM, *MLSSA,* 242.

60 RM, *Journal,* 8.6.1854, (*MJ1,* 165).

61 A mission station school for the Xhosa was started in 1824 at a town later known as Alice in the Eastern Cape. By 1841 it had developed into the Lovedale Missionary Institute, and was one of South Africa's earliest African schools, originally for the training of teachers and clergy. James Stewart (1831-1905), Scottish missionary, minister, educator, and explorer, was responsible for making Lovedale an important centre of education. He insisted that all students undertake some form of daily manual labour, including the construction of roads, watercourses, dams, and work in the fields. The purpose of this was to show that Christianity and idleness were not compatible. In 1878 he wrote that all colours and nearly all tribes of South Africa were found among Lovedale's students. It remained a mixed college for blacks and whites until 1926. The work at Lovedale started in the 1820s, the same time as Kuruman, but over the next fifty years it outstripped Kuruman in taking education to a higher level. However, Lovedale was not on the edge of the Kalahari with its sparse population, nor was it far from other centres of population. Resources were available which Kuruman never had.

was a hands-on person, and he valued educating the population in practical skills, horticulture and agriculture. Even allowing for a certain amount of laudatory comment, John Mackenzie's description of Kuruman in 1870, the year Moffat left Africa, gives a helpful picture:

> I found that most of the people living at Kuruman have considerable knowledge of agriculture and the ordinary management of a garden. The hoe has largely given place to the plough, and in such cases the work of the garden ceases to belong to the women, and is performed by the men. .... As the land at this station belongs to the Missionary Society, the apportionment of the gardens rests with the missionaries, and is perhaps not the most pleasant of their offices. It is required that the occupant be a well-conducted man and the 'husband of one wife.[62]

Mackenzie's latter point—that the apportioning of the gardens on LMS land rested with the missionaries—is important. This gave the missionaries significant authority, and itself could be a tool in enforcing a pattern of life according to missionary standards. It was certainly an incentive.

The Missionary as Activist

The missionary as activist was supremely important to John Philip. He quoted with approval Thomas Chalmers' statement: 'What the man of liberal philosophy is in sentiment, the missionary is in practice.'[63] Was Moffat of the same stamp? We have already noted Ross's judgment that Moffat viewed concerns about justice as a distraction from the 'true missionary vocation.'[64] And it is true that though Moffat wrote admiringly of Van der Kemp as being a defender 'of the rights of the Hottentots'[65]—as he also did of Philip[66]—there is no doubt that he was slower to become involved in the political rights of the indigenous peoples than they had been. But there is enough evidence to demonstrate that his concerns were the same.

There is an unfortunate ambivalence in Moffat's appraisal of the two men. He lauded Van der Kemp and Philip in *Missionary Labours,* which was

62 John Mackenzie, *Ten Years North*, 70.

63 Philip, *Researches in South Africa (1828)*, xxxiii. Thomas Chalmers' Christian philosophy focused on the qualities and potential of human benevolence, following the eighteenth-century Scottish philosopher, William Hutcheson. The ability of humanity, under God, to change the world for the better, also reflected the optimism of the time.

64 Ross, 'Robert Moffat', (*DSCHT,* 598).

65 RM, *MLSSA,* 41

66 Cf. in an unpublished note, written to a friend, Moffat gave directions to the grave of John Philip: 'There lie the remains of the late Dr and Mrs Philip, the great friend of the Hottentot race.' (RM, *Notes on Traveling in South Africa:* NLS/20317/184).

written for a public audience;[67] but in his personal *Journals* and *Letters* he was far less complimentary. Moffat criticised Van der Kemp 'going native' in his lifestyle, and Moffat criticised Philip for stirring up trouble with the Cape Government and putting at risk the freedom to continue the mission work so carefully and painstakingly being nurtured at Kuruman. Despite this criticism of style and practice—and sometimes Moffat's criticisms of Van der Kemp and Philip were devastatingly and rudely hostile—Moffat agreed with their root principles regarding the dignity and rights of the indigenous peoples. But why was he slower to become involved on the political level? Several reasons present themselves:

1. Moffat was a different kind of person. When needed, he had great moral courage as well as physical courage, yet it was not in his personality to be a revolutionary.

2. Though Moffat had an instinctive sense of 'unfairness', he did not consciously operate within a framework of 'rights'. The distinction is subtle, but nonetheless real. A sense of unfairness propels a person to righting unfair situations one by one as he comes across them, whereas an overall framework of 'rights' propels a person to changing the underlying system. Moffat was inclined to the former rather than to the latter, though, as the years passed, he became involved in the latter. His faith principles concerning all humanity as having a common origin, equality and dignity, always had the potential to make him apply the Gospel on a wider canvas. The situation of oppression and repression, which he encountered, eventually brought this to the surface and impelled him to engage directly in political debate.

3. Moffat believed that the work which he was doing at Kuruman needed a long and settled period of input over decades, not just years, and would be at risk if he became politically active. The Cape Governor might not

---

67 RM, *MLSSA,* 38: 'Dr Van der Kemp having, with true Christian benevolence, pleaded the cause of the oppressed ... the great struggle commenced which terminated, through the persevering exertions of the Rev. Dr Philip, on July 17th, 1828, in the effectual emancipation of the Hottentots.' Yet for Moffat the emancipation of the Hottentots became a bitter-sweet experience, when some of the land they were given following their emancipation was taken from the Xhosa [Kafirs]. Cf. RM, *MLSSA,* 43: 'The author does not wish it to be understood that he approves of the policy which deprived the Kafirs of that rich and fertile portion of their territories, and gave it to the Hottentots.' Moffat's disapproval of Van der Kemp was so strong that he could not withhold criticisms: 'It is only right to admit that the Doctor was eccentric; and many, very many, of his personal hardships were self-inflicted' (*MLSSA,* 41).

allow him to stay if he became objectionable.[68] Moffat alluded to this fear many times. He could not risk this, so he separated his missionary activity from overt politics but retained sympathetic views underneath.

4. Bogue's teaching, and LMS official policy, was one of non-interference in political matters. It was Philip who broke new ground. It was Moffat who acted in line with accepted LMS doctrine.

5. Moffat objected in principle to the idea of the LMS sending someone, such as John Philip, to be an overall Superintendent for the mission stations.[69] Consequently, he was reluctant to accept Philip's authority, or to support his policies.[70] Moffat saw the office of Superintendent as Episcopacy in all but name. Moffat was Congregationalist in his ecclesiology, believing that each mission station (church) had full control of its own affairs. He believed that this was the freedom given by the LMS system, and he was stubborn in his unwillingness to acknowledge a man in Cape Town as his superior.

Points (3) and (5) were the main reasons as to why Moffat gave Philip little support. Moffat was not a political animal. Even when, later in life, he became more so, it was not his natural vocation. He was prepared to publish his views in *Missionary Labours,* which was not only intended for the British

---

68 There were examples of missions, promisingly started, being stopped because the authorities refused permission for missionaries to continue in that area (*MLSSA,* 47).

69 JSM saw this as the main problem which his father had with Philip: '[My father] had a stout Nonconformist objection to the principle of a superintendency. He protested against it from the first as 'putting Pope into new clothes.' 'It was well that the remoteness of the Bechwana Mission practically isolated it from the doctor's regime.' (JSM, *Lives,* 64).

70 W.M. Macmillan, *Bantu, Boer and Briton: The Making of the South African Native Problem,* (Oxford: Clarendon, 1963), suggested that Moffat's antipathy to Philip, plus Moffat's a-political stance, was why Philip avoided the Transvaal issue. Macmillan further suggested that if Philip had been involved then the British Government would not have turned a blind eye to what was happening, and perhaps the *Sand River Convention* and the *Bloemfontein Agreement* might never have occurred (334f). Macmillan was possibly overstretching his argument. E.g. on page 358 he stated: 'Moffat, and even Livingstone, failed to keep the Government informed of what was happening under their eyes. So it came about that, in sheer ignorance of the real situation Her Majesty's Government in 1852 left the unfettered control of all these Bantu fragments to the emigrant Boers.' This is wrong. Moffat gave regular reports to the LMS, which was expected to apply pressure in Britain. Livingstone also sent back detailed reports. Macmillan's book has several inaccuracies: e.g. page 357 where he cited an 1847 letter of Moffat's, referring to Sechele receiving missionaries from the Boers. This was not until 1857.

public in general, but was dedicated to the Queen's Consort, Prince Albert.[71] Yet publishing such views in 1842 was not a radical step. By that time, the British Government had already recognised native rights, at least in theory, largely due to the determined pioneer activism of men such as Philip, to whom Moffat had given little support.[72]

Moffat was not a player in the political battle which John Philip waged on behalf of the indigenous peoples, but his convictions were the same. When an opportunity came for him to make a public stand against the authorities, he did so unequivocally in the context of the *Sand River Convention*. By that time, he was revered in the eyes of the British public, and no Cape Governor would dare remove the 'lamp of the Gospel' from Kuruman or expel the most famous missionary station in Africa. Moffat was no longer afraid of the consequences, and he intervened directly on behalf of the people, maintaining the struggle until the end of his life. This homologates Steve de Gruchy's statement that the allegations of Moffat being pietistic and other-worldly do not do justice to Moffat and need to be corrected 'if we are to evaluate his legacy in this generation'.[73]

---

71 RM, *MLSSA,* i.

72 Briggs & Wind, *The Harvest and the Hope,* 36: 'Philip's first real clash with authority was over the terrible plight of the 1820 settlers, when drought and flood had reduced them to desperation. ... Overnight he became the settler's hero. ... Then things changed just as rapidly, and those who had praised him to the skies began to vilify him. He had turned his attention to the plight of the Hottentots, and his tampering with their cheap labour market roused the antagonism of the colonists, Dutch and British alike. ... When *Ordinance 50* of 1828 was ratified by the House of Commons, giving full legal status and civil rights to the Hottentots, the white attitude towards Philip settled into unyielding enmity.'

73 De Gruchy, 'Alleged Political Conservatism of Robert Moffat', 21. De Gruchy has rehabilitated Moffat's political dimension: 'Moffat discerned that a clear priority for him was making the Bible available to the BaTswana, and he focused much energy on this, even to the point of undermining his health. It was, moreover, a priority that was recognised by John Philip when he assigned the press to Kuruman.' (p. 24). ... 'All of this meant that Moffat did not have the time or energy to be active in the kind of work that Philip and Van der Kemp were involved in.' (24). Moffat opposed political involvement because it would detract from other things, and had same attitude to trading (p. 25). Also, Moffat would act as interpreter but refuse to represent the British Government to the chiefs (p. 25; cf. *MJ1,* 78). De Gruchy commented: 'In his book *Missionary Labours and Scenes* Moffat deals with the question of roles in an honest and open way and not (as has been inferred) in a pietistic manner. In much the same way that Archbishop Desmond Tutu in 1994 called on priests in the Church of the Province of Southern Africa (Anglican) not to join political parties lest their role be confused, and in the same way that the successor body to the LMS in southern Africa, the UCCSA, has disciplined ministers for holding political office because of the confusion of roles and authority, so Moffat felt after clear personal experience at Griqua Town with Anderson and later with Peter Wright, whose work as missionaries was severely undermined by their appointment as government agents, that 'more than 20 years' experience among aborigines beyond the boundary of the colony has convinced the writer that the 2 offices ought not to be held by the same person'.

The Centrality
of
Jesus Christ

Chapter 17

The Love of Jesus

> A heathen chief [said] to me, 'We all love you as much as if you were our own father; and we would love you abundantly more, if you would not talk to us about that man, you call Jesus; just leave us to go on as we are.'[1]

FOR ROBERT MOFFAT, as for any missionary from the Evangelical Revival tradition, the centre of his faith was a pietist love for Jesus Christ. Christian ethical principles were built on this centre, but Jesus Christ was the focus for faith and life. When referring to Moffat's Christology, this is of major importance. The influences of the Evangelical Revival in his childhood home and in his conversion experience, ensured that the primary characteristics of pietism, namely affection and love for Jesus, were central to his faith. Conversion—within the context of the Great Awakening and Evangelical Revival—involved 'touching the affections of the heart' otherwise it was not deemed to be a true conversion. The 'love of Jesus' motif was reflected in Moffat's writings, though, being from the Victorian era with its characteristic reticence in expressing emotion, he rarely articulated these sentiments.

Classical Christology is mainly concerned with Patristic creedal statements concerning the person of Christ. In Moffat's writings there is little discussion of the doctrines formulated at Nicaea, Constantinople or Chalcedon, though there is no doubt that he assented to them. Moffat did make a brief allusion to Christ as he in whom 'God became man',[2] and he also composed SeTswana hymns which had the couplet 'Jesus Jehovah', echoing Roby's predilection for the phrase, with its strong assertion of the divinity of Christ.[3] However, Moffat's Christology was not one which dealt with ontology but was one of the heart. Yet it was no less powerful a Christology because of that. In Jesus Christ, Moffat found the grace and the love of God, and, unsurprisingly, the

---

1 RM, *Africa,* 41.

2 RM, *Speech to the LMS Directors,* 1.8.1870, (Walters, *Life and Labours of Robert Moffat: Missionary in South Africa,* 212).

3 Moffat's SeTswana hymn, 'Yehova Yesus moluki', *Lihela Tsa Tihelo Ea Morimo,* (Ldn: Unwin, 1843). Cf. Roby, 'The body of man may be said to have been created in the image of God, likewise because it was made after the form of that body which *Jesus Jehovah* had determined to assume in the fullness of time.' (*Theol. Lect.* 37, 'The Creation of Man').

most quoted hymn in Moffat's writings was Robert Robinson's *'Oh to grace how great a debtor'*.[4]

Knowing Jesus

In reading Moffat, the foremost impression is of a man whose purpose in life was to promote the cause of Jesus Christ, and for whom all was dedicated to that end. Moffat's writings, such as *Missionary Labours*, were not always well organised but they were full of accounts of conversations, preaching, and discussions, all concerning the Christian faith, the need to respond to the Gospel, and the reactions of people to the message. There was a dedication and intensity of purpose in Moffat's writings which we do not find in Thomas Morgan Thomas or in David Livingstone. Their works lack this single-minded concern. Some might view Moffat's driving-force as obsessive. Others might see it as the natural outcome of the spiritual passion and *raison d'etre* of his whole life.

Thomas' book, *Eleven Years in Central South Africa*, was an account of his time among the Ndebele, from the start of the Ndebele Mission in 1859 until 1870, an exciting period of pioneer missionary activity. Yet very little of Thomas' book was about evangelism. Thomas gave excellent insights into Ndebele culture, language, society, and history. He also provided detail on the plant and animal life of the area. Our feeling is that if Moffat had written the book, the emphasis would have been different. Thomas delights the cultural anthropologist, but his relative silence on the work of the mission perplexes the theologian. It is true that during these years there were no conversions at Inyati. At Kuruman, during most of the 1820s, there were no conversions either, but Moffat's Kuruman *Journal f*or the 1820s still focused on his message, on conversations, and on people's reactions to the Gospel. A Moffat account of Thomas' Inyati years would have been a record of discussions, dialogues, and descriptions of individuals to whom he spoke, and who come alive to the reader through Moffat's vital interaction with them. Above all, it would have been a record of a burning desire to communicate Jesus Christ.

For Moffat, the heartbeat of the Gospel defined and circumscribed his whole horizon. However much Thomas shared the same Christian faith, what he wrote did not convey this zeal with anything like the same intensity. The

---

4 'Oh, to grace how great a debtor; Daily I'm constrained to be; Let thy goodness like a fetter; Bind my wandering heart to Thee. Prone to wander Lord, I feel it; Prone to leave the God I love; Here's my heart, O take and seal it; Seal it for Thy courts above.'

same comment can be made of Livingstone's *Missionary Travels.* The depth of Livingstone's personal faith is not in doubt but he had other interests, and these other interests intrude and dominate, especially in his later writings. In our view, the single-mindedness of Moffat is lacking in both Thomas' and Livingstone's writings. It was not hyperbole when Moffat wrote:

> I once said to [Moselekatse] that if I returned to the Kuruman without having preached to him and his people about Jesus the Saviour of the world, I should return with a heavy heart, never to see him again, till he and I and all the dead should rise from their graves.[5]

A closer parallel to Moffat is found in the Wesleyan missionary Barnabas Shaw who arrived in southern Africa around the same time as Moffat. Shaw's *Memorials of South Africa* is much nearer in style and content to Moffat's work, with a similar pietist approach. This may not be a coincidence. Moffat and Shaw were both influenced by Methodism which had even stronger pietist traits than other traditions which had been touched by the Evangelical Revival. It may be that this background, plus their individual personalities, made them express their faith and work in the way they did.

LOVING JESUS

Moffat's motive for mission came from a desire to serve Christ, and his message focused on establishing the reign of Christ. In Moffat's piety, death for the Christian involved, above all else, going to meet Christ in confidence and love. This future hope was not an abstract notion of eternal life but was meeting the Saviour. Christological piety lay deep within his soul. When Moffat described the last moments of the missionary Abraham Albrecht, he wrote: 'Shortly before he fell asleep in Jesus, he read a chapter and conversed on its contents. To the inquiry how he felt, he replied, "*I go to Jesus*; I am a member of his body."'[6] Eternal life was not simply life after death; it was going to be with Jesus. In writing as he did, Moffat was not just repeating conventional idioms of Evangelical religious sentiment: he was expressing the core of his own faith. This Christological focus, especially in the face of death, was also articulated in his account of the death of an old female convert during his early years in Africa. Moffat described a scene of deep piety:

> The subject was a venerable mother, a member of the church, and one of the fruits of Mr Anderson's labours when on the Orange River. Entering her hut, and asking how she felt, she looked upwards with an expression of sweet

5 RM, *Journal,* 20.9.1854, (*MJ1,* 309).
6 RM, *MLSSA,* 84, (our italics).

> composure, 'I am looking for the coming of the Lord Jesus', was her reply. Observing me addressing her unbelieving daughters, who were weeping around her bed, she remarked, 'Yes I have called them that they might see a Christian die'; and a few hours after, she was called to the bosom of her God.[7]

Eighteenth and nineteenth-century books on missionary work made a feature of the pious death of native converts. To a certain extent, Moffat was simply continuing that tradition. But, apart from echoing contemporary practice, his descriptions of death-bed scenes point to his own inner piety. The death-bed was regarded as the place where a person's true convictions were confessed, hence the focus, during these centuries, on the 'last words' of public figures.

For Moffat, and other missionaries, the deepest convictions of converts were those expressed near death. When last words were about their relationship with God, about their peace at the prospect of death, and about their excitement at soon meeting the Jesus who had captivated their hearts, then their testimonies justified all the hardships which the missionary had had to endure. Precious fruit had been produced. The sweetness of the fruit was the clear love which such converts had for their Lord. In the pietist tradition, Christ was only 'conqueror' if he captured the affections of the heart. Religious conquest through subjugation of a culture by means other than through the heart was alien to true evangelical activity.

There are other examples of Moffat writing about love of Christ and heart religion. In describing a convert in 1830, he wrote that she 'has also yielded obedience to the sceptre of Christ and her [life] and general deportment forms a most desirable transcript of one *who loves the Lord Jesus'*.[8] He then added: 'Another Mochuana, a young man, has also produced very pleasing fruit indicating a real change of heart. He became serious, addicted to prayer, and attentive to the preaching of the Gospel.'

In 1835, on his second visit to Moselekatse, Moffat observed some Ndebele men and women who brought food to him: 'They seemed to exhibit great joy on seeing us. They are all as happy as one could wish them, *if they only knew and loved the Lord Jesus Christ*.'[9] In employing this phrase Moffat showed that he was not concerned with simply 'Christianising' a people, but with introducing a piety which touched the affections. In 1840, when he preached in London at the LMS annual meeting, he remarked concerning missionaries: 'Clad from the armoury of heaven, and constrained by *love of*

---

7 RM, *MLSSA,* 115.

8 RM, *To Orme, LMS,* 28.3.1830, (SOAS/CWM/SA/Box12/ 1/B).

9 RM, *Journal,* 31.5.1835, (*MJ1,* 60), (our italics).

Jesus, [they] are becoming more devoted.'[10] Then, when remarking on the conversion of Africaner, Moffat stated: 'The *love of Christ* transformed [him] into a humble messenger of peace. He would take from his pocket his well-worn testament and tell his countrymen of *the love of Jesus* and appeal with tears to his [own testimony as proof].'[11]

A few years later, in an 1847 letter to Arthur Tidman, Moffat described some prospective church members: 'There were about 20 candidates who, however, were not received till they had given further proofs of *their love of the Saviour* by persevering in learning to read his word.'[12] What Jonathan Edwards termed the 'affections', Moffat called 'heart religion'.[13] This 'heart religion' defined conversion. Conversion was not simply knowledge, obedience, and singing hymns. It involved a 'heart religion' in which the deep affections were warmed and captured by Jesus Christ.[14]

The same sentiments and expectations were applied to the Moffat family. In an 1871 letter to his friend Jessie Watt, Moffat expressed his personal feelings in regard to Christ. Writing in the third person, he said that he 'loves the Lord Jesus and has been his servant to the sable sons and daughters of Africa.'[15] Moffat's own anticipation of heaven centred on being with Christ: 'All we need, all we can desire, is to be ready for heavenly eternal years *in the presence of our dear Redeemer*.'[16] Concerning his own daughters, Elizabeth and Jane, who became full members of the church at Kuruman whilst he was absent, setting up the Ndebele mission, Moffat wrote: 'I had the delightful satisfaction of hearing that my own two daughters had also *given themselves to the Lord*.'[17]

---

10 RM, *Africa,* 29, (our italics).

11 RM, *Africa,* 35, (our italics).

12 RM, *To Tidman, LMS,* 23.3.1847, (SOAS/CWM/SA/Box23/1/A), (our italics).

13 Cf. RM, *To Tidman, LMS,* 11.1.1864, (SOAS/CWM/SA/Box 33/3/A).

14 Bosch, *Transforming Mission: Paradigm Shifts in Theology of Mission,* (New York: Orbis Books, 1991), 286-291, had an important section on this topic, entitled 'Constrained by Jesus' Love'. Bosch identified a negative side to the focus on 'love', as it fostered a preoccupation with individual response and individualisation. In our view, there is little evidence that Moffat and other LMS missionaries individualised the Gospel in this sense. This was because they also had a strong notion of the transformation of society by the reign of Christ.

15 RM, *To Jessie Watt,* 13.6.1871, (SOAS/CWM/Africa/Moffat/Pers/4).

16 RM, *To Miss Sapworth,* 22.12.1880, (SOAS/CWM/Africa/Moffat/Pers/4).

17 LMS, *Report to the 67th Annual Meeting, 1861,* 64, (our italics). Robert Unwin Moffat, (Moffat's grandson), wrote about his own father, John Smith Moffat, going to churches on deputation work: 'There was one common bond in all cases: *the love of the Master*, and the desire that the good news that He brought into the world should be proclaimed to all sorts and conditions of men.' (RUM, *JSM,* 124).

SHARING JESUS

Pietism is sometimes viewed as an inadequate basis for missionary activity, in contrast to missiologies which incorporate social issues and cultural interactions. In previous chapters, we have demonstrated that Moffat's theology did include social concerns and cannot be viewed as being a limited form of pietism. However, the general assumption that pietism had little to contribute on its own requires examination. The essence of pietism, in a missionary context, is that the missionary is primarily motivated by the Saviour's love and has the aim of bringing others into a personal experience of Christ. But it is arguable that if pietism posits love of Jesus as the main motivation behind missionary activity, then this actually adds integrity to the missionary task. This is because the pietist missionary looks for conversions one-by-one, rather than through a mass movement, initiated perhaps by the autocratic decision of a chief who has decided that his people will now be Christian,[18] or by the desire of a colonising authority which wishes subject peoples to adopt its form of religion.

A pietist missionary was rarely guilty of adopting methods aimed at a mass Christianisation of society. That was anathema to those who set high value on men and women coming to an individual commitment to Christ, with accompanying evidences that the affections of the heart had been touched. The pietist missionary might be criticised—often unjustifiably—for neglecting the corporate life of society by insisting on individual conversion. However, it was that very emphasis which could act as a bulwark against 'imperialist missionary activity' in which cultures, traditions, and religions were displaced by fiat and not by conviction. A pietist missionary came, first and foremost, as the ambassador of Jesus, rather than as the representative of an ecclesiastical structure or of a colonial authority extending its empire. The pietist method was slower, more painstaking, but in the end carried greater depth and integrity.[19]

---

[18] Many BaThlaping became Christian long before their chief, Mothibi. Conversely, Sechele, chief of the BaKwena, professed Christian faith, though his people did not. A disjunction between the faith of the people and the faith of their chief created problems within tribal society. However, theologically, it carried the advantage of faith being a matter of individual conviction, rather than of convention. The debate has many facets, but the pietist approach had strong points in its favour which are often overlooked.

[19] Even the frequently disapproving Setiloane admitted that early missionary societies were not connected with imperialism, though from the mid-nineteenth century things changed. Setiloane, *The Image of God among the Sotho-Tswana*, 244.

PREACHING JESUS

If Jesus is the ruling affection of the heart, then he should also be the very centre of the missionary message. In the LMS there were discussions on how best missionaries, in previously unevangelised regions, should communicate the Gospel. This debate was reflected in Bogue's *Missionary Lectures,* where Bogue discussed whether a missionary to such areas should commence with general teaching concerning the nature of God, or whether the missionary should immediately preach about Christ and the cross.[20] Bogue considered methods used by various missionary groups such as the Church of Rome, Danish Missionaries, American Missionaries, and the Moravians.

Bogue noted that, in Greenland, the Moravians had begun by giving an orderly introduction to the nature and perfections of God, but that, 'afterwards they preached on the sufferings of Christ, from which great effects followed.' However, it is not clear whether Bogue meant that it was *after* the Moravians first taught on the nature and perfections of God that they then moved onto Christ and the cross as the next logical step, or whether they abandoned the 'systematic' approach as unfruitful, in order to concentrate on the cross as an alternative to their former method.

When Moffat, in *Missionary Labours,* alluded to the Moravian methodology, he clearly thought that the Moravians had abandoned the gradual, logical unfolding of Christian theology, and that they had dramatically switched to a Christological focus, believing it would carry the power of God more effectively to make converts:

> [The Moravians in Greenland] had been in the habit of directing the attention of their hearers to the existence and attributes of God, the fall of man, and the demands of the Divine law; hoping thus, by degrees, to prepare the minds of the heathen for the more mysterious and sublime truths of the Gospel.
>
> As, however, this plan had been tried for five years with no success, they now resolved, in the first instance, simply to preach Christ crucified to the benighted Greenlanders; and not only were their own souls set at peculiar liberty in speaking, but the power of the Holy Ghost evidently accompanied the word spoken to the hearts and consciences of the hearers; so that they trembled at their danger as sinners, and rejoiced with joy unspeakable in the appointment and exhibition of Christ as a Saviour from the wrath to come.[21]

---

20 Bogue, *Miss. Lect.* 3, 'On Preaching (1)'.

21 RM, *MLSSA,* 299. In the following pages, Moffat elaborated and confirmed this theme. The Moravian change of methodology was also noted by the nineteenth-century writer Charles Bridges, *The Christian Ministry with an Inquiry into the Causes of its Inefficiency, (1830),* (Republished, Edin: BOT, 1967 edn) 242.

Bogue was reluctant to lay down strict principles on this issue. He believed that God's Spirit could work through a variety of methods:

> The apostolic method should be followed. The best modes used by faithful missionaries are certainly that which comes nearest to the divine pattern. Those who would argue with scholastic accuracy, may say men cannot know themselves as sinners till they know God, his holiness and law, nor Christ as a saviour till they know themselves as sinners and feel their need of a saviour.
>
> [Yet] from the success attending the labour of missionaries who began different ways, we may infer that the mode of beginning is not so important as some may suppose. If the pure truth be preached – that is unspeakably more important than with what particular truth a missionary may begin. The spirit of God does not always begin with the same truth; he puts all in due order; perhaps not one truth in the Scripture which was not the first truth to some individual.
>
> All true missionaries aim at the same thing—to bring sinners to know a saviour—with whatever truth they begin, their design is to lead to Christ – may go from cause to effect and from effect to cause, from principle to consequence, etc.[22]

Bogue refused to systematise the work of the Spirit: even though it might be held that a person needed to understand the nature of God before they could appreciate the concepts of sin and salvation from sin, the Spirit could use any order. Hence, he maintained that missionaries should not be inflexible in their preaching patterns. Effective preaching and evangelism were not bound by a fixed formula. The object of preaching and evangelism, especially from an evangelical background, was to bring a person into encounter with Jesus Christ. Within that encounter, God, in his freedom, would bring to bear whatever aspect of faith or belief was most relevant. Fundamental themes of sin and salvation were, of course, of the essence of the faith: but it was *encounter* with Jesus Christ which brought conviction, not a formulaic presentation of ideas or doctrines.

In *Missionary Labours*, Moffat accepted that 'Christ and the Cross' should be the primary focus of preaching.[23] But he also believed that general teaching on the nature of God, from a Christian and biblical perspective, was a proper prologue to truths concerning Christ and redemption, citing Paul in Athens (Acts 17) as a prime example.[24] In Moffat's view, preaching 'Christ and the Cross' did not mean that the doctrines of God, creation and

---

22 Bogue, *Miss. Lect.* 3, 'On Preaching (1)'.
23 RM, *MLSSA,* 299.
24 RM, *MLSSA,* 300.

providence were to be ignored. But preaching 'Christ and the Cross' did mean that Christology and soteriology had to be part of the message from the start.

For Moffat, there was no initial period of weeks, months or years, when general notions of God, Law and Sin were the *exclusive* subject of missionary discourse. If these doctrines were mentioned, they were always to be taught in relation to 'Christ and the Cross' and they were given their significance from that perspective. The central theme of 'Christ and the Cross', came early for anyone who listened to Moffat. He saw this as the Pauline pattern. As such, his standard presentation of the faith was to initially mention God the creator, the providence of God, and the immortality of the soul, but to move on immediately to connect these with redemption in Christ, and the future day of judgment before God. In 1876, he was asked what his core message had been during his fifty-three years of missionary work. He answered:

> In reference to preaching to heathens such as those the Moravian missionaries met with in Greenland, and Williams in the Islands of the Southern Ocean, I can only say that I did what I presume they did, and [proclaimed] the love of God to a rebel world. They told them that God so loved the world as to send His Son to die for sinners. The question must instantly rise in their minds: 'What God? What is the God you refer to?' 'You say that the son of that God died for sinners: who are sinners?' and 'Against whom have we sinned?' [These] are questions which must as a matter of course arise in their minds.
>
> For me the Gospel cannot be understood without telling the ignorant degraded heathen the character of that God who compassionated a world lying in wickedness. Such was the preaching of the Apostle to the Gentiles. I may not comprehend the exact object of your enquiry, but, to me nothing is plainer than the example of those who preach Christ crucified. Crucified for what? For sin! Against whom? Against God! Such teaching I have taught and that has produced the power of God and the salvation of thousands.'[25]

How did Moffat balance general teaching about God with an emphasis on Christ and the Cross? Moffat's most vivid reports of his preaching come from the *Letters* and *Journals* which he wrote in the field. He often penned these accounts only a few hours after preaching or conversing, giving them an immediacy which his reports in *Missionary Labours* sometimes lack. Some of the accounts come from his earliest years, and from the time he spent among the Namaqua as well as the Tswana.

Other accounts, and indeed the most detailed records, come from his theological encounters with Moselekatse and the Ndebele. In these, there are several striking examples of Moffat concisely summarising the essentials

---

25 RM, *To Rev. W.B. Woodman,* 9.10.1876, (SOAS/CWM/Africa/Moffat/Pers/4).

of his faith. Three of these are quoted below. The first comes from 1818 and concerns Moffat's preaching to the Namaqua. The second is from 1829 and records his very first conversation with Moselekatse. The third records an encounter from 1854, Moffat's third visit to the Ndebele but the first one on which he was permitted to preach openly to the whole people.

1. In 1818, Moffat wrote to Burder of the LMS: 'During our stay [among the Namaqua] I preached frequently, particularly from Paul's address to the Athenians. I also conversed with them on particular points, some replied, 'If it is so—that we are all the children or descendants of one Father Adam—how is it that you are white and we nearly black?' This I explained. I also spoke on the existence of God, the creation and fall of man, the immortality of the soul, the redemption by Christ. All this was a new thing, neither could it enter into their ears, according as they expected it, or, more properly, they could not believe it.'[26]

2. In 1829, Moffat's very first presentation of his faith to Moselekatse was on similar lines: 'I told him that I was a teacher from God, who was the creator of all things and the governor among the nations, and in visiting him I had also in view the time when his people also might receive messengers from God, to tell them of another and a better world beyond the grave.'[27] In another 1829 entry, Moffat gave a fuller outline: 'The next conversation I had with [Moselekatse] I explained to him the first principles of our religion, man in his natural state, asserting his immortality, the redemption of the soul by the death of Christ, the resurrection of the dead and the state of rewards and punishment beyond death. The last two particulars particularly arrested his attention.'[28]

3. In 1854, Moffat summarised his first open preaching to the Ndebele: 'I gave a general view of creation, providence and redemption, and concluded with death and immortality. I delivered the truths as they stood in the pages of divine revelation.'[29] Moffat's outline of this 1854 presentation is virtually identical with that of 1829. This consistency of record, plus fragments from elsewhere, indicates that, throughout his missionary life, Moffat held to the same pattern: Creation, Providence, Redemption, the Final State. What is noteworthy is that although Moffat had to wait 25 years before gaining permission to preach to Moselekatse's people, he was confident he would have more opportunities, as proved the case. There was no sense of him

---

26 RM, *To Burder, LMS,* 20.8.1818, (SOAS/CMW/SA/Box 7/5/A).

27 RM, *Journal,* 1829, (*MJ1,* 15).

28 RM, *Journal,* 1929, (*MJ1,* 16).

29 RM, *Journal,* 24.9.1854, (*MJ1,* 312).

feeling that he had to move to the Cross quickly in case no more opportunities come along. Nevertheless, though he was not under that constraint, he moved rapidly to the Christian revelation.

Moffat saw himself as having a Christological centre in his presentation of the faith. This did not mean that nothing else was mentioned, or that other aspects were unimportant. It simply meant that Christ, Cross, Redemption and Judgment were introduced from the outset alongside other theological truths, and gave these their meaning and significance. As so often, Moffat's record of his dealings with Moselekatse carried his heart theology. In 1854, when it seemed that he might never be given permission to preach generally to Moselekatse's people, Moffat spoke directly to the chief on the issue, and emphasised the love of God at the heart of his message:

> I told Moselekatse that if I were not permitted to speak to him or to his people about God and his love to us sinners, as I did among the other tribes, I could not be happy. ... I should tell them the good news which would do their hearts good, and it would do my heart good also, for I knew God and loved him and all, for God was love.[30]

[30] RM, *Journal,* 5.8.1854, (*MJ1,* 254). RM, *Journal,* 6.8.1854, (*MJ1,* 256), also recorded that Moselekatse attempted to avoid the matter: 'I try to persuade him to allow me to talk to him and his people about God and eternal life, and rather than put his veto on it, or say it must not be done, he sticks himself away in his harem.' This placed a restriction on Moffat. Not only did he lack permission to preach, but the people could not listen: 'As to talking to the people about serious things, it is out of the question. They can, they will, do nothing without the royal orders or permission. From childhood to youth their minds are imbued with fear of him. No gradation of punishment or fines. It is death at once, and perhaps in a horrid form.' Moffat was frustrated at not being allowed to talk to them about 'the soul's salvation'. Trusting that courtesy might open doors in the future, he waited his time. It did.

Chapter 18
The Reign of Jesus

ESCHATOLOGY IS NORMALLY treated toward the end of a work on theology. For Moffat, and his colleagues, the doctrine so profoundly affected their missionary enterprise that it requires to be treated earlier. Moffat's eschatology was not an addendum to his theological outlook but its driving force, moulding and energising his whole outlook. His eschatology focused on the *reign of Christ* and issued out of his Christology. For Moffat, Christ was not only the Saviour, but was the coming King whose millennial reign was close at hand. Christ was the One whose Kingdom was soon to be established upon the earth. Decisively, Christ was he who would come as the glorious Prince of Peace.[1] In 1838, Moffat wrote to the Rev. George Browne, Secretary of *The British and Foreign Bible Society*, expressing confidence concerning the coming reign of Christ, and stating that translation, reading, and study of the Bible would be major instruments initiating that reign:

> We take courage and feel a kind of triumph when we look to your venerable and majestic society as our magazine of invincible armour destined to conquer the world with love and make all the kindreds of the earth hail the meek and lowly Jesus as their God and King. ... [In the Scriptures] Jesus and the Apostles teach and heal without any scholastic flourish intruding between them and the hearts of the hearers. The great principles of the Bible Society are exemplified here. The simple reading and study of the Bible alone will convert the world.[2]

It was not accidental that some of Moffat's strongest statements concerning the coming King were made in letters to the *BFBS* since, in his theology, the Bible as the 'sword of the Spirit' was the means through which the Kingdom of God would be established.[3] In 1851 Moffat wrote: 'The Bible Society lives,

---

1 Discussed in Ch. 19, 'The Peace of Jesus'.

2 RM, *To Browne, BFBS,* 3.7.1838, (CULBSA/Browne/1838/4/40).

3 The question: 'What means will be used to bring about the Millennium?' received a wide variety of answers. For Moffat, it was the spread of the Word of God in the Scriptures. William Carey believed that trade and exploration could help. John Campbell, mindful of prophecies that, 'in gospel times, waters shall break out in the wilderness and streams in the desert' suggested that the coming of the Millennium would be aided by the new successful technique of boring for water by use of hydro-screws, cf. Campbell, *The Progress of the Kingdom of Christ, the Great End of Divine Providence: A Sermon preached in George Street Chapel, Glasgow, on Thursday April 4th 1833, on Occasion of the Twenty-First Annual Meeting of the Congregational Union of Scotland,* (Glasgow: Gallie, 1833), 11.

and doubtless will live until the whole earth shall be covered with the glory of the Lord, and all flesh shall see His salvation, preparing the way for the reign of peace and love, which will never be the case till the Bible shall be laid on every Family Altar.'[4] A year later he returned to the same theme:

> '[The Bible is] God's book of life to a sick and dying world. How little, yea how insignificant [are] all other enterprises when compared to this. They have their results, and some of them are made subservient to great and important ends in the providence of God; but it is to the Bible we are to look as the only means of directing human invention to the best of causes and thus transform a world of sin and evil into an abode of righteousness, peace and love. This is a theme familiar to your heart. It is one that never cloys nor ever dies ... our delightful anticipations of the coming glory of the *Messiah's Universal Reign* which your Society is the great instrument of advancing.[5]

Moffat referred to his ideals, hopes, and vision for the future, as a future in the glory of the 'Messiah's Universal Reign'. These fed his dream of a transformed world under the reign of Christ. Bible translation would be at the heart of this process of transformation, enabling that reign to come to pass. Two important points may be noted at this juncture.

Firstly, for Moffat, since it was through the ministry of the Word that the triumph of Christ, the *Messiah's Universal Reign*, would be precipitated, he placed the highest importance on God calling someone to minister the Word. Whereas the highest calling for a sacramentalist might be ordination, enabling them to celebrate the sacraments; the greatest vocation in Moffat's view was being appointed as a teacher to spread the message of the Bible, the living and transforming Word of God.[6]

Secondly, Moffat's emphasis on the anticipated *reign of Christ* was not the same as an emphasis on the *return of Christ,* or Second Coming. The paradigm which Moffat worked with was an Old Testament model of the rule of Jehovah being established upon the earth. Moffat rarely quoted New Testament texts which referred to the *Parousia,* but he frequently referenced Old Testament texts such as Psalm 46:10 and Isaiah 9:7 which

---

4 RM, *To Browne, BFBS,* ?.11.1851, (CULBSA/Browne/1851).

5 RM, *To Browne, BFBS,* 22.11.1852, (CULBSA/Browne/1852/M).

6 Moffat ordained no Africans to the ministry, but he did train many to be Teachers of the Word and gave them responsibility for evangelising in villages and nurturing converts. For Moffat, the ministry of the Word was the highest honour in Christian ministry. Putting that into native hands was a strong affirmation of their role.

referred to the *reign of God*. Moffat's main focus was on the coming *reign* rather than the coming *return.*[7]

For Moffat, the reign of God was the reign of Christ. He referred to 'our Redeemer's kingdom'[8] in the same way as he referred to Jehovah's coming reign upon the earth. The reign of God and the reign of Christ were one and the same. The task of the missionary was to participate in the work of God which brought the realisation of this reign. It was no accident that the standard edition of Moffat's *Missionary Labours* concluded with a picture of an African kneeling in prayer with the caption 'Thy Kingdom Come'.[9]

A Glorious Future

At the heart of Moffat's view of the future was a postmillennialist theology. And at this point it may be helpful to clarify the concepts of: postmillennialism, premillennialism, and amillennialism. Postmillennialism is the belief that Christ's second coming will occur after (post) a period of widespread Christian influence and prosperity, known as the Millennium. Premillennialism believes Christ's return will occur before the Millennium. And amillennialism sees the Millennium simply as a symbolic period. The concept of the Millennium is built on a relatively speculative interpretation of Revelation 20:1-6.[10] As we shall see, Moffat was a postmillennialist. And for Moffat, it was the Word of God which would be the means of spreading the knowledge of God over all the earth, creating the conditions necessary for the millennial reign of Christ. But what would that reign be like? When

---

7 Cf. RM, *Journal,* 27.10.1859, (*MJ2,* 203). Moffat directly linked Jesus' promise and great commission *'Go ye! Lo I am with you'*, with the triumphant Reign of God as expressed in Psalms and Isaiah. He instinctively combined Jesus' promise 'Lo, I am with you' with the OT expectation of God's reign, rather than with the Second Coming. He believed in the Second Coming, but it did not dominate his horizon.

8 RM, *To Mrs Pye-Smith,* 8.3.1883, (SOAS/CWM/Africa/ Moffat/Pers/4).

9 RM, *MLSSA,* 620.

10 Rev. 20:1-6: 'I saw an angel coming down out of heaven, having the key to the Abyss and holding in his hand a great chain. [2] He seized the dragon, that ancient serpent, who is the devil, or Satan, and bound him for a thousand years. [3] He threw him into the Abyss, and locked and sealed it over him, to keep him from deceiving the nations anymore until the thousand years were ended. After that, he must be set free for a short time. [4] I saw thrones on which were seated those who had been given authority to judge. And I saw the souls of those who had been beheaded because of their testimony about Jesus and because of the word of God. They[a] had not worshiped the beast or its image and had not received its mark on their foreheads or their hands. They came to life and reigned with Christ a thousand years. [5] (The rest of the dead did not come to life until the thousand years were ended.) This is the first resurrection. [6] Blessed and holy are those who share in the first resurrection. The second death has no power over them, but they will be priests of God and of Christ and will reign with him for a thousand years.'

would it happen? Why was it an important aspect of contemporary theology? From the brief extracts already quoted it is clear that Moffat looked forward to this coming reign with positive emotions. His vision of the future was encouraging and affirmative. It was an optimistic vision in which, despite this broken world being 'sick and dying', God's plan in Christ was for things to get better and better under his sovereign authority.

1. Social Optimism. Social and theological factors can inter-twine, and the late eighteenth century's anticipation of a coming golden-age on the earth was not only fed by religious roots but by general feelings of confidence which pervaded society. There was a philosophy of improvement, and this, in conjunction with religious factors, provided a powerful forward impetus. For example, if we consider lowland Scotland, where Moffat came from, several social factors encouraged this life-view.

Firstly, there was the idea of progress and transformation which permeated Scottish society in general, and Moffat's boyhood area of Bothkennar and Falkirk in particular. Later commentators might dissent from the optimism surrounding the Industrial Revolution, drawing attention to the negative aspects of urbanisation, such as appalling housing, slave-like wages, miserable conditions, exploitative employers and general wretchedness linked to Industrialisation. However, in the early stages of change, during the late eighteenth century and early nineteenth century, the developments were widely welcomed as part of God's purpose for the transformation of society on earth.[11] Factories were not yet viewed as 'dark satanic mills'. A paradigm of progress had become an inherent part of the world-view of eighteenth-century Scotland.

Secondly, Moffat's parents were brought up near the village of Ormiston in East Lothian and started married life there. Along with others, they were part of an experiment in social progress. Ormiston village was a model village for a new age and a new era. Working people lived in neat, planned houses, set in a neat, planned village, which was a hive of neat, planned industry, whether from traditional employments such as agriculture or from cottage industries such as spinning, carding and weaving.[12] Their housing conditions were paradisal compared to the hovels most working-class people had. Lord Cockburn had also introduced new horticultural and agricultural methods for his Ormiston estate. This meant that the ethos surrounding the Moffat and

---

11 Mechie, *The Church and Scottish Social Development: 1780-1870,* (Ldn: OUP, 1960).

12 Phillipson & Mitchison, *Scotland in the Age of Improvement,* 93.

Gardiner families was of improvement and progress through hard work. Allied to hard work was a piety in which godliness and industry were understood to improve a person's position in life.[13]

It was an era of hope for the future. People realised that life could be different, and that the future was not the prisoner of the past. The mental hurdle was broken of fatalistically accepting that the way things had 'always been done' would be the way things 'always would be done'. Though many families still experienced poverty and a low standard of living, there was an awareness that this could be changed through hard work, holiness and general progress. Robert Burns, the Ayrshire poet, and Robert Moffat (Snr), both transitioned from agricultural worker to junior civil servant in the excise industry. They typified the conviction that 'upward' change was possible. 'Progress' became embedded in the mind-set of society.[14] The presence of Napoleon on the Continent, and the danger of French invasion, did foster a flicker of uncertainty. But generally, belief in progress and betterment displaced the scenario of a doom-laden future.

2. Religious Optimism. Although optimism through secular factors was important, there were powerful religious forces also operating. In the mid-eighteenth century the Great Awakening in North America, with Jonathan Edwards at its centre, brought a new vision of the future. Along with a spiritual turning to God, a spirit of confidence swept through the whole movement. This fostered a Christian eschatology different from a paradigm of impending doom and destruction. It stressed an eschatology in which an age of godly righteousness would be established before the Second Coming of Jesus. Baumgartner has pointed out that, instead of seeing the human race progressively worsening, as had previous generations of preachers, those of the Great Awakening believed that the Church was becoming stronger and purer, and that the New Kingdom was close at hand.[15] Edwards moved away

---

[13] The belief that godliness and industry combine to produce personal improvement had various implications. In the missionary context, a sign of true conversion (godliness) was seen as the 'improvement' in a person's appearance, manners, habits, cleanliness etc.

[14] Cf. E.G.K. Hewat, *Vision and Achievement 1796-1956: A History of the Foreign Missions of The Churches United in the Church of Scotland,* (Edin: Nelson, 1960), 2f.

[15] F.J. Baumgartner, *Longing for the End: A History of Millennialism in Western Civilisation,* (New York, Palgrave, 1999), 128. Cf. Klaus Fiedler, *Shifts in Eschatology: Shifts in Missiology,* (2004 staff colloquium, TRS Department, Chancellor College, Malawi), who pointed out that Edwards stressed that the 'millennial kingdom will finally come about through divine intervention, *but not* as a sudden intervention, but as the culmination of a process in which missions (and reform movements) will play a leading role.'

from the notion that catastrophic events would reveal the approach of the Day of the Lord. Instead, Edwards maintained that the outpouring of the Holy Spirit on human hearts, so powerfully experienced during the Revival, would produce a change in society which would anticipate the nature of the coming Kingdom. In Edward's eschatology, Christ would indeed return in his physical body: but this would be *after* the Millennium (postmillennialism).

Unlike some eschatologists who speculated from Revelation 20 that Christ would come twice—once at the start of the Millennium to take away believers, and a second time at its close to judge all—Edwards taught that the first resurrection mentioned in the book of Revelation referred symbolically to the regeneration of the Church which would lead to the first defeat of Anti-Christ. He believed that this regeneration of the Church was taking place at the time of the Awakening and that the Millennium was being ushered in. In the Millennium, Satan's power would be restricted, the Church would grow, and an era of godly righteousness would be established over the earth.[16] This would be the time of the *reign of God* upon the earth.

Edwards' eschatology had a progressive view of the future, allowing for the gradual improvement of humanity during the coming era.[17] Consequently, postmillennialism *tended* to carry within itself a 'can-do' push to transform society here and now for the glory of God. This contrasted with premillennial thinking, which *tended* to minimise the importance of the transformation of society, since society, along with all things belonging to 'this present age' would soon cease to exist. The Evangelical Revival in Britain, in the wake of the American Great Awakening, largely adopted this optimistic interpretation of near-future history. It anticipated a coming golden-age which would be in historical continuity with the present time.[18]

Missionary societies, such as the LMS, adopted this positive postmillennial eschatology. They believed that, before the Second Coming of Christ, the reign of God would be established upon the earth for a significant period of time, perhaps a literal thousand years, and as missionary societies they would be directly involved in bringing it about. This gave a thrilling sense of purpose to everyone who was involved. Excitement of adventure was

---

16 Koester, *Revelation and the End of all Things,* (Grand Rapids: Eerdmans, 2001), 3f, pointed out that Justin Martyr and Irenaeus held a similar view. Cf. Irenaeus, *Adv. Haereses.* 5/32/1.

17 Baumgartner, *Longing for the End,* 129. Cf. S.J. Stein, *J. Edwards: Apocalyptic Writings,* 52f.

18 Needham, 'Millennialism', (*DSCHT,* 562ff). At the same time as Edwards and his fellow Puritans developed the thought that, with divine aid, the human race would progressively improve during the Millennium, a group of mostly French secular thinkers were proposing that human progress, even without divine aid, would lead to the perfection of humanity (Cf. Baumgartner, *Longing for the End,* 133).

blended with a feeling of privilege in being chosen by God for a glorious task. Moreover, it was a task which anticipated achievement and success, not failure; and enterprises which anticipate success are far more energising than ventures which anticipate failure.

Questions still surrounded the nature of this coming reign. When would it start? How many years would it occupy? To what degree would that reign be clear and visible to all? Yet, despite many unanswered theological questions, the missionary societies were convinced of their vocation to establish the Kingdom of God on earth. Their mission was much bigger than simply being a 'rescue operation' for saving individual souls from destruction. Their mission included the making of a new world.

INDEPENDENCY AND POSTMILLENNIALISM

Postmillennial theology dominated Protestant thinking from the middle of the eighteenth century well into the nineteenth. This was a departure from the usual theology of the Protestant Reformation which had an a-millennial eschatology.[19] North America was fertile soil for postmillennialism. Many colonists had emigrated from Europe to America because they wanted new opportunities: they were future-orientated people, with an optimistic pioneer-mentality. During the sixteenth and seventeenth centuries, religion in Europe had been closely associated with war and impending doom, whereas religion in North America was associated with new starts and new hope. Then, when religious revival broke out in America in the 1730s, the transformation of individual lives, and a parallel improvement in society as a whole, added to this positive feeling. The dominant feeling in colonial society was of new beginnings and a hopeful future. A *new* world is not a *doom* world, but a world of opportunities and hope.

One other factor, valid on both sides of the Atlantic and a possible catalyst in the development of postmillennialism, was the effect which generations of exclusive use of the Psalter in worship had had on Reformed theology. In the Psalms there is a strong theme of the coming age of the reign of God upon the earth. This coming age was viewed as being in historical continuity with the present time and not separated from it by an apocalyptic

---

[19] Klaus Fiedler, *Shifts in Eschatology: Shifts in Missiology.* Cf. Needham, 'Millennialism', (*DSCHT,* 562f): 'They did expect a future for the believer in the eternal Kingdom of Christ, but they did not expect an earthly kingdom of a thousand years. 'Chiliasm' was left to that wing of the Reformation which the mainstream Reformers disparagingly called the 'Enthusiasts'. In their a-millennialism the Reformers basically followed the lead of the Catholic Church as expressed for example in the theology of St. Augustine.'

catastrophic event. Certainly, by Moffat's time the Protestant eschatological paradigm had changed from the amillennialism of the Reformers to a dynamic postmillennialism. All the theologians who were part of Moffat's spiritual education were resolute postmillennialists.

Belief in the coming reign of Christ, interpreted within a postmillennial schema, was particularly strong within the Congregationalist/Independent tradition. The Haldanes were postmillennialists.[20] Many others who moulded Scottish Congregationalist theology, after the Haldanes left over the issue of baptism, were of the same view. For example, in 1797 Greville Ewing published his address, *A Defence of Missions.* This was first delivered to the Edinburgh Missionary Society in the wake of the 1796 rejection by the General Assembly of the Church of Scotland of direct involvement in foreign missions. Ewing argued that the Church must read the 'signs of the times':

> We anxiously turn to the page of prophecy that seems now to be unfolding and ask the mysterious questions [Revelation 11] ... The Kingdoms of this world are become the Kingdoms of our Lord ... and He shall reign for ever and ever.[21]

Ewing believed that the time of the reign of Christ over the earth was at hand, and that the missionary enterprise was God's instrument in the ushering in of this glorious Millennium which would last until the Second Coming. This was the prevailing theology in missionary circles. Some in the established Kirk shared this theology, but it was within Scottish Congregationalism that it first became the official doctrine for a Scottish denomination. Unanimity of view within Scottish Congregationalism was predictable, since its original leaders were men like Ewing, who were enthusiastic about world evangelism, but who felt that their vision had been spurned by the Kirk, and who left it to form a new denomination.

It was to the Congregationalist Church in Falkirk that Ann Gardiner took her family. Though no sermons by the Falkirk minister, Robert Caldwell, are extant, addresses by his fellow-churchmen give a flavour of the thinking within Scottish Congregationalism. In 1823, the Congregational Church in Scotland published a book entitled, *Sermons by Ministers of the Congregational Union of Scotland.*[22] Among the contributors were men such as Aikman, Ewing and Wardlaw, all of whom were official tutors at

---

20 Cf. R. Haldane, *Exposition of the Epistle to the Romans,* 3 Vols, especially on Romans 11.

21 Greville Ewing, *A Defence of Missions from Christian Societies to the Heathen World: An Address to the Edinburgh Missionary Society,* 2.2.1797 (Edin: Ritchie, 1797), 17.

22 Joseph Gibb, 'The Millennial Reign of Christ and His Saints' in: Aikman, Ewing & Wardlaw (ed.): *Sermons by Ministers of the Congregational Union of Scotland,* (Glasgow: Curil, 1823).

theological colleges for Congregational ministers. The publication was designed to express the Congregationalist position on various theological issues.

1. John Gibb. The congregationalist minister in Banff, John Gibb, contributed an important sermon to this publication, entitled, *The Millennial Reign of Christ and His Saints: Revelation 20:4-6.* As will be seen, Moffat's presentation of his own eschatology, scattered through his writings,[23] is so much in line with Gibb's methodical account that an exposition of Gibb's position helps to give structure to Moffat's beliefs. Gibb divided the Book of the Revelation into seven sections: Epistles, Seals, Trumpets, Vials, Millennium, the Tribulation, and the New Jerusalem. It is the fifth of these sections, the Millennium, which is relevant to this chapter. Gibb taught that, during the Millennium, the witnesses of Jesus would reign in conjunction with Jesus, who was their head. They would reign with him over the earth, and exercise power over the nations. This promise would be fulfilled *during* the Millennium. It would not be a reign through direct political power,[24] but through the power of righteousness and peace. Jesus would judge among the nations and abolish war, and judgment on the earth would be delegated to his faithful witnesses.[25] During this Millennium the immortal departed saints would also reign with Christ over the earth, but the presence of Christ would be spiritual until the end of the Millennium when the Second Coming would take place:

> There is good reason to believe that during the reign of Christ when righteousness shall abound among mankind many mortal saints shall be advanced in stations of civil power and authority ... yet the dominion of these mortal saints who shall be thus invested with civil authority will be of a secular and worldly nature, ... distinct from that of Christ and his exalted witnesses.[26]

Though the Millennium was the time of Christ's reign, his people were to seek service, not power:

> Those who shall be converted from sin, to fill the church militant during the Millennium, shall be called to imitate the Christians of former generations, by taking the lowest place, denying themselves, and bearing their cross. They

[23] Not all the picture is present in Moffat's writings. But what we present in this chapter is consistent with the available data, and harmonises with known interpretations of the time.

[24] Gibb retained a subtle distinction between political power and the reign of Christ—even during the Millennium—preserving Congregationalist reluctance to be involved in politics.

[25] Gibb, 'The Millennial Reign of Christ and His Saints', 84-91.

[26] Ibid, 94.

cannot share the dominion of Christ until the termination of their mortal and imperfect state.[27]

The glorified saints would reign with Christ in an incorporeal and invisible manner. During the Millennium, Satan would be 'bound'[28] and the souls of the saints would reign with Christ with various degrees of authority.[29] Gibb taught that it was a justifiable ambition for a Christian to aim to be one of those chosen to reign spiritually with Christ, the qualification being outstanding holiness of life.[30] The Christian worked for God with the possibility of gaining this great prize, a prize which could be won or lost even if one's actual salvation were assured. Thus a Christian could desire to be one of the holy souls involved directly in the reign of Christ *before* the final Day of the Lord, the Second Coming, rather than simply being an 'ordinary' righteous soul who must wait in the intermediate state of paradise.

2. Ralph Wardlaw. One of the pioneers of the Glasgow Congregational College was Ralph Wardlaw.[31] He also published a sermon on the Millennium. This provoked a strong response from William Cunninghame who, in 1813, had published his *Premillennial Advent of Christ demonstrated from the Scriptures,* which took an opposite view, and which was one of the first modern treatises advocating a premillennial theology. We have been unable to source a copy of Wardlaw's sermon, and so our discussion depends upon Cunninghame's critique of Wardlaw's address.[32]

Cunninghame profoundly disagreed with Wardlaw, and this should be borne in mind when interpreting Wardlaw through him. Given Cunninghame's premillennialism, it can readily be seen why he disagreed with Wardlaw's view that the commencement of the reign of Christ (the Millennium) was separate from the event of the return of Christ (the Parousia). This is the pivotal issue in Cunninghame's critique of Wardlaw's

---

27 Ibid, 95.

28 Ibid, 102.

29 Ibid, 105-111. The 'Millennium' was a 'very long period', not exactly one thousand years.

30 Ibid, 115.

31 Ralph Wardlaw (1779-1853) officiated at the ordination of Robert Caldwell in Falkirk in 1803. In 1857, RM, *To Mary Moffat,* 22.8.1857, (*MJ2,* 39), declared: 'What a man! How little and ugly one looks beside such a giant!' That was after reading a biography of Wardlaw. After retirement, Moffat corresponded with the Wardlaw family.

32 William Cunninghame, *Review of Rev. Dr Wardlaw's Sermon on the Millennium: with an answer to His arguments against the millennial resurrection and reign of the Saints and Martyrs of Jesus Christ,* (Glasgow: Smith, 1830). Wardlaw's *Systematic Theology,* posthumously published in 1857, also shed light on his eschatology. See: Wardlaw, *Systematic Theology: Vols. 1, 2, 3,* (Edin: A&C Black, 1857).

Sermon, and his treatment of the issues gives insight into the debate concerning millennial theories at that time. He wrote:

> If we next enquire what the great body of our modern Protestant Divines hold and teach to the people on these points we shall find in the first place that they flatly contradict the Apostle Paul by affirming that beside the one great ecclesiastical event mentioned by him, viz. the appearance and reign of the Man of Sin, various other ecclesiastical events of no less importance, namely FIRST the destruction of that power, SECONDLY the conversion of the whole world to Christ by the ordinary means of preaching and teaching; THIRDLY a Millennium of spirituality; and FOURTHLY and lastly the rebellion of Gog and Magog, are all to be expected before the second personal advent.[33]

Wardlaw's stages, as cited by Cunninghame, correspond closely to Gibb's thinking. In contrast, the premillennialist Cunninghame wanted to view the commencement of the reign of Christ and the Second Coming as one event, as in premillennialism. It is to Cunninghame's credit that he represented Wardlaw's postmillennial view with reasonable accuracy. The second and third stages which he cited as part of Wardlaw's scheme were central to the prevailing postmillennial paradigm in the missionary societies: 'There would be the conversion of the whole world to Christ by the ordinary means of preaching and teaching' and there would be 'a Millennium of spirituality' *before* Christ's Second Coming.[34] This Millennium would be a time of peace and blessing in which the reign of Christ would be manifest in every nation. This was the glorious vision of the near future which flowed out of the eighteenth-century revivalist tradition, energising missionary movements. Wardlaw's fuller eschatology, as worked out in his *Systematic Theology*, supplies a passage which is useful for understanding terminology:

> The final resurrection of all the dead is most explicitly taught by our Lord Himself (John 5:28,29). No terms can be more explicit than these; and they are in harmony with the entire doctrine and many express intimations of the apostolic writings. And while the passage decides the universality of the resurrection, it is no less decisive of their rising simultaneously. It is the same 'voice' at the same 'hour', which all are to hear; both those who rise to life, and those who rise to damnation. The millennarian view of the first and second resurrection—the resurrection of the righteous at the

---

[33] Cunninghame, *Review of Rev. Dr Wardlaw's Sermon,* iv. The capitalisation is in the original publication. Wardlaw was accused by some of interpreting the Second Coming purely in symbolic terms. Wardlaw did not accept that his postmillennial eschatology implied that the Second Coming would not be a real future historical event.

[34] Cunninghame commented: 'They [the postmillennialists] teach a thousand years of spiritual light are to intervene between his destruction and the coming of our Lord.' (vi); and that the second personal advent of Christ does not take place until the end of the Millennium (Cunninghame, *Review of Rev. Dr Wardlaw's Sermon*, 1).

> commencement, and of the wicked at the close of the thousand years (Rev 20:4-6)—depends greatly on the question whether that passage, on which this view is founded, ought to be interpreted literally or figuratively. I am perfectly satisfied that on no ground consistent with either the symbolical character of the book, in which it occurs, or with the representations of the plainest points of Scripture, is the literal exposition at all defensible.[35]

Wardlaw argued that there was ONE resurrection which occurred at the close of the Millennium and which was coincident with the Second Coming. He argued against the premillennial notion of TWO resurrections: one at the start of the Millennium, and one at the close. The merits and demerits of Wardlaw's and Cunninghame's divergent opinions need not concern us, but what is important, especially when we interpret Moffat, is Wardlaw's use of the word 'Millennarian'. For Wardlaw and for Moffat, the term 'Millennarian' was used to describe a person who held a premillennialist theology, and who, within that theological system, believed in the concept of two resurrections.[36]

Postmillennial eschatology flourished in England as well as in Scotland. The two figures in English Independency who most influenced Moffat—William Roby and David Bogue—both published works on the Millennium. Moffat was also influenced by Methodism, especially around the time of his conversion experience, and Methodism had also settled on a postmillennial eschatology after an uncertain start. Bogue 'impressed a generation of his students with a postmillennial vision of missionary enterprise and expansion.'[37] Though there appear to be no extant copies of Bogue's *Discourses on the Millennium* (1818), a brief indication of what he wrote on the subject comes in the anonymous introductory memoir to Bogue's reprinted *Sixth Discourse, On Universal Peace*, in which he painted a picture of a paradise on earth.[38]

Though William Roby did not deal with the Millennium or eschatology at

---

[35] Wardlaw, *Systematic Theology, Vol. 3,* 651.

[36] RM, *Journal,* 22.9.1857, (*MJ2,* 70f), wrote that he was 'no millennarian'. This explains why Moffat conceded that, if he were a Millennarian he would not have to face the prospect of his body decaying in the grave and becoming food for worms.

[37] Needham, 'Millennialism', (*DSCHT,* 563).

[38] Cf. Bogue, *On Universal Peace*: 1813, *Tract VI* of the Society for the Promotion of Permanent and Universal Peace, (Ldn: Ward, reprinted 1839). The cited extract is from its anonymous *Preface,* (4). Excitement in anticipation of the coming Millennium, rather than fear at an impending apocalyptic crisis, comes out in a sermon by James Sabine, who took part in the devotional exercises on board the first LMS missionary ship before it sailed down the Thames. See: Sabine, *The Relation the Present State of Religion bears to the Millennium: A Sermon delivered in the Old South Church Boston, before the Foreign Mission Society of Boston and the Vicinity, 8 January 1823,* (Boston: Crocker & Brewster, 1823).

any length in his *Theological Lectures,* he addressed the topic in *The Glory of the Latter Days* (1814),[39] in which he adopted a typical postmillennial line, dedicating his pamphlet, 'to the blessing of Him whose millennial reign is now rapidly approaching.'[40] Roby saw humanity as originally created with the purpose of being the priest of creation, and 'offering to Jehovah the praises both of the animate and inanimate creation.'[41] He held out the hope that, despite the Fall, the divine glory would shine in the earth in an illustrious way during the last ages of the world. Roby underlined that the 'glory of the latter days is foretold in many parts of Scripture, especially the 45th and 72nd Psalms, the Book of Isaiah (chiefly from the 60th chapter), and the Book of Revelation.'[42] Though Roby warned of too much conjecture in this whole area, he looked at several questions.

What will be the nature of the Millennium? Roby gave a multi-layered answer: it will be the reign of Christ; the presence of Christ will be spiritual during this period; the Babylon which will be destroyed will be Islam in the East and Rome in the West; national governments will still function during this period and many will regard the word of Christ as the law of the state; Satan will be totally subdued for a thousand years; there will not be the scourge of war; human longevity will be enjoyed; the earth will become extraordinarily fertile; and there will be domestic happiness arising from religious knowledge.[43]

How will the Millennium come about? Roby was clear that it would not be by military force. He had the forced imposition of Christianity by conquest in mind, especially in some Roman Catholic countries. Instead, it would come about by 'the general distribution of the scriptures and by the preaching of the gospel in every part of the habitable globe.'[44] The 'effectual means of introducing the glory of the latter days will be an extraordinary outpouring of the Holy Ghost. Nothing else has energy sufficient for this purpose.'[45]

When will the Millennium commence? Roby conceded that this was a difficult question: 'Very probably the glory of the latter days will be thus gradually introduced; but several passages of Scripture seem to intimate that a period is fixed when, after it has advanced considerably, it will burst like a

---

39 Roby, *The Glory of the Latter Days: A Discourse delivered in the Independent Chapel, Mosley-Street, Manchester,* 12.1.1814, (2nd edn, London: Condor, 1814).
40 Ibid, 3.
41 Ibid, 5.
42 Ibid, 7.
43 Ibid, 10, 12, 15, 18, 22, 23, 24f, 26, 27-30.
44 Ibid, 33.
45 Ibid, 35.

flood of light upon the astonished world with overwhelming splendour; and *there are various reasons to believe that this time is not far distant*.'[46] Roby speculated that, given the signs of the times (the Church of Rome tottering on its throne, wars and rumours of wars shaking the world, infidels being increasingly impudent, plus the emergence of means to evangelism such as Bible Societies and Missionary Societies) many 'are expecting the glory of the latter days to appear in the course of fifty or sixty years.'[47]

Also significant is that Roby thought in terms of a short time of tribulation after this millennium of glory. During that period the restraint on Satan would be withdrawn, but then would come 'the day of general judgment'.[48] Intriguingly, Roby did not explicitly mention the event of the Second Coming, though there is no reason to infer that he did not believe in it. Believers were to pray for the millennial reign of Christ to come soon.[49]

Roby's pamphlet on the Millennium was published a year before Moffat met him. The themes he emphasised nearly all find an echo in Moffat, especially the coming reign of Christ, peace and harmony being established on the earth, and the belief that the means to accomplish this would be the distribution and knowledge of the Word of God in the Scriptures. The task of mission, within a postmillennial eschatology, involved no less than the transformation of all human society and culture through the benign reign of Christ. This was to be accomplished by spiritual means, not by force or imposition. The Spirit of God would transform the inner heart, though the reign of Christ would affect all areas of society. This was the high missionary vision and purpose for which Roby stood.

MOFFAT AND POSTMILLENNIALISM

Postmillennial thinking was a dominant force in Moffat's spiritual ancestry, and he knew and admired several of the individuals whose postmillennial theology has been described above. Given this weight of evidence, it is

---

46 Ibid, 40, (our italics).

47 Ibid, 41. Fifty or sixty years after the publication of Roby's pamphlet was the mid-1860s or 1870s. Moffat retired from the mission field in 1870. If he followed Roby, he would not be surprised that the Millennium had not yet come with full force during his time in Africa. Yet see his letter, RM, *To Emma Pitman,* 5.12.1879, (SOAS/CWM/Africa/Moffat/Pers/4), for his perplexity that it had not yet come by 1879. Roby was aware that others mentioned 200 years as the possible time period. Roby also connected the outpouring of the Holy Spirit under Jonathan Edwards, with people weeping and in distress, as a sign of the Spirit coming in power as a harbinger of the latter days (Roby, *The Glory of the Latter Days*, 84).

48 Roby, *The Glory of the Latter Days,* 42-44.

49 Ibid, 48.

tempting to conclude that he was an out-and-out postmillennialist. But to what extent is there direct evidence from Moffat's own writings? Though Moffat only made a few references to the Millennium, he did refer repeatedly to the 'reign of Christ' and the 'reign of God' upon the earth. This emphasis was consistent with the postmillennial theology operating within Congregationalism and the LMS. There are also specific references in Moffat's writings.

In 1843, at the Barbican Church in London and near the end of his furlough, Moffat gave an overall analysis of history. He stressed a steady march from darkness to light, and from the rule of evil to the rule of Christ. He spoke of the incredible excitement of being engaged in an activity which was transforming the whole world.[50] Moffat exemplified the positive hope for the future which was so important in contemporary missionary activity and philosophy. That this remained his position, is proven by what he wrote almost thirty years later:

> It is, however, all right if what we are doing tends either directly or indirectly, to advance the blessed and glorious reign of Him whose we are and all that we have. We must all sing 'Oh grace how great a debtor' which expresses the feeling of every new born soul. It will pass beyond time into eternal ages.[51]

Writing to Emma Pitman in 1879, having been in Africa for 53 years, in retirement for nine, but still waiting for the glorious reign to start, he wrote:

> After 50 years and more in the interior of Africa, now the heart feels for the thousands in this rich and sumptuous land, who are shivering and dying from sheer want. When we think of these things and look on the present state of [Christian] nations, *the Millennium seems still far*, but who can set bounds to omnipotence and the overwhelming power of the love of God? But we must pray. *HE must reign*.[52]

One of Moffat's strongest affirmations of his continued expectation of the coming Reign of God is expressed in an 1882 letter to William Dickson:

> The world is still moving on and developing changes and scenes one could never have dreamed, all leading to one great end – the reign of our Redeemer in the world which is still to a fearful extent under the power of the Evil One. It is most gratifying to witness the progress of your Free Church.[53]

---

50 RM, *Barbican Sermon,* 22.1.1843, (*Farewell Services,* 104-106).

51 RM, *To William Dickson,* 10.12.1871, (EUNCL WD9/3/1).

52 RM, *To Emma Pitman,* 5.12.1879, (SOAS/CWM/Africa/Moffat/Pers/4), (our italics). Moffat had *'He must reign',* rather than *'He must come.'* He focused on the Millennium rather than on the Second Coming. He also allowed *praying* for the reign of Christ to come.

53 RM, *To William Dickson,* 29.11.1882, (EUNCL/WD9/3/22/Box 2).

These extracts show that Moffat's vision of the approaching millennial reign remained strong throughout his life, though occasionally he appeared to have doubts. For example, in 1880, in a letter to Olive Helmore,[54] he seemed resigned to things getting worse, not better: 'I was thankful to hear from you, and especially the welfare of you all in this sick and dying world.'[55] Did Moffat's phrase 'sick and dying world' reflect the pessimism of an old man? Or was Moffat expressing his disappointment at the way Britain was ruining Africa, a theme he dwelt on during his later years?

It is unlikely that Moffat's phrase pointed to a serious abandonment of a millennium vision. The letter to Dickson was not a theological treatise, with every phrase weighed before being committed to print, and perhaps the phrase simply reflected Moffat's frame of mind on the day he wrote the note. The previously quoted letter, to Emma Pitman, written nine months earlier, was from a man still convinced about Christ's millennial reign, though puzzled that it had not yet arrived.

In none of these extracts is reference made to the return of Christ. Thus, none of these extracts, by itself, is sufficient to prove beyond logical contradiction that Moffat expected that the return of Christ would be at the *close* of the Millennium rather than at its *start*. However, if there is no proof beyond *all* doubt of Moffat's postmillennialism, there is certainly proof beyond *reasonable* doubt. Firstly, as already adduced, there is the context of his spiritual heritage. Secondly, as we shall see, he did explicitly declare that he was not a 'millennarian'.[56] Thirdly, the relative absence in Moffat's writings of an emphasis on the Second Coming was not unusual for a postmillennialist.

Moffat believed in the Second Coming, but it was not the event which dominated his thinking, nor was it the event which first came to his mind when he considered the future: that was reserved for the anticipated 'reign of God'. Moffat looked to order, rather than to cataclysm. He looked to the increasing influence of the divine rule, rather than to an apocalyptic crisis.

---

[54] Along with the missionary Roger Price, young Olive Helmore and her brother were the only European survivors of the tragic 1859-60 mission to the Makololo. Moffat corresponded with Olive for the rest of his life.

[55] RM, *To Olive Helmore,* 8.9.1880, (SOAS/CWM/Afr./Personal Box 1/30).

[56] For millenarian premillennialism, see: RM, *Journal,* 11.10.1857, (*MJRM- 2,* 94).

The Paradigm Change of Premillennialism

We have already mentioned that the eighteenth century brought both an increase in postmillennialism and a reduction of emphasis on dramatic and apocalyptic eschatology. Medieval theology had constructed bizarre visions of apocalyptic events and, whilst Reformation scholars largely bypassed these, it was Enlightenment thinkers who consciously rejected them. The intellectual climate of the eighteenth and early nineteenth centuries was not conducive to apocalyptic catastrophe. At the same time, the doctrine of the Second Coming was in the New Testament, and it would force itself to the forefront of theological reflection even after a period of neglect. What would happen when Christians recovered an interest in the Parousia? How would Moffat relate to it?

The classical missionary societies saw their task in positive terms of establishing the Kingdom of God on earth. In this, they tended towards an emphasis on positive societal transformation rather than on apocalyptic catastrophe. Later missionary eschatology, which adopted a premillennial emphasis, tended towards 'crisis', in which the apocalyptic 'day of the Lord' might break in at any moment. That later shift of focus from the *reign of God* to the *return of Christ*, was closely related to a shift from postmillennialism to premillennialism. Which was cause, and which was effect, is difficult to determine. An arguable hypothesis is that increased interest in the Second Coming precipitated the change.

What we have seen is that, for Moffat, his focus was not on the *return of Christ* as such, but on the *reign of God* which would precede it. The *reign of God* dominated his world-view. When preoccupation with the *reign of God* was then ousted by a preoccupation with the *return of Christ*, there was no change of fundamental beliefs, but there was a change of perspective. Focus on the *return of Christ* marginalised other aspects of eschatology. The future *return of Christ* then dominated the horizon so much that it started to be regarded as an event which was *imminent,* resulting in the publication of a plethora of dates on which that *return* would occur. Thus, though, at the close of the eighteenth century, many Christians had a positive view of the future, others had a different outlook. Hylson-Smith has argued that as the nineteenth century began, more Evangelicals became convinced that the latter days were beginning and that the end of the world was not far off.[57]

---

[57] Kenneth Hylson-Smith, *Evangelicals in the Church of England: 1734-1984,* (Edin: T&T Clark, 1988), 94ff. Hylson-Smith referred to, S.C. Orchard, *English Evangelical Eschatology: 1790-1850,* (Cambridge University PhD, 1968).

Among other factors, the French Wars created a fearfulness, feeding an interest in prophetic views. Some worked these into traditional postmillennial theology, but others, such as James Hatley Frere[58] and Henry Drummond,[59] adopted the growing belief that Christ's coming would precede the Millennium rather than follow it. This encouraged a shift from a postmillennial to a premillennial theology.[60] However, when Moffat left for Africa in 1816, postmillennial theology was still the dominant hypothesis, and the subtle theological changes which later emerged do not appear to have ever penetrated Kuruman.

William Cunninghame's 1813 publication, with its premillennialist teaching has already been mentioned, but it was Edward Irving who boosted the doctrine through the 1820s and 1830s, with Irving part of a prophetic movement influenced by Cunninghame's 1813 document. Moffat knew about Irving and, when Irving died in 1835, Moffat noted it in a letter to Mary and referred to him as being 'many tongued',[61] clearly aware of Irving's interest in the gifts of the Spirit. However, Moffat made no reference to Irving's premillennialism, nor did Moffat refer to premillennial thinking during his furlough in Britain from 1839 to 1843. This should not take us by surprise since the LMS, and the missionary minded audiences to which he spoke, were largely composed of men and women who operated with the postmillennial missionary hypothesis.

The first references in Moffat's writings to premillennial writers and premillennial eschatology occur in 1857. These come as brief comments on books which he read during his fourth expedition to Moselekatse. Moffat

---

58 Cf. James Hatley Frere, *A Combined View of the Prophecies of Daniel, Esdras, and St. John,* (2nd Ed. Ldn: Hatchard, 1815). Though Frere had been working on his interpretation of prophecy since 1797, he only committed his ideas to writing in 1813, after studying Cunninghame among others. Frere's book has a Prophetic Chart which anticipates the conversion of Islamic nations by 1847, and the conversion of pagan nations by 1867, when the Millennium would start. 1822-1867 would be the Period of the Progress of the Kingdom of Christ. 1867 onwards would be the period of the Perfection of the Kingdom of Christ. The Second Advent would precede the Millennium (214ff.). Frere's book was dominated by three threats: Islam, Rome, and Bonaparte.

59 Henry Drummond MP was a banker and a founding member of the Catholic Apostolic Church. His mansion in Albury, Surrey, was the venue for a series of conferences on prophecy from 1826-1830, at which Edward Irving and premillennialism assumed prominence. He should not be confused with Henry Drummond, author of *The Greatest Thing in the World*.

60 Hylson-Smith, *Evangelicals in the Church of England: 1734-1984,* 95. Edward Irving's emphasis during the 1820s and early 1830s, was on prophesy, gifts of the Spirit, and the Return of Christ. He was excommunicated from the Church of Scotland because of his Christology. He then formed the Catholic Apostolic Church.

61 RM, *To Mary Moffat,* 19.5.1835, (*MJ1,* 50).

took a small collection of books with him, reading them on the ox-wagon as the miles passed. Each day he recorded his impressions, either in his *Journal* or in a letter to Mary. He was eager to know her thoughts on the same books, and this correspondence, sent randomly back to the Kuruman, gives valuable insight into the religious ideas which occupied his mind.

Moffat read at least two prominent premillennialists on that journey. They were Dr John Cumming and Henry Dunn—who wrote under the pseudonym of 'Delta'. Moffat did not supply the title of Cumming's work, but the book by Dunn was Dunn's well-known, *The Revelation of St. John, Simply Analyzed and Briefly Expounded.*[62] Moffat was complementary about both writers, describing Cumming as 'very able'[63] and Delta as well worth reading.[64] However, before examining Moffat's interpretation of Cumming and Delta, we discuss Irving's relationship with the LMS.

1. Edward Irving. A controversial sermon was preached by Edward Irving at the 1824 LMS Annual Meeting.[65] At that time, he was one of the most famous preachers in London, and the LMS expected that a powerful sermon would create even more support for the Society. The LMS were taken aback when Irving did not give a conventional address, but one which was critical of the LMS, and which challenged the LMS to become a mission whose missionaries relied solely on *faith* rather than on allowances sent by the parent body. Irving's premillennial theology went hand in hand with a call to 'faith missions'. When Irving made his notorious address to the LMS, he was still working out the implications of his reading of Scripture,[66] and his sermon

---

[62] Delta, *The Revelation of St. John, simply analyzed and briefly expounded,* (Ldn: Nisbet, 1850); also known as *Delta on the Revelation.* . Moffat read both books in Sept. 1857.

[63] RM, *Journal,* 12.9.1857, (*MJ2,* 62).

[64] RM, *Journal,* 22.9.1857, (*MJ2,* 70).

[65] There are no extant copies of Irving's original sermon, though he did publish an expanded version of 127 pages, titled, *For Missionaries after the Apostolical School: A series of Orations in Four Parts*' (Ldn: Hamilton, Adams & Co., 1825), dedicating it to the poet Samuel Taylor Coleridge who was a mystic with apocalyptic leanings. The LMS Record for 1824 is missing from the SOAS library. The LMS *Missionary Chronicle* for June 1824, gives a diplomatic account of Irving preaching at the LMS meeting: 'This immense edifice was extremely crowded at an unusually early hour.' Irving preached on Matthew 10:7, endeavouring, 'to prove that these instructions were intended to be of perpetual use and obligation in all future missions ... *the unusual length of the sermon obliged the preacher to pause twice during its delivery when the audience sang two or three verses*,' (our italics). Coleridge was one of several English romantic poets with apocalyptic-style beliefs. Morton D. Paley, *Apocalypse and Millennium in English Romantic Poetry,* (Oxford: Clarendon Press, 1999), pointed out that a major theme in Romantic poetry was the imminence of an apocalypse, succeeded by a glorious Millennium.

[66] In 1827, Irving became fully convinced that all the spiritual gifts of the original apostolic age (including tongues) should still be in operation. Cf. Dallimore, *The Life of Edward Irving,* 48; & Strachan, *The Pentecostal Theology of Edward Irving,* (Ldn: Darton, Longman & Todd,

was primarily driven by his expectation of an imminent Second Coming. Irving came to believe that not only would the coming of Christ be soon, but that the primitive Church would be restored once more before the end.[67] It may have been his belief in the nearness of the Parousia which pushed him to emphasise 'relying on faith alone'. Certainly, an imminent Parousia left no space for a thousand-year Millennium still to happen before Christ returned.

Irving's rambling 1824 discourse was ill-judged, ill-timed, and ill-received. It was resented by the LMS, who believed, with some justification, that Irving either deliberately ignored, or was completely unaware of, the sacrifices made by missionaries, and that he discounted the great 'step of faith' they took each day in dangerous situations, often hundreds of miles from any source of help. William Orme, later an LMS Foreign Secretary, wrote a blistering reply to Irving's Sermon.[68] Orme was particularly annoyed that Irving called on missionaries to live without material support from the LMS, whilst Irving enjoyed the living of one of the richest and most fashionable churches in London.

2. John Cumming. Dr Cumming was a Scottish divine, widely known for his writings on the interpretations of prophecy. He established the Church of Scotland congregation of Crown Court in London as a centre of popular London evangelicalism. Cumming held strong anti-Roman Catholic views and he connected these opinions with a detailed historicist premillennialist application of the prophetic books of Scripture.[69] He was also a staunch defender of the Church of Scotland against the Free Church.[70] In eschatology, Cumming was a clear premillennarian, teaching that Christ's Second Coming and the last resurrection were coincident, preceding the final Millennium.[71] His premillennial views coincided with strong belief in an imminent Parousia,

---

1973), 15. It was also in 1827 that Irving published his translation of the South American Jesuit Manuel de Lacunza's *The Coming of Messiah in Glory and Majesty (1812)* strongly advocating a premillennial eschatology, prefaced by 200 pages of Irving's own views.

67 Klaus Fiedler, *'A Revival Disregarded and Disliked',* 6.

68 William Orme, *'An Expostulatory Letter to the Rev. Edward Irving occasioned by his Orations for Missionaries after the Apostolical School'*, (Ldn: Holdsworth, 1825). Orme emphasised the sacrificial faith of LMS missionaries. He also disclaimed any disjunction between apostolic gifts and current spiritual gifts which Irving claimed the LMS had: if God called missionaries to heal the sick and speak in tongues, the LMS had no problem with that.

69 RM, *To Dr Bruce, Newcastle,* 9.6.1855, (JSM, *Lives,* 313), considered that apostate Rome and the Papacy would be destroyed in the latter days. In an 1855 letter, he wrote to his friend Dr Bruce of Newcastle: 'We heard through John [Smith Moffat] some time since that you had visited Rome. ... According to some students of prophecy it is one day to be destroyed or swallowed up by a fiery deluge.'

70 J.R. Wolfe, 'John Cumming', (*DSCHT,* 228).

71 Cumming, *Apocalyptic Sketches, Vol. 2,* (Ldn: Hall, 1858), 459ff.

but his reputation was ruined by the non-fulfillment of his conviction that 1867 would see the last vial of the Apocalypse poured out.[72] Though Moffat read Cumming in 1857, expressing appreciation of his work, Moffat made no specific comment on his eschatology.[73] Cumming's major work *Apocalyptic Sketches* (1858) had not yet appeared, though he had already published many writings on eschatology. Why did Moffat not comment? Did Moffat agree with Cumming? This is unlikely, given Moffat's reaction to Dunn which we examine below. The remaining possibility is that Cumming did not cover eschatology in what Moffat read.[74]

3. Henry Dunn. Lack of comment was not the case when Moffat came to Henry Dunn (Delta).[75] When, on his trek to Moselekatse, Moffat read the introduction to Delta's *The Revelation of St. John, Simply Analyzed and Briefly Expounded,* Delta's emphasis would have impressed him. This was because Delta emphasised that all prophecy 'treats the *moral* condition of those to whom it is presented.'[76] To a man like Moffat, for whom the establishment of moral righteousness in a nation was central to mission, these sentiments would be welcomed. But there were some aspects of Delta's eschatology which Moffat could not accept. He saw that Delta presented a premillennial scenario, different from his own beliefs.[77] He termed Delta a 'millennarian', and emphasised that he and Mary did not hold that theology:

> I have just finished *Delta on the Revelation.* It is worth reading. It has failed to make me a millennarian, and I entertain very little fear of it making you [Mary] one. It contains some exceedingly good remarks calculated to excite enquiry. I think the author fails sometimes in making a distinction between the literal and the symbolic portions of the book. However much people differ about the time and nature of the awful events foretold in this book, I have only one thing to say, that the more I read the Book of the Revelation the more I am

---

72 A premillennialist runs the risk of giving a wrong date for the Second Coming. A postmillennialist is safer since it will be at least a thousand years before a date can be verified! Cumming's reputation faded as 1867 passed without the Parousia. Frere also specified 1867.

73 RM, *Journal,* 12.9.1857, (*MJ2,* 62).

74 Moffat was not reading a book exclusively written by Cumming, but a collection of *Lectures* by Cumming and others. See: RM, *Journal,* 12.9.1857, (*MJ2,* 62): 'I have also read the lectures with which Massie's book was sent for Mr Wilson. Cumming's is very able, so is Binny's and that of Dr Raffles.'

75 Henry Dunn has been claimed by the *Millerite* and *Watch Tower* movements. In reading Dunn for ourselves, we have found nothing which indicated that he thought the Millennium had already started. Cf. Delta, *The Revelation of St. John,* 231-234; H. Dunn, *The Destiny of the Human Race: A Scriptural Enquiry, Vol. 1,* (Ldn: Simpkin, Marshall & Co., 1863), 388.

76 Delta, *The Revelation of St. John,* ix.

77 Delta's work was not written as a Systematic Theology, but as a commentary on the Book of the Revelation. A postmillenarian could read vast chunks of it with approval. And when Delta introduced premillenarian aspects they were not always obvious.

> convinced that it is inspired and intended for the instruction of the Church of Christ till the end of time.[78]

A 'Millenarian' was someone who held premillennialist beliefs. Later, on the same journey, Robert wrote to Mary:

> I am no millennarian, but to avoid that stinking, that putrefying, that dust-becoming destiny inscribed on every child of Adam, I feel, I always shall feel, as if I were the merest iota compared to the hosts, the thousands of myriads of saints and martyrs who have died and passed into glory through deaths too horrible to describe. Yet there is a lingering horror of becoming the food of worms.[79]

This fitted with Delta presenting a premillennarian theology, combined with an imminent return of Christ, which would, in a premillennarian scenario, coincide with the resurrection of the body. In writing 'I am no millennarian' Moffat was not meaning that he did not believe in the idea of the 'Millennium'. Quite clearly, he did. He was simply referring to a strand of millennarian thinking which held to the imminent return of Jesus Christ. Delta had described the attractive prospect that, at the Parousia, all believers who were alive at that time would be 'transported' to be with God without going through the process of death and decay; and all believers who had died would experience the resurrection of the body.[80]

A further point of interest is that, early in his reading of Delta and whilst he was still trying to place Delta's theology, Robert wrote to Mary:

> I see he (Delta) understands the seven epistles to the seven churches as symbolical of seven great eras of the church.[81] This is plausible enough, and consistent with the symbolical character of the whole of Revelation. One thing however staggers me, that is, the last era, indicated by the state of the Laodicean church, which was hateful in God's sight, does not agree with our ideas of millennial glory and blessedness of the last days, without that he indicated under the preceding era of the Philadelphian church. But I may understand him better when I have read all. But I must leave you to make your own comments when you read the book.[82]

Moffat's comment, that some of Delta's interpretation of the Book of the Revelation, did not agree with his ideas of millennial glory and blessedness of the last days, may point to Moffat expecting a golden era before Christ

---

78 RM, *Journal,* 22.9.1857, (*MJ2,* 70f).

79 RM, *Journal,* 11.10.1857, (*MJRM- 2,* 94).

80 Delta believed in a Millennium of blessedness *following* the Parousia. Cf. Delta, *The Revelation of St. John,* 231-234.

81 Delta had a historicist approach to the Book of the Revelation, identifying seven epochs which made up all history.

82 RM, *Journal,* 13.9.1857, (*MJ2,* 63).

came again, *without* envisaging a time of tribulation following the Millennium of glory. If this is a correct interpretation of Moffat's theology, then his postmillennial eschatology lacked the dimension of tribulation which was common to nearly all eschatology. However, there is insufficient evidence to be clear on Moffat's thinking on this point. It may be noted, however, that nowhere did Moffat refer to a future time of tribulation. He may have had in mind a seamless transition between the Millennium, the Second Coming, and the everlasting Glory of the New Jerusalem.

Of interest also, is a reference which Moffat made to the Moody and Sankey evangelistic crusades of 1881-1882. In an 1882 letter to William Dickson, Moffat wrote concerning Moody's approach: 'The Church of Christ ought to be for such renewed means of the advancement of the Redeemer's reign.'[83] Moffat was a postmillennialist, whereas Moody's theology was premillennialist.[84] Thus Moffat expounded 'transformation eschatology' with a vision of betterment of society in the here and now, whereas Moody preached a 'crisis apocalyptic eschatology'. Moody specifically stated: 'I do not find any passage in which God says the world is to grow better and better, and that Christ is to have a spiritual reign on earth of a thousand years. But I find that the world will grow worse and worse.'[85] Such differences were unimportant for the aged Moffat. Whatever helped the advancement of the Redeemer's reign, interpreted in the widest possible way, was all that mattered to him.

THE GLORY OF THE KINGDOM

In Moffat's theology, the glory of the Kingdom would come in two ways. Firstly, the glory of the Kingdom would consist in the transformation of society here on earth into a more godly society. This was already happening, but would peak in the Millennium, during which, though society would not be perfect or sinless as it would become in heaven, it would be a society where the reign of Christ was its hallmark and characteristic feature. Secondly, the glory of the Kingdom would also consist in the consummation of all things in the Second Coming of Christ and in what followed that Second

---

83 RM, *To William Dickson,* 5.1.1882, (EUNCL/WD9/3/21/Box 2).

84 The American D.L. Moody (1837-1899) had evangelistic campaigns in Britain in 1873-1875, 1881-1882, and 1891-1892. Moody took premillennial eschatology from Henry Moorhouse, the boy-evangelist of the English Brethren. Moody, Moody, *The Second Coming of Christ,* (Ldn: Morgan & Scott, undated), 26f, expected the Millennium to break in as the result of Christ's coming: 'The Word of God nowhere tells me to watch and wait for the coming of the Millennium, but for the coming of the Lord.'

85 Moody, *The Second Coming of Christ,* 27.

Coming: judgment, hell and heaven. But there was much work to be done even before the first of these scenarios came to pass. Moffat took very seriously the notion that the Gospel had to be preached to all peoples before the Millennium. On his return journey from Moselekatse in 1854, he wrote:

> When one looks at the tens of thousands of such people scattered over an immense extent of desert country, we are ready to conclude that the Millennium is a good way off yet.[86] But is there anything too hard for God? How the knowledge of the character of God makes one smile at what are called impossibilities.[87]

Moffat believed that the Millennium would come when the Gospel had been preached in every corner of the earth. This was a popular interpretation of Matthew 24:14: 'The kingdom shall be preached throughout the whole world, for a witness unto all nations, and then shall the end come.' From a postmillennial perspective, the Greek word *τελος* [end], could refer to the start of the final *process* of God's purposes, and thus include both the time of millennial reign and the event of the Second Coming. Alternatively, from a premillennial perspective, it might only refer to the specific final *event* of the Second Coming.

Moffat's daughter-in-law, Emily Unwin, interpreted 'end' in the latter sense. In an 1858 letter, penned as she travelled slowly from Cape Town to Kuruman, she wrote: 'If Africa is destined to be Christianised and civilised at bullock-wagon pace, the end of the world cannot be so near as some believe.'[88] Whereas her father-in-law rarely referred to the 'end of the world', Emily appeared to have had in mind the premillennialist scenario of an imminent Parousia. She came from a new generation, having just left Britain in 1857, with more opportunities to be exposed to the 'new thinking'.

Which interpretation of Matthew 24:14 did Moffat have in mind? In writing that 'the Millennium is a good way off yet', did he mean that the millennial reign of a thousand years, which preceded the actual Second Coming, would not commence until all the nations of the earth had heard the Gospel? Did he use the term Millennium in a loose sense, simply indicating

---

86 Whereas Moffat felt that events referred to in Matthew 24:14 were far off, the premillennialist, William Miller, 'believed that the progress made by missionary societies was a proof that the Great Commission of Matthew 28:18-20 and the prophecies of Matthew 24:14 and Revelation 14:6-7 had been fulfilled'. Cf. Stefan Höschele, *From the End of the World to the Ends of the Earth: The Development of Seventh-Day Adventist Missiology,* (Zomba: Kachere, 2004), 15. Premillennialist thinkers were not united on this: the Brethren did not see Matthew 24:14 as being already fulfilled, and were convinced they had to do their share to speed the coming of the kingdom.' Cf. Fiedler, *Shifts in Eschatology: Shifts in Missiology*.

87 RM, *Journal,* 19.11.1854, (*MJ1,* 344).

88 Emily Moffat, *To James Unwin,* 11.9.1858, (Northcott, *Robert Moffat,* 279).

the 'last things' in general? Or did he use the term Millennium as a synonym for the event of the Second Coming? Our view is that Moffat's intended reference was to the millennial reign itself. He believed that the great millennial reign of Christ, though imminent, had not yet started, and would not start until all the nations of the earth had been reached by the Gospel.

The belief that the Second Coming would not occur until the gospel had been preached to every people in every land had a lengthy pedigree. It was alluded to at the start of the Scottish Reformation in the opening preface to the 1560 *Scot's Confession*, which quoted Matthew 24:14 in full. The Westminster Divines also wrote of the need to have the 'Gospel propagated throughout the world and *hasten* the time of his Second Coming.'[89]

Moffat believed that the evangelisation of the world would trigger the millennial reign, and only *after* that period would the Second Coming take place. This adaptation of the earlier Reformed emphasis came from the influence of postmillennialism through the revivalist traditions. Moffat noted that all of these things may be a long way off, and there was much to be done in the interim. There is no indication of Moffat believing that any human activity, apart from prayer, could hasten God's timing. He simply noted that there was much to be done, and therefore the Church should proceed diligently with its important task. Everything was under God's sovereignty.

Moffat saw the future as a future of hope. His vision of a coming glory provided resilience to deal with setbacks. Nevertheless, as the years passed, the immensity of the task became increasingly obvious, and he occasionally mused on discouragements which still had to be faced. In 1883, aged 87 and only a few months from the end of his life, Moffat wrote to Dickson contemplating the state of the world and the hardship of the Tswana at the hands of the Boers: '[It] makes one feel as if the time when the knowledge of the Lord which is to cover the earth is still distant', but then he immediately went on to state: 'But He who has promised cannot lie.'[90]

Moffat understood his work as helping to establish God's rule on earth. That rule would bring closer the day of justice and righteousness to peoples who had lived with darkness, tyranny and oppression. It was natural for Moffat to want to change 'barbaric' systems, and have societies transformed by the principles of the Word of God. The rule of God was to be established here and now. The time of the reign of God was not dependent on there first having been an apocalyptic crisis in history before that reign began. Indeed,

---

89 *The Larger Catechism,* Qu. 191.

90 RM, *To William Dickson,* 13.3.1883, (EUNCL/WD9/3/22a/26/Box 2).

the establishment of the *reign of God* was the task of the Church and of the missionary. The Marxist critique of history berates religion for teaching that the oppressed should endure oppression with resignation and simply hope for joy in heaven. But the early-nineteenth-century postmillennial emphasis on social transformation contradicts that Marxist critique.

Jesus Christ was the Coming King. What Moffat focused on was the *reign* of this King, not his dramatic *return*. The reign which Christ would establish was that spoken of in the Psalms and Prophets. It was a reign whose time would be in continuity with the present time. It was a reign which would be characterised by the knowledge of God covering the earth, and by all nations acknowledging the Lord. Yahweh would be exalted. His enemies, including false religions, would be scattered in the coming eschatological reign of the Messiah. Moffat was convinced of the supreme importance of change to benefit humanity here and now. One issue stood out above all others: peace. The coming reign of Christ must be a reign of peace. This was so important in Moffat's thinking that it requires separate treatment.

Chapter 19
The Peace of Jesus: Idealism

AN LMS MISSIONARY was an ambassador of the Prince of Peace, with peace seen as the fruit of the reign of Christ upon the earth. Peace could be spiritual peace between God and humanity in terms of reconciliation through Christ, and it could also mean inner personal peace for an individual. For example, in his 1843 *Barbican Sermon*, Moffat spoke at length concerning the impression made on a young Tswana girl of the peaceful eschatological image of the lion lying down with the lamb. In Moffat's view she totally understood its message: 'Was I not like the wolf? Did not I possess just the very qualities of the lion, and the poison of the *sheushane* before the Gospel changed this heart of mine?' 'Ah!', remarked Moffat, 'She was a noble commentator.'[1] However, what Moffat had in mind most frequently when he referred to peace, was peace between communities and nations.

JESUS, PRINCE OF PEACE

Moffat regularly used the title 'Prince of Peace' when referring to Christ, and missionary work was frequently styled as work on behalf of the 'Prince of Peace'.[2] Moffat's vision for non-Christian communities was that they would come under the reign of the 'Prince of Peace'.[3] He described communities which had become Christian, and hence were subject to the reign of Christ, as being under 'the banner of the Prince of Peace'.[4] Moffat clearly portrayed Christianity as a religion of peace.[5] Thus, individuals and communities turning from war to peace was major evidence of a work of grace, with Moffat stressing this change whenever possible. In his book, *Missionary Labours*, he

---

1 RM, *Barbican Sermon,* 2.1.1843, (*Farewell Services,* 122-124).

2 E.g. RM, *MLSSA,* 210.

3 Cf. RM, *To Tidman, LMS,* 5.9.1859, (SOAS/CWM/SA/ Box31/3/B): 'The Matabele tribe is desperately savage and wicked, and the nature of their government presents a fearful barrier to the gentle and loving reign of the Prince of Peace, but we know that if the promised influences of the Holy Spirit is granted, the strongest ramparts of Satan's kingdom will fall before the Word like the walls of Jericho.'

4 RM, *MLSSA,* 91. These included Africaner's Namaqua tribe.

5 Moffat stressed this was the message of all true missionaries. Describing how Van der Kemp had once been an army officer, Moffat wrote that he came 'from the army to instruct the fierce savages the tactics of a heavenly warfare under the banner of the Prince of Peace' (*MLSSA,* 31).

emphasised that achieving peace was the outward manifestation of the triumph of the Gospel: 'Already the warrior has exchanged the hoarse war song for the anthems of peace and love.'[6] Not infrequently, he described the Gospel as the 'Gospel of Peace',[7] so strong was his identification between the Gospel and the theme of peace.

In similar fashion, he described Christian converts as 'sons of peace',[8] using the designation as a direct equivalent for 'sons of God'. He was able to treat 'sons of God' and 'sons of peace' as synonymous because, in his theology, 'peace' described the essence of what being Christian meant. It was a defining characteristic applicable to both the individual and the community. As such, he believed that one of the benefits which accepting Christianity would bring would be the establishment of peace between peoples who had been enemies for generations.

Moffat often referred to the bloodshed which existed between tribes, graphically describing appalling practices in which terrible revenge was wrought on enemies, with cycles of violence, retaliation and revenge having no end. In conversation with Mahura, a BaThlaping chief, Moffat stated: 'I told him to throw a burning coal into the grass and tell me where the burning would end.'[9] Another time, he mused on the lifestyle of Moselekatse, with whom he formed such a strong bond: 'Nothing but the Gospel can restore man. O Lord, pity the natives! Why should one mortal be allowed to make countless thousands mourn? "Justice and judgment are the habitations of thy throne." "Thou wilt scatter the people that delight in war".'[10]

One of the arguments which Moffat used to commend missionary work to the British political authorities—who could be suspicious of missionary work—was that missions brought peace and changed warlike tribes into

6 RM, *MLSSA,* 48

7 RM, *MLSSA,* 112, 181, & passim.

8 RM, *Journal,* 10.8.1857, (*MJ2,* 23); and, *Journal,* 14.8.1859, (*MJ2,* 171).

9 RM, *Journal,* 13.5.1835, (*MJ1,* 38).

10 RM, *Journal,* 4.8.1854, (*MJ1,* 252). Moffat's quotations in this extract are favourites of his, especially Psalm 68:30. Both quotations come from Psalms emphasising that God is a God of righteousness who will establish justice upon the earth in his coming reign, cf. RM, *Journal,* 5.10.1854, (*MJ1,* 322f). Moffat applied that future reign—or at least the visible signs of it—to immediate temporal history. For Moffat, these Psalms conveyed the idea that, even though evil men may appear to triumph here and now, the justice of God will ensure that, in the end, his rule will prevail. This confidence in the ultimate triumph of God, enabled Moffat to patiently plod on in his work, confident that the kingdom of God would come. Confidence in the ultimate Divine triumph is seldom mentioned in works on the missionary movement, but is clearly present in Moffat, dovetailing with his postmillennialism.

peaceful ones. When he wrote to his parents in 1818 and mentioned his plan to take the converted chief Africaner with him to Cape Town, he stated:

> I have much reason to believe that this unexpected event will be the means of doing much good, both in a political and ecclesiastical point of view. The Government will see the fruits of our labours and be convinced that we are indeed messengers of peace.[11]

If creating a reputation for missionaries establishing peace was important in relation to the Colonial government at the Cape, it was also important in relation to tribal chiefs. Moffat wrote that, 'Muteebe[12] brought Tsousan (Maccaba's son) with him to church. He remarked that it was indeed true, what he had always heard, that we were men of peace, that Muteebe had also given him an account of our proceedings, with which he was much pleased.'[13] A message which promoted peace not only elicited a favourable attitude from the Cape but commended itself to most tribal leaders.

At the same time, it has been asserted that Moffat, and other missionaries, were themselves part of a European issue which contributed to the problem of war. It has been argued that missionaries were inextricably bound up with European settlement in southern Africa, and that it was European presence which created the problem of conflict between tribes in the first place.[14] What is claimed is that before missionaries, traders and settlers arrived, the tribes lived in relative peace, and that it was the intrusion of an alien population and culture which destabilised society, creating situations of conflict. Was it not European colonisation of southern Africa which resulted in tribal displacements, migrations, conflicts over contested land areas, and access to natural resources, all of which led to wars? Was it not the case that tribal wars, originating through the domino effect of colonisation, were a problem created by some Europeans (the colonists) which other Europeans (the missionaries) claimed to have an answer for?

This analysis contains a serious critique. There is no doubt that increasing European presence in southern Africa did bring displacement and migration, and that some hitherto relatively peaceful tribes were thrown into conflict as they contested the remaining land and resources left to them. A considerable proportion of nineteenth-century wars in southern Africa did have, as a trigger, the European problem.[15] But did all tribal conflicts occur because of

---

11 RM, *To his Parents,* 15.12.1818 (JSM, *Lives,* 42).

12 *Muteebe* was *Mothibi,* a senior BaThlaping chief. *Maccaba* was Mothibi's brother.

13 RM, *Journal,* 19.4.1822, (*AAK,* 50).

14 Setiloane, *The Image of God among the Sotho-Tswana,* 123.

15 The series of conflicts between the Xhosa and the Cape Colonists (the Kaffir Wars) which extended over 100 years from the late eighteenth century were unequivocally caused by European colonisation. But the *Mfecane,* which resulted in enormous tribal displacements in

that?[16] Questionable also is the assumption of widespread peace before the European presence had its effect. In Africa, as in Europe, war and bloodshed had a long history.

Whatever the ultimate causes lying behind conflicts occurring in southern Africa during the first half of the nineteenth century, LMS missionaries, such as Moffat, found that it was essential to relate the gospel to a situation of war, and to present the Prince of Peace as a central element of their Christology. This was not a diversion from the task. Missionaries believed that the millennial reign of Christ would be marked by peace. Therefore, ministry which brought peace was in line with the purposes of God.

The Philosophy of Peace

Within the LMS, the connection between the Millennium and peace was explicit. Peace, as an active principle, had been promoted in LMS circles from its inception. When Greville Ewing—one of the early supporters of the LMS, and brother-in-law to David Bogue—delivered his keynote 1797 Edinburgh speech, *A Defence of Missions,* one of his primary arguments for the extension of Christian missions was that the ultimate aim was 'universal and eternal peace'.[17] A year later, when John Cockin of Halifax preached at the LMS Annual Meeting on 9 May 1798, he described the coming rule of Christ on earth, underscoring the connection between Christianity and peace:

> The prevalence and establishment of Christianity will introduce a general peace into the world. *They shall beat their swords into plough-shares, and their spears into pruning-hooks;* instruments infinitely more useful and much better adapted to the service of man; *neither shall they learn war any more.* The times of innocency will then return to the world, after an absence of ages. Nothing can effect this but the Gospel of Jesus Christ, which must be received for the purpose, not in profession only, but in its real and saving power on the heart. *Peace is the very nature and design of the Gospel*, and when men imbibe its true spirit, the tranquility which they feel in themselves will make them peaceable towards all men.[18]

At LMS leadership level, no one exploited the connection between missionary activity, the millennial reign of Christ, and the establishment of

---

the 1820s and 1830s, with accompanying conflicts, had as its ultimate cause Chaka's over-riding ambitions. But were Chaka's ambitions prompted by European presence?

16 Moffat, and several LMS missionaries, worked well beyond the frontier of Cape Colony. Many of the conflicts they came across had a genesis long before direct or indirect European presence created a domino-effect through tribal displacement.

17 Greville Ewing, *A Defence of Missions,* 18.

18 Joseph Cockin, *Sermon: God's Declared Designs: A Motive to Human Endeavours* 79: *LMS Proceedings*, 1798, (Ldn: LMS, 1798), (our italics).

peace, more than its most influential theologian, David Bogue. He made concern for peace an essential hallmark of missionary work, fusing peace with the Millennium.

As well as his commitment to the LMS, Bogue was an active member of the *Society for the Promotion of Permanent and Universal Peace*, seeing an essential unity between its pacifist aims and Christian mission. In 1813, he gave a series of addresses on the Millennium, delivering his sixth discourse, *On Universal Peace,* in October of that year. The whole series was published in 1818 as *Discourses on the Millennium.* A year later, the *Society for the Promotion of Universal and Permanent Peace* asked permission to print the sixth discourse on its own as *Tract VI* of the Society's publications.[19] Bogue readily agreed, especially since, in his sixth discourse, Bogue had urged the creation of a Peace Society: 'As we live in an age of societies to combine individual efforts for public benefits, why should not one be formed for promoting peace among the nations of the earth?'[20]

The *Society for the Promotion of Universal and Permanent Peace,*[21] also known as the *London Peace Society,* was founded on 14 June 1816. The first step in setting it up had been taken on 6 June 1814 at a meeting held at the home of a London Quaker merchant and philanthropist, William Allen. Nearly all of the members of the Society came from Protestant denominations, and Quaker influence was strong.[22] The context behind this yearning for peace was the French/Napoleonic Wars which, with brief respites, had afflicted Europe for almost twenty years.

In its first *Address* to the public, on 9 January 1817, the Society declared that it was principled against *all* war. It had an unambiguous pacifist stance. Its aim was to print and circulate tracts, and to diffuse information which showed that war was inconsistent both with the spirit of Christianity and the true interests of humanity. The Society aimed to promote permanent and universal peace on the basis of *Christian* principles. It sought to spread the principle of peace, to influence public opinion against war, and to combat prejudice against the possibility of establishing permanent peace. Yet, though its official platform was based on an absolutist pacifist stand, its

---

19 David Bogue, *On Universal Peace*: 1813, *Tract VI* of the Society for the Promotion of Permanent and Universal Peace, (Ldn: Ward, reprinted 1839).

20 Ibid, 22.

21 For the SPUPP, see Peter Brock, *Pacifism in Europe to 1914,* (Princeton: PUP, 1972).

22 Bogue considered that if, during the eighteenth century, all European leaders had been Quakers things might have been better (*On Universal Peace,* 20). He said this in 1813 when the Napoleonic Wars were at their height. Brock argued that Bogue was influenced by Thomas Clarkson's, *Portraiture of Quakerism,* (Brock, *Pacifism in Europe to 1914,* 377).

members included peace workers who did not accept a full pacifist position. In its first year the Society printed and distributed 32,000 tracts, and in the following years it published a vast number of pamphlets and leaflets. From 1819 it issued a monthly journal, *Herald of Peace.* The Society was centred in London, but aimed at being a truly national movement with the main burden of its work carried out by auxiliary societies throughout the country.[23]

David Bogue was at the heart of the peace movement. He was also the official LMS tutor, training 115 missionaries for the LMS. As such, he was influential in moulding the mind-set of LMS missionaries and in laying down LMS principles. As such, it is critical to understand his arguments on the central issue of peace which was closely related to the millennial thinking behind the LMS philosophy.

In *Tract VI: On Universal Peace,* Bogue took Micah 4:1-4 as his text, and expounded his vision of the kingdoms of this world becoming 'the kingdom of our Lord and of His Christ.'[24] In support of the primacy of peace as an absolute principle, Bogue cited the advent message of the angels 'peace on earth', and prophecies concerning the kingdom of the redeemer (e.g. Psalm 72:3-7). He connected all of this with a postmillennialist eschatology, and, referring to Isaiah 11, stated: 'That the season of these joyful events is to be connected with the glory of the latter days, when the religion of Jesus shall be universal, is demonstrated from the words which follow "for the earth shall be full of the knowledge of the Lord as the waters cover the sea."'[25]

In Bogue's view, the cause of the Gospel depended on 'the feet of God's servants being shod with the preparation of the Gospel of Peace'. He lamented the failure of national Christendom to be exemplars of peace: 'Look at the face of Christendom. There is not a nation upon earth which professes to believe the holy Scriptures to be the Word of God, but is engaged in war; and, while they are carrying on the contest with each other, all the

---

23 Later, the *Society* opposed the Boer War. It also opposed the power diplomacy of the pre-1914 period but declined in influence thereafter. In World War I it played no perceptible role in the anti-war movement. By 1930 it had taken the name of the International Peace Society, uniting with the International Christian Peace Fellowship.

24 Micah 4:1-4: 'But in the last days it shall come to pass ... they shall beat their swords into ploughshares, and their spears into pruning-hooks: nation shall not lift up a sword against nation; neither shall they learn war any more. But they shall sit every man under his vine and under his fig tree and none shall make them afraid: for the mouth of the Lord of hosts hath spoken it.' This quotation is placed adjacent to an image of a man sitting 'under his vine and under his fig-tree'; i.e. a settled, agricultural, horticulturally focused community. This explains why some missionaries believed that the advent of peace would be aided by tribes changing from a semi-nomadic hunting lifestyle to a settled agricultural one.

25 Bogue, *On Universal Peace,* 7.

Mohammedan and Pagan kingdoms are living at peace.'[26] He noted that 'the power of politicians and the skill of science is being used for war and conquest and killing'.[27] In stark contrast to the atrocious example set by 'Christian' nations, peace should be a natural result of the Gospel.[28]

Bogue argued that peace, when it became central, would result in the true nature of Christianity being better understood.[29] As such, he advocated non-aggression by individuals even in self-defence: 'Christians are men of peace and should never disturb the peace of society; their religion will teach them that, in evil times, if they are not allowed to be passive, their duty is to suffer injury themselves, in order to avoid doing injury to others.' Bogue believed that pursuit of peace would result in evil principles, deeply rooted within individuals, to be destroyed (James 4:1,2) and would contribute enormously towards the moral and spiritual transformation of individuals.

Bogue extended his argument from the individual to the nation. He claimed that what happened on an individual level could also happen on a national level, and that when nations pursued peace, then good principles would regulate the conduct of nations in their relationship to other nations. He argued that active benevolence as national policy had never been tried by governments, and to those who believed that such ethics, if applied at a national level, would leave a nation defenceless, he argued that God in his providence would protect such a nation.[30] Bogue repeatedly stressed that Christian principles had never been applied at a national level, hence no one could object to his argument on the basis of history.[31]

Bogue lamented that 'Christian' nations had lost their 'Christian' identity: 'From the prevalence of a pagan spirit, multitudes that profess Christianity have lost sight of the peaceful genius of the Gospel and became the advocates of bloodshed and war.' Bogue's reference to a 'pagan spirit' reflected his opinion that heroic warlike ideals from classical antiquity had supplanted the gospel ideals of Jesus Christ in the educated mind. He regarded the contemporary fascination for, and admiration of, Greece and Rome as a flawed exercise, with a resultant glorification of the barbaric, and

---

26 Ibid, 5.

27 Ibid, 8f.

28 Ibid, 9. Also, Matt 22:37-39; 5:43-44, and Romans 12:19-21.

29 Ibid, 11.

30 Ibid, 15.

31 Ibid, 12: 'No one nation ... ever administered a system of government according to Christian principles, or pursued a regular succession of political measures under the influence of Christian benevolence.'

a loss of a true Christian identity.[32] It was at this point, arguing that Christian principles should be fully applied at national and international level, that Bogue proposed one of his most radical proposals. What should a Christian nation do when attacked? Instead of sending ships-of-war for retaliatory action, a Christian nation should send envoys to offer help and friendship. The Christian response should be *bread* not *bullets*:

> Let us suppose that, instead of such an armament [fleets, fire-ships, bombs and armed men] our [British] rulers were to commission ships laden with corn, and clothes, and money, at only half the amount of expense – and to accompany the gift with a letter to the government of a neighbouring country to this effect: 'Through the goodness of God, we have had an abundant harvest, and hearing that you have not, we send a present of corn to the widows and the fatherless, the orphan, the blind, and the lame. As many of them may be unprovided with raiment for the inclemency of winter, accept the clothing which will be delivered to you by our fleet, and divide among those who are in the greatest distress, the money which our messengers carry in their hands.'
>
> What influence would such conduct have upon the people of that country? Would it leave any stings behind in their souls? No, it would conciliate the esteem and affection of all. Tell them after this, 'Britain wishes to injure you.' No, they would say. It cannot be. It is impossible that the people of that land should desire to do us harm. Command them to buckle on their armour and wage war with the English: they would answer: 'We cannot fight them: the weapons would drop from our hands: we love them too well to hurt them: continue in peace.' If any State would act in this way to its neighbours, it would have no enemies: the sound of war would not be heard in its dominions.[33]

The rest of Bogue's majestic *Tract VI* is replete with similar sentiments, arguing passionately that grace should triumph over violence at every level, whether personal or national.

A recurring theme is Bogue's desperate concern that the missionary message lost credibility if nations, yet to be evangelised, came to know the conduct of so-called Christian nations. This fear was carried over into Bogue's *Missionary Lectures.* In Lecture Six, 'On Reasoning about Religion with the

---

32 Ibid, 18f: 'The ancient writers of Greece and Rome are the idols of modern times ... in what veneration are they held! From them, among other evils, the youth imbibe a pagan morality ... this pagan morality—far from inculcating or possessing humility, meekness, benevolence and peace—is selfish, proud, ambitious, savage, hates other nations, despises the mass of mankind, and seeks distinction and honour in the field of battle ... Such is the morality which is most commonly found in the speeches of the most eloquent public men: and the maxims generally recommended and adopted, accord much more with the sentiments of the Grecian and Roman classics than with the spirit of the evangelists and apostles of Christ.'

33 Ibid, 14.

Heathen', Bogue pointed out that one of the questions which the heathen might ask is: 'Whether Christians in Europe live as wicked as those in the East Indies?'[34] For Bogue, those who preached peace and love must live out peace and love, and those who preached grace must live out grace. Bogue's stance anticipated that of Martin Luther King in the 1960s who, in his sermon from Birmingham Jail, Alabama, argued that the Ends of Peace must be achieved by the Means of Peace. Bogue's fundamental conviction was:

> The religion of the New Testament is a religion of peace; and that for the blood of every man slain in war, the Almighty Ruler of the Universe will demand an account from those who direct the affairs of nations, and decree violence and war, and not pursue peace with their whole hearts.[35]

Bogue was adamant that God would protect any nation which employed absolute pacific principles. He argued that active benevolence was an untried principle. Because it was untried, then all the usual arguments against pacifism were irrelevant: 'If this be the doctrine of the New Testament, how much is it to be lamented that multitudes who profess to be Christians, are opposed to it, both in sentiments and practice.'[36] Bogue taught high principles. But could they be put into practice? Could they be adopted in real life in the mission-field at remote stations? What happened in the field? What compromises from Bogue's ideals were made?

The Promotion of Peace

Bogue was driven by an absolutist pacifism, though not all LMS members were.[37] But Bogue's stance demonstrates the close connection between proclamation of the Kingdom of God and promotion of peace, which existed in the missionary movement. The expectation of a millennial reign of peace was a powerful force. Even the Poet Laureate, Lord Tennyson, expressed this eschatological hope: *'Ring out the thousand wars of old; Ring in the thousand years of peace; Ring out the darkness of the land; Ring in the Christ that is to be.'*[38] Moffat certainly viewed peace as a sign of grace operating in individuals

---

[34] Bogue, *Miss. Lect.* 6, 'On Reasoning about Religion with the Heathen'.

[35] Bogue, *On Universal Peace,* 21.

[36] Ibid, 19. Bogue did not advise what to do if pacific overtures were rejected.

[37] Livingstone was sceptical about the Peace Society. After describing Boer attitudes he commented, 'We wonder how the Peace Society would manage them' (Livingstone, *To British Banner,* 14.11.1849: *DLSAP,* 18). Livingstone also made slighting comments about the Peace Society in letters to family members, (*DLFL,* Vol. 2, 159, 186, 194 and 259).

[38] Tennyson, *In Memoriam,* (1850), cvi.

or communities. When Jager Africaner and Berend Berends[39] became Christians, their change of relationship, from one of absolute hatred to acceptance of each other as brothers, was viewed as a mammoth witness to the Gospel: 'Though these two chiefs dreadfully harassed each other, neither conquered; but continued to breathe against each other the direst hatred, till, by the gospel of peace, they were brought to "beat their swords into ploughshares, and their spears into pruning-hooks"'.[40]

Change of lifestyle—from war to peace—was central, with Moffat celebrating 'the standard of the Prince of Peace reared in the very village of the man who once breathed out threatenings and slaughter against not only his fellow heathen but against the saints of the Most High'.[41] When Moffat took the converted Africaner to Cape Town in 1819, they had to pass through Pella which was inhabited by people from Warmbath who had fled when Africaner destroyed Warmbath years earlier. The transformation of relationships was extraordinary. Moffat described it in expansive language:

> Men met who had not seen each other since they had joined in mutual combat for each other's woe. They met, warrior with warrior, bearing in their hands the olive branch, secure under the panoply of peace and love. They talked of Him who had subdued both, without a sword or spear, and each bosom swelled with purest friendship, and exhibited another trophy destined to adorn the triumph of the Prince of Peace.[42]

Unsurprisingly, when he summarised the nature of a Christian community he wrote: 'We want to see progress by aggression on the dominion of Satan; we tell our converts that a church of true believers is a fighting and a conquering church under the banner of the Prince of Peace.'[43]

Moffat also prioritised peace as a focus for prayer. The Reports to the LMS in London, which Moffat sent from Kuruman, have frequent references to

---

39 Like Africaner, Berend Berends had been violently hostile towards Europeans. He professed conversion around 1812. The LMS *Reports* mention that 'Berend Berends' was appointed an 'assistant preacher of the Gospel' in August 1814, at the same time as Andries Waterboer, and was subsequently attached to the Mission at Griqua Town. Moffat, *Journal,* 11.7.1824, (*AAK,* 123f), was unimpressed, seeing him as a 'secret enemy to the cause he once espoused'.

40 RM, *MLSSA,* 77. Cf. 181: 'Being now converts to the faith, all their former animosities were melted away by the Gospel of peace and love. These chiefs sat down together in our tent with a number of people, all united in singing a hymn of praise to God, and listening to an address, from the invitation of Jehovah to the ends of the earth to look to him, and him alone, for salvation. After which, they knelt at the same stool, before the peaceful throne of the Redeemer'. In *MLSSA* (1842), Moffat did not allude to Berends' 'apostasy'.

41 RM, *MLSSA,* 91.

42 RM, *MLSSA,* 174f.

43 RM, *To Tidman, LMS,* 14.11.1855, (SOAS/CWM/SA/Box 29/3/A).

annual seasons of prayer which had peace as their emphasis. These seasons of prayer did not come about because of a particular threat to Kuruman—as had been the case in the 1820s—but were organised as part of a worldwide call in evangelical societies for times of prayer for peace in Christendom. Out of several references in successive LMS *Annual Reports*, the one pertaining to the 1868 season of prayer may be cited:

> Although the number of the *Evangelical Christendom* to inform of the subjects of the first week of prayer has not been received, subjects which were deemed the most important to be prayed for were given out to our church.[44] The attendance was beyond expectations, large and animatory to everyone who had come to pray for the *peace* and prosperity of the Redeemer's reign, the numbers attending and the earnestness in prayer offered by so many members of the church were tokens of the influence of the Holy Spirit.[45]

In evaluating his own work, Moffat placed peace high in his list. When, in *Missionary Labours,* he described the long-term effect of the work at Kuruman, he cited the visible transformation of lifestyle which had taken place. He claimed that crowds were now assembling, not to hear tribal leaders arousing them with 'revenge and war, but the heavenly message of peace and love'.[46] Similarly, in a speech made at Port Elizabeth, in May 1870, before leaving for Britain at the close of his life in Africa, Moffat summarised his fifty years of toil, with the advancement of peace the feature which he highlighted above all:

> When I first went to the Kuruman scarcely an individual could go beyond there. Now they travel in safety to the Zambezi. Now it is safe to traverse any part of the country, and traders travel far beyond the Kuruman without the slightest fear of molestation. Formerly men of one tribe could not travel through another's territory, and wars were frequent.[47]

Moffat believed that change had come for one reason: the influence of Christianity. He may have exaggerated the extent to which peace had been established in the regions he had in mind, but that does not detract from the

---

[44] *Evangelical Christendom* was published by the *Evangelical Alliance* (formed 1846). It organised Seasons of Prayer: e.g. 'January 5th, 1862: Preached in the morning from First Peter. Read to the congregation the arrangements made for the following week for special prayers to be held each day as recommended by the *Evangelical Alliance*. Mr. Ashton preached in the afternoon ..., both sermons intended to prepare the minds for the devotional services of the week. Mr. Price expounded in the evening.' Cf. RM, *Occasional Journal: 1860-1862, 1868,* (SOAS/CWM/Africa/Moffat/Personal/4).

[45] RM, *To Mullens, LMS,* 15.1.1868, (SOAS/CWM SA Reports/Box 1). Moffat rarely mentioned the Holy Spirit. For him to do so here may indicate times of deep significance.

[46] RM, *MLSSA,* 242.

[47] RM, *Speech at Port Elizabeth, 1870*, (Deane, *Robert Moffat,* 183).

fact that, in his own thinking, he *believed* peace had been established, and that the establishment of peace was central to mission. The importance of peace meant that social implications were at the heart of missionary work. It could not be otherwise, since a missionary such as Moffat came to establish the Redeemer's reign in every area of life.

Jesus as the 'Prince of Peace' and the Gospel as a 'Gospel of Peace', were central in Moffat's missionary theology. Jesus' own teaching on peace, the stories of Moravian missionaries and their endeavours—which his mother had read to him—and the teaching of David Bogue with his powerful influence on the ethos of the LMS, all had a similar emphasis.[48] With such powerful factors, it is unsurprising to see peace featuring highly in Moffat's thinking. But were high ideals consistently put into practice in the mission field? In the field, theoretical issues became existential ones. Mission stations were vulnerable places. Hostile forces sometimes lived nearby. In Britain, Bogue could treat the Government as 'them', but in the field the 'government' was 'us'. The LMS missionaries were themselves the 'government', if 'government' is understood as the body which had responsibility for the safety and well-being of people who live on the mission station. And a primary responsibility of any government is the protection of its people.

It was relatively easy for Bogue to demand absolute pacifism from secular Government, when he did not have responsibility for the defence of the nation. But at remote stations, how was the reign of the Prince of Peace to be applied? What happened when wife and family might be victims? Did LMS missionaries put Bogue's advice into practice? Did they *really* believe that God would protect such a nation (mission station) without taking steps for self-defence? What advice could a missionary give to a new Christian village or even to a non-Christian village which felt vulnerable and at the mercy of hostile forces? Bogue made his radical statements with deep sincerity, but also from a position of security and comfort. What was it like at the front line? How was theory to be translated into practice? How was idealistic theology to be applied on the ground? At Kuruman the theology of peace required tailoring to the situation.

---

48 During the eighteenth century, the Moravians were granted exemption from military service by most states in which they settled. In Europe, the Moravians were associated with pacifism, though in America they bore arms, and some of their mission stations were armed. Brock, *Pacifism in Europe to 1914,* 250ff, argued that Moravian non-combatancy derived primarily from a desire to live separately from the world rather than from principled non-resistance, and, whereas the Czech Brethren were absolutely pacifist, not all Moravians were.

Chapter 20
The Peace of Jesus: Pragmatism

DAVID BOGUE'S IDEALISM WAS most exposed when it came to self-defence under attack. Bogue was convinced that God would give providential protection, but for LMS missionaries in the field a change of judgment took place. A critical illustration of Moffat's theology on this matter, as theory was put into practice, came in his strategy during the 1823 Mantatee invasion of the Kuruman area. Rumours had reached Kuruman about the fearsome activities of a large group called the Mantatee, who were advancing from the east.[1]

THE MANTATEE CRISIS

The Mantatee, as Moffat named them, were a mass of refugees, who had been displaced by Moselekatse's early campaigns and who were fleeing westward.[2] In mid-1823, Moffat set out to visit the BaNgwaketse, but *en route* heard news of Mantatee attacks on tribes and villages ahead of them. He also heard of Mantatee activity toward the rear of their missionary party, causing his party to immediately retrace their steps to the missionary base at Lattakoo where an emergency public meeting was called. News of Mantatee atrocities was alarming, and there was considerable panic. Moffat advised the assembly that the missionaries and Tswana by themselves could not resist the Mantatee, and that there were two choices before them. They could flee to the Cape Colony; or they could call in the aid of the Griqua at Griqua Town whose chief, Andries Waterboer, had been educated by the missionaries, and who, before his election as a chief had been set apart as a

---

1 For Moffat's account see RM, *MLSSA,* 354ff, and RM, *Journal*, (*AAK,* 80ff). In 1857 Moffat came across a veteran enemy combatant who had taken part in the battle, cf. RM, *Journal,* 3.10.1857, (*MJ2,* 81): 'I told him what my object was in being there, not to fight but to try to make peace and prevent bloodshed, and how they acted and how I narrowly escaped with my life.' The encounter with the veteran occurred at Moselekatse's town. In that context, it was important for Moffat to stress his role in promoting peace.

2 Moselekatse was a vassal of Chaka, but incurred Chaka's wrath by keeping back part of the booty won on an expedition. To escape execution Moselekatse fled with his remaining army over the mountains to the High Veldt. Only the BaSuto withstood Moselekatse's attacks. Other tribes were incorporated into the Ndebele, or exterminated, or driven westward.

native teacher. Moffat also pointed out that John Melville, a Government agent, resided in Griqua Town, and might give assistance.[3]

The meeting agreed on the second option, and Moffat set off for Griqua Town. Andries Waterboer readily promised assistance. Eleven days later, Waterboer, Melville and one hundred Griqua horsemen armed with guns arrived at Lattakoo. Meanwhile the Mantatee had reached Letakong [Dithakong], only thirty-six miles away. Prayer was held, with the hope that shedding blood might be avoided, but arms were also made ready.[4] A small force was deployed as far as the Matlaurin River, about half way to Letakong. Waterboer, Moffat, and eleven others rode ahead.[5] The next day they saw the Mantatee, who had divided into two groups—one holding a town, and the other lying on the hills to the left of the town.

According to Moffat, the Mantatee did not respond to peaceful overtures, and it was clear that battle was imminent. Moffat rode back to confer with Melville and the other Griqua chiefs, including Cornelius Kok. The whole party advanced the next morning, met up with a scouting group, and moved to less than two hundred yards from the enemy, hoping that this show of force would intimidate the Mantatee and make them retreat. Instead, the Mantatee attacked.[6] A fierce battle ensued, with the Griqua the victors. In the aftermath of the battle some Griqua started to slaughter Mantatee women and children as well as Mantatee warriors.[7]

Moffat claimed to have concentrated on trying to stop the Griqua from their gratuitous killing-spree. He later told a London audience: 'I have, at the peril of my life, shielded mothers and children from the bloody war-axe of the unfeeling conquerors!'[8] Also, according to his own version, Moffat took no personal part in the fighting.[9] Melville and Moffat collected many

---

3 The Cape Governor appointed John Melville as Government Agent to the Griqua in 1823. Melville unsuccessfully tried to unite all the Griquas under Andries Waterboer. He resigned his position in 1826 and became an LMS missionary.

4 RM, *Journal,* 23.6.1823, (*AAK,* 90), wrote: 'Monday. Ammunition was got in readiness. It is what has been collected from each of the missionaries, there being no powder of any consequence in the country, with the addition of 8 pounds of powder kindly given by Mr. Thomson, and which was all he possessed.'

5 RM, *Journal,* 24.6.1823, (*AAK,* 91). We follow Moffat's account in this narrative.

6 RM, *Journal,* 26.6.1823, (*AAK,* 92).

7 RM, *Journal,* 26.6.1823, (*AAK,* 94).

8 RM, *Africa,* 27

9 RM, *Journal,* 26.6.1823, (*AAK,* 94), claimed: 'As fighting was not my province, I of course avoided discharging a single shot.'

Mantatee women and children and took them to the mission station where they could be looked after and kept safe.[10] The battle saved the mission.

At that time, immediately after the battle, it was feared that the Mantatee might regroup and attack Lattakoo after the Griquas left, and so there was a temporary evacuation to Griqua Town. But it was found that the Mantatee had left the neighbourhood. The Tswana were grateful that the missionaries had stayed with them when they might easily have fled to the Colony, leaving them to face the Mantatee alone. Despite this genuine gratitude, Moffat noted that the attendance at the mission church on the Sunday immediately following the successful battle was thin.[11]

Events following this action introduced a factor which accelerated the split between Moffat and John Philip. When Moffat sent his account of the events to Philip, he included the fact that some of the Griqua 'converts' had started to kill Mantatee women and children and that the Griqua had pursued fleeing Mantatee with bloodthirsty enthusiasm. In his note, Moffat used the phrase 'alas they are heathen still'.[12] This was embarrassing for Philip since, for some years, the LMS had given significant publicity to its Christianising success among the Griqua. Philip objected to the phrase and advised the LMS in London to remove it from Moffat's published report.[13]

---

[10] De Gruchy has discussed Julian Cobbling's bizarre allegation that Moffat was actively engaged in slavery, and that, together with co-conspirators from the Cape Colony, Moffat engineered an attack on a defenceless village (Dithakong) in order to secure slaves to trade for arms and ammunition. Whilst Cobbling's questioning of Mfecane theory has been adopted by the uncritical, that Moffat was a slave trader has been comprehensively refuted by Elizabeth Eldridge and Guy Hartley, cf. De Gruchy, 'Alleged Political Conservatism of Robert Moffat', 18f. De Gruchy referred to Cobbling, *Mfecane as Alibi,* 487-519; Eldridge, 'Sources of Conflict in Southern Africa c1800-1830,' (Hamilton, *Mfecane Aftermath,* 123-161); and, Hartley, *Battle of Dithakong,* 395-416. See also, Jacobs, *Environment, Power and Injustice,* 63.

[11] RM, *Journal,* 6.7.1823, (*AAK,* 99).

[12] RM, *Journal,* 27.6.1823, (*AAK,* 96), and fn. Moffat referred to the gratuitous slaughter of those still alive. But there were Bantu traditions connected with the aftermath of battle which may be relevant. With the Zulu (and some other Bantu) a warrior must cut open the corpse of his dead foe before it begins to swell. Neglect of this renders the warrior liable to being possessed by the avenging ghost. This practice was misunderstood during the Zulu War of 1879, giving rise to reports of 'atrocities' and 'mutilation of the dead' (Alice Werner, *Myths and Legends of the Bantu,* 100).

[13] Cf. John Philip, *To LMS,* 23.8.1823, (SOAS/LMS 9/1/C), cf. *AAK,* 96 and fn. Philip was an administrator; Moffat was a missionary. Philip was a political activist; Moffat was a Pastor and a Shepherd. Philip's ministry was on behalf of the native peoples; Moffat's ministry was directly to the native peoples. Philip challenged the attitude of Europeans; Moffat challenged the practices of native Africans. Philip was never an evangelist, never directly had to face the problems of a new born and growing church and never dealt with converts who had had no Christian tradition: Moffat did. It was vital for Philip to extol and laud all the positive features of native converts in order to impress the home audience, whereas Moffat had to deal with

This was not the only time when Philip wanted to alter Moffat's written submissions. Moffat objected to Philip's attempt to change his reports. He resented the sanitised picture Philip wanted to convey to the home public. He did not like being edited by a man who had not been there.

The battle of 1823 repulsed the Mantatee threat for a time, but the danger was not eliminated. There was always the possibility that they would resume their westward migrations, and that Kuruman would again be threatened. From time to time, rumours reached Kuruman that the Mantatee were re-advancing. Sometimes the missionary families moved south to Griqua Town, and sometimes they stayed. During this period, when the Kuruman mission faced the possibility of attacks on a regular basis—both from the Mantatee and other groups—there is no question but that the missionaries built defences with the intention of repulsing the enemy by force. In 1825, Moffat made the following entry in his *Journal*: 'As there was reason to expect that they would attack the station, the men were all armed and a watch set.'[14] The mission station also helped to distribute gunpowder and ammunition to Mothibi to help protect his BaThlaping from the menacing marauders.

Moffat may not have fired a shot in the 1823 battle, but he was clearly pro-active in preparations for possible battle at Kuruman in 1825, and on other occasions. His willingness to use arms in self-defence is also clear from a conversation with Moselekatse in 1829. Moffat pointed out to Moselekatse that the violence which the Ndebele warriors were associated with meant that he [Moffat] had to be prepared to act in self-defence: 'I was under the necessity in two instances to keep myself and men ready armed while passing places where many had been torn to pieces.'[15]

---

the reality of new Christians, the mixture of advance and slippage, the need for discipline and the heartbreak of disappointment as well as joy over real progress. Philip was minister to a European congregation in Cape Town, whereas Moffat was spiritual leader of a native congregation in a remote area which was feeling its way through a multitude of problems. For further comment on Philip's editing and Moffat's reaction see: Legassick, *The Griqua, the Sotho-Tswana, and the Missionaries, 1780-1840: the Politics of a Frontier Zone, Parts 1 & 2* (PhD dissertation, University of California, 1969), 453ff. Legassick pointed out: 'Until 1825 John Philip had not visited the Griqua of whom he had written with such confidence.' (Part 2, 456).

14 RM, *Journal,* 1.5.1825, (*AAK,* 182). Moffat adopted a policy of being ready-armed when passing through hostile territory to Moselekatse in 1829, cf. *Journal,* 1829, (*MJ1,* 15).

15 RM, *Journal,* 1829, (*MJ1,* 15).

Self-Defence for Kuruman

In 1823, the Griqua came to the aid of the mission station in the battle against the Mantatee. But in 1828, some renegade Griqua, who were part of a group of marauding 'bandits', threatened it.[16] In his *Journal,* Moffat described the group as a collection of 'mountaineers' plus the Coranna. Moffat used the term 'mountaineers' to refer to the Bergenaars, a group of Griqua bandits. The Coranna were part of the Khoikhoi, and one of their leaders was a man named Paul whom Moffat had known from his early work in Namaqualand.

According to Moffat, this bandit group left a trail of death, plunder and rapine, and arrived at the gates of the mission station on 11 August 1828. To prevent them discovering the weakness of Kuruman's defences, Moffat met the leaders at a distance outside the entrenchments.[17] During negotiations, Moffat appears to have said to the bandits that he would not use firearms against them at Kuruman:

> I requested him [Paul, the Coranna chief] to view me in the same light in which he was wont to do [when Moffat had known him years earlier in Namaqualand], and I should speak to him as one who feared God rather than man. I then glanced at [i.e. referred in speech] the deeds of robbery, rapine, and bloodshed perpetrated by the Mountaineers and Corannas on the unoffending Bechuana. I appealed to his conscience, and directed his attention to that tribunal before which we should both shortly appear to render an account; that if he had any fear of God, any respect for one who pitied his immortal soul, if he had any sympathy for the natives who were already reduced to comparative poverty, he would not only relinquish his wicked intentions, but return all that had been taken that morning; and should he refuse, *I should not resist with firearms*, but, like one of old, lay the matter before the Lord, and implore his interference.[18]

Moffat's declaration that he would not resist was left untested, since the bandits withdrew. Providence had answered! At first reading it appears that Moffat was following Bogue's absolute position of non-violence. However, the clear preparations which Moffat had made in preceding years to repulse any further Mantatee threat by force indicates that he was not totally committed to Bogue's pacifist principles. In fact, as the bandits approached Kuruman, Robert and Mary had not only prayed earnestly, 'to Him who has said "Call upon me in the time of trouble, and I will deliver,"'[19] but had also placed twelve armed men in the entrenchments which had been prepared

---

[16] This incident is covered in *AAK,* 283-289, and *MLSSA,* 485-492.

[17] RM, *To the LMS Directors,* 26.8.1828, (*AAK,* 286).

[18] Ibid, 288 (our italics)

[19] Ibid, 286.

during previous times of danger.[20] In a letter written by Mary to her father, only days beforehand, she stated: 'ammunition is to be granted for the defence of the station.'[21]

It is beyond doubt that the Moffats were not practising Bogue's absolute pacifism. Their stance was more in line with Oliver Cromwell's 'Trust in God and keep your powder dry!' In the end, Moffat persuaded the bandit leaders to negotiate, and the personal influence he had over his one-time acquaintance, Paul, proved adequate to avert disaster.

It may be that Moffat *had* to negotiate since he knew that a mission station with only twelve guns could not repel such a powerfully armed group. It may also be that Moffat's decision to negotiate did not come from pacifist idealism but from the knowledge that if fighting started then the defenders could only lose. Yet, in 1823 before the battle with the Mantatee, Moffat had also attempted to avert bloodshed by negotiation, and on that occasion, with 100 armed Griqua at his back and facing a large but vastly inferior armed enemy, he had no need to parley unless he had a sincere desire to avoid conflict.

What is clear is that defending a mission station and having responsibility for one's own wife and children brought a vivid compromise with the idealism of absolute pacifism. Moffat's policy was a 'common-sense' position. But Bogue had not argued for a 'common-sense' position. Bogue had argued for an absolute ideal: 'Christians are men of peace: their duty is to suffer injury themselves, in order to avoid doing injury to others'.[22]

Self Defence for Villages

What emerges from Moffat's philosophy, and becomes clearer when the advice he gave to converts is considered, is that Moffat, as an ambassador of the Prince of Peace, applied three principles when faced with the moral and theological problem of the use of force which might result in bloodshed and killing. Firstly, a Christian should never initiate violence. Secondly, where possible *flight* is preferred to *fight.* Thirdly, if flight is impossible then force may be used to defend *life* but not *property*. Moffat quoted with approval a

---

[20] RM, *To the LMS Directors,* 26.8.1828, (*AAK,* 288): 'Though [the Bandits] were four times the strength of the shooters on the station, they were so alarmed that they begged me to prevent any attack being made on them during the night. Surely this was the Lord's doing. He sent a fear into their hearts, nor did he suffer them to do us harm.'

[21] Mary Moffat, *To James Smith,* 28.7.1828, (*AAK,* 285).

[22] Bogue, *On Universal Peace,* 10f.

passage in which Van der Kemp described an attack on the missionary settlement at Bethelsdorp:

> We always had instructed our people that it was their duty rather to part with their earthly goods than to save them by killing another; and that it was not the duty of a Christian to kill anybody but [except] when the safety of his own life, or that of a third party should render it absolutely necessary.[23]

Moffat's opinion was that native converts did not always receive Van der Kemp's guidelines favourably, since, 'they had obtained a certain degree of pleasure in fighting'. Van der Kemp's principles were clear in his own mind, though they left Bogue's pacifism far behind. But how did Moffat apply these principles when advising village leaders? Moffat stressed to converts that they must not continue to be involved in tribal wars: that was an elementary characteristic of new Christian life-style. But what advice did he give when villages were under threat? Fight or flight?

1. Flight. Sebobi was a native teacher, trained at Kuruman, whom Moffat sent to minister at the village of Sechele of the BaKwena. In 1854 Moffat instructed Sebobi in the following terms:

> He was in duty bound to fulfill his promise, even were it to his own hurt; that, should war arise, he was on no account to take up arms to fight, but to make his escape as best he could; that as a soldier of the Prince of Peace he must use the sword of the spirit only, and fight with sin and the devil with all his might, but on no account shed man's blood.[24]

Moffat's advice to Sebobi was 'flight' not 'fight'. However, this was advice given to an individual. Sebobi was not a chief with responsibility for a clan or tribe. He was a religious teacher sent from Kuruman, and he had the option of simply abandoning his post and fleeing back to Kuruman when danger threatened. A chief did not have that option. What would happen if flight were not a choice? What if an individual had a responsibility not just to himself, but to others? What would be the advice concerning non-violence in such a situation? How would such advice tally theologically with a gospel of peace? What constituted legitimate self-defence? Did this policy allow pre-emptive action? In the case of Andries Waterboer of the Griqua, who took pre-emptive action against some neighbouring hostile tribes, Moffat

---

[23] Quoted by RM, *MLSSA,* 36. The first LMS missionaries to Mothibi's Tswana were Read and Hamilton They had had to deal with this issue at the start of their time at Lattakoo. In 1816, when they sought permission to stay in Mothibi's village, they were informed by the Chief that they should aid the people in 'their expeditions to plunder the BaNgwaketse. The missionaries refused, but 'assured them that, should an enemy invade the town, assistance would be given by the missionaries' (RM, *MLSSA,* 235).

[24] RM, *Journal,* 5.6.1854, (*MJ1,* 156).

appears to have regarded his actions with approval, though there are indications in Moffat's account which point to unease concerning what took place.[25] In the end, Moffat wrote a favourable record of Waterboer taking 'such measures as might put a stop to the system of depredation [which the Bergenaars] were carrying on against the tribes around them'. At the time, Waterboer was a 'native teacher' of the Christian faith, and it seems that Moffat saw no contradiction between his actions and the Gospel of Peace. Common-sense triumphed over idealism.

2. Fight. Though Moselekatse was not a Christian, Moffat's conversations with him reveal Moffat's mind concerning the arming of Africans, whether Christian or non-Christian. During Moffat's embarrassing conversation with Moselekatse in 1854, concerning the British agreement with the Boers to an embargo on selling guns or ammunition to Africans north of the Vaal River, it is clear that, in disagreeing with British policy, Moffat was not imagining guns and ammunition being used only for hunting, whoever the recipients were. Moffat envisaged the tribes being armed for self-defence, and he believed it to be right that they were. Moffat expressed indignation at the injustice of the law, and the resultant inability of the Africans to defend themselves against the Boers. He also contrasted the aggression of the Boers towards the British with the attitude of the native tribes: 'The [African] has yet to be found, in these interior regions north of the Vaal, who has intentionally shed the blood of an Englishman.'[26] Why arm those who had been hostile to Britain, yet make impotent the Africans who had given no cause for offence? Moffat made the explicit point that it was unjust to deprive a people of the means of self-defence. He wrote to Tidman, 'For the sake of a handful of malcontents, these [Africans] must be deprived of the means of self-defence and left to be trodden down by the oppressor.'[27]

For Moffat, the British policy lacked both common-sense and justice. Yet, though he regarded the policy as indefensible, he obeyed it. Thus, in 1857, on the outward leg of his Fourth Visit to Moselekatse, he recorded: '[An African from Motito] would have liked a share of my ammunition as a reward, but we happened to be in the wrong latitude.'[28]

---

[25] RM, *MLSSA,* 202. Moffat looked on Waterboer's actions with a kindly eye since he had helped to instruct Waterboer in the principles of law, the history of nations, and political economy (in rudimentary fashion) when Waterboer became leader of the Griqua. Moffat was quick to point out the magnanimous spirit Waterboer showed in 'victory'.

[26] RM, *To Tidman, LMS,* 10.5.1855, (*MJ1,* 373).

[27] Ibid.

[28] RM, *Journal,* 2.8.1857, (*MJ2,* 11).

THE THEOLOGY OF SELF-DEFENCE

Moffat did not have an absolute pacifist stance, despite peace being important in his theology. What justification did he have for this, apart from an appeal to 'common-sense'? It is here that traces of Moffat's Calvinist heritage may be detected. The clue comes in a phrase which Moffat used in his early writings concerning Africaner, the converted Namaqua chief. The phrase was *'the sword of the magistrate'*. Africaner, as a converted chief, had civic responsibilities towards his people, including protection. And in this context there was available to Moffat, over against Bogue's pacifist Christianity, a ready-made theological system.

Calvinist Scotland had *The Westminster Confession of Faith* as its theological basis, within which there was a clear theology of the duties of the civil magistrate within a Christian society. It was this theology, or something similar, which Moffat applied to the responsibilities of a Christian chief. As a Christian, Africaner was now a man of peace, and his village was under 'the banner of the Prince of Peace'. But as a chief he had to shield his people. It was in this circumstance that Moffat referred to 'the sword of the magistrate':

> [Africaner] was a man of peace; and though I could not expound to him that the *'sword of the magistrate'* implied that he was calmly to sit at home and see Bushmen or marauders carry off his cattle and slay his servants, yet so fully did he understand and appreciate the principles of the gospel of peace that nothing could grieve him more than to hear of individuals or villages contending with one another. [29]

The phrase 'sword of the magistrate' is within inverted commas in Moffat's book, suggesting that Moffat regarded the concept as taken from another context. Though the exact phrase does not occur in *The Westminster Confession of Faith,* the two words 'magistrate' and 'sword' appear in close proximity within it, and the teaching of the *Confession* is what Moffat adopted in regard to Africaner's responsibilities:

> God, the supreme Lord and King of all the world, hath ordained civil magistrates to be under Him over the people, for His own glory, and the public good; and, to this end, *hath armed them with the power of the sword*, for the defence and encouragement of them that are good, and for the punishment of evil-doers.[30]

---

[29] RM, *MLSSA,* 112.

[30] *The Westminster Confession of Faith,* Ch. 23/1 (Italics ours). This coincides with what Calvin taught concerning the duties of a Christian ruler (*Institutes,* IV, xx, 11).

This understanding of the role of the Christian civil magistrate was almost unquestioned in Scotland. Even though Congregationalism tended to detach Church from State more than did the Kirk, it did not question this general assumption. Moffat viewed Africaner as the civil magistrate. As such, he had the 'power of the sword', though that power was only to be used for defence of the people. This was the ready-made theological answer to the question about the relationship between a chief's responsibilities and the Gospel of Peace. The Calvinist tradition did not adopt the idealism which identified peace with absolute non-violence. Bogue made that identification. Moffat did not. He adhered to a different theological model.

If the theology of the civil magistrate gave Moffat a freedom to incorporate self-defence into his theology of peace, it was a two-edged sword. This was because defence of a community might be offered by an outside authority, such as the government of the Cape Colony. Did that mean that the outside civil authority also had the right to demand responsibilities from those whom it protected? Kuruman was outside the bounds of the Cape Colony for all the years Moffat worked there, and so the issue did not arise at Kuruman itself, but it had been a problem elsewhere. In *Missionary Labours,* Moffat discussed the matter in reference to the vexed question of compulsory military service being demanded by the Colonial Government.

The Dilemma of Obligations

In 1814, the Cape Government decided that tribes, which enjoyed its protection, should contribute towards that protection by providing men to serve in the Cape forces. Moffat recorded that William Anderson, the LMS missionary to the Griqua, 'received an order from the Colonial Government to send down to the Cape twenty Griquas for the Cape regiment.'[31] Moffat added that the missionaries to the Griqua were surprised by this move. They thought that their missionary work, which had the side-effect of pacifying otherwise potentially hostile tribes, would have been noted with appreciation rather than be exploited by the Cape Government. Anderson, as the principal missionary to the Griqua, was in a dilemma. He felt that circumstances compelled him to present the proposal to the Griqua.[32] However, his action in conveying this request resulted in him being viewed

---

[31] RM, *MLSSA,* 197. Cf. JSM, *Lives,* 93.

[32] Anderson felt that non-compliance could result in the Cape Government preventing missionaries from crossing the northern border of the Colony. This would threaten a large area of missionary work (RM, *MLSSA,* 197). Moffat was aware of the danger of losing permission to work at Kuruman. It was a major factor in his early a-political policy.

by the Griqua as a Government agent. This all but destroyed a relationship which had been built up over many years, as the Griqua intensely resented the order. Moffat sympathised with their reasons. As well as the proposal assuming a tacit authority over them, the order from Cape Town threatened their own security:

> The only wonder was that the people did not stone [Anderson], when he made the proposal, to which duty compelled him. Was it possible that a people just emerging from barbarism, and scarcely able to defend themselves, would send twenty of their best men to serve at the Cape?[33]

The Griqua were now convinced that Anderson was simply a Government agent. His previous work with them counted for little. He had preached peace to them: he was now perceived as trying to persuade them to fight for an alien power. His life was threatened, and he had to leave that mission.[34]

It was partly because of this incident that Moffat decided, from an early stage, not to act in any way that might involve him being seen as an agent of the Cape Government. He attempted to completely separate missionary work from political work. This was another reason why he could not be as politically active as Philip. For Moffat, the continuance of the work at Kuruman was all-important.

As a missionary in the field, Moffat saw a need to be apolitical because of two main reasons. On the one hand, the mission must not be threatened by creating hostility between himself and Africans, due to being viewed as a Government agent. On the other hand, the work must not be threatened by creating hostility towards the Cape Government by being unduly politically active. After recording the Anderson incident Moffat concluded: '[These events] prove to a demonstration that it is not the duty of the missionary to take an active part in political affairs.'[35]

---

33 RM, *MLSSA,* 197. Clinton, *The South African Melting Pot: A Vindication of Missionary Policy, 1799-1836,* (Ldn: Longmans, 1937), 5, noted: '[Van der Kemp] was willing that, in common with other inhabitants, the Hottentots should assist in the defence of the Colony against external enemies. He actually suggested this to Colonel Janssens. But he constantly maintained that they should not be compelled to serve as soldiers, nor that they should serve in that capacity against their own nation or the Kaffirs.'

34 RM, *MLSSA,* 198.

35 RM, *MLSSA,* 199. Moffat saw an exception to this in the case of Andries Waterboer, Chief of the Griqua. Waterboer was not a missionary, but he did combine both a 'spiritual office' and a 'political office'. Moffat wrote, 'He has always continued to preach, as well as to exercise his office as a magistrate; and though in the eyes of many this union of offices is inexpedient, he has ever maintained his cause; and having obtained a liberal salary and ordnance supplies from the Colonial Government, he is able to present the Griquas in an aspect his enemies never contemplated', (*MLSSA,* 203f). Despite some benefits of Waterboer's dual offices,

It may be argued that being politically active in campaigning against some of the racial policies of the Cape Government is not the same as being politically active as an agent of the Cape Government. But as far as Moffat was concerned, the same risk—of being forced to leave Kuruman—was attached to both. As a gardener, he thought of the long term: time to plant, time to grow, time to nurture, time to reap. Interference in Cape politics could threaten that strategy. Moffat also noted that, after Anderson left, the Griqua mission became disorganised. Moffat never wanted that to happen to Kuruman. Part of his original task in being sent to the Griqua as a young man had been to set the mission on its feet again following the Anderson incident. Moffat's analysis of the causes of the problems cemented the conviction of his early years that the missionary should be apolitical.[36]

The Dilemma of Non-Interference

There was a further rule which Moffat took from the Anderson incident: missionaries should not interfere in tribal government. He wrote: 'In order to save the mission from ruin, it was necessary to make a vigorous stand against interference on the part of the missionaries with the government of the people'.[37] Moffat saw the missionary as a visitor who stayed at a mission by a double permission. He needed permission from the Cape Government, and he also needed permission from the local people. He had to respect the way

---

Moffat had strong reservations: 'It is not without reason, however, that many judicious persons deprecate the effects of what they consider an unhallowed union, in the missionary's holding among the Griquas the office of *Confidential Agent to the Colonial Government.* There may be apparent advantages arising from this measure in accordance with the sentiments of those who hold up the benefit effected by missionary labours to be more of a political than a religious nature, and who maintain that it is far more convenient for Government than appointing distinct agents; but the fact is, it has no warrant from Scripture, and the question is, what does experience say? Let us take South Africa for an example. The preceding statements demonstrate that the cause of Mr Anderson's removal was his government agency; and though his not having had a precedent is an apology, the principle and the consequences of that agency cannot but be deprecated', (203). Moffat cited two missionaries, Brownlee and Thompson, who unsuccessfully tried to combine the two offices. Moffat stated that suspicion that he himself worked on behalf of the Government had threatened his own position. He and other missionaries could not risk being viewed as spies (*MLSSA,* 206f).

36 RM, *MLSSA,* 119f.

37 RM, *MLSSA,* 199. Moffat not only felt that Anderson's scenario was incompatible with the relationship between missionary and people, but believed that John Campbell had interfered wrongly in the 'internal affairs' of the Griqua, forcing 'Christian' civil legislation upon them, and manipulating the election of Waterboer as their leader.

the local people governed themselves, and he should never become, or appear to become, a Colonial policeman.[38]

At times, this meant that Moffat had to sit on the sidelines and watch whilst trials leading to executions took place. He was prepared to reason and remonstrate with a chief such as Moselekatse in private, but he took the view that he had no role in publicly interfering with the internal affairs of a tribe. This policy became more complicated when the missionary himself became the spiritual and moral guide of a converted people, but Moffat strove to maintain this position.[39] But being a Government agent, seeking to impose the rule of law by Government authority, was one thing; being a missionary and acting in according with the principles and convictions of your faith was quite another.

Moffat insisted that every missionary had a duty to give, 'pacific counsel and advice when those among whom he labours require it'.[40] Similarly, if possible, a missionary might be an arbiter who helps to hush the 'din of war arising either from family interests or national claims'.[41] The missionary might, very occasionally, even intervene in tribal matters when life was at stake, or be a mediator or an intercessor for someone who was at risk of unjust or excessive censure. Moffat gave an example:

> I once seized the right arm of an enraged chief of no little power, who grasped a weapon, which, but for this interference, would have been plunged into the breast of a victim, who had grievously offended. I did no wrong, nor did the chief think so, for when the paroxysm was over he said to me 'I thank you father.'[42]

Nevertheless, this was an exception to the general rule. Moffat saw a world of difference between *political* authority exercised by a *Government Agent,* and *moral* authority exercised by someone who had earned the respected title *father.* One was an alien authority from outside; the other was earned authority in a structure of trust and relationships built up from within.

---

38 Moffat followed the traditional non-conformist theology of separating Church and State as far as possible. Moffat conceded that the missionary may—indeed should—be willing to act as 'interpreter or translator' in political situations, but only in that capacity (*MLSSA,* 207).

39 Cf. *Kuruman Church Records* where Moffat left 'criminal law' to the tribal *Pico* and simply dealt with ecclesiastical discipline. The *KCRB* for 2.10.1863 illustrates this. That day, three members were 'cut off' from the congregation for the 'murder of Moroengane'. This censure was the only one given by the church. The church meeting meted no punishment which might be viewed as assuming an authority in civil law.

40 RM, *MLSSA,* 207.

41 RM, *MLSSA,* 208.

42 RM, *MLSSA,* 208. Moffat argued mitigation. He did not challenge the judicial system.

Could Christian principles be applied in non-Christian environments? There is a strand of evangelical thinking which holds that communities cannot be transformed until the majority of its individuals are converted. On this basis it would be futile to try and persuade non-Christian communities to apply Christian principles. Moffat did not hold this view. For Moffat the primary purpose of mission was the establishment of the reign of God upon the earth: and, in second place—albeit important in its own right—came conversions. Of first concern was the honour and glory of *God.*[43] Then came the benefits accruing to humanity.

The work of the kingdom was to ensure that the righteousness of God was made manifest upon the earth. That principal aim applied in all spheres, Christian or non-Christian. Even if individuals were not 'saved,' the manner of life which a community followed should conform to the divine plan, and should be something which did not offend God but gave Him honour and glory. In theory, the task should be easier if individuals, especially leaders within a community, were themselves converted and transformed. But even if they were not, the imperative to establish the righteousness of God in all corners of the earth still stood. Lifestyles and practices which did not conform to a biblical model of divine government should be supplanted by those which did. Two examples may be cited. One is advice given to Mothibi of the BaThlaping. The other involves Moselekatse of the Ndebele.

Firstly, in 1822 Moffat wrote that Mothibi—at this stage an unconverted chief—had heard that a commando was in agitation against the Bushmen. What Mothibi meant was that some of his men were on an aggressive campaign against the San, following a murder: '[Mothibi] informed us of their design. He asked if there was any harm or evil in so doing. We replied that to seize the murderer and punish him was just, and according to the laws of God, but to destroy the innocent with the guilty was surely evil.'[44] For Moffat, the 'sword of the magistrate' theology applied to Christian and non-Christian leader alike. Moffat simply pleaded that proportionate legal action be taken, and that the exercise did not become an excuse for an orgy of blood-letting.

Secondly, as early as 1829, at the start of his connection with Moselekatse, Moffat insisted to the Ndebele monarch that the values of the Kingdom of God should be applied to his people. Jehovah was God of all the

---

43 Calvin, *Institutes of the Christian Religion,* III, xx, 43.

44 RM, *Journal,* 3.7.1822, (*AAK,* 52).

earth. He was not a local tribal deity. Therefore, the rule of Jehovah should be established in all places amongst all peoples:

> I next explained to him the nature and extent of divine government, a particular and retributive providence even among those like the Matabele, who knew not God.[45]

The context is a conversation between Moffat and Moselekatse in which Moffat criticised the aggressive warring and plundering carried out by the Ndebele:

> I took this opportunity of pointing out to him the horrors of war, and at the same time directing his attention to a depopulated country, once swarming with inhabitants … that I had only met with a few solitary wretched individuals, the remains of all the multitudes who must be either destroyed or scattered.[46]

Moffat's concern was twofold. He wanted to see peace where there had been war: this was part of his Gospel of the transformation of society that he, as a postmillennialist held as important. Also, he wanted to warn Moselekatse personally about the risk hovering over him from the retributive judgment of God. In this, Moffat was not thinking of the last judgment, but of God's anger being put into action now. There was a 'retributive providence' to be experienced here on earth in this life. The events which followed Moffat's 1835 visit gave apparent credibility to his message that God would judge those who scorned peace. In 1837, Moselekatse's Ndebele were overwhelmed at their Mosega headquarters by the Boers. It was this heavy defeat and the loss of many men which made Moselekatse relocate hundreds of miles to the north. Moselekatse never forgot that Moffat's predictions came true. The catastrophe of Mosega gave Moffat's 'peace-message' enormous authority.

A 'retributive providence' being fulfilled in the here and now, brought an element of 'realised eschatology' into Moffat's theology of the Kingdom. The ruler who did not pursue peace would receive judgment on this earth. Similarly, the Kingdom of God would be established here and now. The reign of God would be made manifest here and now. The justice of God would also come here and now. The Kingdom of God was breaking in, with both grace and judgment.

For Moffat, Moselekatse would have to stand before God on the Day of Judgment at the end of time; but the Kingdom also came *now*, and since

---

45 RM, *Journal,* 1829, (*MJ1,* 15).

46 Ibid.

peace was an essential attribute of that Kingdom then God would indeed 'scatter the people that delight in war'. Before Mosega the cocksure Moselekatse was prepared to argue the matter, and protest his innocence, despite all the evidence to the contrary, with his defence against Moffat's rebukes being along three lines. Firstly, he was not to blame for all the wars. Secondly, he was in fact very humane. Thirdly, he was more considerate than some white men.[47] But Mosega changed him. Before Mosega, Moffat and his message of peace was merely interesting. After Mosega, Moffat was, for Moselekatse, a prophet whose word was to be weighed with respect.

Moffat believed that his repeated appeals, in 1829 and 1835,[48] for Moselekatse to abandon a warrior culture effected a fundamental change in Ndebele attitudes, especially after the 'judgment of the Lord' in retributive providence at Mosega. Thus, in the 1850s, we find Moffat recording his satisfaction that Moselekatse promised no more unprovoked aggressive warfare. *En route* to Moselekatse in 1854 Moffat met Chief Sekhomi[49] who said to Moffat: 'Everybody knows Moselekatse is your friend, that he wishes to see you, and that you will speak *peace* to him'.[50] Moselekatse had heard that Moffat was coming to see him after they had not met for nineteen years, and sent a message of welcome in which he specifically focused on *peace*. Reflecting on Moselekatse's salutation, Moffat recorded: 'He wished to see me, as all that I had said to him about bloodshed, and how that God would

---

47 RM, *Journal,* 1829, (*MJ1,* 15f).

48 In 1835, Moffat's appeals to Moselekatse were particularly strong. Moffat frequently expressed his abhorrence of the warlike ways of the Ndebele and of the change that the Gospel could bring to them. Moselekatse often invited Moffat to a 'review of his warriors', which involved the performance of war dances and battle rituals which Moffat found difficult to take. He recorded several such occasions: (i) RM, *Journal,* 13.7.1835, (*MJ1,* 112): 'I returned to my wagon, right thankful that I was not born among such a people, inured to war, whose every song and gesture partakes of war. Truly their feet are swift to shed blood. The verses from 10 to 18 of the 3rd of Romans are strikingly applicable to them,' (ii) RM, *Journal,* 14.7.1835, (*MJ1,* 112f): 'About two hours were taken up in the men coming forward to near where he sat ... declaring how many persons [they had] driven out of the world with their spears [and] showing how manfully they perpetrated the deed. ... While witnessing the scene, often did my heart sigh and say, 'Lord, scatter the people that delight in war'. (iii) Another example is: RM, *Journal,* 20.7.1835, (*MJ1,* 119). What weakened Moffat's pleas was that white people had made war against the Ndebele: this was an inconvenient truth which led Moffat to make weak denials, cf. RM, *Journal,* 10.7.1835, (*MJ1,* 106f): '[He] said that among the slain of Berend's commando [who attacked his people] there were white men. I assured him that those who told him so had told him lies.'

49 Sekhomi, Chief of the BaMangwato. His territory lay between Kuruman and the Ndebele.

50 RM, *Journal,* 20.6.1854, (*MJ1,* 192).

punish him and scatter him and his people if he did not live in peace and cease from shedding human blood, had come to pass.'[51]

What Moselekatse highlighted in his greeting, and what had stayed with him down through the years, was Moffat's emphasis on peace, and on the judgment of God if that were not followed. Moselekatse, as king and ruler of his people, related to an aspect of the Christian message which had to do with government and way of life. This penitent and wistful message, from an apparently war-weary Moselekatse, gave Moffat hope that true conversion might now take place in the soul of the old warrior:

> What a miracle it would be to see such an one plucked as a brand from the burning! Is there anything too hard for the Omnipotent whose arm is not slackened and whose ear is not heavy?[52]

Moffat's highest hopes were not to be realised. But the weariness of Moselekatse with his bloody lifestyle was unmistakable. He wanted something different and better. He yearned for it. The message brought by Moffat, many years before, seemed the best prospect for a new way of living. Moffat believed that the Moselekatse of 1854 was 'tired of war, and well he may, for he must have been the means of sending to eternity many thousands of men, women and children.'[53] But was Moselekatse weary with his lifestyle because it brought hardship for his people? Was it because he personally feared the judgment of God? Did he see the Gospel as a transforming influence for his people, or as a way of escape from the wrath of God? It is difficult to decide which was the major factor. Perhaps Moselekatse was never sure himself.

1n 1854, after many weeks with Moselekatse, Moffat again emphasised God's requirement of peace: 'I repeated the text which I had repeatedly done before, that God had declared in his word that he would "scatter the people that delight in war"'.[54] Moselekatse seemed to take Moffat's advice and warnings seriously, at least within the parameters of the 'obligations' of a chief with a warlike reputation to maintain. He told Moffat that he had not taken revenge on Sekhomi, despite Sekhomi murdering sixteen men whom Moselekatse had sent to him on a 'friendly' mission. Moffat commented:

> I told [Moselekatse] that, as he had withheld his wrath against the Bamanguato on my account, I hoped he would for my sake allow it to die altogether, that war was hateful to Jehovah, and it was impossible to carry on

---

51 Ibid, 195.

52 Ibid, 195.

53 RM, *To Mary Moffat,* Aug. 1854, (*MJ1,* 360).

54 RM, *Journal,* 5.10.1854, (*MJ1,* 322f), (Psalm 68:30).

war, even on the smallest scale, without shedding innocent blood, which would raise his ire. On hearing this remark on a topic I had already frequently pressed on his attention, he put his hand on my arm and said 'Enough! I have not forgotten the fulfillment of the warnings you gave me at Mosega.'[55]

By 1860 Moffat was able to write to Tidman of the LMS: 'Moselekatse seems to have become entirely averse to aggressive warfare, and appears to be proud in making his boast that since my visit in 1854, he has in no instance attacked any tribe.'[56] On the same day, Moffat wrote to Sir George Grey, the Cape Governor, with the same message using exactly the same words.[57]

Moffat really believed that Moselekatse had changed. But future events proved otherwise. John Smith Moffat did not share his father's optimism, making various references to Moselekatse's continuing aggression. For example: '[Moselekatse's] commando has returned from attacking the unhappy MaShona' and, 'I on principle refuse to mend guns or to supply ammunition of any kind to the Matabele or to Moselekatse, and shall maintain this position until I am satisfied that they have ceased to carry on aggressive warfare.'[58] The reign of the Kingdom had not yet taken root. Moselekatse wanted to please his old friend Moffat. He had not really bowed the knee to the Prince of Peace.

Contradictions to Peace

A major problem which Moffat had to face was that peace—at the heart of his Christianity—was repeatedly contradicted by professing Christians. In *Missionary Labours* he recorded that the first encounter which the Tswana had of white people came in a series of three violent raids upon them. Firstly, they were visited by a colonist with a party on a predatory expedition. Secondly, after a time of respite, due to the disapproval of the Colonial Government concerning such raids, 'they were again visited by these white plunderers'. Thirdly, they suffered:

> From the marauder Bloom, a Dutch farmer. He was accompanied by a considerable number of similar characters, who committed sad havoc on the herds and flocks of the Bechuanas, butchering great numbers of the comparatively defenceless inhabitants.[59]

---

55 RM, *Journal,* 8.10.1854, (*MJ1,* 328).

56 RM, *To Tidman,* 2.10.1860, (*MJ2*), 273.

57 RM, *To Sir George Grey,* 2.10.1860, (NLS/Ms/10780/mf/4/3/474).

58 JSM, *To James Unwin,* 24.7.1861, (*MM,* 152).

59 RM, *MLSSA,* 214f. Moffat felt that the negative view of white people was softened by the decency of the traders Somerville and Truter who contacted the BaThlaping c. 1801.

Moffat claimed that the Tswana had done nothing to justify such raids. He frequently returned to this contradiction between the missionary's foundational principles, and the actions of supposedly God-fearing European Christians. A typical comment comes in a few lines which Moffat penned during his 1835 visit to Moselekatse. His companion, the scientist Dr Andrew Smith, was urging Moffat to persuade Moselekatse to show a real desire to live in peace, and Moffat's response demonstrated his awareness of the contradiction which missionaries lived with. He wrote: 'The Doctor is sanguine enough to suppose I can influence a pagan king to do what few Christian kings will perform [i.e. live in peace.]' [60] In the southern African context, examples of 'Christians' indulging in violence came from three main groups: Boers, British, and Africans themselves.

1. Christian Boers. The first major problem was that of the Boers. They too were Christians. Yet the Boer farmers were capable of violent reprisals against natives by whom they felt threatened. Sometimes these actions were in response to real attacks inflicted on the Boers. Sometimes they were pre-emptive. Whatever the cause of Boer aggression in particular situations, the fact remained that, though they carried the name of Christian, they were not viewed as a people of peace. The ambiguity between Christian theory and Boer practice was expressed with memorable eloquence to Moffat by Sechele's brother Khosilintse at Sechele's camp in 1854:

> 'Have not the English the word of God, and have not the Boers the word of God? Do their teachers teach them with the same book?' – pointing to a New Testament. 'Are we only to obey the word of God because we are black? Are white people not to obey the word of God, because they are white?[61] We know much of what the word of God teaches, but we are not allowed time to think about our souls while the Boers are seeking to kill us.'[62]

Khosilintse's complaint: 'Are we only to obey the word of God because we are black? Are white people not to obey the word of God because they are white?' went deep. Were Christian principles to be observed rigorously by Africans under the guise of devotion to God, but really in order to allow the European to dominate?

---

60 RM, *Journal,* 28.7.1835, (*MJ1,* 123).

61 The unhappy opposition of white to black, which Khosilintse despairingly mentioned, was alluded to in *The Times* review of Moffat's life at the time of his death: 'It would seem, indeed, that it is only by the agency of such men as Moffat and his like that the contact of the white and black races can be anything but a curse to the blacks. It is the missionary alone who seeks nothing for himself.' (Deane, *Robert Moffat,* 181).

62 RM, *To Tidman, LMS,* 10.5.1855, (*MJ1,* 378).

In 1854, as he journeyed north, Moffat heard stories from tribe after tribe of predatory Boer actions. Sometimes these were punitive raids, but often they were unprovoked. This was in the aftermath of the *Sand River Convention*. What Moffat feared was coming to pass. At Kuruman, he had noted rumours, but hearing the accounts at first hand made a deep impression. The saving feature was that the Africans, whom he met, knew that the Boers hated the missionaries as much as they hated the Africans. That maintained the integrity of the missionaries. Khosilintse also said:

> They will not spare you. We have seen what they have done to Livingstone, our teacher, and to Edwards, the teacher of the Bakhatla, and to Inglis, the teacher of the Bahurutse. ... Every one of my tribe fears the Boers. Little children fear the Boers.[63]

David Livingstone's station at Kolobeng, in Sechele's country, was attacked and destroyed by Boers, led by Marthinus Pretorius, on 28 August 1852. In the same year, the Boers expelled Roger Edwards from his station at Mabotsa, and drove Walter Inglis from his station at Matebe.[64] Even allowing for Moffat enhancing Khosilintse's speeches, there is no reason to think that the essence of what Khosilintse said was much different from Moffat's record. Khosilintse put his finger on an enormous inconsistency between the deeds of the Boers and the teaching of the missionaries.

2. Christian British. Convenient as it might be to blame all white atrocity on the Boers, such musing has little foundation. It is true that, during Moffat's time at Kuruman, British forces were less engaged in war against Africans. The high-profile Zulu War and Matabele Campaigns came after he had returned to Britain. But the Xhosa Wars, which erupted at regular intervals, showed the British, and not just the Boers, indulging in unchristian acts of

---

63 Ibid.

64 David Livingstone, Rogers Edwards and Walter Inglis were all LMS missionaries who, through Kuruman, moved on to establish new mission stations. Edwards came from Theopolis and joined Moffat in Cape Town, assisting in the printing of Luke's Gospel in SeTswana. He then went north with Livingstone in 1843 and established a site at Mabotsa. When a lion had attacked Livingstone, Edwards nursed him until Livingstone could return to Kuruman. After Livingstone returned to Mabotsa with his bride, Mary Moffat, he and Edwards clashed. Livingstone left Mabotsa. Inglis then joined Edwards. The Boers claimed that they found a workshop on Livingstone's mission station for the repair of guns, plus arms and ammunition, which proved the missionaries were arming the Africans and were responsible for raids on Boer farms. Livingstone vehemently denied this. The controversy over what was, or was not, found at Kolobeng continues to this day. Cf. Livingstone, *To Mary Livingstone*, (*DLFL,* Vol. 2, 184-186). For an evaluation of both Livingstone's and the Boer claims, see: *DLSAP,* 21-48.

violence.[65] In an 1851 letter to Tidman, Moffat reflected on being associated with British actions which made Africans less inclined to become Christians:

> Everyone [i.e. Africans] tells you he has enough to do to think about his own safety, where terror, rapine, war and bloodshed are being carried on by white men, the subjects of that very nation from which the missionaries emanated with the message of peace and love. Were any one at the present time to attempt a mission among the Bechuanas, circumstanced as they now are—that is supposing that no mission had been commenced—it would be like the doings of a maniac. The Bechuanas, I mean those not reduced to vassalage by the Boers, are proud and independent, and instead of bowing assent will hold out the finger of scorn to the *British* and to the colonist and say, 'go and convert your own countrymen and then try your hand on us.'[66]

Moffat referred to British actions which Africans were aware of, and which hindered his work. In his retirement, Moffat returned to this flaw at the heart of Christendom. In 1878 he commented on the Congress of Berlin:[67]

> It is very sad to think that in this enlightened age the nations should be so prone to live a life of Bulldogs, planning who is to be the greatest. [They] think only of bringing over ... a host of Indian warriors to fight our battles. We can only hope and pray that the spirit of peace may persuade the counsels of the countries now assembled. The great powers of Europe, armed to the teeth and betrothed with the weapons of destruction, what a painfully distressing sight to angels and to all who from the very bottom of their hearts love and adore the Prince of Peace who was born to send peace on Earth and good will among men. I wonder if that august assembly, the Congress of Berlin, have a prayer for Divine Wisdom to aid them in their deliberations. I wonder! Except the Turks they profess to be Christian.[68]

But was he only interested in events in so far as they could affect gaining future converts? Not so. The missionary also had a personal spiritual life, and Moffat was genuinely depressed by the conduct of 'Christian' Europeans who indulged in non-Christian conduct. He did not object simply because they

---

65 The Xhosa [Kafir] Wars, also called Cape Frontier Wars, between 1779 and 1879, involved intermittent warfare between the Cape colonists and the Xhosa agricultural and pastoral peoples of the Eastern Cape. They were one of the most prolonged struggles by African peoples against European intrusion. The struggle ended in the annexation of Xhosa territories by the Cape Colony. Initially these were conflicts between the Xhosa and the Dutch. After the British took control of the Cape, they were between the Xhosa and the British. In 1834-35 fighting erupted in what is termed the 6th Kaffir War, and for the first time the war moved into the territory of the Gcaleka Xhosa. The Gcaleka paramount chief, Hintsa, was shot while in British custody. Moffat may have had similar crimes in mind.

66 RM, *To Tidman, LMS,* 3.11.1851, (SOAS/CWM/SA/Box 26/1/A), (our italics)

67 The Congress of Berlin (1878) took place after the Russo-Turkish War of 1877-1878. The Congress of Berlin (1878) should not be confused with the Berlin Conference (1884-1885) which initiated the 'scramble for Africa'.

68 RM, *To Mrs Wilson,* 14.6.1878, (NLS/20311/71).

made his work more difficult, but because it grieved him to see 'Christian' nations acting contrary to the religion which they professed. He was also bemused: how could the Redeemer's reign be at hand if even 'Christian' nations were conducting themselves in such a way?

3. Christian Africans. In Moffat's view, the main problem with Christians acting in a manner contrary to Christian principles lay with the Boers, and, to a lesser extent, with the British. However, there was also the problem of some Africans who had professed conversion indulging in violent raids on neighbouring tribes. Moffat knew of these, and he knew that non-Christian Africans were aware that some groups which terrorised them were professedly Christian. There was the chronic problem of Griqua bandits who had been brought up under the Gospel at Griqua Town. Mothibi pointed out this contradiction.[69] Another instance of contrary practice among 'converts' came in the example of the enigmatic Sechele who promoted himself as a teacher of the Gospel, yet who sent his BaKwena to attack other tribes. Moffat dealt with this at length in his *Journal.*[70] Notwithstanding these examples, and others, the main problem lay squarely with the conduct of European Christians. For Moffat, a great part of the glory of the Gospel was the emphasis on peace. Unfortunately, therein also lay its Achilles' heel.

The Legacy of Peace

As a retired missionary, Moffat viewed British policy in southern Africa with increasing concern. After a man leaves a place where he has worked for many years, it can be tempting for him to view what follows as a deterioration, and Moffat was not immune from that tendency. Yet facts supported his gloom. Amongst peoples, with whom he had worked for so long to achieve a state of peace, there was now war. It came to a head in the Zulu Wars of 1879-1880, initiated by the Cape Governor Sir Basil Frere, in a blundering attempt to give the Boers confidence in British administration and British protection against resurgent Zulu nationalism. But other, smaller, conflicts between Africans and British had also taken place.

Moffat put the blame squarely on his own British Government. He believed that their flawed policies were responsible for creating distrust, unrest, and agitation. He viewed British policy as unwise, unfair, heavy-handed, insensitive, and destined to promote enduring suspicion and hatred. At the 1885 unveiling of the Moffat memorial in Ormiston Village, John Smith

---

69 RM, *To Alexander Moffat,* 9.12.1824, (*AAK,* 165).

70 RM, *Journal,* 13.12.1859, (*MJ2,* 242ff).

Moffat referred to the state of affairs in South Africa following his father's departure. The *Haddingtonshire Courier* stated:

> Remarking on the political service rendered by Dr Moffat in promoting peace where there had been war, he [JSM] stated that he did not wish to say much about that now, because things that his father did were being undone, and unhappily, by political blundering, we [British] had done a great deal of harm lately there. When his father left the country, the people gathered around him and said: 'Now the wall is broken down, and now there is no one to stand between us and the white man.' Well, that was quite true. From that day there had been a steady disintegration.'[71]

During the 1870s, Moffat expressed distress over the deteriorating situation in Bechuanaland. In letters to Miss Isabel Cunningham of Brighton, he made several references to what was unfolding in Africa: 'My dear Bechuanaland, now alas the scene of war, desolating war and bloodshed';[72] 'I need not refer to the terrible carnage in South Africa; it affects me deeply.'[73] In another letter, he criticised the politicians Frere and Disraeli (Beaconsfield):

> You will see that Sir Basil Frere with all his ability and goodness has made a sad mess of affairs in South Africa over which I mourn; and Beaconsfield's 'scientific frontier' is confusion worse confused.[74]

With such scenarios unfolding year by year, it is not surprising that Moffat wondered when the promised Millennium would dawn, in which the glorious reign of the Prince of Peace would truly be established. Moffat's eschatological vision, of the ever-improving effects of the reign of Christ upon the earth, especially in the establishing of real and lasting peace, was not fulfilled as he imagined. This perplexed him. But his response to perplexity was simply to trust more, believe more, and reaffirm his fundamental expectation that God would reign. It was war which depressed

---

71 JSM, *The Unveiling of the Moffat Memorial,* (*Haddingtonshire Courier,* 24.4.1885).

72 RM, *To Isabel Cunningham,* 12.10.1878, (SOAS/CWM/Africa/Moffat/Pers/4). Kuruman was technically beyond the boundary of the Cape colony. As such, there was little interference by the Cape authority. However, the situation changed as the century progressed. In 1885, British Bechuanaland was created, following complaints from principal Tswana Chiefs that Transvaal Boers were invading their territories. This invitation to protect dovetailed with the imperial expansionist policy of the 1885 Berlin Conference.

73 RM, *To Miss Isabel Cunningham,* 23.4.1879, (SOAS/CWM/Afr./Moffat/Pers/4).

74 RM, *To Isabel Cunningham,* 5.11.1880, (SOAS/CWM/Africa/Moffat/Pers/4). Sir Basil Frere (Sir Henry Bartle Edward Frere) was Governor of the Cape from 1877 to 1880. He approved Shepstone's annexation of the Transvaal in 1877. Most Cape politicians were opposed to any form of federation with the other Boer republics to the north, but Frere felt that if he defeated the Zulu in battle then his policy of federation would be made easier, since the Boers would believe that the British could protect them. Frere thus precipitated the Zulu war of 1879.

him most, especially war waged by 'Christian' nations in a land in which he had striven to bring the Gospel of Peace.

Occasionally, in his later correspondence, we glimpse an old man succumbing to moments of pessimism. In an 1878 letter to a Mrs Wilson of Falkirk, he shared his sickening disappointment at the conflicts taking place in southern Africa, commenting: 'This sickly dying world, which, as is well said in the English Prayer Book, "In the midst of life we are in death".'[75]

*

In Moffat's account of his conversations with chiefs such as Africaner, Berend Berends, Mothibi, and Moselekatse, he gave a prominent place to the gospel of peace. He stated that these chiefs seemed to want the blessing of peace, and he gained the impression that it was this aspect of Christianity which appealed to them most. They may have had difficulty with concepts of atonement, judgment after death, and other doctrines, but were convinced of the benefits of a religion which could bring peace here and now—if it really could. This was the crux of the matter. Could it? Christianity as peace-bringer was potentially one of the central advantages in evangelism, if not the most important one. Moffat himself claimed:

> I once heard a chief from the interior telling his friends that the doctrines of God were worthy of all acceptation, were it only for the principles of peace they inculcated. 'Look' said he, 'to the Kuruman (Lattakoo) and look at Motito; when we visit those places we can sleep from night till morn, while among our heathen neighbours we often lie down fearing that we may be killed, or awake with our house in flames'[76]

Commitment to a 'peace mindset' involved a huge step of faith for converts. The pressures of 'realpolitik', plus the lack of role models among European Christian communities made it difficult for chiefs to pursue that path.

One other point may be made. Moffat's approach, especially his profound disagreement with the British policy of not allowing indigenous peoples to be armed for self-defence, shows that his emphasis on peace had little to do with getting the indigenous peoples 'tamed' so that they could be colonised more easily. Peace was for the glory of God and the blessing of humanity, not for the ambitions of the powerful.

---

75 RM, *To Mrs Wilson,* 14.6.1878, (NLS/20311/71).

76 RM, *Africa,* 42.

Chapter 21
The Hope in Jesus

IF LATER GENERATIONS TENDED to stress the imminent return of Jesus Christ as the crisis event which might break in at any moment, for Moffat the crisis was death. It was death which might come in an instant. It was death which might find a person unprepared. Questions 112 to 115 of *Brown's Catechism* stressed this crisis with chilling directness:

> Q&A 112: Do you know when you will die? No.
>
> Q&A 113: May you die very soon? Yes: though I am well today, I may be dead before tomorrow.
>
> Q&A 114: Should you be preparing [making ready] every day to die? Yes: I should try to spend every day as if it were to be my last.
>
> Q&A 115: May you delay [put off] preparing for death until you are dying? No: for I may then have no opportunity: I may be killed by some accident without any warning; or I may be so sick, that I may not be able to think about anything.

This was the Catechism which Moffat translated into SeTswana, which he memorised, which he taught in evangelistic situations, and which he used in educating new converts. It was death which was the ultimate and inevitable apocalyptic crisis. It was the inexorable approach of death which provided urgency to the evangelistic task.

In traditional culture at Kuruman, death was not viewed as an inevitable fact of nature. There was an assumption that, but for some unforeseen accident, or some piece of carelessness or willful disobedience, people need never have died at all. Any death whose cause was not understood must be due to witchcraft.[1] Moffat was aware of this: 'As for death, they [Tswana] suppose, as a chief informed me the other day, that no man can die of himself naturally; that he must be killed or bewitched by another.'[2] This philosophy came to sharp focus when Peclu, heir-apparent to Mothibi of the BaThlaping, died suddenly. Moffat went to console Mothibi:

> We made some remarks on the importance of submitting to the divine will, 'who was too wise to err', etc. These remarks gave rise to an argument of

---

1 Alice Werner, *Myths and Legends of the Bantu,* 39.
2 RM, *To Alexander Moffat*, 25.2.1822, (*AAK,* 55).

> some length. When any person, especially of note, dies, it is generally attributed to some person or persons whom the relatives charge with having bewitched the deceased. Notwithstanding the knowledge of Christianity which Mothibi and his relatives possess, in this case superstition predominated; and a family in the vicinity of the town, with whom Peclu had some little misunderstanding, was charged with being guilty. The persons charged, it appears, had fled, which seemed to confirm Mothibi in his groundless suspicions.[3]

Moffat well understood that, in indigenous thought, the causes of death were not left to the inscrutable will of God, but were connected with malevolent agencies.

The Crisis of Death

Death was a taboo subject among many whom Moffat encountered. This created a key obstacle for a missionary whose message majored on the conquest of death through Jesus Christ. Several times Moffat touched on this unwillingness to discuss death. In 1857, he told Moselekatse that when he, Moffat, was no longer able to serve Christ he would seek tranquility in solitude and prepare his soul for heaven. Moselekatse was shocked:

> [Moselekatse] stared at me, his wives stared at me. Poor things. They wonder how easily I can talk of age and death. Moselekatse said, 'You old! You are young! I saw your activity and boldness when you shot sea-cows in the Kame River, and you seem the same now as then.' I interrupted – no subject dare do so – by saying, 'No, no. You may think so, but I do not feel so, and I am most anxious to do for you and your people all I can before I die'. He rejoined, 'Atch, atch, atch' – no, no, no – 'you must not talk of your dying'.[4]

Moselekatse's discomfiture with the topic of death was not simply due to wishing that his friend should live long, but sprang from his own intrinsic fear of the subject. This comes out clearly when Moffat refers to Moselekatse's refusal to go through a town where one of his wives had died, fearing that death might capture him there also.[5] It was not only Moselekatse and the Ndebele who had this aversion. In 1854, Moffat recorded a conversation he had with the wife of Makaba, chief of the BaNgwaketse. He had met her many years before, and her ageing was evident, as was his own:

---

3 RM, *Journal,* 4.4.1825, (*AAK,* 180). Shillington suggested that grief at Peclu's premature death in 1825 may have contributed towards a 'developing sense of disillusionment with the missionaries.' (Shillington, *The Colonisation of the Southern Tswana:1870-1900,* (Braamfontein: Ravan Press, 1985), 12). It was not until 1828 that Mothibi left Kuruman. In the 1840s he announced his conversion to the Christian faith.

4 RM, *Journal,* 16.11.1857, (*MJ2,* 118).

5 RM, *Journal,* 19.12.1859, (*MJ2,* 249).

> How altered! She was a good-looking [woman] then, but now an aged but yet comparatively strong old woman. She shook hands and spoke of days of old, when I was what she called a youth. ... I began telling her how age was causing me to follow her with rapid step to where all mankind had gone and where all must go. This she understood. But when I asked how she felt about death, she could not understand and only wondered that I should talk of death. ... After saying some more, I left her, with a deep sigh for the aged among the heathen.[6]

On the same journey, Moffat noted the answers of the native guides, who attended Sabbath worship, when they were quizzed about what they heard:

> When pushed a little close, it will be found that words which refer to death generally first strike their attention. They are accustomed to view death as they do a lion—a dangerous enemy and a disturber of their peace.[7]

When Moffat arrived at Moselekatse's town, the conversation came round to the same topic, with similar reactions: '"You are young" said [Moselekatse], "You march and jump as you always did". I shook my head and added, "No, no! Though I am still strong, I feel I am old and must soon die." "No, you must not die", said he.'[8] Years earlier, Moffat had found the same dread of death among the San.[9] Death was a taboo subject. This raises the question: when the central concern of the Gospel is met by a central taboo of indigenous culture, how can the gap be bridged? To consider this we first examine Moffat's view of the relationship between body and soul.

Roby taught that humanity has a bipartite constitution of body and soul, and made no reference to a tripartite concept of body, soul and spirit.[10] Roby's emphasis was in line with mainstream Calvinist teaching, and reflected both the *Thirty-Nine Articles* and the *Westminster Confession of Faith.* Also, in Roby's theology the soul was not a part of God, nor was it a 'divine spark' in humanity, nor was it an aspect of human temperament. Instead, the soul was a distinct creation of God: it was a spiritual, immortal, and thinking 'substance' though 'not pure thought as such'.[11] Whenever Moffat referred to the spiritual constitution of humanity he assumed Roby's bipartite model of body and soul, hardly ever making reference to 'spirit'. When he did, it was with the understanding that 'spirit' was a synonym for 'soul', but 'soul' was Moffat's preferred term. Consequently, when referring

---

6 RM, *Journal,* 4.6.1854, (*MJ1,* 151f).

7 RM, *Journal,* 2.7.1854, (*MJ1,* 206).

8 RM, *Journal,* 22.7.1854, (*MJ1,* 231).

9 RM, *MLSSA,* 59.

10 Roby, *Theol. Lect.* 37, 'The Creation of Man'. Cf. Roby, Lect. 66, 'On the Immortality and the Separate State of a Soul', where he used 'soul' and 'spirit' as synonyms.

11 Roby, *Theol. Lect.* 37, 'The Creation of Man'.

to death, where some might write in terms of a man or a woman giving up their 'spirit', Moffat stuck with 'soul'. Thus, in 1859, commenting upon Mrs Ashton's death, Moffat wrote: 'She breathed her soul into the hands of Him who gave it.'[12]

'Soul' is notoriously hard to define in English and is equally difficult to render in another language. Hammond-Tooke has pointed out that the southern Bantu term *moya* does not correspond exactly with the Christian notion of the soul, though it is often assumed to do so:

> They [the southern Bantu] made a distinction between the physical body on the one hand, and aspects which somewhat resemble western concepts of the soul on the other. ... There was the *moya,* a term that could also mean 'wind' or 'breath', which was used to refer to the essence that leaves the body at death. It thus seems to be best translated as 'life force' or simply 'life'. Writers on African religion often translate *moya* as 'soul' but it is doubtful whether this is justified. ... Most importantly, the concept was not identical with that of ancestor spirit, which was accorded quite a different term .... It seems that the term *moya* was not confined to the breath, but was thought of as suffused throughout the whole body, being especially associated with the lungs, liver, genitals, head and hair.[13]

The distinction between *moya* as a 'life-force' on the one hand, and *soul* on the other hand, is subtle but important. *Moya* is what which makes life possible in all creatures, whereas *soul* is what constitutes the 'spiritual' nature of a human being. In Bantu thought *moya* is that which enables physical life to exist.[14] In traditional Christian thought *soul* is united to body until the dissolution brought by death: but *soul* is not the body's physical life force. The body's physical life force is in itself. Notwithstanding semantic difficulties, of which Moffat may not have been fully aware, Moffat sought to communicate standard Reformed teaching concerning the nature of the soul, and the relationship between soul and body.

For Moffat, 'immortality' was an attribute of the human soul which came from God's act of *creation*, rather than from his act of *salvation*. Salvation did not confer immortality. Immortality existed already. Indeed, it was humanity's inescapable immortality which made salvation necessary, since eternal existence could not be avoided, and eternal existence under God's

---

12 RM, *To Tidman, LMS,* 23.2.1859, (SOAS/CWM/SA/Box 31/3/A).

13 Hammond-Tooke, *Roots,* 149.

14 It may be argued that, in traditional African thought, there is not the same division between 'physical' and 'spiritual', or between 'body' and 'soul', which is common in European thought. Thus, if *moya* is the 'physical' life force, then, because the 'physical' and the 'spiritual' are one, it is also the 'spiritual' life force and hence reasonably equivalent to 'soul'. Whatever the merits of this perspective, it seems that *moya* and soul are not identical.

condemnation was a state to be feared. An 1818 letter illustrates the sequence of thought in Moffat's theology, with Moffat placing 'immortality' prior to 'redemption'.[15] The same order is repeated in his 1829 *Journal.*[16] In Moffat's theology, immortality was a quality of the human soul in virtue of creation, and hence part of the permanent nature of humanity.[17] Humanity did not get immortality because of salvation, but required salvation because of immortality. But what did this mean? On this, there were two lines of thought: the Classical and the Reformed.

1. The Classical Approach. 'Immortality' meant that the soul not only would exist for ever into the future but had existed forever in the 'past' with 'God'. But this was a Platonic and Stoic concept, rather than a biblical one. In strictly biblical terms, the soul is not eternal, if eternity is understood as involving an eternal pre-existence. Instead, the soul is created within time just as the body is created within time. This was Roby's understanding, and also Moffat's.

2. The Reformed Approach. Roby and Moffat interpreted 'immortality' as eternal existence into the future.[18] Immortality was bestowed on men and women in virtue of their creation. Thus, immortality was the gift (or curse) of every man and woman, granting their soul an existence which would never end at any point in the future. With this understanding, Moffat lamented that Moselekatse's people had no idea of their true destiny, and he commented sadly on the tribal dancing arranged by Moselekatse for his visitors:

---

[15] RM, *To Burder, LMS,* 20.8.1818, (SOAS/CWM/SA/Box 7/5/A): 'During our stay [among the Namaqua] I preached frequently, particularly from Paul's address to the Athenians. I also conversed with them on particular points, some replied, if it is so—that we are all the children or descendants of one Father Adam—how is it that you are white and we nearly black? This I explained. I also spoke on the existence of God, the creation and fall of man, the immortality of the soul, the redemption by Christ. All this was a new thing.'

[16] RM, *Journal,* 1929, (*MJ1,* 16): 'The next conversation I had with [Moselekatse] I explained to him the first principles of our religion: (1) man in his natural state, (2) asserting his immortality, (3) the redemption of the soul by the death of Christ, (4) the resurrection of the dead and (5) the state of rewards and punishment beyond death. The last two particulars particularly arrested his attention.'

[17] Cf. *The Larger Catechism* Qu.17, and *The Westminster Confession* 4/ii and 32/i.

[18] Though Roby rejected the Graeco-Roman view of the immortality of the soul, he cited classical philosophers in support of its immortality. Roby accumulated many arguments, not all of which were biblical. He pointed out that human reason has inferred the truth of the idea from various principles, such as dread of annihilation, the justice of God, the universal consent of nations both civilised and barbarous, the testimony of celebrated heathen philosophers such as Cicero, Seneca, Socrates, Pythagoras, Plato, and occasional appearance of separate spirits (Roby, *Theol. Lect.* 66, 'On the Immortality and the Separate State of a Soul').

> These scenes, which gave so much apparent joy to them made my heart sad to see so much time and strength devoted to pleasures so gross, while not one of the thousands who were dancing down to the gulf of black despair had the slightest idea of their immortality, the being of a God, or a future state.[19]

Moffat was convinced that the Ndebele lacked a notion of immortality or of life after death. In his 1840 London *Sermon*, he stated this starkly, this time in relation to the Tswana:

> It is generally believed that all the nations of the globe have some indistinct notions respecting a future state. Not so with the Bechuana tribes inhabiting the interior of Southern Africa; for among them there did not exist one single idea on the subject of immortality. That man possessed a never-dying soul, and that man should rise again and live forever, was to the Bechuanas preposterous in the extreme.[20]

Moffat went too far. There was an idea of a 'future state' among both the Tswana and the Ndebele, though it appears to have been a limited concept. Livingstone, who heard Moffat in England before he himself left for Africa, initially accepted Moffat's statements. Livingstone later changed his mind and reverted to the thinking of Thomas Dick, whose writings influenced him significantly, and who was typical of several theologians of his day in teaching that a universal belief in the doctrine of immortality had obtained in all ages and among all peoples.[21] Livingstone was more ready to presume that such belief was universal, than was Moffat.[22] Moffat believed that, for some

---

19 RM, *Journal,* 1929, (*MJ1,* 21).

20 RM, *Africa,* 22f.

21 Dick, *The Philosophy of a Future State,* (Glasgow: Collins, 1828), 32. Dick wanted to demonstrate that Christian beliefs were universal beliefs: if doctrinal truths could be proved to be universal, then they had a stronger foundation than if they arose only from revelation. This apologetic was developed in response to the criticism of revelation by rationalism.

22 Livingstone, *To Charles Livingstone,* 16.3.1847, (*DLFL, Vol. 1,* 192f), wrote that the Tswana, 'have parables from which we—who are better informed—can gather the idea of a future state. The knowledge of some of these parables is universal, and, if we can believe testimony, it was so of old. Here is one. God sent a chameleon to say to men: 'Though you die you do not vanish or become annihilated, you will return again'. The chameleon being a slow walker was outstripped by the little black lizard sent by another, and the latter came first to man. The black lizard said to men 'One will come after me and tell you that when you die you will not perish but will return again. It is all a message of lies. When you die you perish as an ox.' When the chameleon came, men stopped his mouth by saying "O we know your message. It is all lies."' As early as 1843 Livingstone cast doubts on some of Moffat's views, and, in a letter to Adolphe Mabille, he referred to the fable of the chameleon and the lizard, as told to him by a Motswana who said, 'Is it not a fact that we Bechuanas of old believed that we should not perish entirely at death? I don't speak of the knowledge the white man has brought. I speak of the knowledge we had of old. God sent the chameleon with a message to man saying, "You must not do wickedly. You must reform, for when you die you will come again"' (Livingstone, *To Adolphe Mabille,* 24.2.1843, in: Smith, *Robert Moffat: One of God's Gardeners,* 107).

indigenous tribes, a concept of personal annihilation, rather than of continuation, prevailed.

The State of Death

A missionary, such as Moffat, considered it a vital part of his duty to prepare men and women for death and for meeting their Creator. It is unsurprising that, in Moffat's first conversations with Moselekatse, he spent considerable time on this subject:

> When I told him that death was only a separation between the soul and the body, he remarked that the soul could not be seen. To which I replied that a pain could not be seen but felt, neither was the wind seen but everybody knew wind and believed in wind. On hearing this he remarked that I must have been born in ancient times.[23]

Moffat's analogy between the unseen soul and the invisibility of pain or wind impressed Moselekatse. Their dialogue occurred within the context of Moffat teaching Moselekatse the Christian concept of resurrection, and in order to explain resurrection more clearly he had to explain the relationship between body and soul. In teaching a separation of soul and body at death Moffat was presenting Reformed doctrine as expressed in the Westminster documents which taught: 'The bodies of men after death return to dust, and see corruption; but their souls (which neither die nor sleep), having an immortal subsistence, immediately return to God who made them.'[24] All Protestant traditions agreed that death brought dissolution between body and soul. Where disagreement entered was the nature of the transitional state between death and the final resurrection, which we discuss later in the section on 'Death and Hades'.

Moffat made a contrast between Christian hope and the perceived indigenous belief in annihilation after death. But to what extent was Moffat correct in his interpretation of African beliefs? And how well did he communicate his own convictions? We have already cited the entry in Moffat's 1829 *Journal,* in which he wrote of thousands dancing down to the 'gulf of black despair'. His conviction, that the prevailing native belief was of

---

[23] RM, *Journal,* 1929, (*MJ1,* 16). Also, RM, *Journal,* 8.8.1824, (*AAK,* 142), had a similar conversation in 1824 in Makaba's village: 'One remarked, 'I have killed man, but I never saw the breath or soul escape.' I referred him to both wind and heat, which were both felt and believed, but invisible. On this Makaba remarked that he was an old man, but never once thought of these things before.'

[24] *The Westminster Confession,* Ch.32.

annihilation, had been expressed on many occasions. In 1823, following the battle against the invading Mantatee, he wrote:

> Imagining that annihilation is the common lot of man, the world is their God. To acquire the things of the world, therefore, they will bear any hardship, break through every tie, and with brutal enthusiasm tear the yet palpitating heart from the breast of their fallen enemy. Methinks these facts are calculated to draw forth the love of God shed abroad in our [the missionary's] souls, which extends to every individual of Adam's fallen race. Nothing but the blood of Christ can heal the breasts, nothing but the word of inspiration can lead them from these 'doleful shades of heathenish gloom'. What a call for missionary exertions to tear away the veil![25]

This conviction was also recorded in 1827, whilst on language study in a BaRolong village:

> Sabbath: I collected the people and preached unto them the Gospel of salvation. They seemed to pay much more attention than last Sabbath, but afterward I was much grieved to hear them making a kind of diversion of some part of the discourse, particularly that which related to a future state of reward. After listening a few minutes, I went and placed myself among them, and resumed the subject in a way of argument; when they changed their tone, especially when I dwelt on the article of death, to them a subject of all others the most unpleasant, and alas, no wonder, for the utmost stretch of their faith in *annihilation*.[26] ... I try sometimes to conceive of the extent of their happiness in this life, supposing, as they do, that *annihilation* envelops all beyond. They seem happy, and that too in a superlative degree, when the fleshpots are full. One remarked a few days ago, 'How ugly the fire looks without a pot'. Surely their highest happiness arises exclusively from animal gratification.[27]

Among other passages, a section in the 1834 *Report* to the LMS is typical:

> We surely have abundant reason to give thanks to God for his blessing on the Mission. ... Some who, but a short time ago, had their dwelling among perfect heathens, with no prospect after death but *annihilation*, now made partakers of the faith of the Gospel, and looking forward with the blessed hope of immortal life with the saints in glory. [28]

Similarly, when Moffat explained African culture to British audiences, during his 1839-1843 furlough, he stressed that the Tswana believed in annihilation

---

[25] RM, *Journal,* 27.6.1823, (*AAK,* 97). Cf. RM, *To Alexander Moffat,* Jan. 1823, (*AAK,* 70), 'Alas! We still hang our harp on the willow, and mourn over the destiny of thousands, *dupes to annihilation*, hastening with heedless but impetuous strides to the regions of woe. They turn a deaf ear to the voice of love, and treat with scorn the glorious doctrine of redemption.'

[26] RM, *Journal,* 15.4.1827, (*AAK,* 246).

[27] RM, *Journal,* 6.5.1827, (*AAK,* 251).

[28] LMS, *Report to the 40th Annual Meeting, 1834,* 96f.

after death: 'They never had an idea of an immortal state; they supposed that when a man died, he ceased forever. They had no prospect but a dark and dreary *annihilation* before them'.[29] But did Moffat confuse Tswana rejection of the Christian concept of resurrection, with Tswana ideas of existence after death? On one occasion, Moffat referred to an African 'of quick and superior understanding' who said to him:

> Friend, I fear greatly that the people will think you are mad, if you continue to teach that there is another world, and that the dead shall arise; the thing was never heard of before, and you must know that the thing is impossible. The people consider that you are wise and good, but what will they think when they hear you talking about dead men living again?'[30]

The speaker rejected Moffat's teaching on resurrection, but did that mean that he also rejected the notion of the 'living dead'? Not necessarily. Moffat's view—that African belief was belief in annihilation, rather than in continued existence after death—was not unchallenged, even in his own life-time. Some of the missionaries who followed him in the same region, questioned his conclusions.[31] Livingstone wrote to Adolphe Mabille, in BaSutoland in 1843, after only two years in Africa, wondering whether the people were really so 'far sunk as has been represented':

> I heard Mr. Moffat say in England that the Bechuana had really no conscience until it was formed by the missionaries ... Besides other fragments of knowledge which I have found among them, they seem to have had the idea of future existence clearly.[32]

Likewise, after twenty-five years in southern Africa, Willoughby, one of Moffat's successors, was convinced that there was a universal Bantu belief in survival after death. Yet at the same time, we note that Willoughby, who was severely critical of Moffat on several issues,[33] made a distinction between the notion of survival after death, and the concept of immortality. Even Willoughby concluded there was no evidence, 'that the Bantu have considered the idea of immortality.'[34] Does this distinction between 'survival

---

29 RM, *Walworth Address,* 1843, (*Farewell Services,* 72).

30 RM, *Africa,* 23.

31 Cf. Northcott, *Robert Moffat,* 74.

32 Livingstone, *To A. Mabille,* 24.2.1843, (Smith, *Robert Moffat,* 107).

33 Cf. Willoughby, *The Soul of the Bantu,* (Ldn: SCM, 1928).

34 Willoughby, *Race Problems in the New Africa,* 64f. Livingstone, Smith and Willoughby viewed the situation after decades of Christian mission, though Livingstone's citation of the chameleon fable did indicate a pre-Christian belief. Moffat made an absolute statement where a relative one would have been better. Willoughby had an agenda, noble in intention, of demonstrating that the native African was the equal of the European. To that end he wished to eliminate anything which may be interpreted as spiritual or intellectual inferiority.

after death' and 'immortality' excuse Moffat? Perhaps not, or at least not fully, since Moffat understood indigenous belief to be belief in *annihilation*, and the concept of annihilation excluded even a reduced notion of a shadowy survival after death, not simply the fuller concept of immortality.

What complicates the issue is that, alongside Moffat's insistence on *annihilation* being the prevailing native belief, he was fully aware that the Ndebele and Tswana prayed to the departed spirits of the ancestors, the *manes* of the dead.[35] How might this contradiction be resolved? What is important is Moffat's style of writing. He did not indulge in fine distinctions. Moffat employed hyperbole for emphasis. Unfortunately, this can mislead. Moffat was a man who used strong words, and who expressed statements in robust terms in order to emphasise his point. This mode of communication is dramatic and arresting. Unfortunately, it can also be misleading. Might native belief include both annihilation *and* continued existence? If so, there may be grounds for partially reaffirming Moffat, and among anthropologists there are a range of views.

Alice Werner stated that in traditional Bantu thought: 'The dead are supposed to go on living for an indefinite time underground, very much as they have done on the upper earth.'[36] Werner also speculated that, though there is a belief in survival after death, there seems also to be the thought that the ghosts go on living only as long as people remember them.[37] If

---

35 Cf. RM, *Journal,* 8.10.1854, (*MJ1,* 327) & RM, *To Tidman, LMS,* 3.9.1854, (*MJ1,* 370f). RM, *Journal,* 11.10.1857, (*MJ2,* 94), also wrote, 'After our service I talked to some Matabele who were present and put a few questions in reference to God, government, immortality, etc. ... They said that the Matabele believed that there was a town underground where Machobane, the [dead] father of Moselekatse, lived and where there were Matabele cattle, etc. The speaker, being one of the more intelligent, was asked if all went thither. This he could not tell. I then enquired if there was another place for those who did not go thither. This also he could not answer. When I enquired if those in that nether region had taken their bones and their flesh with them, he seemed at a loss, and then answered he thought not. ... Moselekatse occasionally offers a sacrifice, or a killing of cattle, to the manes of his departed father, and pretends to ascertain coming events, or obtain information on points on which he is at a loss, by intercourse with the dead. This gives him no little influence over the minds of his people.' Also, 'I have been induced to think what I have written [about death (above)] from the strange, the mysterious sights I see from day to day. ... To them the future is shrouded in darkness. They have some glimmering that, when man dies, he goes down to where the manes of the dead are. Some think they become serpents, but after much enquiry I find that their hope or confidence in the future is of an evanescent description, so evanescent that they or their language fail to give an idea on which one can fix the mind. It is Moselekatse, and nothing but Moselekatse. At his orders they will at any day rush into death, die for Moselekatse, the son of Machobane. This is all their glory.'

36 Alice Werner, *Myths and Legends of the Bantu,* 19.

37 Ibid, 18.

Werner was correct, then ideas of life after death *and* annihilation did sit together. This dualism is represented in Werner's book, in which she stated unequivocally: (i) 'The core of Bantu religion ... is the cult of the dead. The belief in a High God is more or less vague – by some tribes it is almost forgotten ... but everywhere among Bantu-speaking peoples the spirits of the departed are recognised, honoured, and propitiated. There is not the slightest doubt that these people believe in something which survives the death of the body.'[38] And (ii) 'Though the ghost survives the body for an indefinite period, it is not necessarily thought of as living on forever. ... Some people state ... that after the lapse of several generations they simply go back to nothingness, except in the case of outstanding personalities. ... In other words, the ghosts last only so long as they are remembered by the living.'[39]

Schapera similarly argued that, among the Tswana, the dominant cult was the worship of the dead: 'A man was buried with his weapons in his hands, a woman with her hoe and some seeds of every cultivated grain; both were also dressed in the clothes they wore when alive. They were then equipped *for their journey to the world of the dead, where a man would continue to herd his grandfather's cattle, and a woman to cultivate the soil*. ... the grave was a round hole, with a niche to one side, in which the body was placed in a crouching position, with the head facing west, so that he was ready to get up and walk to the place where the souls of the other dead had gone.'[40] Yet Schapera also hinted at a dualism:

> [In modern times] professing Christians have accepted the Church doctrine of immortality, with the associated conceptions of Heaven and Hell. Some of the heathens retain the ancient belief that the soul goes underground to the world of the dead ... *others maintain that it is simply blown away by the wind, so that when a person dies he is annihilated*.[41]

In relation to the ancestors, their importance as deities was determined by the status they had enjoyed on earth.[42] In practice, worship was directed only to those most *recently dead*, such as father or grandfather, whose personal peculiarities were known and remembered.[43] Only the 'recently dead' were relevant. Hence, if the *memory* was annihilated, it is a moot point whether the person was also deemed to be 'no more', lacking even a shadowy existence in the spirit-world.

---

38 Ibid, 81.
39 Ibid, 81f.
40 Schapera, *The Tswana,* 59 (our italics).
41 Ibid, 61.
42 Ibid, 59.
43 Ibid, 59f.

Hammond-Tooke has admitted that studying this whole area is difficult since detailed evidence is lacking, especially among the Tswana, who had largely ceased to practice the ancestor rituals by the time anthropologists studied them.[44] However, he did state: 'All southern Bantu believed in a life after death, although their ideas about it were vague' and, 'there was little or no speculation as to what happened to the *moya* at death, and no conception of rewards or punishments in an afterlife. Importantly, a concept of the *moya* having future existence was not identical with that of ancestor spirit, which was accorded quite a different term.'[45]

The lack of a conception of rewards or punishments in an afterlife may have contributed to Moffat concluding that indigenous peoples believed in annihilation. Hammond-Tooke claimed that what *was* truly important was the belief that *some*—not necessarily all—became ancestral spirits at death and continued to take an active interest in their descendants. The belief in the spirits of the ancestors lay at the heart of traditional religion. If Hammond-Tooke was correct, then it is only *some* people who go on to become ancestral spirits. Concerning the rest, what happened to their *moya* after death is vague.

There is little doubt that Moffat, wittingly or unwittingly, exaggerated the lack of a concept of life after death in native belief. Yet, it was not easy to connect the indigenous concept of existence after death with Christian ideas on the immortality of the soul. Part of the problem lay not just in the ability of one culture to listen to another, but in the concept of 'time' and hence of 'eternity' which a culture carries. Hendricks argued that the African concept of time is so different from a non-African one that mutual understanding may be impossible. Hendricks stated, following Mbiti, that in African philosophy, eternity or endlessness is inconceivable.[46] However, this introduces a host of debatable issues, especially given the enormous interest which some Africans have in time-charts relating to future apocalyptic events.[47]

Moffat wanted to give a message of hope so that his listeners might not be bound by the idea of nothingness at death. However, they already had a corpus of ideas about the presence in this life of spirits of departed ancestors. And for them, annihilation was more reassuring than an immortality under condemnation! That was why Moselekatse was uncomfortable with Moffat's doctrine. Their alternative theology of death was something which Moffat

---

44 Hammond-Tooke, *Roots,* 151.

45 Hammond-Tooke, *Roots,* 149.

46 Jurgen Hendricks, *Studying Congregations in Africa,* (Wellington SA: NETACT, 2004), 126.

47 Cf. Baëta, *Christianity in Tropical Africa,* (Ldn: OUP, 1968), 149.

needed to address. Any Christian theology of eternal life had to engage directly with these beliefs, positively or negatively.

DEATH, HADES, AND THE INTERMEDIATE STATE

Moffat held the notion of an Intermediate State after death. In an 1838 letter to the *BFBS*, he wrote that he had used two different terms to distinguish between Hades and Gehenna.[48] Put simply, Moffat believed that both the saved and the unsaved first go to Hades after death, writing in 1854: 'I never hear of [vilification] without thinking how soon we shall see each other face to face in the Hades, for good and bad go there *in the first place*.'[49] Yet, mainstream Reformed theology taught that there was no Intermediate State. It did not teach communication between, or awareness of, persons in Hades before the Judgment. *The Shorter Catechism* stated: 'The souls of believers are at their death made perfect in holiness, and do immediately[50] pass into glory; and their bodies, being still united to Christ, do rest in their graves, till the resurrection'.[51] This gave no basis for Moffat's idea of a conscious existence after death in Hades, shared by believer and unbeliever alike. So, where did Moffat get his theology from?

The word 'Hades' did not occur in Moffat's English bible, the King James version (AV), since the AV consistently translated the Greek *άδης* as 'hell'. The term *άδης* occurs ten times in the Greek New Testament, two of which are in Luke, and include one of the most dramatic parables involving the 'Hades' concept, that of the Rich Man and Lazarus. Luke was the first part of the Bible which Moffat translated into SeTswana. When this is allied to the fact that Moffat tried, whenever possible, to translate from Greek directly,[52] this may partly account for Moffat's recognition of the specific term 'Hades'

---

48 RM, *To Browne,* BFBS, 3.7.1838, (CULBSA/Browne/1838/4/40). Cf. Northcott, *Robert Moffat,* 123. In his SeTswana translations of the NT, Moffat used *bobipo* for άδης (Hades); and *molete* for γεεννα (Gehenna). The AV translated both Greek words as 'hell'. Matumo, in the English-SeTswana section of his *Dictionary* (536), gives both *bobipo* and *molete* as equivalents for 'hell'; but in the SeTswana-English section, he defines *bobipo* as 'a place where things are hidden; a place of darkness'; and he defines *molete* as 'a deep natural hole or pit; a dungeon; an abyss; hell'. To a certain extent, Matumo preserves Moffat's distinction between the terms.

49 RM, *Journal,* 31.8.1854, (*MJ1,* 283), (our italics).

50 The *Shorter Catechism* emphasises that this final 'being made perfect' is immediate. It is not a process during a time of waiting.

51 *Shorter Catechism,* Qu. 37. The *Larger Catechism,* Qu. 87, gives almost exactly the same answer, as does *The Westminster Confession,* Ch. 32.

52 By 1820 Moffat was working on Greek and SeTswana together. See: RM, *To John Philip,* 19.9.1820, (*AAK,* 10), 'I also hope to be making progress in my Greek and the Bootchuana [SeTswana] language.'

as distinct from 'hell', both in his translation work and in his espousal of a theology of the Intermediate State.[53] When Moffat wrote: 'We shall see each other face to face in the Hades, for good and bad go there in the first place' he was simply musing in his *Journal*.[54] However, a similar theme occurred when Moffat discussed with some Ndebele the following Sabbath, and he jotted down his record of the exchange:

> "[Moselekatse] saw my Testament edging out from under my coat and moved off ... Of course I left him to his council, and we proceeded without. A few of the Matabele were with us, to whom I put a few questions after service in reference to God, immortality, etc., and endeavoured by answering my own questions to diffuse a little light into their darkened understandings.
>
> They said that there was a town underground to which the dead went. I could not make out that they had the shadow of an idea of a resurrection.[55] When I told them that good people go to the same place as bad people, I was asked where they went to. I replied, to heaven, to an abode of happiness. They promptly replied that Moselekatse had a house in heaven where he made rain and other good things".[56]

If we did not have a quotation from Moffat which stated: 'we shall see each other face to face in the Hades, for good and bad go there in the first place', we might assume that Moffat simply meant that both good and bad could get to heaven: i.e., justification by grace, not by works. However, the quotation in question indicates that the 'good' and 'bad' referred to believers and unbelievers, and not to different categories of saved sinners. Thus, for Moffat, 'Hades' included both the saved and the unsaved. But what theology lay behind Moffat's position on this matter?

An Intermediate State was denied in the dominant Presbyterian traditions in Scotland. When we examine the various strands which influenced Moffat's theological development, Methodism may have been the only one which could have given him this doctrine. There is, of course, the possibility that he derived it simply from his own study of the Scriptures, but usually an individual's theological position has a history behind it. There were three major traditions which influenced Moffat: Reformed theology in the Westminster tradition, Congregationalist theology, and Methodist theology.

---

53 Moffat's concept of Hades echoes the use of the word 'Hades' in the biblical period. See: Joachim Jeremias, 'Hades', *Kittel's Theological Dict. of the New Testament, Vol. 1,* 146ff.

54 RM, *Journal,* 31.8.1854, (*MJ1,* 282f).

55 This statement must be borne in mind when interpreting Moffat's use of 'annihilation'. Moffat was aware that the Ndebele had the notion of some kind of existence after death, but he refused to equate it with the idea of resurrection.

56 RM, *Journal,* 3.9.1854, (*MJ1,* 287f).

The *Westminster Confession of Faith* gave no encouragement to speculations concerning an Intermediate State.[57] In the list of scripture texts officially appended to the *Westminster Confession,* the phrase 'immediately return to God who gave them' is linked with to Luke 23:43: 'Today you will be with me in paradise'. The *Confession* countenanced no Intermediate State, no soul sleep, and no soul death. It taught immediate transportation into the presence of God. The strength of opposition from the Reformed tradition to the idea of an Intermediate State was considerable.

The Burgher minister, John Brown of Haddington, had a theology exactly in line with the *Confession.* His comments on the issue came in the context of his criticism of Methodism. He deplored Methodism's tendency toward Arminianism, and he specifically objected to Methodist teaching of an Intermediate State of Hades between death and final resurrection. In his view this was too close to the notion of purgatory.[58] John Brown was a Burgher, and in 1847 the United Presbyterian Church became the Burgher Church's successor. It therefore comes as no surprise that, in 1871, the UP Church arraigned the Rev. Fergus Ferguson on a heresy charge because he was suspected of teaching an Intermediate State.[59] A straight line can be drawn from the *Westminster Confession,* through the Burgher Kirk, to Ferguson's heresy trial. Given Moffat's Burgher connections, it is intriguing to speculate on what might have developed, had he become a minister of the UP Church but held such views!

For Congregationalist theology, Ralph Wardlaw was the leading Scottish Congregationalist theologian of the time. Wardlaw, like Moffat, taught that humanity had a two-fold constitution of body and soul, and that death brought dissolution between soul and body.[60] But where Moffat varied from Wardlaw was in what happened after death. Wardlaw taught that after death there was no Intermediate State.[61] Wardlaw did discuss the concept of 'Hades',[62] but without affirming an Intermediate State. Indeed, one of the criticisms made by Cunninghame, in his critique of Wardlaw's 1830 sermon

---

57 *Westminster Confession of Faith,* Ch. 32.

58 John Brown, *An Historical Account of the Rise and Progress of the Secession,* (Edin: Guthrie & Tait, 1819 edn), 63. *Brown's Catechism* did not affirm an Intermediate State.

59 J.E.H. Thomson, *The Present Heresy Case in the United Presbyterian Church with Statement by Rev. Fergus Ferguson,* (Edin: Elliot, 1878). Cf. J.H. Leckie, *Fergus Ferguson: His Theology and Heresy Trial,* (Edin: T&T Clark, 1923), & G.C. Scorgie, 'Fergus Ferguson', (*DSCHT*, 318).

60 Wardlaw, *Systematic Theology, Vol. 3,* 644.

61 Ibid, *Vol 3,* 645.

62 Ibid, *Vol 2*, 597.

on eschatology, was the lack of a theology of Hades.[63] Cunninghame interpreted Wardlaw as teaching that the souls of all believers who 'fall asleep in Jesus' at once passed into glory. Wardlaw's theology was in line with traditional teaching, whereas Cunninghame's theology was not.[64] Cunninghame was convinced that a doctrine of the Intermediate State was demanded by Scripture. For him, Hades was not Hell. It was Paradise. But Paradise was not Heaven, it was an Intermediate State. Under this interpretation, when Jesus said to the dying thief, 'Today you will be with me in paradise' Jesus was not promising that the crucified criminal would be in heaven, but in Hades, waiting for the final resurrection. This is closer to Moffat's understanding, but is nowhere near the Congregational tradition which Wardlaw typified. Thus Moffat did not derive this doctrine from the mainstream Congregationalist/Independency theological tradition in Scotland or in England.[65]

There remains Methodism. In John Wesley's thinking, Paradise was the Intermediate State of the souls of the godly between death and the final resurrection: 'As happy as the souls in paradise are, they are preparing for far greater happiness. For paradise is only the porch of heaven; and it is there the spirits of just men are made perfect.'[66] Wesley's statement—that in Paradise the spirits of just men 'are made perfect'—came from his belief that the final process of sanctification and cleansing for the justified took place during this intermediate existence. It was this teaching which John Brown of Haddington criticised as simply being another version of purgatory. Also in Wesley's thinking, Paradise was a section within Hades but reserved for the godly. His Sermon 'On the Rich Man and Lazarus' shows that he conceived of Hades as the Intermediate State for both the godly and the ungodly, with Paradise the specific 'section' within Hades for the godly.[67] That Wesley interpreted Hades as a 'place' for both the godly and the ungodly between death and the final resurrection—of which Paradise was a particular

---

63 William Cunninghame, *Review of Rev. Dr Wardlaw's Sermon on the Millennium: with an answer to His arguments against the millennial resurrection and reign of the Saints and Martyrs of Jesus Christ* (Glasgow: Smith, 1830).

64 Ibid, 14f.

65 There is nothing in Roby's *Theological Lectures* on this issue. In his book on Protestantism, Roby homologated the Westminster approach: 'The Scriptures speak plainly of two states beyond the present, heaven and hell, and the eternity of both.' Roby, *Protestantism: An Address particularly to the Labouring Classes in defence Of the Protestant Principle 'that the Scriptures, not Tradition, are the Rule of Faith',* (Ldn: Westley, 3rd Ed. 1822), 102.

66 John Wesley, *Sermon 73, 'On Hell'*. See also, Wesley, *Notes on Luke 23:43*, and *Notes on 2 Corinthians 12:4.* Calvin, *Commentary on Luke* 23:43, was more cautious, 'We ought not to enter into curious and subtle arguments about the place of paradise.'

67 John Wesley, *Sermon 112, 'On the Rich Man and Lazarus'.*

section—is strengthened by some of his notes on other Bible passages.[68] Wesley stated that the soul abides in Hades during this Intermediate State. But it was Christ, not Peter, who decided who in Hades would be 'released' to enter Heaven. Heaven and Hell were the final permanent states for the saved and the unsaved respectively.[69]

In our opinion, the references to Hades in Moffat's writings are much closer to Wesley's model than to any other. This may well be because Moffat's conversion experience was under Methodist influence.

---

68 John Wesley, *Notes on Revelation 1:18.*

69 John Wesley, *Sermon 73, 'On Hell'.*

Chapter 22
The Cross of Jesus

DURING HIS TRAVELS IN 1854, Moffat recorded preaching to those who were with him on the journey: 'Our company is not large, but by far the greatest majority are *without God* and *without hope*, but God is here with all his compassion and with all his love'.[1] The Reformed emphasis on God as the faithful, gracious, covenant God was embedded in Moffat's frame of mind. God was a covenant God who kept his promises:

> Reflecting on what has taken place we cannot but feel a lively sense of the goodness of our *covenant God* and Saviour. We feel like people taken by surprise or rising from a dream. [God is] directing heathen minds to a sense of their [sin and] to the blood of atonement.[2]

God's faithfulness and love were critically important to Moffat, precisely because so many men and women were without hope. The lostness of humanity was one of the most compelling motivations in evangelical missions, with evangelicals maintaining a firm belief that the personal destiny of every individual was linked to acceptance or rejection of God's revelation, and physical death took on eschatological dimensions for evangelicals because it was seen as the end of any opportunity to respond to the Gospel.[3]

Moffat was such an evangelical missionary. The revival movement, which cradled his spiritual development, emphasised the importance of saving the souls of men and women before it was too late. When recounting one of his encounters with the San, Moffat wrote: 'I could say but little to them about Him who came to redeem the poor and the needy'.[4] Moffat's concern was that a lost humanity needed to be saved. During the Moffats' furlough in Britain, Livingstone heard Moffat describe how he had '*sometimes seen, in the morning sun, the smoke of a thousand villages, where no missionary had*

---

1 RM, *Journal*, 18.6.1854, (*MJ1*, 187), (our italics).

2 RM, *To Orme, LMS*, 6.3.1829, (SOAS/CWM/SA/Box11/3/B). Cf. RM, *To Burder, LMS*, 20.12.1824, (SOAS/CWM/SA/Box9/2/F), in which he wrote similarly : 'Through the goodness of our *covenant God* we all enjoy a tolerable share of health at the present time'.

3 Philip L. Capp: 'Eschatology: It's Relevance to Mission from an Evangelical perspective', *Missionalia*, Vol. 15, No.3, Nov. 1987, 111.

4 RM, *MLSSA*, 157. The Comaroffs, *Revelation and Revolution, Vol. 1*, 273, insisting that Moffat neglected social and political issues facing the indigenous people, wrote disparagingly of his emphasis on saving souls and of similar other-worldly promises of the church.

ever been'.[5] That galvanised Livingstone: thousands were perishing who had never heard the Gospel. Livingstone had been bound for China, but Moffat's dramatic appeal, plus the difficulties raised by the Opium War in the Far East, changed everything.

In 1843, before returning to Africa, Moffat preached in the Barbican Church London, and restated the primacy of the message of salvation:

> The theme of heaven is man's salvation. For that, heaven has groaned. I might say: for that, heaven has bled. It was for this object that the Lord of life and glory left the heavenly world, became a man of sorrows, and acquainted with grief, and lived in the form of a servant among men, tabernacled among men, was the servant of men, was the victim of men's rage. It was for the salvation of the world that he lived and groaned and bled and died.[6]

In preaching to an evangelically minded congregation this was the theme which any agreeable preacher would stress. He wanted them to know that their concerns were his concerns. But there was no question of Moffat's words being tailored for his audience. The salvation of souls was central in his personal missionary vision. From start to finish of his life's work he had a vision of countless numbers of men and women without Christ going to everlasting loss.[7] In a letter to the LMS, written in the final stages of over fifty years of missionary work he wrote:

> When we think of the flood of vanity of vanities *which is sweeping thousands to perdition*, can eternity of life ever be compared? Though old, my heart is warm and my step firm, but it is time for me and the partner of so many years labour, to retire and give place to youth and energy. When I look to the interminable regions beyond of heathen darkness, my heart melts and I wish I was young again.[8]

Yet surprisingly, though salvation of souls was so dear to his heart, Moffat rarely referred to the Cross of Calvary. There can be little doubt that in his own faith the Cross was extremely important, but in his records of preaching

---

5 When Livingstone arrived at Kuruman in 1841, he was disappointed to find a small population. This differed from Moffat's dramatic sentence. But see RM, Journal, 3.8.1824, (AAK, 135), where he wrote: 'Lifting our eyes northward we were astonished at the number of towns which lay scattered in the valleys.' It may have been these scenes, north of Kuruman, which Moffat had in mind, rather than Kuruman itself.

6 RM, *Barbican Sermon,* 22.1.1843, (*Farewell Services,* 100).

7 One of the clearest affirmations of this soul-burden comes in John Smith Moffat's biography of his parents: 'To people like the missionaries, whose whole heart was in their work, who believed that all said in the New Testament about the solemn eventualities of another world was literally true and no mere figure of speech, who looked at the heathen around them and felt they were verily perishing, it was a sore trial of faith to go on year after year with their message burning in their hearts.' (JSM, *Lives,* 152).

8 RM, *To Mullens, LMS,* 22.4.1869, (SOAS/CMW/SA/Box 35/2/D).

and teaching the Cross is seldom mentioned. For Moffat, the 'mechanism' behind salvation, whether that of ransom, substitution, or some other interpretation of the Calvary-event, was unimportant. Much more important than the mechanism of atonement was the fact that the grace of the Gospel—salvation—was located in the person of Jesus Christ, and grace is made ours by seeking Him and receiving freely from Him: 'O to grace how great a debtor!'

THE CROSS OF CALVARY

Though explicit references to the Cross are infrequent in the records of Moffat's evangelistic work, they are not totally lacking. In 1827, recording his experiences in the BaRolong village on language study, he wrote:

> In the evening, I had some conversation with a number of men who were partaking the benefit of the fire. Their ignorance in divine things cannot have a parallel. The doctrine of the Cross was a subject of loud laughter. I saw this with much pain of mind but could not prevent it. O! When shall the light of knowledge [of] God shine into their hearts?[9]

Moffat mentions the doctrine of the Cross, but gives no indication as to how he explained it. If he followed the pattern of *Brown's Catechism,* then his emphasis would have been that Jesus was punished for our sins so that we might not be punished.[10] For evangelical missionaries, penal substitution was a common way of explaining the atonement. But if so, and if Moffat explained the cross in these terms, how would this theology be received? Moffat referred to Christ's atoning death in some of his conversations with Moselekatse, but there is no record that Moselekatse, among the multitude of questions he asked, ever made any comment on the person or work of Christ. Moselekatse was interested in the consequences of the message: immortality, resurrection, rewards and punishments. But there is no record of him enquiring about the Saviour, the Cross, or the logic of someone taking a penalty on behalf of another. Moselekatse appears to have been uninterested in Christian soteriology.[11]

The meagre number of references to the Cross in Moffat's Ndebele *Journals* contrasts with a much richer vein in *Missionary Labours.* When, in his book, Moffat described the conversion of some of the Khoikhoi he stated that they

---

9 RM, *Journal,* 2.5.1827, (*AAK,* 250).

10 *Brown's Catechism* had only two Questions on Calvary: 'Qu. 60: Why then did God make him suffer all these things? It was for our sins. Qu. 61: Why did Jesus Christ suffer the punishment of our sins? It was to save us from being punished on account of them.' It cited Isaiah 53 in support of Qu. 60. These verses were printed as an appendix and learned by heart.

11 E.g., RM, *Journal,* 1829, (*MJ1,* 26, 27).

were 'aroused by the voice of love, and drawn by the attractions of the Cross'.[12] Again, when Moffat described meeting up with his old friend, the Coranna chief named Paul, Moffat wrote that he was 'glad of this renewed opportunity to preach, and he was glad to hear again the message of divine grace'.[13] Moffat regularly used the term 'the word of grace' to describe the Gospel.[14] In *Missionary Labours,* Moffat also described the brotherly meeting of the former enemies Africaner and Berends:

> Being now converts to the faith, all their former animosities were melted away by the Gospel of peace and love. These chiefs sat down together in our tent with a number of people, all united in singing a hymn of praise to God, and listening to an address, from the invitation of Jehovah to the ends of the earth to look to Him, and Him alone, for salvation. After which, they knelt at the same stool, before the peaceful throne of the Redeemer.[15]

All of these examples, taken from *Missionary Labours,* were couched in the form of words an evangelical readership would expect. But the same phraseology does not occur so frequently in the *Journals* which were written in the immediate, on-the-spot, situation. In *Missionary Labours* did Moffat overstress the impact which the Cross made? This may be the case, but if so, only to a certain extent. This is because it should also be noted that many of Moffat's *Journals* were written in the context of interaction with Moselekatse's Ndebele who remained unconverted, whereas most of *Missionary Labours* focused on the Namaqua and Tswana, many of whom did embrace the Gospel. Thus, when we turn from Moffat's Ndebele *Journals* to his earlier *Journals* and *letters* dealing with the Namaqua and Tswana, there are some entries which centre on the Cross. For example, in the early 1820s, Moffat wrote to the LMS Directors asking them to send new missionaries to Africaner's Namaqua:

> I have seen men, once the dupes of ignorance and vice, sweetly falling asleep in Jesus; others exulting, as they depart out of life, and saying, 'it is finished for guilty me.' Sometimes my solitary moments are interrupted with their doleful complaints – 'You have snatched us from heathen darkness; discovered to us the enemies of our never-dying souls; pointed us to the *lamb of God* and withdrawn the curtain of the eternal world. We see the crown that awaits the faithful, but why have you left us to finish the warfare alone?'[16]

---

12 RM, *MLSSA,* 213.
13 RM, *MLSSA,* 150.
14 RM, *MLSSA,* 166.
15 RM, *MLSSA,* 182.
16 RM, *MLSSA,* 187. Cf. the 1822 case of Jason in, RM, *Journal,* 30.1.1822 &4.2.1822, (*AAK,* 43): 'This evening Jason, a young man whom we had often visited, sent for me. For some time past he has been afflicted with the white swelling in the leg. ... I found him extremely weak. When I enquired into the state of his mind, he stated that death was too cunning for him, that

Another important reference to the atonement came in a letter which Moffat and Hamilton wrote in 1829 to the Rev. Richard Miles in Cape Town:

> About four months ago several females were carried off by a disease called *Tluatsi* which is very fatal in this country. Among these there was one, a married woman, who was, previous to her sickness, an enquirer after Divine things and vigilant in the means of grace. Before the disease began to take a fatal form, she spoke very clearly on the importance of the doctrines to which she had lately paid so much attention and professed a lively hope of eternal life through the atonement of Jesus.
>
> After a few days when she felt the harbinger of Death beginning to arrest her powers, she called her husband and friends to whom she spoke in language at one striking and arousing, exhorting them to believe the word of Jehovah and take their refuge to Jesus the only saviour. 'I am going to die' said she, and paused, some appearing affected. She resumed 'Weep not because I am going to leave you. Weep for your sins. Weep for your souls. With me all is well. Do not suppose that I die like a beast or that I shall sleep for ever in the grave. *No! Jesus died for my sins. He has said He will save me. I am going home. I am going to heaven, that happy place, to be forever with Jesus my Saviour.*'[17]

Idealised or nor, this account portrays exactly what an evangelical missionary would hope for. Moffat closed the narrative: 'Shortly after bearing this testimony, she expired. Blessed be God for his rich mercy to so poor and ignorant a sinner, which was her state a few months before.'

The Resurrection of Easter

After analysing the Cross, it is natural to discuss the Resurrection. Yet Moffat rarely mentioned the Resurrection of Christ. Moreover, when he mentioned the resurrection of men and women, he did not connect it directly with *Christ's* resurrection, but with the immortality of the soul. In Moffat's theology it was the inherent immortality of the soul which made future existence certain for an individual. Existence after death was based on the doctrine of the immortality of the soul, not on immortality having been made possible through Christ's resurrection. Moffat accepted as obvious that all humanity would rise and face the Judgment, because immortality was granted along with creation. The critical issue was the nature of the

he was much afraid of dying, etc., etc. I pointed him to Christ, as having taken away the sting of death. I made as plain as possible the way of a sinner's acceptance. At the conclusion I asked a few questions, but alas! he seemed entirely ignorant of the nature of what I had been speaking. ... [5 days later] This morning poor Jason closed his eyes in the sleep of death. Towards the close his mind became gradually more incapable of digesting or even retaining what he heard."

17 Moffat & Hamilton, *To the Rev. R. Miles,* 12.8.1829, (SOAS/CWM/SA /Box11/3/D).

inevitable eternal existence which a person had. The Gospel was good news, not because it conferred immortality, but because it made immortality a blessing rather than a curse.

Moffat recorded that Moselekatse was spellbound by the idea of resurrection, and asked in wonderment: 'Shall Machobane, my father, rise from the dead?'[18] Moffat replied in the affirmative: 'All the dead and all that should die would rise at the last day'. What struck Moselekatse initially was not so much the moral and spiritual consequences of the resurrected standing before God—which was Moffat's concern—but the sheer impossibility of such a cosmic event. 'Shall all rise?' he asked with 'apparent wonder'.[19] Moffat explained: 'All the dust of human bodies which bespangled his dominions would rise to life and be judged by the Son of God.'[20] Moffat was trying to get Moselekatse to think seriously about the consequences of his killings, to appreciate that actions had eternal consequences, and to realise that he would have to answer for his actions before God with the evidence of a host of murdered victims being present to accuse him.

Future conversations with Moselekatse show that Moselekatse's personal concern was how Moffat's teaching squared with his own cultural beliefs on the nature of his ancestors' existence after death. Nevertheless, he was not immune from concern as to how he, with blood on his hands, might fare at the day of judgment. On a subsequent occasion, during the 1829 visit to Moselekatse, Moffat wrote:

> I spoke much on man's ruin, and man's redemption. 'Why' he asked, 'are you so earnest that I abandon all war, and not kill men?' 'Look on the human bones which lie scattered over your dominions,' was my reply. 'They speak in awful language, and to me they say, "Whosoever sheddeth man's blood, by man also shall his blood be shed."' This was fearful language in the ears of such a murderer. 'You say, he added, 'that the dead will rise again'. My remarks on this subject were startling in the ears of a savage, and he interrupted me by hastily assuring me that he would not go to war.[21]

Moffat's teaching on the evils of war and the reality of a judgment, affected Moselekatse. It certainly made him reluctant to discuss the military side of his activities: 'Of the countries his warriors had visited, I could learn little from him, as he seemed to wish me ignorant of his marauding disposition,

---

18 RM, *Journal,* 1829, (*MJ1,* 16).
19 Ibid.
20 Ibid.
21 RM, *MLSSA,* 551f.

particularly after I had spoken on the evils of war and the guilt of those who shed innocent blood.'[22]

David Bogue had taught that one of the difficulties facing an evangelical missionary came from the nature of the Gospel, in that it offered its chief promises in a future state rather than in the present.[23] Bogue thought that the offer of heaven might not help in converting people who wanted blessing here and now. What Moffat also found was that the idea of a future state was deeply off-putting to a man such as Moselekatse who felt he might be called to account in a Christian vision of the future. Christianity offered immortality. But to Moselekatse's discomfort it went hand in hand with judgment. And it was a judgment based on holiness and morality, not on warrior status or bellicose valour. It was probably he who remonstrated: 'The words of a resurrection are too great to be heard. I do not wish to hear about the dead rising again! The dead cannot arise! The dead shall not arise!'[24]

There was similar reaction to Moffat's teaching on the immortality of the soul during his 1827 stay in a BaRolong village. On that occasion his message about the immortality of the soul brought alarm. Moffat reckoned this was because the doctrine brought disturbing news concerning judgment after death, rather than the panacea of a comforting annihilation:

> About a dozen women, principally the wives of chiefs had come to the wagon. I continued on the subject [death]. They smiled at first, but when I spoke of the immortality of the soul, the coming of Christ, the events of that day, and the burning of the world and all things therein, they seemed really alarmed.
>
> At intervals I made a pause, to allow them to make remarks or ask questions ... One seemed much concerned to hear that the oxen etc. would be destroyed with all other earthly things, and particularly that there would be none in heaven. 'What would become of beads, ornaments, etc., when the world was on fire?' asked another, and one asked (as if in some degree acquainted with scriptural language), 'And we who remain alive at his coming, what shall become of us?' Paul's words were a ready answer.
>
> Some, on [the] other hand, looked up as if they were afraid of the dreadful event taking place at that moment. One of a roughish character, who had heard the gospel at the Kuruman, remarked that they [had] thought that these things were lies, but having lately seen many persons die she was now afraid. On hearing one say that she would like to be able to pray, I took from

22 RM, *Journal,* 1829, (*MJ1,* 17).

23 Bogue, *Miss. Lect.* 14, 'Difficulties attending Missions'.

24 RM, *Africa,* 25.

> my pocket a prayer in Sechuana which I had just composed, and read it, which appeared to please them much.[25]

A similar reaction occurred in 1824. When Moffat enumerated some of the works of Jesus, one listener exclaimed: 'What an excellent doctor, to raise the dead!' But, 'When I referred them to a place of rewards and punishments, they seemed not so well pleased.'[26] Reflecting on this, Moffat reasoned that the lack of a notion of resurrection resulted in the lack of a notion of judgment, which in turn resulted in a lack of accountability and conscience.[27] This logic was one of the factors leading him to say that many Tswana had no concept of a *conscience* before they heard the Gospel: a conclusion with which Livingstone strongly disagreed.

The Judgment of Eternity

In the Old Testament the *judgment* of God was closely related to the *justice* of God. Whereas earthly rulers may judge with partiality, the Lord would judge with justice and righteousness, and His judgments would be true and fair. For the godly man or woman, the judgment of God was therefore an event to be welcomed, whereas for the unrighteous it was an event to be feared. Translated into a Christian perspective this meant that for some individuals the eschatological judgment brought an eternal hope; for others the same judgment brought eternal despair.

1. The Person of the Judge. In his *Theological Lectures* Roby made a direct equation between Jehovah and Jesus Christ, and this identification was at the root of Roby's doctrine of the Trinity.[28] Roby's explicit identification of the two is unusual, not because it breaks the logic of orthodox Christian theology, but because most Christian theologians hesitated in applying the Hebrew designation 'Jehovah' to Christ as the second person of the Trinity. The Greek equivalent of Jehovah (*κυριος* or Lord) was applied without hesitation, but it was not traditional to apply the Old Testament holy name so directly. Nevertheless, Roby did, and rightly in our view. As such, Jesus became Jehovah, the eschatological Judge. Christ as Judge was clearly taught by the New Testament writers, and this role was emphasised by Moffat, who taught that all would meet before the judgment seat of Christ.[29] *Brown's Catechism*

---

25 RM, *Journal,* 21.4.1827, (*AAK,* 248). See also: RM, *To Mary Moffat,* 25.4.1827, (*AAK,* 265).

26 RM, *Journal,* 8.4.1824, (*AAK,* 142).

27 RM, *Africa,* 27.

28 E.g. Roby, *Theol. Lect.* 37, 'The Creation of man': 'The body of man may be said to have been created in the image of God, likewise because it was made after the form of that body which *Jesus Jehovah* had determined to assume in the fullness of time.'

29 RM, *Journal,* 6.10.1854, (*MJ1,* 324).

also underlined this strong doctrine of Jesus Christ as the eschatological Judge of all the nations.[30]

2. Eternal Hope. It was the aged Moffat who mused over his own eternal hope. In 1880, on the day following his 85th birthday, he wrote to Emma Sapworth: 'All we need, all we can desire, is to be ready for heavenly eternal years in the presence of our dear Redeemer.'[31] What is significant in this tiny extract is that for Moffat heaven was Christ-centred. This corresponded to his pietist outlook. The attraction of heaven was not immortality in itself, but being with Christ. Jesus was the focus of the Christian hope, and theology was personalised in the person of Jesus. It was this faith which the evangelical missionary sought to communicate to others, that they might also know Jesus and his love.

3. Eternal Reward. Side by side with his expression of confidence in the future outcome, Moffat betrayed a whimsical perplexity concerning the heart of faith and life. On his death bed in 1883, 'he talked with wonderful vigour of the mysteriousness of Providence and was evidently clinging to the hope of the restitution of all things, but wound up with the words, "It is all a mystery. Will not the Judge of all the earth do right?"'.[32] Despite such wondering, there was appreciation of having victory in the struggle in which he had been engaged. The Psalm which Moffat looked to during his last days was Psalm 34, which celebrates the victory of the servant of God over forces which had opposed the Lord's work. The note is triumph and achievement. The enemies of God are scattered. The Kingdom has come, in the life of the Lord's servant. The judgment of God is faced in confidence, though the reward will be proportionate to what has been achieved. As Moffat said, many years earlier: 'Meet again some of us never shall, till we meet at the bar of God to receive our reward according to the deeds done in the body.'[33]

4. Eternal Loss. If the believer anticipates eternal glory, the unrepentant sinner is faced with eternal loss. In his 1840 LMS *Sermon,* Moffat insisted that those who had not heard the Gospel would go to hell.[34] The young Moffat in 1822 also had firm beliefs concerning the lost: 'As to Jehovah, a Saviour, Heaven, Hell, the Soul's immortality, and a day of retribution, which they [Tswana] hear from the missionaries, [these] are neither understood nor

---

30 *Brown's Catechism,* Qu. 47 & 48.

31 RM, *To Miss Sapworth,* 22.12.1880, (SOAS/CWM/Africa/Moffat/Pers/4).

32 JSM, *Lives,* 425.

33 RM, *Barbican Sermon,* 22.1.1843, (*Farewell Services,* 99).

34 RM, *Africa,* 45.

believed by any.'[35] In 1829, Moffat had commented that the thousands *dancing down to the gulf of black despair* had not the slightest idea of their immortality, the being of a God, or a future state.[36] The 'gulf of black despair' was a future without Christ and without salvation. A few days later Moffat repeated this concern: 'Lord, enlighten their darkness. Deliver them from going down to the pit.'[37] In 1835, among the Ndebele, he wrote: 'It excites a gloomy reflection to think that all these people are dancing headlong to everlasting *torment*. Their ignorance is deplorable."[38] Moffat did not hide the solemn doctrine of hell behind ambiguous words. As previously cited, in 1827, whilst living among the BaRolong, he jotted:

> This afternoon, sitting on my fore chest, I entered into conversation with a young widow, who seemed more sprightly than wise. My first question was: what would become of her after death? She stared at me with the utmost astonishment, as if she had said, 'Shall I die?' repeating my question, assuring her that death would spare neither of us, she at last answered, that she knew not.
>
> I gave her a plain scriptural answer, namely that *she should go to hell if she died in her present state. I added that the wicked would be turned into hell, etc., etc.,* and pointed out that she was really of the number that forgot God. She looked at me, and added, 'You are a man of wisdom, how can you talk in that way?' I put the same question to an old man who stood by, who replied that he thought he should not die, because he would not think of it. I made a few remarks about the certainty of death, when he walked off.[39]

Elsewhere, Moffat wrote of missionaries 'weeping over immortal souls, who, after having been brought within sight of the haven of eternal rest, despising the day of their visitation, have perished'.[40] On another occasion he added: 'I tell the Bakuenas who hear me that if they will not listen to divine instructions and learn to read, they will continue ignorant, will die in ignorance of the Saviour, die miserably and go to perdition'.[41] Moffat's message was no different from what was being preached in Scotland, and no different from the doctrine stated in *Brown's Catechism* which was designed for children. The message for Africa was the same as that for the home front.

Moffat's anxiety over this issue is strongly reflected in an entry in which he expressed frustration at being unable to communicate directly with

---

35 RM, *To Alexander Moffat,* 25.2.1822, (*AAK,* 57).
36 RM, *Journal,* 1829, (*MJ1,* 21), (our italics).
37 RM, *Journal,* 14.1.1835, (*MJ1,* 113).
38 RM, *Journal,* 1829, (*MJ1,* 111).
39 RM, *Journal,* 21.4.1827, (*AAK,* 247f). See also the entry for 21.5.1827, (*AAK,* 253f).
40 RM, *MLSSA,* 212.
41 RM, *Journal,* 6.6.1854, (*MJ1,* 170).

Moselekatse: '[He] paid me a very short visit in the evening when the interpreter was absent. It is a terrible barrier, not to know the language of a people who are dancing on to everlasting *destruction*.'[42] Death would bring an irreversible finality. In 1857, he mused: 'To die and be the next moment in the overwhelming radiance of the divine glory *or in unquenchable flames*, startles and alarms. A single moment, and a destiny eternal is fixed.'[43] There is little doubt that Moffat would preach in similar fashion, using dramatic metaphors. The phrases have signs of polished usage, presumably through frequent preaching on the utter finality of death. In 1859, he wrote that some of Moselekatse's subjects whom he knew before were now dead, commenting: 'Some two or three more whom I knew are gone, *forever*. Shall we know the destiny of such in the other world?"[44] The Day of Judgment would bring divine wrath and punishment upon the unsaved Sinner.

The Sovereignty of God

Did Moffat adopt the doctrine of predestination which was predominant in Reformed theology? There is no doubt that Moffat had a strong doctrine of the Sovereignty of God, with that powerfully expressed in his understanding of divine providence. Mary was of the same mind, writing in 1823: 'Mr. Wright may come to the people for which he was *destined*.'[45] Robert also alluded to God's detailed plan for each life in an extract written in 1857, in which, reflecting on the dangers he faced, he wrote:

> There is an old saying and a true one, 'Never ventured, never won'. Although it is [a] duty to adopt all the means of self-preservation in our power, we find [it] absolutely necessary to exercise unshaken faith in the Divine promise and Divine government. For, as Dr Cumming justly remarks, 'There are no trifles in the biography of man'. Saith the Scripture, 'Man's goings are of the Lord'. *Every little link, no matter how small, makes up the chain of events in human life*.[46]

It would be unreasonable to take his expression 'every little link, no matter how small, makes up the chain of events in human life' as indicating a deterministic fatalism. The phrase does not warrant that. Moreover, Moffat's comments on Van der Kemp's perceived extreme notions of predestination also point away from such a conclusion.[47] And when we consider Moffat's

---

42 RM, *Journal*, 19.7.1835, (*MJ1*, 118f).
43 RM, *Journal*, 11.10.1857, (*MJ2*, 94).
44 RM, *Journal*, 1.11.1859, (*MJ2*, 210).
45 Mary Moffat, *To James & Mary Smith*, 1.9.1823, (*AAK*, 108).
46 RM, *Journal*, 31.8.1857, (*MJ2*, 49), (our italics).
47 RM, *MLSSA*, 42.

theology in relation to the extreme Calvinist view that Christ only died for specific individuals who were predestined for salvation, then there is little evidence of Moffat holding such a doctrine. Moffat believed that Christ died for everyone:

> Were we always able to have a lively view of the myriads who are descending to the horrible pit, our zeal would be proportionate. Much depends on us who have received the ministry of reconciliation, assured that God our Saviour willeth the salvation of all.[48]

Nowhere in his writings did Moffat make any reference to a chosen number being the only ones who could respond to the Gospel. It is true he wrote that divine 'omnipotence' is the only power able to bring salvation and to convert obdurate hearts,[49] but there is no suggestion that his notion of 'omnipotence' was based on irresistible grace or divine determinism:

> Let each remember that great as is Jehovah's arm, and great as is the redemption purchased by Christ, this will avail nothing without the labour of man. Omnipotent as Jehovah's arm is—and I know that what I am saying is not heterodox—he saves only by means. These means have been put into your hands, into my hands, and into the hands of the church [prayer] ... I do not quote one text in the way it is sometimes quoted: 'Paul MAY plant and Apollos may water.' It is a simple and historical fact that 'Paul planted, Apollos watered, and God gave the means'. I will, however, say again, that God will not give the increase unless we labour, unless we work.[50]

Within the omnipotence and sovereignty of God, Moffat believed that active human agency was required in mission work. But what about assurance? Moffat often wrote positively concerning his future hope of eternal life, but there were occasions when he seemed to doubt the certainty of his salvation. These moments may have been exceptions to his settled view, but they demonstrate that he did not always enjoy an unshakeable assurance. Whilst at Moselekatse's kraal in 1857, he wrote at great length one evening on

---

48 RM, *To Richard Moffat,* 28.7.1834, (JSM, *Lives,* 181f).

49 RM, *Journal,* 6.8.1854, (*MJ1,* 256f), wrote concerning Moselekatse: 'The conversion of such a man seems stupendous, but nothing is too hard for omnipotence; but where the ears are hermetically sealed against knowledge conversion is impossible.' 'Omnipotence' was referred to again by Moffat only a few days later when he wrote on the status of women among the Ndebele. Cf. RM, Journal, 24.8.1854, (MJ1, 268): 'The females were observing [our evening worship] and making their remarks on our peculiar custom; at least it must appear such to them, the last to be reached when the Gospel shall obtain a hearing among this people. Alas, the prospect is dark, but Omnipotence has declared: "I shall be exalted among the nations"'. The Scripture reference is Psalm 46:10: texts from Psalms came readily to his mind.

50 RM, *Barbican Sermon,* (*Farewell Services,* 125f).

death and his attitude to it. This extended meditation reveals much of Moffat's reflection on his faith:

> I only hope and pray that these single seeds of divine truth may yet spring forth and bear a harvest, when you, dear Mary, and I are—where? What an awful thought! The moment after death settles our destiny forever. Forever![51]

When Moffat pondered, 'When you, dear Mary, and I are—where?', was he wondering where he and Mary would be on earth when the seed of the gospel finally flourished among the Ndebele? Or was he pondering his and Mary's eternal destiny? The sense of the sentence, especially the last few words, favours the latter interpretation. Did he not have full assurance concerning his salvation? His form of words could, of course, simply be a humble way of describing one's eternal future. It may have been considered presumptuous to vaunt spiritual assurance. It may have been that even a person who, theologically and spiritually, had no doubts about being in Christ, would speak of the future only tentatively. But Moffat was writing to Mary, his wife, and we would expect him to be direct with her. This tentative way, in which Moffat wrote of his eternal future, was expressed even more intensely in some sentences written later in that day's entry in his *Journal*:

> But, Mary, there are mysteries to me overwhelming, and depths unfathomable in the dispensation of God's mercy to the world. I know the Scriptures, and you will say I ought to know them, and in all my childish ignorance and perplexity there is no text that affords me more consolation than that of *John 3:16* and what Paul calls a 'faithful saying'.[52] With these blessed words *I think I can enter death and enter heaven with a hope resting alone on the Lamb of God*. But who can help being perplexed when they gaze of the untold myriads of stars with which the whole heavens are bespangled … what is man![53]

These hints, that perhaps Moffat doubted his eternal destiny are, in our opinion, fleeting exceptions to a fundamental assurance concerning his salvation. These are the doubts which almost every believer has at one time or another. Much deeper than doubt was a foundation of positive Christian hope. Indeed, having just expressed the above, Moffat continued:

> It is good to think of death. I often do so: perhaps oftener than people who see me daily can possibly think. The impression is sometimes so

---

51 RM, *Journal,* 11.10.1857, (*MJ2,* 93).

52 The Pauline letters have five 'faithful sayings', four of which are relevant to assurance.

53 RM, *Journal,* 11.10.1857, (*MJ2,* 95). In the Westminster tradition 'assurance' was considered to be of the essence of true faith. Paradoxically, this created within Presbyterian piety a culture of doubt as to the certainty of eternal security.

> overwhelming that I wonder if I am still in the body. I feel as if I would like to leap to glory – Paul's wish.[54]

As his life approached its end, Moffat had peace about what was to come: 'I feel a growing desire to spend my future in praise and prayer. Of course, it is natural that one at my age should be frequently looking at the 'goodly land' beyond the 'narrow stream'. The prospect is sublimely grand.'[55]

---

54 RM, *Journal,* 11.10.1857, (*MJ2,* 93f).

55 RM, *To William Dickson,* 19.7.1883, (EUNCL/WD9/3/24/Box 2).

The Creation of a Christian Church

Chapter 23
The Essence of a Church

IN RUTH TUCKER'S VIEW, a weakness of some missionary organisations was that they established mission stations rather than churches.[1] The validity of her argument depends upon which definition of 'church' is being considered. It is arguable that the polity of Congregationalism, which Moffat and most LMS missionaries promoted, meant that a mission station was automatically regarded as a Church in the full sense. Presbyterianism requires a system of church courts. Anglicanism requires a hierarchy of deacon, priest and Bishop.[2] But Congregationalism simply requires there to be a group of Christian believers, meeting together under rudimentary rules, for a church to be constituted, with leadership, discipline, and ordination carried out under the authority of the local congregation, which is itself subject to no external authority.[3] If LMS mission stations were looked at through the eyes of an Anglican, Lutheran, or Presbyterian, they may well seem only to be 'mission stations'; but if viewed by an Independent Congregationalist they were fully fledged churches.

THE FORMATION OF A CHURCH

Part of the opposition from the Moderate faction, at the Church of Scotland 1796 General Assembly, towards Missionary Societies was the suspicion that such Societies would eventually constitute themselves as churches in their own right. This was why, when Greville Ewing later defended the formation of Societies dedicated to foreign mission, he argued that Missionary Societies

---

1 Ruth Tucker, *From Jerusalem to Irian Jaya,* (Grand Rapids: Zondervan, 1983).

2 In Anglican missions the church was only considered as truly existing where there was a bishop: 'Where is the bishop, there is the church.' Cf. J.W. Barrow, *A Brief History of the Bloemfontein Mission, South Africa, from its Commencement to 1876, Part 1,* (Ldn: Hayes, 1876), 5.

3 Wardlaw, *Congregational Independency,* 232, defined Congregationalism/ Independency as, 'The full competency of every distinct Church to manage, without appeal, its own affairs.' Klaus Fiedler, *The Story of Faith Missions,* pointed out that Churches established by Congregationalist missionaries usually developed a Presbyterian-like form of governance, through copying the structures of the mission organisation which had given it birth. A local church which had started as a mission station, tended to see itself still within a chain of authority.

were not churches, and that they could not, and would not, take upon themselves the authority to ordain ministers.[4] The LMS followed this policy.

When Moffat was ordained on 30 September 1816[5] in the Surrey Chapel London, the ordination was carried out by ministers acting in their capacity as members of the Congregational Church, and not as members of the LMS—even though all of them were LMS stalwarts. Similarly, in 1840, Livingstone was ordained by the Congregational Church and not by the LMS.[6] In this way the LMS sought to defuse suspicion and sought to fulfill its ecumenical vision of accepting ministers from all denominations. At the founding of the LMS in September 1794, the Church of England clergyman, the Rev. Dr Haweis, had preached on Mark 16:15f, setting out an encompassing ecumenical vision:

> No scheme of worldly advantage, no project of vain ambition, no selfish ends or aims, contaminate our views. The petty distinctions among us, of names and forms, the diversities of administrations, and modes of church order, we agree shall this day all be merged in the greater, nobler, characteristic name of Christians.[7]

Next day, at another session of the LMS founding conference, David Bogue expressed the same sentiment, employing a memorable phrase which stated that the conference delegates were: 'assembled with one accord, to *attend the funeral of bigotry*, and I hope it will be buried so deep, as never to rise again.'[8] Bogue's inspired oratory was received with thunderous acclaim by the packed gathering.

As the years passed, and as specific denominations formed their own strategies for mission, the original all-inclusive nature of the LMS gradually changed, and it became more markedly linked with Congregationalism. This drift was unsurprising since many of its founders were already of that

---

4 Ewing: *A Defence of Missions from Christian Societies to the Heathen World: An Address to the Edinburgh Missionary Society,* 2.2.1797 (Edin: Ritchie, 1797).

5 JSM, *Lives,* 415, stated, concerning a visit made to Manchester by Moffat in 1881: 'The most interesting service was the one at Grosvenor Street, where 65 years before he had been *ordained* to mission work by William Roby.' Other records indicate that Moffat's formal ordination was at the service in Surrey Chapel London. JSM used the term 'ordination' loosely, in the sense of being commissioned to missionary work.

6 The certificate of Livingstone's 20 November 1840 ordination in London makes it clear that he was ordained by ministers of the Congregational Church in virtue of his membership of the Congregational Church in Hamilton, Scotland (NLS/10778/13). Though most of the ministers who officiated at his ordination ceremony were in the LMS, the ordination was carried out in virtue of their denominational qualification, not their LMS connections.

7 Haweis, *Sermon on Mark 16:15, 16,* (21.9.1794), quoted by Ellis, *The History of the London Missionary Society, Vol. 1,* (Ldn: John Snow, 1844), 25.

8 Bogue, *Sermon on Haggai 1:2,* 22.9.1794, (Ellis, *The History of the LMS, Vol. 1,* 30), (our italics). Cf. LMS, *Transactions, Vol. 1: 1795-1802,* (Ldn: LMS, 1804), xv.

persuasion. Nevertheless, the ecumenical founding principles of the LMS did attempt to break down barriers between denominations and amongst Christians of an evangelical persuasion; the LMS had noteworthy success in that direction. Throughout its existence, it remained a society with which Christians from many Protestant denominations felt they had an affinity.[9]

Before the LMS was formed, the Particular Baptist Mission had already been created through the influence of William Carey. In contrast to that society, the LMS was explicitly an paedo-baptist organisation. Thus in the 1820s, when William Orme redrafted the form of questions to be put to candidates who sought service with the LMS, he made it clear that candidates must be comfortable with infant baptism. Apart from Baptists, the LMS embraced a wide Protestant catholicity. Given that ecumenicity, the LMS adopted the following fundamental principle at its Annual Meeting in May 1796, regarding the establishment of churches in the field:

> As the union of Christians of various denominations, in carrying on this great work, is a most desirable object; so, to prevent, if possible, any cause of future dissension, it is declared to be a *fundamental principle* of the MISSIONARY SOCIETY, that its design is not to send Presbyterianism, Independency, , or any other form of Church Order and Government (about which there may be differences of opinion among serious persons) but the glorious Gospel of the blessed God, to the Heathen: and that it should be left (as it ought to be left) to the minds of the persons whom God may call into the fellowship of his Son from among them, to assume for themselves such form of Church Government as to them shall appear most agreeable to the Word of God.[10]

In theory, this meant that converts could choose their own form of church polity, but in practice this choice would rest with the missionary. John Philip, the LMS Superintendent in South Africa, confirmed that LMS missionaries could organise a station according to their preferred ecclesiology:

> It is altogether contrary to my principles, which I have learned from the New Testament, and contrary to the regulations of the London Missionary Society, for the agent [Philip] of that Society to interfere with the discipline of the Church of Christ in Africa. The Directors send out Lutherans, Presbyterians, and Independents, and allow them to form Churches and regulate them according to their own views. Any interference on my part with the discipline of one Church would at once violate the fundamental rule of the Society, and open a door to great abuse ... I have no more connection with the receiving or exclusion of members from the church at Lattakoo, than Mr. Moffat has to

---

[9] The LMS began in 1795 as The Missionary Society. Soon it became The London Missionary Society. In 1966 it became The Congregational Council for World Mission. From 1977 has been The Council for World Mission.

[10] LMS, *Transactions, Vol. 1, 1795-1802,* xx.

> do with the receiving or exclusion of members in the church with which I am connected at Aberdeen, or with Mr. Roby's church at Manchester. The church at Lattakoo has the sole power in the matter.[11]

The said 'Mr Moffat' agreed with Philip on the ecclesiastical independence of each mission station/church. But 'Mr Moffat' would also, with the same logic, question the policy of the LMS in setting up Philip as a 'Superintendent' over such churches. Had the LMS set in place a Bishop? The argument that Philip was simply the LMS agent in southern Africa, helping to connect the parent body with missionaries in the field, did not impress Moffat.

It is important to note that Moffat's objection to one person—rather than a body of believers—having overall authority, predated Philip's arrival in Africa. As early as 1817, at the Cape Town 'Synod' there had been consideration of Van der Kemp's rule: 'Every missionary station must be under the direction of one missionary to whom, from time to time, as many brethren shall be added as assistants as the state of the settlement may require.' Moffat immediately objected: 'I disapprove of this rule as being contrary to the spirit of the Gospel.'[12]

At the heart of Moffat's objection was his dislike of the notion that *one* missionary should have such authority. Moffat's position was supported by his fellow missionary Pacalt, who was recorded as saying: 'To put all missionaries under one is to establish a Bishopric or Church of England, and most of the Directors are dissenters. It is inconsistent with the Word of God.' That discussion sheds light not only on Moffat's overall ecclesiology, but also on the roots of his later antipathy to Philip's superintendence role. Yet, as Northcott has wryly pointed out, in view of Moffat's own dislike of committees and his 'tendency to autocracy', Moffat's intervention was amusingly inconsistent![13]

THE CONSTITUTION OF A CHURCH

Moffat's early introduction to Independency/Congregationalism through his mother taking him to Robert Caldwell's Bank Street congregation in Falkirk was reinforced by his later membership of William Roby's congregation in

---

[11] Philip, *To Robert Hamilton,* 18.1.1822, (*AAK,* 69, fn. 43). When Philip arrived in Cape Town as LMS Superintendent, he also agreed to become minister of the Calvinistic Society Church, on condition that the first claims on his time were his missionary duties, and that, in the congregation which he served, the church meeting would be the governing authority. It was named Union Church because initially Congregationalists and Presbyterians together comprised its membership (Briggs & Wing, *The Harvest and the Hope,* 38).

[12] 1817 Synod Minutes, 13.8.1817, (SOAS/CWM/Box 7/2/C).

[13] Northcott, *Robert Moffat,* 35f.

Manchester. Roby argued that, according to Scripture, true churches are not Parochial, Diocesan, Provincial, National, Presbyterian or Methodistical, but simply Congregational.[14] In Roby's theology, Congregationalism brought a restoration of the original simplicity of the New Testament pattern. The fact that this ecclesiology was termed Congregationalist was unimportant. Far more important to Roby was his belief that this was how the New Testament Church had organised its life under the guidance of the Holy Spirit. Moffat followed Roby, claiming that the form of discipline operative at Kuruman was 'exercised according to the example of the ancient Church.'[15]

Bogue, as the LMS theological tutor responsible for training men who had come from various denominations, had a more ecumenical approach. This was despite being personally convinced of Congregationalism, having left the Church of Scotland on that specific principle prior to his licensing. When, in his *Missionary Lectures,* Bogue gave advice for the organisation of a mission station, he attempted to give non-denominational guidelines, only stressing that 'simplicity in Church government is an excellence to be sought for'.[16] Albeit a Congregationalist by conviction, Bogue did not object to the offices of Bishop and Deacon, so long as these were applied in what he regarded as a simple New Testament way: 'There should be as little about regulation of the church to awaken ambition and covetousness as possible'.

Bogue built his ecclesiology on what he saw as a Scriptural pattern. Yet he believed that there was one vital difference between the New Testament era and the present time. He held that, in the New Testament Church, the Holy Spirit enabled astonishingly rapid advances in spiritual maturity, whereas in the contemporary mission situation more time was required: 'As there were in the Apostolic Churches extraordinary gifts bestowed on men for the work of the ministry, it will now require a much longer time before persons be qualified for offices in the Church than in that age.' Accordingly, Bogue discouraged rapid promotion of new converts, despite being convinced of the importance of indigenous leadership.

Bogue taught that great care had to be taken in the nurture of converts, and that the missionary should not underestimate the task involved in converts fully changing from heathenism to Christ. Nevertheless, his aim was to produce local leadership, with local teachers, and local ministry. However, only converts of the highest calibre should be given responsibility: 'So much depends on the gifts and graces, zeal and piety of bishops; everything should

---

14 Roby, *Theol. Lect.* 77, 'Church Fellowship', 431.

15 RM, *Journal,* 29/31.7.1821, (*AAK,* 20).

16 Bogue, *Miss. Lect.* 21, 'Establishment of Churches among the Heathen'.

be done so that they might be men of God.'[17] Bogue felt free to use the term 'bishop', attempting to be consciously ecumenical. Equally importantly, Bogue considered established LMS mission stations as churches, even though the LMS was not one itself. Given that Bogue's ecclesiology was a Congregationalist one, there was no theological hurdle for Bogue to cross for him to declare mission station fellowships as 'proper' churches.

Like Bogue, Moffat worked with Congregationalist principles. The ruling body in church life at Kuruman was the church meeting, and the book used as the *Kuruman Church Record Book* was an official Congregationalist publication.[18] There is no doubt that Moffat viewed Kuruman mission station as a church in the fullest sense, modelled on a Congregationalist and Independency ecclesiology. It was a community with ordained ministers, where the Word was preached, the sacraments dispensed, and discipline exercised.[19]

Moffat regularly used the term 'church' when referring to Kuruman, meaning the people, not the building. In 1854 he wrote to Mary: 'Kind regards to the Ashtons and the Fredoux, and also to the members of the church and domestics'.[20] In that extract, 'church' clearly referred to the community of believers. Yet the physical church building, as the 'house of God', was also important, giving a locus for Christians to meet as a congregation and fulfill all the features of regular church life. Whilst at Moselekatse's headquarters in 1854, Moffat wrote: 'I often think of the Kuruman, but [I feel the] absence from the house of God and its ordinances,

---

17 Ibid.

18 The *Kuruman Church Record Book (KCRB)* is held in the archives of the *Kuruman Moffat Mission Library* (Box A3: KCRB-A3). It has data from 1825 to 1880, with most entries in Moffat's handwriting. His last entry was 6.3.1870, thereafter the majority were by JSM. The book was an official Congregationalist publication, with several printed pages expounding Congregationalist principles. The printed inside title of the *Record Book* states: RECORDS OF THE CONGREGATIONAL CHURCH ASSEMBLING AT [Here Moffat wrote: '*Chapel of the L.M. Society Seoring-Kuruman, and of the Out-stations thereto belonging*] WITH THE DECLARATION OF FAITH AND CHURCH ORDER PUBLISHED FOR THE CONGREGATIONAL UNION OF ENGLAND AND WALES. There is then a printed statement that: 'The Declaration of Faith and Church Order was adopted in 1833 ('as a Declaration only and not as a Test or Creed for Subscription')'. This is followed by a 'Declaration of Faith and Church Order', printed over the next few pages. The *KCRB* is clearly a standard church *Record Book* for any Congregationalist Church in England and Wales. Whilst dates range from 1825 to 1880, the book may only have come into operation in 1852, with earlier data inserted from previous records.

19 Scottish Presbyterianism defined a Church as existing where: 'The Word was rightly preached, the sacraments rightly celebrated, and discipline rightly exercised.' These were the standard *nota ecclesia* of Reformed ecclesiology.

20 RM, *To Mary Moffat,* 11.6.1854, (*MJ1,* 180).

the people of God and their well-known voices in prayer and praise.'[21] Moffat was describing a church, not simply a mission station. Other examples could be cited, and it is difficult to see how Ruth Tucker's point that mission stations were not churches applied to Kuruman. In Moffat's view, Kuruman required no extra ecclesiastical superstructures to qualify as a church.

THE ECUMENICITY OF A CHURCH

As a young man Moffat experienced a wide range of denominations: Presbyterianism, Scottish Congregationalism, Methodism, Anglicanism, and English Independency. The LMS also encouraged a catholicity of spirit. Moffat's own ministry at Kuruman was never seriously threatened by the intrusion of a rival mission or denomination, and so his instinctive bonhomie toward other Christians and missions was never put under strain by competing interests in the local situation. In Africa, Moffat had good relationships with Wesleyans (especially Barnabas Shaw), Moravians, and other mission groups. He also had warm fellowship with individuals of the Dutch Reformed Church, despite a strong antipathy toward what the Boer community stood for.[22]

1. Anglicans. As a young gardener in England, Moffat had been unimpressed by Anglicanism. Yet it was in the Anglican St George's Cathedral, Cape Town, that Robert married Mary on 27 December 1819. As time passed, the influence on South African Anglicanism by the Oxford Movement, plus its emphasis on baptismal regeneration, reinforced seeds of suspicion in Moffat's mind concerning the denomination. He shared the evangelical aversion to ritual, and this resulted in him also having reservations about German Lutheran missionaries who worked with Sechele's BaKwena in the 1850s, though he eventually developed a working relationship with them.

---

[21] RM, *To Mary Moffat,* 30.7.1854, (*MJ1,* 247). On another Sabbath, whilst traveling beyond Moselekatse's headquarters, Moffat wistfully reflected on the Kuruman church. See: RM, To Mary Moffat, 27.8.1854, (MJ1, 275): 'While in all probability you, with the Kuruman friends, are assembled in the house of God, either singing his praises, engaged in prayer, or hearing his voice, here I am sitting in my wagon.' Following his reluctant decision to go no further in his attempt to find Livingstone, he wrote dejectedly, 'I think enough about the Kuruman and your assemblies there on the Sabbath for the whole week. "How lovely are thy tabernacles"', see: RM, *To Mary Moffat,* 10.9.1854, (*MJ1,* 296f).

[22] This included a brief connection with the Murrays of Stellenbosch, staying with them whilst travelling from Cape Town to Kuruman. Cf. Ben Conradie, *Andrew Murray no Honderd Jaar,* (Stellenbosch: Christen Studenten Verenigingmaatskappij, 1951), 8,27. The obstacles which Boer racism put in the way of the LMS fellowshipping with the Dutch Reformed Church did not stop Moffat from arguing that it should be consulted on the work of Bible translation into SeTswana. Cf. RM, *To Bergne, BFBS,* 18.10.1869 (CULBSA/ BFBSEC/ Inwards/7/107).

2. Roman Catholics. If Anglican theology was suspect, Roman Catholicism was totally unacceptable! There was no Roman Catholic mission anywhere near Kuruman during Moffat's entire ministry, and this was just as well since his attitude to Roman Catholicism was decidedly antagonistic. In Moffat's view the Church of Rome was 'Babylon the Harlot', a moniker which echoed Presbyterian and Congregationalist antipathy toward Rome:

> Had it not been for British power and British sympathy,[23] under the favour of Heaven, Africa, to this day, with scarcely one exception, might have had the tri-coloured flag waving on her bosom, bearing the ensigns of the mystery of Babylon, the crescent of the false prophet, and the emblems of pagan darkness, from the shores of the Mediterranean to the Colony of the Cape of Good Hope.[24]

Moffat identified three powerful spiritual forces which, in his view, brought darkness instead of gospel light. The 'tri-coloured flag' bearing the 'ensigns of Babylon' was French colonisation with its attendant Roman Catholicism. The 'crescent of the false prophet' was Islam. The 'emblems of paganism' referred to African Traditional Religion. Of all these dangers, the first-mentioned, and the most important, was Catholicism.

3. Wesleyans. Moffat owed much to Methodism and had warm feelings toward any of its missionaries. Robert and Mary's children, after being schooled for a few years at Kuruman, were sent to a Wesleyan School near Cape Town. In 1877 Moffat wrote to a Methodist friend: 'I have always felt an attachment [to Methodism]; and have had the honour and the privilege of much delightful intercourse with the missionaries of that society since the days of Barnabas Shaw.'[25] Wesleyan missionaries shared a common evangelical piety with Moffat, creating an instinctive oneness of spirit.

4. ABCFM. In 1836, some missionaries from the *American Board of Commissioners for Foreign Missions (ABCFM)* came to live and work with Moselekatse's Ndebele, although their enterprise was short lived. Moffat gave them all the assistance he could, and they stayed at Kuruman for some months on their outward journey. Among the American missionaries were

---

23 Moffat alluded to British victory in the Napoleonic wars. The threat of Napoleon and the possibility of French Catholic domination was the threat Moffat feared for the first twenty years of his life. This was part of the background of his spiritual formation. Scottish schoolmasters had to take an Oath of Allegiance, specifically against the background of revolutionary tendencies coming from France.

24 RM, *MLSSA,* 2. The same three evils of Paganism, Islam, and Roman Catholicism, were cited in: RM, *Africa,* 28.

25 RM, *To a Wesleyan Minister,* 7.1.1877, in: Jabez Marrat, *Robert Moffat: African Missionary,* (Ldn: Woolmer, 1884), 4.

Alexander Erwin Wilson and his wife Mary Jane Wilson, whose first-born daughter, Martha Smithey Wilson, was born at Kuruman on 15 January 1836. Sadly, Mrs Wilson died on 18 September later that year, in Moselekatse's country. On Moffat's 1835 visit to Moselekatse he had tried to prepare the Ndebele chief for the coming of the missionaries: 'I went in and sat a long time [with Moselekatse] in the afternoon, and had a long conversation on several important points, the coming of the American brethren, their treatment, what he is to expect from them, the doctrine they will teach when once sufficiently acquainted with the language.'[26] The fact of people coming from a different land than Moffat's land, yet with the same doctrines, beliefs and aims, led Moffat to discuss the concept of the 'communion of saints' with Moselekatse:

> This led me to explain in some measure to him the communion of saints, a subject which he, of course, could scarcely comprehend. I assured him that we had one feeling and object in our lives, professing one spirit of one God, our only Father who was in heaven and whose kingdom ruleth over all.[27]

Moffat's God was presented as the Lord over all, with Moffat describing God as beyond tribal boundaries. This would be proved by the fact that different people, from different and widely scattered lands, all followed him and worshipped him. A universal ecumenicity of faith pointed to the universality of the God who was followed. However, the *ABCFM* mission to Moselekatse's Ndebele was soon over. Boer raids during 1836, and especially in 1837, made the missionaries abandon the work in panic as the situation deteriorated. Moselekatse eventually moved hundreds of miles to the north.

5. PEMS. Kuruman had cordial relationships with workers from the *Paris Evangelical Missionary Society.* Robert and Mary's daughter Ann married Jean Fredoux, the *PEMS* missionary at Motito, which was about thirty-six miles from Kuruman. After his retirement, Moffat was invited to Paris to address the *PEMS* in April 1877, which he did to an enormous audience.

6. Hanoverian Lutherans. From the 1840s the LMS worked with Sechele and his BaKwena, with Livingstone and his wife Mary stationed at Kolobeng among the BaKwena from 1847 until 1852. Moffat also sent one of the very first Kuruman converts, Paul, to work full-time (on an LMS salary) with the BaKwena, both during Livingstone's time and after Livingstone left. However, Sechele hankered after a European missionary, not deeming Paul to be a 'proper' Christian worker. When the LMS were unable to supply a European teacher Sechele turned to the Hermannsburg Hanoverian Lutheran Society,

---

[26] RM, *Journal,* 2.8.1835, (*MJ1,* 127).

[27] Ibid.

even though he knew that they were favoured by the hated Boers.[28] Accordingly, in 1857 when Moffat re-visited Sechele's village on the way to the Ndebele, he was surprised to find European missionaries in place. To begin with, Moffat thought they were Moravians and was delighted to meet them. Then it became evident that they were not.[29] Moffat's perplexity had started when he saw a crucifix 'in a rather darkish corner of the missionaries' house on a box.'[30] Despite this, he developed a respect for these 'simple-minded, excellent men'[31] and, on subsequent journeys through Sechele's land, such as in 1859, he readily accepted the Lutheran's hospitality and shared worship.

Apart from the *PEMS*, the Lutheran missionaries were the society working geographically closest to Kuruman, and Moffat's relationship with them is therefore of particular interest. Though their theology differed from Moffat's—especially on the issue of baptism where Moffat feared they held a doctrine of baptismal regeneration[32]—he recognised their work as valid Christian mission. But Moffat had to deal with three main issues concerning the Lutherans: possession of LMS 'property', possible absorption into the LMS, and co-operation in the work of Bible translation.

After 1857, Moffat took the view that since the Lutheran missionaries were now working with Sechele, then no rival missions should work with the same tribe. Accordingly, he withdrew Paul. Nevertheless, the Lutherans were

---

28 Sechele's strange step of approaching the hated Boer Transvaal Government was referred to in a letter to Moffat from the Rev. Dr Augustus Hardeland, Superintendent of the Hanoverian Mission: 'In the year 1857 Sechele, through the Dutch government of the Transvaal, appealed to the Hermannsburg mission for some missionaries. Four missionaries were sent who have erected there three stations; one at Sechele's, Liteyana; one at Nohila's, Linokane; and one at Sekhomi's, Shoshong.' Cf. Hardeland, *To RM,* 17.4.1863, (SOAS/CWN/SA/Box 33/1/B).

29 A clear account of this was given by JSM, *Journal,* 3.6.1863, (*MM,* 202f). JSM stressed that his father was surprised to discover the missionaries with Sechele since, 'their taking possession of the station, ... was a contravention of the principle observed by evangelical missionary societies; for the place was occupied by a paid native agent [Paul] of the LMS who was obliged to withdraw.'

30 RM, *Journal,* 22.8.1857, (*MJ2,* 38).

31 Though the Boers were keen for Sechele to receive the Lutheran missionaries, Moffat did not regard the Lutherans as Boers themselves. Cf. RM, *To Mary Moffat,* 17.8.1857, (*MJ2,* 29f). He saw them as: 'simple-minded, excellent men'. His policy was that if these missionaries were working with Sechele, then Paul should stop his work there, since the policy of missionary societies was not to overlap on each other's fields, (MJ2, 30). Moffat 'enjoyed their society' and taught the missionaries SeTswana so that they could work more effectively (*MJ2*, 32).

32 RM, *To JSM,* 1.9.1860, (*MM,* 114, fn. 2). As well as unease over baptismal regeneration, he would be aware of Roby's view that Lutheran theology on Consubstantiation was as erroneous as Transubstantiation. Cf. Roby, *Theol. Lect.* 76, 'The Lord's Supper'.

worried that the LMS might return to this 'Lutheran sphere of operations'. This fear increased when there was dissension within the Lutheran mission. With that situation in mind, Dr Hardeland, who had overall responsibility for the Hermannsburg Society in South Africa, wrote to Moffat in 1863 seeking an assurance that the LMS would not re-occupy the stations.[33] Moffat had already decided on a policy of non-competition; but in his reply he sharply reminded Hardeland that much of the property, which the Lutherans discovered when they originally arrived, was LMS property.[34] Moffat was content for such resources to be used by others; but in his view the property still belonged to the LMS.

The disagreement within the Lutheran mission brought the possibility of some of the Lutheran missionaries—discontented with Hardeland's type of superintendence—joining the LMS. Moffat saw problems with this if it ever became a concrete proposal. In a letter to John Smith Moffat at Inyati, he wrote: 'Did I inform you in my last that the Hanoverian missionaries whom we know are now living on their own resources as they—I think most justly—will not submit to the superintendent sent out to Port Natal (Durban) with almost unbounded powers. I should not wonder at their offering themselves to our Society, but some of their tenets, especially baptismal regeneration, would be in the way.'[35]

Moffat completed his translation of the Bible into SeTswana in 1857. This translation, including issues of orthography, was subsequently revised by a Kuruman committee which was set up in the 1860s. Moffat knew that the Lutheran missionaries were also working on a translation into SeTswana, and he was anxious that the Tswana enquirers should not be confused by two versions. Hence, he tried to persuade the committee to involve the Lutherans and wrote to the *British and Foreign Bible Society* on the same issue:

---

33 Hardeland, *To RM,* 17.4.1863, (SOAS/CWN/SA/Box 33/1/B).

34 Cf. RM, *To Hardeland,* 8.6.1863, (SOAS/CWN/SA/Box 33/1/B): 'When your missionaries [first] arrived at Liteyana they took possession of a mission station belonging to our society. They found a chapel, a number of church members, and a school supplied with books and lessons etc., and a paid agent conducting the public services and carrying on the school, of which, namely the latter, there now remains little more than a shadow. Your missionaries, when they came, could not hide their surprise at finding things as they saw them, nor did they attempt to deny that they were taking possession of another Society's mission station. This they evidently felt was not the thing, and one which societies have ever felt very great delicacy. They however apologised, by informing me that their Superintendent had written to the Directors of our Society on the subject and that Pastor Thoms was also in communication with our board and that I should have due information on the affair. These letters must never have been received, or I should have been informed.'

35 RM, *To JSM,* 1.9.1860, (*MM,* 114, note 2).

> I had before, and at the Committee, suggested the propriety of those brethren [Hanoverians/Dutch Reformed Church] being consulted. The proposal was not agreed to, which I regretted, for although the Hanoverians who are High Lutherans, differ from us on some points, they have no fault whatever to find with the translations ... and have been a long time in the country.[36]

Moffat grew in respect for the Lutheran missionaries. Though he never lost his unease with their 'rituals', he respected their commitment and viewed them as genuine co-workers in the Gospel.

THE OFFICE OF ORDINATION

Roby was of the view that authority to minister the sacraments went hand in hand with commission to preach the Word. In his *Theological Lectures* he asked: 'Who have a right to dispense the Lord's Supper?' His answer was: 'They who have a commission to preach the gospel'.[37] Yet Roby does not seem to have taken on board the full implications of his position, in which appointment to preach was equivalent to full ordination. In practice, he held that a ceremony of ordination, validated by a congregation, was required before a minister could celebrate the sacraments. It was, of course, of the essence of Congregationalism that the *congregation* validated ordination, and not a Presbytery, Bishop, or any kind of 'higher' authority. Moreover, in Congregationalism, ministers who officiated at such ordinations were mere agents putting into effect the will of the congregation, and they did not, in themselves, carry authority to ordain.[38] Roby also argued in his *Lectures* concerning the appointment and ordination of Church officers: '[Ordained ministers] cannot thrust themselves upon a Church. They ought not to be imposed upon a Church by others. In the primitive Churches they were chosen and appointed by common suffrage.'[39]

Moffat also saw ordination as involving more than simply a licence to preach, and he accepted the propriety of having a regularly ordained person to administer the sacraments. This view was underlined in a letter to his friend James Kitchingham, in which he stated that 'it would not be prudent,

---

36 RM, *To Bergne, BFBS*, 18.10.1869, (CULBSA/BFBSEC/Inwards/7/107).

37 Roby, *Theol. Lect.* 76, 'The Lord's Supper'.

38 Wardlaw, *Congregational Independency,* 318, on the relationship between ministers and congregation: '[Congregationalism] is not properly a system of popular rule, but of pastoral direction and *popular concurrence* in the application and execution of the laws of Christ. The submission enjoined is submission to the preaching and directing pastor or pastors, as the divinely authorised organ, by whom, in each case, the law of Christ is to be pointed out, and, with the concurrent judgment and voice of the church, to be carried into execution.'

39 Roby, *Theol. Lect.* 77, 'Church Fellowship'.

nor in some respects scriptural, that unordained missionaries should administer the ordinances where there are opportunities of being scripturally ordained.'[40] This introduced two issues.

Firstly, by 'scripturally ordained' Moffat meant being ordained by decision and consent of a congregation of believers. Yet, given the opportunities which this accorded to congregations, why were so few indigenous converts ordained by churches which sprang from LMS mission stations? The LMS could not ordain. That was understood. But a church at a mission station, constituted on Congregationalist principles, had authority within itself to ordain its members to the full ministry of word and sacrament. Yet the freedom to do this was never put into effect during Moffat's time at Kuruman. Moffat had several long-standing native teachers whom he respected, such as Paul who worked with the BaKwena. But Paul was never ordained. The first ordained native African to work at Kuruman was Maphakela Lekalake, who was in charge of the Station from 1911 to 1947. Perhaps Moffat regarded Kuruman as having a plethora of ordained European missionaries, and saw no need to ordain more. But ordination of Africans would surely have encouraged the development, growth, dignity and self-esteem of African Christians. This question, and related issues, is further examined when we consider native teachers in Moffat's missiology in chapter 31.

Secondly, Moffat's phrase, 'where there are opportunities', indicates that *in extremis* Moffat might approve of an unordained person administering the sacraments. What does a totally isolated lone missionary do? Does he serve himself with the bread and wine of the Lord's Supper? Moffat felt this was inappropriate. In 1818 he had written to the LMS directors explaining his predicament as he worked totally on his own among Africaner's Namaqua:

> You will recollect that though I am daily engaged in exhibiting the excellency and power of our Redeemer's blood and righteousness, yet I am not permitted to enjoy the privilege of a common Christian in England, I mean the receiving of the Lord's Supper. I know that this is not the wish of the Directors, nor was it when they appointed me to labour with an ordained Brother; but now I am alone. I ask, must I continue so or expect an ordained Brother?[41]

Moffat was a low-churchman. Nevertheless, he believed that regularly constituted ordination, carried out according to the polity of a recognised denomination, was important for good order in the Church. In Moffat's theology, ordination was for functional purposes relative to the sacraments,

---

40 RM, *To Kitchingham,* 27.10.1818, (Le Cordeur, *Kitchingham Papers,* 54).

41 RM, *To Burder, LMS,* 22.6.1818, (SOAS/CWM/SA/Box 7/4/B).

and did not confer any higher authority, since authority lay with the congregation, and not with individuals. At the same time, ordination was still important.

For Robert Moffat, the task of the evangelical missionary was not to bring the Church as an institution, with its multiplicity of offices, to a people. The task of the missionary was to do the work of the church, which was to sow the seed of the Word of God. And for Moffat, if a person were engaged in the ministry of the Word, then there was no need to aspire to 'higher' office. There was none.

Chapter 24
The Life of a Church

WHAT WORSHIPPING COMMUNITY existed at Kuruman? Though a description of church life at Kuruman by the Rev. John Mackenzie comes from 1859, which is a comparatively late date, there would be no essential difference from what happened then to events in any year. Mackenzie depicted a typical Sabbath at the station. Many of the worshippers brought a large bag. Some carried a chair on their shoulder. The bag contained the three-volume Sechuana Bible and their hymn book. After the people assembled, the minister of the day ascended the pulpit, and the service started with praise. The service then proceeded with the reading and exposition of Scripture, succeeded by solemn prayer. A sermon or lecture followed, in which the preacher strove 'to reproduce some incident in the sacred narrative – some parable or doctrine, so as to impress its lesson on the minds of his audience.'[1]

In 1859 there were three such services on a Sunday, all in SeTswana. The evening one was attended chiefly by cattle-herders, bird-frighteners at the gardens, and others who could not come during the day. During the week there was also a public evening service conducted by one of the missionaries, and another entirely in the hands of one of the indigenous believers.

THE SACRAMENT OF BAPTISM

The Kuruman Baptismal register—contained within the *Kuruman Church Record Book (KCRB)*—reveals a mixture of African names and Biblical names, but mainly African ones. There is no evidence that Moffat compelled converts to take new names. This is supported by the names carried by native teachers from Kuruman, who were mainly referred to by their African appellations such as, Mebalwe, Sebobi, Mosaise, etc. One or two, including Paul and Aaron Josephs, had biblical names, with Aaron Josephs adopting that name at his baptism, being formerly known as Arend Josephs, but that was unusual.[2] Regular use of African names also occurs in the Kuruman records for church discipline. Those disciplined were all church members and baptised believers, yet the names they carried as Christians were

1 Mackenzie, *Ten Years North,* 72ff.
2 Cf. JSM, *Lives,* 155.

overwhelmingly indigenous.[3] The LMS had a relaxed approach to indigenous names. 'High Church' mission organisations, such as Anglicans and Roman Catholics preferred, and in some instances insisted, that a 'Christian' name replaced the indigenous name upon baptism.[4]

Moffat was an ordained minister of the Congregational Church, with a low-church understanding of baptism, rejecting any notion of baptismal regeneration, and working comfortably within LMS paedo-baptist theology.[5] Not only did he baptise the infant children of the missionary community,[6] but he also baptised the children of African converts. For example, on 1 March 1829,[7] the baptism of the first adult African Christian to be baptised at Kuruman, Aaron Josephs, was accompanied by the baptism of his three children.[8] Aaron's wife Rachel was baptised a few weeks later. Baptism of another Christian couple, Paul and Sarah, was also soon followed by the baptism of four of their children, Isaac, Paul, Sara, and Hendrek.[9] Two issues emerge when considering the Baptismal section of the *KCRB.*

---

3 *KCRB,* passim.

4 At the opposite extreme, the German missionary Bruno Gutmann, profoundly influenced by Romanticism, positively forbade converts from giving non-African names to their children at baptism. Cf. Fiedler, *Christianity and African Culture: Conservative German Protestant Missionaries in Tanzania 1900-1940,* (Blantyre: CLAIM-Kachere, 1999). Later he had to accept Biblical names as well, by decision of the Mission, but no English names.

5 Baptisms carried out by Moffat were recognised by other denominations. RM, *To Mr Scott,* 10.3.1876, (NLS/10708/160), has an intriguing sentence in which he stated: 'Tomorrow off to Chelmsford to take part in the *recognition services* of one whom I baptised.'

6 Cf. RM, *Journal,* 4.2.1826, (*AAK,* 210f): 'This evening Mrs Hughes was safely delivered of a fine boy'. On 5.3.1826, Moffat recorded that the 'son of Mrs Hughes was baptised Isaac.'

7 The LMS *Annual Report* for 1830 (85), dealing with the events of 1829, stated that Aaron Josephs and his three children were baptised on 1.5.1829. This date is repeated by Schapera (*AAK,* 292: fn. 67), and by JSM (*Lives,* 155). However, 1.5.1829 was a Friday, not a Sunday. Examination of the original manuscript of Moffat's letter to the LMS, in which he described Aaron Josephs' baptism, reveals that Moffat wrote the date as 1.3.1829, a Sunday, see: RM, *To Orme, LMS,* 6.3.1829, (SOAS/CWM/SA/Box11/3/B). The LMS transcribed incorrectly: a mistake perpetuated by both JSM and Schapera. The LMS *Annual Report 1830* correctly recorded that Rachel, Aaron's wife, was baptised on a Sunday, 'the first Sabbath of July'.

8 The epoch-making baptism of Aaron Josephs is not recorded in the *KCRB,* but *is* recorded in Moffat's 1829 report to the LMS (LMS, *Report to the 36th Annual Meeting, 1830,* 84f). Similarly, the baptism of Paul and Sarah is not in the baptismal section of the *Record Book,* but is alluded to in the section on church membership. The 1829 entry in the baptismal section of the *Record Book* lists seven baptisms: the three children of Aaron Joseph and his wife, and the four children of Paul and Sarah. Just as Aaron Josephs' baptism is missing from the KCRB, so is the baptism of Helen, Robert and Mary Moffat's infant daughter, who, according to tradition, was baptised on the same day.

9 Cf. *KCRB* for 1829. Two more of Paul and Sarah's children were mentioned at later dates: Hese, in 1837, and another Sara in 1842. Care must be taken when consulting the KCRB since

Firstly, the *KCRB* had a column for the parents' names, and usually both father and mother were entered. Several entries have only the mother's name.[10] More surprisingly, some have only the father's name. It appears that the church meeting followed the principle that one believing parent was sufficient for a child to be presented for baptism. This was the doctrine implicit in the Congregationalist 'statement of faith' printed in the opening pages of the book, where *Article 18* stated that for an infant to be baptised 'a parent'—note the singular—had to be a believer.

Secondly, the *KCRB* displays further evidence of the oneness of the church body at Kuruman. Children of African converts and children of European missionaries were baptised in the same church, at the same time, and their names entered in the same book. The names of Ashton, Fredoux, Moffat, Livingstone and Price children jostle side by side with those of the African children of the church family. A glaring omission is that the baptism of none of Robert and Mary Moffat's own children is recorded in the *KCRB,* though names of their grandchildren are. This is the case even though tradition holds that Helen (b. 1829) was baptised on the same day as Aaron Josephs whose baptism is also omitted.[11]

In the early nineteenth century, LMS missionaries baptised converts almost immediately on conversion, without a probationary period to test their spiritual change. When Africaner was converted through the ministry of Mr Ebner, baptism was virtually immediate: 'In the course of a short time, Africaner, his two brothers, David and Jacobus, with a number of others, were baptised'.[12] Though Ebner baptised Africaner almost immediately, he

---

data pre-1852 was probably inserted in 1852. Despite inevitable copying inaccuracies, and despite some data being out of sequence, the KCRB gives invaluable information.

10 The list of 'single' mothers includes a young woman referred to elsewhere in the KCRB as 'dear Dina'. Dina was frequently under church discipline! Almost as frequently, she presented children for baptism!

11 Mary (b. 1821), Ann (b. 1823), Robert (the first of that name, b. 1825), and Robert (second of that name, b. 1827), were all born and baptised before the entries in the KCRB begin. Helen (b. 2.2.1829), according to tradition was baptised as an infant on the same day as Aaron Josephs was baptised as an adult (1.3.1829): neither she nor Aaron Josephs are mentioned in the KCRB. Elizabeth (b. 1831) was born in Cape Town and presumably baptised there. We do not know where James (b. 1833) was born. John Smith Moffat (b. 1835) is the one name which we might definitely expect to see in the KCRB as he was born at Kuruman. Elizabeth (b. 1839) was born in Table Bay, Cape Town, as the family prepared to leave for England, and Jane (b. 1840), was born in England. Thus, there is only one name, that of John Smith Moffat, which we would definitely expect to see in the KCRB, but which is missing.

12 RM, *MLSSA,* 93. The practice of 'early baptism' was changed later to a policy of 'baptism after a probationary period' though, as Clinton pointed out, such a period was emerging as early as Van der Kemp's day. A notable example was Van der Kemp's own wife Sara Janse,

was under no illusions that a significant change of lifestyle was yet to occur. He warned Moffat that they were a 'wicked, suspicious, and dangerous people, baptised as well as unbaptised.'[13] The problem of granting baptism too early was discussed at the 1817 Cape Town 'Synod':

> What are we to consider in reference to this holy ordinance? Much evil having resulted in some missions, particularly at Bethelsdorp, and it is to be feared in other missions also, by baptising heathens who have not given proper evidences of conversion [i.e. in 'deeds' rather than in 'words'], and not proper time having been allowed to prove the sincerity of the religious impressions. This meeting therefore earnestly recommends to the Directors to lay the most solemn injunctions on all the missionaries here not to administer this holy ordinance so early and indiscriminately as has been the custom by some missionaries.[14]

Moffat took this seriously. In the Kuruman Awakening of the late 1820s, and despite having waited years to see conversions, he stuck to a cautious policy in granting baptism. This was noted by John Smith Moffat: 'Great as was the change, the missionaries did not dismiss their northern caution. It was only after careful examination that, from the many who pressed forward, they selected some six in the first instance to receive the rite of baptism':

> On the 1st of May 1829,[15] a man belonging to one of the aboriginal tribes, with his three children, were received within the pale of the Christian church by baptism, when he assumed the name Aaron Joseph. This solemnity, which, as regards the natives, was the first of the kind ever performed at Lattakoo [Kuruman], appears to have made a deep impression on the congregation assembled on the occasion.
>
> On the first Sabbath of the following July, six more of the Aborigines, (among whom was the wife of Aaron Joseph) were admitted to baptism, together with six of their children.[16] These persons were selected by the missionaries out of a larger number, who were apparently under serious impressions, as exhibiting more decided fitness than the others, as candidates for that rite.[17]

The later baptism of Ma-Sebele, wife to Sechele, chief of the BaKwena,

---

formerly a slave, whose baptism he delayed for some time.' Cf. Clinton, *The South African Melting Pot,* 39f.

13 RM, *MLSSA,* 103.

14 1817 Synod Minutes, 18.8.1817, 31f, (SOAS/CWM/Box 7/2/C).

15 It should be 1.3.1829. JSM perpetuated an LMS error of transcription.

16 This explains some of the baptismal and membership entries in the *KCRB,* which does not start with the baptism of Aaron Josephs in March 1829, but with the July baptisms.

17 JSM, *Lives,* 155.

illustrates other aspects of Moffat's approach to baptism.[18] Sechele had been baptised by Livingstone on 1 October 1848, to the consternation of his tribe who saw themselves losing their rain maker and cultural leader. Sechele learned to read the Bible, refused to make rain, renounced all his wives except one, and almost forfeited his chieftainship as a result. However, neither Sechele's remaining wife, Ma-Sebele, nor any of his children were baptised on that occasion.

It was six years later, in 1854, that Ma-Sebele's baptism took place. By that date Livingstone had left, and it was Moffat who performed the ordinance when he visited Sechele's village *en route* to Moselekatse. Consistency of lifestyle, as well as profession of faith, was essential for Moffat before he would baptise. For evidence of this, Moffat relied on Paul, the native teacher from Kuruman, who had been with the BaKwena since 1847. Moffat wrote:

> [Ma-Sebele] had another daughter since I saw her. Found her clean and well dressed, as well as the child, though she did not expect me. Had a long conversation with her about her soul: her experience clear and consistent, her views scriptural, and, from all I could understand, her conduct blameless. Felt great pleasure and satisfaction in conversing with her on the things of God. Promised to be back next morning and baptize her and her children.[19]

Moffat listed the features which were essential before someone could be considered for baptism. He noted that Ma-Sebele: was clean and well dressed; had a clear and consistent experience [testimony]; had scriptural views on basic doctrinal matters; and had blameless conduct. In his interview with her, Moffat was able to ask questions on her understanding of Christian faith and doctrine. And, though he had no way of making his own judgment concerning Ma-Sebele's lifestyle over a significant period of time, he was content to accept Paul's word on this important issue. With no church-meeting existing in Sechele's one-convert village, Moffat took responsibility for accepting Ma-Sebele for baptism. Having satisfied himself that the conditions were met, baptism took place the next morning:

> I found all things neatly in readiness, a table placed in the *loluapa* [forecourt] at which Sechele sat down, read a chapter (the 11th of 1st Corinthians) and then gave us a very long prayer. This, I presume, was family worship. I then took my stand behind the table, explained a few passages of scripture which had a reference to baptism, the duties and responsibilities of those who were

---

18 Ma-Sebele was the mother to Sechele's son Sebele, hence her name. In a similar way Mary, Moffat's wife, was known as Ma-Mary, not after her own name, but after the name of her first-born who was Mary, later Mary Livingstone.

19 RM, *Journal,* 21.11.1854, (*MJ1,* 346).

> members of Christ's body. I then asked Ma-Sebele a few suitable questions and baptised her and her three children and concluded the service with prayer and singing, feeling perfectly satisfied with what I had done.[20]

Sechele himself had been suspended by Livingstone, for the fault of taking back one of his former wives, and when Moffat met him in 1854 he was still in a state of suspension, though he was preaching each Sunday to his people. Why did Sechele read *1 Corinthians 11*? The chapter deals with marriage relationships and with the Lord's Supper. It may be that Sechele was thinking about being head of his family and yet disciplined from the Lord's Supper.

Admission to Membership

Two things stand out concerning church membership at Kuruman. Firstly, no one became a church member because they were ordered to become so by a chief. Such an approach was antithetical to an evangelical missionary's whole understanding of faith. For the evangelical missionary, faith involved personal conviction, personal commitment, and a personal walk with God. The communal aspect of a believing community was recognised, but individual faith was regarded as essential. Secondly, despite many applying for membership, few were admitted by Moffat and the church meeting. Many men and women attended church membership classes, but of these only a few were admitted to full communion.

In theory the criteria set for church membership, and the judgment as to whether or not individuals had satisfied these criteria, was under the control of the church meeting, as was normal in Congregationalism. In practice, Moffat's influence was formidable, because of his personality and because of his position as leader at the mission. Given his prominence we can assume that the policy of the church at Kuruman was identical with Moffat's own policy, unless strong reasons indicate otherwise. Moffat was rigorous, as had been his mentor William Roby. Dissatisfied with what he saw as a lax approach to membership in the Church of England, Roby determined to set high standards, and he listed the following criteria for applicants:[21]

1. That they signify their desire of communion with the Church in its spiritual privileges.

---

20 RM, *Journal,* 22.11.1854, (*MJ1,* 347f).

21 Roby, *Theol. Lect.* 77, 'Church Fellowship'.

2. That they give satisfactory evidence that they are possessed of experimental religion—with their faith altering their way of life—and fit to become members of a Church of Christ.
3. That proper allowance be made for those who are weak in the faith.
4. That their admission be by general consent of the members.

Roby's criteria were clearly operative at Kuruman. But what concerns us in this section are the additional conditions which Moffat introduced. He decided that a church which mainly comprised of first-generation Christians required even more stringent standards. Reporting to the LMS in 1866, he gave the following illuminating account of his requirements:

> Many there are who have no objection to becoming members of our churches, indeed they would greatly prefer being so, could they be received without being questioned as to their motives and ability and it is astonishing and sometimes rather ludicrous to hear the excuses some make for their backwardness in learning to read and as a consequence their ignorance of Divine things. There are those who regularly attend all the means of grace and are most anxious to join the enquirers.
>
> When such are asked how long it is since they were led to feel a concern for their soul's salvation, they will probably refer to a year or two ago. 'You are of course learning to read, or rather *can* read by this time?' 'No, I am only in the ABC'. 'Have you been trying daily to teach yourself or get others to do so during that time?' 'Yes, but my eyes are tender, and do not see as well as the others do'. As if this excuse is made to appear not to be true, they will then excuse themselves on the ground that their heads are not capable of being taught to read, though they are constantly mingling with all ages who can read with fluency, some of whom they would account dunces compared to themselves.
>
> Such characters give us much trouble, for though we cannot help manifesting courtesy and giving them *Line upon Line*[22] we cannot allow them to think they are what they are not. It is surprising to see some men and women, shrewd and sensible enough about worldly affairs, who, while trying to take the kingdom of heaven by force, cannot be made to commit a verse of a hymn or

---

22 *'Line upon Line'* was a catechical aid. The edition which we consulted was *Line upon Line,* (Ldn: Hatchard & Co, 1866, 2nd Series, part 1). Of its 348 pages, the first 310 retell in simple words various Bible stories from the Pentateuch. Pages 311 to 340 consist of questions relating to the previous chapters. These are mainly questions of fact rather than of interpretation. Pages 341 to 348 consist of Scripture verses to be memorised, each relating to a question or a statement, for example: 'Who loves God? *He that hath my commandments and keepeth them, he it is that loveth me.'* (John 14:21). Though the book has 348 pages, it is a small volume, with clear, large type. *Line upon Line* was translated into SeTswana and printed in 1850 (Parts 1 and 2), with a second edition in 1854. The 1850 edition was for children. The 1854 edition was for adults. Cf. Bradlow, *Printing for Africa,* 33f.

> a passage of scripture to memory even though hymns of which the natives are exceedingly fond are sung very frequently both in and out of doors. But above these nondescripts there are those who stand out in bold relief and shew by their works that they have got the root of the matter in them and will adorn the doctrine of their Saviour.[23]

Moffat highlighted important principles which he and the church meeting considered before admitting a person to full communion. What were their motives in seeking membership? Were they able to read and thus feed themselves with the Word of God? Had they memorised Scripture passages and hymns? Had they a concern for their soul's salvation? Had they shown by manner of life that they had 'the root of the matter' in them? After conversions started in 1829, only a few, out of many who presented themselves as enquirers, were admitted to full membership. Far more people attended church than were members. Many who regularly attended all 'the means of grace', including prayer meetings as well as services, had not even reached the enquirers group.[24]

Year	**1829**	**30**	**31**	**32**	**33**	**34**	**35**	**36**	**37**	**38**	**39**	**40**	**41**	**42**
Enquirers	n/r	n/r	n/r	n/r	84	80[25]	n/r	nr	60-70	n/r	n/r	n/r	n/r	n/r
Admissions	7	0	3	5	14	0	13	10	14/47[26]	89	28	35	60	61
Members	7	12[27]	n/r	n/r	n/r	29	40	35[28]	55	143	181	200	200	n/r

---

23 RM, *To Tidman, LMS,* 17.1.1866, (SOAS/CMW/SA/Box 34/1/A).

24 Livingstone had a similar approach. Cf. Livingstone, *To Janet Livingston,* 31.1.1849, (*DLFL,* Vol. 2, 19): 'We do not encourage a hasty profession. We are Congregationalists, and many whom a Presbyterian would admit are kept back for years by the missionaries, who are decided for purity of communion.'

25 Northcott, *Robert Moffat,* 149: citing RM, *To Ellis,* 16.9.1835.

26 We cannot reconcile these figures. *KCRB* lists 47 admissions: 1 in February; 9 in March; 1 in April; 5 in July; 12 in November; 19 in December. The LMS *Annual Report* explicitly states 14 new members. Did Moffat confuse baptisms (including infants) with admissions? However, this does not work for other years where there is a problem. We know that Moffat completed one of the LMS annual returns forms in August (1836). Conflating Kuruman statistics with figures from out-stations is also possible.

27 The 1829 membership statistic of 7 only include the new African converts, whereas the 1830 statistic of 12 presumably includes the missionaries on the station.

28 Decrease in membership was due to: death, transfers, discipline. Readmission of previously 'cut off' members also complicates the yearly totals. In 1836 Mary Moffat wrote

Available statistics from the period following 1829 illustrate the disparity between enquirers and the number admitted to full membership, with N/R signifying 'no statistical return' for that year.[29] The membership figures, as tabled above, are mainly taken from LMS *Annual Reports.* Initially, all members lived at, or near, Kuruman itself. As the years passed, out-stations developed and church members worshipped at these out-stations rather than at Kuruman, though they were still regarded as 'Kuruman members'. However, as even more time passed, some out-stations became regarded as full congregations in their own right, and membership of these new 'churches' meant that a person was no longer deemed to be a Kuruman member. Details of 'transference' are recorded in the *KCRB.* Not all new members were African converts. Sometimes numbers would increase because of visiting Europeans connecting themselves with the congregation.

From the outset, and as early as the 1820s, Moffat was concerned about the motives of those who sought church membership, knowing that material benefits could be a substantial temptation. In 1821 he wrote:

> A blind Bootchuana girl has been baptised since the Mission commenced, but there is reason to fear that the loaves have influenced her to embrace Christianity. She found that the missionaries, like the kings of Israel, were merciful. She, having no home, found one in the Mission, but her knowledge is so erroneous and superficial that it seems hardly scriptural to believe the extent of her knowledge is capable of changing the heart. At present she is absent from the station.[30]

Moffat tried hard to ensure that spiritual motives were why a person sought membership. This was one reason why he sought to ensure that Kuruman never became a trading station. At the same time, it is undeniable that material advantages were associated with church membership and in having good relationships with missionaries. Jacobs has argued that, during the late 1820s and early 1830s, poverty led many Africans to seek employment from Moffat, and, as they worked the land on and around the mission station, their wealth increased alongside other benefits.[31] There is no doubt that close ties with the mission station brought advantages including security, wealth and

---

that several members had been disciplined and, as a consequence, some had left the mission station. Cf. Mary Moffat, *To her Father,* 18.7.1836, (JSM, *Lives,* 211).

[29] Moffat rarely recorded the numbers of enquirers. More often he simply stated that X had been baptised or admitted 'out of a much larger number'. He was in Britain, 1839 to 1843.

[30] RM, *Journal,* 5.8.1821, (*AAK,* 21).

[31] Nancy Jacobs, *Environment, Power and Injustice*, 64. Not only did their wealth increase, but their culture changed from a pastoral-nomadic culture to a settled-agricultural culture, exactly what Moffat hoped for: cf. Ch. 19: 'The Process of Civilisation'.

status. Others sought church membership, not for selfish reasons but out of respect for Moffat. It was politeness and good manners to join the church which he represented and which had brought them blessing. Moffat tried, with varying success, to untangle these motives in an attempt to identify who had truly been touched in their souls by the claims of Christ and the obligations of the Gospel.

Moffat's 1866 letter to Tidman laid great emphasis on prospective members being literate.[32] Moffat regarded learning to read as essential for vital Christianity. The Word of God in the Scriptures was the paramount means of grace and, in order to mature as a believer, an ability to read the Bible was essential. Moffat did not rule that a person was forever barred from full communion if they could not read, but the tenor of his letter pointed in that direction. This position was also expressed in his 1854 *Journal*:

> I tell the [BaKwena] who hear me that if they will not listen to divine instruction and learn to read, they will continue ignorant, will die in ignorance of the Saviour, die miserably and go to perdition.[33]

Moffat allowed no excuses. He believed in the intellectual equality of African and European. He had high expectations that all Africans who sought church membership could, if they tried, become fully literate. This was a powerful statement about Moffat's notions of human equality, as well as being a clear assertion concerning his criteria for church membership. A prospective member had to show evidence of having committed a suitable amount of Scripture to memory, plus some verses of hymns, as signs both of piety and of seriousness. Moffat had recommended memorisation as a catechical tool from the early 1820s onward, encouraging his listeners to learn *Brown's Catechism* which he had translated into SeTswana, plus the Scripture verses which were published alongside it. After 1835 the *Assembly's Catechism (Shorter Catechism)* was also available in the language. Committal to memory, originating as a catechical instrument, became a membership criterion. Thus, apart from public worship on Sundays, the chief instrument of instruction was the catechetical meeting during the week, when either *Dr*

---

[32] Cf. RM, *To Tidman, LMS,* 17.1.1866, (SOAS/CMW/SA./Box 34/1/A), (quoted above). There was a similar emphasis at Bethelsdorp, cf. Clinton, *The South African Melting Pot,* 38f. This conviction concerning equality was anathema to most Boers.

[33] RM, *Journal,* 9.6.1854, (*MJ1,* 170). Cf. RM, *To Tidman, LMS,* 25.10.1847, (SOAS/CWM/SA/Box23/1/B): '30 belong to the Bible Class, the rest not yet being able to read; they come simply to listen; but to encourage them, after the reading and explanation are over, they too are taught the catechism, hymns, etc. They of the first class have committed to memory and repeated the whole of the Assembly's Catechism with proofs.'

Brown's or the *Assembly's Catechism* was drummed home to the thirty or forty attenders who were able to read.[34]

At Kuruman, 'the condition of souls was more important than the condition of crops, and the health of the church more to be desired than a large membership.'[35] It was of the essence of evangelical piety that a convert had a concern for his or her soul. If the Gospel had not moved a person in their feelings, then it had not truly penetrated their life. The 'affections of the heart', in terms of *conviction of sin* on the one hand, and *love of Jesus* on the other, had to be touched. This, perhaps the most important criterion of all, was the most difficult to apply since it was difficult to evaluate a person's inner spiritual life. Nevertheless, in Moffat's theology, this was precisely the task which the church, guided by the Holy Spirit, required to do in examining prospective members. Discerning the inner heart-attitude is illustrated by Moffat's comments on the 1859 journey to the Ndebele, concerning some Tswana enquirers who had accompanied the expedition as helpers:

> *Marilole* is consistent and gives evidence of grace and discretion. *Masin*, I think, is sincere, but I may have more to say about her in a day or two. I fear that *Magari* does not understand that which constitutes a Christian. *Khaneile* ditto, and our latest addition of *Morolon* adds to the anomalies of Christian profession. He is prompt to tell of his wishes to be saved. One hour he is sitting with me, as grave as if he sat on a coffin, and the next you may find him on his hobby-horse – fun. He is light-hearted and he gives way to it – too much for one who professes to feel something of the powers of the world to come. He may turn out well eventually, but he requires a watchful eye to be upon him; he is easy minded and would perhaps make a better Christian at home than abroad.[36]

---

[34] Northcott, *Robert Moffat,* 149.

[35] Ibid, 149. Northcott underlined that, at Kuruman, there was rigorously controlled entry to membership: 'By 1834 the number of communicants was only 29 despite the congregation on Sunday morning being 340, 130 on weekdays, and candidates under instruction numbering 80.' (Northcott, *Robert Moffat,* 149: citing RM, *To Ellis,* 16.9.1835).

[36] RM, *Journal,* 10.12.1859, (*MJ2,* 238). 'Enquirers' were termed *baipoberi*. Moffat gives more information about this group in his *Journal* for 27.10.1859, (*MJ2,* 202): 'There are four *baipoberi* with whom I converse regularly. I give their names as they stand in my reputation. *Marilole, Masin, Mogori* and *Khaneile.* The first promises to be, I think, an excellent character, has good scriptural knowledge and clear views. I have lately called on him to take his turn with us in our evening family prayers when a chapter is read and a hymn sung. He appears to have a good gift in prayer. I have heard none pray better. Sebolai and Tolai take their turn, the former improving, leaving a dozen or so of his *Khosis* out. The latter speaks rapid, difficult to be heard and withal long, and has been induced to dispense with many of his *khosis ee tserilen.* The two girls give perfect satisfaction. Mogori's profession is rather unstable and Khaneile more so. I gave the former last night a few texts to meditate upon.'

Admittance to membership of the church required evidence of a true and lasting change in lifestyle. From many extracts which could be cited, the following passage from an 1868 letter to the LMS illustrates the point:

> To the church here there has been added [in 1867] eight, four men and four women, besides five restored to church fellowship, from this and other churches. As to the thorough conversion of those received we have no doubt. One, whom those who know him, would have thought that his quarrelsome, haughty and most vexatious disposition would have been the last to undergo a radical change, to the surprise of all became, through divine grace, so entirely altered a character that those who have no faith in Christianity admired the change.[37]

In Moffat's thinking 'manner of life' and 'soul concern' were closely linked. Together, they should be marked by a 'love for Jesus'. This was what he found in the wife of one of the converts:

> [She] has also yielded obedience to the sceptre of Christ and her [life] and general deportment forms a most desirable transcript of one who loves the Lord Jesus. Another Mochuana, a young man, has also produced very pleasing fruit indicating a real change of heart ... he became serious, addicted to prayer, and attentive to the preaching of the Gospel.'[38]

Moffat employed the phrase 'the sceptre of Christ'. This referred to the surrender of a person's faith, lifestyle and heart to the rule of Jesus Christ. All mission work for Moffat was carried out to further the reign of Christ and the glory of God. If criteria were met, admission to full church membership was granted by decision of a meeting of the congregation. In 1830, in a letter to William Orme of the LMS, Moffat described such a group:

> [The 6 new members of 1829] continued to adorn their profession with a walk and conversation consistent with their privileges. ... We had also the prospect of other individuals who were likely to be proposed as candidates, but these have not yet given all that satisfaction requisites towards giving them the right hand of fellowship.[39]

Moffat also described the reception of candidates in 1847, mentioning some of the criteria which, in being fulfilled, enabled the church to admit them:

> There were about 20 candidates who, however, were not received till they had given further proofs of their *love of the Saviour* by persevering in learning to read his word. On the Sabbath afternoon, 115 sat down to commemorate

---

[37] RM, *To Mullens, LMS,* 15.1.1868, (SOAS/CWM SA Reports Box 1).

[38] RM, *To Orme, LMS,* 28.3.1830, (SOAS/CWM/SA/Box12 /1/B).

[39] RM, *To Orme, LMS:* 28.3.1830, (SOAS/CWM/SA/Box12 /1/B).

the dying love of their redeemer' whilst 'Satan's motley group', [those involved in the circumcision rite] 'gathered near the church and danced etc.'[40]

Membership to full communion meant a radical and abrupt change of religious allegiance. 'Love of the Saviour' had to replace the traditional ceremonies which were associated with non-Christian religion. On a formal level, three actions were involved in transitioning from being an enquirer to being in full communion: baptism, decision of the church meeting, and being given the right hand of fellowship. Baptism was administered in face of the congregation on a Sunday at a regular morning service. The church meeting, which took the formal decision to grant full membership, took place usually on a week-day, often a Friday but occasionally on another. It is uncertain when the 'right hand of fellowship' was given. The most likely time would be following the church meeting, or even during the church meeting itself.

An interesting feature about the creation of a church community at Kuruman is the way in which this new type of community was able to exist alongside existing communities which already had traditional structures of leadership, seniority, and discipline. At Kuruman the church community did not seem to have been viewed as a direct threat to existing tribal structures. This felicitous situation was perhaps due to the fact that, for many years, most of the church at Kuruman consisted of men, women and their families who had been displaced from their original tribes and hence were not, at the time of their conversion and admission into church membership, under an existing strong tribal authority. Credit should be given to Moffat, as he tried to separate authority exercised by the church on disciplinary matters from that exercised by the indigenous community.

The potential for a conflict of status was never far away. This was especially the case if, in the church community, an 'ordinary' person was given the status of an 'elder' or 'deacon', and someone, who in the tribal setting was regarded as of higher importance, was not given that status. Wisdom was required. One tempting way to avoid difficulties was to elevate only those who were also elevated in the tribal community. But Moffat seems not to have been bound by this, especially since some of his early outstanding converts such as Aaron Josephs and Paulo were men with no status of any significance in the indigenous community.

There are two main sources for membership statistics at Kuruman. Firstly, the *Kuruman Church Record Book* supplies not only baptismal lists, but also minutiae of church meetings, with details as to how many people were

---

40 RM, *To Tidman, LMS:* 23.3.1847, (SOAS/CWM/SA/Box23 /1/A).

admitted by profession of faith at each meeting. Secondly, there is also data in the annual reports to the LMS, which stated how many members were admitted during the year. The figures derived from these two sources usually, but not always, match each other. Variations are hard to explain. As previously noted, in the *KRCB,* entries from before 1852 were inserted later, and the transmission of data may not have been perfect. It is also possible, though unlikely, that sometimes baptisms and admissions were conflated. Membership figures were also affected by deaths, transferences, and suspensions. It should also be kept in mind that it was only after many years had passed that those baptised as infants proceeded to full membership.[41]

Years	**Baptisms**[42]	**Men Admitted**	**Women Admitted**	**Total Admitted**
1829-34	29	12	17	29
1835-39	114	77	106	183
1840-44	260	97	145	242
1845-49	160	31	60	91
1850-54	96	12	18	30
1855-59	59	3	6	9
1860-64	101	N/R	N/R	40
1865-70	123	N/R	N/R	N/R
Total	942	232	352	624

With these caveats in mind, the figures in the table above, covering the years from 1829 to 1870, are roughly dependable. But what was wholly inaccurate was Livingstone's assertion that, when he arrived at Kuruman, there were no more than 20 members. Livingstone's widely erroneous statistic has been reproduced at the Blantyre (Scotland) Livingstone Centre, and is read by tens of thousands of visitors every year. In contrast to Livingstone's statement,

41 E.g. *KCRB:* '5th August 1853: 4 admitted, 3 baptised as infants'; '7th May 1854: 4 admitted, 2 baptised as infants'; '5th August 1855: 1 admitted, 1 baptised as infant'; '1st January 1858: 1 admitted, 1 baptised as infant', and '29th December 1859: 5 admitted, 5 baptised as infants.'

42 The number of baptisms included both infants and adults.

Moffat wrote in 1839 that the number of members belonging to the church at the Kuruman alone was about 150.[43] Moffat's figure corresponded with data derived from the sources alluded to. As the years passed, statistics became more complicated since Kuruman out-stations were not always included in the figures, especially if these out-stations had been elevated to missions or churches in their own right.

The Sacrament of the Lord's Supper

The original missionary policy of immediate baptism for new converts waned as the nineteenth century progressed. There was a parallel caution on admitting the baptised to the Lord's Supper. At the 1817 Synod some discussion took place respecting the immediate admission of baptised adults to the Lord's Supper. Several of those present argued that it was not necessary that baptised adults should be immediately admitted to the Supper. Others said they should.[44] It is not recorded what Moffat said on that occasion, but at Kuruman, where his policies reigned unchallenged, the process of admittance to baptism for adult converts was so lengthy and strict that those who qualified for baptism were already usually well qualified for church membership and to receive Holy Communion.[45]

Moffat had no hesitation in calling the Kuruman group a church, and it celebrated the Lord's Supper on the first Sunday of most months. For example, in 1821 Communion was celebrated on 5 August, 2 September, and 7 October.[46] Communion was also due to be held on Sunday 4 November, but a problem deferred it until the next week,[47] with the regular pattern re-established on Sunday 2 December,[48] continuing into 1822 and beyond. After 1829 the baptism of new members was also on the first Sunday of a month, and the settled practice appears to have been: baptisms in the morning followed by the Lord's Supper in the evening.[49] Baptism was a public

---

43 RM, *To Kitchingham,* 8.2.1839, (Le Cordeur, *Kitchingham,* 205).

44 1817 'Synod' Minutes, 18.8.1817, 31f, (SOAS/CWM/Box 7/2/C).

45 Cf. the case of Aaron Josephs, the first African to be baptised at Kuruman. He was baptised on Sunday 1.3.1829, but not received into church membership until 5.7.1829, along with Paul, Sarah and others who had been baptised a few days earlier (*KCRB,* 114).

46 RM, *Journal,* (*AAK,* 21, 23, 27).

47 RM, *Journal,* 4.11.1821, (*AAK,* 31).

48 RM, *Journal,* 2.12.1821, (*AAK,* 35).

49 Approval by a church meeting for candidates to proceed to baptism was usually given a few days prior to the appointed Sunday, most often on the Friday. An examination of church meetings for the 1850s reveals that the Friday prior to the first Sunday of the month was the normal day on which candidates were admitted by the church meeting. The Kuruman procedure was: (i) approval of candidates by the church meeting; (ii) baptism of candidates

ordinance, observed by all who attended the morning service, both believers and unbelievers. This is illustrated in Moffat's account of the July 1829 reception of converts:

> After prayers and deliberation, we choose six candidates from among a goodly number who appeared to be under conviction. These, to our great joy, continued to give us the most satisfactory proofs of a real and saving change in their souls. After a period of more than 3 months, during which they were repeatedly examined individually, we felt it our duty to give them the right hand of fellowship. They were baptised on the first Sabbath of July. ... After a sermon on John 1:29 [in SeTswana] a suitable address was given to the candidates, and on a number of questions being asked, they were baptised with five of their children. Brother Hamilton addressed Rachel, the wife of Aaron in the Dutch, she being more conversant in that language. The other five were Bechuanas. In the evening, we sat down together to commemorate the death of our Lord. The season was interesting, cheering, and encouraging to our souls.[50]

In 1821, whilst at Griqua Town, Moffat made an entry in his *Journal,* the terminology of which was repeated frequently during the Kuruman years: 'This evening our little church met to *commemorate the death of our Redeemer*.'[51] Moffat's sacramental theology was simple. The Lord's Supper was the *commemoration*, or *remembrance*, of Christ's death. Moffat never strayed from viewing the Lord's Supper primarily as a simple commemorative ordinance, but yet to be approached with solemn holiness and godliness of life. He was not as adventurous as Van der Kemp who, at Bethelsdorp, also introduced the Agape Feast.[52] Moffat was aware of the Agape Feast concept from his time with the Methodists whilst a gardener at High Leigh in Cheshire, but there is no sign that he introduced it at Kuruman.[53]

Though Moffat had a low-theology of the Lord's Supper, framed in the modest terms of 'commemoration', it was for him a holy ordinance, to be approached with awe and reverence. As a means of grace, it was able to bring joy and refreshment to a believer's soul. The Supper as a 'means of grace'

---

on the Sunday morning; (iii) church members (including the new members) sharing Holy Communion on the Sunday evening. Friday was the favoured day of the week for all church meetings.

50 RM, *To Rev. R. Miles, Cape Town,* 12.8.1829, (SOAS/CWM/SA/Box11/3/D). Moffat is clear that the Lord's Supper was celebrated on the same day as the converts' Baptism/Admission.

51 RM, *Journal,* 2.9.1821, (*AAK,* 23), (our italics).

52 Cf. Clinton: *The South African Melting Pot,* 41.

53 RM, *To a Wesleyan Minister,* 7.1.1877, (Marrat, *Robert Moffat,* 4): 'From curiosity I once went to Warrington to see a love-feast. I had comparatively little intercourse with the Wesleyans, but the more I knew of them the more I admired them for their Gospel simplicity, love and zeal.'

was the old Presbyterian theology of the Lord's Supper, familiar to common piety in Moffat's Scotland, whether in the established Kirk, the Secessionist tradition, or the newer Congregationalism. This view of the Supper was alluded to by Moffat at Griqua Town in 1821: 'This evening I administered the Lord's Supper. Our number together was twelve. I believe it was a season of refreshing.'[54]

That the Supper was an ordinance to be approached with solemnity and seriousness, is seen in Moffat's disgust at Christians who absented themselves from the holy table. For Moffat, the absence of some members of the missionary community from the Lord's Supper 'disturbed the peace of our minds, and rendered the solemn season the less impressive.'[55] By 1822, still at Griqua Town, Moffat noted that the number of church members attending the Lord's Supper was declining month by month. This, plus Christians living lifestyles which required discipline, convinced Moffat that too many had been received into membership on flimsy grounds:

> This evening, we again commemorated our Lord's death as usual. Our number continues to decline. Sanna, the sister of Frederick [who was under discipline], seems to have taken offence at her brother having to be sent away, and evinces very little concern about either the ordinances or worship of God. Alas! Too many of the members of our South African Churches are of this description. Having been received into church communion on very loose grounds, feelings and frames supply the want of real knowledge, and, when all continues smooth, words supply the want of works, and thus make a tolerable show, till they find themselves a little crossed and disappointed, when human nature bursts forth and exhibits a degree of pride perhaps unparalleled among what many be term civilised Christians.[56]

It was not only African converts who absented themselves. In the latter months of 1821, Mrs Ann Hamilton, wife of Moffat's colleague Robert Hamilton, rarely attended Holy Communion. The Griqua Town mission was an unhappy place at that time. Moffat had been sent there by the LMS with the task of restoring some order and proper discipline within that Christian community, and his draconian severity in applying church discipline alienated many, both African and European. Moffat believed that the troubles at Griqua Town had arisen because people had been accepted as converts too early, without testing their profession over a suitable probationary period. His policy, for the remaining years of his time in Africa, was cemented in the Griqua Town experience. True faith should bring with it a profound change

---

54 RM, *Journal,* 5.8.1821, (*AAK,* 21).
55 RM, *Journal,* 7.10.1821, (*AAK,* 27).
56 RM, *Journal,* 6.1.1822, (*AAK,* 40).

of lifestyle. In future years Moffat was determined to thoroughly test a person's conversion before admitting them through baptism and profession of faith to church membership and Holy Communion.

It is pertinent to mention what Moffat regarded as a miraculous providence in July 1829. Some years earlier, Mary Moffat had been asked by a Mr and Mrs Greaves of Sheffield, England, if there was anything the mission station needed. Mary replied that, though there were no converts, could they send Communion Vessels believing that 'we shall need them someday'. The consequent events of July 1829 are described in Robert's words:

> It is perhaps worthy of observation that on Friday evening previous to the Sabbath, among other things which arrived from our friends in England and Scotland we received communion vessels and pulpit candlesticks from Mr and Mrs. Greaves of Sheffield, the esteemed friend of Mrs. Moffat. This arrival just at the very juncture when really wanted, was rather remarkable for, when the want of them was suggested by Mrs. M, it was indeed a season of darkness, and we believe it was seven-fold darkness to Mr and Mrs. G. when they sent them from Sheffield.
>
> But faith has always a sure reward as it is not governed by sensible appearance, but pierces the gloomy cloud and relies on the immutable secrets of the invisible, ever-present, and faithful Jehovah. We cannot feel otherwise but sincerely grateful to Mr and Mrs. Greaves for their Christian kindness and love to the work of our Lord and Master. May they be richly rewarded from the overflowing goodness of Jesus Christ.[57]

Communion vessels, asked for long-before, arrived at Kuruman two days before the first Tswana converts were baptised into the Christian faith. The spiritual impact which this had on the Kuruman community should not be underestimated. It further deepened and strengthened the evangelical piety of Robert and Mary Moffat.

---

57 RM, *To Rev. R. Miles, Cape Town,* 12.8.1829, (SOAS/CWM/SA/Box11/3/D).

Chapter 25
The Discipline of a Church

CHURCH DISCIPLINE WAS important for Moffat, as it was to anyone heavily influenced by Scottish church life of the early nineteenth century. The importance of right discipline is seen in Moffat's attitude from the start of his missionary life, especially in the way he ran the Griqua Town station in the early 1820s. The Moffats were at Griqua Town for two reasons. Firstly, they were waiting for permission to live and work among the BaThlaping. Secondly, they had been sent by the LMS with the task of setting the mission station in good order after a period in which, under James Read, it had lapsed from high standards.[1] In 1820 the church at Griqua Town was well attended, but Moffat was disturbed at the quality of life lived by those professing faith:

> It is true of late we have been delighted to see a full church. ... But alas! Too many of these have stains upon their garments but of such a nature as not to bring them under church discipline. Heretofore this important duty has not been exercised to that extent that Paul would have done had he been here. The result of such a neglect is that our church is a mixed heap of which the major part is rubbish. They have a name, and they lead a course of life which exhibits neither a devil nor a saint. Within the last month a number of these dead members have been amputated from the body, and their examples have the very effect which the Scriptures intimate: 'others fear' and dread to commit crimes which they would otherwise have done with impunity.[2]

Moffat was strict, even severe, in his application of church discipline, and this has provided ammunition for critics who label him as dictatorial. But what he did was no different from how discipline was exercised in Scottish churches, and his standards were applied to all: European and African alike.

---

1 James Read, LMS missionary, was accused of having committed adultery with a Khoikhoi woman. This was discussed at the 1817 Synod. That was not the only charge: his general conduct and allowing lax moral behaviour among converts were also criticised. Ross argued that the charges were artificial and that Moffat exaggerated. But Read's adultery is admitted by Ross; and it was not Moffat who brought the charges. Elsewhere, Moffat wrote warmly about Read's work, (Le Cordeur, *Kitchingham Papers,* 78ff). Ross's book divides people into pro-Philip or anti-Philip. Philip and Read were friends.

2 RM, *Letter,* (c.1820) (JSM, *Lives,* 95).

When the Moffats left Griqua Town and arrived at New Lattakoo[3] in 1821 discipline was again rigorously applied. John Smith Moffat wrote: 'In a few months after Robert Moffat's arrival a course of stern discipline had purged the little community; and, though the band that met around the Lord's table was reduced to a mere fraction, yet it was a lesson to heathen onlookers that must have told its tale.'[4] Most of those disciplined were Khoikhoi converts from Bethelsdorp who were helping at Lattakoo, but who, in Moffat's view, were bad exemplars of the faith. Europeans were also placed under discipline for their careless attitude in not attending the Lord's Supper. Among those disciplined was Mrs Ann Hamilton, the wife of Robert Hamilton who was to be Moffat's colleague at Kuruman for over thirty years. She left shortly after this unhappy period, returning to England where she lived apart from her husband for the rest of her life. As is clear from LMS correspondence, her troubles started before the Moffats arrived on the scene and it seems she was unsuited for the mission field. These factors were not recognised by Moffat and so the application of discipline to Mrs Hamilton was, in hindsight, unfair.[5] Yet it shows that Moffat applied his rules without discrimination.

Moffat's status as undisputed leader at Kuruman meant that Kuruman church policy was effectually Moffat's policy, though he was not always present when disciplinary sessions took place. Whilst on furlough in Britain, or when he was on his long visits to Moselekatse, the functions of church life continued in his absence. Also, though Moffat often visited out-stations, and took part in the church meetings whilst there, at other times the native teachers appointed by Kuruman were well able to bring the membership together and exercise discipline without a missionary being present.

The Categories of Censure

Moffat exercised three types of census: Reproof; Separation; Cutting Off.[6] He nowhere explains the distinguishing features which classify the three

---

3 The LMS mission to the BaThlaping moved as the tribe moved. Before 1810 the BaThlaping were at Old Lattakoo [Dithakong]. By 1817 they were at New Lattakoo [Maruping]. In 1824 the mission moved seven miles south of New Lattakoo, to Seoding [Kuruman] which became its permanent base, independent of the main BaThlaping tribe under Mothibi. Throughout the 1820s, Moffat frequently referred to Kuruman as Lattakoo.

4 JSM, *Lives,* 101.

5 Cf. Karel Schoeman, *'A Thorn Bush that grows in the Path': The missionary career of Ann Hamilton, 1815-1823,* (CT: NLSA, 1995). Schoeman was scathing of Moffat's treatment of Ann Hamilton. This echoed Schoeman's position in his book, The Mission at Griquatown, 1801-1821, (Griquatown: GTV, 1997).

6 The full range of terms in the *KCRB* include: Reproof, Separation, Cut Off, Suspended, and Dissolution. At Kuruman the term 'suspended' was, in our opinion, the same as 'separation'.

forms, but examination of the *Kuruman Church Record Book* indicates the approximate differences between them, though it must be stressed that censures over a forty-year period were not always consistent.

Reproof	Reproof was admonishment for a minor offence, such as missing the Lord's Supper (Holy Communion) once without reason. Reproof usually carried the punishment of suspension from Holy Communion for one occasion. Reproof was not often mentioned in the minutes of the church meeting. It may be that in Moffat's system 'reproof' was the admonishment usually given privately to an erring member which, if accepted, meant that the matter had no need to come to the church meeting at all (Cf. Matthew 18:15,16).
Separation	Separation was for more serious offences or repeated minor offences. It involved being formally suspended from Holy Communion for an indefinite period until due repentance had been made and until the church meeting was satisfied that the contrition and good intentions were genuine.
Cutting Off	Cutting Off was for the worst offences, and involved being removed from church membership. It was the equivalent of excommunication. Readmission to church membership was still possible by decision of the church meeting. Cutting off was for serious repeated sins such as reversion to heathenism, etc.

There was also a corporate censure of *Dissolution*, applicable to a whole congregation. There are extant records of Moffat applying dissolution on at least two occasions to congregations at errant out-stations. Both times the BaTlaro were involved, and it appears that Moffat acted either on his own authority, or under the authority of the area committee. If the latter were the case then it strengthens the view that, in the field, Congregationalist-type churches operated with a Presbyterian-type polity, recognising an area authority. Moffat himself never referred to carrying out the decision of a 'higher court'. It is possible that in these cases he acted on his own authority:

Dissolution was first applied to the BaTlaro congregation in 1851 when they refused to subscribe to the Auxiliary which raised money for the wider work of the LMS. Moffat wrote to Freeman of the LMS:

> You will remember when you were here that a chief of the BaTlaros with the native teacher made application for a European missionary. They appeared satisfied with the reasons you gave for them not getting one. Soon after my return from you, the application was renewed, and, finding their demands could not be granted, the church there—numbering about 70—influenced by the chief (yet a heathen) or the chief influenced by the church, resolved not to subscribe to the auxiliary. The consequence was the church was dissolved while we continued our preaching visits regularly as hitherto fore.[7]

Moffat concluded his letter: 'After a time they came to their senses, saw their errors, confessed their faults, and were again received into our mission'.

Dissolution was again applied to the BaTlaro congregation in 1853, when it refused to discipline some of its members who had been dealing in stolen cattle. The congregation refused to separate eight persons who had been to Namaqua and traded in cattle which they knew to have been stolen. Sometime later matters were rectified, the congregation reconstituted, and regular individual discipline applied to the wayward members.[8]

THE SCOTTISH ROOTS OF CENSURE

The three levels of Kuruman discipline (Reproof, Separation, Cutting Off) had their roots in the modes of discipline operating in Scottish Presbyterianism. Following the 1560 Scottish Reformation, the *First Book of Discipline (1561)* and the *Second Book of Discipline (1578)* supplied blueprints for good order in a Reformed church. This helped to fulfill the third of the crucial *nota ecclesia* of the Reformed tradition: the Word rightly preached, the Sacraments rightly administered, and Discipline rightly exercised. Yet both *Books of Discipline* gave little detail on the application of the process at local level. It was the lesser-known *Form and Order of Excommunication and of Public Repentance (1563)* which tackled procedures in congregations. In the seventeenth century, the *Form of Church Government* of the Westminster documents gave some details as to how principles should be applied.

It was, however, the *1707 Form of Process* which provided definitive actions which a congregation could follow. The *1707 Form of Process*, adopted by the Church of Scotland in discipline cases, had the following gradation of censures:[9]

---

7 RM, *To Freeman, LMS,* 20.3.1851, (SOAS/CWM/SA/Box 26/1/A).

8 *KCRB,* 25.11.1853. Congregation reformed: 9.7.1855.

9 See: (i) Church of Scotland, *The Form of Process in the Judicatories of the Church of Scotland,* (Glasgow: Bryce, 1780). (ii) I.M. Clark, *A History of Church Discipline in Scotland,*

1. Admonishment
2. Lesser Excommunication (suspension from Sealing Ordinances)[10]
3. Higher Excommunication (being 'cut off' from the church)

A promise of true amendment of life had to be accepted by the Kirk Session for the latter two censures to be cancelled, and sometimes a person had to declare their contrition in front of the congregation. The three forms of censure provided for in the *1707 Form of Process*, are close to the three censures which were operative at Kuruman. In Presbyterianism, it was the Kirk Session which had the authority to exclude or readmit, whereas at Kuruman the church meeting did so. Moreover, in Congregationalist polity, church discipline was independent of any secular authority, whereas the established Church of Scotland retained the right to call on the civil magistrate if her own discipline failed to be effective.

The procedures set up by the *1707 Form of Process,* reaffirmed in 1780 by the General Assembly of the Church of Scotland,[11] provided the disciplinary framework for most Scottish Presbyterian churches, and these remained in force until the 1902 General Assembly. Thus, throughout the eighteenth and nineteenth centuries, the 1707 provisions provided the basis for Kirk Session disciplinary cases, though fine distinctions of penalty began to be lost as time passed.[12] Nineteenth-century Kirk Session records reveal that disciplinary procedures became one-dimensional, not simply in relation to the censures carried out, but also in relation to the cases with which Kirk Sessions involved themselves. Church discipline concerned itself overwhelmingly with pregnancy cases. A case in point is the Kirk Session records for Polmont Old Parish Church during the years that the young Robert Moffat attended

---

(Aberdeen: Lindsay, 1929), 143. (iii) Henry Sefton, 'Discipline', (*DSCHT,* 244ff). There was an ecclesiastical *Form of Process,* and a parallel civil *Form of Process* in the Scottish judiciary.

[10] The 'sealing ordinances' were Baptism and the Lord's Supper.

[11] The 1780 Act of Assembly stated that, in accordance with the Act of General Assembly 1707, private admonition and amendment of life is the first preference, as advised in Matthew 18:15. This corresponds closely to Moffat's concept of 'reproof'. The 1780 Act also emphasised that there should be a clear distinction between the Lesser and the Greater Excommunication. The sentence of Lesser Excommunication was suspension from the benefits of the sealing ordinances. To make amends under Lesser Excommunication there should be appearance in the presence of the congregation to be rebuked. In some cases, this could be commuted to private admonition. The serious censure of Greater Excommunication was after 'manifest contumacy' and 'obstinate continuance' in sin. Under the Greater Excommunication, if a person continued in clear contumacy they were 'cut off' from the society of the faithful. Importantly, excommunication did not dissolve civil or natural relationships such as marriage.

[12] Recording of disciplinary cases in particular Kirk Session Minute Books did not, in practice, always correspond to the categories created by the 1707 *Form of Process.* However, in overall terms, the three-stage model, under a variety of terminologies, was put into effect.

Patrick MacFarlan's ministry. The Polmont records are almost exclusively devoted to discipline in relation to pregnancies outside marriage.[13] The records have no variety of offences, such as later found at Kuruman where disloyalty, gossip, and backbiting, were treated with the same seriousness. Also, in the Polmont records there is no variety of punishments such as later found at Kuruman. At Polmont, the formula was simply suspension, admonishment and rebuke before readmittance to full fellowship.

This concentration on sexual misdemeanour was considered inadequate by some evangelicals. Thus, though the *1707 Form of Process* gave a helpful framework, the evangelicals who left the Church of Scotland to form the Congregational Church in Scotland felt that questions of real discipline had not been addressed properly. When the was made the first Congregational Church in Scotland in 1799, Robert Haldane stated that strict discipline on a much wider basis would be applied.[14] He believed that sins issuing from bad relationships between church members—such as quarrelling and disloyalty—were as detrimental to the body of Christ as sexual immorality. In effect, this was a return to the outlook of the 1563 *Form and Order of Excommunication and of Public Repentance,* which included fornication, drunkenness, swearing, cursing, chiding, fighting, brawling, common contempt of the church, and breaking of the Sabbath. These should also be taken seriously.

In southern Africa, it was this extra dimension which Moffat put into practice at Kuruman. Whilst Presbyterian Kirk Sessions in Scotland had before them a series of young girls made pregnant outside marriage—and only occasionally a man as a guilty party—at Kuruman Moffat brought every aspect of relationships into the process.

What types of faults resulted in discipline being applied at Kuruman? The most complete set of Kuruman church meeting minutes available are those from after April 1852. The following list is composed from decisions mainly taken in the ten-year-period, 1852 to 1862.[15]

---

13 Polmont Old Parish Church Kirk Session Minutes: 1810-1834, (FHRC/CH2/ 1134/3). In the Polmont minutes there are, unexpectedly, very few cases dealing with Sabbath breaking.

14 Haldane, *Address to the Public,* (Haldane, *The Lives of Robert and James Haldane,* 236).

15 *KCRB,* 1ff.

Sexual Faults	Fornication. Taking another woman. Allowing your house to be a rendezvous for illicit relationships. Seeking medicine to induce an abortion. Absconding with the husband of another woman. Refusing to acknowledge guilt in committing fornication. Sleeping in the house of a woman who is not your wife. Disgraceful sexual conduct with English traders.
Parental Faults	Not providing clothing for the children. Not sending them to school. Persuading a daughter to leave her husband to become the wife of another man. Causing a man's wife to be put away in order that he may marry your daughter. Fighting with your children. Beating your daughter-in-law. Neglecting the children.
Religious Faults	Not attending the Lord's Supper recently. Being absent from the chapel on Sabbath. Extended absence from the Lord's Table. Refusing to contribute to the auxiliary fund.[16] Joining with the heathen in singing heathen songs when working in the garden. Going to live among the heathen. Allowing or sending boys to the Bogwera (male initiation ceremony). Making karosses for boys going to the Bogwera. Allowing a daughter to go to the Boyale (female initiation ceremony). Accusing people of having bewitched you. Accusing someone of causing the death of your husband.
Raiding Bushman Communities	Many examples before 1852 of Church members being suspended and cut off for this.
Lifestyle Faults	Generally bad conduct. Telling lies. Abusing a person. Slighting the missionaries. Disputing about a garden. Going into the interior for a year seeking ivory. Being drunk, lying, deceit, etc. Taking the wife of another man to be the wife of your servant. Abusing people. Stealing from Mr Moffat during his absence. Living in constant quarreling and bitterness. Making wine or beer and acting outrageously. Abusing the teachers who cut off your wife from the church. Being in bad company.

[16] The LMS encouraged its missions to be financially independent. Many formed Auxiliary Associations which aimed to raise money to aid the LMS rather than vice versa. Initially there was aid both coming *from* the LMS and aid going *to* the LMS simultaneously. It was important to make the local church aware of, and supportive of, the world-wide work of mission.

This table gives a brief snapshot of the issues which came under the auspices of discipline during Moffat's fifty-year missionary labours. Several points merit consideration.

1. The Kuruman situation was quite different from a Scottish Parish. Kuruman had to deal with first generation Christians and the ever-present influences of African Traditional Religion. Even after taking these factors into account, it is clear that Kuruman, under Moffat's leadership, applied church discipline over a far wider orbit of life than the average Scottish Kirk Session.

2. Moffat was confident in the power of the Gospel. Accordingly, he felt no need to be soft on discipline, or to fear that converts so slowly and painfully won might be lost. He believed that if the right thing were done then, under God, right results would follow. The church meeting was to do the 'right thing'. Consequences were left with God.

3. Though the list appears intimidating, the number of church meetings for disciplinary matters was relatively small. The number of members readmitted was also large. It is also likely that many members of the community, both indigenous and European, would secretly enjoy the 'soap-opera' drama of suspensions, separations, and readmissions.

4. As discussed below, the church meeting only applied church law, not civil law. Thus, in 1847, Moffat recorded: 'We separated from the church twenty individuals all for the same offence: going with the heathen who attacked a kraal of Bushmen and killed the men and took away the women and children. The Bushmen are continually stealing their cattle.'[17] Though the men were guilty of murder, Moffat could only apply church discipline, and his strongest sanction was cutting them off from membership. The local community, as an independent civil authority, dealt with any penalties relating to criminal charges. Moffat divided the two jurisdictions.

The Scriptural Basis of Censure

Though the Scottish model lay behind Moffat's disciplinary processes, he regarded his procedures as ultimately having a biblical basis in Matthew 18. Moffat believed that his mode of applying church discipline was not a Congregationalist/Independency pattern, but followed the practice of the

---

17 RM, *To Tidman, LMS,* 25.10.1847, (SOAS/CWM/SA/Box23/1/B).

New Testament Church. Like Roby, he believed that Congregationalist polity recreated the tradition of the Apostles:

> [29 July 1821, Sabbath]: 'I preached on the nature and order of a Christian church. This I did to prepare the minds of the members for the exercising [of] church discipline.'
>
> [31 July 1821, theory was put into practice] 'In the evening, after a prayer meeting, we held our church meeting, when one of the members, Knecht, was suspended for public misconduct. The conduct of other two of the brethren was considered, but no decision made till they should return, they being on a journey. All the members were fully satisfied with what had been done, and the necessity of church discipline being exercised according to the example of the ancient Church.'[18]

The significant phrase is, 'according to the example of the *ancient church'*. By this, Moffat meant the New Testament Church—and the text appealed to most often as providing the model for discipline was Matthew 18:15-17.[19] Congregationalism believed that its method of discipline, as well as its overall ecclesiastical structure, was that of the 'ancient' or 'primitive' church.

In his lectures, William Roby had taught that the rule of discipline had to be the word of Christ only (Matthew 18).[20] In his view, this was in opposition to all human prescriptions whether legislated for in Synods, in Councils, or by church custom or tradition. Roby also argued that, because admission to membership was by consent of the church members, then discipline should also be carried out by the same body. He discussed excommunication under several heads: the nature of excommunication (nothing to do with civil penalties); the persons who should be excommunicated; the medium by which excommunication was to be effected; the purpose of excommunication, and the conduct which a church owed to those who were excommunicated.

Roby did not deal with gradations of censure such as Reproof, Separation and being Cut Off. He only discoursed on the one censure: excommunication.

---

18 RM, *Journal,* 29&31.7.1821, (*AAK,* 20). There were no more details on Knecht.

19 Matthew 18:15-17: '(15) If your brother sins against you, go and show him his fault, just between the two of you. If he listens to you, you have won your brother over. (16) But if he will not listen, take one or two others along, so that every matter may be established by the testimony of two or three witnesses. (17) If he refuses to listen to them, tell it to the church; and if he refuses to listen even to the church, treat him as you would a pagan or a tax collector.' Roby, *Theol. Lect.* 77, 'Church Fellowship', had these verses in mind: 'The Rule of Discipline: this is the word of Christ only.' For application of Matthew 18 by Moffat see our later discussion on Younker.

20 Roby, *Theol. Lect.* 77, 'Church Fellowship'

It may be that he applied this one censure in a graduated form, but that is not indicated in his lecture.

In terms of the mechanism for applying censure, Ralph Wardlaw, the Scottish Congregationalist theologian, went as far as to state that, since the theology underlying Congregationalism was founded on the idea that the whole church was the body of Christ, then, in some instances, the church could be deemed to have the power of the Lord. Wardlaw wrote concerning discipline in a Congregationalist setting:

> The separation of an offender from the communion of the church – the highest act of ecclesiastical discipline ... is described [in Corinthians] as [the church] having 'the power of the Lord Jesus Christ' and in the legitimate exercise of that power is enjoined to 'put away' from its sacred fellowship 'the wicked person'.[21]

Unlike Roby, Wardlaw alluded to degrees of censure. He wrote of, 'the highest act' of ecclesiastical discipline, implying that other levels existed below it. As noted earlier, gradations of censure in Presbyterian Scotland had become somewhat flattened and merged by the nineteenth century, and so the re-emergence, in Congregationalism, of distinct levels of censure, differed from the current Scottish trend.

THE EFFECTS OF CENSURE

What were the effects of church discipline as exercised in the African context of Kuruman? Did its implementation create problems in attracting new converts? Was there a tension between ecclesiastical authority and traditional authority?

Roby taught that there were four major reasons for discipline: the glory of God; the purity of the church; the warning of fellow-members; and the eventual spiritual advantage of the person disciplined.[22] Moffat was at one with Roby on all these points. That being so, we can see that Moffat would not, in any way, entertain any modification of disciplinary processes in order to make Christianity more acceptable. On the contrary, he understood the exercise of right discipline as an *aid* to spiritual progress rather than as an *obstacle*. In this sense, discipline was viewed as an 'evangelical' instrument. The protection of the glory and honour and holiness of God came first, whatever the reaction to the expected high standards. From many examples in Moffat's ministry, the following illuminate his approach.

---

21 Wardlaw, *Congregational Independency,* 316.

22 Roby, *Theol. Lect.* 77, 'Church Fellowship'.

1. *The Younker Case (1821).* Moffat discussed Matthew 18:15-17 in relation to the case of a young Christian Khoikhoi convert named Younker. Younker had not attended the Lord's Supper because, as he explained to Moffat, he had decided to marry a Tswana woman who was a non-Christian. Some of Younker's friends had also not attended the Supper, their reason being that they had been arguing with Younker, trying to change his mind. Moffat's view was that they acted incorrectly. They should not have absented themselves from the Supper, since the matter was one for the church meeting to deal with, not them.

Moffat interpreted verses 15 and 16 of Matthew 18 as applying to problems between individuals which were resolvable by individuals, whereas verse 17 applied to sins against God which were only resolvable by the church body. In Moffat's view, Younker had sinned against God. As such, the matter came under verse 17, and had to be dealt with by the church body. Younker's friends should not have tried to deal with the matter by private admonition:

> I explained to them that their conduct [being absent from the Lord's Supper through arguing with Younker] was nothing else than a determination to sin against Christ by disobeying his command, because they could not mould another person's mind into their views. For a rule of duty in that case I referred them to *Matthew 18:15-17*, which I had more than once read and explained to them. After hearing my remarks, they professed and appeared to be very penitent for having deviated so far from the path of duty.[23]

Moffat had 'more than once read and explained to them' the text in question. The necessity for discipline, and the form of discipline, was clearly something at the forefront of the teaching Moffat gave on the nature of church life. The Younker case also throws light on the relationship between the mission station and the community, whose local BaThlaping chief was the still-to-be-converted Mothibi. African converts were under two authorities: the discipline of the church, and obligations to the chief. So Moffat made a point of explaining to Mothibi what was happening:[24]

> [23rd October 1821] We explained to [Mothibi] the rules of our church, and that on account of Younker's having publicly deviated from these rules he was to be separated from our church tomorrow evening. ...
>
> [24th October 1821] In the evening we held our church meeting. All the members were unanimous that Younker be separated. ... He [Younker] has

---

23 RM, *Journal,* 8.10.1821, (*AAK,* 27).

24 Moffat was concerned to stress that, in these early days, the village chief Mothibi, agreed with what the missionaries were doing in such disciplinary cases. Cf. RM, *Journal,* 15.11.1821, (*AAK,* 33). What would have happened if the chief had not agreed is uncertain.

become very hardened.[25]

Moffat respected the traditional authority which Mothibi had over Younker, and kept Mothibi informed as to what was happening. The sympathetic understanding of the chief was critical, since a sanction of being 'separated from the church' could sometimes mean exclusion from the ground, property and privileges of the mission station. The chief, as the one who, on behalf of the tribe, had granted the LMS its right to the use of the land, was interested in who was or was not allowed to live there. What happened next was that Younker's 'hardened' attitude—as Moffat termed it—resulted in him seeking forgiveness from his traditional BaThlaping community, but not from the church. He had not only broken church rules by planning to marry a non-Christian, but he had broken tribal custom by having sexual union with her before marriage. In traditional BaThlaping culture sexual union before marriage was believed to hinder rain-making for the whole community. Younker only sought forgiveness for his sins against tribal custom. And after he had been separated from the church for some time, Moffat noted:

> [Younker] submitted to be washed according to the Bootchuana custom, in order to be purified from his uncleanness, which he had contracted from having illicit connections with a young female whom he intends marrying. The object of this ceremony is that the rain is not hindered.[26]

In Moffat's view, Younker had reverted to heathenism. Making amends to the BaThlaping community for a sin against tradition was acceptable. But doing so in order not to hinder the rain-making was heathenism.

2. *The Khoikhoi Convert (1821).* In 1821 Moffat recorded a discipline case in which a Khoikhoi convert, who had impregnated a servant girl, was 'driven from the station'.[27] But was Moffat imposing alien rules of morality and sexual behaviour? Moffat defended his position by pointing out that in Tswana custom a girl who had a baby outside marriage was obliged to kill it, and that he wanted, as much as possible, to discourage such circumstances.[28] Moffat never saw himself as bringing a European morality. He viewed himself as introducing biblical precepts which transcended culture since God was Governor of all nations. In such a situation, Moffat saw

---

25 RM, *Journal,* 23&24.10.1821, (*AAK,* 30f). Younker's judgment was given on 23.10.1821.

26 RM, *Journal,* 25.1.1822, (*AAK,* 43). According to Jacobs, (*Environment, Power and Injustice*), the 1820s was a time of drought in the Kuruman area. It is likely that Younker was put under immense pressure by the BaThlaping community to atone for his sin in order that the rains might return. Moffat's emphasis on agriculture through a system of irrigation eventually helped to break the power of the rain-makers and tribal dependence on them.

27 RM, *Journal,* 12.8.1821, (*AAK,* 22).

28 Ibid.

Christian practice bringing liberation. Schapera, who is often critical of Moffat's understanding of indigenous culture, agreed on the fact of infanticide: 'Until very recently it was still considered a serious offence among the BaTswana for an unmarried girl to become a mother, and infanticide in such cases was fairly common.'[29]

Congregationalism was reluctant to mix church discipline with civil law. In this it differed from the Presbyterian tradition. Ever since the Reformation, Presbyterianism reserved the right to call on the aid of the civil magistrate to enforce church discipline.[30] Congregationalism rejected this philosophy, and Roby resisted any idea of the church being formed by or sustained by the power of the civil authority.[31] The Younker case had brought to the fore a distinction between ecclesial and community censure, and Moffat tried to respect that division. It was in his interests to respect cultural procedures whenever possible.

Moffat would occasionally intervene by pleading a case. For example, in 1824 he successfully persuaded Makaba to commute the punishment of a man who had killed an ox.[32] And, as time passed, Moffat became less averse to invoking the authority of the chief for Christian purposes. Thus, if the moral authority of the missionary was not enough to keep order—though usually it was—then, as a last resort, appeal might be made to the BaThlaping chiefs.[33] Moffat was pragmatic. It is no surprise to find him in 1821 being prepared to use physical force to stop a man named Cedras from beating his wife.[34] In that instance, Moffat was also aware that Mothibi, the chief, approved his actions.

Readmittance after Censure

The disciplinary pages of the *Kuruman Church Record Book* detail many men and women re-admitted into full church membership and fellowship. Moffat was serious about discipline. But he was also serious about its intended purpose of enabling a person to see the error of their ways, repent, and grow into Christian maturity. For example, in 1849 the LMS *Annual Report* recorded the following about a Kuruman out-station:

---

29 *AAK,* 30, fn. 31. Schapera cited his, *Handbook of Tswana Law and Custom,* 171ff, 261f.

30 Cf. *1707 Form of Process,* 8:18. Also, *Westminster Confession of Faith,* Ch. 23/3.

31 Roby, *Theol. Lect.* 77, 'Church Fellowship'.

32 RM, *Journal,* 2&3.8.1824, (*AAK,* 134, 136).

33 Cf. JSM, *Lives,* 356.

34 RM, *Journal,* 4.11.1821, (*AAK,* 31f).

> On several of the church-members discipline had been exercised on account of their taking part in the destruction of a Bushman village. [After discipline] their whole deportment had given entire satisfaction to the native teachers and believers, on whose testimony they were again received with deep thankfulness and joy into the bosom of the church.[35]

It surprised Moffat in 1821 that, despite the mission disciplining people, despite no rain, and despite much 'ill-feeling', more Tswana attended church.[36] It may be noted, however, that, at that time, most of those disciplined were Khoikhoi from elsewhere, and the number of Tswana disciplined was minimal. Notwithstanding that factor, why did more attend church? Did the Tswana appreciate the 'fairness' of the missionaries? Were the Tswana afraid of losing missionary patronage if they did not submit to the rules which the missionaries brought? Whatever the reason, discipline frequently had a beneficial effect on attendance. In 1822 Moffat wrote:

> The attendance at Church on the weekdays has considerably increased since we spoke so decidedly on the case of Cedras. It is evident that they dread our displeasure ... nor would they sanction our departure from them.[37]

Discipline was not always welcomed. In 1836, after several members had been disciplined for having 'grievously departed from the path of rectitude', Mary Moffat wrote:

> The school is not flourishing as it was, and we can scarcely account for it, except that some few families have left the place on account of the discipline which it has been necessary to exercise.[38]

*

Such were the vicissitudes of life on a front-line mission station. Robert and Mary were of one mind in this matter, as with most others. It never came as a surprise to him that discipline was required. The sins of Christians were unwelcome but never unexpected. The practical, gardening man took the anomaly of 'ungodly things occurring among God's people' more in his stride than someone with an academic or idealist cast of mind. Gardeners knew that even the best soil, with the best preparation, and sown with the best seed, might still produce an imperfect crop!

---

35 LMS, *Report to the 55th Annual Meeting, 1849*, 104.

36 RM, *Journal,* 30.12.1821, (*AAK,* 39). By 24.2.1822, he noted: 'The attendance at church seems again on the decline. On the Sabbaths a few come, but during the week almost none.'

37 RM, *Journal,* 18.1.1822, (*AAK,* 42).

38 Mary Moffat, *To her Father,* 18.7.1836 (JSM, *Lives,* 211).

Chapter 26
The Community of a Church

IN CHRISTIAN THEOLOGY, the Holy Spirit is understood to be the enabler of spiritual maturity, discipleship, sanctification and obedience. It is also the Holy Spirit who brings success in spiritual warfare, contending against other spiritual forces. Though Moffat had only a few references to the Holy Spirit, he did have some. For example, he taught it was the Holy Spirit who changed otherwise implacable hearts. Hence, when he heard that Moselekatse was making overtures of peace to once sworn enemies, he commented: 'To me the peaceful message of Moselekatse to Sekhomi is somewhat mysterious: or can it be that the Divine Spirit may have caused my sermons to have a deep impression on the heart of the Matabele king.'[1]

Moffat regarded the Holy Spirit as the only enabler who could transform diligence into astonishing fruitfulness. He noted that, though the work at Kuruman was done dutifully, 'the interests of the mission continued to fluctuate, without any decisive evidences of the influences of the Holy Spirit being poured out'.[2] For Moffat, 'decisive evidences' were mainly understood as changes in moral behaviour. He did not have extraordinary gifts of the Spirit—such as speaking in tongues—in mind. The Reformed emphasis was moral and ethical. The Spirit was the *Holy* Spirit. The Spirit established holiness and righteousness of life.[3] Bebbington has pointed out that, for nineteenth-century Calvinist evangelicals, a holy life had four characteristics: conversion, the cross, the Bible, and fervent zeal and activity.[4] To these we could add holiness in terms of moral living. That was the understanding with which Moffat worked.

A holy God requires a holy people. Salvation of lost souls was not the sole motivation for mission. The ultimate goal was to produce a holy people for God. Conversion was only the first step. Next came discipleship. Converts had to be strengthened in righteousness in order that God might be glorified. The

---

1 RM, *Journal,* 27.8.1857, (*MJ2,* 44).

2 RM, *MLSSA,* 238.

3 Not the same as the 'holiness movement', which focused on a spiritual experience subsequent to conversion, variously called holiness experience, sanctification, second conversion, or entering the higher/deeper/victorious Christian life. For Moffat, holiness was not an additional spiritual experience, but the outworking of a moral life which honoured God.

4 Bebbington, *Holiness in Nineteenth-Century England,* 36-41.

glory of God was the primary motive for conversion. It was also the true motive for discipleship, since God was to be honoured in sanctified lives. This is illustrated in Moffat's ministry to two early converts: the Namaqua chief Africaner, and the Khoikhoi woman Francine.

THE FAITH OF JAGER AFRICANER

Jager Africaner was the 'trophy of grace' *par excellence* for early LMS work in South Africa.[5] Though Africaner professed Christianity before he met Moffat, it was Moffat's ministry which cemented his faith.[6] Africaner became chief of his tribe at an early age. His people originally dwelt within 100 miles of Cape Town, but settler expansion drove them north. Then Africaner killed a Boer farmer and his two children, after which he fled with his people towards the Orange River, as an outlaw with a price on his head. Commando parties sought him out but were unsuccessful. He then initiated a campaign of murderous harassment, principally against white farmers to the south, but also against tribes to the north. His name became a byword for terror.[7]

Remarkably, he made non-hostile contact with Abraham and Christian Albrecht of the LMS, who had crossed the Orange River in January 1806 and set up a mission station at Pella. Africaner, 'listened with attention to the first principles of the doctrine of Christ'.[8] Initial interest did not mean immediate conversion. Nor did it mean instant change of lifestyle. He still attacked farms and mission stations. Then, in 1812, new missionaries, including Johann Ebner, who had married Abraham Albrecht's widow, came to the area. With

5 Campbell, *The Life of Africaner: A Namaqua Chief of South Africa,* (Ldn: Religious Tract Society, 1830); RM, *MLSSA,* 73ff. See also: Briggs & Wing, *The Harvest and the Hope,* 26f.

6 Moffat recognised Albrecht and Ebner as instrumental in Africaner's conversion (*MLSSA,* 183). There were four Africaner brothers: Jager, Titus, David and Jacobus. Titus never made a Christian profession. David and Jacobus became believers along with their brother Jager. Campbell wrote: '[Mr. Ebner] proceeded to Africaner's kraal, where he immediately commenced his labours. We are not acquainted with the particulars of what passed, but the preaching and conversation of this Missionary were blessed of God; for, some time afterwards, Africaner expressed himself to the following effect: 'I am glad that I am delivered. I have been long enough engaged in the service of the devil, but now I am free from his bondage. Jesus has delivered me' ... several other natives were converted to God ... The missionary, Mr. Ebner, ... was succeeded by Mr. Moffat, who was instrumental in building up the new converts in their faith, and adding to their number, and maintaining peace amongst them.' (*Life of Africaner,* 27-29).

7 Cf. RM, *MLSSA,* 92: '[He] found in every village through which he passed, the terror of Africaner's name, and ... a trembling, lest he should pay them a visit.'

8 RM, *MLSSA,* 84.

great courage the Ebners left the main station at Pella, and settled at Africaner's kraal itself. It was there that he was converted to Christianity.

In accordance with the practice of the early LMS, Africaner's baptism was performed immediately without a probationary period. The authenticity of his conversion was put in doubt soon afterwards when he appeared to connive with a thieving runaway slave called Peterson.[9] This blip passed, and Africaner's conversion was accepted by the missionaries as genuine. But, if the missionaries were convinced, the farmers who lived within the boundary of the Cape Colony were not. To them, Africaner was a refugee from justice, with the enormous bounty of £100 on his head.

Though Johann Ebner achieved remarkable results, the strain of the work took its toll and, after six years beyond the Colony, he yearned for the comforts of pastoral work nearer the Cape.[10] Consequently, when Moffat arrived in southern Africa, he was sent to relieve Ebner at Africaner's village. On his way north, Moffat found that the farmers were totally sceptical about Africaner's reported conversion, warning Moffat of the appalling things that would happen to him if he approached the terrible outlaw.[11] Then, on 26 January 1818, Moffat arrived at Africaner's kraal. The atmosphere was unwelcoming. The chief was cool and reserved. Titus, his unconverted brother, hated missionaries, and he insulted and threatened Ebner, whilst Africaner seemed indifferent to his brother's hostile behaviour. The Ebners had had more than they could cope with. Moffat was soon alone at Africaner's kraal. What Africaner needed now was consolidation and deepening of his Christian profession. That was what Moffat supplied.

Moffat understood that discipleship was a process in which set-backs as well as advances took place. As a gardener, he knew that sown seed needed ongoing attention if it were to grow well rather than be stunted or barren. This was why he was unafraid to apply discipline. As plants needed to be pruned, so Christians required discipline. Moffat had an empiricist view of conversion, accepting that it did not produce the full fruit immediately, but simply initiated a discipleship process. Throughout his life, he employed two main tools to facilitate Christian maturity. One was grounding a convert in

---

9 RM, *MLSSA,* 93f.

10 Northcott, *Robert Moffat: Pioneer in Africa,* 46.

11 RM, *MLSSA,* 94: 'One said he would set me up for a mark for his boys to shoot at; and another, that he would strip off my skin, and make a drum of it to dance to; another most consoling prediction was, that he would make a drinking cup of my skull. I believe they were serious, and especially a kind motherly lady, who, wiping a tear from her eye, bade me farewell saying "Had you been an old man, it would have been nothing, for you would soon have died, whether or no; but you are young, and going to become a prey to that monster."'

the Word. The other was applying discipline where necessary. All was covered by prayer, but application of the Word and discipline were the primary methods. With Africaner, the emphasis was on steeping him in the Word through a one-to-one pedagogical relationship.

As a foundation Moffat conducted daily morning and evening services: 'the custom of our missionaries at that period'.[12] He also held school classes for three or four hours during the day. Africaner attended all of these. Two results emerged from this intense grounding in the Word, both of which were crucial in the maturing of Africaner's Christian faith.

1. Study. Africaner started to read the New Testament—a Dutch version—'with all the assiduity and energy of a youthful believer'.[13] It became 'his constant companion'. Sometimes, for a whole day, he would sit 'under the shadow of a great rock' or in his hut, 'perusing the pages of divine inspiration'. Moffat described Africaner's ability in not only remembering passages of Scripture but having a facility to compare them: 'He had no commentary, except the living voice of his teacher, nor marginal references, but he soon discovered the importance of consulting parallel passages which an excellent memory enabled him readily to find'.[14] When Moffat took Africaner to Cape Town in 1819, 'his New Testament was an interesting object of attention; it was so completely thumbed and worn by use'.[15]

2. Discussion. Added to a focus on the New Testament—prodigious for a man learning to read—there were numerous nights spent with Moffat, discussing 'creation, providence, redemption, and the glories of the heavenly world'.[16] If this list identifies the actual topics which were important to Africaner and Moffat, then it gives another window into Moffat's core message. Firstly, God has made all things. Secondly, God is the Governor or Ruler who provides all things. Thirdly, God has provided salvation from sin. Fourthly, God has a future for us, even beyond the grave, since we have immortal souls. Elsewhere Moffat summarised his ministry to Africaner:

> [The Word of God] was his daily companion, and often has he sat with me at the door of my hut from night until dawn of day, eagerly listening to my

---

12 RM, *MLSSA,* 108.

13 RM, *MLSSA,* 109.

14 RM, *MLSSA,* 109.

15 RM, *MLSSA,* 180. Moffat, *Journal,* 9.6.1854, (*MJ1,* 170), recorded a similar devotion shown to the Bible by Sechele of the BaKwena.

16 RM, *MLSSA,* 109.

answers to his numerous inquiries on the great subjects of creation, providence, and redemption'.[17]

Moffat emphasised the impact which the first two topics had on Africaner: God as Creator, and God as Governor of all things. From the Bible, and from his conversations with Moffat, Africaner appears to have experienced a new experience of the reality of God as seen in the natural world:

> He was led to look upon the book of nature; and would regard the heavenly orbs with an inquiring look, cast his eye on the earth beneath his tread, and, regarding both displays of creative power and infinite intelligence, would enquire about endless space and infinite duration.[18]

Africaner appeared to be fascinated by the 'descriptions given of the 'majesty, extent, and number of the works of God.' Moffat reported this as an novel experience for Africaner, implying that such thoughts about God and the created Universe had not occurred to him before his eyes were opened to them by Christian teaching and by reading the Bible. Whether this was in fact the case is difficult to determine, but Moffat believed it to be so. Moffat saw Bible teaching opening up Africaner's perception of the natural world. It was not that contemplation of the creation led to an awareness of the Creator, but that contemplation of the Creator led to a deeper awareness of the Universe God had made. This sense of wonder and awe appeared to aid Africaner's spiritual development. Intriguingly, Moffat did not report a similar amazement at the message of the Cross.

Wonder and awe, whether inspired by God's works of creation, or by his works of redemption, or by both, seemed to affect Africaner's soul and conscience, producing a genuine deep repentance and amendment of life. Ebner sowed the seed. Moffat's labours brought the fruit, with Africaner developing a profound sense of contrition. Moffat recorded that, on one occasion, when he mentioned to Africaner that he now found it hard to picture how formerly he had led a life of fire and sword, 'he answered not, but shed a flood of tears'.[19] In Calvinist Scotland, evidence of true fruit of repentance was critically important. That was why Moffat emphasised the new walk with God and changed lifestyle which Africaner now had: 'During the whole period I lived there, I do not remember having occasion to be grieved with him, or to complain of any part of his conduct; his very faults

---

17 RM, *Africa,* 35.

18 RM, *MLSSA,* 109. Africaner had only one wife, so no complications with polygamy. His brother, the unconverted Titus, was the only individual on the station with two wives.

19 RM, *MLSSA,* 111.

seemed to lean to virtue's side.'[20] According to Moffat, the formerly brutal Africaner now tried to solve inter-tribal difficulties by negotiation rather than by war. And, since Africaner understood and appreciated 'the principles of the gospel of peace',[21] then his conversion was deemed to be deep and authentic as far as Moffat was concerned.

In 1819 Moffat persuaded Africaner to go with him to Cape Town.[22] The prospect horrified Africaner since, in the eyes of the Cape Government, he was still a wanted man: 'I had thought you loved me, and do you advise me to go to the government, to be hung up as a spectacle of public justice? Do you not know that I am an outlaw, and that 1000 rix-dollars have been offered for this poor head?'[23] As it happened, Africaner was pardoned. On the journey, Moffat encountered the same farmers who had warned him in 1817 that he would die at the hand of the murderous bandit. Most would not believe that Africaner was truly converted: 'My testimony as to the entire reformation of Africaner's character, and his conversion, was discarded as the effusion of a frenzied brain.'[24]

Moffat gleefully described one farmer, who had been convinced by rumours of Moffat's death at the hands of Africaner and thought the figure before him was Moffat's ghost! When Moffat remonstrated that Africaner's conversion was real, he quoted the farmer as replying: 'I can believe almost anything you say, but *that* I cannot credit; there are seven wonders in the world, that would be the eighth'.[25] When the 'meek and lamb-like' Africaner was introduced to the sceptical Boer he exclaimed, 'O God, what a miracle of thy power! What cannot thy grace accomplish?' This crowned Moffat's account of the transformation of the once-feared chief. Africaner was a 'trophy of grace'. He had all the classic signs of true conversion: fascination

---

20 RM, *MLSSA,* 111. Moffat gave examples of Africaner's conduct, especially his sympathetic tenderness towards the needy: 'It may be emphatically said of Africaner, that 'he wept with those that wept' for wherever he heard of a case of distress, thither his sympathies were directed; and notwithstanding all his spoils of former years, he had little to spare, but he was ever on the alert to stretch out a helping hand to the widow and fatherless.'

21 RM, *MLSSA,* 112.

22 RM, *MLSSA,* 179: 'My object in coming to the Colony was twofold; to procure supplies, and to introduce Africaner to the notice of the Colonial Government'. He wanted the Cape Governor, Charles Somerset, to see this 'trophy of grace' and have a higher view of mission work. If impressed by Africaner's conversion, there would be less risk of him withdrawing permission for mission stations to continue, and he might encourage more to be set up.

23 RM, *MLSSA,* 173.

24 RM, *MLSSA,* 176.

25 RM, *MLSSA,* 177.

with the Word of God, sorrow for sin, change of life, a steadfast commitment to the way of Christ.

At Cape Town Moffat was directed by the LMS to a new field of operations among the Tswana, and Africaner made the journey home without Moffat. They never met again, but he remained in Moffat's thoughts. In nineteenth-century piety, the record of a believer's dying was viewed as an important witness to their walk with God. Hence, when Africaner died in 1822, his last words, as related by the Wesleyan missionary the Rev. J. Archbell, were portrayed as the perfect epitaph of the model convert:

> 'My former life is stained with blood; but Jesus Christ has pardoned me, and I am going to heaven. Oh! Beware of falling into the same evils into which I have led you frequently; but seek God, and He will be found of you to direct you.'[26]

Archbell highlighted Africaner's focus on forgiveness of sins through Jesus Christ. Yet, when Moffat recorded his conversations with Africaner, what Moffat focused on was Africaner's awareness of the majesty of God and the immortality of the soul. The Cross was implied, but rarely made explicit. This may evidence Moffat's style, though the scarcity of references to the Cross is puzzling. In fact, immediately after recording Archbell's account of Africaner's last words with their *Christological* emphasis, Moffat described his own early conversations with Africaner, but the aspect he focused on was again Africaner's growing awareness of the *Creator* God:

> His thoughts were frequently occupied while looking around him, and surveying the 'handy-works' of God, and asking the question 'Are these the productions of some great Being? How is it that His name and character have been lost among the Namaquas, and the knowledge of Him confined to so few?[27]

At the very point where we might expect Moffat to put into the mouth of Africaner some comment on Christ dying for him, what Moffat featured was Africaner's growing wonder concerning the Creator God as he came under increasing Christian influence. Why did Moffat move so quickly to God the Creator? Or was the Cross and the mercy of God in Christ, as understood by Africaner, a derivative consequence of there being such a Creator God? Did Moffat focus mainly on man's duty toward his Creator, with all else flowing

---

26 RM, *MLSSA,* 182.

27 RM, *MLSSA,* 183. In Moffat's *Journal*, written at the time in comparison to *Missionary Labours* written 20 years later, Moffat did allude to redemption. Cf. RM, *Journal,* 3.7.1822, (*AAK,* 52), on hearing of Africaner's death: 'I feel as one deprived of a near relation, especially when I call to mind the many happy hours I spent in his company, performing the delightful exercise of infusing into his growing understanding the doctrines of Redemption.'

from that? Or did Moffat have a gardener's predisposition to focus on the works of God in creation? Whatever the reason, Moffat's work deepened Africaner's discipleship, and the main method was grounding him in the Word of God, especially relating that Word to what made a deep impression upon Africaner—the creative power of the Almighty.

The Faith of Francine

Francine (or Fransinna) is another example of spiritual growth.[28] In her case, it was the application of church discipline which aided her progress in faith. Francine and her husband Fridrick were Khoikhoi converts, who came from Bethelsdorp around 1820 to help in the new work at Griqua Town. Fairly or unfairly, Moffat was displeased with the quality of life displayed by many of the Bethelsdorp converts, and the first mention of Francine occurs in 1821, when Moffat wrote of her being unhappy at Fridrick being disciplined and expelled from the mission: 'It appears that Francine, the wife of one of our Hottentots, is displeased at Fridrick's being sent from the Station.'[29] Francine's resentment resulted in her becoming, in Moffat's view, 'hostile' to the mission. Moffat had enforced the first stage of church discipline: admonishment applied on a personal basis. He then visited Francine:

> I visited one of our members, Francine, who a little before behaved in a manner very hostile to the cause. She appears to be heavily affected. I inquired into the state of her soul, and found her deeply convinced of the evil of her conduct in her late hostile attempt to subvert our power as missionaries. I gave at once a scriptural view of her conduct by quoting passages relative to her own actions, and pointed out the evil effects which resulted from what she had done, that the whole was a source of much sorrow to us all, and had almost terminated in the total subversion of the cause of Christ in this place.
>
> She confessed her crime, and begged that we might forgive her, to which I cordially assented, pointing her to the blood of atonement, assuring her that nothing less than firm reliance on the testimony God had given of his love could save her soul, viz. the end of the Law for righteousness to every one that believeth; that as it was possible that she might be hurled into eternity before long, it became her to pray without ceasing, that she may experience the peace-speaking blood of Christ applied to her soul. We united in prayer.[30]

---

28 Schapera, *AAK,* 36, fn. 42, identified 'Francine' as the 'Fransinna' of *MLSSA,* 302. Moffat's *MLSSA* has an altered version of Francine's death from *AAK,* 46. Moffat polished accounts for his book, giving a more positive version in order to encourage his readers.

29 RM, *Journal,* 3.12.1821, (*AAK,* 36).

30 RM, *Journal,* 10.1.1822, (*AAK,* 41).

The phrase 'one of our members' shows that Francine was already regarded as a Christian.[31] Suggestively, in this extract, and as an exception to Moffat's normal paucity of references to the cross, Moffat made the cross and the 'blood of Christ' central in the counseling which he gave, pointing Francine to their power to take away resentment and hostility, and in their place to create peace. Moffat's counseling method was thus: going to Scripture, challenging the person directly, warning them of the imminence of death, pointing them to the Cross, and praying for them. Francine responded immediately. There was no need for discipline to be taken to another level. She showed grief and conviction of sin.

In a previous *Journal* entry Moffat had discussed the problem of superficial converts who had little conviction of sin. Francine's response was in sharp contrast. Following this counseling, it was only a few weeks later that Francine died and, like Africaner, the manner of her dying was viewed as a witness to the maturity and strength of her faith in Christ. As she weakened, Moffat wrote: 'Visited Francine. Found her getting much weaker. Her disease is of a peculiar nature. She professes a firm reliance on the righteousness of Jesus Christ.'[32] Seven weeks later he recorded:

> This afternoon Francine died. For several months her body has been the object of a most tormenting disease. For more than a month the left leg up to the knee has been consigned to the dust, and the remaining part has been gradually decaying. But while worms were actually destroying her body, she knew in whom she believed, for from the commencement of her affliction her soul has been renewed day by day.
>
> As may be seen from the preceding part of this journal, previous to her illness she had wandered from God, and done things to the grief of our souls and the injury of the cause. She had also used her endeavours to persuade her husband and the other men who are from Bethelsdorp to abandon this station and return. (Her enmity to the missionaries originated chiefly in church discipline, which she thought was too severe). While yet in the midst of her fiery zeal of opposition to us, the Lord showed her that he had a controversy with her, by visiting her with affliction. Thrice happy was it for her who heard the rod, and Him who did appoint it. ...
>
> [She] took refuge in the blood of Christ, which cleanseth from all iniquity. She made a full, free, and public confession of all her iniquities. Some time before her death, recollecting the injury she had attempted to do by persuading the men to leave the station, she called them together, and, as her dying advice, entreated them not to forsake the Mission, however accumulated their privations might be. During the whole of her illness not a murmuring word

---

31 Also indicated by the phrase 'wandered from God', which Moffat used of her in *AAK,* 46.
32 RM, *Journal,* 26.1.1822, (*AAK,* 43).

> was heard to pass her lips. Resting on the imputed righteousness of Christ, she gloried in the cross. A lively gratitude to God, who had redeemed her through the blood of atonement, beamed forth in her whole experience. ... [33]

About an hour before Francine died, Moffat was called. Accompanied by Mary, Moffat found Francine apparently asleep, and she breathed her last, 'without a sigh, a struggle, or a groan'. Moffat regarded his whole dealing with Francine, including her composed death, as 'a remarkable display of divine providence in his government of his church, however small, and his jealousy for the honour of his own cause'.

With Francine, Moffat included phrases such as: 'the imputed righteousness of Christ', 'she gloried in the cross', and 'the blood of the atonement'. These were missing when he discussed Africaner. The reason may simply lie in the type of conversations which Moffat had with each. Moffat encountered Africaner as a newish convert who required instruction about God, whereas he encountered Francine as a backslider whose need was to put away her sins of hostility and resentment. Africaner and Francine both needed to grow into deeper Christian maturity: but, for each, the means to advance in discipleship were slightly different. One matured through an obedient repentance in response to feelings of awe and wonder when faced with the majesty of the Creator God. The other progressed through focusing on the blood of the cross, which brought both conviction of sin and release from guilt. Both situations illustrate the basic approach which Moffat had when assisting converts toward spiritual maturity: focusing on the Word of God in which God the Creator and Redeemer was revealed, and applying discipline where necessary.

The Holiness of the Christian Life

Soon after Francine's death in 1822, Moffat wrote at length on what he saw as the shallow Christianity of many of the Khoikhoi from Bethelsdorp who came to assist in Griqua Town. Moffat admitted that it was impossible to do the work without the help of three or more men from the Colony, and yet there were dangers in having them around. Moffat lamented that all but one had disgraced the cause, with adultery, fornication, and even incest, their reigning crimes. Deeply affected, he commented, 'Their conduct has

---

[33] RM, *Journal*, 16.3.1822, (*AAK*, 46). See also the next day's entry: 'This morning the remains of Francine were committed to the dust. In the evening, I improved her death from Revelations 14:13.' ('Improved her death' meant: applied lessons from her death).

successively wounded our souls, but indeed little else could be expected from a religion founded on feelings and frames, visions and dreams.'[34]

Did Moffat slur Bethelsdorp converts because of an antipathy toward James Read and others?[35] But it had been the church, not Moffat, which had judged that many of the Bethelsdorp Khoikhoi required discipline. Moffat's conclusion was that the Bethelsdorp converts had not been grounded in the Word of God, and that their faith was, 'founded on feelings and frames, visions and dreams'. Correct or not, what is significant is that Moffat cited a lack of grounding in the Word as the reason for lack of Christian maturity and holiness. Moffat was aware that even missionaries had to feed deeply on the Word to retain their personal spiritual appetite. The previous year, 1821, he had recorded his thoughts on the necessity of missionaries having regular in-depth teaching:

> This measure [of having a Sunday evening service totally in Dutch with no translators—i.e. directed specifically towards the missionaries] is also of greater importance to the missionaries themselves, who are accustomed to study and preach on little more than the first principles of the doctrine of Christ, for alas! The Bootchuanas have not learned these. Under such circumstances, the soul [of the missionary] either loses a relish for stronger food, or finds itself impoverished for want of more knowledge and more enlarged views of the doctrine of the Cross, the Christian warfare, etc.[36]

Moffat saw that a missionary needed to grow in faith. And if solid teaching were not given regularly, then even a missionary could become shallow and demotivated, with a danger of never getting beyond the 'A,B,C' of the Gospel, or having 'enlarged views' of the heart of the faith.

Moffat frequently used the term 'transformation' to describe the effects of the Gospel. In discussing the changed lives of chiefs 'who have laid their weapons of war at the feet of the Prince of Peace', he stated: 'We have only to glance over our missionary records to be convinced of the *transforming* effects of the Gospel'.[37] Intriguingly, Moffat noted that transformation could take place not only with those who had become Christians, but with some who were still 'strangers to the inward teachings of the Spirit of God'. Transformation, effected by the Gospel, spread much further than the circle of professed Christians. The Gospel had a considerable 'salting' effect: 'We

---

34 RM, *To James and Mary Smith,* 20.8.1822, (*AAK,* 64).

35 Ross, *John Philip 1775-1851*. Moffat was not alone. A correspondent, writing to the *South African Commercial Advertiser* on 10.3.1824, raised serious questions concerning Bethelsdorp, though his criticisms were dismissed in the 17.3.1824 edition.

36 RM, *Journal,* 18.6.1821, (*AAK,* 18).

37 RM, *MLSSA,* 210f.

have entered the kraal of the filthy and lazy Hottentot, and have witnessed the transforming influence of the Gospel effecting a change in his character and state, which neither the might nor the policy of an empire could achieve'.[38] Moffat's words may be indelicate, even offensive, but his message was clear. The Gospel brought a fundamental transformation of lifestyle. For Moffat, the call to repentance and conversion was ethically based. The marks of Christian maturity and the work of the Spirit would be seen in lives showing a new ethical holiness. In Moffat's opinion, one of the problems faced by ordinary Africans was that they were compelled to live lives of cow-towing deceitfulness in order to survive the totalitarian claims made by their chiefs. Consequently, instilling deeply-rooted moral awareness was an enormously difficult task:

> They are the vassals of the chief in whose country they dwell. If they are successful in killing an elephant, they must convey the tusks to the chief. ... If they have beads on their persons, a thing I have rarely seen, they are [asked] if seen by their superiors, where they got them ... Of course, they take care to keep coveted things out of sight of their superiors.
>
> With them truth and falsehood are terms synonymous. With us they only break out into a loud laugh when convicted of telling untruths. Tell them that to tell lies is to make crooked or go away from a straight line; but tell them it is a moral evil, a sin against God, this they do not understand, and [it] excites another laugh. ... They become from this slavish life habituated to intrigue and lying and deceit of every description.[39]

Moffat reckoned that one of the reasons why a chief, such as Moselekatse, resisted the teaching of Christianity amongst his peoples, was because it undermined his absolute power and encouraged notions of liberty and individual responsibility.[40]

1. *Holiness and Prayer.* Prayer was at the centre of Moffat's spirituality. Intercessory prayer was what he mostly had in mind, and he normally wrote about corporate prayer, rarely discussing his private prayer life. In evangelicalism, prayer-spirituality was traditionally fostered through prayer-meetings, and this emphasis was prominent at Kuruman. From the start, there was a weekly prayer-meeting for believers. Then, when the 1829 Awakening occurred, the first converts organised their own Friday prayer-meeting. Other examples are numerous. Thus in 1859, at Moselekatse's after Sabbath services, Moffat wrote:

---

38 RM, *MLSSA,* 213.

39 RM, *Journal,* 2.7.1854, (*MJ1,* 206).

40 RM, *Journal,* 6.8.1854, (*MJ1,* 256).

In the evening, we had a prayer meeting among ourselves in the tent. We need divine counsel, and without prayer we cannot expect it. We are living in painful, galling, soul-wearing-out suspense. I could easily put up with it were I alone. I never open the bible without looking for something like an answer to prayer.'[41]

When Moffat made that entry, things were going badly for the expedition. And for Moffat, the mature Christian response was to pray and turn to the Scriptures. Twelve days later, a similar entry was made: 'In the evening we had our English prayer meeting in the tent, a season I think all enjoy. We had need to pray for divine direction and help, for I suspect we shall find the need of it before patience shall have its perfect work.'[42] Spiritual maturity and progress in discipleship were marked by commitment to intercessory prayer. At Kuruman the whole Church was encouraged to take part in the annual week of world-wide prayer organised by the *Evangelical Alliance.* The following entry from 1862 is typical:

January 5th, 1862: Preached in the morning from First Peter. Read to the congregation the arrangements made for the following week for special prayers to be held each day as recommended by the 'Evangelical Alliance'. Mr. Ashton preached in the afternoon ... both sermons intended to prepare the minds for the devotional services of the week. Mr. Price expounded in the evening.[43]

The extract refers to formal communal times of prayer, and the type of prayer which, at Kuruman, was deemed to be important for an individual's walk with God was alluded to by John Mackenzie:

I have been struck with the touching manner in which some, in leading the prayers of the congregation, have besought the help of God's Spirit to assist them in their struggle with temper, habits and passions.[44]

Though the prayers which Mackenzie referred to were made as part of public worship, it seems that the burning mention of 'temper, habits and passions' sprang from deep individual anxiety. Prayer was seen as an important way to deal with these problems, and to progress in the walk with God. Prayer as an expression of heart-religion was expressed by Mackenzie in the following:

Few prayers are offered by the Bechuanas in which the Scripture is not introduced: 'God so loved the world that he gave his only begotten Son that

---

[41] RM, *Journal,* 8.11.1859, (*MJ2,* 211). The weekly prayer meeting at Kuruman was mentioned by Mary Jane Wilson, wife of the ABCFM missionary Alexander Erwin Wilson (Wilson, *Letter,* 21.3.1836: https://www2.wheaton.edu/bgc/ archives/docs/wiltxt.html).

[42] RM, *Journal,* 20.11.1859, (*MJ2,* 226).

[43] RM, *Occasional Journal: 1860-1862,1868*, (SOAS/CWM/SA/Moffat /Personal/Box 4).

[44] Mackenzie, *Ten Years North,* 76.

> whosoever believeth in him might not perish but have everlasting life.' Even the most ignorant of the members of the church, those who have become Christians in advanced years, have got fast hold of a few leading truths. God loves them. Christ died for them. God will help them if they cry to Him. ... They hope that when the journey is over 'Yesu' will allow them to go with the rest to green pastures and beside the still waters of the heavenly land.[45]

2. *Holiness and the Sabbath.* Observing the Sabbath as a day of rest from labour, and as a day of devotion to God, was important for Moffat. His adherence to Sabbath rest was nowhere more striking than in his resolve to observe it despite the threat of invasion and slaughter. Traveling on the Sabbath was only permissible in cases of absolute necessity. On his 1823 journey to meet Chief Makaba, of the BaNgwaketse, he heard alarming reports of the approaching pillaging Mantatee, and decided to return to New Lattakoo. Yet he did not consider the reasons so pressing as to justify Sabbath traveling:

> Sabbath: Remained here and held divine service twice. Feel extremely anxious to get home, but cannot see it to be a duty to travel on a Sabbath, without it be a case of urgent necessity.[46]

Even after returning to New Lattakoo, and after the emergency meeting which was held to consider the threat, and after he set out for Griqua Town to get armed help, he still stopped for a whole Sabbath at Kramer's Fountain: 'I preached twice and spent most of the day in religious conversation.'[47] The next year, 1824, after the Mantatee crisis, Moffat resumed the aborted visit to Makaba and, on the journey, still observed the Sabbath as a rest day. By agreement, so did his Griqua companions.[48]

Moffat made few exceptions to his Sabbath. If setting out to raise help for the defence of the mission station was no justification for Sabbath travel, what might be? Moffat did mention a few occasions when his rule was broken. In 1827, on his journey to spend several months in a BaRolong village for language study, he was reluctantly compelled to travel a short distance on a Sabbath because not only was there a lack of water, but bold and aggressive lions were in the vicinity.[49] In 1857, necessity again intervened: Moffat was on a new route, water had not been found on the Saturday, so Sabbath became a day of hard labour:

---

45 Ibid.

46 RM, *Journal,* 1.6.1823, (*AAK,* 86).

47 RM, *Journal,* 8.6.1823, (*AAK,* 87).

48 RM, *MLSSA,* 381.

49 RM, *Journal,* 1.4.1827, (*AAK,* 240).

The oxen suffering from thirst and but a moderate portion for ourselves, for we had never doubted [the previous day] finding water. ... We proceeded as best we could. ... The toil of running back and forwards and hewing down trees, rolling stones out of the way, kept me in a state of constant perspiration till reaching where we now are at one o'clock p.m. Such a Sabbath of labour I never spent before, and hope and pray that I may never be under the necessity of spending such another."[50]

On other occasions Moffat made it clear that not even preliminary work was to be done on the Sabbath. When he prepared to leave Sechele in 1854, the Monday departure was delayed by the previous day's Sabbath observance: 'All the friends came to salute us before we started and, no preparations having been made on [the] Sabbath, according to law, we were not able to get off so early as we intended.'[51]

What lay behind his strict Sabbatarianism? Contemporary Scottish Church life placed high value on Sabbath observance, and Moffat carried this over into his missionary work. But he was not simply copying the practices of his homeland. He believed there were important principles lying behind them.[52] He alluded to these in an 1835 conversation with Moselekatse:

> On the first Saturday I was there I told Moselekatse that the next day was a holy day which we kept at the command of the Lord, and that I should prefer having no intercourse with anyone except on subjects that referred to the honour of God, whom I served. This led me to explain to him the law of the Sabbath, that it was binding politically as well as in a religious point of view on all nations. He replied as usual, 'Good, good!'[53]

In Moffat's theology, the Sabbath, as part of the Decalogue, was a law of God for all humanity and not restricted to Christians. Moffat saw himself as presenting God's original blueprint for all humanity. He never saw himself as importing an alien religion. On the contrary, he viewed Christian faith and morals as reuniting everyone with their true spiritual home. Thus, the Sabbath applied to all cultures in the same way as prohibitions on murder, theft, and adultery applied to everyone. Christian mission did not conquer

---

[50] RM, *Journal,* 6.9.1857, (*MJ2,* 54). After they reached water the whole group, animals and men, slaked their thirst and rested exhausted. Then a short service of worship.

[51] RM, *Journal,* 12.6.1854, (*MJ1,* 181): 'According to law' refers to the Law of God, especially the Ten Commandments which Reformed theology saw as universal and permanent.

[52] Roby concentrated on two issues in relation to the Sabbath: why *Sunday* is the Christian Sabbath, and the duty of Christians to meet for public worship on that day. Roby did not discuss Sabbatarianism (Roby, *Theol. Lect.* 79, 'Public Worship').

[53] RM, *Journal,* 1829, (*MJ1,* 22).

nations, but liberated them to be what God had originally created them to be.[54] And this Sabbath liberation applied in several ways.

To begin with, the Sabbath liberated men and women to reflect on spiritual matters. 'How much more thankful ought intelligent and immortal beings [to] be for the entire cessation of worldly thoughts and cares, and the enjoyment of one day in seven to reflect on the past and contemplate the future: how strange to think that man, believing himself to be immortal, should devote all [his] time and his energies to mortal things!'[55] The Sabbath also liberated animals from the captivity of daily labour. Thus, the Sabbath was a blessing for 'both man and beast'.[56] It was for the benefit of all creation. On his 1854 journey Moffat wrote: 'Could the dumb oxen speak, how thankful they would be for the day of rest!'[57] On the 1857 journey he commented: '[Saturday] But tea is tempting and will just help one to get ready for Sabbath, which both man and beast will thoroughly enjoy, for neither have much time, the way we are traveling.'[58]

Moffat was so confident of the God-given benefits of the Sabbath that he referred to it in evangelistic discussions.[59] In Moffat's view, the issues relating to the Sabbath—God's Law, reverence for God, the beneficial effect of the Sabbath on the whole community—had evangelical persuasive power. Sabbath emphasis enabled Moffat to stress that all men, even chiefs, had a

---

54 Livingstone taught Sechele of the BaKwena the same principles. For Sechele not fighting on the Sabbath when the Boers threatened him, see Sechele's 1852 letter to Moffat. Cf. Sechele, *To RM,* Sept. 1852, (*DLSAP,* 134): 'They came on a Saturday and prepared to fight on the Sabbath; but I besought them not to fight on a Sabbath and they listened.' This is corroborated by Boer correspondence in Schapera (ed.), *op cit.,* 156 etc. Livingstone also wrote concerning Sechele's Sabbath principles. Cf. Livingstone, *To William Thompson,* 27.9.1855, (*LMC,* 286): 'Sechele asked the Boers on commando not to fight on Sunday. The former beat the Bakwains [BaKwena] hollow in lying and meanness, and it would be an insult to compare the honesty of the Bakwains with the dishonesty of the Boers.'

55 RM, *Journal,* 1.7.1854, (*MJ1,* 205). Elsewhere Moffat wrote about 'dark shades' which afflicted life, concluding that times of shadow make: 'more prominent the brighter lines which point to a rest; or, more correctly, a *sabbatism*, from the Greek *sabbatismos*, and as rendered in the margin of our English Bible, a keeping sabbath, which the Holy Spirit assures us, remains for the people of God.' Cf. RM, *Journal,* 8.11.1859, (*MJ2,* 21).

56 RM, *Journal,* 24.5.1835, (*MJ1,* 54).

57 RM, *Journal,* 1.7.1854, (*MJ1,* 205).

58 RM, *Journal,* 29.8.1857, (*MJ2,* 48).

59 Moffat arrived at Moselekatse's headquarters on Saturday 22.7.1854. The next day was a Sabbath. Moffat spoke to Moselekatse in quiet entreaty regarding his spiritual state: 'I spoke to him about divine things, and how good God was to spare us to meet and that we ought therefore to love him. To everything he responded, and enlarged on it to those standing by, so that I could scarcely get a word in at times.' Cf. RM, *Journal,* 23.7.1854, (*MJ1,* 231), also entries for 29 & 30.7.1854.

duty to God.[60] Moffat saw it important in evangelism to underline that there was a higher authority, and a higher Being, to whom all must bow. The Sabbath, with its regular weekly intrusion into time, publicly demanded that duty to One who was higher. This fitted with Moffat's Calvinist approach to evangelism in which his emphasis was man's duty to God. This was a God-centred evangelism, rather than a human-centred evangelism. Moffat did sometimes expound on the subjective benefits of Christian faith for individuals and for communities, but at the heart of his evangelical message were the objective glory, honour, and duty owed to God. This was of first importance, and Sabbath observance underlined it.

Sexual morals, marital faithfulness, and conduct such as not stealing, were all part of basic Christian living, but in closing this section we can consider two other matters of interest. On one of his journeys Moffat introduced a series of 'fines' in order to discourage swearing among his helpers. This innovation seems to have been introduced with good humour and general acceptance: 'The English swearers had unanimously agreed to pay a half stick of tobacco for every oath. It was on a Sabbath, and when the characters are considered, one will forgive such a contract on such a day. Next day's produce was seventeen and a half sticks = thirty-five oaths. The most notorious lost only one and a half sticks. The number of fines decreased so rapidly that the treasurer is out of employ, except keeping what he has got. I comfort them by stating that they will have all the fewer oaths to account for in the Day of Judgment.'[61]

Concerning beer-drinking, Moffat had no fundamental objection to drinking alcohol in the form of native beer, though he personally chose not to do so. For example, in 1854 when Moffat arrived at Moselekatse's headquarters, Moselekatse sent him a gift:

> While I was laid down [due to an inflamed and painful knee] Moselekatse sent out to my wagon some six or seven large calabashes of beer – I should think eight gallons. I sent word that though I felt thankful for his kindness, he must remember that I do not drink beer, [and] that milk was my beer when I could get it. He sent in reply that he knew I did not drink it, but it was for my company, and that he had given orders for milk to be brought, as no milk-cows were kept in this town.[62]

60 RM, *Journal,* 30.7.1854, (*MJ1,* 247).
61 RM, *Journal,* 24.5.1835, (*MJ1,* 54).
62 RM, *Journal,* 23.7.1854, (*MJ1,* 231).

Moffat did not drink beer, but was happy to give it to others.[63] He especially noted that the drinking of beer did not rouse the Ndebele to violence, as often happened among Europeans who took wines and spirits.[64] He also mused on the possibility that beer kept away fever: 'Messrs. CW and L drink no beer, or at least next to none, and they have had fever enough. Messrs. E, the G's and T drink it plentifully and never had a touch of fever; but so far as self is concerned, I think I am better and more comfortable without it.'[65] Moffat knew that alcohol was a problem in his own country and, on one occasion, he described an African being as 'drunk as a piper',[66] referring to drunkenness in Scotland. Moffat did not teach that a Christian lifestyle meant 'thou shalt not drink beer'. However, the *Kuruman Church Record Book* does record that, at least once, Kuruman disciplined church members who actively promoted beer production.[67]

---

63 RM, *Journal,* 25.7.1854, (*MJ1,* 236).
64 RM, *Journal,* 16.8.1854, (*MJ1,* 261).
65 RM, *Journal,* 16.8.1854, (*MJ1,* 262).
66 RM, *Journal,* 25.7.1854, (*MJ1,* 236).
67 *KCRB,* 9 (3.5.1861): '[2 people] separated on account of disgraceful conduct, living in constant quarrel and bitterness, besides making wine or beer and acting outrageously'.

Chapter 27
The Gifts of a Church

SHOULD THERE BE A DIVISION between the 'ordinary' spiritual gifts such as leadership, wisdom, compassion, and those often designated as 'extraordinary' such as miracles, healing, tongues and prophecy? If so, does that point to a dualism in theological thinking, rather than indicating separate forms of activity by the Holy Spirit? Putting these wider questions aside, how did Moffat understand such gifts?

Mainstream Reformed theology rejected the Anabaptist claim that the age of extraordinary spiritual gifts such as healing, speaking in tongues, and prophecy was still with the Church. There were several reasons behind the Reformed 'cessationist' position: there was a desire to curb Anabaptism; there was a concern to ensure that the centre of attention was the Bible alone; there was unease that a medieval emphasis on miracles wrought by saints had led to superstition rather than true faith; and, most of all, there was very little experiential evidence of miracles in the current life of the Church. Reformed theology thus tended to teach that extraordinary spiritual gifts were restricted to the apostolic age, though this was challenged by the likes of Edward Irving, with whom the LMS had an uncomfortable relationship. The LMS 'official position' was illustrated in a sermon preached by William Chaplin in May 1823 at the LMS annual meetings, and published by the LMS Directors in the same year. Chaplin stated that extraordinary spiritual gifts had,

> Ceased at an early period and that of course no signs of this description are to be expected by us. But although miracles have ceased, and although apostolic signs are not granted to us, yet we are far from being left without signs of another description.[1]

What were these new signs? Chaplin listed several: the destruction of idolatry; the extensive translation and dispersion of the Holy Scriptures; the progress of knowledge and the advancement of civilisation; and the fruits of righteousness. These were the extraordinary, even miraculous, works of the Holy Spirit in contemporary missionary work. In Chaplin's analysis, the

---

1 William Chaplin, *The Example and Success of Primitive Missionaries: A Sermon Preached before the London Missionary Society,* 14.5.1823, (Ldn: Holdsworth, 1823), 20ff.

'miraculous' was still occurring, but the Holy Spirit was producing different signs for a different age.

The Gift of Miracles

The argument that miracles were *a priori* impossible, since they broke God-established laws of nature was an argument of the Enlightenment, rather than of the Reformation century. David Bogue was a cessationist but not a 'miracle denier.' However, he taught that, though the missionaries of the New Testament had extraordinary powers, miracles ceased after the days of the Apostles.[2] Moffat endorsed this view. At the same time, when coping with so many difficulties when evangelising the Ndebele, he wrote wistfully:

> I could not help wishing I could work a miracle. But the best of men, whose shoe latchet I am not worthy to unloose, say the day of miracles is past, and other men of grand minds have tried in vain. Faith, faith, faith, I believe is now our only motto. When the mission was commenced among the Bechuanas, it was like an ant attempting to reach the summit of a stupendous mountain, but it has been gained, and why should we doubt of the Matabele.[3]

Moffat was discussing the possibility of conversions among the Ndebele which seemed to need a miracle if any were to occur, but his comments also related to miracles in general. When he wrote 'Faith, faith, faith', he had in mind his own faith, notably his trust that through the ordinary means of prayer and preaching people would be converted. Mary Moffat may have been more open to the possibility of the openly miraculous, perhaps due to Moravian influences in her childhood. In an intriguing 1859 *Journal* entry, Robert described the claim of a Methodist to have seen a miracle:

> I think sometimes if I could but work a miracle! If it were required in the infancy of Christianity, among an enlightened people, cradled in theology, with gleams of prophecy resting on the high places, and its voice heard anon in the synagogues of Israel, one would think how much more among a people like this. ... Mr. Sykes was telling us some days or weeks ago of a Methodist preacher who wrought a miracle!
>
> > *[He then related a story, about an apparently miraculous provision of wind for a windmill].*
>
> Now, what do you say to this! 'Nothing too hard for almighty power, nothing living, beyond the bounds of infinite love' you will say. No indeed! I am well aware the one thing lacking is *faith.* 'Have faith in God' says Jesus, and the words which follow are of startling import, I fear read by few without the

---

2 Bogue, *Miss. Lect.* 26, 'Advantages of Ancient and Modern Missionaries compared'.

3 RM *Journal,* 16.11.1857, (*MJ2,* 118).

> conviction that they come short of the mark, while there seem no bounds to the encouragement they are intended to convey.[4]

The words 'Now, what do you say to this', may indicate that he considered that Mary had a more open attitude to modern miracles.

The Gift of Healing

Christians in every age have accepted the possibility of God granting healing. Even churches which are avowedly non-charismatic have prayers for the sick. Reformed theology never rejected that possibility. What it rejected was a continuance of the Apostolic era, when a specific healing power was manifest, often through the laying on of hands, resulting in dramatic occurrences of immediate demonstrable physical healing. For the avoidance of confusion, we term that as 'apostolic style healing'. It was that phenomenon which mainstream Reformed theology judged had ceased.

Moffat certainly believed in supernatural healing through the prayer of faith, and he attributed all healing—including healing through the skill of doctors—as a work of God. For example, he wrote in 1835: 'Dr Smith found me suffering from a severe attack of intermittent fever, but by the divine blessing on his medical skill, I was soon restored.'[5] Around the same time, Mary gave birth to a son and was very ill, even, 'brought to the very gates of death'. Moffat gratefully recorded Smith's medical skills, setting them within the healing power of God:

> [Dr Smith] watched for several successive nights with fraternal sympathy, what appeared to be the dying pillow of my beloved partner, nor did he leave before she was out of danger. While we devoutly acknowledge His hand 'who healeth all our diseases' we cannot but record how much we owe to this intelligent and enterprising traveler, for the untiring assiduity with which he exercised his professional skill.[6]

Moffat acknowledged supernatural healing power, and was of the view that God exercised that ministry through the medical skill given to men and women. Such intervention came from God's sovereign will, and the miracle was a miracle of a gracious and loving providence, with God choosing to work through natural means and natural gifts. This view was not due to deism, but because there was no clear evidence of ongoing 'apostolic style healing'.

---

4 RM, *Journal,* 27.10.1859, (*MJ2,* 201f).

5 RM, *MLSSA,* 577. Smith led an 1835 scientific expedition from CT to explore the interior. He stayed at Kuruman for some weeks before going to Moselekatse with Moffat.

6 Ibid.

Moffat had little time for African traditional medicine or African traditional doctors.[7] When treating Moselekatse for a gout-like illness, Moffat noted with satisfaction that Moselekatse placed high value on Moffat's medicines: 'If he was attached to me before, he is now more than ever, for he suspects I can keep him alive. He finds my medicines more potent than his native charms'.[8] Moffat told Moselekatse that, 'with very few exceptions all native medicines were mere charms.'[9] The phrase 'very few exceptions' does indicate Moffat accepting that *some* traditional and natural medicines were effective. He had a positive attitude toward homeopathy.[10] Unlike Livingstone, Moffat received no formal medical training, nevertheless, during his missionary career he was in demand to give medical assistance.[11] Moffat's simple skill with medicines, and his kindness in giving help, was an important factor behind the respect he received:

> [Moselekatse said] 'You gave medicine to the sick and you have cured my beloved (favourite) wife. All the doctors in the land have been called. They could do nothing. I pay and feed doctors, but they are fools. My wives say, 'Let us have Moshete'. You assist those who do not like to ask, and you have done many things for me and my people of which I only heard when they were done.'[12]

The Gift of Prophecy

Prophecy includes both proclaiming the word of God to a contemporary situation, and interpreting the will of God for the future. The former aspect—proclaiming the word of God to the present-day situation—was foundational in all of Moffat's missionary work. The latter aspect—ability to foretell the future—requires more analysis. Moffat discovered that Africans were very interested in future prophecy, and converts coming from a background in which foretelling was an important activity, had questions in this area. Moffat's starting-point was that knowledge of the future, *as far as God wishes us to know the future*, had already been given. It was not a secret

---

7 Traditional doctors were classified into horned doctors and hornless doctors. Both treated diseases. The horned doctors diagnosed through divining bones. The hornless doctors relied on examination of the patient (Schapera, *Tswana,* 62).

8 RM *Journal,* 10.8.1854, (*MJ1,* 258).

9 RM, *Journal,* 28.11.1857, (*MJ2,* 127).

10 RM, *Journal,* 9.11.185, (*MJ2,* 215). Also *Journal,* 10.12.1859, (239): 'I forget at the moment what our homoeopathists recommended. I think *aconite,* a panacea with tyros.'

11 Moffat used several medical works to assist him. Cf. RM, *Journal,* 10.12.1859, (*MJ2,* 239): 'I have been employing leisure moments in the perusal of Spencer Thompson's *Domestic Medicine.* It contains much worth knowing, but does not come up to my expectations [though] there are fewer technicalities than are found in most books of the kind.'

12 RM, *Journal,* 5.12.1857, (*MJ2,* 134).

which required to be divined. It was revealed in the Word of God. This put Moffat in direct opposition to magicians who claimed they could foretell the future, by using dice (*bola*) or by other methods. In 1854, whilst at Sechele's village, Moffat recorded an absorbing discussion on the subject:

> Sechele introduced a subject I had partially explained on the preceding day. It was on prophecy and if prophets still existed. ... I told him [of] the age when Old Testament prophets and prophecy ceased, never to be renewed, and that those in the New Testament were the whole revelation of God, and what He would do till the last trumpet should call the dead from their graves; that henceforth no human being could foretell an event; the spirit of prophecy had ceased to be imparted; that God's whole counsel was now written, and it was that, and that only, we were called to believe.
>
> We could only reason and deduce from circumstances and appearances, as the Saviour remarked about rain and fair weather; that preaching was called prophesying. For example, I tell the Bakuens who hear me that if they will not listen to divine instruction and learn to read, they will continue ignorant, will die in ignorance of the Saviour, die miserably and go to perdition. To tell of events – apart from revelation – which will take place to individuals or nations, was beyond the power of man.
>
> Pointing to a man who had the *bola* (prognosticating dice) around his neck, I said, 'That poor dark benighted mortal will persuade himself that he can foretell with those play-things if he will kill game or, if he is going to a town, if he will get his stomach filled when he gets there'. 'Quuaa!' ejaculated Sechele, 'they are children.' I said I had seen people laugh outright to see the Bechuana throw their bones and look at them with the gravity of a funeral; but I could not laugh, but sigh, for they looked like men robbed of their understanding.[13]

This section of Moffat's *Journal* has the mark of a record written as soon as the session with Sechele finished, with Moffat's head still buzzing with the discussion. Moffat wanted to present orthodox Christian teaching on the nature of prophecy, and to give a theology which undermined the role of the 'magician' or 'soothsayer'. The Reformed view of prophecy gave him what he wanted. Moffat made a series of theological assertions:

Prophecy has ceased and is never to be renewed.
The Scriptures give the whole revelation of the plans of God.
God's whole counsel is now written.
It is that written counsel, which we are called to believe and trust.
At most we can deduce a few things from the 'signs of the times'.
Prophesy is now called preaching.

---

13 RM, *Journal,* 9.6.1854, (*MJ1,* 169f).

The magician's claim to prophesy was therefore false.

Moffat's theology was built foursquare on the belief that the age of prophecy—in terms of new revelation from God—was over. For his view, he again had a ready-made theological model at hand. Reformed theology in Scotland was moulded by the Westminster documents which were clear on this matter. The *Form of Presbyterial Church Government and of Ordination of Ministers agreed upon by the Assembly of Divines at Westminster,* stated:

> The officers which Christ hath appointed for the edification of his church, and the perfecting of the saints, are: some extraordinary, as apostles, evangelists,[14] and prophets *which are ceased:* others ordinary and perpetual, as pastors, teachers, and other church-governors, and deacons.[15]

Some nineteenth-century figures dissented from this, but Moffat reflected the dominant position. This gave him a theology to counter the claims of magicians from a Christian standpoint. He believed that his theology was able to account for all aspects of the presented phenomena. Because his theology focused attention on the exclusivity and sufficiency of Holy Scripture, he saw no need to take the visions of a seer seriously. The only serious thing that needed to be done was to study God's Word.

The Gift of Tongues

Calvin had generally interpreted the gift of tongues in the light of Acts 2, in which the Apostles at Pentecost were able to speak to people gathered from many nations in their own tongue. In this sense, the 'gift of tongues' had not disappeared, since, through translation activity, the Church continued this ministry. Bogue adopted Calvin's argument. And for Bogue, the miraculous ability of the Apostles to speak in another language without training and education had passed. Bogue did not discuss the second form of the gift of tongues—angelic languages with no earthly counterpart. Bogue taught:

1. Tongues were given as evidence of the truth of Christianity.
2. Tongues were given for a more rapid progress of the gospel.
3. Tongues were given for the peculiar encouragement of the first preachers and missionaries.[16]

---

14 The LMS rarely called its workers 'evangelists'. It preferred terms such as, 'missionary', 'teacher', or 'teacher of righteousness'.

15 The 'Form of Presbyterial Church Government and of Ordination of Ministers agreed upon by the Assembly of Divines at Westminster' (1645).

16 Bogue, *Miss. Lect.* 2, 'Employment of a Missionary: Learn the language of the Heathen.'

Bogue then asked: 'What are we to think of the opinion of those who conceive that these gifts will be *restored* to the church for the more effective spread of the gospel?' His answer: 'It is not probable, because the same reasons do not remain'.

Without committing ourselves to either side of the debate, we suggest that Bogue's answer was inadequate. He gave three reasons for the gift being given originally: credibility, evangelism, and encouragement. It is difficult to see how any of these reasons were no longer relevant. But Bogue's position was the LMS position, and the early LMS generally regarded the biblical gift of tongues in terms of the ability to speak foreign languages. Supernatural enabling in speaking new languages had been given to the very first apostles, but now that enabling was through more natural means.

The *Introduction* to Volume One of LMS *Transactions* stated that two things contributed greatly to the success of missionary labours in the apostolic era. One was the vast extent and general laws of the Roman Empire, which gave free access to all its provinces. The other was the gift of tongues, which enabled the missionaries to address the different nations in their own language.[17] Edward Irving introduced a new element, though it was only in 1827 that Irving became convinced that all extraordinary spiritual gifts should still be in operation.[18] Moffat was aware of Irving, and noted Irving's death in his *Journal,*[19] but there is no evidence that Irving's Pentecostal theology influenced Moffat or the LMS in this matter.

Moffat belonged to the early-nineteenth-century classical missions. The Pentecostal influence on missions had to wait until later. It may be trite to claim that much modern evangelical activity, heavily influenced by Pentecostalism, points converts to the *experiential* 'gifts of the Spirit', whereas classical missionaries pointed converts to the *ethical* 'fruit of the Spirit'. But if this observation carries any legitimacy, then a challenge in contemporary mission is to return to principles which concentrate upon holiness of life, transformation of society, establishment of Christian virtues and Christian character, and to a conviction that these things glorify God to a far greater extent than spectacular phenomena.

---

[17] LMS, *Transactions, Vol. 1: 1795-1802,* Introduction, iv (possibly written by Bogue).

[18] Dallimore, *The Life of Edward Irving,* 48. Also: Strachan, *The Pentecostal Theology of Edward Irving,* 15.

[19] Cf. RM, *Journal,* 19.5.1835, (*MJ1,* 50). Moffat wrote to Mary from Manapane *en route* to Moselekatse: '[The *Commercial Advertiser*] announces the death of ... the many-tongued Rev.. Edward Irving at Glasgow.'

THE APPROACH TO MISSION

Chapter 28
The Power of the Word

DIAMONDS WERE NOT DISCOVERED around Kimberley until after 1869, and the Moffats left Africa in 1870. Moffat was not in Africa for wealth, but to bring souls to salvation. His clear motivation was a concern to warn sinners about 'the wrath to come'. One of the few English language devotional books which Moffat translated into SeTswana was John Bunyan's *Pilgrims Progress,*[1] the plot of which is built on the warning given by Evangelist to Christian to 'flee from the wrath to come.' Moffat's decision to translate *Pilgrim's Progress* was not accidental. It summarised his personal incentive for mission: rescuing men and women from judgment.

In 1859, whilst establishing the Ndebele mission, Moffat wrote: 'The question always rises in my mind: "What would the world be without Christianity?"' He answered his own query: 'It would be as if one built and furnished an expensive factory for no earthly use, and in which not a bobbin was ever expected to be spun.'[2] With this conviction in the importance of the Christian faith, Moffat saw mission as the central task and *raison d'etre* of the Church. He believed that if the Church lost its sense of mission then it lost its identity. That was his message during his deputation furlough:

> Of those prosperous churches, planted by the apostles themselves, not one remains (the churches of Revelation especially): and why? Because they lost the Spirit of their Lord and Master. Because they lost their first love. They did not continue to be missionary churches and therefore they withered, therefore they died – Pray![3]

Moffat affirmed the importance of mission. But did he believe that the Christian Gospel was applicable to every tribe and nation? He was clear:

> Already we have seen that the Gospel is suited to the depths of human misery, that it transforms the most barbarous and the most rude; that it changes the lion into a lamb, and the raven into a dove. Can we despair? Dare

---

1 Moffat (translator), *Loeto los Mokereseti lo lo coan batsin yenu ...* [The Journey of a Christian from this world to the world which is to come], (Kuruman: 1848, printed for the Religious Tract Society). Translating, printing and publishing the main part of *Pilgrim's Progress* took three years. The sales were sluggish! (Bradlow, *Printing for Africa,* 33).

2 RM, *Journal,* 12.11.1859, (*MJ2,* 218).

3 RM, *Barbican Sermon,* 22.1.1843, (*Farewell Services,* 127).

we despair? Oh no![4]

In 1829, when Moffat rejoiced in the first Kuruman converts, he noted that since they 'profess a tolerable share of scriptural knowledge with the love of Christ in their souls, they may, through the divine blessing, *be instrumental in warning and instructing others*.'[5] But as Moffat became increasingly preoccupied with translation and printing, he regretted that:

> The work of conversion, or endeavours to convert sinners, is not so much the primary object of our souls as it ought to be. If I speak for myself I must say that I do not feel that sympathy for the awful condition of my fellow-men which their state ought to excite in every Christian bosom. When I look at the Man of Sorrows, His toilsome days and midnight prayers, and the burning zeal of the first ministers of the gospel, I feel as if I had not the same mind or spirit.[6]

Despite his growing preoccupation with Bible translation, a concern for 'lost souls' never left him. And even if he felt that he imperfectly carried out the imperatives attached to 'soul concern', then that 'soul concern' itself never departed. Nor did a full church at Kuruman dilute his desire for there to be a *quality* of evangelical experience to complement the *quantity* of people who gathered on the Sabbath. Through the years, what beat most strongly in his heart was his original desire for the conversion of 'lost souls'. In 1856 he wrote to Arthur Tidman of the LMS:

> We have no reason whatever to complain of [full] benches either in church or school ... but we do not see the things for which we long, and for which we pray without ceasing – the sinner's broken, contrite heart – the heaving sigh – the agonising cry 'what shall we do to be saved?' – the fervent breathings of deep compassion for perishing souls – and the tangible tokens in each who bears the Christian name that feels he is really his 'brother's keeper'. We are authorised to expect these things. We have, blessed be God, been permitted to see these things.[7]

In penning these words, Moffat was casting a wistful eye back to the events of the Kuruman Awakening of 1829. In the 1850s he longed for a repetition of these times. And, as always for him, the true signs of revival or awakening centred on a profound sense of sin before the holiness of God and seeking God's provided remedy. Moffat sought conversions based on man's moral standing before God, with demonstrable signs of a new way of living.

---

4 RM, *Barbican Sermon,* 22.1.1843, (*Farewell Services,* 125).

5 RM, *To Miles,* (CT), 12.8.1829, (SOAS/CWM/SA/Box11/3/D).

6 RM, *To Mary Moffat,* 23.12.1835, (JSM, *Lives,* 205).

7 RM, *To Tidman, LMS,* 28.10.1856, (SOAS/CWM/SA/Box 30/1/A).

THE WORD IN MISSION

Moffat's focus on Bible translation was directly linked to his understanding of mission. But how was that mission to be carried out? Moffat held that the God-appointed method was to make the Word of God in the Bible available to men and women. He believed that the power of God was mediated through the power of the Word: 'It is to the Bible we are to look as the only means of directing human invention to the best of causes and thus transform a world of sin and evil into an abode of righteousness, peace and love.'[8] Moffat looked at Africa and at Europe, and saw each in critical need of the transforming message of the Bible:

> How like these barbarians are to some of the civilised nations of Europe who love robbery, dominion and oppression! Wherever such things are perpetrated: whether here or in civilised Europe, they must be classed among the dark places of the earth. Nothing but the Bible can save man from these woes.[9]

The Bible was the foundation of Moffat's faith. 'It was only yesterday,' he wrote in his 1859 *Journal,* 'after laying down the Bible, that I wondered what kind of mind I should have had, if I had not the Book of God, the Book containing the astounding idea of "from everlasting to everlasting."'[10] For Moffat, the Bible was where men and women learned the concept of an 'eternal unlimitedness', culminating in the dazzling wonder of the Lamb of God. What Moffat was expressing was the notion that it is the Bible which lifts the human spirit above the finite limitedness of ordinary existence into an eternal, transcendent realm, the centre of which is Jesus Christ; and, in so raising the human spirit, gives a sense of meaning, value, dignity and purpose to human existence.

There is no trace in Moffat's writings of a missiology based on inculturation. That concept was unknown to him and, even if he had been aware of the idea, it would have been uncongenial to his thinking. Later missionaries, such as Smith and Willoughby,[11] who worked in the same geographical area as Moffat only a generation or two later, have, not without cause, criticised Moffat's lack of sensitivity to cultural issues and especially his lack of awareness of how indigenous culture could have aided his work. It would be disingenuous to make Moffat into what he was not: a modern,

---

8 RM, *To Browne, BFBS,* 22.11.1852, (CULBSA/Browne/1852/M).

9 RM, *Journal,* 9.6.1854, (*MJ1,* 168).

10 RM, *Journal,* 28.11.1859, (*MJ2,* 234f). Cf. RM, *To Mullens, LMS,* 19.5.1868, (SOAS/CMW/SA/Box 35/1/A).

11 Cf. Smith, *Robert Moffat, One of God's Gardeners.* Also: Willoughby, *The Soul of the Bantu.*

culture-affirming missionary, with methods to match. Our exposition of Moffat's missiology follows a different path. Our exposition must also proceed despite the lack of any work written by Moffat on the subject. Moffat did not set out a philosophy of mission, believing that others, more able than he, had already done so:

> The present writer has indulged but slightly in philosophical disquisition, as he deemed it in his province principally to supply facts. He leaves it to men of leisure and reflecting habits to analyze, compare, and deduce from those facts such doctrines as they supply.[12]

Though discussion of missiological methods was not his aim, Moffat did offer occasional comments which give insight into his thinking. At the heart of his missiology was a conviction that the Word of God, the Scriptures, had within itself the power to penetrate hearts, change lives, and accomplish the divine purposes. Moffat wrote to the *British and Foreign Bible Society*: 'The simple reading and study of the Bible alone will convert the world.'[13] This was Moffat's missiology. The task of the missionary was to make that Word known, and to give the Word opportunity to accomplish its goals through its inherent power. In another letter to the *Bible Society,* he wrote:

> I have frequently listened with surprise to hear how minutely some, who were unable to read, could repeat the story of the Woman who was a sinner; the parable of the Great Supper, the Prodigal Son, and the Rich Man and Lazarus; and date their change of views to those simple but all-important truths, delivered by the great Master Teacher.[14]

Moffat believed that there was little need for specialised training, or for the development of methods of evangelism. The Word would do its own work. It only needed to be set free.[15] Human wisdom, arguments, and culture were unimportant. The duty of the servant of God was simply to liberate the Word to accomplish its task. Any missionary achievement was due to the power of

---

12 Moffat mentioned: 'the luminous works of Dr Campbell and Harris, and Messrs. Hamilton, Noel and others, by whom the subject of Missions has been so learnedly and eloquently illustrated.'(RM, *MLSSA,* v.).

13 RM, *To Browne, BFBS,* 3.7.1838, (CULBSA/Browne/1838/4/40).

14 RM, *To Browne, BFBS,* 20.11.1836, (CULBSA/Browne/1837/2/11). This points to Moffat using *story* in presenting the Gospel, but always undergirded by his Calvinist theology. In the New Testament the *narrative* of the Gospels links with the *theology* of the Epistles.

15 Livingstone expressed this point well. Cf. Livingstone, *To William Thompson,* 27.9.1855, (*LMC,* 286): 'The Word of the living God has been brought in contact with their hearts and minds. This word has life and power. Few human souls can withstand its force, and no hatred, however deep, can quench its power.'

the Word.[16] Any superficiality or lack of depth was due to 'a religion founded on feelings and frames, visions and dreams.'[17]

A concentration on the primacy of the Word had long moulded Scottish theological thinking. Even today, in Calvinist and Presbyterian circles, preachers speak more often in terms of 'preaching the Word' than 'preaching the Gospel'.[18] The latter is subsumed under the former. Indeed, when Moffat referred to the Christian Faith he frequently spoke of the '*Word* of Life'.[19] The Spirit worked through the Word: and, since humanity is body, *mind,* and soul, conversions occurred when the Word first transformed the mind, leading to a spiritual and moral change in an individual. As Moffat expressed it: 'Knowledge changes the heart'.[20]

THE EFFICACY OF THE WORD

For Moffat, the Word had power because the Word was God's chosen instrument to effect change in the mind and hearts of those who heard it and surrendered to it. An alternative understanding of why the translated Word had this power has been offered by Paul Landau[21] and the Comaroffs[22] who have questioned Moffat's reasons as to why the Word was so effective.

---

16 E.g. RM, *To Bergne, BFBS,* 18.7.1866, (CULBSA/BFBSEC/Inwards/4/259): 'The Word of God has taken too firm a hold on the native mind to allow us for a moment to doubt as to its extending influence among Africa's trodden-down children. It is the means and the only means by which the Redeemer is to conquer the world by bringing all to the obedience of faith' On another occasion Moffat focused on the Holy Spirit: 'We see, and may God grant that we may ever feel, that it is not the missionary, it is not the Bible, but the Spirit of the Lord.' (RM, *Africa,* 47). Also: 'The mystery to those who are still in their native state, is, how an invisible agent [the Bible] can produce such a change [of lifestyle]. Also: RM, *Africa,* 40: 'If they ate their books' say they, "there would be some reason for their getting new hearts."'

17 RM, *To James and Mary Smith,* 20.8.1822, (*AAK,* 64). This was Moffat's possibly unfair critique of what was going on at Bethelsdorp. The converted Khoikhoi from Bethelsdorp who worked at Lattakoo had, in his view, 'low moral quality'.

18 When John Campbell, LMS Director and Moffat's Scottish contemporary, wrote about the progress of Christianity in southern Africa, he framed his remarks in terms of what the *Word* had achieved: '[A chief said] "Before the *Word* of God came to the Griquas, the Corannas (who live beside them) were continually attacking us and killing us and taking away our cattle; but since the *Word* of God came to the Griquas I have never been molested: wherefore I consider it to be a good *Word,* so that I cannot refuse its coming to my people."' (Campbell, *The Progress of the Kingdom of Christ,* (1833), 5.

19 E.g. RM, *Journal,* 24.5.1821, (*AAK,* 18).

20 RM, *Journal,* 5.8.1821, (*AAK,* 21).

21 Paul Stuart Landau, *The Realm of the Word: Language, Gender and Christianity in a Southern African Kingdom,* (CT: David Philip, 1995).

22 Comaroff, *Revelation and Revolution, Vol. 1.*

Landau and the Comaroffs rejected Moffat's premise that the Word was effective because *God* was in the Word. They sought other factors.

1. *Landau*. Paul Landau focused on the importance in missionary work of the Biblical text as a religious given, with the text having a status underscored by its physical reality as a printed entity. Landau pointed out that, in their initial meetings with evangelists, the Tswana heard many different kinds of messages, with little supporting these messages except the status of the bearers. However, following the translation of the Bible into SeTswana by Moffat, the message had greater credibility. The printed text, precisely in being a *visible printed* text, became authoritative, with missionaries and evangelists mediating this text, refracturing it many times with new interpretations.[23] What Landau was arguing was that the message which Moffat brought had little persuasive power until it became associated with the authority of a printed text. Thereafter, its authority was enormous, even if the interpretation of the Word evolved over generations. Landau explained that what he wanted to do was to shift away from a story about the actions of missionaries and the reactions of Africans, to a story about orchestration of power based on the elaboration and reverberations of a printed text.

For Landau, Moffat unwittingly utilised an ethos expressed in GammaNgwato as *thuto.*[24] Landau wanted an explanation of how a religion introduced by one culture was accepted by another culture, whilst excluding any supernatural factors—though it was only at the end of his book that he admitted this presupposition: 'I want to end, as so many begin, with a confession. It may be that the only way truly to privilege Christians' own experiences and expressions is to share in their faith. This my analysis could not do.'[25] At the centre of Landau's comment was a fundamental question: do sociological, psychological and cultural factors precipitate religious changes, or does the Spirit of God do it? Landau sought non-supernatural explanations. Yet his academic honesty made him recognise that, from a different worldview, his conclusions may be disputed.

2. *The Comaroffs.* The Comaroffs went further. In their politicised interpretation of history and culture, they viewed Moffat's work—of translating and printing the Bible in SeTswana—as the colonisation of language. For the Comaroffs, 'word power' was at the root of missionary success, with 'word power' an extension of European colonialism. Through translation and printing, Moffat took control and ownership of the language.

---

23 Landau, *The Realm of the Word,* xxi.

24 Ibid, 208, also 27f.

25 Ibid, 219.

Words, previously only spoken, were now written and read. This written word was 'possessed' by the missionary, and thus under the control of the missionary. And if language is a major factor in the identity of a people, then, when their language is 'colonised', the hearts and minds of the people follow.[26] The Comaroffs' thesis was that the Tswana were dispossessed of their own language, and, because language expresses identity, they had to follow their language into the new culture and religion which had taken possession of it. Hence the missionaries' success.

It is not surprising that Landau and the Comaroffs, writing from secular perspectives, came to their conclusions. What is at issue is the well-known matter of a theological interpretation of history. The Christian theologian may be convinced of the hand of God in historical events, but the secular scholar cannot introduce such a factor. Even the theologian may feel constrained to work with secular axioms in order to preserve his or her academic reputation, it being assumed that 'objectivity' requires personal faith assumptions to be set aside.

The question of what constitutes true objectivity is too wide to discuss here, but how might Moffat have responded to the Landau and Comaroff critiques of the 'power of the Word'? The type of analysis offered by Landau and the Comaroffs was unknown in Moffat's day, but it is safe to say that he would have insisted on acknowledging a supernatural work of God. Moffat claimed that a chief once said to him: "Is it the precepts of that book' (pointing to the Gospel of Luke which I held in my hand) 'which have made you what you are? Is it that *mahuka a molemo* (good news) which has made your nation new, and clothed you; compared with whom we are like the game of the desert?"[27] Moffat's presuppositions were considerably different to those of Landau and the Comaroffs. He believed that the Spirit of God changed the hearts of men and women by the word of truth, not through social or psychological manipulation, intended or unintended.

The Proclamation of the Word

Moffat insisted on a regular pattern of morning and evening worship. This was the case whether at a mission station or on a journey. Out of numerous passages in his writings we refer to two striking incidents. In 1823, whilst journeying to visit Makaba, Moffat recorded that, about two hours after dark, the group halted by a pool where there were a few bushes to give

---

[26] Comaroff, *Revelation and Revolution: Vol. 1,* 218f, 152.

[27] RM, Moffat, *Africa,* 33.

shelter from the piercing wind: he then read a chapter from the Bible, and commended the group to the care of the covenant God.[28] On another occasion Moffat's group were bivouacked at a small pool and had just closed evening worship, the Bible still in Moffat's hand and 'the closing notes of the song of praise' scarcely finished, when the roar of the lion was heard.[29] These incidents illustrate the invariant practice of Moffat's daily life. Fellow-travellers, and the people whom he visited, noticed this consistent seriousness of piety concerning the things of God. Even Moselekatse, who remained unconverted, enjoyed sharing in Moffat's evening Bible reading and prayer. The event impressed him.[30]

Regular worship was not simply a devotional exercise for individual benefit. It was also a public witness to the majesty of God. It was deliberately public, and not something done secretly or in isolation. In being a public act, God's name was 'exalted among the heathen' and right honour was ascribed to him in the 'midst of the nations'. This public ascription of glory was a powerful declaration of faith, which Moffat believed God would use to speak to those watching and listening. Though its primary purpose was to worship God for His own sake, public worship was an evangelistic tool. In Scottish theology the term 'means of grace' was applied to any action which brought a person closer to, or deeper into, the things of God. The 'means of grace' might be Bible reading, prayer, the sacraments, or the act of worship itself. Moffat employed the phrase in the latter sense when describing his ministry among Africaner's Namaqua:

> The means of grace, however, were well attended, and a delightful unction of the Spirit realised, especially in our Sabbath convocations: and so strong was the attachment of the people that, although I was contemplating a visit to the Cape, I dared not mention the subject.[31]

Baptism and the Lord's Supper were also 'means of grace', but were applied differently. Baptism at Kuruman was carried out at the public act of worship on a Sabbath morning as a witness to the power of the Gospel to change lives, and believers, enquirers, and non-believers were all present. The Lord's Supper was celebrated in the evening, with possibly only members of the church being present.

The most common way in which the Word was used in evangelism was through preaching. The *content* of Moffat's message is the subject matter of

---

28 RM, *Journal,* 15.5.1823, (*AAK,* 76). Also: RM, *Journal,* 6.6.1854, (*MJ1,* 162).

29 RM, *MLSSA,* 131.

30 RM, *Journal,* 26.8.1854, (*MJ1,* 274).

31 RM, *MLSSA,* 172.

this whole book, but in this section our concern is to examine the approach Moffat had to preaching. In nineteenth-century Scottish Presbyterianism, a typical Sabbath service included two addresses. The first address, near the start of the service, was an expository lecture, explaining the meaning of a Scripture passage point by point or verse by verse. The second address, often termed the 'sermon', was more wide-ranging, possibly thematic, and sought to apply the Christian faith to individuals and the community. This was the form of service offered by Ebenezer Brown of Inverkeithing whose ministry was well known to Moffat, and it was a form widely observed elsewhere.

Kuruman replicated this model with one major variation. At Inverkeithing and other Scottish Kirks, both types of address were delivered in the one service, whereas at Kuruman the differing forms appear to have been assigned to separate diets of worship on the Sabbath. Thus, in 1868 John Smith Moffat wrote that at Kuruman: 'My custom, in the regular way, is to give New Testament reading in the morning, a topical sermon in the afternoon, and Old Testament exposition in the evening.[32] Moffat alluded to a similar pattern in his 1862 *Occasional Journal*.[33]

There are no extant copies of sermons preached by Moffat at Kuruman.[34] The scraps of sermon material which are accessible come from his accounts of preaching as documented in his *Journal* or letters. Most of these are concerned with preaching to non-Christians and are evangelistic sermons, therefore not necessarily of the same style as sermons for his 'settled congregation'. Nevertheless, despite the paucity of evidence available, there are enough clues to confirm that Moffat's 'congregational preaching' was expository, and his 'evangelistic preaching' was thematic: though these categories were not mutually exclusive.

---

32 JSM, *To the LMS Directors,* 12.10.1868, (Deane, *Robert Moffat,* 165).

33 RM, *Occ. Jour: 1860-1862, 1868,* 26.1.1862, (SOAS/CWM/SA/Moffat /Personal/Box 4). The LMS *Annual Report* (1850), 81f, alluded to a fourth service in Dutch 'for the benefit of the scattered Griqua.'

34 In the SOAS Archives there is a bundle of undated 'sermon notes' in English, 'believed' to have been written by Moffat (SOAS/CWM/SA/Moffat/Personal/Box 4). We have not drawn on that material. The provenance is uncertain, and though some are in handwriting similar to Moffat's, there are, in the same batch, notes in a different hand (similar to that of Roger Price). Moreover, the sermon notes are in outline only, not a full text, and there is little to be gained from their contents. Though it may be tempting to use the material, we judge that there is no advantage to be gained from assuming Moffat's authorship. The SOAS archives do hold a copy of the sermon Moffat composed on board ship *en route* to Africa in late 1816: the sermon of a student 'just qualified' rather than the sermon of the more experienced missionary.

PREACHING TO BELIEVERS

When instructing or encouraging fellow workers, Moffat's style was to expound a text or passage of Scripture. On the 1859 expedition to the Ndebele, Moffat described preaching to the group who accompanied him from Kuruman, and supplied the following illuminating statement: 'It being my turn, I *preached* or rather *lectured*, going through Matthew's Gospel.'[35] To go through Matthew's Gospel verse by verse would require a preaching series covering months, or years, and Moffat was only referring to his preaching on one Sabbath. It would seem that his sermon was an overview of Matthew, systematically identifying the main themes and implications of Matthean teaching. In the quotation cited, Moffat explicitly preferred the term 'lectured' to the term 'preached'. This demonstrates two things. Firstly, he saw a subtle difference between the two. Secondly, the 'lecture' or 'systematic exposition' was important to him. To prepare his companions for their forthcoming work, Moffat prioritised expository teaching.

Moffat's predilection for the term 'lecture'—viewing it as a synonym for 'expounding'—occurs in another extract. This was in 1857, when his fellow travellers needed encouragement. Sunday, 6 September 1857, was one of the few Sabbaths on which Moffat travelled on the day of rest. The previous day, the group had failed to find water near where they camped for the night, and men and oxen were in dire need of water. For the whole of the Sabbath morning until mid-day the party cut its way through woodland until, in the early afternoon, they came across water. Moffat recorded that after the group was refreshed, 'I took the 107th Psalm and *lectured* on it, or rather, *expounded* it, for the edification of myself and people. I prayed, and then Sebolai, and we were not forgetful to return thanks for many mercies.'[36] The apt content of Psalm 107 helps to explain why much of Moffat's preaching was expository. Psalm 107 is a lengthy Psalm, but the first few verses show its relevance:

> Give thanks to the LORD, for he is good; his love endures forever. Let the redeemed of the LORD say this - those he redeemed from the hand of the foe, those he gathered from the lands, from east and west, from north and south. Some wandered in desert wastelands, finding no way to a city where they could settle. They were hungry and thirsty, and their lives ebbed away. Then they cried out to the LORD in their trouble, and he delivered them from their distress (Psalm 107:1-6).

---

35 RM, *Journal,* 20.11.1859, (*MJ2,* 226).

36 RM, *Journal,* 6.9.1857, (*MJ2,* 55).

What Moffat did was to select a portion of Scripture which perfectly described the day which had just been experienced. He came from a tradition which believed that the Scriptures covered every situation in life and spoke to every context. Finding an appropriate passage was no surprise to him. This was why evangelical preaching was based on exposition of the Word. It was believed that the Word was able to engage with *every* circumstance in life.[37] Hence, for the people of God as a people under the Word, expository preaching was seen as the basic form of all preaching.

An emphasis on exposition was also present when Moffat described preaching to the BaNgwaketse in 1854. The tribe had been evangelised for some time, and Moffat recorded that, 'They all appeared very attentive to my discourse from these words, "God is not mocked". I had read a chapter and *expounded* it as I usually do among such people.'[38] On this occasion, Moffat probably preached from Galatians 6:8ff, especially the section: 'Do not be deceived: God cannot be mocked. A man reaps what he sows. The one who sows to please his sinful nature, from that nature will reap destruction; the one who sows to please the Spirit, from the Spirit will reap eternal life.' The passage was practical, direct, challenging, and led on to the imperative of living a new kind of life.

In his preaching, Moffat consistently emphasised a new and better way of life. His favoured method was to describe and condemn the old way of life, using the sermon as a mirror in which his hearers saw themselves and their current mode of living,[39] then he pointed to something better which, he believed, his hearers were secretly yearning for. In this example, the content of Moffat's message (living a new life) was clearly presented from within a method based on exposition of the Word.

---

37 The *power* of the Word linked to its being *relevant* to every circumstance was illustrated in a letter from Robert to Mary in 1859. The context was one of increasing frustration among the Kuruman group as they waited for Moselekatse to give them permission to build houses to form a mission station at Inyati. See, RM, *To Mary Moffat,* 8.11.1859, (*MJ2,* 211): 'I never open the bible without looking for something like an answer to prayer. By daily reading I have gone through the Psalms, and I am now in Proverbs. I remember you telling me of a minister who, in his experience, always found a word of comfort or encouragement in *Proverbs.* On Sabbath, when I was feeling a good deal perplexed, my eyes happened to fall on *Proverbs,* 21, 1st verse.' The verse stated: '*The king's heart is in the hand of the Lord,* as the rivers of water; he turneth it whithersoever he will' (AV).

38 RM, *Journal,* 26.11.1854, (*MJRM-I,* 354).

39 Scripture as a *mirror* in which we see our sinful nature reflected, is alluded to by Moffat on an 1824 journey to the north, during which he preached to his traveling companions: 'Once or twice every weekday I illustrate and apply a portion of scripture. I cannot complain of want of attention, but alas, how many see their face as in a *glass* and straightaway forget!' See: RM, *Journal,* 11.7.1824, (*AAK,* 124).

He followed a similar pattern when preaching on discipleship issues to the same tribe in 1857. He spent a Sabbath at Kanye village, near where Sebobi, a native teacher from Kuruman, worked among the BaNgwaketse:

> The people were called, and I had a congregation just large enough in open air to be reached with my voice at the highest key. My subject was Psalm 33:12. I spoke long, loud, and earnest too, for I could not help feeling grieved to see them, as I saw them in the days of Makaba, except for some five or six readers or learning to read. Four, including Gasiitsive,[40] can read tolerably. I saw two or three more in the spelling book. They (about seven hundred) listened attentively. I kept talking to the chief and some of his principal men during the whole interim.[41]

Moffat's message was yet again set within a context of expounding the Word. The psalms were especially rich ground, stressing the universal reign of God, underlining that the LORD was God of all the nations of the earth, and bringing into sharp focus the state of humanity—believers and unbelievers—before such a God. Psalm 33:12 stated: 'Blessed is the nation whose God is the Lord, the people he chose for his inheritance.' These sentiments fitted an important facet of Moffat's theological emphasis: his concern with the transformation of a nation, not simply the conversion of individuals.[42]

Whenever he was on a missionary expedition, Moffat's companions were regularly described as 'my people', and almost invariably he described his preaching to 'my people' in terms of expounding the Word. Whilst among the Ndebele in 1857 he wrote: 'Felt great comfort while expounding to my people the 13th chapter of 1st Corinthians—the principles the very opposite to those of the people among whom I sojourn.'[43] In this extract 'my people'

---

[40] Gasiitsive was the grandson of Makaba who was chief of the BaNgwaketse when Moffat visited him in 1824.

[41] RM, *Journal,* 10.8.1857, (*MJ2,* 22). Exposition was central when Moffat preached to Sechele's BaKwena in 1854. Initial attendance was small—only Moffat's traveling group, Sechele, his wife, his children, plus a few domestics—though, after the service started about two dozen more filtered in. RM, *Journal,* 11.6.1854, (*MJ1,* 178) wrote: 'I read from the 17th chapter of 2nd Kings and commented chiefly on the subject of the 13th, 14th and 18th, 19th and 20th verses.' This was not an evangelistic sermon, but a call to deeper discipleship. It took the style of exposition which was Moffat's format when preaching to the 'church'. A similar emphasis on didactic exposition is conveyed in Moffat's account of a second service he had in Sechele's village that day: 'The mass, including the children outside, was perfectly silent. I read the 19th of Matthew, with a word of explanation here and there, and preached—or rather *expounded*—from verses 24 to 27 of the 16th chapter of Matthew. The chief men were there from nearly all the different villages, and listened with marked attention.'

[42] The preceding verses in the Psalm (33:8-11) gave Moffat the biblical setting for his sermon. The verses following verse 12 provided applicable theological content, with emphasis on the sovereignty and uniqueness of God, and God's knowledge of every detail of human life.

[43] RM, *Journal,* 22.11.1857, (*MJ2,* 122f).

referred to traveling companions from Kuruman, whereas 'the people among whom I sojourn' were the Ndebele. Earlier on the same visit, Moffat used almost identical terminology:

> This forenoon expounded to my people from the 11th verse to the end of 1st Thessalonians 4. Many Matabele, most of whom could not understand me, drew near, and sat with great decorum during the whole service. In the afternoon I had a large attendance, and felt an indescribable pleasure in unfolding to them the common salvation. It is pleasing to address people who evidently take a deep interest in what is said.[44]

Each time, the ministry to 'my people' is described as 'expounding' the Word. This was the form of ministry which Moffat deemed appropriate for the people of God. It was what he gave to believers whilst on expeditions, and it was what was given to believers at Kuruman.

PREACHING TO NON-BELIEVERS

In evangelistic situations, Moffat's style was doctrinal and thematic. This is demonstrated in his record of one of his earliest sermons, which was to the Namaqua in 1818:

> During our stay there I preached frequently, particularly from Paul's address to the Athenians. I also conversed with them on particular points, some replied, if it is so—that we are all the children or descendants of one Father Adam, how is it that you are white and we nearly black? This I explained. I also spoke on the existence of God, the creation and fall of man, the immortality of the soul, the redemption by Christ. All this was a new thing, neither could it enter into their ears, according as they expected it, or, more properly, they could not believe it. [45]

The doctrines which Moffat listed are consistent with his account of other evangelistic sermons, such as in 1854 when he summarised preaching to the Ndebele: 'I gave a general view of creation, providence and redemption, and concluded with death and immortality. I delivered the truths as they stood in the pages of divine revelation.'[46] This was thematic and doctrinal preaching, though rooted in 'the pages of divine revelation'. Moffat made it clear that his message came from Scripture, but concentrated on explaining themes rather than expounding the Word directly. The above quotations, one from the start and one from the mid-point of his career, are complemented by an

---

44 RM, *Journal,* 25.10.1857, (*MJ2,* 105).

45 RM, *To Burder, LMS,* 20.8.1818, (SOAS/CMW/SA/Box 7/5/A). Kitchingham, *Journal,* 30.11.1817, (Le Cordeur, *Kitchingham Papers,* 47), who worked with Moffat at this time, recorded Moffat preaching to the Namaqua from John 10.

46 RM, *Journal,* 24.9.1854, (*MJ1,* 312).

1876 letter to the Rev. Woodman, in which he discussed the nature of the message he had spent a lifetime proclaiming:

> In reference to preaching to heathens such as those the Moravian missionaries met with in Greenland, and Williams in the Islands of the Southern Ocean, I can only say that I did what I presume they did, … proclaiming the love of God to a rebel world. They told them that God so loved the world as to send His Son to die for sinners. … For me, the Gospel cannot be understood without telling the ignorant degraded heathen the character of that God who compassionated a world lying in wickedness. … Such teaching I have taught and that has produced the power of God and the salvation of thousands.'[47]

When Moffat described the sermons he gave the Ndebele, he often referred to having focused on core doctrines, the source of which was the Word:

> Had a large congregation today: I referred to our parting, which [I] had expected before this time. Referred to separation at death and the eternal separation at the last day; put them in mind of what I had spoken to them during the repeated opportunities I had had of addressing them on the great and eternal truths of God's Word which they saw in my hands, and which would testify against them in the day of judgment if they refused to believe.[48]

On the 1859-60 visit, Moffat's final sermon to the Ndebele was concisely summarised by John Smith Moffat: 'He walked up to the chief's kraal for the purpose of speaking to Moselekatse and his people for the last time on the great themes of *life, death, and eternity*.'[49] This thematic doctrinal evangelistic preaching was delivered with a passionate urgency:

> I addressed the [Ndebele] with the prospect of it being the last time[50], perhaps the last time in this world; exhorted them not to forget what I had taught during my sojourn among them, as they would have to give an account on the last day when we should see each other again, not to hear me entreating them to believe in the Son of God, but to receive from him everlasting reward or punishment according to the deserts of each. I have repeatedly observed how strange some of them look at me, and I suppose wonder how easily I can talk about death.[51]

Whilst with the Ndebele in 1857, Robert wrote home to Mary, musing on the utter finality of the destiny a person met after death: 'To die and be the next moment in the overwhelming radiance of the divine glory, or in unquenchable flames, startles and alarms. A single moment, and a destiny

---

47 RM, *To Rev. W.B. Woodman,* 9.10.1876, (SOAS/SA/Moffat/Pers/4).

48 RM, *Journal,* 6.12.1857, (*MJ2,* 135).

49 JSM, *Lives,* 347, (our italics).

50 Moffat visited the Ndebele again in 1859.

51 RM, *Journal,* 28.11.1857, (*MJ2,* 129).

eternal is fixed.'[52] Though this extract is taken from a letter to Mary, and not from a sermon, it is reasonable to assume that Moffat preached in similar terms, using similarly dramatic metaphors.[53] The phrases were strong, with signs of polished usage through frequent usage in Moffat's preaching. The irreversible finality of death, with its accompanying finality of human destiny, was presented in a correspondingly dramatic style.

We note one further point concerning Moffat's homiletic methodology. This comes from an 1818 letter to James Kitchingham in response to questions Kitchingham posed concerning preaching:

> As to the questions which you propose, I would just state my own thoughts. 1st, I have addressed the people in a methodical manner, but very seldom indeed have I found plain illustration of the passage to be the most effectual plan to attract, entertain, and edify the hearers. When the text divides itself, I show them that, but seldom more.[54]

The key-phrase is 'plain illustration'. In Moffat's view 'plain illustration' was insufficient. Simple *explanation* was not the same as *expounding* the Word. Expository preaching required a deeper approach. It was more than simply preaching on a text. It was allowing the sense and logic of the Word to reveal itself. It also included the application or 'improvement'[55] of the doctrine involved, in which moral and spiritual imperatives were as important as doctrinal indicatives. It was here that exposition and doctrine came together. A passage must be taught systematically, but behind any adequate exposition there had to be a theological system acting as a tool to expose the coherence of the fullness of the faith rooted within the passage.

EMBEDDING THE WORD: SINGING

Moffat came from church traditions in which proclamation of the Word was understood in terms of the preacher delivering his address whilst the congregation listened in submissive quietude. Church members would then take the message home to meditate upon as individuals, or perhaps to discuss with neighbours during the following week. Contemporary accounts record that it was a source of pride amongst sermon-hearers to be able to recite from memory all the headings and sub-headings which made up the

---

52 RM, *To Mary Moffat,* 11.10.1857, (*MJ2,* 94).

53 E.g. Moffat's preaching to some BaThlaping in 1835. RM, *To Mary Moffat,* 2.12.1835, (JSM, *Lives,* 201): 'I addressed them from 'How shall ye escape etc.' All were attentive; every eye seemed to continue fixed on me. I think I continued speaking for nearly an hour. After they had dispersed, several spoke to me about their souls.'

54 RM, *To Kitchingham,* 27.10.1818, (Le Cordeur, *Kitchingham Papers,* 54).

55 'Improvement' referred to the practical application of a doctrine in the believer's life.

address. In addition to preaching there was of course catechising. But in Africa, Moffat discovered song and discussion as allies to the task.

Whilst with the Ndebele in 1854—and before permission was given to preach to Moselekatse's people—Moffat held Sabbath services for his Kuruman group in the open. He noted: 'A number of warriors stood near and appeared to be attracted by the singing'.[56] Christian singing, both as an observed phenomenon and as a participative activity, had proved to be effective in evangelism from the early years at Kuruman. Spiritual progress had been slow during the initial period at the station, but a significant advance took place when hymns were sung in the vernacular, a suggestion first made by Richard Miles, the LMS agent in Cape Town. Miles argued that singing of Christian hymns in SeTswana would enable the great truths of salvation to become imperceptibly written on the minds of the people.

This suggestion was adopted, and Moffat prepared the first hymns in the language. Printed spelling-books also arrived, enabling the missionaries to open a school in the SeTswana language.[57] By 1828 Moffat cited real signs of encouragement despite the dangers caused by Griqua Civil Wars raging around the Kuruman area, and he particularly highlighted the effect of vernacular hymn singing: 'We also commenced singing hymns in the language, which had a very pleasing effect.'[58] He reported the same encouragement, citing the same reasons, in a letter to his brother Richard, writing: 'The school is doing well. The hymns I compose in the language are soon acquired, and sung well, which has a very pleasing effect on public worship. Some of the natives also sing them in their families.'[59]

In 1830 a visit to Cape Town to print the first SeTswana version of Luke's Gospel also resulted in the printing of a small hymn book in the SeTswana language. Thereafter, the translation, composition and printing of hymns became an indispensable feature of the work at Kuruman.

We have cited Moffat's account of the attractive effect of hymn-singing in 1854 on the Ndebele. He noted the same impact in 1857: 'I had service with my company. Many Matabele drew near, attracted by the singing, which

---

56 RM, *Journal,* 20.8.1854, (*MJ1,* 264).

57 Deane, *Robert Moffat,* 97f.

58 RM, *To Miles,* 30.1.1828, (*AAK,* 279). Smith, *Robert Moffat: One of God's Gardeners,* 144, quoted an undated letter by Miles: 'Something like hymns in the native language, which being constantly sung, the great truths of salvation would become imperceptibly written on the minds of the people.'

59 RM, *To Richard Moffat,* 30.12.1828, (*AAK,* 290).

they seem to enjoy exceedingly.'[60] Three years later in 1860, as the Ndebele Mission became established, Moffat wrote:

> Mr. Sykes accompanied by Mr. Thomas and John went to [Moselekatse's] headquarters and took all the people with them; Moselekatse wishing to hear more singing. Mr. S. attracted a large congregation to his great satisfaction; and, as the king requested a second service in the afternoon Mr. T. went and found a still larger gathering. The events of the day gave much pleasure to those who witnessed it.[61]

On the return journey from the Ndebele in 1860, he recorded:

> [We] went to the two villages which lie at a considerable distance from each other among the hills. All the people readily assembled to hear the word of God preached to them. All perfectly understood the Sechuana and appeared to pay great attention. ... As I was accompanied by all the people of my own camp, some of whom being tolerable singers, *the music appeared to please*.[62]

A sociologist or psychologist may offer non-theological reasons for hymn singing aiding evangelism. But Moffat saw it as simply another avenue of the Holy Spirit working through 'means of grace'. After Miles had persuaded Moffat of the value of vernacular hymn-singing, Moffat used it to the full, realising that hymn-singing was a way of bringing the Word and a sense of the presence of God, to those who gathered together. Praise sung in public, not just in private gatherings of believers, became a powerful channel for the work at Kuruman. As well as translating established hymns into SeTswana, Moffat composed his own in the language, as did Livingstone.[63] The modern edition of *Dihela* ascribes one-third of the hymns to Moffat as either composer or translator. One hymn which he composed has the verse:

Ye the followers of Jesus,
Ye who dwell in heavenly light,
Come and help us we are dying,
Rescue us from heathenish night.[64]

---

60 RM, *Journal,* 15.10.1857, (*MJ2,* 99).

61 RM, *Occ. Journal*, 6.5.1860, (SOAS/CWM/SA/Moffat/Personal /Box 4).

62 Ibid, 1.7.1860: Returning from Inyati after helping to set up the Ndebele Mission.

63 RM, *Journal,* 3.12.1857, (*MJ2,* 132): 'I have been confined to my wagon most of the day, reading, correcting the New Testament, and composing hymns in Sechuana.' The hymns were used in the Kuruman school, where daughter Jane taught. In 1859, writing from Moselekatse's kraal to Mary, Robert, *Journal,* 12.11.1859, (*MJ2,* 222) stated: 'I am thankful for Janey's note and glad to find that the few attempts at translating hymns have been acceptable. When an opportunity offers to send letters, I dare say I shall write a few lines to her. It does my soul good to learn that the school is still carried on with vigour.'

64 In: SOAS/CWM/SA./Moffat/Personal/Box 4 (Moffat's translation of a SeTswana hymn).

Moffat used standard Scottish hymns, metres and tunes, as well as writing new hymns in SeTswana which also used Scottish metres and tunes. He also adopted the Scottish style of having a precentor to lead the singing, either by having the congregation singing along with the precentor, or by the congregation following the precentor as he gave out the hymn, line by line. Moffat referred to the latter practice in 1857, at a Sabbath service in Sechele's village where Paul, the resident native catechist from Kuruman, acted as precentor.[65]

Despite Moffat claiming that the Christian hymn-singing which he introduced had a pleasing and positive effect, Setiloane has been highly critical of Moffat's hymnody, contrasting the dour singing of the Scottish tradition with traditional African *joie de vivre*:

> In the hymns which were written and translated into Sotho-Tswana at this time (they are still the hymnology of most of the Church there, even today) one searches vainly for the ebullience of the native people and the '*xaira*' (joy), expressed in African tones, of those who have found 'Salvation'. The result is that this solemn, gloomy character of Christianity has been bequeathed not only to the Church in Sotho-Tswana-land, but also to the people in their general deportment and carriage.
>
> This is true more among BaTswana, especially in those who have lived longer under the influence of the missionaries ... than among BaSotho. ... Salvation is expressed in their hymns in a mood of wonder and marvel at the grace of God. The emphasis is on the abject sinfulness and undeservedness of the worshipper. ... They are therefore a good indication of what the missionaries transferred to the people as their experience of salvation. There is very little record of the peoples' own expression of what they experienced as happening to them.'[66]

As if to forestall a defence of Moffat, Setiloane added that the missionary account cannot be relied upon.[67] There is no doubt that there is much in Setiloane's critique which is valid. The hymn quoted above, with its emphasis on death and gloom, would seem to confirm all of his worst fears.

However, in our view Setiloane misjudged the core emotion at the heart of evangelical hymnody. The evangelical believer certainly sang many verses which focused on his or her unworthiness and sinfulness, but these were sung in the light of the message of the Gospel. Thus, though some verses reinforced the picture of a dark and bleak humanity, they did so to contrast the overwhelming love and grace of God which had so profoundly touched

---

65 RM, *To Mary Moffat,* 22.8.1857, (*MJ2,* 33f).

66 Setiloane, *The Image of God among the Sotho-Tswana*, 118ff.

67 Ibid, 120.

the feelings of the heart. Thus, even whilst singing about death and sin, the believer felt an inner joy. That was missed by Setiloane, but was at the heart of evangelical worship. Within an evangelical piety that was what constituted a positive affirmation of dignity, worth and joy before God. We can ourselves testify feeling inward joy whilst singing hymns or psalms to slow traditional tunes such as 'The Old Hundredth' which Moffat used at Kuruman.[68] It is the meaning of the words which bring joy.

Setiloane has to answer several questions. What did new believers, at Kuruman, *feel* when they sang these hymns? Does Setiloane have evidence that they, at that time, were not *celebrating* their faith? These questions cannot be answered by referring to African hymnody today. It may also be asked: what was the mode and mood of Tswana praise songs to a chief in Moffat's day?[69] Setiloane's methodology requires assessment. On the one hand he has no written or oral accounts of how the contemporary Tswana *felt* whilst singing, yet he has argued that they *must* have felt mournful. On the other hand, he *did* have contemporary accounts by the missionaries, which spoke positively of the pleasing and welcome effect of the hymns which were introduced, but he dismissed such accounts as unreliable.

EMBEDDING THE WORD: DISCUSSING

In Africa Moffat learned that whatever value there was in a monologue, it required to be supplemented by dialogue, as in cultural custom. In Moffat's little-known manuscript on *Bechuana Customs,* he noted: 'Among the Bechuana in public meetings and in discussion there is great freedom of speech'.[70] Moffat described the *Khotla* where this took place:

> *Khotla* is the public fold where all the assemblies meet for discussion: Parliament House, where chief men pass much of their time working and discussing the topics of the day—a barber's shop—great talkers, and it is

[68] The hymns and psalms which Moffat translated had Short Metre, Common Metre, or Long Metre rhythm. These fitted nearly all the traditional psalm tunes from Scotland. Though such tunes are seen by some modern Christians as dirges, they were not so regarded in the nineteenth century. JSM mentioned a range of hymns which Moffat loved: *Oh, to grace how great a debtor; Why was I made to hear His voice? Our best friends and our kindred dwell; And Christ our Saviour reigns; The sands of time are sinking; Come thou fount of every blessing; How sweet the name of Jesus sounds; At even when the sun was set; Nearer my God to Thee; Abide with me; I long to hear the story; Hail sovereign light* (JSM, *Lives,* 400-425).

[69] We are informed by friends from northern Malawi that a praise song to a Chief had to convey solemn dignity and gravitas as well as energy. In accordance with African tradition, Christian hymns to God should also convey a profound sense of dignity, expressed by solemn gravitas. Serious dignity was valued. Solemnity was not non-African.

[70] RM, *Bechuana Customs*, (SOAS/CWM/SA/Moffat/Personal/Box 4).

> difficult to conceive from whence they derive matter of thought. During public meetings women are not allowed to enter, but can stand outside and look over the fence and enjoy the discussion. Speakers succeed each other in the arena.[71]

The Tswana fondness of debate and discussion spilled over into how they related to Moffat, especially in the early years when his ministry was more evangelistic. Though his sermons would be listened to with great politeness, it was only when he defended his ideas in open discussion that they went home. This was new to him, since his own tradition identified the 'authority' of the Word with 'no questions to be asked'.

Despite coming from a similar tradition as Moffat's, the far-seeing David Bogue had taught the value of discussion and conversation. In his lecture 'On Conversation,' he stated: 'From the circumstances of the heathen, this method becomes absolutely necessary.'[72] Even though Moffat transcribed all of Bogue's lectures, it took years before he appreciated the implications of Bogue's advice. But once he realised the necessity of this method, he committed himself to it, supplementing preaching with discussion after preaching. In 1827, whilst on language study among the BaRolong, he wrote:

> I collected the people and preached unto them the Gospel of salvation. They seemed to pay much more attention than last Sabbath, but afterward I was much grieved to hear them making a kind of diversion of some part of the discourse, particularly that which related to a future state of reward. After listening a few minutes, I went and placed myself among them, and resumed the subject in a way of argument; when they changed their tone, especially when I dwelt on the article of death, to them a subject of all others the most unpleasant, and alas, no wonder, for the utmost stretch of their faith in annihilation.[73]

This discovery, that people gave more attention when engaged in dialogue, than when listening to a sermon, became an important part of Moffat's strategy. From the same village, he wrote:

> I committed the whole of the Catechism etc., to memory, which also became better stored with a variety of words, by which I find that I am able to reason with and address them in a way pretty well understood. Indeed, to reason with them, so as to allow them time to make remarks and ask questions, is undoubtedly the best way of impressing truths on their minds, that is when

---

71 Ibid. In his deputation speeches Moffat frequently underlined how intellectually sharp the arguments were. E.g. RM, *Walworth Address,* 1843, (*Farewell Services,* 75).

72 Bogue, *Miss. Lect.* 7, 'On Conversation'.

73 RM, *Journal,* 15.4.1827, (*AAK,* 246).

they will reason.[74]

Though dialogue was the 'best way' of engaging in deep communication, Moffat still found it awkward, since the questions he asked were sometimes treated with hilarity:

> Sabbath: Had service as usual, in which I was very much annoyed with a person who kept laughing during the whole time. *I feel most happy when I can get them to contradict or doubt of the truth of what is stated.* I find that information by way of dialogue makes the deepest impression on their minds. Seldom do I enjoy this pleasure, for in general my questions are only mimicked and laughed at.[75]

Nevertheless, Moffat regularly combined preaching with discussion. For example, the record of his last Sunday among the BaRolong gives an account of the combination of didactic discourse and conversational dialogue:

> Early this forenoon about seventy people collected, when I addressed them on John 3:16. After sermon, I continued the subject at some length, it being perhaps the last time I might ever stand between God and their immortal souls.

In the traditional Protestant view of preaching, the 'proclaimed Word' was seen as a spiritual exercise in its own right. It was believed that passively listening to the Word created a receptivity of mind and heart in the hearer, which dialogue—in which parties might be more eager to argue than listen to God's speaking—did not. This was a conviction, and Moffat never totally abandoned it. The 'proclaimed Word' was never totally replaced by dialogue, but was complemented by discussion. Moffat accepted the difficulties and vulnerability which this brought, since the fruit was worthwhile.

Embedding the Word: Catechising

The LMS missionary George Thom of Cape Town, in the biography of his late wife, Christiana Thom, gave an insight into the philosophy behind catechical instruction and its relationship to preaching: 'Catechising is an admirable auxiliary to preaching. When this religious exercise is performed by the pastor of the church, or by pious catechists, public discourses have a much

---

[74] RM, *To Mary Moffat,* 25.4.1827, (*AAK,* 264). Cf. Bogue, *Miss. Lect.* 6, 'On Reasoning with the Heathen'): 'As it would occupy too much of the missionary's time to answer the cavil of every disputant, it might be advisable to have particular sessions set apart for this purpose.'

[75] RM, *Journal,* 6.5.1827, (*AAK,* 251). Moffat's intentions could be misunderstood, not knowing local customs. On one occasion, Moffat indicated that he wanted to 'gather the people together' on a Sabbath to preach to them. An older person explained that 'gathered together' was misinterpreted, since the phrase was associated with portents of death. See: RM, *Journal,* 30.5.1825, (*AAK,* 191).

greater effect upon the minds of the young.'[76] We have already discussed how catechical instruction moulded Moffat's own faith.[77] Moffat applied the same principle in Africa. In 1825 he wrote:

> We visit the Bechuanas regularly, and every Sabbath a catechetical meeting is held in their language.' A year later he further comments: 'For a considerable time past we had appointed the Tuesday evening expressly to instruct the Bechuana resident on the station, who are chiefly poor, and several of them strangers. The attendance has hitherto exceeded our expectations, so that they also attend on the other nights when service is held. As it regards these objects, we labour in hope, recollecting how in the Apostolic age the glorious Gospel was first received by the poor, and frequently by the despised. 'Not many noble', says the Apostle.[78]

Formal catechical instruction was given to serious 'enquirers'.[79] This was in addition to Bible instruction given at Sunday school for both adults and children before church. The nineteenth-century missionary would think it absurd to do other. Preaching and catechising—these were essential, home and abroad.

The above extract not only acknowledges the patient teaching given by the missionaries, but indicates the nature of the indigenous community around Kuruman in the later 1820s. It was a diverse collection of poor families and fragments of various tribes. In the next chapter, 'The Awakening at Kuruman', we discuss how this semi-refugee community, distinct from a regular chief-centred tribe, helped to facilitate a break-through. Catechical instruction remained important in all the years at Kuruman.

---

76 Thom, *Memoir of Mrs Christiana Louisa Thom,* (Ldn: Nisbet, 1822), 4.

77 Ch 2, 'School, Catechism and Church in Scotland'.

78 RM, *Journal,* 23.5.1826, (*AAK,* 220).

79 Moffat initially taught *Brown's Catechism.* After the mid-1830s he taught the '*Assembly's Catechism'.* In an important passage, Moffat described the rapid advance after using the vernacular become standard at Kuruman. Cf. RM, *To Richard Moffat,* 15.2.1828, (*AAK*, 281): 'Mr. Miles having brought the Sechuana school books etc., with him, I was enabled shortly after his return [September 1827] to commence school in that language, and the number which attend, and the progress they have made, exceeds our expectations, especially when the circumstances of the country are taken into consideration. There are already four Bechuanas who are reading the Rev. Mr. Brown's Catechism in their own language, and in a short time I trust to be enabled to put a number more into that class. I have also commenced night school, which does well; the attendance, chiefly adults, has risen to forty, while that of the day is nearly fifty (including fourteen of Jan Karse's children and domestics, who are learning Dutch). We have also begun to sing hymns composed in the language, which is very enlivening. ... The attendance at public worship is on the whole very good, though we do not yet see any real fruit of our labours.'

TRANSLATING THE WORD

As a young missionary, Moffat realised that no effective work could be accomplished without proficiency in the indigenous language. Some missionaries used Boer Dutch for communication, but few indigenous Africans knew Boer Dutch, and the amount they did know was usually insufficient for the deep work which Moffat had in mind. When he moved north from Cape Colony to the BaThlaping kingdoms he first had to preach in Boer Dutch which was then translated into SeTswana, but he was never certain whether his ideas were getting across. He commented: 'Many inauspicious changes take place through ... an interpreter who not unfrequently moulds the matter after his own ideas.'[80] This problem was unsurprising since, while the indigenous translator might be reasonably fluent in trade-Dutch, he might not have vocabulary suitable for theological truths. Direct communication in the language of the people was essential.

The history of Bible translation at Kuruman is well covered elsewhere, and there are bibliographies of all works printed in SeTswana with which Moffat was involved.[81] Our task is not to rehearse well-chronicled facts, but to discuss issues lying behind Moffat's translation activity and how it affected his theology in general and his missiology in particular. Translating the Bible, catechisms, hymns and tracts, as well as educational material to be used in school, was a major achievement of Moffat's career, and where possible he translated from the original languages. Moffat was not an expert linguist, but he had a usable knowledge of several tongues.

For example, in 1854 he mentioned he had not brought his Hebrew Lexicon on the journey,[82] and in 1857 he noted that the term 'sons of peace' which he used to describe Christians should really be 'sons of blessing 'for the word is a *Hebraism*.'[83] Again, in 1859, whilst waiting for permission to

---

80 RM, *To LMS Directors,* 30.1.1828, (SOAS/CWM/SA/Box11/1/A). Earlier Moffat wrote: 'I would say from heartfelt experience that where interpreters are necessary to the communication of the truths of the Gospel, it proves a great barrier which cramps the heart of the speaker and tarnishes every idea before it reaches the objects to whom it is spoken. ... I highly disapprove of interpreters. But the question is: what can I do till I have learned their language? Better speak one word through an interpreter than a thousand in an unknown tongue.' See: RM, *To Kitchingham,* 27.10.1818, (Le Cordeur, *Kitchingham Papers,* 54).

81 See: (i) Bradlow, *Printing for Africa.* (ii) Margaret Brownlee, *The Lives and Work of South African Missionaries: A Bibliography,* (CT: University of Cape Town Libraries, 1952). (iii) Marguerite Andrée Peters, and Matthew Mathêthê Tabane, *Bibliography of the Tswana Language: A Bibliography of books, periodicals, pamphlets and manuscripts to the year 1980, (Bibiliokerafi ya Puo ya SeTswana),* (Pretoria: The State Library, 1982).

82 RM, *Journal,* 27.7.1854, (*MJ1,* 241f).

83 RM, *Journal,* 10.8.1857, (*MJ2,* 23).

build houses for the Ndebele Mission at Inyati, he wrote: 'If this suspense continues a little longer, I shall set to … revision and correction of translations. I regret that I did not bring my Hebrew books with me'.[84] He knew not only Hebrew but some Greek, writing to John Philip in 1820: 'I also hope to be making progress in my Greek'.[85] In addition, he referred to his Dutch Bible in a marginal note,[86] and he alluded to French and Latin in correspondence with the Bible Society: 'Thanks for the Vulgate and the French Bible.'[87]

In his translation work Moffat was ably supported by fellow missionaries Robert Hamilton and Isaac Hughes. There was also considerable assistance given by Africans, but we do not have their names.[88] By 1843 he was able to say to a British audience: 'Go into a house: you will find the Word of God; you will find hymns and catechisms in their language; you will find Christian names, and you will find a light.'[89] The immense labour put into translation was because of the conviction that use of the 'mother tongue' was essential.

At the height of the Scottish Enlightenment the Scottish Law Lord James Burnet, (Lord Monboddo), published a weighty six-volume-work on the nature of language, entitled *Of the Origin and Progress of Language.*[90] Burnet stated that speech was not only the mere words or sounds of a language, but the conceptions of the mind that are signified by such sounds;[91] and that language was the *expression of the conceptions of the mind* by articulate sounds.[92] Monboddo understood that the language of a people was more

---

84 RM, *Journal,* 28.11.1859, (*MJ2,* 234).

85 RM, *To John Philip,* 19.9.1820, (*AAK,* 10).

86 RM, *Journal,* 14.10.1854, (*MJ1,* 331).

87 RM, *To Browne, BFBS,* Nov. 1851, (CULBSA/Browne/1851).

88 Sundkler, *A History of the Church in Africa,* (Cambridge: CUP, 2000), 429 incorrectly stated: 'From 1857 [Moffat] devoted himself to the translation of the Tswana Bible. He was dependent on his African assistants in his work. One was his interpreter 'William the Griqua, the only individual through whom I could speak freely to his [Moselekatse's] people on the things of God'', referring to: RM, *Journal,* 30.10.1859, (*MJ2,* 205). Sundkler was inaccurate. First, Moffat's translation into SeTswana was completed in 1857, not *started*. Second, William the Griqua was Moffat's translator in later conversations with Moselekatse who spoke SiNdebele. He was a Griqua whom the Ndebele captured at the Vaal River in the 1830s, and Moffat first met him in 1835 during his second visit to the Ndebele. Cf. RM, *Journal,* 23.7.1854, (*MJ1,* 232) and Schapera's fn. 3. There is no evidence that William the Griqua was involved in translating the Bible into SeTswana at Kuruman.

89 RM, *Barbican Sermon,* 22.1.1843, (*Farewell Services,* 121).

90 James Burnet, *Of the Origin and Progress of Language: In six Vols, Vol. 1, 1773,* (Edin: Kincaid & Creech, 1773). Monboddo was one of several eighteenth-century thinkers on the nature and origin of language.

91 Burnet, *Of the Origin and Nature Of Language, Vol. 1,* 1.

92 Ibid, 5.

than simply their vocabulary. It involved the expression of a people's thoughts, emotions and world-view, and, as Baëta pointed out, if language is the expression of thought patterns then important indices to the mind of a people are embedded in their language.[93] David Bogue underlined this in his *Missionary Lectures,* stressing that the missionary's first task was 'to learn the language of the Heathen':

> When a missionary has a prospect of spending his days in a place, he should by all means make himself master of the language; and is greatly deficient in his duty if he does not. This is an important part of the first year's labour.[94]

For Bogue, it was language which opened doors, being, 'the key to open to them all the treasures of heaven, which without it will continue shut'. It is possible to interpret Bogue's comments simply in terms of the functional practicality of learning and using the indigenous language, but Bogue would have been aware of the eighteenth-century emphasis on mother-tongue. This went beyond seeing language simply in practical terms. The mother-tongue of any people was the medium of communication which resonated most powerfully with them, and was key to unlocking hearts and minds.

During his first years in southern Africa, Moffat did not know where the focus of his ministry would ultimately lie, and there were many indigenous languages. When it became clearer that his permanent work was to be among the BaThlaping, the insufficiencies of relying upon a translator soon became apparent. He always insisted that it was Mary who crystallised the fundamental problem of not being able to communicate directly in the BaThlaping dialect of SeTswana, which was the local mother-tongue. At Edinburgh, in 1842, he recalled the initial barren years at Kuruman:

> I remember, at an early period of our toils in that distant land, one day I felt peculiarly melancholy at the gloomy prospect which lay before us, and said to my wife, 'Mary, this is hard work.' 'It *is* hard work', she said, 'but take courage; our lives shall be given us for a prey.' 'But think', I replied, 'how long we have preached the Gospel to this people, and no fruits yet appear'. She answered, 'The Gospel has never yet been preached to that people; they have heard it only through interpreters, who have no understanding of, or love for, the truth. We need not expect the blessing to any extent till you are able to give from your own lips the everlasting Gospel into their ears'. From that hour I gave myself with untiring diligence to acquire the language.[95]

---

93 Baëta, *Christianity in Tropical Africa,* 144.

94 Bogue, *Miss. Lect.* 2, 'The Employment of a Missionary'.

95 RM, *Edinburgh Address,* 3.11.1842, (*Farewell Services,* 19f). Cf. Mary Moffat, *To James Smith,* 28.8.1827, (*AAK,* 267): 'They now hear the Gospel direct from Moffat in their own language, and it does appear to affect them somewhat more than through an interpreter.

It was not only evangelism, but education in general which required full use of the vernacular: 'Nothing can be done in the school till books are used in the native language.'[96] Throughout the rest of his ministry, Moffat wrestled with SeTswana. The task of translating Christian works into it became the central pillar of his work. After acquiring the beginnings of the language, Moffat moved in 1827 to a BaRolong village and lived there for several months, cut off from contact with outsiders with the clear aim of becoming more fluent.[97]

Moffat initially felt that SeTswana would be inadequate for theological concepts: 'The language, which is barren and barbarous enough, and which of course is perfectly consonant to their ideas, will hardly admit a shade of theology.'[98] But by 1838 he had changed his mind. He commented positively on both the scope of the vocabulary and the beauty of SeTswana, though he still felt that some concepts translated with difficulty:

> The Sechuana language, though exceedingly copious, is of course deficient in theological terms; being according to the character and genius of the people, who know nothing of God or immortality. This at first occasioned considerable difficulty; but research has convinced me that the language itself possesses an ample source of suitable words to convey, with wonderful clearness, the language and meaning of the Scriptures.[99] ... [Sentences

---

With regard to some truths, they say they did not believe them before, they thought the interpreter was telling lies. They come in great numbers to hear the word, and are more attentive. They appear to understand it perfectly well, and will often repeat for him all that he has said, if he requires it, which is a proof that they understand well. We do indulge a hope that the spirit of grace will descend ere long.'

96 RM, *To Burder, LMS*, 20.5.1826, (*AAK,* 226). Once the mother-tongue was used, the changes were dramatic. Moffat informed the Rev. Miles in Cape Town of the developments. See: RM, *To Miles, CT,* 30.1.1828, (SOAS/CWM/SA/Box10/3/B).

97 Cf. RM, *Journal,* 28.3.1827, (*AAK,* 237ff). Moffat wrote, after conversing with some of the village women: 'The season above described gave me inexpressible pleasure, but at the same time pain, that I could not fully and freely disclose the grand attractions of the Cross. I felt as if incompetency in the language only prevented me from converting them.' See: RM, *Journal,* 21.4.1827, (*AAK,* 248f).

98 RM, *To Alexander Moffat,* 25.2.1822, (*AAK,* 57).

99 Bogue considered several of these issues in his *Miss. Lect.* 4, 'On Preaching': '*One*: What shall a missionary do when the language does not furnish a suitable word to express his ideas? Answer: See if any other word or phrase conveys the same idea. If not, then coin a new word and explain it to the heathen. *Two*: When a missionary finds the heathen using words to express their false ideas in religion should he make use of the same word to denote the true God? What was the practice of the Apostles? The words *Theos* and *Kurios* which were in common use among the heathen were retained by the Apostles to denote God and Lord. ... There is a danger, when the heathen word is used, lest the heathen should attach it to heathen ideas. When a missionary finds it necessary to coin a new word and phrases of the heathen, they should be well expressed for fear of mistake. In some instances, it might be edifying to

> expressing the numerical system are] an exception to the general neatness and perspicuity of the language. The numerous forms and conjugations of the verb, varied by prefixing or adding one or two letters at most, is a great beauty in the language, whereby much can often be expressed with the greatest brevity and clearness.[100]

By 1842 Moffat was reflecting upon new and exciting possibilities for SeTswana: 'We look forward to the time when this people shall have a literature of their own; no unworthy counterpart of Africa's far-famed literature in times of old.'[101] Moffat's optimistic prediction has been fulfilled, despite Livingstone's fear that SeTswana might become a dead language![102] Today, it is the native tongue of over eight million people in southern Africa. For Moffat, translation became a life's work, and he frequently testified to its huge importance to him.[103] In 1838, when he had been translating for more than ten years, he reflected on his methodology in a letter to the Rev. G. Browne of the *British and Foreign Bible Society*:

> I have laboured hard at the work but much still remains to be done; for it was not until the translation was made that I finally settled in my mind the appropriate use of numerous words of importance, which I had left undecided until I should very thoroughly discover their meaning and their parallels in the Scriptures. Of course, this obliges me to re-examine the whole very closely in order to obtain something like uniformity.[104]

Even twenty years later, when he had mastery of the language, he took pains to try and capture the original flavour of an English phrase in SeTswana:

---

retain the original word from the Scriptures [Jehovah or God] when it bears to their language. This may be done taking these words that are most like the heathen.'

100 RM, *To Browne, BFBS,* 3.7.1838, (*35th Annual Report of the BFBS,* 1839).

101 RM, *Edinburgh Address,* 3.11.1842, (*Farewell Services,* 18). Moffat had in mind the early North African Fathers. Starting in October 1857, another Kuruman missionary, William Ashton, tried to establish a regular local language newspaper which was 'occasionally contributed to by natives', cf. Mackenzie, *Ten Years North,* 43. In the first edition, Sept. 1857, there was a letter by Morisanyane, a native teacher at Borigelon. The newspaper ran for two years with 20 editions. All editions may be found in the NLSA, CT, (Grey/10/c/22/4). Moffat does not appear to have contributed. Cf. Bradlow, *Printing for Africa,* 32f.

102 Livingstone, *To RM,* (*DLFL,* Vol. 2, 263).

103 RM, *To Jowett,* 8.4.1841, (CULBSA/Jowett/1841/2/28), wrote to the Rev. Jowett (*BFBS*) in 1841: ' [The NT and Psalms in SeTswana] are works which will ever yield satisfaction infinitely more that the duties of flying through the country preaching and speech-making, which will hereafter appear merely like a tale that was told, while the Scriptures in the Sechuana language will in public, and in private, be giving instruction which maketh wise unto salvation, enlightening, comforting, and establishing believers and making sinners see and feel their wretched state; the need of a change of heart, and the value of Jesus Christ for salvation.' He made the same point even more strongly in: RM, *To Bergne, BFBS,* 22.5.1867, (CULBSA/BFBSEC/Inwards/5/198).

104 RM, *To Browne, BFBS,* 3.7.1838: *35th Annual Report of the BFBS,* 1839.

'"This awful God is ours." I have tried this beautiful expression in Sechuana Hymnology, but I fail. But I shall try again.'[105] As a linguist, Moffat was determined rather than brilliant. But perseverance made him effective. As Tore Janson and Joseph Tsonope have pointed out, Moffat's labour of love in translating Christian literature into SeTswana became the foundation for all written SeTswana, and since his SeTswana was in the BaThlaping dialect, it became the literary standard of the language. Religious literature, largely written in the nineteenth century, still constitutes a considerable portion of what is published.[106]

The Word as Process

In Jesus' parable of the Sower, the broadcasting of the Word did not always result in fruit. A missiology based upon expecting that the Word would accomplish a deep and lasting change in individuals was a missiology requiring patience and perseverance. Christianisation by political settlement or by colonial imposition was a sharper, more clearly defined process: whereas evangelisation through individual conviction was slower and less predictable. But communal tribal conversion at the command of a chief was anathema to Moffat.[107] He sought to build the kingdom one soul at a time, as individuals were convicted by the Word.

The twentieth-century evangelist, Reinhardt Bonnke, admired classical missionaries such as Moffat, but viewed their ways as sluggish![108] Bonnke's answer was mass evangelism and displays of the power of the Holy Spirit, including the manifestation of extraordinary spiritual gifts. In contrast, and as a gardener by profession, Moffat accepted the methodical cycle of sowing, tending and waiting before reaping. Soul husbandry required the same

---

105 RM, *Journal,* 21.11.1857 (*MJ2,* 122).

106 Tore Janson and Joseph Tsonope, *Birth of a National Language: The History of SeTswana,* (Gaborone: Heinemann Botswana, 1991), 45, 83.

107 The Moffat philosophy was well-expressed by his grandson, Robert Unwin Moffat, who quoted his father, John Smith Moffat, '[In mission] there are three alternatives: the open aversion of the chief to the new teaching; or his indifference; or his active goodwill. The first of these practically shuts out the possibility of a mission at all, and the last suggests the danger that the people, in making a Christian profession, may be doing so in a time-serving spirit, and merely in deference to the chief's influence. This danger is accentuated when the chief himself is a mixed character such as Sechele was. Upon the whole, the middle alternative is likely to be the more favourable where the chief maintains a friendly neutrality. We can then gauge with some approach to certainty the genuineness of the profession made by those who avow themselves as believers in Christ.' (RUM, *John Smith Moffat,* 144f).

108 Reinhardt Bonnke, *Evangelism by Fire,* (Eastbourne: Kingsway, 1994), 7. Bonnke's reported conversion rates of tens of thousands rarely produced measurable church growth.

meticulous care as plant-husbandry. Nevertheless, the patience which his missiology of the Word required could be frustrating. Moffat himself stated: 'We have all eternity in which to enjoy our victories, but only one short life in which to win them.' Yet Moffat knew that a crop would only yield fruit in its season, and should not be manipulated into forced growth. Faith and dogged perseverance were essential. He wrote:

> Brother Hamilton and I visit the neighbouring villages alternately, but with no apparent fruit to our labours. It is often with great difficulty that we can prevail upon them to collect in one spot. Every excuse is urged, but we persevere in the strength of our Redeemer, assured that his word shall not return to him void, but will accomplish the end for which it is sent.'[109]

Moffat's temperament helped him persevere when there was no obvious progress. A gardener had to wait and care for the soil, even when no visible changes were taking place.[110] But what the gardener believed was that if the right seed were sown in the right soil and nurtured in the right way, then growth and fruit would inevitably come.[111] That fortitude was sorely tested over the years of little fruit. At times Moffat despaired when regress, rather than progress, seemed to be taking place.[112] During these barren times he developed a theology of patience which moulded his whole ministry:

> I often find myself much at a loss what to say relative to the Kingdom of Christ at this station. Sameness marks the events of each returning day. No conversations, no enquiring after God, no objections raised to exercise our powers in defence. Indifference and stupidity form the wreath on every brow; ignorance, the grossest ignorance, forms the basis of every heart. Thoughts earthly, sensual, and devilish stimulate to motion and mirth, while the great concerns of the soul's redemption appear to them like a ragged garment in which they see neither loveliness nor worth. O, when shall the day star arise in their hearts? We preach, we converse, we catechize, but without the least apparent success.[113]

Realism enabled Moffat to place resignation and hope side by side. On his visit to Moselekatse in 1835, he was able to cope with his despair over Moselekatse's 'diabolical tyranny', through a resolute confidence in God:

> I feel very gloomy when I look at the dreadfully degraded state of his people:

---

109 RM, *Journal,* 26.8.1821, (*AAK,* 23).

110 RM, *MLSSA,* 241.

111 Moffat, *MLSSA,* 30, described Van der Kemp as, 'introducing the gospel plough, and casting the seed into an ungenial soil, where, though in some instances it remained long buried, it eventually produced "an abundance of corn in the earth upon the top of the mountains!"'

112 RM, *MLSSA,* 284.

113 RM, *Journal,* 15.5.1822, (*AAK,* 51).

> how impossible for the Ethiopian to change his skin or the Leopard his spots, were it not that heavenly power. How much it becomes us to be instant in prayer while we use the means! Can these dry bones live?'[114]

An absolute unshakeable conviction that he was where God wanted him to be, gave him his missiological convictions. 'Success' was not the decisive factor. His calling was to be obedient:

> I feel half melancholy tonight ... but I have no wish to be anywhere else ... I believe I am in the path of duty, and though I may not live to see my hopes realised, I firmly believe that my wanderings here ... are not in vain. The heathen is the inheritance of him before whom every knee must bow, and every tongue confess.[115]

When he penned these words he was far from Kuruman; Moselekatse was impervious to the Gospel; he had seen bodies of men and women tortured and executed by the Ndebele chief; and his pleas to Moselekatse to set free the daughter of Peter David had fallen on deaf ears. Moffat admitted his depression. But he also stated the bedrock of his whole mission, namely, that God *is* the Lord before whom every knee shall bow. In his theology, resignation and hope were both rooted in the sovereignty of God.[116]

> We must patiently wait, and look upward from whence help cometh. It is our consolation to know that there is 'no wisdom, nor understanding, nor counsel against Jehovah. Today, after the usual course of readings, I opened on the psalms 120 and 121. They were seasonable.[117]

Whilst in Britain on furlough, Moffat referred several times to this theology of patience and perseverance: 'I have seen the blessed result of going to this village and persevering there; and going to that village and persevering there.'[118] It was the same conviction which prompted Mary to request communion vessels when there was still no company of believers with whom to celebrate the sacrament. At the very heart of Moffat's faith was belief in

---

114 RM, *Journal,* 5.7.1835, (*MJ1,* 100f).
115 RM, *Journal,* 10.7.1835, (*MJ1,* 108).
116 The sovereignty of God and patient waiting for spiritual fruit, was alluded to by John Campbell, *The Progress of the Kingdom of Christ,* 10: 'The sovereignty of God is often manifested in his communicating or withholding his influence—as in the case of the Moravian brethren who laboured 10 years in Greenland without an instance of conversion; the Missionaries at Otaheite in the South Sea, 16 years without fruit, and at Lattakoo, 10 years equally fruitless.'
117 RM, *Journal,* 22.11.1859, (*MJ2,* 228). This was from a difficult time during the fifth Visit. Moselekatse was awkward, uncooperative and procrastinating. For a time, the mission group was virtually abandoned by their host. They had few available resources, and the promised oxen did not come. On Moselekatse's orders no milk was supplied from neighbouring villages. No assistance of any kind was to be given. The party were not to shoot game.
118 RM, *Walworth Address,* 1843, (*Farewell Services,* 87).

the sovereign rule of God. All things would happen in God's time. Mission was obedience driven, not results driven.

Alongside a conviction in the sovereignty of God, lay the Moffats' inner belief that they were in the right place, doing the right thing. Robert and Mary were realists. Lack of fruit was not due to disobedience, unfaithfulness, or error: despite awareness of their own fallibilities, they were convinced that delay in spiritual fruitfulness was not due to them. They were called to Kuruman. God in his time would fulfill His purposes. This was expressed by Moffat on his 1854 visit to Moselekatse: 'I felt more than ever satisfied that I was in the path of duty'.[119] This was not boasting. It was quiet assurance of being in the centre of God's will. If that were so, then anything could be endured.

Yet there had been times of severe doubt, especially when Moffat was isolated. During his first years in southern Africa, Moffat was alone at Africaner's kraal, and the utter isolation and loneliness of this situation had led him to extensive soul-searching as to whether he was in God's will or not:

> Circumstances led to great searching of heart, to see if I had hitherto aimed at doing and suffering the will of Him in whose service I had embarked. Satisfied that I had not run unsent, and having, in the intricate and sometimes obscure course I had come, heard the still small voice saying, 'This is the way, walk ye in it,' I was wont to pour out my soul among the granite rocks surrounding this station, now in sorrow, and then in joy.[120]

Moffat believed that conversions amongst the Tswana and other peoples of southern Africa required a total change of both beliefs and lifestyle.[121] Verbal profession of belief was not enough. A new way of living and thinking had to take place, requiring the establishing of deep roots. Given this, Moffat saw himself as there for the long-haul, and had no problems with God's work through the Word requiring time for its accomplishment. He was, after all, a gardener.

---

119 RM, *To Mary Moffat,* 31.5.1854, (*MJ1,* 145).

120 RM, *MLSSA,* 108.

121 RM, *MLSSA,* 267.

Chapter 29
The Period of the Awakening

WHEN MOFFAT COPIED OUT David Bogue's *Missionary Lectures,* it is unlikely he imagined that Bogue's assertion, 'God has never allowed any zealous, faithful missionary to labour seven years in vain',[1] would be tested in his own life. But at Kuruman the Moffats waited eight years before the first conversion took place.[2] During that time there were occasional signs of slight advance,[3] but these were often followed by discouragement. Once, after reading about positive growth elsewhere in the world, Moffat depressingly recorded: 'Here is nothing to encourage; but everything to the contrary.'[4] He was so discouraged that in January 1828 he wrote to the LMS Directors about traveling further afield, among the BaKwena and BaRolong, perhaps even setting up a temporary house there.[5] Though not abandoning Kuruman, Moffat was seriously contemplating concentrating his labours elsewhere. But the events which soon followed were to be in complete contrast to what had gone before. During the dark years, Mary had kept hope: 'We may not live to see it, but the awakening will come as surely as the sun will rise tomorrow.'[6]

When, in 1823, the missionaries stood with the local community against the Mantatee invasion, this act of solidarity gained respect for the mission, though in its immediate aftermath there was little discernable increased interest in the Christian faith. Yet Du Plessis has judged that, after 1823, the tide of popular feeling began to flow in favour of the intrepid missionaries.[7] But it did not yet evidence itself in 'true' conversions, that touching of both heart and mind which the evangelical missionary saw as essential to the

---

1 Bogue, *Miss. Lect.* 15, 'Encouragements to Missions'.

2 The eight barren years start in 1821, when the Moffats began work among the BaThlaping. The LMS mission to the tribe commenced four years earlier in 1817, with no conversions during that period either. Mary wrote in 1822: 'Five years have rolled on since the missionaries came, and not one soul converted, nor does anyone seem to lend an ear. All treat with ridicule and contempt the truths which are delivered'. See: Mary Moffat, *To her Parents,* 29.08.1822: (JSM, *Lives,* 103). Cf. RM, *To his Brother,* 1822 (JSM, *Lives,* 105).

3 RM, *Journal,* 30.9.1821, (*AAK,* 26).

4 RM, *Journal,* 8.2.1822, (*AAK,* 44).

5 RM, *To LMS Directors,* 30.1.1828, (SOAS/CWM/SA/Box11/1/A).

6 JSM, *Lives,* 153.

7 J. Du Plessis, *A History of Christian Missions in South Africa,* 160.

adoption of real Christianity.[8] When the Awakening did arrive, it arrived dramatically, with remarkable scenes of deep emotion, creating a situation which was totally new for Moffat and his co-workers.

The LMS *Annual Report* for 1828 makes it clear that a zephyr of change was beginning to blow over Kuruman.[9] 1828 started inauspiciously, with a group of bandits threatening to destroy the mission. This was averted, and, apart from Kuruman being menaced by Corannas later in the year, there was relative peace. Spiritually, the missionaries were 'encouraged by observing the unremitting attendance of the people on the preaching of the word.'[10] Each Sabbath, before the forenoon service, Moffat catechised the children and adults, and read to them a chapter from one of the Gospels. The singing of hymns in the vernacular was also proving to be an encouraging and enlivening practice. The LMS *Report*, based on Moffat's submissions, also noted the pleasing news that many of the 'poor people engage in secret prayer.' These were heartening signs.

For Moffat, however, attendance at worship, the ability to learn the catechism by heart,[11] and even a desire for prayer,[12] were not enough. These signified an increasing seeking after God, but they did not equate with real fruit. Moffat would be satisfied with nothing less than an intense moving of the affections of the heart, accompanied by a deep sense of sin, and manifested by a profound surrender to, and love of, Christ. But in the midst of the large number now attending church Moffat saw one man

---

[8] Moffat believed that the low-quality of converts on some mission stations was because becoming a Christian benefited them materially and in other ways. He contrasted that with situations elsewhere, in which becoming a Christian brought persecution and difficulty. He possibly had India in mind. Cf. Bogue, *Miss. Lect.* 14, 'Difficulties attending Missions'. RM, *Journal,* 6.1.1822, (*AAK,* 40f), also pointed to a lack of conviction of sin among converts on some stations. He usually had Bethelsdorp in mind. Conviction of sin was vital in his theology.

[9] LMS, *Report to the 35th Annual Meeting, 1829,* 81f.

[10] Cf. RM, *To Richard Moffat,* 30.12.1828, (*AAK,* 289): 'The attendance, particularly on a Sabbath, is good, and if it continues so, it will be requisite to have a large place of worship built. We are cheered with the sincere attention paid by many to the truth of the Gospel.'

[11] Mary Moffat, *To James Smith,* 30.12.1828, (*AAK,* 292): 'Attendance on public worship is very good. A chapel must soon be built, Mr. Hughes' dwelling house being much too small. The singing goes on charmingly, and to hear many of them repeat [Brown's] catechism, with copious extracts from scripture, is very gratifying. The fixed and serious attention of some of them to the preacher induces us to hope that the Spirit is at work in their hearts.'

[12] RM, *To his Father,* 18.2.1828 (JSM, *Lives,* 144): 'There are also some things calculated to cheer and encourage, and we have no doubt but ultimate success will crown our labours. At a small distance are two Batlaro villages, and on the station there are at least 50 families. All these from time to time have the gospel of salvation preached in their own language; and though we as yet see no immediate fruit of the Spirit, yet it is a consolation to know that their knowledge in Divine things is increasing, and there are several who have begun to pray.'

who seemed to have the 'root of the matter' in him. He wrote to his brother Richard:

> One person stands a candidate for baptism, and being a person possessed of a little influence his example and zeal may through the divine blessing prove useful to others. He was a slave, but purchased his freedom; has been long in the country; is industrious and respectable.[13]

On 30 December 1828, the same day as Robert wrote to Richard expressing that hope for the future, Mary wrote to her father, also voicing positive sentiments concerning the same former slave.[14] He was called Arend, but later took the name Aaron Josephs.[15] He was Khoikhoi, not Tswana, and had not always been regarded favourably by the Moffats. Moffat's first recorded impression of him was in 1823, and was unflattering: 'Several things show that Arend is not a very honest man.'[16] Five years later, Moffat had changed his opinion. On 1 March 1829, Arend became the first convert baptised at Kuruman.[17] Even so, the Moffats never dreamed that the steady progress they noted, and the hopes attached to Arend, would burst into fulfillment in the dramatic way in which they did in 1829. But a powerful happening soon swept through the mission station. If 1828 brought a zephyr of spirituality, then 1829 brought hurricane and tempest. Men and women, previously only politely interested in the faith, were seized by the message and responded spectacularly. Richard Lovett, official historian of the LMS, described the Kuruman Awakening in the following terms:

> It was not until 1829 that the hearts of the patient and persistent workers were cheered by signs of the success they most desired. The congregations began to exhibit marks of spiritual awakening. The awakening came, as such

---

13 RM, *To Richard Moffat,* 30.12.1828, (*AAK*, 290).

14 Mary Moffat, *To James Smith,* 30.12.1828, (*AAK,* 292): 'We have at present a candidate for baptism, who, though not a Mochuana, may prove the beginning of a Christian Church among them. It is Arend, of whom you have heard formerly: a slave who ran away and sojourned many years in the interior, has some years ago purchased his own freedom with ivory, has since lived near the station, and has lately seen the necessity of a decided profession. He is an industrious pushing man, and we have reason to believe that he will be a good example, and that ere long there will be some of our poor people inclined also to come out and be separate.' Mary described true discipleship as 'coming out and being separate': converts must break with the past, their former religion, and former way of living.

15 Aaron Josephs had been a runaway slave from the Cape Colony, who led a wandering life, partly in company with the notorious Boer renegade Coenraad Buys, and became relatively wealthy through trade. He ultimately bought his own freedom from his former master. Cf. *AAK,* 106, fn. 7, and RM, *MLSSA,* 496f. Arend had been of great help when the mission station was threatened during 1828.

16 RM, *To Mary Moffat,* 13.8.1823, (*AAK,* 106).

17 Not 1 May 1829 as Schapera stated (*AAK,* 106, fn. 7). Schapera followed the LMS *Annual Report* for 1830. Moffat's date was transcribed incorrectly by the LMS.

> things do come, without any human or visible existing cause. There was a wave of tumultuous and simultaneous enthusiasm. In a few months the whole aspect of the station had changed.[18]

The Kuruman meeting-house was now crowded before the service had begun. 'Heathen songs and dancing had ceased, replaced by the songs of Zion and the outpouring of impassioned prayers'. The missionaries were 'beset even in their own houses by men and women seeking fuller instruction in things which had become to them all at once of paramount importance'.

THE ACCOUNT OF THE AWAKENING

Isaac Schapera's otherwise admirably edited *Apprenticeship at Kuruman* stops short of the 1829 Awakening, with his last item dated 30 December 1828. He did not include the joyful letters which told the story of spiritual birth at the mission, despite the Awakening being the culmination of the Moffats' prayers and hopes throughout the previous years. Why did he make this editorial decision? Was it because he was an anthropologist, and more interested in letters which related to politics and culture than to piety? The same might be said of Wallis, who edited *The Matabele Journals of Robert Moffat.* Both editors reveal in footnotes that they intentionally omitted passages which were mainly concerned with religious sentiments. Yet the Awakening was also a cultural event. It marked the start of an important transition among Tswana, from traditional religion to Christianity. Moreover, Schapera was clearly interested in missions, as evidenced by his editing large collections of Livingstone's papers. Whatever his reason for stopping short of the watershed year of 1829 it is regrettable that he did so, since material from that *annus mirabilis* would have crowned his collection.[19]

Our main primary source for the events of the Kuruman Awakening is the manuscript copy of the Robert Moffat and Robert Hamilton letter of 6 March 1829 to William Orme of the LMS.[20] This joint report is a foundational document since all subsequent descriptions of the Kuruman Awakening are dependent upon it, though it is rarely cited directly. Historians usually quote

---

[18] Lovett, *History of the London Missionary Society:* 1795-1895, Vol. 1, (Ldn: Froude, 1899), 587. Lovett drew much of his material from JSM, *Lives,* 154f.

[19] The *Preface* to *AAK* (ix) indicates that whilst Schapera had direct access to Moffat papers in Harare, his access to LMS London papers was indirect. H.V. Hiller, chief archivist of the Harare Archives, whilst in London, microfilmed documents to take back to Schapera.

[20] Moffat/Hamilton, *To Orme, LMS,* 6.3.1829, (SOAS/CWM/SA/Box11/3/B), (Italics ours). Cf. Moffat/Hamilton, *To Miles, Cape Town,* 12.8.1830, (SOAS/CWM/SA/ Box11/3/D). The same events are mentioned by Mary Moffat, *To her Father,* Oct. 1829, (JSM, *Lives,* 158).

from the extracts which were published in the 1830 LMS *Annual Report,*[21] supplemented by the description of the Awakening in John Smith Moffat's *Lives.* In order to have a basis for theological reflection on the Awakening, we shall cite extensive portions of the Moffat/Hamilton *Report*. The Report opened by referencing difficulties of the past:

> It is with peculiar feelings that we now take the pen to address you; for, through the tender mercies of our God, we feel called upon to write in a strain rather different to that which has hitherto been the burden of our conversations. The contents of our former letters, like Ezekiel's roll, we only calculated to suppress the spirits and lower the hopes of such as longed and prayed for the prosperity of the Bechuana Missions. Thanks be to God for that gracious aid by which He has ever kept His feeble servants from sinking into despair. ... Under repeated disappointment, it afforded some consolation to know that the acquisition of the language was going on. Knowledge of serious things was becoming more extensively widespread; and, from many influences and examples on the stations, many families, *originally poor and others who had been plundered of all*, were tolerably well supported from grounds which never before yielded food for man. ...
>
> We have studiously attended to the temporal interests of the natives. ... In attending to this secondary object, we have always had an eye not only to arresting the attention of a people whose minds are exclusively alive to the wants of the present hour, and to whom the past and the future are things of little moment; but we have also looked to the advantages which we hope will accrue to the Society in a reduction of that expenditure which the stations would otherwise require.[22]

Moffat and Hamilton then recorded a change of mood, of extraordinary religious phenomena, and of a deep hunger for the Gospel:

> From these preliminary remarks we trust that you will not be influenced to expect more than what we are now about to communicate. From former letters you would see that for near the last 12 months the attendance on divine service was not only pretty regular, but continued imperceptibly to increase, and our hearts were often gladdened to see that riveted attention to the speakers, which to us seemed a prelude of something real. Our congregations also began to assume that decorum and solemnity which we were wont to behold in our native land. Whether this arose from respect to their teachers, or the force of truth, we were for a time at a loss to know.
>
> A few months ago, we saw for the first time two or three who appeared to exhibit the marks of an *awakened conscience*. This feeling became gradually more general (and in individuals the least expected) till it became demonstrative that the divine blessing was poured out as the word of Grace.

---

21 LMS, *Report to the 36th Annual Meeting, 1830,* 84f.

22 Moffat and Hamilton cited success in persuading locals to take up productive agriculture. This meant that the station did not have the financial burden of supporting them.

To see the careless and the wicked drowning the voice of the missionary with their cries, and leaving the place with hearts overwhelmed with the deepest sorrow, was a scene novel enough to the unthinking heathens. ... Two men (natives), the most sedate in the station, who had long listened to the word with unabated attention, came and declared their conviction of the truths of the Gospel, and professed how deeply sensible they are of their ruined and lost condition. One of these was a chief of the Bashuta which was first driven by the Caffres and afterwards plundered of all by the Mountaineers.

The Report then moved on to Aaron Josephs, the former runaway slave from the Cape Colony, who, after buying his freedom, had settled at Kuruman:

> About eight months ago, Aaron Josephs, who had removed to the station from no other motive but to get his children educated, and to acquire for himself the knowledge of writing, was soon after aroused to a sense of his awful state by nature. Being able to read, he possessed a tolerably extensive knowledge of divine things, which made it the more easy for us to direct him to the Lamb of God who taketh away the sins of the world. About three months ago he became a candidate for baptism. On Sabbath last he with his three children were publicly baptised.
>
> The scene was very impressive and more easily conceived than described. Our meeting-house was, as usual, too small for the congregations. It was with difficulty that order could be maintained from the sobs and cries of many who felt the deepest interest in what they saw and heard. Aaron's wife, who is a respectable and industrious woman, and who had for a long-time stifled conviction, could now no longer restrain the pangs of a guilty conscience. An old Hottentot (he was with Mr. Campbell in his first journey), and a Mochuana who had apostatised when at the old station, saw the enormity of their guilt and were cut to their heart. The former, in particular, for a time seemed inconsolable.

The intense phenomena spilled over into other meetings where, as well as at Sabbath Church services, deep emotions were released:

> On Monday last we held our Missionary prayer meeting. The attendance was great, and the whole presented a most affecting scene. Many, independent of any remonstrances, were unable to restrain their feelings and wept aloud so that the voice of prayer and singing was lost in that of weeping. It became impossible for us to refrain from tears of gratitude to our indulgent Saviour for having thus vouchsafed some tokens of his presence and blessing.
>
> These things are not confined within the walls of the sanctuary. The hills and dales, the houses and lanes, witness the strange scenes. Sometimes three and four at a time are waiting at our houses for counsel and instruction. For some time past the sounds which predominate in our villages are those of singing, prayers and weeping. They hold prayer meetings from house to house occasionally to a very late hour; and often before the sun is seen to gild the mission they will assemble at some house for prayer and continue ... to go forth to labours. It has often happened lately that before the bell was rung,

the half of the congregation was assembled at the doors.

Moffat and Hamilton noted a strong desire on the part of Aaron Josephs and others to give their time freely to the mission as an expression of gratitude:

> But we have to record more, for we have the happiness to see some fruits, the results of a real change of disposition. Several weeks ago, Aaron, with two more came and proposed to take upon them the labour and expense of building a school-house which for a long time would also serve for public-worship, till one for that especial purpose was necessary. All (they said) that they required on the part of the Missionaries was to give the plan and dimensions and make the door and windows with their frames. These, they said, they would also willingly do, but they lacked ability. We were no little astonished at this proposal, it being entirely voluntary, without so much as a single [suggestion?] on our part. We of course most cordially agreed to their wishes, entertaining no doubt as to their competency to the task, Aaron being by trade both a builder and [carpenter?].
>
> We had scarcely laid down the plan (37 feet long and 16 feet wide) when Aaron set all in motion, took his own wagons and oxen and procured timbers for the roof at some distance. Brother Hamilton has been busily employed preparing frames, lintels etc, and had it not been 2 weeks interruptions from heavy rains, the roof-work would have been commenced before this time. However, if no unforeseen hindrances occur in the course of two weeks more, we expect this will be the case. This new building will be of especial use, both for school and divine services, the one which we now occupy being not only small but inconvenient. If it pleases the Lord that the work should continue to prosper with that influx of natives to the Kuruman which we do expect, we shall soon find it necessary to have a still larger building for a meeting-house, but not before circumstances really demand it.

Moffat and Hamilton then took stock of the remarkable series of events, and the new spiritual direction which the mission was taking:

> Reflecting on what has taken place we cannot but feel a lively sense of the goodness of our covenant God and Saviour. We feel like people taken by surprise, or rising from a dream. ... To pour in the balm of consolation to wounded souls has hitherto been to us a strange work, but we look by faith and prayers to Him who giveth liberally and upbraideth not. ... Satan, our adversary, who hitherto reigned with potent sway will now see violence done to what he deems his ancient rights and attack us on fresh ground, but the Lord omnipotent reigneth. The Lamb shall overcome and [reign?]; while the prayer of the Church is, 'Kingdoms wide that sit in Darkness, Grant them Lord the glorious Light.[23]
>
> The experience of some of those who are but emerging from heathenish

---

[23] Taken from the hymn 'O'er those gloomy hills of darkness' by the Welsh hymn-writer William Williams. Cf. RM, *Journal*, 12.8.1854, (*MJ1*, 259).

gloom is of course very simple, and great discrimination on our part is necessary on receiving members at a season when there is so much to operate on the feelings. Some describe their state to be like one who knows that he is walking in darkness and tries in vain to find the road; others say that their hearts are awake from an awful death broken to pieces with the multitude of their sins. Some can scarcely find words to describe their state; like a young man of volatile disposition who came and stated that he knew and felt that all was wrong with him, but what was the matter he could not explain.

One man said that he had seen for some time past that he must be the greatest sinner, for every sermon applied to him and brought to his mind sins which he thought he had forever forgotten. ... He remarked with great feeling that when he reflected on his past life and the love of God to sinners, his head flowed waters and slumber departed from his eyes.

While writing these remarks, the old Hottentot ... sent his son with a bible with the request that Mrs. M. might sound out the chapter (Hosea 14) which she had read to him the day before. When we see and hear these things we cannot but recognise the workings of the Spirit of God. Among those under [alarm?] there are Batlapis, BaRolong, Mantatee (Bakuena) and Bashuta. Let us hope and pray that the present may be but the beginning of a glorious day of Grace.

The Awakening, with its associated phenomena, continued through the year. In July 1829, six more converts were admitted to church membership.[24] They were a small part of a much larger number who wanted to be baptised, but whose profession the missionaries wished to test more thoroughly. John Smith Moffat, drawing on family table-talk, further described the emotion attending the Awakening:

The missionaries did not dismiss their northern caution. It was only after careful examination that from the many who pressed forward they selected some six in the first instance to receive the rite of baptism. ... The Bechwanas pride themselves in the suppression of all outward emotion. ... But if their feelings do gain the upper hand they are shown by uncontrollable outbursts, and in ways almost painful to witness. Thus, it was that at times the little meeting-house at Kuruman was filled with a storm of sobs and cries which made it almost impossible to proceed with the service. As time went on these manifestations moderated and the converts settled down to steady work.[25]

---

24 Referring to these converts, Moffat stated: 'It was truly gratifying to observe the simplicity of their faith, implicitly *relying on the atonement of Christ*, of which they appeared to have a very clear conception, considering the previous darkness of their minds on such subjects.' (Deane, *Robert Moffat,* 102).

25 JSM, *Lives,* 154f. Emotional response was at its height in 1829. Though intensity lessened thereafter, it remained a factor. When Robert visited Moselekatse in 1835, Mary, *To RM,* 25.6.1835 (JSM, *Lives,* 196), wrote: 'I must now give some account of this place and

THE ASSESSMENT OF THE AWAKENING

In considering the Moffat/Hamilton Report it is illuminating to note the issues which they emphasised. These reveal how Moffat and Hamilton interpreted what was happening.

1. An Attentive Listening. Before the Awakening broke upon Kuruman, there was a mesmeric attention to the Word of God, and a hunger for more of it: 'Our hearts were often gladdened to see that riveted attention to the speakers which to us seemed a prelude of something real.' The Word was the primary missiological force in Moffat's thinking, and he would not be surprised to see a deep hunger for it as a prelude to spiritual awakening.

2. A Serious Spirit. The mood of the people changed: 'Our congregations also began to assume that decorum and solemnity which we were wont to behold in our native land.' In Moffat's piety, an attitude of quietness, solemnity, and sober decorum, was seen as a sign of the Spirit working in people. For Moffat, the Spirit brought order, seriousness and awe.

3. An Awakened Conscience. The Report continued: 'We saw for the first time two or three who appeared to exhibit the marks of an *awakened conscience*.' The word 'awakened' not only inspires the title to this chapter, but connects the Moffat/Hamilton Report with the evangelical concept of a 'spiritual awakening' which was primarily an awakening of the moral conscience. 'Awakening' was not intellectual enlightenment. It was a realisation of the state of sinful humanity before a holy God. 'Conscience', together with 'awakened', underlines that in Moffat's theology true religion was not based in the discovery of new spiritual truth *per se,* but in the realisation of the sinner's standing before God. Emotion was not based on religious ecstasy, but on contrition. Evangelical mission majored on moral repentance. The conscience was awakened. Evangelical missionaries made a distinction between people who professed conversion out of duty, politeness, self-advantage, fervour or gratitude, and those who exhibited signs of an 'awakened conscience' in heart-felt weeping over sin.

4. A Conviction of Sin. This was the litmus test which proved whether a person was truly under the influence of the Holy Spirit or not. Moffat's description is of enormous significance: 'The careless and the wicked drowning the voice of the missionary with their cries, and leaving the place

---

neighbourhood. ... The congregations are exceedingly large ever since you went, and the brethren never so much encouraged with appearances among the Batlaro. The numbers who attend are great, and there is *considerable emotion* among them such as was never before observed.'

with hearts overwhelmed with the deepest sorrow.' Other passages in the Report refer to profound weeping. In Moffat's theology, Word and the Spirit combined to bring conviction of sin to the unsaved soul. True conversion was accompanied by deep sorrow over sin, before any expression of joy over salvation. The expression of strong emotion would not surprise Moffat and Hamilton, so long as it was rooted in deep-seated moral repentance. Weeping over sin was evidence of grace. But when emotion was disengaged from repentance then that prompted unease. The *Report* stated that Aaron Josephs was awakened to the realisation that he was sinful 'by nature'. Moffat and Hamilton saw it as important that people understood that they were affected by original sin,[26] not simply by personal sinful acts. Humanity was in a state of sin. It was not just that people were doing sinful things.

5. A Desire for Prayer. The Moffat/Hamilton Report underlined the strong desire for prayer which the Awakening brought: 'They hold prayer meetings from house to house: occasionally to a very late hour; and, often before the sun is seen to gild the mission, they will assemble at some house for prayer'. The emphasis on prayer continued well after the *anus mirabilis.* The 1832 LMS *Annual Report* recorded: 'The prayer-meeting conducted by Aaron Joseph at his house on Friday evenings, is generally crowded to excess, and many retire from it, as they do from the house of God, to repair to the bushes in order to pour out their hearts to God in earnest supplication.'[27] Even before the Awakening, and before individuals professed conversion, Moffat noted an increasing number of men and women engaging in prayer. Within evangelical theology this pre-conversion prayer was regarded as a sign of the Spirit moving in a person's soul, creating a seeking after God. The prayer emphasis which followed the Awakening was seen as the response of a child of God who has entered a new relationship with their heavenly Father.

6. A Desire for Service. The Report made a strong point out of Aaron Josephs, and others, voluntarily offering their services in the development of the Mission Station. Moffat and Hamilton were deeply moved by that. It helped seal the genuineness of what happened at Kuruman: 'We have the happiness to see some fruits, the results of a real change of disposition'.

---

[26] *Brown's Catechism* taught in Q&R 28, 29 that Adam's sin 'hurts all children as soon as they are born' and 'makes us come into the world sinful and miserable creatures.' The same wording is in the SeTswana version (Grey/9/c/3/8, 6).

[27] LMS, *Report to the 38th Annual Meeting, 1832,* 92f.

The Emotion of the Awakening

Kuruman was not the first place in southern Africa to experience an Awakening attended by strong emotional phenomena. In 1815, Joseph Williams, who stayed at Hooge Kraal en route to Bethelsdorp, described a similar type of revival which was sweeping the village.[28] At Kuruman, the emotional intensity subsided as 1829 drew to a close, and was less pronounced thereafter.[29] But the Awakening left its mark, setting a benchmark of what happened when the Spirit of God worked in power: 'The Spirit of God has commenced His operations, and surely He will go on.'[30]

Moffat was not surprised when men and women broke down and wept over their sins. This fitted his theology, in which conversion was understood in terms of 'new life in the soul',[31] and for that new life to be born there had to be a profound realisation of, and repentance over, sin. True repentance had a deep emotional aspect. But what brought some discomfiture to Moffat was the extreme degree of the emotion. For Moffat, godliness and decorum went together, and decorum should be observed even when weeping over sin. Such tears were right and proper and expected, but excessive demonstration of emotion was not. John Smith Moffat pointed out that Moffat and Hamilton were not men who encouraged such 'excesses'. He described them as two sober-minded Scotsmen by disposition, not willing to lend themselves to any movement which might have the taint of sensationalism.[32] It comes as no surprise that in August 1829 Moffat wrote to Richard Miles in Cape Town:

> Those marks of acute feeling exhibited in bitter cries and hysteric emotions have greatly subsided; we having repeatedly, in public and private, disapproved of anything whatever which interrupted the solemn decorum

---

[28] Briggs & Wing, *The Harvest and the Hope,* 21. In 1842 Livingstone used the term 'awakening' when referring to events taking place at the French Mission Station at Motito, cf. Livingstone, *To Mr and Mrs Livingston,* 13.7.1842, (*DLFL,* Vol. 1, 61).

[29] Mary Moffat, *To her Father,* Oct. 1829 (JSM, *Lives,* 157): 'The converts are going on well, and though the general commotion in the minds of the people has is great measure subsided, we have solid reason to believe that there are many persons who are the subjects of an abiding conviction of their condition as sinners before God'. Cf. LMS, *Report to the 37th Annual Meeting, 1831,* 81f: 'The strong excitement that at a former period prevailed for a season, has indeed abated, but there is reason for believing that the work of grace is going on in the hearts of many, and that their convictions will end in conversion.'

[30] Mary Moffat, *To her Father,* Oct. 1829, (JSM, *Lives,* 157).

[31] In 1851, looking for a 'new awakening', Moffat, *To Freeman, LMS,* 20.3.1851, (SOAS/CWM/SA/Box 26/1/A), noted that, though earnest attention was paid to the preaching, so far there had been little evidence of 'movement in the soul.'

[32] JSM, *Lives,* 154f.

which should ever characterize divine worship. [33]

In a marginal note Moffat added that though he did not condemn 'feeling', he recommended to those who felt themselves overcome by emotion during a service to retire from the church, and to sit near the doors so that they might be able to relieve themselves of their feelings without disturbing others in the congregation! The intensity of the Awakening took Moffat and Hamilton by surprise. It was something they had never encountered before. Yet, it was not unknown in Evangelical revivalist history. But whilst so much around him was in turmoil, Moffat's answer was to steer a course spiced with 'Scottish' theological sobriety.

But how 'Scottish' was Moffat's reaction? Was the 'sober-minded' and hard-headed' response, which John Smith Moffat referred to, truly typical of Scottish evangelicalism? The Burgher tradition, to which Robert Moffat was exposed through Ebenezer Brown in Inverkeithing, and which may have been his mother's spiritual home, certainly treated such phenomena with suspicion. William Brown, brother of Ebenezer Brown, and author of *Brown's Catechism,* published his *History of the Propagation of Christianity among the Heathen* in 1854. In his book, Brown commented specifically on the Kuruman Awakening, focusing on the emotions displayed:

> Of these awakenings we confess we entertain great doubts; at all events, they are probably to be taken for much less than the representations originally given of them. It has indeed been remarked, in reference to such outbreaks of feeling - and we doubt not with some truth - that among an uncivilised people, there is scarcely any medium between not feeling at all and giving full vent to the expression of their feelings.[34]

Brown dismissed the 'excesses' of the Kuruman experience as something to be expected from 'uncivilised' people, who were unable to moderate their feelings. Yet, as we explore below, there were many instances in Scotland of experiences similar to what happened at Kuruman.

Evangelical faith, especially that which was influenced by the American Great Awakening under Jonathan Edwards, had an ambiguous attitude toward the type of manifestations which took place at Kuruman in 1829. Around 1740, Edwards described phenomena in New England similar to those at Kuruman ninety years later. He noted that it was a frequent thing to see a house full of outcries, faintings, convulsions, and 'such like', both from

---

33 Moffat/Hamilton, *To Miles,* 12.8.1830, (SOAS/CWM/SA/Box11/3/D).

34 Brown, *History of the Propagation of Christianity among the Heathen, Vol. 2,* (Edin: Blackwood, 1854), 239. Brown was deeply sceptical of converts who converted quickly.

distress and from joy.[35] Edwards judged these to be genuine marks of the work of God's Holy Spirit. However, he was also aware that opponents of the revival, such as Charles Chauncy, were attributing such phenomena to excesses and extravagancies, and that they were dishonouring to God. Edwards had to tread a fine line between defending what he considered to be the effect of the Holy Spirit among converts, and disapproving of ungodly excesses. He had to develop a theology which recognised a distinction between ecstatic experiences which were of God, and those which were not. Edwards' *Treatise concerning the Religious Affections* was devoted to this issue, taking the form of a lengthy commentary on 1 Peter 1:8: 'Whom having not seen, ye love: though now ye see him not, yet believing, ye rejoice *with joy unspeakable and full of glory.'* Iain Campbell has discerned a development in Edwards' writings on this matter. In 1737 Edwards wrote almost uncritically concerning extraordinary spiritual experiences. In 1742 Edwards had to defend many of the ecstatic phenomena which came with revival against criticisms from Chauncy. Finally, in 1744, in his *Treatise concerning the Religious Affections,* Edwards cautioned supporters of the revival who previously had been uncritical of every spiritual experience.[36]

Though Edwards never repudiated the validity of the experiences which converts had during the high days of the Great Awakening in New England—believing that the Holy Spirit prompted them—he agreed that Christians had to be wary of counterfeit phenomena. Yet, notwithstanding Edwards' position, the Chauncy doubts concerning ecstatic phenomena became the doubts not only of non-evangelical churchmen, but of several evangelical bodies. The Scottish Secessionist and Burgher tradition, with a history of suspicion towards other forms of evangelicalism, followed Chauncy.[37] With this background, William Brown's antipathy toward 'Awakenings' is unsurprising.

---

35 Edwards, *An Account of the Revival of Religion,* in: Iain D. Campbell, 'Jonathan Edwards' *Religious Affections* as a Paradigm for Evangelical Spirituality': *SBET,* Vol. 21, No. 2, 2003, 170.

36 Ibid, 172. Cf. Jonathan Edwards, *To James Robe,* 12.5.1743, (Campbell, 173): 'Many among us have been ready to think that all high raptures are divine: but experience plainly shows it is not the degree of rapture and ecstasy (though it should be up to the third heavens) but the nature and kind that must determine us in their favour.' Edwards' reference to the 'third heaven' (2 Corinthians 12:2) is intriguing. In a letter from Robert Moffat (Snr.) to Robert his son around the time Robert became involved with Methodists in England, there was a warning to young Robert about being over fascinated with 'third heaven' experiences. Cf. Moffat (Snr), *To RM,* (JSM, *Lives,* 14). Was there a distrust in the Moffat household concerning ecstatic phenomena? Did it link in with Robert's 'sober-minded' and 'hard-headed' approach in 1829?

37 Cf. John Brown, *An Historical Account of the Rise and Progress of the Secession*, 60f. The Burghers had been reluctant to work with either Wesley or Whitfield.

Yet at the Cambuslang Revival in 1742 there had been extraordinary scenes of emotional outpouring. And Cambuslang was not a one-off. John Gillies of Glasgow gathered a mass of information which told the story of revivals both overseas and in Scotland.[38] His aim was to collect authentic narratives describing contemporary spiritual awakenings, which collection was first published by himself in 1754.[39] It was then republished by Horatius Bonar in 1845, under the title *Gillies' Historical Collections,* with Bonar adding material to cover the period to 1840. *Gillies' Historical Collections* leaves no doubt that, during revivals in Scotland, times of intense weeping and high emotion were not unusual. Bonar supplied numerous additional instances in Scotland of revival attended by intense emotion. In particular, he referred to 'remarkable awakenings during the last half century: at Moulin in 1798 and 1800; and on the island of Skye in 1812 and 1814.'[40] Moffat may have heard of these before leaving for Africa in 1816.

Donald Meek has argued that, within certain sectors of Scottish evangelicalism, there is still a tendency to ignore the physical impact of revivals, and an anxiety to preserve 'spiritual decorum' at all costs.[41] Like Gillies and Bonar, Meek maintained that ecstatic phenomena were no strangers in the Scottish context, with the Skye Revival of 1841-42 showing that such occurrences were not restricted to so-called 'primitive' nations:

> McQueen, pastor of the small Baptist Church at Broadford on the Isle of Skye gave vivid accounts of the events in the late autumn of 1841 and the spring of 1842: 'I hear that ... hundreds fell down as if they were dead. This usually commences with violent shaking and crying out with clapping of hands.' In March he wrote: 'As to the revival things are more moderate. The crying and fainting are dying away in most places, but the desire to hear is the same. ... Other pastors experienced the same phenomena, including screaming.[42]

---

38 John Gillies, *Historical Collections relating to Remarkable Periods of the Success of The Gospel,* (Publ. 1754, revised 1845. BOT edn, Edin: 1981). For Gillies see: *DNB,* Vol. 7, 1246.

39 Gillies (477, 479) cited similar phenomena in David Brainerd's *Journal.* He also cited John Wesley (487f), and noted the same phenomena on the continent (490f), quoting a 1750 letter from a minister in Holland to a Scottish minister: 'At last the preaching of the gospel began to be attended with such awful power, that several were made to cry out aloud with many tears, and a bitter, painful sense of their fearful distress and misery. ... There was a great lamentation; rivers of tears gushed out, and several fell trembling and astonished to the earth, unable to stand, by reason of the agony and agitation of their spirits.'

40 *Gillies,* 556. The extract mentions similar phenomena during revivals on the Island of Lewis in 1824 and 1836, plus events at Kilsyth (near Glasgow) in 1839.

41 Donald Meek, 'Falling Down as If Dead: Attitudes to Unusual Phenomena in the Skye Revival of 1841-1842', (*SBET, Vol. 13, No. 2,* 116). Cf. Haykin, *Revival, Signs and Wonders: Some Evangelical Perspectives from the Eighteenth Century* (Ontario: Richmond Hill, 1994).

42 Meek, 'Falling Down as if Dead', 117f.

One Skye schoolmaster wrote that the cries of weeping from the meeting house could be distinctly heard at the distance of half a mile.[43] It was the fruit which followed, which convinced many that the phenomena were from God. Gross sins were abandoned. Carnal levities were given up. And a deep interest was felt, and shown, in salvation and the serious things of God.[44]

Was William Brown unaware of these events? Unlikely. He was full-time secretary of the Scottish Missionary Society. He had his finger on the spiritual pulse of the nation. It seems that, when Brown wrote about emotionalism at the Kuruman Awakening, he wrote with a deliberate eye on events in Scotland of which he did not approve. Putting the later Skye Revival aside, it seems improbable that Moffat had not heard of, or read about, such phenomena occurring at recognised evangelical revivals. It may be that his discomfiture with extreme weeping, was not through ignorance of revivalist history, but through the influence of a form of Presbyterianism with which he had been attached. Admittedly, he did not forbid such expressions; he simply wanted to retain the 'gravity' and 'decorum' of worship.

One further observation. Although few cited *joy* as a God-given ecstatic spiritual phenomenon, all focussed on weeping over sin. This was the Kuruman experience. Loud cries and sobbing accompanied a realisation of sinfulness. But Moffat did not judge every form of religious ecstasy as having come from God. He saw religious ecstasy in tribal dances, but he made a vast contrast between ecstatic phenomena encountered in African Traditional Religion and the moving of the Holy Spirit within the soul. If any feature were to 'authenticate' an ecstatic expression, it would be 'weeping over sin'. Moffat expected weeping over sin, even if its unrestrained expression took him aback. Yet, individuals weeping over their sins was a new experience for the indigenous people at Kuruman. Beforehand, there had been fear lest sins offend the ancestral spirits. But weeping tears of repentance under conviction of sin toward God was something new.

---

43 Ibid, 121.

44 See also, Alexander McCrae, *Revivals in the Highlands and Islands in the 19th Century* (Stirling: Mackay, undated). McCrae examined periods of revival in highland Scotland, citing remarkable phenomena and judged these as genuine manifestations of the Holy Spirit. Cf. 'There were sobs, groans and cries to be heard among the awakened in this place; but the work of God's Spirit, in convincing of the evil of sin, and the sinner's need of a hiding place from the storm, was particularly manifest in floods of tears on every cheek.' (143).

Chapter 30
The People of the Awakening

THE AWAKENING TOOK PLACE among a mixed group of indigenous peoples who lived around Kuruman. Many were BaThlaping, but there were a number of others, resulting in a heterogeneous population. Though the LMS Kuruman Mission originated as a mission to the BaThlaping, by 1829 a demographic change had taken place. In order to appreciate the 1829 situation, we need to outline the history of the LMS and the BaThlaping in that area.

Mothibi, later Senior Chief or Kgosi[1] of the BaThlaping, was born around 1780. During the period 1801 to 1817 the BaThlaping, under his leadership, settled in four main locations before moving nearer the Kuruman River. In 1805 Lichtenstein visited the region, followed by Burchell in 1812.[2] In 1813 John Campbell of the LMS opened up negotiations for the settlement of missionaries with the BaThlaping, to which Mothibi responded positively. Evans and Hamilton then left England in 1815, reaching Lattakoo on 17 February 1816. However, they were directed by Mothibi to settle at the Kuruman River, thirty miles away. Disappointed, they returned to Griqua Town. Evans gave up on the mission, but Robert Hamilton and James Read made another attempt. This time permission was given for them to live with the chief and his people. This was the first LMS Tswana mission.[3]

In June 1817, when Mothibi moved his tribe to the Kuruman River, the missionaries accompanied them. In due course Hamilton was left on his own, waiting for Moffat, who, with his young bride, Mary, arrived at the end of March 1820 along with the returning Campbell and Read. Campbell and Read then set out on a journey to the BaHurutse, almost two hundred miles to the northeast of Lattakoo, while Robert and Mary remained with Hamilton in

---

1 The following offices existed: (i) *Kgosi* (Chief); (ii) *Borangwanakgosi* (Chief's uncles); (iii) *Bagakolodi Ba Kgosi* (Councillors); (iv) *Dikgosana* (Headmen); (v) *Bomonna Dikgosana* (Sub-headmen). Mothibi was *Kgosi* to the BaThlaping, Sechele was *Kgosi* to the BaKwena. Less important BaThlaping chiefs whom Moffat cited may have been *Dikgosana* who were also on the Chief's council. Within their wards, headmen had their own councils.

2 The anthropologist W.H.C. Lichtenstein explored several areas of southern Africa in the early nineteenth century. He was interested in the Tswana, and authored, *Foundation of the Cape & about the Bechuanas: 1807,* which was translated by O.H. Spohr from Liechtenstein's *Ueber die Beetjuanas* (CT: A.A. Balkema, 1973). W.J. Burchell was a British naturalist/explorer. Burchell's zebra was named after him.

3 Deane, *Robert Moffat,* 58f.

order to gain the confidence of Mothibi and his people. The home of the missionaries moved to the present-day mission station site in 1824. Then in 1825, having lived adjacent to the Kuruman River for many years, Mothibi suddenly moved, with most of his BaThlaping, to a new permanent site near Philippolis, a considerable distance away. Mothibi was weary of the raids to which his people were subject at the hands of their eastern neighbours. At Philippolis he was under the aggressive protection of Adam Kok's Griqua.[4]

The Kuruman Awakening thus took place amidst Tswana who had no local high-ranking leader.[5] Many were BaThlaping, but Mothibi, their senior chief, was distant. John Smith Moffat was of the opinion that, when Mothibi left the Kuruman area, the BaThlaping who remained—though a much-reduced number under Mothibi's nephew Mankoroane—were more amenable to the influence of the missionaries.[6] After 1825 this reduced BaThlaping population had been supplemented by various small groups who came into the district. Additions continued as the years passed, and Du Plessis has pointed out that, during 1828, the drift of scattered groups toward Kuruman increased significantly. They were often refugees from smaller interior tribes, dispersed by raids from Ndebele and Mantatee. Du Plessis also commented that, in the Gospel as proclaimed by Moffat and Hamilton there was something which strongly appealed to these impoverished and homeless fugitives.[7] Lye and Murray agreed that, as a refuge for dispossessed peoples, the Kuruman settlement proved important.[8]

The LMS station at Bethelsdorp under Van der Kemp's ministry had also been a magnet for the poor and the displaced. Bethelsdorp was criticised by some who perceived it as an illegal safe-haven for runaway slaves and malcontents from within the Colony. But Kuruman, well beyond the boundaries of the Colony was never accused of being a refuge in that sense, though it did become a draw for uprooted people.[9] During the 1820s

---

4 In 1835 Moffat made a visit to Mothibi at his new site. Mothibi was absent but his Queen, Mahuto, invited Moffat to preach. Cf. RM, *To Mary Moffat,* 2.12.1835, (JSM, *Lives,* 201): 'She then with many others begged me to tell them about God and their souls.' Mahuto converted before Mothibi.

5 Mackenzie, *Ten Years North,* 58, discussing the period of missionary success throughout the 1830s wrote: 'The BaThlaping tribe had been broken up, and were scattered all over the country under 'head-men'; the power of the supreme chief being considerably in abeyance.'

6 JSM, *Lives,* 129.

7 Du Plessis, *A History of Christian Missions in South Africa*, 160f.

8 Lye & Murray, *Transformations,* 51f. Lye and Murray noted that, with the Missionary Societies, conversions came slowly, and often to the 'lesser' members of the community (66f).

9 Setiloane, *The Image of God among the Sotho-Tswana,* 123ff, believed that the 'Foreign Teaching' brought by the missionaries eventually took root because *refuge* and *compassion*

drought, famine and war made life difficult in that remote area. At such times, in contrast to the aridity affecting so much of the area, Moffat was transforming Kuruman into a land of plenty by his horticultural revolution.[10] Moreover, despite Mothibi's decision to seek stronger protection elsewhere, Kuruman was still viewed as a relatively safe place, giving security against migrant tribes, bandits and raiders. Kuruman was regarded as both an oasis and a refuge. Even before Mothibi left the area, non-BaThlaping people had been allowed to live on the land which Mothibi and his elders had granted to the LMS. After Mothibi left it was even easier to absorb non-BaThlaping into the community. This population, though predominantly Tswana and BaThlaping, was a collection of 'nations',[11] including the Khoikhoi Aaron Josephs and his family. The safe-haven concept, which mission stations created inadvertently, ensured the physical survival of many poor and weak groups who otherwise would have disappeared.[12]

The 1829 Indigenous Community

Demographic changes, after Mothibi left with most of the BaThlaping in 1825, meant that the remaining indigenous population, though mainly BaThlaping, were a varied range of peoples, many from the poorer sections of society.[13] The indigenous community around Kuruman, after Mothibi's departure, had the following characteristics:

1. It had no strong local tribal leader.
2. It comprised of the poorer part of the BaThlaping and others.

---

were provided. On missions making progress among refugee groups and displaced or fragmented societies, see: Sundkler & Steed, *A History of the Church in Africa,* (Cambridge: CUP, 2000), 311, 368.

10 Cf. Nancy Jacobs, *Environment, Power and Injustice*, 61.

11 Noted by Livingstone, who saw it as God's plan: 'The providence of God fixed the residence of the translator on a spot which became a city of refuge for individuals and families from nearly every tribe in the country' (Livingstone, *Notes of a Tour of the River Sesheke in the Region north of Lake Ngami,* in: *South African Commercial Advertiser,* 7.4.1852: *DLSAP,* 114).

12 Cf. Du Plessis, *The Evangel in South Africa,* 31.

13 The *LMS* 1830 Report, 84f, based on information supplied by Moffat, referred to the mixed nature of the Kuruman community: 'Several persons ... belonging to various aboriginal tribes, manifested a serious concern for the salvation of their souls; those persons belonged to the following tribes: Batlapees, Borolongs, Mantatees (or Bakuens), and Bashutas.' The Report for 1834 also underlined the heterogeneous nature of the community, making the additional point that non-BaThlaping were the most amenable to the Gospel: 'They are mostly poor, but a spirit of industry prevails; and abundance of labourers can be obtained when in our power to employ them. It is also worthy of remark, that of all the members and candidates there are, strictly speaking, no Batlapis among them; their society being composed of the following interior tribes, viz.: Bakuena, Bashuta, BaRolong, Batau, Batlatla, and some Batlaru who were formerly in Mathibee's jurisdiction.' LMS, *Report to the 40th Annual Meeting, 1834,* 96f.

3. It was a heterogeneous mixture.

It was among this diverse and structurally weak populace that the Awakening took place, with conversions first occurring among ordinary people rather than the tribal aristocracy. Setiloane noted this, commenting that the first converts to Christianity were certainly not the members of the royalty in any tribe, and that chiefs and people of rank and standing were not zealous to accept the teaching of the missionaries: 'For a long time Christianity was accepted as something in which the women and lesser members of society could indulge.'[14] This was not 'top-down' conversion to Christianity. It was conversion among the unimportant, the poor, and the powerless.[15]

Was the lack of the presence of a senior chief a necessary precondition for conversions to occur? Did Moffat become substitute-chief and vicarious father-figure? These are difficult questions to answer. Mothibi never opposed the missionaries, and indeed he aided them considerably. And at Mothibi's new base, many of his tribe converted, though it was only in the early 1840s that Mothibi himself did so. This indicates that Mothibi did not place obstacles in the way of individuals within his tribe converting to Christianity even before he did. Thus, though the Awakening occurred in the aftermath of Mothibi's removal, it should not be deduced that his presence had been an obstacle. Moreover, in the years immediately following his 1825 departure, there was no sign that the missionaries had an easier task.

Nevertheless, though Mothibi's departure may not have been a factor in enabling the Awakening to take place, it did affect the nature of the Awakening when it did occur. It was an Awakening among those who had little power, little wealth, little influence, and little status. This may—and we stress *may*—have had several consequences. Firstly, it may have contributed to Moffat having enormous freedom in moulding converts as he felt they should be. In later years Moffat did become a powerfully influential father-figure: benevolent paternalism suited him! Secondly, the absence of a senior chief may also have resulted in the Kuruman Church polity and exercise of discipline not being in direct opposition to a strong locally based tribal

---

14 Setiloane, *The Image of God among the Sotho-Tswana,* 140, 141, 143. But the list of members in the *KCRB,* indicates that men, just as much as women, became converts.

15 Also noted by Livingstone. Cf. Livingstone, *To Freeman, LMS,* 24.8.1850, (*LMC,* 148): 'The first success [Moffat] had at Kuruman was among a small tribe of Balala called Bachaine (of which Paul and Mebalwe here are members) and a lot of refugees from the interior. But the seed had been sown in the hearts of the Batlapi too'. Livingstone wrote from Kolobeng. 'Balala' is the generic Tswana name for 'serfs, servants, inferior people'.

structure.[16] Thirdly, and negatively, it may also have meant that the relatively low social status of Kuruman converts contributed to them not being readily accepted as evangelists to their own people.[17] When the LMS in southern Africa had had a mass commissioning of native teachers in 1814—before Moffat arrived—most of those selected were men of status, and many of them later had a conflict of interests between their Christian calling and the secular leadership roles which their social position required. But fourthly, the lowly status of converts meant that their lives were not complicated by other responsibilities, with the risk of compromises between these roles.

INDIVIDUAL, TRIBE AND CHIEF

The Kuruman Awakening started among the poor and the displaced within a fragmented society. In no sense were conversions chief-led or imposed from above. The LMS Directors appear to have initially thought that any advance at Kuruman would have been chief-led through Mothibi, but such was not to be the case.[18] It is true that Mankoroane, the nephew of Mothibi, was still near Kuruman, but he was not a significant figure. Yet, despite the Awakening being mostly among people of low status in society, there were signs that Kuruman missionaries did make an impact on some senior families.

Peclu, the heir-apparent son of Mothibi, was significantly affected by the missionary message. Unfortunately, he died at a young age in 1825. Moffat gave a lot of time to Peclu, at that stage being convinced that evangelism would be more effective if conversion took place at the head of the tribe. Even before Mothibi was converted, two of his sons with their wives were already members of the church. And Mahuto, Mothibi's own wife, had also been baptised.[19]

In the Moffat/Hamilton joint report to William Orme of the LMS, there is also reference to a chief of the 'BaShuta' [BaSuto], 'who had long-listened to the word with unabated attention' and who 'came and declared [his]

---

[16] Later in the nineteenth century, the missionary successes of Robert Laws in northern Malawi took place with strong local chiefs near at hand. Cf. John McCracken, *Politics and Christianity in Malawi 1875 – 1940: The Impact of the Livingstonia Mission in the Northern Province*, (Zomba: Kachere, 2008).

[17] Yet all converts were not only baptised but were admitted to Holy Communion. As such, they were given important status, which even a chief was denied if he were not also a church member. Allowing this to happen points to a remarkable openness on the part of the chiefs.

[18] LMS, *Report to the 40th Annual Meeting, 1834,* 96f: 'The Gospel was first sent to the Batlapi, and to the palace of the King; but Mathibee and his tribe are now in a hopeless condition, and far removed from the means of grace.'

[19] RM, *MLSSA,* 606.

conviction of the truths of the Gospel, and professed how deeply sensible [he was] of [his] ruined and lost condition'.

In 1831 Moffat mentioned that, among the 300 attending Church each Sabbath, 'there is an old woman, the wife of a chief, who, with her eldest daughter, comes generally a whole day's journey to attend the Sabbath services: there is reason to hope that these individuals are earnestly and sincerely seeking the way to Zion.'[20] Presumably that lady was the wife of a *Dikgosana*. What is noteworthy is that she felt that she had the freedom to come to Kuruman and hear about this new religion, and was not prevented from doing so by her husband or by the tribal elders. It may be that she was one of those mentioned in the 1837 LMS *Annual Report*:

> In November [1836] 8 natives were added to the number who assemble on the first Sabbath of the month around the table of the Lord. Three of the new members are the *wife*, the *sister*, and the *daughter* of a Batlaru chief, and, from the influence they possess over their tribe, the public profession of their faith in the Redeemer has made a deep impression in the native village where they reside, and in the neighbouring hamlets.[21]

The freedom which such prominent people had to become full members of the church indicates that Christianity was not at that time seen as a threat to traditional religion or culture.[22] This signals a remarkably generous outlook on the part of some local tribes. Elsewhere, when prominent tribal members became Christians, life was not easy for them. The 1840 *Annual Report,* compiled from information submitted by Robert Hamilton and Roger Edwards (Moffat was in Britain) stated, concerning converts:

> One of these is a son of a barbarous chief who hates the Gospel, and now looks upon his son as dead. This young man has been much persecuted by his father and friends, but has hitherto stood firm, and is determined, through promised grace, not to be deterred from serving the Lord.[23]

---

20 LMS, *Report to the 37th Annual Meeting, 1831,* 81f.

21 LMS, *Report to the 43rd Annual Meeting, 1837,* 107.

22 On the other hand, Mackenzie, *Ten Years North,* 58, pointed out that, during the 1830s: 'One whole village—*with the exception of its old chief* and 2 or 3 of his counselors—professed themselves disciples of the new faith.'

23 LMS, *Report to the 46th Annual Meeting, 1840,* 91. This is probably a reference to the persons mentioned in Moffat's 1840 *LMS Sermon*: ''Look', said a stern and veteran chief, in an assembly convened to consult what measures ought to be adopted to prevent the work of conversion, 'Look', said the father, 'there is my son' who was present, 'he is not my son, he is changed into another being. I know him not. He is my heir, my first-born, but he is lost; he is the representative of my fathers, but he is dead.'' (RM, *Africa,* 40). When Sechele, of the BaKwena, converted under Livingstone, his tribe was appalled.

The extent of the freedom of individuals, whether low-born or high-born, to respond to Moffat's Gospel message was inextricably bound up with notions of tribal communality, and the expectation within a community that all members of that community would be committed to, and practise, the traditional religion as an expression of the homogeneity of the community. John Mbiti famously expressed the concept, stating that in African society: 'I am because we are, and, since we are, therefore I am; the individual is united with the rest of his community, both the living and the dead, and humanly speaking nothing can separate him from this corporate society.'[24] In contrast, Moffat believed that individuals, as individuals, were accountable to God on the day of judgment and therefore individuals, as individuals, must make profession of faith one by one. This approach is criticised by scholars who wish to stress the communal nature of African society. But how did it work in practice? Did Moffat's focus on individual response make sense among the major people groups with whom he engaged, the Ndebele and the Tswana?

No Awakening took place among the Ndebele in Robert Moffat's time. Northcott has argued that this was because Moffat preached a personal salvation to a society where, for a man to think of himself as the object of divine favour *individually*—apart from his tribe—would seem absurd and impossible.[25] It was certainly the case that without Moselekatse's despotic 'nod' no Ndebele would dare adopt the new religion. Even after Moselekatse gave permission for the Ndebele Mission to be established in 1859-60, no conversions took place in his lifetime. It was not until he died in 1873 that his people felt free to engage directly with the missionaries. Moselekatse permitted preaching and attended services, but his overpowering presence created a barrier between the missionaries and the people.

Significantly, on the first Sunday after Moselekatse's death, hundreds came to church. Even so, in all the years of the Ndebele Mission few professed Christianity. The mission had only two baptisms by 1887.[26] This was in contrast to what Moffat looked for and expected. He believed that the manly discipline of the Ndebele, though sometimes a barrier to the Gospel, would result in high quality Christians once conversions began. In his farewell speech at Port Elizabeth in 1870, he expressed great hopes concerning the Ndebele: 'Our advanced station at the Matabele is in a very prosperous state, and I quite expect that the Matabele will become one day a great nation.

---

[24] John Mbiti, *African Religions and Philosophy*, (Oxford, Heinemann, 2nd edn, 1990), 113. The context of Mbiti's statement is a discussion of Ndebele and Sonjo initiation rites.

[25] Northcott, *Robert Moffat,* 241.

[26] Northcott, *Robert Moffat,* 291, and RUM, *John Smith Moffat,* 103.

They sternly obey their own laws, and I have noticed that when men of fixed principles become convinced of the great truths of Christianity they hold firmly to the faith, and their fidelity is not lightly to be shaken.'[27]

Moffat saw clearly that the authority of an absolute monarch was in competition with that of Jesus Christ.[28] The situation is illustrated by a problem which his son, John Smith Moffat, encountered one Sabbath whilst preaching to the Ndebele. On that day, he taught that anyone, anywhere, had direct access to God through prayer. Moselekatse was furious, and stormed out of the service in a terrible rage.[29] The idea that ordinary people could by-pass him as the channel to the Supreme Being was anathema to Moselekatse. This homologated Robert Moffat's belief that Moselekatse was definitely a major obstacle to evangelism. Moselekatse expected his people to regard himself as, *de facto*, the ultimate and absolute being, to be obeyed, reverenced, worshipped, adored, and to be regarded as the source of every blessing, with total power of life and death over each and every subject. Moffat believed that in the day-to-day lives of his people Moselekatse *was* the Supreme Being. The God of whom Moffat spoke was not seen as a threat to an actual Ndebele god, or even to the ancestral spirits: the threat was to Moselekatse. It was impossible for an individual Ndebele to profess allegiance to another 'Supreme Being' whilst Moselekatse lived. Only one could hold that office. Allegiance to Christ was in direct opposition to allegiance to the chief, as allegiance was interpreted by a Moselekatse.

The Tswana were not ruled by chiefs as powerful as Moselekatse, and among the Tswana there did seem to be freedom for individuals to make individual commitment to the Christian faith. Moffat had noticed, as early as 1823, that Mothibi of the BaThlaping had 'little authority over his subjects'.[30]

---

[27] RM, *Speech at Port Elizabeth, 1870,* (Deane, *Robert Moffat,* 184). JSM, writing 17 years later, was less positive: 'Moselekatse, faithful to his promise, was a steady friend to the new missionaries; and in this respect his son, Lobenguela, has followed in his steps, but the mission has as yet been without visible success. Time will only tell what has been the meaning of this strange history. It is more than fifty years since Moffat first visited the Matabele.' (JSM, *Lives,* 348). In 1890, JSM revisited Inyati: 'The native service was attended by seven people outside of the missionary group. This is a poor show after thirty years ... I could still trace the foundation of the little cottage where Emily and I had our first home.' (JSM, *To Miss E. Unwin,* 10.12.1890: Baxter & Burke, *The Historical Manuscripts of Rhodesia,* 320).

[28] Bogue taught: 'The unbinding nature of Christianity which required universal fidelity to Christ and forbids compliance with that which is evil, renders it very disagreeable to the rulers of this world' (Bogue, *Miss. Lect.* 13, 'Opposition to be expected by Missionaries').

[29] RUM, *John Smith Moffat,* 100f.

[30] RM, *Journal,* 17.7.1823, (*AAK,* 100). Cf. RM, *To Alexander Moffat,* 22.9.1824, (*AAK,* 163), 'Matabee has the name of king, but he is destitute of the influence and wisdom which should characterize his office.'

The concept of chieftainship among the Tswana appears generally to have been non-despotic. Perhaps this was why individuals felt free to take their own decisions. Their concept of communality was fluid enough to allow for individual decision making in regard to religion. In particular, the heterogeneous group around Kuruman did not have a strong communal identity, and were more amenable to a change of religious paradigm. Weak chiefly leadership was also alluded to by Moffat in 1856:

> Hitherto the progress of the gospel has been, as it has always been, among the poor and middling sort of folks. Our chiefs are sordid and sottish. Yantye of Lekatlong is one who has influence, but he has not much energy. However, he has around him a Christian community, under the ministrations of our worthy brother Helmore. Though there may be a solitary village whose chief might refuse a native instructor, there is no chief in the whole country, from here to the Zambezi River that would refuse the services of a missionary.[31]

Mothibi's conversion—whilst Moffat was in Britain—demonstrates the principle of individual response in Kuruman evangelism.[32] When Mothibi came for baptism he claimed no privileges, waiting in line to take his turn.[33] In allowing him to queue, were the missionaries disrespectful? More likely, Mothibi wanted to come as an 'ordinary' child of God, and not because of any status he had—and continued to have—within his community.[34] It was

---

31 RM, *To one of his Children,* 20.8.1856 (JSM, *Lives,* 317), in which Moffat wrote warmly and positively about Sechele. Legassick, an aggressive critic of Moffat, argued that, because Moffat was himself a domineering person—'a hardly repressed authoritarian'—he was attracted to others of the same type, and despised weak personalities especially BaThlaping chiefs who had to govern in a more 'democratic' system through discussion in council (Legassick, *The Griqua, the Sitho-Tswana, and the Missionaries, 1780-1840, Vol. 2,* 448f).

32 Livingstone, *To the Livingston Family,* 29.9.1841, (*DLFL,* Vol. 1, 39): 'Old Moteebe, our chief, was here [Kuruman] a few weeks ago for the purpose of being baptised and admitted into the church, a feeble decrepit old man, tottering into the grave. After he had carelessly heard the offers of mercy for about 25 years, we trust he has now turned to the Lord. His baptism has caused great excitement through the whole country, particularly among the violent opponents of the gospel. I hope it will lead others to think of their state and look for mercy before it is too late.' Mothibi's baptism is described by Edwards in the LMS *Chronicle*, Vol. 6, (1842) 41.

33 Cf. RM, *MLSSA,* 606ff.

34 Livingstone, *To Livingston Family,* 29.9.1841, (*DLFL,* Vol. 1, 40), described Mothibi's piety after his conversion: 'When talking to [him] of his past life, he always commenced crying like a child. This is remarkable for a Bechuana, and particularly for a king. They never weep until the Spirit works upon their hearts, and then they weep like children. Sometimes in the chapel they hide their heads in their karosses and creep under the forms to avoid the eyes of the preacher. This however won't do. They then scream out, and occasionally rush out of chapel fleeing with all their might. It has often made me wonder, for in performing most severe surgical operations they sit, both men and women, as if they had no feeling. In one case of fungous, 4 inches in length and nearly 2 in breadth, nearly ½ in height, I employed a severe but quick mode of getting rid of it. During the operation I expected him to get up and dance

not an easy step for a chief to become a church member. Being admitted to membership also meant becoming subject to the disciplinary procedures of congregational life, with the possibility of being judged at a church meeting consisting of men and women from his own tribe. Sechele of the BaKwena was prepared to live with this possibility. However, none of Sechele's tribe converted, so no one had to sit in judgment over him.

There are wider questions. Does a strong cultural notion of communality mean that a missionary should never think in terms of individual conversions? Northcott argued that, while compulsory conversion was not within the plan of any of the Kuruman missionaries, 'the idea of mass conversion was not beyond the conception of Livingstone who saw more deeply into the relationship of community life than did Moffat.'[35] However, there is little evidence that Livingstone applied a principle of mass conversion. He was more amenable to traditional customs than Moffat was, but when it came to conversion, we find no evidence that he operated with any other notion than that of men and women coming to faith one by one.

But what did Northcott have in mind? He may have envisaged a model similar to that described by Alan Tippet who, in his study of Oceanic people, described communal conversion as a 'group movement', though not a 'mass movement'.[36] What he envisaged was a conversion-process whereby a people was separated from an old context, and incorporated into a new one. It would be a multi-individual experience, 'whereby the group changes from one conceptual and behavioural context to another, within the operations of its own structure and decision-making mechanisms regardless of whether or not the external environment changes.'[37] Tippet maintained that he was still concerned with individuals, though within groups rather than in isolation. He had in mind a process of Christianisation through a combination of community consent and the authority of the leadership of the community. Through this process the group decides that the new way is what they, as a community, now believe.

However, Tippet's model must address a number of questions from an evangelical perspective. Was he describing the final phases of a process of evangelisation rather than pioneer work? Did he envisage *no* individual

---

from the pain. But no, he sat immoveable and talked with as composed a countenance as if he felt nothing. 'A man like me never cries', he said 'It's only children who cry'. The spirit of God alone can affect their hearts. Without his aid all our efforts must be ineffectual.'

35 Northcott, *Robert Moffat,* 182.

36 Tippett, 'Conversion as a Dynamic Process in Christian Mission', (*Miss.,* 5/2, 1977), 204.

37 Tippett, 'Conversion as a Dynamic Process in Christian Mission', 205.

conversions taking place at all, until the group changed together? But if adopting Christianity is more than Christianisation, and involves specific belief in, for example, one God, the resurrection of Christ, and atonement through Christ's death, what happens—even within Tippet's idealised group movement—when some individuals do *not* believe these new things? Are individuals, as individuals, allowed to believe or not believe by their own decision, without breaking the overall concept of communality?

Such questions may of course be avoided by stating that they all come from an individualistic mind-set! Nevertheless, was Tippet describing a cultural religious identity, or a living personal faith? Tippet would also have to respond to Moffat's primary requirement, that men and women, individually, be convicted of sin. Moffat looked for the 'affections of the heart' being touched by the Gospel. Moffat would also ask about the Last Judgment: are *individuals* lost or are *groups* lost? And if individuals are lost, on the basis of individual response, then to what extent can evangelisation avoid being focused on conversions one by one?

The evangelical missionary did not see himself as manager of a cultural change. Evangelical missionaries saw themselves as *prophets of crisis*. The crisis was the coming judgment which all men and women, from every nation, must face before God. As such, the evangelical missionary saw himself as a channel through whom the Word of God could break into all cultures, all societies, and all belief systems, seeking a response of heart and soul signifying the sinner seeking grace. The missionary's calling was to be a prophet, not an enabler of a new culture. Humanity was humanity in *crisis.* The need, for individuals and nations, whether European or African, was to 'flee from the wrath to come'.

THE LEGACY OF THE AWAKENING

The Awakening continued throughout 1829, and was sustained, if not always with the same intensity, through the next few years. During the 1830s membership of the Kuruman congregation by profession of faith grew considerably. This was without any reduction of the stringent criteria for admission, and despite strict discipline being exercised. The missionaries were less concerned with reporting great numbers than with assessing purity of heart and soul, in order that any work may be built on solid foundations. The following table illustrates the growth:

Year	1829	30	31	32	33	34	35	36	37	38	39	40
Full Members	7	12	NR	NR	NR	29	40	35	55	143	181	200

In 1838, the large Kuruman Church, roofed with timber beams from Moselekatse's country, was officially opened, and the picture of church life at Kuruman for that year, as portrayed in the LMS *Annual Report*, was animating and lively, though the report began with a cautionary remark:

> The Directors have heard with no small regret that some of those lately added to the Church are suffering persecution on account of the open profession they have made of their faith in Christ. ... 'Our Church is composed of people from ten different tribes, and it is an animating sight to see them all uniting in ascribing praise and glory to the Lamb who has redeemed them with his blood, and gathered them into the fold of God' ...
>
> The outward appearance of the people, considering their limited means, is stated to be rapidly improving. They are all anxious to obtain decent clothing, and many purchase when opportunities offer, but this is very seldom. Grateful mention is made of the supplies of apparel from friends in Manchester. ... On the 2nd of November [1838] the new chapel was opened. Four services were held on that day, and the congregations each time numbered about 800 persons.'[38]

If Moffat's figures are at all accurate, then, over four services, about 3000 people attended church on the day the new building was opened. On our visit to Kuruman in 2003, we estimated the capacity of the church building to be about 300, using modern benches. With no benches, uncrowded seating on the floor would allow about 450. With no benches, and with people crammed together the figure could rise to around 600. Moffat's figure of 800 may be a slight exaggeration, but if he included people outside, listening through open doors and windows, then 800 could easily be the case. Many attendees would be native dignitaries from surrounding villages. There would also be scores of the curious, especially since such a huge building had never been seen before. Some would attend more than one service.

The fact that there were only 143 full members of the congregation out of that great multitude is evidence of the care which Moffat and his colleagues exercised when admitting men and women to full membership. Steady progress, not spectacular advance, was the maxim. By 1840

---

[38] *LMS, Report to the 45th Annual Meeting, 1839,* 95f.

membership had risen to 200, even though the missionaries began to record that less people were living at or near the mission station:

> Of late years, since the cessation of the commandoes, the people have begun to wander more about the country, and to reside at a greater distance from the station. In so doing, many of them believe that their cattle will increase more abundantly, and not a few are influenced by a desire to escape from the effects of the Gospel, which they dread, as being fatal to their heathenish customs; thus showing the enmity of the carnal mind to God—its antipathy to the only means of salvation – and a wish to shut out from their minds the dreadful prospects of the impenitent.[39]

On the one hand, the necessity for refuge had declined. On the other hand, tension between Moffat's evangelical Christianity and indigenous culture was becoming more pronounced. Additionally, though the threat posed by traditional commando groups may have subsided, fear created by hostile Boers increased during the next decade. Northcott was of the view that, by the late 1840s, Moffat saw two dangers to the future of Kuruman. One was Kuruman's lack of a resident chief or chief's son to keep the people together. The other was fear of insurgent Boers. The two dangers were intertwined.[40] This is not to say that Kuruman was becoming deserted.[41] Nor was Church attendance sluggish: in 1843, over 400 sat down to Holy Communion.[42]

Nevertheless, as the 1840s melted into the 1850s, and as twenty years passed since the great days of the Awakening, Moffat looked back wistfully: 'We long for a season of revival such as we witnessed when the work of faith

---

39 LMS, *Report to the 47th Annual Meeting, 1841,* 91f. The information was supplied by Hamilton and Edwards, since Moffat was in England. Livingstone arrived in 1841, and it was this population movement which he encountered, causing him to comment on the relatively sparse population around Kuruman. Cf. Livingstone, *To Freeman, LMS,* 23.9.1841, (*LMC,* 1ff).

40 Northcott, *Robert Moffat,* 186. Livingstone, in typical forthright style, argued that, because fewer people lived at Kuruman in the late 1840s, then Moffat should move elsewhere, cf. Livingstone, *To RM,* 2.9.1848, (*DLFL,* Vol. 1, 256). In the *KCRB*, from the 1840s onwards there are numerous reference to members 'now under the care of Mr. Helmore', or 'now under the care of Mr. Ross', etc. A positive view of what was still happening at Kuruman was conveyed to the Livingstones by the native teacher Paul, and alluded to in a letter two months later than the one already quoted: 'Paul gave such a glowing account of the numbers and state of your young people we felt quite cheered.' See: Livingstone, *To RM,* Nov. 1848, (*DLFL,* Vol. 1, 259).

41 Moffat, *Edinburgh Address,* 3.11.1842, (*Farewell Services,* 19), stated: 'There was a time when I longed to see a little church formed ... I saw that accomplished, and the little one has increased, till now we have 300 members at the Kuruman alone'. The actual Kuruman membership in 1842 was about 240.

42 RM, 'Return to Kuruman': *The Juvenile Missionary Magazine, October 1844,* 99ff. The membership at Kuruman in 1843 was much less than 400. The large attendance at Holy Communion, on the Moffats' return after four years in Britain, would include well-wishers who came from a wide area. The *KCRB* and LMS *Annual Reports* reveal healthy numbers admitted to church membership during the 1840s, with a membership of 400 in 1850.

commenced here.'[43] By 1851 he began to record concern at the *quality* of Church life:

> It has not for the last 20 years fallen to our lot to have so little to say about the saving influences of the Gospel in the hearts of the people among whom we labour. While we are labouring in season and out of season, and by all means within our reach to make known a Saviour's love to perishing sinners, and to build up in the faith those who have believed, we are compelled to mourn our want of success. True, we have invariably good congregations. Indeed, it seems a thing taken for granted that everyone within a reasonable distance must go to the Church, keep the Sabbath – at least refrain from all public labour. Yea, the appearance of our congregation is even animating, from the cleanliness, decorum and attention to the great truths sounded in their ears.
>
> A great change has been effected in their entire appearance and deportment; but we do not see that fervent piety, that ardent zeal in believers for the salvation of others, and that devout anxiety to honour that worthy name by which they are called, which we think we might now look for.[44] We are aware that we need not expect that this generation, nor perhaps the three or four to come, will come up to that standard of pious zeal which we find among educated people. We are too well acquainted with the slow progress made even by the Caucasian in civilisation for hundreds of years to feel much disappointment with what we witness among this of the human race, who are universally allowed to be less apt to learn than their white neighbours.'[45]

Apparently thriving church life brought little satisfaction. Moffat's mission was not to extend the empire of the church as an institution. As a young man in Scotland, he had himself been a regular church attender and Bible reader, but his mother had never seen these as enough. In her view it was only when faith burned with love for Christ that faith was real. That moulded Moffat's whole outlook. The church building might be full, but was it full of the redeemed or was it full of the lost? Moffat looked beyond numbers. He was concerned with the 'things of the soul', and the inner relationship men and women had with God. His worries continued through the 1850s:

---

43 LMS, *Report to the 57th Annual Meeting, 1851,* 92. Moffat felt that a new Awakening was starting. Cf. RM, *To Tidman, LMS,* July 1852, (SOAS/CWM/SA/Box 27/1/A).

44 This sentence represents Moffat's consistent desire to see true marks of evangelical faith: affections of the heart surrendered to Christ, and exhibited in a profound personal piety centred on the Saviour. 'Churchianity' was never satisfactory.

45 RM, *To Tidman, LMS,* 3.11. 1851, (SOAS/CWM/SA/Box 26/1/A). Moffat rarely compared the quality of Christian life among new African converts to that of believers elsewhere. But here he did. He saw that time was needed for a new way of living, separate from old customs, to become deeply rooted. Several converts, admitted to full church membership, were still dealing in stolen cattle and taking part in raids on the San.

> To any visitor from a Christian church in Britain everything would appear all that was lovely and of good report. But all this is far away from what we think we ought to see. We want to see progress by aggression on the dominion of Satan;[46] we tell our converts that a church of true believers is a fighting and a conquering church under the banner of the Prince of Peace.[47]

In another letter, he wrote: 'Our present prospects are anything but bright. There is a general deadness over which we mourn. We feel we need the kindling influences of the Holy Spirit.'[48] We suspect he would have expressed the same sentiments had he been a minister in Scotland.

John Smith Moffat wrote that, by 1857, the Bechwana Mission was 'already almost abandoned'. He did not mean that the station was dead, but that little pioneer work was taking place.[49] Moffat's translation work was important, but it tied him down. Visitors always commented favourably, but Moffat wanted more, much more. He longed for the supernatural days of 1829. Despite many converts, he was burdened for the lost souls whose eternal future was uncertain. Success in the past was never enough for Moffat, and on his 71st birthday he was in reflective mood:

> What we now see, churches gathered – the Bible translated – more than 30 places where there are missionaries, teachers and schools and thousands who can now read in their own language – the wonderful works of God. He has done great things for the Bechuana tribes. I have much to gladden besides having my own children in the work – but there is much to sadden. ... [I] have not seen all nor the half of what I expected to see of the influence of the Gospel. Compared to the multitudes to whom the word of God has been spoken, the number of believers are few.
>
> I had been now 50 years in the service of the heathen; of these 47 the servant of the Bechuanas. I had lived 71 years and could not be expected to do much more for the situation of those who were still in unbelief. *I looked on grey headed sinners before me with sorrow.* They had heard my voice for many long years prating them in Christ's stead to be reconciled to God. I should now cease to warn and exhort and leave some worse than I had found them, but

---

46 'Dominion of Satan': Moffat expressed this verdict on some indigenous cultural practices, especially rainmaking, initiation ceremonies, and polygamy, which he viewed as antithetical to the values of the kingdom of God.

47 RM, *To Tidman, LMS,* 14.11.1855, (SOAS/CWM/SA/Box 29/3/A).

48 RM, *To one of his Children,* 20.8.1856 (JSM, *Lives,* 316).

49 JSM, *Lives,* 320. Cf. JSM, *To Unwin,* 21.3.1859, (*MM,* 54): 'I cannot say much for the state of things ... My father's whole energy has been devoted to the translations, and now his heart is in Moselekatse's country. Long absences have occurred, and, when here at all, his time and thoughts have been pre-occupied with preparations for another start. Consequently, he does but little for the people of the station. ... There is the usual organic growth indicative of spiritual progress, but that is rather the fruit of the truth sown in former years than the preparation of still deeper culture.'

> there were those whom I hoped to be my joy and crown of rejoicing in the day of Christ.[50]

Moffat concluded his birthday speech by saying to the company that 'they were my witnesses and the witnesses of MaMary that we had laboured all these years, often by night as well as my day, to administer to their temporal as well as to their spiritual wants.' His closing words were an entreaty to all: 'Prepare to meet God, which, prepared or unprepared, we must soon all do'.

---

50 RM, *Remarks on his 71st Birthday,* 21.12.1866, (SOAS/CWM/SA/Moffat/Personal /Box 4), (our italics). The occasion at Kuruman was attended by the older people on the station and beyond, who were invited to a tea meeting in the chapel.

Chapter 31
The Potency of Opposition

ROBERT MOFFAT VIEWED African Traditional Religion as existing in a realm of 'charms' and superstition.[1] He saw a battle between the Gospel and indigenous beliefs in which any compromise would be a betrayal of the faith. Spiritual warfare was core to mission. He did not work with the notion of traditional religion being a *praeparatio evangelii* or 'primal vision' of God and the Gospel, and in which some rites, if not all, could be interpreted as pointing to himself. On the contrary, Moffat stated that traditional religious beliefs and practices had their origin in the mind of Satan.[2] He saw Satan as an opposing force, working through non-Christian religions:

> The Matabele tribe is desperately savage and wicked, and the nature of their government presents a fearful barrier to the gentle and loving reign of the Prince of Peace, but we know that if the promised influences of the Holy Spirit are granted, *the strongest ramparts of Satan's kingdom will fall before the Word* like the walls of Jericho.[3]

Moffat mentioned Satan/Devil only a few times. When he did, he regarded Satan as having objective existence. In 1827, after Kuruman had been established for some years, he wrote that 'Satan still maintains his throne in the hearts of the natives.'[4] On that occasion Moffat was lamenting continued indifference towards religious instruction, increased use of firearms among Africans in raiding, and the custom of still consulting rainmakers.

References to Satan are then sparse in Moffat's writings until the 1857 expedition to Moselekatse. On that journey he stopped for a Sabbath at the village of Kanye. In the evening, he wrote to Mary, referring to tribal dancing in the nearby village: 'I can hear, cold as it is, the Devil is having his dance upstairs. Alas!'[5] Significantly, most of Moffat's references to Satan occur in the account of the 1859 mission. That expedition was crucial. Its goal was one which he had cherished for thirty years, of establishing a permanent

---

1 A brief unpublished manuscript displays Moffat's awareness of 'charms' etc. See: RM, *Charms,* (SOAS/CWM/Africa/Moffat/Pers/4).

2 RM, *Africa,* 2. Many of Moffat's notions of heathen religion came from what he learned of unpalatable religious practices in India and the South Seas, (RM, *Africa,* 14).

3 RM, *To Tidman, LMS,* 5.9.1859, (SOAS/CWM/SA/Box 31/3/B).

4 RM, *To Mr and Mrs Moffat (Snr),* 6.2.1827, (*AAK,* 233).

5 RM, *Journal,* 10.8.1857, (*MJ2,* 23).

mission station among the Ndebele. The importance of the enterprise is reflected in the seriousness of Moffat's writing, and in increased references to the 'Wicked One'.[6] As the missionaries waited for week after week, as Moselekatse stalled over a possible mission site, Moffat wrote:

> Whatever may be the results of our attempt to introduce the gospel among the Matabele, we are all, I believe, of one mind not to be scared by appearances, but resolved, through divine help, to bear patiently and see what the Lord intends us to do – to remain or return. Satan may make a desperate effort, which we need not wonder at, but we must be still assured that Jehovah will be exalted among the heathen.[7]

The possible failure of such an important expedition, plus the weeks of delay and obstacles, caused Moffat to record: 'I have my melancholy hours, though nothing like fear. Satan is making a desperate effort to shut the door against the blessed Gospel.' Then he added, quoting Scripture: 'We are troubled, verily, but we are not distressed; we are perplexed, but we do not despair.'[8] Elsewhere he noted: 'By perseverance in faith [we] shall overcome these obstacles, of which Satan is making a lively improvement.'[9] Moffat used 'Satan' to describe the Devil as a personal spiritual being. He was not using the word to describe Moselekatse. And his acceptance of the reality of Satan was in line with nineteenth-century Scottish evangelical piety:

> It is a desperately difficult thing to be a rascal and an honourable character at once. [Abe] beats Old Nick[10] himself, for his attempts, beginning at Paradise, have been foiled times without number. Would his head (his power and pride) have been bruised, as it has been, and his punishment increased, as it will be, if he had not played the rascal with our first parents? But oh, the million woes which are borne on every breath of air from human hearts since the dire catastrophe! How it makes one shudder, divine vengeance, eternal punishment, on poor old Devil! But what saith the Scriptures, 'Reserved in everlasting chains'.[11]

Dancing and Witchcraft

What were some of the symptoms of Satanic influence among the unconverted as far as Moffat was concerned? One was dancing. Moffat never viewed tribal dancing simply as a form of African culture expressing joy, celebration or enthusiasm. For Moffat, such dancing always had religious,

---

6 RM, *Journal* 12.11.1859, (*MJ2,* 220).

7 RM, *Journal,* 19.11.1859, (*MJ2,* 226).

8 RM, *Journal,* 24.11.1859, (*MJ2,* 232). Cf. 2 Corinthians 2:8.

9 RM, *Journal,* 10.12.1859, (*MJ2,* 242). 'Improvement' = 'use' or 'application'.

10 'Old Nick' is a Scottish name for 'Satan' or 'The Devil'.

11 RM, *Journal,* 31.8.1854, (*MJ1,* 282).

sexual, or warlike undertones. As such, the dances were the devil's dance.[12] The sound or sight of native dancing invariably left him feeling depressed. One quotation in particular expresses a sentiment mentioned on other occasions: 'The little time I had for sleep last night was disturbed by Bechuana dances in different villages, which made me melancholy.'[13] Moffat could not see the dances but he could hear the music, and he knew that one accompanied the other. That he heard such sounds in some Tswana villages after so many years of ministry distressed him.

Another symptom of Satanic influence was witchcraft. Yet, though Moffat believed in Satan as an objectively real spiritual person, he did not have the same attitude toward witches and witchcraft. In his view, these were empty phenomena, lacking reality. In 1821 he told Mothibi that 'sorcery and witchcraft were nothing more than names, the fruit of imagination, which were the cause of much mischief in putting to death persons who, they ignorantly suppose, possess such power.'[14] Moffat had the same attitude to what he called 'fairy-folk', 'spirits' or 'ghosts'. These also were non-existent. After dogs howled through the night, Moffat commented: 'My people, with others who sleep in the midst of them, feel no disturbance with a noise enough to frighten ghosts, if such things existed.'[15] We can see Moffat's Scottish lowland roots in his attitude to these phenomena. Protestant lowland Scotland had a strong belief in the reality of Satan, but Catholic highland Scotland had a greater acceptance of the reality of fairy-folk. It may have been this that the lowland Moffat had in mind to when, in 1826, he wrote, after the visit of a hyena one night:

> This is not a land for ghosts or fairies. The climate perchance does not suit them. Be it as it may, it is well (though Ariel) that they are not beings of passage, or else many myriads of wizards and fairies could have migrated to these fairy-less regions during the last 1000 years.[16]

Did Moffat link the fairy, ghost-like figures—of which he had heard in Scotland—and the spirits of the ancestors of which he heard in Africa? Moffat rarely referred to ancestral spirits, though he did mention the topic when meeting Moselekatse in 1829. The context of the conversation was Moffat pressing Moselekatse on his concept of God:

---

12 RM, *Journal,* 10.8.1857, (*MJ2,* 23). Cf. RM, *To Tidman, LMS,* 23.3.1847, describing celebrating the Lord's Supper, whilst other villagers, 'Satan's motley group', who were involved in a circumcision rite, gathered near the church and danced in order to disturb them.

13 RM, *Journal,* 29.7.1857, (*MJ2,* 6).

14 RM, *Journal,* 25.9.1821, (*AAK,* 25).

15 RM, *Journal,* 21.10.1857, (*MJ2,* 101).

16 RM, *Journal,* 28.3.1826, (*AAK,* 214).

> He appeared to have some shadows of ideas respecting an influence possessed by separated spirits, especially those of great men. He stated that he prayed to *Molimo,* [Setutu] but from what he said, it appeared that he prayed or spoke to the late Machobane, his father.[17]

There is no clear evidence that Moffat connected 'separated spirits' with the fairies and ghosts with which he was familiar.

Why was Moffat so strong in his belief in the objective reality of Satan, whilst rejecting reality to witches, wizards, fairies or ghosts? The answer may lie in a changed view of witchcraft in his homeland. Witchcraft had been a serious crime in Scotland as early as the seventh century,[18] but it was Protestant Scotland which introduced the 1563 Witchcraft Act, in which practising witchcraft or consorting with witches was declared a capital offence. It is estimated that from 1563 until 1735, around 1500 women died as witches in Scotland, compared to only about 1000 in England, despite England's much larger population.[19] The lowlands of Scotland, rather than the highlands, were especially zealous in hunting out and executing witches.

It was in 1727, only sixty-eight years before Moffat's birth, that the last capital sentence was carried out against witchcraft. The intellectual classes had begun to question whether such women were actually consorting with the Devil, and whether witchcraft existed at all. During the eighteenth century, medical skill began to ascribe to nerves, hysteria, or catalepsy, what previously had been assigned to other forces.[20] In 1735 Scotland legally decided to burn no more witches,[21] though that did not immediately imply non-recognition of witchcraft. It was simply that the sentence was reduced, though, technically, the crimes remained. Nevertheless, a wind of change not only brought in a more compassionate treatment toward suspects, but began to dispel any belief that there was reality in witchcraft at all. Enlightenment thinking, and an emphasis on natural causes for phenomena, all influenced a new way of seeing the world.

Given Scotland's appalling record in the execution of so many witches, it is understandable that contemporary Scottish society wanted no truck with the concept. It comes as no surprise that Scottish missionaries in other lands campaigned against belief in witchcraft, seeing it as distinct from belief in

---

17 RM, *Journal,* 1829, (*MJ1,* 16).

18 Cf. Wilkins Rees, 'Witchcraft and the Kirk', in: William Andrews (ed.), *Bygone Church Life in Scotland,* (Ldn: Andrews, 1899), 163.

19 Wormald, 'Witchcraft', (*DSCHT,* 879f).

20 Graham, *Social Life of Scotland in the Eighteenth Century,* 487.

21 This change of mind occurred within the Kirk, as well as outside of it. Cf. Andrews, *Bygone Church Life in Scotland,* 167f. The most effective agents of changed thought were lay-persons.

Satan. East Lothian, the area in which Moffat's parents were born and raised, had been to the fore in the execution of witches. Local oral tradition was strong on the issue, something of which both the Gardiners and the Moffats would have been aware.[22] Between the passing of the 1563 Act and its repeal, records show that the number of people executed in East Lothian alone for witchcraft and associated crimes was not less than 290.[23] This history fostered a desire in Moffat's generation to have nothing to do with such things. Accordingly, while there remained acceptance of the reality of Satan, there was scepticism concerning the powers and existence of witches and wizards. This was where Moffat came from, and his writings witness to it. On the one hand, Satan was active against the work of Christ. On the other hand, witchcraft was an empty phenomenon: Moffat viewed with disdain local beliefs, such as the ability of sorcerers to turn themselves into lions.[24]

RAIN-MAKING CEREMONIES

In southern African culture, the power of making rain was widely viewed as being invested in the chief.[25] Both Sechele of the BaKwena, and Moselekatse of the Ndebele, had important duties to fulfill for the benefit of the whole tribe when rain was required. This was one reason why Sechele's BaKwena were distraught when their chief was baptised. They knew that if he were true to his baptism then he would no longer carry out these vital functions. Missionaries such as Moffat were aware of this. They knew that the chief had a role which loaded important responsibilities upon him, and that Christianity

---

22 It is likely that Ann Gardiner, brought up in the village of Ormiston, would have been aware of the events of 1678 when four witches were executed by strangulation in Ormiston (Lyell, *Ye See it A': The Ormiston Story,* 20).

23 Anon, *Witch-Hunting in East Lothian,* (Haddington: East Lothian Library, 1976), 9. In October 1705, Spott Kirk Session recorded: 'Many witches burnt on the top of Spott loan' (7).

24 RM, *To Burder, LMS,* 20.8.1818, (SOAS/CMW/SA./Box 7/5/A): 'During our stay [among the Namaqua] I preached frequently, particularly from Paul's address to the Athenians ... The following account will abundantly prove the awful ignorance into which they are sunk. The lions are very numerous and troublesome. The day before our arrival one entered the kraal and killed some of their cattle – also one of ... spouses. They immediately imputed this occurrence to their sorcerer, who they are taught to believe is the lion. They accordingly make hideous and shoutings and addressing themselves to the Lion, saying 'what have we done that you should come and take our cattle etc.? Accordingly, they are afraid of doing any harm to those sorcerers, fearing lest he should revenge them by paying them a visit in his lion garb. I desired to see one of them, but they always take good care to absent themselves when Christians and particularly missionaries are present.'

25 Schapera, *Tswana,* 60: 'Rainmaking was everywhere held to be an attribute of chieftainship, and a chief's reputation and popularity were often determined by the nature of the rainfall during his period of rule.' Moffat's 1857 *Journal* indicates he thought he had persuaded Moselekatse that only God sends rain, cf. RM, *Journal,* 3.12.1857, (*MJ2,* 132).

interfered with essential aspects of traditional tribal life. But, as part of their missiology, they taught that a clear break had to be made. Yet, should a missionary publicly pray for rain? Like Elijah, should he put his faith on the line to show that Jehovah was more powerful than the forces to which unbelievers prayed? Sometimes missionaries were invited to stay with a tribe in order that their prayers might assist in bringing rain.[26] But even if missionary prayer was followed by rain, that could be a mixed blessing. It could convey the concept of a stronger 'magic', rather than fostering humble reliance upon Jehovah whatever Jehovah decreed.

Moffat, with his theology of passively accepting the providence of God as part of Christian obedience, wanted converts to trust God through good and bad times, through times of blessing and times of withholding. He did not want professions of faith simply because his 'god' seemed more powerful than other spiritual forces. He wanted people to believe because of the Word, rather than because of 'signs and wonders'. A believer was to walk by faith in the Word, and humbly trust in the general providence of God. Nevertheless, Moffat occasionally agreed to pray for rain. One early example was in 1822 during a prolonged period of drought, and after an imported rain-maker failed.[27] On 14 January 1822 Moffat recorded: 'I assured them that next morning we should appropriate [gather] to pray to God for rain."[28] Heavy rain then fell on the 15th and 22nd. Yet that did not guarantee faith in the missionary's god, since the Tswana were still continuing with their own rain-making and counter-rain-prevention ceremonies.

The importation by the Tswana of another rain-maker later in 1822 was a critical event in Moffat's early work, resulting in Moffat debating at length with the Tswana. When the rain-maker failed in his task, he sought sanctuary at the Moffats' home. Sanctuary was granted, but eventually he was caught and killed. In 1823 it was with some relief that Mary wrote home about a

---

26 The 1820s had repeated drought in southern Africa. Tribes welcomed any factor which might add to the spiritual potency of rain-bringing, unless it contradicted traditional methods. Cf. RM, *Journal,* 28.7.1824, (*AAK,* 129): '[An African] remarked, 'You must come and make rain for us.' RM, *MLSSA,* 388, referred to his colleague, Hamilton, who, when he stayed in a village was viewed as a rain-maker: 'And as it had rained very heavily during his visit, he was viewed in the very imposing light of a rain-maker, they having requested him to pray for rain, which he did.' In *MLSSA* 114, Moffat gave a positive view on missionaries praying for rain.

27 RM, *To Alexander Moffat,* Jan. 1823, (*AAK,* 70).

28 RM, *Journal,* 14.1.1822, (*AAK,* 42). When rain fell Moffat told the Tswana that the thunder was the voice of God, and that 'His voice was love to men and answering prayer.' (RM, *Journal,* 22.1822, 43).

decrease in the people seeking a rain-maker, alongside the breaking of other taboos.[29]

In Tswana culture, several reasons were given for the lack of rain: the presence of missionaries;[30] because the missionaries had brought salt;[31] because the missionaries' God 'hid the rain';[32] because a tribal member had illicit sex;[33] because women had gone to work in the field when the sky was cloudy;[34] or because the rain-maker or his assistants had sexual activity during the rain-making period, spoiling communion with the ancestral spirits,[35] etc. These were all attempts to find an explanation in terms of cause and effect. Over against these 'causes', which were accepted by the Tswana as rational science, Moffat appeared to offer little but faith. And if Moffat's God did not provide rain, the only reason Moffat was prepared to give was that it was not God's will. From a Tswana point of view, Moffat was asking them to live by 'blind trust', rather than by reference to a known 'rational' system which had been handed down through trusted tradition.

Moffat could not point to clear 'causes'. He could only appeal to the inscrutable will of God, though occasionally he did offer a cause. For example, during the 1821 rain-maker controversy, he wrote: 'God was determined to teach them [Tswana] that it was he alone who had power to give or withhold rain as he pleased.'[36] The sovereign will and purposes of God overrode everything for Moffat. God himself was never on trial. The believer was simply to trust, come what may. But for a Motswana, reared in traditional religion, with its accepted array of 'reasons' for events, it required a great leap of faith to move to Moffat's position. Moreover, from a Tswana perspective the strong 'rationality' of traditional thought meant that, with some converts, the old 'reasons' were never fully abandoned. It was faith

---

29 Mary Moffat, *To James & Mary,* 1.9.1823, (*AAK,* 107f): 'Last year we had the pleasure of informing you of the downfall of rain-making superstition. Now another is broken through. Indeed, they now seem to fear denying Robert anything. I suppose no Bechuana living can recollect a spadeful of dung being taken out of their calf fold ... but now the missionaries have got permission to take as much as they will – and it is four or five feet deep!' It was thought that if manure were removed from the cattle-kraals, the cattle would die of disease, (*AAK,* 108, fn. 15).

30 RM, *To John Melvill,* Jan. 1821, (*AAK*, 12).

31 RM, *Journal,* 25.12.1821, (*AAK*, 39).

32 RM, *To Alexander Moffat,* 25.2.1822, (*AAK,* 56).

33 RM, *Journal,* 25.1.1822, (*AAK*, 43).

34 RM, *Journal,* 19.8.1821, (*AAK,* 24).

35 Lye & Murray, *Transformation,* 122.

36 RM, *Journal,* 14.10.1821, (*AAK,* 28).

versus reason, but in a different context from that of Enlightenment Europe. The missionary urged 'faith'. Traditional religion offered 'reasons'.

When Moffat confronted the Tswana about their fears concerning rain-making and rain-prevention, he found that he was in an area where the power of tradition, and fear of breaking that tradition, had immense force. Rain, rain-making, and any factor which promoted rain-prevention, affected a core need of society: that of survival. Consequently, shibboleths surrounding the subject were enormously strong. Moffat's theological response was to teach about the power of God the Creator:

> I found that they firmly believed that, were the women to work [in the fields] when the sky was cloudy thus, the clouds would immediately depart. I asked if he [Bromella] had ever tried the experiment. His answer was that their forefathers taught them, and on that account [he] believed. I pointed him to a small stream within a few feet of where we stood, and asked if it were not the power of God which made that stream to issue from the rock, as well as cover the heaven with clouds. This he acknowledged.
>
> I then enquired if he believed the stream would dry up were a person to cultivate ground along its banks. He found it hard to answer this, but referred me to what their forefathers believed. How, like many in England, who censure everyone who is not of the same religion as their forefathers! How difficult to promote the spirit of religious enquiry: that people may judge for themselves! Very few arguments are necessary to silence the heathen in these quarters, and we are only sorry that they neither propose questions nor raise objections.[37]

Moffat realised that tradition was powerful: 'The laws of their forefathers, however ridiculous, are to them like the laws of the Medes and Persians.' Even when the rain-maker departed, the falling of rain was ascribed to causes such as 'the churning of a milk sack.'[38] 'Causes' trumped 'faith'.

Initiation Ceremonies

Among the Tswana, the *boguera (Bogwera)* was the male initiation ceremony, and the *boyale* the female counterpart. Moffat opposed Christian converts participating in traditional initiation ceremonies, and church members were disciplined for allowing their children to participate. They were also disciplined if they provided food for the ceremonies. Yet, within traditional society, it was expected that the whole community would support and provide for the ceremonies, and so Moffat's missionary principles cut through the social glue of society. But did Moffat establish an unnecessary

---

37 RM, *Journal,* 19.8.1821, (*AAK,* 24).

38 RM, *To Alexander Moffat,* 25.2.1822, (*AAK,* 56).

rule? Did he adopt a policy which was excessive, and which needlessly opposed traditional African social systems? Livingstone had a more liberal view. In a letter to John Smith Moffat, Livingstone wrote: 'Is there anything really irreligious in the *boguera*? Or is it anything more than a political rite?'[39] Moffat's line was quite different. But what did he think happened at initiation events? In an 1849 letter to his friend Thomas Barnes, he set out his view of the ceremonies as they were practised by the BaThlaping:

> The natives have two ceremonies by which youths are made men, and girls are made women. Circumcision of course is that of the masculine, and the females have their *boyale*, when the girls are selected from the bulk and dressed most fantastically or most ugly and lubricated and marched about and taught to sing and obey their husbands when they get married. And after a couple of months have passed in these private exercises in their enclosures apart from the common rabble they are regularly anointed and are sent forth wearing the dress of a woman. ... It had been agreed to years ago that no believer should be coerced.[40]

By the phrase 'no believer should be coerced', Moffat presumably referred to an agreement between the missionaries and the tribal leadership, that Christian young men and women would not be forced to attend. However, as Moffat found out with Sechele's family, young people, even within a Christian household, were keen to do what their friends were doing. Moffat's position may have been stronger if he had specified in more detail why he opposed initiation ceremonies, but his overall view seemed to be that these ceremonies were associated with alien religious rites, hence participation implied acceptance of an alien religion. Moffat saw himself as entering a land of false religion which had to be swept away by the Gospel light.[41] This mind set was what lay behind the title of his address to the LMS in 1840: '*Gospel light shining in the Midst of Heathen Darkness*.'

The issue of young people participating in initiation ceremonies came to a head with Sechele's family. During the early 1850s, Sechele was the sole convert within his tribe, the BaKwena. This created pressures on Sechele, and

---

[39] Livingstone, *To JSM,* 16.4.1858, (*MM,* 11).

[40] RM, *To Barnes,* 25.6.1849, (SOAS/CWM/SA./Moffat/Personal/Box 4).

[41] Moffat, *MLSSA,* 236, wrote: 'What wisdom, what meekness, are necessary to (the missionary) who proposes to introduce the elements of a spiritual empire, to sweep away refuges of lies, to prostrate idols and altars in the dust, to abolish rites and ceremonies, to transform barbarous and antiquated judicial systems, and, after apostolic example "to turn the world upside down"'. In 1854, Moffat told Moselekatse that Africans at the Kuruman had given up their old customs: cf. RM, *Journal,* 26.8.1854, (*MJ1,* 274): 'I added that the people [at the Kuruman] were God's people, and though Bechuanas, or BaSutos, as all the southern and western tribes are called by the Matabele, they had thrown away all their old customs and were learning God's word and law.'

the missionaries felt that at times he compromised his faith. Moffat visited Sechele in 1854, and recorded an exchange involving himself, Sechele, and Sebobi, the native teacher:

> [Sebobi said]: 'You sanction every heathen custom among your people. You are chief and as such you are the fountain; good and not evil should flow from you if you are a believer: but you are only a fountain of rain-making, *boguera* and *boyale*. You teach your people to do these things: does the Word of God tell you to do so? If you have embraced the Gospel and if you are a Christian chief, why do you not do as others have done? Look at Jantje of Lekatlong and Lephui! They have a large number of people under them, and they have no more of these heathenish customs among them'. 'These', said Sechele, 'are villages and not towns'."[42]

Even if Moffat's record does not reproduce the exact words which were used, it shows how he viewed the *boguera* and *boyale*. There had to be a clean break from native customs for the true convert! Sechele's response revealed the quandary that a convert chief had. If he were to retain his authority as an important *Kgosi*—in charge of towns, not just villages. Could he really put aside tribal traditions? If he were to live as a true Christian, would he have to leave his tribe? This latter option was raised by Sechele's wife, Ma-Sebele. She asked if Sechele had to go out from the BaKwena and live apart.[43] Sechele was in a desperately difficult position. Conversion of chiefs had advantages, but it also brought dilemmas. Hence, though in 1848 Livingstone wrote of Sechele being converted and baptised, by 1852 he described Sechele as an 'apostate': 'I believe Sechele is an apostate. He cannot be referred to as a trophy of grace'.[44] Livingstone wrote with a heavy heart, for he had seen signs of a deep discipleship only a few years previously: 'Never did man bid fairer for years to enter the Kingdom of Heaven than he.'

---

42 RM, *Journal,* 5.6.1854, (*MJ1,* 156f).

43 RM, *Journal,* 5.6.1854, (*MJ1,* 157). Ma-Sebele may have had in mind a suggestion made by Sechele himself at the time of his conversion and baptism in 1848, as recorded by Livingstone, *To Tidman, LMS,* 1.11.1848, (*LMC,* 119): 'The greatest sacrifice he had to make was the renunciation of polygamy. [The circumstances] made his parting with [his wives] assume the appearance of ingratitude, and led him to propose to remove to some other country for four years, in order that they might in the interval forget him and become married to others.'

44 Livingstone, *To Tidman, LMS,* 26.4.1852, (*LMC,* 202). Sechele's 'old ways' restarted soon after his baptism, cf. Livingstone, *To William Thomson,* 12.10.1852, (*LMC,* 225). Though Moffat initially accepted Livingstone's testimony, he began to doubt if Sechele had sinned as Livingstone described. Moffat double-checked with Jan Khatlane. Cf. RM, *Journal,* 11.6.1854, (*MJ1,* 178): '[Khatlane] bore the same testimony as Khosilintse ... that he knew nothing of the report [of having taken another wife], that he believed nothing of the kind existed in his thoughts, but that he acted, as far as he saw, with all due tenderness to Ma-Sebele [his official wife].' Was Sechele unjustly judged by Livingstone?

If Sechele stumbled, why did he? Livingstone blamed the negative influence of other missionaries—whom he disliked.[45] Another issue was that Sechele could not accept monogamy but returned to his former wives. Yet these factors were but symptoms of deeper cultural difficulties relating to his chieftainship. At the time of his conversion and baptism, as is clear in Livingstone's account, Sechele's tribe were dumbfounded that their chief took the step he did, undercutting almost everything he meant to them as chief in relation to their traditional customs. Livingstone's description of the fateful morning after Sechele's decision to be a Christian is revealing. Sechele's people viewed the change in their chief almost as a bereavement:

> On the morning after it was known that Sechele had renounced his wives on account of the Gospel, a general consternation seemed to have seized both young and old. The town was as quiet as if it had been a Sunday. Not a single woman was seen going into her garden. Picos [tribal assemblies] were held during the night in order to intimidate him and make him renounce his purpose. But after having been tried in various ways for two months, we proceeded to administer the ordinance of baptism. Many of the spectators were in tears, but these were in general tears of sorrow for the loss of their rainmaker, or of grief at seeing some of the ties of relationship to him completely broken.[46]

If the putting away of his wives was seen by Sechele's people as a symbol of deeper issues, then returning to his wives—if he did—was also a significant symbol. It concerned his core role as the chief of his people. He was their chief, their rainmaker, and the custodian of the customs which gave them their identity. To break with such things involved breaking the structure of his peoples' lives. If their chief abandoned their customs, then a death had taken place: their death as a people.

In 1854 Sechele still considered himself a believer. Moffat's account of the meeting of Sebobi and Sechele shows a man torn apart by two great forces in his life: his people with their customs versus his Christian faith. Moffat, perhaps unfairly, described him as 'perverse Sechele'.[47] Yet, as time passed, Moffat was prepared to give Sechele the benefit of the doubt.[48] In this, he

---

45 Livingstone, *To Tidman, LMS,* 26.4.1852, (*LMC,* 202).

46 Livingstone, *To Tidman, LMS,* 1.11.1848, (*LMC,* 120).

47 RM, *Journal,* 5.6.1854, (*MJ1,* 158).

48 Later visitors, such as Emily Moffat, had a good impression of Sechele. Even Moffat began to doubt the bad reports spread by Livingstone. Moffat confided to Mary that he was beginning to question rumours about Sechele apostasising. Cf. RM, *To Mary Moffat,* 11.6.1854, (*MJ1,* 179). On the same journey Moffat discussed Christianity with another chief, Sekhomi, in which Moffat drew positively from the example of Sechele: cf. RM, *Journal,* 20.6.1854, (*MJ1,* 191). Sechele, even 'under discipline' was held up as a trophy to other Africans.

was more generous than Livingstone. Concerning initiation, Moffat recorded a long conversation he had with Sechele, in which Sechele explained that he had really tried to show his people a better way:

> He laboured to convince them of [the] foolishness of sending children to *boguera* and *boyale;* but none—no, not one—would listen, adding that he and other chiefs had no power over the people, who would kill them if they opposed them.[49]

Moffat then delivered the full force of his opposition to the initiation rites, warning of a judgment from God if they were not stopped. Sechele defended himself by saying that it was his children themselves who chose *boguera* and *boyale.* Moffat countered by stressing the difference between permitting a child to exercise freedom of choice to embrace *positive* moral practices, and exercising freedom of choice to embrace *negative* immoral practices:

> I entered fully into the case and, taking the New Testament, pointed out his duty to his children and, referring to Joshua's disobedience, also Lephui's and Jantje's,[50] where these immoral customs had ceased, and asked if the Bakuena were better or more noble than they. I remarked also that if his children were in a land, or like Englishmen, who each earned his living by some calling, it would be wrong in him positively to hinder one from seeking to live by trading ... or to sketch and measure hills and dales like our Robert, or work in wood or iron.
>
> All these were moral sciences, but *boyale* and *boguera* were immoral customs and imparted nothing but pride and impudence. I had been a witness of these beloved customs of the Bechuana for more than thirty years, and I had been in the *loluapa* among a set of *boyale* girls, some old enough to be married, all stark naked, and would he allow his daughters, who could read the word of God and sing his praises in their own language [and] who had been nurtured in the knowledge of divine things by Ma-Mary to wallow in such obscenity?[51]

Moffat was uncompromising. And Sechele emerged as an unhappy figure, struggling with the old and the new. For Moffat the *boyale* and the *boguera* were not customs which harmlessly gave an identity to a people, but were religious practices in direct opposition to Christian values. Moreover, they involved degrading nakedness. In Moffat's view, b*oyale* and *boguera* involved spiritual forces in opposition to the transforming purity of the Word of God. Accommodation within Christianity was impossible. Weaning from

---

[49] RM, *Journal,* 8.6.1854, (*MJ1,* 164). Sechele reminded Moffat that the people had killed Mochoasele, Sechele's own father. Sechele said: 'If I were like the Matabele chiefs, I would do so (compel the people to learn to read); but as I am, no one will listen to me'.

[50] Lephui and Jantje were seen as examples of how Christian chiefs had done away with *boguera* and *boyale* in their communities. See: (RM, *Journal,* 5.6.1854, (*MJ1,* 157).

[51] RM, *Journal,* 8.6.1854, (*MJ1,* 164f).

such practices was painful, but a total transformation of faith and life was the inflexible goal of mission. Moffat called the initiation rites 'immoral customs' and named them obscene. He also commented that they imparted 'pride and impudence'. This actually corresponded with the observations of others, who noted that, after the initiation ceremonies, the young people acted arrogantly, aggressively, and with little self-restraint.[52] Moffat considered that the ceremonies fostered a hostile and arrogant attitude which was unbecoming for a Christian community. Above all else, the *boguera* and *boyale* involved a form of non-Christian worship,[53] and Moffat could not compromise on that. Moffat's reasons were not trivial. He believed that at stake was the whole issue of whether the Gospel was being allowed to transform not just individuals, but whole communities.

Later, on 10 June 1854, Moffat spoke to five of Sechele's young people about the ceremonies—three girls and two boys. Some of them had lived at Kuruman for a time, and Moffat's record is enlightening:

> I told them that both you [Mary] and I felt a deep interest in their welfare, that their father [Sechele] had done for them what no chief in the country had done for his children [sent them to Kuruman for education], that they had possessed advantages that no one else in the country had, and that great pains had been taken to make them wise and good, that they not only could read God's word, but they could understand it too, that I was surprised and grieved to hear that they wished to enter the *boyale.*
>
> I described the Batlapin *boyale* and supposed that of the Bakuena was the same, and asked what it would do for them. I referred them to the women of the Kuruman and other Bechuana towns, to my daughters Mary and Ann, and asked them if the *boyale* would make them better wives and mothers than those were. I described a Christian and a *boyale* girl. The ludicrous picture of the latter made them laugh a little. After a solemn talking about death and eternity, I concluded by saying how sorry I was, and how sorry you would be, to hear that they were opposing their father who was determinately against their going to that heathen custom. [54]

Moffat used ridicule. But ridicule could never undermine the prospect of an exciting experience. Argument was no match for desire. Sechele himself

---

52 In Tswana initiation ceremonies the youths had to compose and sing praise-songs in praise of themselves. If Moffat had known this, he would have found even more reason to see the exercise as anti-Christian. Cf. Livingstone, *To the British Quarterly, 1851*: *DLSAP,* 102: 'Each Mochuana has his own hymn of praise which he first publicly rehearses when circumcised. These hymns are essentially self-adoration'. Schapera discussed the praise-songs in: Schapera, *Praise-Poems of Tswana Chiefs,* (Oxford: 1965), 1-7.

53 Willoughby, *The Soul of the Bantu,* 298ff.

54 RM, *Journal,* 10.6.1854, (*MJ1,* 173). The Christian BaThlaping near Kuruman had largely abandoned initiations, perhaps due to the fragmented nature of their community.

intervened, referring Moffat to the Old Testament institution of circumcision, making the point that circumcision was abrogated under the Gospel, and asking Moffat to explain this to the young people.[55] Sechele then spoke directly and personally to his children, after which they were challenged as to their response. The young people were divided, with the girls still expressing a desire to go, but the boys not. Ope, the elder girl, claimed that her father was oppressing her and she clearly wanted to go to the boyale. Kiribolecae said that if Ope went she would go too. Kuanteng said the same as Kiribolecae. However, Sechele's son, Sebele, said that he did not want to go to the circumcision; and another son, Bantsang, was of the same mind as Sebele. Sechele spoke again, with great earnestness, to those who wanted the *boyale,* putting them under massive parental pressure, as Moffat recorded: "You eat my food, you wear my clothes, you are under my care. You are mine. I – am – your – father." This he said with great emphasis. "Dare to run away, to grieve me, and to put me to shame before those who have taught me and taught you other things"[56] Later Moffat heard the *boyale* note sounding in the hill villages. Did Sechele's daughters obey their father? No indication is given.

The Victory of the Christian Life

Moffat was aware that spiritual forces, real or imagined, had power over people. In 1854, on a journey undertaken along with Moselekatse towards Sekeletu's country, he recorded his disdain of the powers of bewitching, to the consternation of Moselekatse:

> Feeling my hair uncomfortably long, I took my scissors and ... cut off a few handfuls and of course threw the hair away. [Moselekatse] happened to be approaching, and begged of me not to throw away my hair, as there were rascals among his people who might take it up and bewitch me. I thanked him for his anxiety on my account, but told him that I should be glad to cut off every bit of my hair and divide it among all the rogues in his dominion and let them try their hand, and would reward anyone. He only replied that he was exceedingly glad to hear that no one could do me harm in that way.[57]

Moselekatse's reply to Moffat shows that while he was prepared to believe that Moffat had power over any attempted bewitching, bewitching still had

---

[55] RM, *Journal,* 11.6.1854, (*MJ1,* 173), wrote: 'Sechele then opened the Old Testament; turned to the 17th Chapter of *Genesis,* handed the book to me, and requested me to read and explain it to them. I did so ... and how it was abrogated under the new dispensation'.

[56] RM, *Journal,* 10.6.1854, (*MJ1,* 174). Sechele further protested his seriousness in this whole matter the following Sabbath, cf. RM, *Journal,* 11.6.1854, (*MJRM,* 178).

[57] RM, *Journal,* 13.9.18754, (*MJ1,* 303).

a power in itself. However much Moffat tried to persuade Moselekatse that 'bewitching' was a groundless fear, Moselekatse saw otherwise. Moffat realised that a subjective belief in witchcraft and sorcery carried its own potency. Witchcraft and sorcery had a derived power, with strong influence in the lives of men and women, fostering a trust in spiritual powers and authorities other than God. On furlough, Moffat told his London audience: 'The church is waging war with the prince of darkness without one emotion of uncertainty as to the result.'[58] But how to oppose Satan in the mission field? Above all, Christians should trust in the Word of God alone, and set loose the living Word of God through prayer, preaching and teaching. In 1819, Moffat wrote concerning congregations in Cape Town:

> On the Sabbath a prayer-meeting is held in this house, also on the Wednesday evenings, when exhortations are given. The two directors (Campbell and Philip) are always present. There are many other meetings in Dutch. Brother Evans preaches in Dutch tonight to slaves, and I have to engage on Sabbath. This you see is the old way and the only way to damp Satan's courage and eventually gain victory. Pray for us all.[59]

In 1821 Moffat came across a sick woman called Delewing. His ministry to her illuminates the same principle:

> I found that they supposed, yea firmly believed, her to be bewitched by a woman who had during the night laid the hand on her neck. ... I embraced this favourable opportunity of explaining to [Mothibi] the inconsistency of such a faith. I turned his attention to the Holy Scriptures as the criterion by which we must think, speak, and act; that peace and resignation were the fruits of sincere obedience to that unerring rule; that the Word of God assured us that life and health were at the disposal of their author, and that sorcery and witchcraft were nothing more than names, the fruit of imagination, which were the cause of much mischief in putting to death, as the Bootchuanas do, persons who, they ignorantly suppose, possess such power, by which innocent blood is shed and they who survive [are] no less than murderers. To what I said [Mothibi] made little or no answer, except that as I was a doctor, as they suppose me to be, I surely must know.[60]

Central to Moffat was total trust in the Scriptures. Gospel light should displace superstitious beliefs. Over the next twenty-four hours, he applied simple medical skills to Delewing. He also stopped female attendants from applying their own 'contrary' methods. In due course, she recovered:

> The attendants, who ... had borne the look of sadness, now seemed quite overjoyed. I conversed some time with them on death and immortality, and

---

58 RM, *Africa,* 5.

59 RM, *To Robert Moffat (Snr.),* 16.4.1819 (JSM, *Lives,* 45f).

60 RM, *Journal,* 25.9.1821, (*AAK,* 25).

> the necessity of faith in Jesus Christ, in order to escape the punishment due for sin and obtain an everlasting salvation. They paid considerable attention, and urged many excuses for their absence from church.[61]

Two weeks later Moffat wrote: 'Delewing, who was so extremely ill, seems nearly recovered. She has more than once attended the church. She seems to be a thinking woman, of whom one would desire to entertain hopes.'[62] The phrase: 'thinking woman', is significant. Moffat sought to replace 'irrational superstition' with 'rational belief' founded upon the Word of God. We bear in mind that, during the time Moffat was attending Delewing, the entire missionary community would be praying that God would restore her to health, in order to be both a sign *for* the Lord, and a sign *against* native beliefs. Moffat did not state that such prayer took place, but it would. A successful outcome would confirm to the missionary community that their theology, practice, and stand against native belief were justified. Important in this battle were integrity, mercy and reason.

1. Integrity. Moffat refused to allow people to think he had supernatural abilities. He wanted his work to have an integrity founded simply upon the truth of his message. In 1854 Moselekatse wanted Moffat to 'purify' some water by touching it. Moffat refused.[63] It was the same concern, of safeguarding the integrity of the missionary, which made Moffat reluctant to pray for rain. His reluctance did not just come from fear of unanswered prayer, but from concern over how it would be interpreted if the petition were granted. He might be regarded simply as another magician. He wanted people to walk by faith in God's word, accepting God's providential rule, and living trustful lives under the sovereignty of God. The question of missionary integrity raises another issue. There was a suspicion, in the minds of some, that missionaries were in Africa because they were fleeing justice in their own country. Moffat explained this to his London audience in 1840.[64] Thus the missionary's character was of immense importance, and Moffat alluded to this on many occasions: 'The missionary character is known and respected many hundreds of miles beyond Lattakoo, and however averse the nations may be in the first instance to the requirements of the Gospel, they will in general look on missionaries as honest men and the real friends and benefactors of their nation.'[65]

---

61 RM, *Journal,* 26.9.1821, (*AAK,* 26).
62 RM, *Journal,* 11.10.1821, (*AAK,* 27).
63 RM, *Journal,* 25.7.1854, (*MJ1,* 235).
64 RM, *Africa,* 38.
65 RM, *Africa,* 41.

2. Mercy. Moffat urged mercy for those 'guilty' of witchcraft. He was appalled that those found guilty, often on rumour alone, were put to death, and he referred several times to such trials. Moffat was aware that, among the Tswana, every death was seen as a result of witchcraft, not natural causes: 'As for death, they suppose, as a chief informed me the other day, that no man can die of himself (naturally), that he must be killed or bewitched by another.'[66] When death occurred the bewitcher had to be caught and punished. This produced a crisis when Peclu, Mothibi's son and heir, died suddenly in 1825. Moffat went to condole Mothibi:

> We made some remarks on the importance of submitting to the divine will, 'who was too wise to err', etc. These remarks gave rise to an argument of some length. When any person, especially of note, dies, it is generally attributed to some person or persons whom the relatives charge with having bewitched the deceased. Notwithstanding the knowledge of Christianity which Mothibi and his relatives possess, in this case superstition predominated; and a family in the vicinity of the town, with whom Peclu had some little misunderstanding, was charged with being guilty. The persons charged, it appears, had fled, which seemed to confirm Mothibi in his groundless suspicions.[67]

In his grief and anger, Mothibi was unwilling to listen to Moffat's theology of submission to God's providential will. The desire to apply a paradigm of cause and effect pointed Mothibi in another direction. As in rain-making, passive submission to the inscrutable will of God seemed a poor substitute to 'scientifically' identifying the 'evil culprit'.

3. Reason. Moffat occasionally tried to invalidate witchcraft and sorcery by encouraging 'rational tests'. For example, on the evening of 24 September 1854, the day Moselekatse finally permitted him to preach to his people, Moffat talked to Moselekatse about witchcraft:

> I introduced the subject of witchcraft and the use of prognosticating dice, which, agreeable to my intention, gave rise to a long conversation. Having witnessed the day before two doctors of the art, foreigners and from different tribes, throwing their dice and prognosticating causes or coming events, I asked him what they said. He replied that they were telling him about cattle which were to prosper, and much more, if he had wished [to] tell it.
>
> I put the question whether such folk ever prophesied evil, and told him that he [Moselekatse] was the cause of any calamity which befell him or his people. He laughed and said that they had no such thing in the country from whence they came; that he only met with such among the tribes he had conquered. I told him that books, and especially the Book of God, told us to

---

66 RM, *To Alexander Moffat,* 25.2.1822, (*AAK,* 55).

67 RM, *Journal,* 4.4.1825, (*AAK,* 180).

> try [test] such men, that I had done so frequently and found them to be deceptive and dangerous men, for they were sometimes the cause of the death of innocent men, which was a very great sin, and referred him to what I said about God. He remarked that he had tried them too …
>
> I said if he would take my advice he would banish all such characters from his dominions, that it was offensive to God to look to men and not to Him for what He only could perform[68], that there were a set of men called rainmakers (I knew I was talking to a reputed 'father of rain') who professed to be able to do what God alone did; that I had seen notable ones try, and offered great rewards to them to let me see their skill and power, but no one was able; that if a land was suffering from drought it was the duty of the people to pray to God for help.[69]

This discussion came after events of 13 September 1854. Moffat had observed Moselekatse who was engrossed in the operations of a *'ngaka* or magician until he became aware of Moffat watching. At that point, Moselekatse changed from wanting to know what the *'ngaka* divined from the cast bones, to putting the *'ngaka* on the defensive. It seems that some of Moffat's arguments had made an impression on Moselekatse, since he used them himself:

> I had been leaning on the wagon-side unobserved while this [casting the bones] had been going on, till Moselekatse, looking up and seeing me trying to stifle a laugh, winked at me to be quiet while he requested that the throwing of the bones etc., be repeated again and again, while he was puzzling him with questions, the very questions I had put to him at a former period to test such characters. The *'ngaka* at last began to perceive that there was something like fun going on between his master and someone else, looked round and seeing me, asked his permission to return his bones and horns into their bag. Moselekatse was well pleased that he had made this wise one feel bewildered, and he was still better pleased to see him at his wits' end to find something to answer my questions.[70]

The questions which tested the sorcerers were described in a later passage:

> I afterwards saw two notables of that craft, who belonged to distinct tribes, catechised by Moselekatse on some points he wished to know. The one who was last called, to see if he would corroborate what the preceding one had stated, sat looking at his scattered *bola* on the ground and then on Moselekatse, with a countenance that bespoke the terror he was in, while the perspiration was rolling down his cheeks in big drops. … Moselekatse, who

---

68 Moffat drew upon an emphasis on the glory and honour of God in evangelism.

69 RM, *Journal,* 24.9.1854, (*MJ1,* 313f). Mackenzie, *Ten Years North*, 52, claimed that Boers accepted 'native superstitions': 'The Boers are superstitious, accepting and absorbing native practices such as consulting dice, use of charms etc.' Livingstone made similar allegations.

70 RM, *To Tidman, LMS,* 10.5.1855, (*MJ1,* 374).

> inclined to be waggish, after asking him what he was afraid of, him or his own *bola,* told him to get some beer to drink.[71]

What Moffat suggested to Moselekatse was for him to ask two *'ngaka,* separately, to foretell the future. Their prophecies should be identical. This put the second in a state of terror. If his was different, then one of them, maybe both, would likely face a gruesome death. Moffat's presence probably prevented that happening, with Moselekatse contenting himself with making fun of them.

*

For Moffat's generation, progress in mission, progress in discipleship, and progress against Satan were measured by the extent to which indigenous peoples were weaned from customs associated with non-Christian practices. These signs were eagerly looked for, and celebrated enthusiastically. An appreciation of what might be the positive elements of indigenous religion would come with a later group of missionaries.

---

71 Ibid.

Chapter 32
The Promotion of Indigenisation

JOHN MACKENZIE, who succeeded Moffat at Kuruman, thought that the development of native agency was the weak point of the Kuruman mission.[1] That was despite indigenous converts taking responsibility for prayer meetings and for catechising others from the outset of the 1829 Awakening. When the perceptive though swaggeringly self-confident Livingstone arrived in 1841, his lack of missionary experience did not inhibit his readiness to submit a report to Freeman of the LMS on what he found. Deficiency in the development of native ministry was high on the list. Livingstone's assessment was that a greater work might have been done if more use had been made of native teachers in evangelism and church planting.[2] Whilst Moffat, on home leave in Britain, was writing *Missionary Labours* with occasional warm mention of native teachers, Livingstone was at Kuruman convinced that Moffat should have taken them more seriously. The increase in references to native teachers after Moffat returned may be attributed to several causes, with Livingstone's promotion of the office a major factor.

Livingstone's letter to Freeman was essentially a quasi-statistical analysis concerning population densities of Kuruman and its surrounding areas, with suggestions for future strategy.[3] On the one hand, Livingstone displayed a budding scientific approach to mission strategy. On the other hand, his conclusions need to be read with an awareness of his wish to have an excuse to travel further, set up his own stations, and pioneer where no one had worked before. These personal yearnings influenced his interpretation of what he saw. Nevertheless, the sharp observations of the raw young

---

1 Mackenzie, *Ten Years North,* 80. Mackenzie stated there were 2 native teachers by 1834, 6 by 1842, but still only 6 in 1869. But he did not include native teachers from Kuruman who worked at new mission stations and were no longer under Kuruman.

2 Livingstone was initially disappointed in what he found at Kuruman, but revised his assessment as he began to understand how difficult pioneer missionary work was. Cf. Livingstone, *To Mr & Mrs Livingston,* 26.9.1842, (*DLFL,* Vol. 1, 66). When he first went to Kuruman he was under the impression that Moffat positively opposed native agency, but later revises that opinion: 'He is not, as I was informed by some that knew him, in the least opposed to native agency', see: Livingstone, *To Mr & Mrs Livingston,* 16.12.1843, (*DLFL,* Vol. 1, 89).

3 Livingstone, *To Freeman, LMS,* 23.9.1841, (*LMC,*1ff).

missionary touched on fundamental principles of missionary policy. Livingstone focused on two main issues.

1. Under-population. Before setting out for Africa, and having been inspired by Moffat's account of the work at Kuruman, Livingstone was enthusiastic about what might yet be done at the station. However, after arrival, and 'having personally inspected most of the surrounding localities in connection with this station', he changed his mind. The problem was a want of population. In Livingstone's view, the station could not itself be the means of converting many, since 'within a circle of 8 or 10 miles around the station there are not a thousand inhabitants.'[4] For Livingstone, the work had to move many miles into the interior if it were to influence a larger population.

2. Under-Use of native teachers. How could the mission engage with great numbers at such distances? Livingstone had a clear view: 'I suggest that we make the most of whatever agents we can find. Although desirable that they have somewhat more than decided piety, it is, I conceive, not absolutely necessary.'[5] In support of his argument, he cited the example of the LMS station at Griqua Town, 'making the most of every man under them seems to have been the reason, by the blessing of God, of the great success of the brethren at Griqua Town.' Livingstone's sentiment, 'Although desirable that they have somewhat more than decided piety, *it is, I conceive, not absolutely necessary'*, marks a decisive difference between his thinking and Moffat's. Livingstone was a risk-taker. Moffat was not. For Moffat, spiritual maturity had to precede commissioning. But what Livingstone correctly assessed was that Kuruman already had spiritually mature converts, men like Paul.

Three months after this letter, and having returned from a 700-mile round trip to the interior along with Roger Edwards, Livingstone was even more convinced that future work would be impossible without 'the machinery of native agency put into vigorous operation.'[6] Writing again to Freeman, he pointed out that native agents enjoyed many advantages, especially, 'their warm affectionate manner of dealing with their fellow countrymen', and 'their capability to bring the truth itself before their minds, entirely divested

---

[4] Livingstone, *To Freeman, LMS,* 23.9.1841, (*LMC,* 2). Toward the end of the 1830s there was a dispersal of the Kuruman population as bandit raids decreased. Livingstone's 'not a thousand inhabitants' is on the low side. When Moffat recorded an accurate census in the *KCRB* (92) for Kuruman and its environs in 1852, the total population (men, women and children) was 3038, with adults comprising half that number.

[5] Livingstone, *To Freeman, LMS,* 23.9.1841, (*LMC,* 3).

[6] Livingstone, *To Freeman, LMS,* 22.12.1841, (*LMC,* 5).

of that peculiar strangeness which cleaves to foreigners.'[7] And he again cited the successes at Griqua Town as directly attributable to the use of native agents.[8] He pointed out that, in places 60 or 80 miles from Griqua Town, native agents had kept up public worship and a school for the children even though no missionary had visited for over 10 months. For Livingstone, the road to success was clear. His comparison between the thriving work at Griqua Town and, in his view, the stalled work at Kuruman, was an indirect criticism of Moffat's methods. Respect for Moffat prevented him from writing more directly on this occasion, but the implication was clear.[9] Yet he was also realising that Moffat was more open to the concept than he had thought:

> But native agency has been tried here [Kuruman] too, as well as at Griqua Town. After Mr. Moffat went to England he seems to have changed a little his opinions on that subject, for he wrote back advising the brethren here to make a trial of two. These were appointed and the consequence has been a large accession to the Church.[10]

---

7 Ibid. Some years later, Mackenzie had discoursed at length on the inherent benefits of native ministry. See: Mackenzie, *Ten Years North,* 78f: 'The best specimens [of professing Christians] are not to be found on the station of the European missionary, but at out-stations occasionally visited by him. On the mission-station, the learning, the skill, the higher civilisation of the Europeans, become overwhelming, almost repelling to the native Christian. An attitude of reverent wonder and ready assent become habitual to him. ... On the other hand, where there are a few Christians under the care of a native schoolmaster, more independent thought is begotten. The Bible is the court of appeal. It is studied with some amount of intelligence. The office of native teacher in these circumstances is no sinecure. ... From what I have seen I am deeply convinced that it is the power of Jesus Christ in his gospel which overcomes men; and that by standing as it were in the way of this specific agency, the European missionary may even retard and deteriorate the work.'

8 Livingstone, *To John Arundel,* 22.12.1841, (*LMC,* 11). Moffat agreed that in the 1830s native teachers had helped transform the Griqua mission (RM, *MLSSA,* 204).

9 Livingstone was not always tactful in relation to his father-in-law. In 1851 he published an anonymous article in the *British Quarterly* concerning 'Moffat's mistake'. Moffat was deeply hurt by the article. Livingstone had not shown it to him before having it published. Moffat wrote privately to Tidman: RM, *To Tidman, LMS,* July 1852, (SOAS/CWM/SA/Box 27/1/A): 'I would refer you to the article which some time ago appeared in the British *Quarterly* on our African Missions. I suppose by this time you are aware that it was from the pen of Mr. Livingston, and, if I am not very far mistaken it was written here in my house during one of his visits. How he came to write as he has done about what is called 'Moffat's mistake' I cannot conceive for all that I ever heard from his lips went to establish all I have written on the subject. ... His remarks on native teachers are exaggerated and some are erroneous. He has had what no missionary has—two native teachers on his station—the two best—the very pick of all.' Livingstone's letter is a long epistle, the bulk of it reproduced in: *DLSAP,* 99-109.

10 Livingstone, *To John Arundel,* 22.12.1841, (*LMC,* 12). The two were Paul and Mebalwe. We have not located Moffat's letter, referred to by Livingstone, in which he encouraged the Kuruman missionaries to do more with native agency, but it must have been written in 1840.

Returning to the Griqua Town model, Livingstone described the work achieved by these native agents, claiming that it was greater in both quantity and quality than that achieved by the official missionaries at Kuruman itself: 'Each at his location has more members under him than are at the station, that is, they have more than 2/3 of the church, and the chief accessions to it are always from their ministry. Add to this they [the converts/congregations] are much more consistent in their deportment than those here and so affectionate to us and to each other it is quite a treat to visit them.'

The Ideal of Indigenous Ministry

Was Livingstone correct? Was he aware of the full history of Kuruman? Did he know about Moffat's suspicion of native ministry owing to past lapses? What had already been achieved with native ministry at Kuruman? Was Moffat truly undergoing a change of mind? How did Moffat really regard the role of indigenous Christians in the propagation of the Gospel? Did Moffat's paternalism inhibit the maturing of indigenous converts to full Christian service? To address these questions, we require first to reflect on missiological issues of that time.

David Bogue was never a missionary in the field, but he had an astute grasp of long-term strategy. He stressed that indigenous converts had to take responsibility for the continuing work of church and mission. He taught that the relationship of a missionary to converts must be a mature one which treated the convert as a true and full member of the Church of Christ, and 'as those who are called to perform important offices in that respect, endeavouring to prepare them as soon as possible to act for themselves in the management of the affairs of the Church'.[11] Moffat was aware of what Bogue taught, having transcribed these very words. And Bogue had taught this policy for some time, predating Anderson and Venn's missiological policies by at least forty years. Bogue emphasised the importance of converts being trained and given responsibility as soon as possible: 'By treating people, especially converts, as children, you make them children; by teaching them as men, and endeavouring to lead them to act as men, you make them men.'[12] Yet Bogue also held that the 'dark spiritual background of converts' might mean that time had to elapse before this ideal state could be realised:

> There are some peculiarities belonging to a newly formed Church among the heathen: The believers are but just called out of heathenish darkness and can have but an imperfect knowledge of the principles of Christianity. Their

---

11 Bogue, *Miss. Lect.* 17, 'Behaviour of Missionaries to different Classes of People'.

12 Ibid.

heathenish habits and ways of thinking may be expected to be overtaking and overcoming them. Besides, their gifts may be rather considered as in the bud or blossom, than as full ripe fruit, so that they are less fit for offices which require men to be examples and to give counsel to others.[13]

Some later missiologists, such as Roland Allen, minimised the risk, arguing for rapid indigenisation, and claiming, like Livingstone, that the Holy Spirit would make good any deficiencies. But Moffat, even as late as 1867, had a cautious view.[14] Piggin has pointed out that much of Bogue's thinking was based on reports concerning India, and when Bogue made his insistence on training native clergy to be missionaries in their own Churches he was mainly thinking of the sub-continent where there was a more advanced educational system.[15] Nonetheless, his general principles could be applied anywhere. Philip, as LMS Superintendent in southern Africa, also argued that native ministry was essential if LMS work were to advance. In 1833, Philip wrote:

One thing is clear, that to carry on and extend the missionary work we must have native agency; and that to procure that agency the work of education among the heathen cannot be begun too soon, nor carried on too extensively ... The gospel can never have a permanent footing in a barbarous country unless education and civilisation go hand in hand with our religious instruction.[16]

Van der Kemp, Read, and Campbell, all championed indigenous ministry, but it was Philip who promoted it as an essential aspect of the work. This was in connection with his emphasis on civilisation through education, rather than through agriculture and industry, which was Moffat's main focus. Ross also criticised Moffat's methods, arguing that Philip's positive vision for native agency was frustrated by Moffat's attitude.[17] Bogue and Philip were both pointing towards missiological strategies which would later be codified by Rufus Anderson and Henry Venn.[18] These would be expressed in three

---

13 Bogue, *Miss. Lect.* 21, 'Establishment of Churches among the Heathen'.

14 RM, *To Mullen, LMS,* 1.1.1867, (SOAS/CWM SA Reports Box 1): 'It requires a long time however to raise a people from barbarism to that state in which they can be safely left to find their way unaided. We have found it so in Africa where so much labour is required to raise the converts above pupilage. We want to see more of that manliness which disdains to be dependent on others for everything. But though we have not seen all that we have longed and prayed for a great deal has been accomplished.'

15 Cf. Piggin, *Making Evangelical Missionaries: 1789-1858,* 178.

16 Philip, *To Purney,* May 1833, (Legassick, *The Griqua, the Sotho-Tswana, and the Missionaries: 1780-1840, Part 2,* 474). Philip's letter was written in 1833, only four years after the Awakening. At that point Moffat might be excused for not yet having instituted regular native ministry. The 'casualties' of the 1814 native agents were in his mind.

17 Cf. Ross, *John Philip 1775-1851,* 218ff & 224ff.

18 For Anderson and Venn see: (i) Gailyn Van Rheenen, *Biblical Foundations and Contemporary Strategies: Missions,* (Michigan: Zondervan, 1996), 182ff; (ii) A. Scott Moreau

principles: self-propagation, self-support, and self-governance. Anderson and Venn were both born in 1796, one year after Moffat's birth. Hence, though their publications came late in Moffat's missionary career, the development of their thought took place when Moffat was active in the field. Yet there was little opportunity for Moffat to be influenced by their writings. Moreover, they were secretaries of great mission organisations, able to survey missions on a world-wide basis, whereas Moffat, in the field, was restricted by his local horizons, his workload, and the energy-sapping day-to-day practicalities of running a mission station church.

Rufus Anderson was an American Congregationalist, and became Foreign Secretary to the *American Board of Commissioners for Foreign Missions* in 1832, remaining so until 1866. Moffat met missionaries from the *ACBFM* in 1836, when the *ABCFM* attempted to set up a mission station among Moselekatse's Ndebele.[19] When the Boers attacked Mosega the *ABCFM* mission collapsed. Wilson, one of their missionaries, wrote to Anderson from Kuruman, reporting that, during a similarly aborted French Mission, 'Moselekatse was at that time engaged in putting to death a number of his people—men, women and children—on account of the death of one of his own children, which he alleged had been caused by witchcraft.'[20] The *ABCFM* missionaries then worked elsewhere in South Africa.

In the 1850s Anderson proposed self-propagation, self-support, and self-governance, over against missionary paternalism, arguing that the apostle Paul established local Churches which were not dependent upon him. Anderson contended that priority should be given to institutions to educate native teachers and preachers, and was firmly committed to the training and

---

(ed.), *Evangelical Dictionary of World Missions,* (Michigan: Baker Books, 2000); (iii) Kenneth Hylson-Smith, *Evangelicals in the Church of England: 1734-1984,* (Edin: Clark, 1988), 216ff.

19 Following the failure of the first mission to the Ndebele, under the *Paris Evangelical Missionary Society*, due to the cattle raids of Berend Berends (a former native teacher commissioned in 1814), and the reprisals meted out by Moselekatse, Moffat wanted to prepare the way properly for the American missionaries. After correspondence with John Philip, it was decided to send two groups to Southern Africa. One group would form the *Maritime Mission* among the Zulus. The other would go to Mosega to work among the Ndebele. They reached Cape Town in February 1835, where John Philip welcomed them. By May, the Ndebele group had reached Griqua Town, where they stayed for seven months to learn the language. Moffat had already left for Moselekatse's kraal to prepare him for their coming. The *ABCFM* missionaries reached Mosega in February 1836. They were soon forced out by a combination of fever and being caught in the middle of a savage conflict that erupted between Moselekatse and the Boers (Briggs & Wing, *The Harvest and the Hope,* 61ff).

20 Wilson, *To Rufus Anderson,* 21.3.1836 (Kuruman): D.J. Kotze (ed.), *Letters of the American Missionaries: 1835-1838,* (CT: Van Riebeck Society, 1950), 104.

ordination of indigenous pastors. Like Livingstone, and like Roland Allen after him, he believed in the possibility of rapid change.

Anderson's criteria were eagerly adopted by Henry Venn, Secretary of the Anglican based *Church Missionary Society* (CMS, who had been thinking along similar lines. Venn's grandfather had been a key figure in eighteenth-century evangelicalism, and his father, John Venn, was the rector of Clapham, working alongside the evangelical social-reforming families of the Clapham Sect. Venn went to Cambridge University in 1814, and after entering the ministry of the Church of England became Secretary to the CMS in 1841, holding the position until 1872. As a missionary statesman, Venn's leading idea was: 'The euthanasia of missions'.[21] Venn saw a foreign missionary as always primarily an evangelist, who had the task of planting churches which would become self-supporting, self-governing, and self-extending. Each church should then develop according to its national character under indigenous leadership, and unencumbered by a continuing European presence. As an Anglican, Venn envisaged a diocese with a local bishop.[22] But his view of the role of the bishop in foreign mission was somewhat different from that of the Tractarian High Church Oxford Movement, which became so influential in southern Africa through Bishop Gray in Cape Town and Bishop Mackenzie in Central Africa. In Venn's opinion, bishops were functionally necessary for confirming, ordaining, and overall oversight, but not essential for mission work and the actual establishment of a Church.[23] For Tractarians, a bishop was *essential.* For evangelicals, a bishop was *functional.*

Unlike Anderson, Venn was a gradualist, but with indigenous leadership as a positive central goal. He expressed his missiological views in the preface to his biography, *The Missionary Life and Labours of Francis Xavier* (1862). Venn's views on indigenous ministry were quickly adopted. For example, though the Anglican Church only established its mission at Bloemfontein in 1863, by 1876 it had a Theological College training both European and African students 'as Readers, Catechists, and Preachers, if not with a view to their actually receiving Holy Orders within the next few years.'.[24] By this date the new thinking was streaming in almost every missionary organisation, including the LMS.

---

21 Hylson-Smith, *Evangelicals in the Church of England: 1734-1984,* 217.

22 Rheenen, *Biblical Foundations and Contemporary Strategies: Missions*, 183.

23 Hylson-Smith, *Evangelicals in the Church of England: 1734-1984,* 217.

24 J.W. Barrow, *A Brief History of the Bloemfontein Mission, South Africa, Part 2,* 13. This contrasts with the slowness of the LMS in establishing a College for ministry training.

In line with the new thinking, in 1855 the LMS initiated two actions which had long term consequences. The first was partly prompted by a joint 1852 letter from Moffat and Livingstone to the Rev. Thompson who was the LMS agent in Cape Town. Moffat and Livingstone had proposed that all mission stations within the extensive boundary of the Colony be treated as self-supporting and independent and needing no missionary.[25] Though Kuruman was outside the boundary, following the Moffat/Livingstone letter the LMS arranged in 1855 for a visitation of all its colonial institutions. This was to see whether, as argued by Moffat and Livingstone, these should now be made independent and no longer dependent on the LMS for finance or personnel. The Moffat/Livingstone letter certainly reinforced a growing concern in the LMS hierarchy concerning the status of long-established 'mission stations' and their continued reliance on European missionaries. The second action was to include in the LMS *1855 Annual Report* some of the LMS provisions for native ministry world-wide. Significantly, southern Africa was not referred to in the list of regions already giving substantial training in this area:

> The number of native agents [world-wide] employed by the Society, including schoolmasters, scripture readers, evangelists and pastors, amounts to about 600. In the appointment of these Agents our Missionaries select the most suitable men in their congregations: but their qualifications are often limited and inadequate; and to meet this deficiency Training Institutions have been formed in *India*, *China*, and the *Islands of the South Pacific*. There are at present in these different seminaries about 100 students; and those who have already enjoyed the advantages they supply are found most efficient labourers in different branches of Missionary service.[26]

That was simply a report. But by the mid 1860s, and fired by the missiological thinking of men like Anderson and Venn, the LMS took more positive steps. In its 1867 *Annual Report,* every contribution, from every LMS mission station around the globe, was presented in a way which highlighted the role of native ministry.[27] This concentration on native ministry in the 1867 *Annual Report* was an editorial decision taken at the highest level.

---

25 Moffat/Livingstone, *To the Rev. Thompson (LMS agent in Cape Town),* 22.11.1822: (*DLSAP,* 111). Moffat totally agreed concerning the need to make such churches fully independent. Schapera (*op. cit.* 112), pointed out that in the original version the letter was signed 'Robert Moffat' and 'David Livingstone' in that order, whereas, when Livingstone transcribed it into his journal, he put his own name first. Following this letter the LMS arranged for a visitation tour in 1855 of all its colonial institutions: the outcome was that the LMS ultimately ceased to give them financial support and gradually transferred all responsibility to the indigenous population, including the freehold of the land which such stations occupied.

26 LMS, *Report to the 61st Annual Meeting, 1855,* 8. Kuruman was one of many LMS Mission Stations in southern Africa.

27 LMS, *Report to the 73rd Annual Meeting, 1867*.

Then in 1868 the new LMS Secretary, Joseph Mullens, sent a series of questions concerning native ministry to all mission stations. These were discussed at a major area conference at Kuruman in February 1869. The central concern of Mullens' questions was the creation of a native ministry in order to speed the pace of an independent Church. It is clear that the LMS leadership was now urgently trying to put Anderson and Venn's missiological principles into practice. It was probably Venn's work, published in England in the early 1860s, which brought the issues to the top of the LMS agenda. Vague notions in the past concerning indigenisation were now becoming formal policy.

How did Kuruman answer Mullens' questions? Northcott has tactfully suggested that the questions were after Moffat's own heart, which he and Livingstone had foreseen in their policy of northward expansion.[28] However, at first glance, it seemed that after forty years of work, there was little to report. At Kuruman itself, there were five native pastors on £10 a year, described as 'not good but zealous'. At Likhatlong there were four 'inefficient', paid £6 each. At Griqua Town, there were four 'uneducated' with reading their only qualification. What was wanted was a school for the training of native pastors.[29] And yet, though Kuruman had embarrassingly little to report, an irresistible drive toward implementing a genuine and effective native ministry was now central in the leadership thinking in missionary societies.

Indigenous Lay-Ministry: Existing Examples

Moffat's work at Kuruman was carried out in parallel to this development of missiological thought. But how far did he progress in mobilising, training and equipping people as leaders of new churches? In this section we focus on the detail of Moffat's use of native teachers. What we shall see is that Moffat did make some headway in developing an indigenous *lay-ministry*, but made no headway in advancing an indigenous *ordained-ministry*. Yet, as we noted previously, ordination was relatively unimportant in Moffat's theology. He came from a tradition in which the ministry of the Word was seen as the highest form of service with which a person might be entrusted. Did Moffat never go beyond the concept of lay-ministry simply because, for him, lay-ministry adequately fulfilled the most important function of all, the preaching of the Word? The evangelical notion that all offices were *functional* rather than *essential* meant that the *essence* of an office was in its

---

28 The 1852 Moffat/Livingstone letter shows that there was some truth in this.

29 Northcott, *Robert Moffat,* 322. Northcott cited *Kuruman Conference Minutes,* 17.2.1869.

function. And so, when Moffat assigned someone to teach and preach the Word, then he was giving that person the highest office and the practice of its most sacred function. This still leaves the question of ordination to be addressed, which we discuss later. But what is clear is that the post of native teacher was important to Moffat. It was not a minor appointment. It touched the very heart of ministry, the holy ministry of the Word.

What was a native teacher? A native teacher or native agent was an indigenous lay-person who had appropriate knowledge of the Christian faith, whose life displayed consistent Christian qualities, and who was given the task of preaching and teaching the Christian faith to his fellow countrymen and countrywomen. Under this definition, the concept of a native teacher, involved in lay-ministry, was not unknown in Britain, and utilisation of lay-ministry was present in most of the traditions which had influenced Moffat.

The Society for the Propagation of Christian Knowledge had used lay-catechists in Scotland from the mid-eighteenth century. This was copied by *The Society for Propagating the Gospel at Home* (SPGH) established by Robert and James Haldane in 1798. The SPGH had imaginative and inclusive methods, especially in its wide use of lay-catechists and lay preachers in addition to ordained clergy. It employed two main groups of 'evangelists'.

1. Catechists. These were pious young men whose duty was to plant, superintend, and teach evening schools in villages, confining learners to the subject of religion. By 1799, there were nearly 40 SPGH Catechists, mostly working in the remote rural areas of Scotland.

2. Ministers. Initially the SPGH and the Independency movement brought in 'Ministers of known character' from England to work alongside Scots. These 'visitors' included George Burder, later to be Foreign Secretary to the LMS, and David Bogue, later to be theological tutor to the same Society. Bogue only stayed a short time, returning to England on health reasons. It is easy to see how Bogue's advocacy of the use of native converts, as taught in his *Missionary Lectures*, was perfectly in line with the principles of the SPGH with which he had been associated.

Moffat would be aware of SPGH methods. It may not be too far from the mark to see the SPGH model as the one to which Kuruman most closely approximated, with Moffat envisaging his native teachers operating as lay-catechists and lay-teachers. He saw them as establishing schools in villages to teach reading and writing. When learners had gained these skills, they would be brought in contact with the Word of God and be converted. Native teachers also conducted religious services which people would be invited to attend: the first seeds of a new congregation.

Scottish Congregationalism, which followed on from the founding of the SPGH, was also sympathetic to lay-ministry. English Independency was similar. William Roby of Manchester trained considerable numbers of lay-preachers at his theological school.[30] Clearly, lay-ministry was not alien to LMS leaders, and it had been in the home mission fields of Scotland and England that the strategy of lay-ministry first flowered. Hence it is not surprising to find John Campbell, an early enthusiast for the SPGH, Congregationalism, and the LMS, encouraging the commissioning of native teachers whilst inspecting LMS stations in southern Africa in 1813.[31]

Though John and Charles Wesley, as Anglicans at heart, had a keen respect for the holy office of ordination, the advance of Methodism in the eighteenth and nineteenth centuries also owed much to lay-preachers. When Moffat was converted under Methodist influence at High Leigh, he not only benefited from the visiting Methodist minister, the Rev. Joseph Beaumont, but from the ministries of lay-personnel who preached at meetings organised by the Okeys. Methodist use of lay-ministry, so prominent in Britain, was also encouraged by Wesleyan Missions in the mission field. Moffat observed the progress of the Wesleyan mission in Namaqualand under the guidance of his friend Barnabas Shaw, noting the 'zeal by which our Wesleyan brethren are distinguished, supported by an extensive native agency'.[32]

With clear home-bred models of lay-ministry behind him, why was Moffat sluggish in implementing a parallel policy? We have already referred to John Campbell, who, during his first visit to southern Africa, encouraged the commissioning of native teachers. This came to fruition in August 1814 when the LMS appointed six indigenous Africans for ministry. The LMS *Annual Report* for 1815 proudly stated that six converted natives, Griquas and Hottentots, were solemnly designated as assistant preachers of the gospel. Their names were: Berend Berends, Jan Hendrick, Andries Waterboer, Peter David, Jan Goeyman, and Cupido [Kakerlak].[33] Thus, by the time Moffat arrived in Africa in 1817, there were existing examples of native ministry. Indeed, the concept was relatively advanced. The LMS had already placed native teachers strategically, some near the Orange River, and some at Konnah and Ramah to instruct the San, as part of Campbell's ambitious project to establish a chain of mission stations leading from Graaff-Reinet to

---

30 Robinson, *William Roby,* 100f.

31 Schoeman, *The Mission at Griqua Town,* 16f.

32 RM, *MLSSA,* 190.

33 LMS, *Report to the 21st Annual Meeting, 1815,* 21. Briggs and Wing, *The Harvest and the Hope,* 20, cite an impressive list of additional names.

Klaarwater [Griqua Town] and beyond.[34] It was in connection with this project that the 1814 commissioning took place.

Indigenous Lay-Ministry: Moffat's Intentions

The 1820s were, for Moffat, fallow years in terms of conversions to the faith, and he could not develop native agency where there were no new converts to work with. And whatever use Moffat made of lay-catechists and lay-teachers during the 1830s—after the Awakening—their involvement at Kuruman was far more significant after he returned from Britain in 1843. Livingstone gave a big push whilst Moffat was absent, but it also seems that Moffat himself, whilst in Britain, began to think more seriously about their role. Was he influenced by discussions with LMS figures, who urged him to take the concept more seriously?[35] Did the discipline of writing *Missionary Labours* make him reflect on the issue? Did the many meetings throughout the country, at which he described missionary achievements, make him realise that lasting success must be connected with indigenous converts assuming more roles? Did his defence of the intellectual abilities of indigenous Africans make him realise that if he were to be true to his argument then Africans must be allowed to take responsibility? And if fear that the remnants of traditional religion still affected converts, did he now believe that enough time had lapsed for mature converts to take that next step? Whatever the reasons, Moffat, post-1843, was more positive.

In *Missionary Labours,* Moffat recorded that he had encountered native teachers on his very first journey, on his way to Africaner's kraal. He recalled meeting, at the Pella Mission Station, Magerman, the native teacher of Warmbath.[36] Moffat also indicated how much the Griqua mission had been enhanced by native teachers, expressing satisfaction at how it was revived after 1829 through Peter Wright and Isaac Hughes, and that fundamental to this success were six native teachers.[37] Moffat acknowledged that it was through the native teachers that the mission had been able to extend its influence, with the establishment of congregations in various places. He also wrote of how sister missionary societies in the southern Africa field benefited

---

34 Schoeman, *The Mission at Griqua Town,* 16f.

35 Northcott, *Robert Moffat,* 172, portrayed Moffat as persuading the Directors rather than vice versa: 'During his four years in Britain Moffat expounded the theory of 'native agency' to the directors of the Society so effectively that he even opened up the idea of training institutions for them, which waited another thirty years, after his retirement, for its fulfillment.'

36 RM, *MLSSA,* 101.

37 RM, *MLSSA,* 204.

from the use of native agents.[38] All of these points were made explicitly. But in his book, Moffat made little reference to the historic 1814 setting aside of native teachers. His silence spoke volumes. Moffat regarded most of that group as abject failures. Since *Missionary Labours* was intended for public consumption it is not surprising that Moffat stressed the positive side of native ministry. Yet, despite his reservations concerning the 1814 group, his increasing interest in native ministry spilled into his speeches. For example, in his *Edinburgh Address* of 1842 Moffat gave a positive spin to the role of native teachers:

> There is a native agency rising up among them, and we look to the time when an academy shall be formed among them, to cultivate their minds and to prepare them for preaching throughout all Africa the everlasting Gospel of the grace of God.[39]

A few months later, in his *Barbican Sermon,* Moffat expanded on the theme:

> Blessed be God, we have not only missionaries on many a continent, and in many an island, but we have native agents who have been raised up by these missionaries, who are going to and fro, and not only reading in their own language, the wonderful works of God, but preaching the Gospel to others, and pointing their countrymen to 'the Lamb of God who taketh away the sins of the world'.[40]

And in his *Valedictory Sermon,* at the LMS Mission House in London, before returning to Africa, Moffat was fulsome on the positive role which native ministry must have, though still expressing some reservations:

> I have had occasion frequently to refer to native agency – the importance of one more extensive, and especially, more effective. I believe the Directors now thoroughly understand the subject and our wants in that respect. I have, it is true, not all the confidence that some, *less experienced*, have in certain kinds of native agency. Native agents may very properly be compared to a body of sepoys, who will fight well while they have good English officers to lead them on. ... They will be centres, and around them native agents will gather and revolve, and guided and sustained by them, do wonders.
>
> But I wish especially to remind you that something effectual ought to be done in the way of the direct instruction of the native agents. I am glad to find that this plan is being adopted ... It is a subject of the utmost importance to prepare natives to carry the Word of God far beyond the regions we now occupy. I do not, however, expect from my knowledge of the native character, that they can do much on new soil; I do not expect that they will be pioneers for some time to come; but this confidence I have in them, that if *you* once

---

38 RM, *MLSSA,* 190.

39 RM, *Edinburgh Address,* 3.11.1842, (*Farewell Services,* 18).

40 RM, *Barbican Sermon,* 22.1.1843, (*Farewell Services,* 103).

> open the way and point out the field where they are to labour, they will be found the most successful labourers in the good and glorious cause of evangelising the interior of Africa.'[41]

Moffat's phrase: 'I believe the Directors now thoroughly understand the subject, and our wants in that respect' requires analysis. The repeated mention of the value of native teachers in successive LMS *Annual Reports,* from long before 1843, makes it plain that the LMS Directors did not need to be convinced of their importance. And so it is unlikely that Moffat was implying that the Directors required to be persuaded concerning the concept. It is more likely that Moffat's conception of native ministry, and the Directors' conception of it, did not totally coincide, and that Moffat was referring to a coming together of views.

Moffat felt that more resources were needed to do the task properly. He was a deliberate man. He was not prepared to take chances as some 'less experienced' were advocating. This certainly accords with what he expressed in the rest of the paragraph. He still had doubts about the leadership qualities of native teachers. He still had doubts about their ability to do pioneer work. He still had doubts whether, unless full training were given, they would progress at all. Andrew Ross avers that all of Moffat's statements about the value of native teachers amounted to no more than 'lip-service'.[42] But Moffat's honest appraisal of what he thought was the true situation should not be confused with 'lip-service'. He was not as bold as Livingstone. Neither was he as positive as his colleague the Rev. William Ross.[43] But as he prepared to return to Africa he was taking the matter very seriously.

INDIGENOUS LAY-MINISTRY: GRADUAL PROGRESS

Two years later, the LMS *1845 Annual Report* mentioned four Kuruman out-stations under charge of efficient native teachers 'supported by friends in England'. These out-stations were equivalent to 'prayer-houses'. They were

---

41 RM, *Sermon at the Mission House,* 23.1.1843, (*Farewell Services,* 148f).

42 Ross, *John Philip 1775-1851,* 224.

43 William Ross wrote: 'At present the state of the mission is very promising, with regard to the native agents employed in teaching and addressing the people. 6 such men are connected with Kuruman, and these, from what I know of them, are, through the divine blessing, calculated to do much good. I am intimately acquainted with them: they all visit this place from time to time, with the exception of one, and are as much encouraged, instructed and assisted, as circumstances permit. It is truly delightful to observe the fervent zeal of these godly men: many such are greatly needed in this dark part of benighted Africa. In my humble opinion, it is the only way by which the interior of the country can have a stated ministry of the Gospel, and it is the imperative duty of all of us to raise up and instruct such men as far as possible.' (LMS, *Report to the 50th Annual Meeting, 1844*, 105).

at Hamhana, Nokaneng, Lingopeng and Borigelon. (The future major Kuruman mission stations of Kolobeng and Likhatlong, where native ministry by Kuruman converts was to be vitally important, were not yet established.) The 1845 LMS *Annual Report* also stated: 'The distribution of the missionary force, of which Lattakoo [Kuruman] may be regarded as the centre, was accomplished shortly after the arrival of Mr. Moffat'.[44] This 'distribution' related not only to a wider native ministry, but also to a wider deployment of European missionaries, such as Livingstone and Edwards. The LMS Directors were willing to give Moffat credit for this new thrust, though Livingstone had pushed for it before Moffat returned.

In the following year, the LMS *1846 Annual Report* maintained its laudatory comments about an extensive Native Agency emanating from Kuruman, with six native teachers in the field.[45] The LMS hierarchy was giving Moffat every encouragement. But Moffat's creative energies were being drained by the task of translation and printing. Nevertheless, a course offering basic training was started at Kuruman, and Moffat gave strong support to native teachers already in place. John Smith Moffat described the situation in 1847 when Moffat visited BaThlaping villages along the Kolong River:

> The advance which had taken place of late years was striking. A severe contest was going on between heathenism and Christianity. A little company of believers had, however, been gathered in each place, and were ministered to by native teachers, who had spent a few months in training at Kuruman. These people were feeling the pressure of the surrounding heathenism, and were proposing, in many instances, to remove to Kuruman.
>
> From this step they were dissuaded by the missionary, who pointed out to them the value of their presence and testimony to the gospel in the midst of a heathen community. The test of their sincerity has no doubt been severe, and has led to many relapses; but greater reliance can be placed on those who remain firm in the midst of some of the more heathen villages in isolated situations, than on those who, under the wing of the missionaries at headquarters, have every inducement to maintain their profession.[46]

John Smith Moffat was a son writing about his father. Even so, he is usually reliable. What he described was Kuruman placing native teachers in the villages, and Moffat encouraging Christians in remoter areas to have faith in these men and not to move to Kuruman for 'spiritual security'. The *Kuruman Church Record Book* makes it clear that preaching, teaching, nurturing and

---

44 LMS, *Report to the 51st Annual Meeting, 1845*, 121.

45 LMS, *Report to the 52nd Annual Meeting, 1846*, 115.

46 JSM, *Lives,* 257f.

disciplining at comparatively remote villages was under indigenous control, directed by native teachers. This homologates John Smith Moffat's account.[47] This may not have been the mass pioneer work which Livingstone envisaged. Nevertheless, it was happening.

The 'few months in training', alluded to by John Smith Moffat, was taken further by the Rev. William Ashton from 1848 onwards. Ashton came to Kuruman in 1843, and the LMS *1849 Annual Report* recorded: 'Mr. Ashton has received a few youths under his care, with a view to the formation of an Institution which the Directors are desirous of establishing at this station for the education and training of native teachers and evangelists.'[48] Moffat was totally preoccupied with his translation activities, and the extent to which that drained his time and energy must not be underestimated. Yet nothing happened at Kuruman without Moffat's approval. Unfortunately, Ashton's programme withered away after a few years. Thus, despite signs of promise, and though Kuruman moved a little in the right direction, it still lacked a real commitment of energy and resources to the scheme. In 1854 Moffat wrote to Tidman of the LMS:

> At present, and for some time past you will have seen that it is no easy matter to give reports of native teachers, and at present there is no prospect whatever of public offers [of] subsidy so as to send native teachers or schoolmasters to stations with any prospect of permanency. But for all that, where there is an opening we must endeavour to enter.[49]

Moffat referred to a lack of funds. Kuruman native teachers were paid a salary. This salary had to come from abroad, usually from well-wishers in Britain. Perhaps Moffat could have circumvented this by other means, and some may argue that the financial problem was an excuse for inaction. But perhaps it was a real barrier. Moffat's concluding phrase, 'where there is an

---

[47] Cf. LMS *55th Annual Report (1849),* 104, referring to Kuruman during 1848: '[At an out-station] discipline had been exercised on account of [several of the church members] taking part in the destruction of a Bushman village … [they were then reinstated] …their whole deportment had given *entire satisfaction to the native teachers and believers*, on whose testimony they were again received with deep thankfulness and joy into the bosom of the church.' Autonomy was given to the local congregations along with their native teachers, to manage the affairs of the church including discipline. For major cases, the local congregation would wait until a missionary were present before proceeding with the issues. Even then, the evidence, testimony and decision, were those of the congregation.

[48] LMS, *Report to the 55th Annual Meeting, 1849*, 105.

[49] RM, *To Tidman, LMS,* 5.4.1854, (SOAS/CWM/SA/Box 29/1/A). Ongoing native ministry among the BaNgwaketse and BaHurutse was referred to in an 1856 letter to Tidman, cf. RM, *To Tidman, LMS,* 28.10.1856, (SOAS/CWM/SAfr/30/1/A).

opening we must endeavour to enter', points to him, in principle, accepting the importance of this type of ministry.

One further factor. This was Moffat's belief that many villages were reluctant to accept an indigenous teacher. Moffat's 1851 letter to Arthur Tidman focused on this problem:

> Seven native teachers have gone from this mission, I may say from this station, and they have done well, considering that they did not commence their labours or their studies in their youth. And, although they appear as if they could not advance themselves, nor of course carry others beyond a given point, they might do very well for the present generation, were their own people satisfied with them. Instead of which the hue and cry is raised: 'we won't have a black teacher like ourselves, we will have a white teacher who can guide and protect us', thus verifying what is written. Of course, it is not the Gospel that they seek in the first instance. They think they will enjoy unusual privileges and that by the presence of the missionary they will increase their intercourse with the whites and increase what is paramount, their riches.
>
> They find these results do not follow the native teacher and from this cause our two native teachers Sebobi and Tlomelang among the Bamanketse are much disheartened and write in a very mournful strain respecting their present circumstances and prospects. The same holds good with the two native teachers among the Bakuena in the absence of Mr. Livingston.[50] They have no influence whatever. ...
>
> Where the native teacher is labouring among a people who are under the eye of the missionary, and who are constantly visited and among whom the ordinances of religion are administered at stated times as is the case with our BaTlaros some 10 miles to the north of this station, the case is very different. Though they have individuals of their own nation who carry on the work of exhortation, schools and prayer-meetings, they still look on the missionary as their own. The same may be said of our native teachers on the Kolong River, but place them alone, they are disregarded, at least such as we have tried.[51]

Moffat wanted the native teachers to be effective. In the above extract, he was not criticising their ability. Nor was he undermining their ministry in order to maintain a dependence upon himself. He was simply reporting their lack of influence through not being fully accepted as 'proper' Christian

---

50 David Livingstone had not yet added the 'e' to Livingston.

51 RM, *To Tidman, LMS,* 3.11.1851, (SOAS/CWM/SA/Box 26/1/A). When Tidman edited the letter for the *1852* LMS *Annual Report,* he put a spin on Moffat's comments: 'From this Mission seven native evangelists have at different times been sent forth into the vineyard; and, notwithstanding the prevalence of an unhappy prejudice among some of the tribes against receiving instructions from their own countrymen, these worthy men have, to a certain extent, been blessed in their labours.' (LMS, *Report to the 58th Annual Meeting, 1852*, 66).

teachers by fellow Africans. A good number of Kuruman converts came from what were regarded as the 'lower' sections of indigenous society. That may have been why some villages were reluctant to accept them. This was the opposite of India, where LMS native teachers were treated with honour by indigenous Indians.[52] Moffat's situation was different. As so often, the 'devil is in the detail', and requires an assessment of individual cases which is the theme of our next chapter.

---

52 LMS, *Report to the 71st Annual Meeting, 1865*, 27.

Chapter 33
The Preachers of the Kingdom

MOFFAT TOOK NATIVE TEACHERS seriously, even though he failed to develop the concept as fully as he might have. Locked in his study, his energies were dedicated to language and translation. If we add to that his natural caution plus difficulties in the acceptability of native teachers amongst their fellows, we can see why he neglected this promising area. But some did emerge, and in this chapter we examine individual native teachers known to Moffat. For example, from an early-stage Moffat used Aaron Josephs and Paul to assist him in the instruction of enquirers. In the ensuing years, they had semi-official status as lay-catechists. In 1834, Moffat reported to the LMS:

> One of the brethren meets alternately every week, with [candidates for baptism] to converse with them; and Aaron and Paulo, the two principal members of the church, have also met with them for the same purpose. The catechetical meeting, held every Sabbath and Wednesday afternoon, is most encouraging. It is attended by persons of all ages and sexes—the number of attendants has amounted even to 84 persons.[1]

Moffat added that several of the people had become so well acquainted with the 'great truths of the Gospel' that they occasionally assisted in catechising others, and reading to them passages of Scripture. Aaron, Paulo, Mebalwe, Sebobi, and Mosaise, came from the growing number of African believers.

KURUMAN TEACHERS: PAUL

Paul was lay-catechist at Kuruman for many years, and was used in a similar capacity in surrounding villages. He was the most outstanding example from Kuruman during Moffat's ministry, with Livingstone describing him as 'our best theologian by far'.[2] Paul and his wife Sarah were converts from the first days of the Awakening, and were baptised and admitted to membership on 5 July 1829. In 1847, he was assigned—with Mebalwe, another Kuruman convert—to work with Livingstone among Sechele's BaKwena at Kolobeng.[3] When Livingstone left Kolobeng in 1852, Paul continued as the resident

---

1 LMS, *Report to the 40th Annual Meeting, 1834,* 96f.

2 Livingstone, *To RM,* 29.9.1847, (*DLFL*, Vol. 1, 214). Extra detail on Paul in: *DLFL*, Vol. 1, 116.

3 Janet Parsons, *Kolobeng: Home of the Livingstones and the BaKwena, 1847-1852,* (Gaborone: Botswana Soc., 1985).

native teacher in Sechele's village despite little enthusiasm on the part of the people. Moffat valued what Paul did there and when, in 1854, Sechele's wife, Ma-Sebele, requested baptism and admission to church membership, Moffat placed full confidence in Paul's testimony as to the consistent blamelessness of her life and the veracity of her profession of faith.[4] It was not Moffat who under-valued Paul's ministry as a native teacher among the BaKwena, but Sechele. In 1857 Moffat recorded that Sechele seemed to despise native teachers.[5] He wanted a European. Livingstone had noted the same reaction several years earlier, with Sechele expressing displeasure when Livingstone promised to provide him with a native teacher, and not a missionary.[6] Though Moffat had full confidence in Paul, Sechele did not. Paul's low social status may have contributed to Sechele's opinion. Apart from that, Paul's ministry faced two particular problems:

Firstly, in Moffat's view, an extra-marital relationship between Paul's youngest daughter and the youngest son of Sebobi, threatened to compromise the Christian integrity of the work. Moffat believed that a Christian teacher must be seen to be head of a clean-living Christian family which stood out as a beacon of godliness within the community. This will be further analysed when we consider Sebobi as a native teacher.

Secondly, Sechele's desire for 'real' teachers resulted in him undermining Paul's position by negotiating with the Lutherans of the Hanoverian Hermannsburg Society, who sent him three missionaries. Moffat was fearful that the Boers could control the Hermannsburg missionaries, enabling the Boers to succeed in ousting all LMS missionaries—with their notions of human equality—from the region. The arrival of the Hermannsburg missionaries resulted in Moffat removing Paul, arguing that different mission organisations should not 'compete' in the same area. In 1858, Moffat wrote to Tidman of the LMS, informing him of this decision, and of his intention of placing Paul with the BaNgwato, whose chief, Macheng, was more open to native teachers.[7]

Further evidence of Moffat's confidence in Paul was demonstrated when Moffat went to the Ndebele in 1859. There was the prospect of leaving no ordained European at Kuruman, but Moffat assigned full responsibility to Paul, expressing total trust in him in a letter to Arthur Tidman:

---

4 RM, *Journal,* 21.11.1854, (*MJ1,* 346).

5 RM, *Journal,* 7.8.1857, (*MJ2,* 21).

6 Livingstone, *To Janet Livingston,* 21.8.1843, (*DLFL,* Vol. 1, 82).

7 RM, *To Tidman, LMS,* 18.6.1858, (SOAS/CWM/SA/Box 31/1/A). Moffat secured the release of Macheng from the Ndebele. Macheng was agreeable to most of Moffat's suggestions.

> As [Kuruman] could remain entirely vacant by my departure, I have sent for our native teacher Paulo who is no longer required where he was labouring among the Bakuena. A better native supply is not to be found. His praise is in all the churches, and his services so far as preaching and attention to the affairs of the church go, are of a superior order.[8]

After reaching the Ndebele, Moffat wrote to Mary, again declaring that he had 'the fullest confidence in Paul's ability and prudence'.[9] Thus from 1859 to 1860 Paul did much of the teaching at Kuruman, sharing it with John Mackenzie who was bound for the Makololo Mission but staying at Kuruman until his wife gave birth. In December 1859, Robert wrote to Mary from Inyati: 'I suppose by this time Mr. Mackenzie is holding forth in the Sechuana so that with Paul, you will lack no desirable means [for Sabbath worship]'.[10]

Preaching the Word of God was, for Moffat, the highest form of Christian service to which a person could aspire. In Paul, and others, Kuruman had indigenous Africans who reached that peak. Yet, despite Moffat's genuine confidence in Paul, if sufficient European missionaries were present at Kuruman it was the ordained European who preached at the main Sabbath services, though there were other services when indigenous preachers preached. As late as 1868, native preachers rarely preached at the main services at Kuruman. With typical honesty John Smith Moffat recorded:

> The early prayer meeting is left entirely to the natives, the three preaching services entirely to the missionaries, and the Sunday school, with the juvenile service, to my sister. There is also a Wednesday evening service, a monthly missionary prayer meeting, a Church meeting, and a prayer meeting on Thursday afternoon. This last is in the hands of the natives. No native takes any part in the preaching on the station, except in extreme cases, when it is regarded as a makeshift. My father and I share the preaching.[11]

KURUMAN TEACHERS: MEBALWE

A gravestone in the Kuruman Mission Cemetery reads: 'Paulo and Mebalwe First Kuruman Teachers'. When the Livingstones went to Kolobeng in 1847, it was Mebalwe, as well as Paul, who accompanied them. Mebalwe was a product of Kuruman, though his elevation to native teacher seems to have

---

8 RM, *To Tidman, LMS,* 22.6.1859, (SOAS/CWM/SA/Box 31/3/B). As things turned out Paul shared responsibilities with John Mackenzie.

9 RM, *To Mary Moffat,* 12.11.1859, (*MJ2,* 216).

10 RM, *To Mary Moffat,* 13.12.1859, (*MJ2,* 240). This extract confirms that when Emily Moffat (JSM's wife) at Inyati wrote to her father, stating that 'Paulo' became ill of fever and, after his slow recovery, returned to the Kuruman, she had another Paulo in mind. See: Emily Moffat, *To JS Unwin,* 24.6.(or July 29th) 1860, (*MM,* 101).

11 JSM, *To the LMS Directors,* 12.10.1868, (Deane, *Robert Moffat,* 164).

been engineered by Livingstone, rather than by Moffat, with Livingstone recognising his qualities and giving him the opportunity he required. Mebalwe continued to give solid service to the LMS even after Livingstone left the area,[12] despite the fact that in later years he had several personal issues. Mebalwe has a unique place in mission history, as it was he who rescued Livingstone when the latter was attacked by a lion in 1844. Afterwards, he was often known as David—since the biblical David also drove off a lion—though his full African name was Mebalwe Molehane. In 1843 Livingstone wrote to Arthur Tidman from Kuruman saying Mebalwe was, 'a deacon of the church here'.[13]

Mebalwe is often mentioned in Livingstone's *Family Letters,* and he first worked with Livingstone just after the Mabotsa mission started. In 1843, before Moffat returned to Kuruman from Britain, Livingstone and Edwards, with the concurrence of the LMS, set up a mission among the BaKhatla at Mabotsa.[14] Mebalwe soon joined them. He may have been a MoKhatla himself since, in the land agreement between Livingstone and the BaKhatla, Mebalwe's name appears as a witness on behalf of the tribe. All other tribal witnesses made their mark (+), but Mebalwe signed his name.[15] His appointment at Mabotsa also highlights the financing of native ministry, which usually came from individual supporters in Britain. Livingstone reckoned that Mebalwe was well qualified to be a native teacher and hence, 'a proper person to receive the assistance rendered by a friend of mine in Scotland'.[16] The donor was a Mrs McRobert, who gave Mebalwe's 'assistance' of £12 per year.

KURUMAN TEACHERS: SEBOBI

The *Kuruman Church Record Book* notes that Sebobi was baptised and admitted to church membership at Kuruman on 4 January 1835. Before his conversion he had been a 'great warrior and inspired terror in the minds of the BaNgwaketse'. Conversion changed Sebobi, and he became 'the man

---

12 Schapera (ed.), *LMC: 1841-1856,* 49, fn. 1.

13 Livingstone, *To Tidman, LMS,* 30.10.1843, (*LMC,* 49). For Mebalwe see: *DLFL,* Vol. 1, 90.

14 Ibid, (*LMC,* 46ff).

15 Ibid, *The Agreement between the BaKhatla Chief and the Missionaries,* (*LMC,* 51).

16 Ibid, (*LMC,* 49). Livingstone was unwilling to call the sum 'remuneration'. He felt it 'undesirable to convey even in a remote way the idea of wages in the Lord's service'. Yet he was paid an LMS salary. Presumably he felt that Mebalwe's work as a native teacher was in addition to his normal employments. Though Livingstone tried to give the impression that he received little financial support: 'No missionary is paid for his work. A bare subsistence is all that is pretended to by the Society'. See: Livingstone, *To Mr Wilson,* 2.10.1853, (*DLSAP,* 122).

who is now teaching them the gospel of peace.'[17] Sebobi's going to the BaNgwaketse as a native teacher, around 1848, appears to have been his personal choice. Moffat wrote to Tidman arguing the rightness of Sebobi's placement with that tribe as a native teacher, since he had already been very effective in Kuruman out-stations.[18] When Moffat met with Sebobi in 1854[19], he tried to persuade him to go to Sechele's village since Moffat was concerned that Sechele was finding difficulty reconciling his two roles of chief and Christian.[20] But though Sebobi lived not far from Sechele he preferred to work with the BaNgwaketse and declined. Sebobi's familiarity with the BaNgwaketse language meant that not only was he effective in his own work, but could also act as interpreter.[21] Moffat wrote glowingly of Sebobi:

> He appears well contented where he is, and Gasiitsive and also Senthuhe no little pleased at having him among them. ... *[Then a description of how Sebobi complemented Moffat's teaching]* ... Sebobi, who was standing near, said, 'There, there! That is what I was telling you last Sabbath, how that Jehovah would ... and repeated with wonderful correctness the 25th, 29th, 30th, 31st, 32nd, and 33rd verses of the 28th chapter of Deuteronomy, on which he appeared to have been lecturing. I was exceedingly gratified to see and hear this. Sebobi is faithful and fearless in his testimony to the truth of the Scriptures.[22]

Was Moffat over-praising a Kuruman product? If so, then, as we shall see, when Moffat felt that Sebobi needed rebuke then he was reproved without hesitation. Moffat was even-handed in his criticism of those who fell from his high standards, whether from Kuruman or elsewhere. On his 1857 journey, Moffat again wrote warmly about Sebobi, who was still busily working among the BaNgwaketse:

> We always thought highly of Sebobi, but my estimation of him is greatly increased, though he is not one given either to puff or to murmur. He has his troubles as a teacher and a father, and manifests a spirit which does honour to his calling. He has to work hard, being poor, and weekly he traverses ... to Kanye to preach twice and instructs the few who are learning to read, and returns home the evening of the Sabbath without tasting a morsel of food.

---

17 Livingstone, *To Janet Livingston,* 20.4.1849, (*DLFL,* Vol. 2, 34).

18 RM, *To Tidman, LMS,* 24.11.1848, (SOAS/CWM/SA/Box23/4/C).

19 RM, *Journal,* 1.6.1854 (*MJ1,* 148).

20 RM, *Journal,* 5.6.1854, (*MJ1,* 156).

21 RM, *Journal,* 4.6.1854, (*MJ1,* 151).

22 RM, *Journal,* 5.6.1854, (*MJ1,* 155f). In Moffat's presence, Sebobi was prepared to upbraid Sechele for compromising Christian standards and 'sanctioning every heathen custom' (157f.).

> No, not for once do they offer him food. He preaches to at least five or six hundred every Sabbath.[23]

Sebobi fulfilled vital criteria for Moffat. He was humble, hard-working, showed initiative, had spiritual motivation, did his work without gain, and was reliable. Negatively, however, Moffat judged Sebobi to be weak as a father. Not considered critical in 1857, this became a problem later. When Moffat visited Sebobi in 1859, Sebobi had such serious family problems that Moffat felt Sebobi's usefulness among the BaNgwaketse was over:

> Sebobi has got a very naughty set of children to deal with, over whom he seems to have little control. How much such hurt a parent's usefulness among those he is appointed to instruct! Sebobi's youngest son has seduced Paul's youngest daughter, which appears to be a sad heart-sore to both Paul and Sara. And Sebobi's wicked daughter has a child. ... I had a long conversation with Sebobi, who seems to be sensible that his usefulness here is at an end. The Banguaketse cannot be otherwise than be disgusted with such a fraternity.[24]

Sexual misdemeanours closed the work even though the sins were the sins of the children. In Moffat's view, a Christian leader should rule his own household well, and so Sebobi's inability to govern his children undermined his calling. Instead of being a witness to the Gospel, Sebobi's family had become a stumbling-block amongst those to whom they sought to minister. For Moffat, the task of a missionary or native teacher was to establish the reign of Christ on earth, and an essential feature of that reign was a community of godly righteousness. The missionary's family was to be a light, illustrating core values of the Kingdom. When a family went astray, the work was compromised. Moffat was strict. When he first came to Africa he supported action against the LMS missionary James Read on account of Read's unquestioned adultery. In later years he applied similar principles to Sebobi, a teacher of his own, and a person whom he had long admired. Whether the party was European or indigenous, Moffat was consistent.

Was Moffat too strict? As a gardener, he believed that good husbandry required the removal of all harmful influences, pruning severely so that there might be a good harvest. He took the same principles into church growth. Several elements combined in Moffat: a natural inclination to discipline and morality; a pietistic conviction that personal holiness was essential if God

---

23 RM, *Journal,* 11.8.1857, (*MJ2,* 24). In 1858 Moffat alluded to difficulties Sebobi faced: 'Sebobi among the Banguaketse I found continuing his services with unremitting attention though he meets with little to encourage in the way of conversions'. See: RM, *To Tidman, LMS,* 18.6.1858, (SOAS/CWM/SA/Box 31/1/A).

24 RM, *To Mary Moffat,* 14.8.1859, (*MJ2,* 173).

were to use a man or his family;[25] a biblical duty based in 1 Timothy 3:4f; a gardener's instincts making him prune severely and weed out the harmful; plus the teaching which he had received from Roby which was strict on family responsibility.[26] Whether Moffat's draconian measures were always right in a pioneer missionary situation is debatable. But he applied discipline impartially. He rejoiced in the abilities, spirituality, commitment and application of men such as Sebobi and Paul. They were Kuruman men, imbued with Moffat's own principles. As such he was prepared to give them responsibility. But when fault occurred there could, in Moffat's eyes, be only one course of action. Sebobi was removed.

Kuruman Teachers: Mosaise and Others

Mosaise came later in Moffat's career. In the LMS 1862 *Report,* Moffat wrote:

> Our Native teacher Mosaise, among the Batlarus, is diligent in his Master's work. He carries on, with the assistance of others, the public services, but the School is what mainly occupies his time and attention. He works hard and says little, while he turns out yearly a goodly number of fine readers. To the Church of which he has the oversight, four young men have been added, and there are about 30 inquirers, some of whom will be shortly examined preparatory to being received into Church fellowship.[27]

Mosaise had full responsibility for this out-station. In Moffat's view, he taught well, led well, catechised well, and the church was thriving. Two years later a similarly glowing report was submitted:

> The church among the Batlaru tribes presents a more encouraging aspect, and to which, from an increasing number of candidates, seven adults have been added. Our native schoolmaster, Mosaise, among the people practices his work of instruction with his wonted zeal, aided by others in public services and visiting neighbouring villages. We continue our visits every alternate Sabbath, preaching at the two principal towns and administering the Lord's Supper about every two months.[28]

Mosaise was not ordained, so there was still a need for the ordained missionary to administer the sacraments. In every other respect Mosaise was the full minister of that congregation.

---

[25] This element of Moffat's theology came from his pietist roots than from the later 'holiness movement', despite his contact with the Murrays of Stellenbosch. The South African 'holiness movement' only became an identifiable force in the second half of the nineteenth century.

[26] See: Roby, *Theol. Lect.* 80, 'Family Religion'.

[27] LMS, *Report to the 68th Annual Meeting, 1862,* 77.

[28] RM, *To Tidman, LMS,* 11.1.1864, (SOAS/CWM/SA./Box 33/3/A).

Other named individuals appear as native teachers in the *Kuruman Church Record Book,* the LMS *Annual Reports',* or Moffat's *Journal* and letters. Though the information is sparse, such persons are clearly designated as native teachers. It can sometimes be difficult to interpret the data, especially in the *Kuruman Church Record Book,* and a full analysis is a task waiting to be done. Despite that caveat, the following material concerning native teachers who were connected with Kuruman, merits notice:

1. *Morisanyane*. Morisanyane was baptised and admitted to membership at Kuruman in 1836. The *KCRB* noted that he became a native teacher at Borigelong. The 1848 LMS *Annual Report* stated that a congregation of 80 existed there.

2. *Hope*. The *KCRB* recorded Hope's (Hopi's) baptism and admission in 1837. It also states that he became a native teacher at Linopen. The outposts of Borigelong and Linopen were disjoined from Kuruman in 1850, and attached to Holloway Helmore's mission station at Dikhatlong.[29]

3. *Morisanyane*. Morisanyane (possibly different from the other native teacher of the same name) was baptised and admitted on 31 December 1837, and he became a native teacher to the BaTluaso. He was cut off from church membership on 26 November 1853, after buying stolen cattle from Namaqualand. Moffat faced up to the faults of his own people. Kuruman native teachers were not appointed casually, and so the decision to discipline him would not be taken lightly.

4. *Gasebirire*. Gasebirire was baptised and admitted in 1839. He later became a native teacher with the Rev. William Ross.[30] Gasebirire was a product of Kuruman, but, because he was assigned to the mission station at Dikhatlong under Ross (who took over from Helmore in 1856), he was rarely included in Kuruman statistics. The same was true of other native teachers from Kuruman who worked with Holloway Helmore.

---

29 See: *KCRB,* 92f. In Livingstone's 1851 letter to the *British Quarterly* in which, among other matters, he touched on the importance and effectiveness of native ministry, he cited Linopen and Borigelon as shining examples of what could be achieved. See: Livingstone, *British Quarterly Letter, 1851,* (*DLSAP,* 108).

30 William Ross arrived at Kuruman with Livingstone in 1841. He went to Taung (Vryburg) in 1844 to work among a branch of the BaThlaping. He worked there until the Transvaal banned all missionary work in their republic. In 1856 he succeeded Holloway Helmore at Dikhatlong, where he remained until he died in 1863. The *KCRB* has frequent references to members who 'went to' or 'came from' the Rev. Ross or the Rev. Helmore, indicating population movements.

5. *Tlomelang*. In 1852 Moffat mentioned Tlomelang,[31] who was a native teacher among the BaNgwaketse along with Sebobi. In a relatively unfruitful situation Moffat wrote warmly of him: 'Tlomelang is a plain simple straight-forward zealous and persevering character and, we conceive, well adapted for the situation he has occupied.'[32] Tlomelang was also mentioned in Moffat's 1851 letter to Tidman concerning the difficulty native teachers had in being accepted by fellow-Africans.[33]

6. *Jan Khatlane.* Jan Khatlane had a brief appearance in Moffat's 1854 *Journals.* Wallis indicates that Khatlane was a native teacher, trained at the Kuruman: 'A half-breed, perhaps Griqua, speaking Dutch, and useful as an envoy from Sechele to the Boers'.[34] Apart from a few references, Moffat gave little information concerning, 'Jan Katlane, the *predikant* [preacher], as Sechele calls him'.[35]

7. *Thabi*. Thabi, who died on the Makololo expedition, was another native teacher originally from Kuruman. Thabi worked with Holloway Helmore for many years, and his outstanding qualities were strongly underlined by Moffat when Moffat wrote to the LMS about the Makololo tragedy.[36]

8. *Serite*. According to Wallis, Serite was also a Kuruman native teacher.[37] In 1859 Moffat noted: 'Serite is prolix, longwinded and wearisome, though possessing good common sense. I saw him once a downright fool, when his monkey was up with Ashton.'[38] Serite is also referred to in the *KCRB* disciplinary section for 28 September 1854, his son having committed fornication. Serite and his wife were also suspended from Holy Communion in 1862 for four months.

We can summarise and illustrate this section by referring to the *Kuruman Church Record Book* entries for 1852, which give a detailed overview of the Mission Station that year, recording several Kuruman native teachers. In the following list, we have retained original spellings. It does not include Paul and Mebalwe, both from Kuruman, who were working among the BaKwena

---

31 We assume that Tlomelang (whose name appears in various Moffat letters) is the same person as Homelan (whose name appears in the *KCRB*). The *KCRB* data should probably be interpreted as meaning that Homelan was baptised and admitted in 1840, becoming a native teacher some years later The *KCRB* adds that he was transferred to teach the BaNuakele.

32 RM, *To Tidman, LMS,* 15.1.1852, (SOAS/CWM/SA/Box 27/1/A).

33 RM, *To Tidman, LMS,* 3.11.1851, (SOAS/CWM/SA/Box 26/1/A).

34 Wallis (ed.), *MJ1,* 156, fn. 1.

35 RM, *Journal,* 5.6.1854, 8.6.1854, & 10.6.1854, (*MJ1,* 156, 162, & 174f).

36 RM, *To Tidman, LMS,* 12.11.1860, (SOAS/CMW/SA/Box 32/1/A).

37 Wallis (ed.), *MJ2,* 216, fn. 1.

38 RM, *To Mary Moffat,* 12.11.1859, (*MJ2,* 216).

under Livingstone. Kolobeng, as Livingstone's station, was deemed a distinct mission station from Kuruman.[39]

Name	Members at their Station	Comments
Kisinoyile[40]	20	Receiving £30 per year from Rev. Binney's Sunday School, Glasgow
Mayonoring (Magonarem)	c. 40	Among the Batluaros
Sebodi (Sebobi)	c. 48	Among the BaNgmaketu. Station destroyed by Boers.[41]
Honelong (Tlomelang)	c. 28	Among the BaNgmaketu. Station destroyed by Boers.
Khauri	c. 50	Schoolmaster at Khata. Not paid.
Molehi	c. 45	Schoolmaster at Malsepole. Not paid.

At outposts which were regarded as mission stations in their own right—including those under Livingstone, Edwards, Ross, and Helmore—the native teachers were nearly always Kuruman men. But though these stations had been planted from Kuruman they were usually excluded from Kuruman statistics. Thus, in the 1852 *Report*, only six native teachers are listed for Kuruman, despite many more operating elsewhere. There may have been many others, also products of Kuruman during Moffat's time.[42]

---

39 Paul and Mebalwe were not regarded as members of the Kuruman congregation whilst they were with Livingstone at Kolobeng. After Livingstone left Kolobeng in 1852, they returned briefly to Kuruman in 1853. Sebobi did the same after the Boers destroyed his Station. Cf. *KCRB,* 1: '*1853, February 4th,* 'Mebale, his wife Catrine and Lelokolae returned with certificates from Mr Livingston. Paulo and Sarah also; Sebobi (his wife) returned bringing with them certificates of membership from Mr. Edwards dated Nov. 27th, 1852'.

40 Kisinoyile may be the same as Kisinogile, mentioned in *KCRB* (5.10.1852 & 4.9.1863). The latter refers to a disciplinary case in which Kisinogile was separated for 'gross lying and deceit'.

41 In 1852, following the *Sand River Convention*, the Boers attacked several LMS Stations.

42 The others may include: (i) *Pomore*: Livingstone mentioned a native teacher named Pomore, see: Livingstone, *To Agnes Livingston,* 4.4.1842, (*DLFL,* Vol. 1, 53). Pomore was not mentioned in any of Moffat's documents. (ii) *Koboeapori*: Koboeapori, who appears in Moffat's later writings, is not named by Moffat as a native teacher, but is by Wallis. In his 1854 *Journal* entry concerning Sabbath worship at Sechele's Moffat wrote: 'I must ask Sechele why he only prayed, and that twice, though Koboeapori and others were there', see: RM, *Journal,*

The Problems of the 1814 Group

Ross stated that Moffat did not trust the native teachers produced by the Griqua churches and the Cape folk-congregations, which had been under the care of James Read and others, with the result that, whilst Moffat paid lip-service to native agency, he never pursued the policy with vigour.[43] Ross argued that when Moffat arrived among the Tswana, he met a people already evangelised extensively by teachers from Bethelsdorp, trained and organised by Read, but as soon as Moffat took over he set about getting rid of them all, *on one pretext or another*. Ross further argued that, in all of Moffat's extensive writing about his life and work, he never gave any credit to the foundations laid by Read and the Cape folk-evangelists upon which he built. In our view these were sweeping and inaccurate assertions.

The crucial phrase employed by Ross was: 'on one pretext or another'. This implies that Moffat used spurious arguments to get rid of many existing native teachers. In our opinion this is far from the mark. Moffat was just as rigorous in applying the highest moral standards to native teachers who were products of Kuruman. Ross made his comments in his book on John Philip, whom he set over against Moffat. Yet Philip himself had reservations concerning the Khoikhoi converts. Even though Philip's policy was to paint as positive a picture as possible of the work done at Bethelsdorp, he was disturbed about the sexual morality of many Khoikhoi converts, and admitted that there were profound problems.[44] What Philip reluctantly admitted, Moffat, in the field, had to take action over. Many of Moffat's letters, referring to converts from Bethelsdorp, highlight the dishonesty and sexual laxity of these converts. Moffat had specific reservations concerning the group of six native teachers who were admitted to that office in 1814 by the LMS, and whose admission had been celebrated as a triumph in the advance of Christianity in southern Africa. In the following paragraphs we examine some of the 1814-six in detail

1. *Andries Waterboer.* As a young man at Klaarwater (Griqua Town), Andries Waterboer came under the influence of LMS missionaries who taught him to read and write, and he was baptised in 1807. Waterboer

---

11.6.1854, (*MJ1,* 177). At Moselekatse's kraal, Koboeapori was mentioned as being present with Moffat during discussions with the Ndebele chief, and on occasion was called on for prayer, cf. RM, *Journal,* 27.8.1854, (*MJ1,* 276). On none of these occasions was Koboeapori given a task of his own. He was Moffat's assistant, with the primary duty of wagon driver, which he was also on the 1854 and 1857 expeditions.

43 Ross, *John Philip 1775-1851,* 224.

44 John Philip, *Researches in South Africa, 1828,* 225f, 228.

became an interpreter for the mission, and then set apart as a native teacher in August 1814. He was subsequently suspended on an accusation of adultery, but in 1818 he was reinstated. Moffat only arrived in southern Africa in 1817, and was not responsible for Waterboer's early suspension. In 1820 Waterboer was elected as chief, which was a victory for the mission party among the Griqua.[45] At first he had the backing of the government at the Cape as well as of the missionaries but, 'in the course of conflicts with his neighbours and some internal disputes, he forfeited the confidence of both'.[46]

Waterboer's character did not impress Moffat, even though Waterboer brought his Griqua to help repulse the Mantatee in 1823. Moffat was critical of the way in which the Griqua behaved towards people after the battle, and was furious that Waterboer's men had shown no concern for the weak and wounded after their victory. It was this which prompted Moffat to spit out the phrase, 'Alas they are heathens still'.[47] In a letter to Mary, he wrote, 'I think that it would help to wash away the indelible stain which will mark the character of [Waterboer], were he to send two humane persons with a couple of wagons to rescue these objects of misery from their painful situation.'[48] And yet, could Moffat really expect warriors in the immediate aftermath of battle—a battle that Moffat himself reluctantly approved of—to turn immediately from fighting to nursing?

During the 1820s, Waterboer drifted further and further from Christian commitment. He joined with Cornelius Kok and led a group of bandits who at one time threatened to attack Kuruman itself.[49] Andries Waterboer was no positive advertisement for one who had been raised to the status of native teacher. In the latter years of his life, his relationship with the Cape Government and the missionaries improved and he became responsible for peacekeeping along the Gariep. He died in 1852.

2. *Berend Berends.* Berend Berends was another who failed to impress Moffat. He also had been set aside as 'an assistant preacher of the Gospel' in August 1814, and had been attached to the mission at Griqua Town.[50] On a

---

45 Cf. RM, *To John Melvill,* probably Jan. 1821, (*AAK,* 12). Also see: RM, *MLSSA,* 200. John Campbell was instrumental in getting Waterboer elected. Moffat, believing that a missionary should not interfere in the internal affairs of a tribe, disapproved of Campbell's actions.

46 Smith, Malherbe, Guenther, Berens (eds), *The Bushmen of Southern Africa,* 47.

47 RM, *Journal,* 26.6.1823, (*AAK,* 96).

48 RM, *To Mary Moffat,* 13.8.1823, (*AAK,* 107).

49 Mary Moffat, *To James Smith,* 8.6.1826, (*AAK,* 227).

50 *AAK,* 124: fn. 17.

journey in 1824, Moffat's party met up with Berends' Griqua group and Moffat noted in his *Journal:* 'Sabbath. My congregation, about forty in number, is indeed a mixed multitude. Some have had a name to live, but are now dead in trespasses and sin. One (Berend, a Griqua chief) was once a preacher of righteousness, but now a secret enemy to the cause he once espoused.'[51] A few years later, Berends, like Waterboer, had become an out-and-out bandit leader, specialising in cattle raids. It was the cattle raiding carried out by Berends on Moselekatse's Ndebele at Mosega, plus the savage reprisals which Moselekatse executed in return, which contributed to the abandonment of the early French mission to the Ndebele.[52]

It may be significant that the LMS used the title 'preacher of the Gospel', whereas Moffat preferred 'preacher of righteousness'. For Moffat, one of the main functions of the Gospel was to bring righteousness and holiness. The Gospel was first and foremost to glorify God, and God was glorified when righteousness was established upon the earth. It was vital, therefore, that righteousness and holiness were characteristic of those who preached. In Moffat's opinion Waterboer and Berends did not show that holiness.

3. *Cupido Kakerlak.* Some have viewed Cupido Kakerlak as one of the brightest stars of early LMS converts in southern Africa.[53] The LMS was keen at an early stage to promote Cupido as a success story, and it proudly published a letter written by him as an example of what the mission had achieved with an indigenous Griqua.[54] Cupido was also one of the six commissioned by the LMS in 1814. However, in 1821 Moffat visited Cupido and what Moffat saw did not live up to his view of what a Christian worker should be: 'The appearance of Cupido's house and family seems strongly to dictate that he does not intend to rise an hair breadth in civilisation above them whom he pretends to instruct.'[55] Two years later, on his way to visit Makaba, Moffat met Cupido again: once more Moffat was unimpressed.[56]

---

51 RM, *Journal,* 11.7.1824, (*AAK,* 123f), (our italics).

52 Briggs & Wing, *The Harvest and the Hope,* 61ff.

53 Briggs and Wing, *The Harvest and the Hope,* 20. Ross was of the same view.

54 LMS, *Transactions of the London Missionary Society, Vol. IV: 1813-1818,* 296.

55 RM, *Journal,* 24.5.1821, (*AAK,* 18). Schapera, (*AAK,* 18: fn.7), gives more information about Cupido in a footnote: 'This man, a Hottentot from Bethelsdorp, had accompanied Campbell on the latter's first journey to the BaThlaping in 1813. In the following year he was appointed an 'assistant preacher' of the LMS at the same time as Andries Waterboer. He was subsequently stationed among the Koranna at Nokaneng, close to 'Old Lattakoo', from which he was driven by the 'Mantatee' invasion of 1823.'

56 RM, *Journal,* 17.5.1823, (*AAK,* 79).

Moffat's standards were exacting. But they were applied to everyone. It was axiomatic in his thinking that true conversion would be evidenced by self-improvement in manners, appearance and custom. This view came not only from spiritual convictions, but from the social experience of Scotland in the late eighteenth and early nineteenth centuries. Within Scottish society many in the 'working classes' had come to believe that education and industry could bring social improvement, and that such improvement was a true sign of civilisation and godliness. Moffat's own family background, in which his father had risen from being a manual worker to being a minor civil servant, was an example. Christianity, more than anything else, was seen as the force which aided, abetted, and energised this 'elevation' of humanity. When Moffat found Cupido still living in unnecessarily wretched conditions, then he doubted the reality of his calling if not his conversion.

The case of Cupido demonstrates the gulf between Van der Kemp's approach at Bethelsdorp, and Moffat's approach at Kuruman. In Moffat's view Van der Kemp had 'gone native', and had not emphasised the need for converted indigenous peoples to improve their manner of life. What might pass at Bethelsdorp would not pass at Kuruman. But Moffat's criticisms of Cupido went further than simply appearance. Moffat was disappointed with Cupido's lack of zeal and lack of initiative. Cupido's appearance simply strengthened Moffat's conviction that offices such as 'native teachers' had been bestowed too freely and too soon. Even if some of Moffat's views concerning dress and life-style confused personal taste with Christian principles, there is no evidence that Moffat singled out Cupido for criticism simply because he was a Bethelsdorp man. At Kuruman, or in Scotland, the same standards would be applied with equal rigour.

4. *Jan Goeyman.* Goeyman was a converted Khoikhoi, also appointed as a native teacher by the LMS in August 1814. By 1825 he had given up preaching and concentrated on farming.[57] But in 1821 Goeyman was still in 'Gospel service' and Moffat wrote sympathetically and generously about him—contradicting Ross' generalisation that Moffat had nothing good to say about these early native teachers: 'The case of Jan Goeyman, who was appointed by Mr. Campbell to commence a mission to the Bushmen at the Kooning fountain, came before us.'[58] Our phrase 'the case of Jan Goeyman' may appear to imply that Goeyman was deemed guilty of fault. Not so. Moffat's

---

[57] Cf. *AAK,* 19, fn. 8. James Clark, formerly a member of Dr Philip's Church at Cape Town, was stationed at Philippolis in 1825 after the resignation of the native evangelist Jan Goeyman, (*AAK,* 235: fn. 35, and LMS *Report,* vol. xxxii, 1826, 82).

[58] RM, *Journal,* 20.6.1821, (*AAK,* 19).

criticisms were directed at Campbell who, Moffat believed, had misdirected Goeyman and given him an impossible mission. Moffat judged that it was evident that Campbell had never 'glanced at the many disadvantages to which the commencement of a mission at that place would be laid under.'[59]

There is no suggestion in Moffat's *Journal* entry that Goeyman was guilty of any moral or spiritual wrong, or that he was not up to the work if given proper direction. On the contrary, he commended Goeyman's energy and initiative: 'he was on that account anxious to be placed in a situation where he in the meantime could be doing something'. Moffat also recommended him for service at Griqua Town.[60] But Goeyman's resignation in 1825 disappointed Moffat, and may have added to his doubts concerning the quality of commitment found in these early native teachers. In his later writings Moffat lauded the achievements of the new generation of native teachers at Griqua Town who did excellent work during the 1830s.[61]

Moffat did have considerable grounds for questioning the quality of the first wave of native teachers appointed by the LMS in southern Africa. His attitude may well have been complicated by his personal feelings concerning Campbell and Read.[62] But he had genuine concerns, and these undermined his confidence in native agency. Of those whom he personally trained at Kuruman, many gave outstanding service. Despite that, Moffat still proceeded hesitatingly in this area when perhaps a bolder stroke was required. He understood indigenisation through language, but he did not pursue with equal vigour indigenisation through personnel. It would be a new generation who would view indigenisation of leadership as a priority issue from the start. The issue was summarised by John Smith Moffat:

> It is easy, looking back over the experience of half a century, to see how things might have been better done. ... There is a hope that in time there may be an indigenous native ministry sufficiently qualified to meet the wants of their own people with little or no guidance from Europeans. ... The Scotch missions in South Africa and in Nyasaland have long pursued this course, as at Lovedale, Blantyre, and the Overton Institute, and we see the fruits in numbers of well-qualified natives.[63]

---

59 RM, *Journal,* 20.6.1821, (*AAK,* 19).

60 RM, *Journal,* 20.6.1821, (*AAK,* 20).

61 RM, *MLSSA,* 204. Peter David and Jan Hendrick, also app. in 1814 are not discussed by RM.

62 Ross believed that James Read was traduced by Moffat. Yet Ross accepted that Read was guilty of adultery and had to be suspended. What Ross seemed unaware of was that when Moffat visited the reinstated Read in 1825 and saw the work he was doing, Moffat wrote to Kitchingham in warm fashion concerning Read, (Le Cordeur, *Kitchingham Papers,* 78ff).

63 RUM, *JSM,* 119f.

Chapter 34
The Pursuit of Sustainability

WHAT OF ANDERSON AND VENN'S THREE PRINCIPLES of self-propagation, self-governance and self-support? Did Moffat devise, or even begin to devise, a platform for the future? The three criteria, already alluded to in passing, we discuss in the following sections.

SELF-PROPAGATION.

If notable progress was made at Kuruman on lay-ministry, none was made on the full ordination of indigenous Africans. When Moffat left Africa in 1870 it was still the European missionary, visiting every few months, who dispensed the sacraments at out-stations where otherwise a native teacher fulfilled all other responsibilities of teaching, preaching, catechising, examining, and guiding the congregation in matters of discipline. The LMS as such did not ordain, since that would make it into a church rather than simply an arm of the churches. But that stricture did not apply to LMS mission stations which regarded themselves as churches in their own right, under a Congregationalist polity. In Congregationalism it was the congregation which decided who should be ordained, without reference to any area or national body. In 1867 the LMS published the followed statistics regarding its ordained native pastors.[1] The statistic for the African mainland is staggering.

Location	China	India	West Indies	South Seas	Madagascar	Africa
Those Ordained	3	24	4	2	6	1

If all Africans objected to having a native teacher rather than a European missionary, then it would have been difficult to introduce ordained native pastors. But not all villages across all Africa complained. Even in the Kuruman area, most out-stations were content with them. Could a start not have been made to promote more to full ministers of Word and Sacrament?

[1] LMS, *Report to the 73rd Annual Meeting, 1867*, 77f.

If Moffat, at Kuruman, erred in this regard, his fault was common to stations across southern Africa. The church at Kuruman had the freedom to nominate persons from among its number for ordination. But there is no evidence that Moffat encouraged that step. It is of course possible that he did encourage the congregation to do so, but that they preferred not to, wanting to have baptism, bread and wine from the hands of venerable missionary patriarchs. Yet there is no evidence for this.

The requirement for extensive theological education before ordination does affect the above figures. India, with a more advanced educational base, had an advantage. Nevertheless, it is astonishing that out of the many LMS stations in southern Africa, and after 68 years of the LMS operating there, the only station with an ordained native pastor was at Tidmanton. Moffat was not such a low-Churchman that ordination meant nothing to him. Things had to be done 'properly' and the sacraments should be administered by someone set aside for that responsibility. He expressed this view in an early letter to James Kitchingham.[2] But it seems that, in southern Africa as a whole, the LMS put few resources into formal theological education. Though Kuruman's remote location cannot be overlooked, any eye for the future should not have been blind to such an important requirement.

SELF-GOVERNANCE

We have seen previously that in the 1860s the LMS London leadership made the issue of indigenous ministry a major policy. Following this, in the 1870s the LMS urged churches which had been mission stations to prepare for a fully independent life. Moffat and Livingstone had earlier argued for this policy among the mission stations within the Cape Colony.[3] And after 1883 the annual accounts of the various mission churches ceased to appear in the annual LMS missionary report.[4] As already stated, it could be argued that any church founded on Congregationalist principles had an ethos of self-governance from its inception.[5] And though European missionaries retained

---

2 RM, *To Kitchingham,* 27.10.1818, (Le Cordeur, *Kitchingham Papers,* 54).

3 Cf. Moffat/Livingstone, *To Thompson (LMS agent in CT),* 22.11.1822: *DLSAP,* 111.

4 Horne, *The Story of the LMS, 1795-1895,* (Ldn: John Snow, 1895), 259.

5 The superintendency of John Philip was resented by Moffat, who saw it as compromising the independence of congregations. In 1843 the affairs of the Griqua and Tswana missions were formally set free from Philip's 'authority' and placed under the direction of a District Committee composed of local missionaries. This Committee was interpreted by most LMS missionaries as having the same role as area-meetings in English Congregationalism where representatives met in free association for mutual benefit. The first meeting of the newly-formed 'District Committee of the Griqua and Bechuana Mission' was held at Kuruman on 6 January 1844. There is no evidence of indigenous members attending early meetings.

considerable influence at Kuruman for many years, in theory they had no extra power in virtue of who they were. It was the church as a body which had authority. Thus, in theory at least, self-governance was established as soon as a congregation was established. This was a situation which was almost impossible in churches arising from Roman Catholic, Lutheran, Anglican or Presbyterian activity.[6] However, it took several generations before the personal influence of the missionaries decreased. This was despite the mission station churches having a Congregationalist structure, with every member 'equally' empowered.

As an aside, it may have been that the Congregationalist style of polity was one reason why Ethiopianism rarely affected Churches which sprang from LMS foundations. Ethiopianism was a religio-political movement in the late nineteenth and early twentieth centuries, which sought to establish African-led churches and promote a sense of African identity and nationalism. Churches affected by Ethiopianism were mostly those with a hierarchical structure.[7] In such churches, power was not located in the local community of ordinary members but elsewhere: in those holding special ordained office, in regional or area central committees, or even in the parent body back in Europe. Resentment over real or perceived foreign control was more liable to emerge in such organisations than in churches where the indigenous members of the congregation already had authority.

SELF-SUPPORT

True autonomy requires financial self-sufficiency. In the remote bush areas of southern Africa this goal was always going to be difficult to attain. Moreover, self-support involves more than money. It also requires a self-sufficiency in food, housing, clothing, etc. Moffat made a great contribution in that direction with his horticultural revolution enabling the Kuruman community to withstand the vicissitudes of a dry climate. However, if we concentrate on financial self-sufficiency the following points may be made:

1. *Native Teachers.* By 1867, Kuruman, by itself, was supporting five native teachers: 'Contributions from the faithful of £47 for the year from the

---

[6] Kuruman out-stations enjoyed considerable autonomy, especially in applying discipline, cf. LMS, *Report to the 55th Annual Meeting, 1849,* 104.

[7] Lye and Murray pointed out, 'A minor incursion [of Ethiopianism] occurred ... in the Tswana country at Taung in 1885. But the Ethiopian movement generally made little progress amongst the Southern Sotho and the Tswana.' (*Transformations,* 129). Lye and Murray further suggested that the lack of Ethiopianism amongst the Southern Sotho and the Tswana may have been because both the *Paris Evangelical Missionary Society* and the LMS had opposed settler intrusion on behalf of their respective African communities.

Kuruman area, almost enough to pay for the five native teachers at £10 each'.[8] The salary each received was not high, given that Mebalwe was already receiving £12 per annum in 1843. Nevertheless, Moffat's satisfaction in the ability of Kuruman members to finance this work is clear to see.

2. *European Missionaries.* The European missionaries at Kuruman were employees of the LMS. They received their salaries from London. The possibility of Kuruman being able to pay for them was never explored. This illustrates another tension between Kuruman as a church trying to exist by its own means, and Kuruman as a mission station, still dependent on the LMS.

3. *The Auxiliary.* At an early stage, Moffat introduced the concept of the Auxiliary. These were common in Britain, existing as supportive local arms of various organisations. The support they gave was both moral and financial. When Moffat introduced the Auxiliary at Kuruman, its purpose was to give support to the wider work of the LMS through prayer and offerings. In this way, Moffat tried to make Kuruman converts see themselves not simply as recipients from London, but as contributors to the world-wide work of mission. Initially, there was aid both coming *from* the LMS and going *to* the LMS. Whilst the greater amount was *from* the LMS to Kuruman—missionary salaries etc.—the contributions which went in the other direction helped to establish the important principle of making the local church aware of, and supportive of, the world-wide work of mission. This was further emphasised by Kuruman's participation in the annual January world-wide week of prayer organised by the *Evangelical Alliance.* At Kuruman, support of the Auxiliary was not optional for converts. It was seen as part of their Christian duty. If contributions were refused then that was a disciplinary matter.[9] In 1848 the Auxiliary raised £48 for the LMS.[10]

4. *The Church Building.* When the large Kuruman church was constructed in the 1830s, Moffat saw it as important that indigenous Africans had direct involvement, not simply through paid labour but through financial commitment. Moffat wrote with satisfaction to Ellis of the LMS attaching a

---

8 RM, *To Tidman, LMS,* 17.1.1866, (SOAS/CWM/SA/Box34/1/A).

9 E.g. RM, *To Freeman,* 20.3.1851, (SOAS/CWM/SA/Box 26/1/A). Cf. *KCRB,* 31.10.1862 (10), 'Magame and his wife Itsineng separated for irregularities of conduct, especially for neglecting the house of God, neglecting their children, and refusing to contribute to the Auxiliary.'

10 Details of annual contributions from the Kuruman church to the LMS can be found in *KCRB,* 99f. There are also detailed records in the SeTswana Kuruman newspaper *Mokaeri oa Becuana, le mulari oa Mahuku*. E.g. in the 1859 February edition there are listed contributions from (a) Ba-Seorin [Kuruman], £25-1-6; (b) BaTluaro, £5-12-8; and (c) BaLikhatlan, £29-1-6, (NLSA/Grey/10/c/22/4). These contributions are named *Phalalo* which, in Matumo's modern *SeTswana-English-SeTswana Dictionary,* means 'contributions to mission work'.

list of 120 subscribers who had raised a total of £20 to its construction.[11] The Moffat family was listed alongside African subscribers.

Apart from the payment of native teachers, the above did not add up to full financial self-sufficiency. Yet, at the same time, if missionary salaries are discounted, the church at Kuruman required little financial assistance from outside. There was also, of course, the work of Bible translation and printing, an integral part of Kuruman ministry, where paper, ink, letter-types etc. were heavily subsidised by the *British and Foreign Bible Society.* When Moffat finished his ministry at Kuruman in 1870 would Kuruman have survived if all foreign funding had been cut off? No. But Kuruman did have a form of church life which minimised the need for financial outlay. In Congregationalism, there was no large ecclesiastical superstructure to support. If a congregation could support itself, then, in Congregationalist polity, the church supported itself. In 1870, Kuruman had not yet reached the point where, from the resources of its own congregation, it could, by itself, support a full-time ministry plus general running costs, but was not far from doing so. But, in terms of belonging to a group of churches, financing a Training College plus the other expenses inevitably incurred by any group or association, then Kuruman had definitely not reached that stage. Nevertheless, Moffat did seek to instill a philosophy of financial responsibility, aiming to take the congregation beyond total dependence upon London.

The Moffat Institute

After Moffat retired in 1870 there was a campaign to establish a Moffat Institute for the training of indigenous Africans. The Moffat family, especially John Smith Moffat, was lukewarm, not because they rejected the concept but because they felt more could have been done by the LMS beforehand. The site chosen for the Moffat Institute was close-by the mission station. Despite good intentions, the Institute had problems. For example, after John Smith Moffat left Kuruman in 1877, local Africans saw themselves as being evicted from their homes to make room for the Institute building. Also, when a local 'rebellion' broke out, the British authorities were given permission to billet troops in the Institute building. Robert Unwin Moffat interpreted this as the Institute, bearing his grandfather's name, being used as a 'laager' for the 'protection' of missionaries and Europeans, and of the station becoming a base for armed men acting against the indigenous population.[12]

---

11 RM, *To Ellis, LMS,* 7.7.1838, (SOAS/CWM/SA/Box16/2/E).

12 RUM, *JSM,* 135f.

The population around Kuruman was decreasing. It was no longer the centre it once was. In its heyday Kuruman was on a major route from the Cape to the interior. But after gold and diamonds were discovered elsewhere, new routes bypassed the old mission station. By the mid-1880s, the explorers' road from Kuruman, pioneered by Moffat, had been bypassed by Cecil Rhodes' great northern railroad one hundred kilometres to the east, running through the Kimberley diamond fields, Vryburg, Mafikeng, Victoria Falls and beyond.[13] Then in 1904 the LMS instituted the Tiger Kloof Institute at Taung (Vryburg), which became a centre for training, under the leadership of W.C. Willoughby. This was built next to the railway and flourished under Willoughby's leadership. By the end of the nineteenth century, in every missionary society working among the Tswana and Southern Sotho, including the LMS, African teachers were prominent.[14]

*

We started our reflections on the development, or otherwise, of indigenous ministry by referring to Livingstone's comments when he arrived at Kuruman. We conclude with him. By the time Moffat returned to Kuruman in 1843, Livingstone had begun to change his mind about Moffat's strategy:

> He is not, as I was informed by some that knew him, in the least opposed to native agency. He is a warm friend to them, but his character has been sadly traduced by many who ought to have known better. He told me the reason of the slander brought against him was his having got an unworthy character turned out of that office ... Nearly all great men have their slanderers and traducers.[15]

---

13 Cf. Mark Irvine, 'Tiger Kloof', *Optima* (February 1996).

14 Lye & Murray, *Transformations,* 67.

15 Livingstone, *To Mr & Mrs Livingston,* 16.12.1843 (Kuruman), (*DLFL,* Vol. 1, 89).

THE VEXED QUESTION OF CIVILISATION

Chapter 35
The Concept of Civilisation

CIVILISATION WAS PART OF the LMS vision. And the LMS—Moffat included—had a very specific understanding of what civilisation was, connecting it with the coming millennial reign of Christ. Later missionaries, such as the German Bruno Gutmann in Tanzania, who did not share the same millennial paradigm as Moffat and his contemporaries, were less sanguine about the benefits of 'civilisation' especially if what it meant was Europeanisation. Gutmann called European civilisation a blatant blasphemy.[1] But the LMS came from an earlier time. It was founded at the close of the Enlightenment century, and infused with ideas of progress and development. The early LMS was confident of the scientific, literary and intellectual achievements of a European culture which, if not identical with Christian values, had certainly been shaped by them. The LMS came from a tradition of 'improvement', whereas Gutmann came from the Romanticist tradition of affirming 'natural goodness'. Yet, as a product of the Evangelical Revival, the LMS never made a direct equation between any culture and Christianity. The doctrine of original sin precluded that possibility, even in a so-called 'Christian' society.

The LMS saw itself as participating in the inauguration of the Kingdom of God on earth, as part of the millennial reign of the Prince of Peace, and it viewed the process of civilisation as falling within that vision. In the opening pages of the very first volume of its *Transactions of the Missionary Society:*

---

[1] Cf. Klaus Fiedler, *Christianity and African Culture*. Gutman's instinct was to affirm cultural practices which had arisen naturally within indigenous traditions, interpreting these as a primal vision of God, even among those who had not yet heard of Christ. He deplored the emergence of the commercial society, seeing it as creating the fragmentation of community and the rise of individualism. In his view, commercialism and industrialisation made people lose their dignified humanity, hence becoming 'uncivilised'. This ran counter to the thinking which emerged in Calvinist, Presbyterian, Enlightenment Scotland. German Romanticism majored on 'feeling' and 'tradition', and an appreciation of the individualities of different cultures. Romanticism tried to be non-Eurocentric, stressing mother tongue, mother culture, as God-given gifts to particular peoples. Gutmann picked up on Schleiermacher's view that folk-hood was part of the divine gift of being in the Imago Dei. He wanted to implant Christianity within traditional society, not uproot individuals from it. He saw European civilisation as a bigger enemy than Islam, because it destroyed the social organisms which were destined by God to be the vessel to receive the gospel. In Gutmann's view, ATR was not an enemy to the gospel, since Christianity brought *fulfillment* to traditional religion, not *conquest* over it.

1795-1802, the LMS made reference to eighteenth-century explorers such as Captain James Cook, commenting that voyages of discovery in the Southern Ocean brought to light unknown countries, and innumerable groups of fertile islands, 'which invite the visits of the humane, to soften, by *civilisation*, the savage customs of their inhabitants, and to communicate to them the inestimable blessings of true religion.'[2] 'Civilisation' and 'true religion' were part of transformational progress, and there was a commonly accepted connection between them. Roby stating in his opening theological lecture: 'Without an acknowledgment of the Being of God civilised society could not exist.'[3] Roby saw correct knowledge of God as the pre-requisite factor to initiate a process toward true civilised life. Evangelism and civilising were inextricably linked.

What constituted a civilised society? This is a controversial question, especially when, in an eighteenth and nineteenth-century context, parts of Europe, including Scotland, were also deemed by some to be uncivilised.[4] John Mackintosh, in his four volume, *The History of Civilisation in Scotland (1895),* argued, somewhat controversially and unfairly, that even into the nineteenth century the Clans of Scotland required civilising.[5] Putting aside Mackintosh's prejudices, what is significant is that for Mackintosh, as for others, it was the factors of peace, security, law, order and learning which defined civilisation, with absence of these indicating a lack of it. It was the perceived deficiency of these specific qualities which prompted some commentators in Cape Town, in the 1820s, to describe even Spain as a 'degraded country'.[6] Such words were not reserved for the interior of Africa.

Law and order, peace and humane behaviour, were regarded as foundational to civilised life. Good religion and good education[7] were important, but it was good law which provided the basis for all else. Only on the foundation of good law could the superstructure of a civilised society be

---

2 LMS, *Transactions,* Vol. 1: 1795-1802, x. Bogue frequently used 'barbarous' as an antonym for 'civilisation', meaning 'total ignorance and cruelty' (*Miss. Lect.* 12, 'Fields of Mission: I).

3 Roby, *Theol. Lect.* 1, 'The Existence or Being of God'. This was on the first page which Moffat transcribed in 1817). Roby's statement saw 'right knowledge of God' (through evangelism) as preceding true civilisation. This was the evangelical position: evangelism preceded civilisation. Cf. RM, *Africa,* 43: 'We might have preached civilisation to the end of our lives; [but] our efforts, without the Gospel, would have ended in mortification.'

4 Cf. Samuel Johnson, *Journey to the Western Islands of Scotland,* (1775): Chapman (ed.), *Johnson and Boswell; Tour to the Hebrides,* (Ldn: OUP, 1933), 23, 31, 49, 45.

5 Mackintosh, *The History of Civilisation in Scotland,* III, (Ldn: Gardner, 1895), 225ff.

6 *The South African Commercial Advertiser,* No. 6, 11.2.1824, 41, (Reprint: CT: NLSA, 1978).

7 Bogue stressed education: 'Knowledge acquired will tend to raise them out of the state of barbarism and bring them towards civilisation.' (*Miss. Lect.* 10, 'Of Setting up Schools').

erected. Though a few people identified 'civilisation' with European culture as expressed in the polite manners of society, this was not the dominant equation. It was more important for there to be law and order, peace and humane behaviour. These were the essential attributes which made for a civilised society. If sometimes civilisation was identified with European culture, it was because it was thought that the attributes of law and order, peace and humane behaviour, were values at the heart of European life. European wars, and other undesirable occurrences, were viewed as temporary interruptions to the settled state of things, which was one of civilisation. This contrasted the state of things elsewhere in the world, in Africa for example, where the settled state of society was viewed as lacking these qualities and hence was uncivilised. The LMS postmillennial theology of the coming reign of the Prince of Peace fitted into this world-view. Mission would not only produce converts, saving them from everlasting loss, but would also establish stable and peaceful societies. What mechanism might stimulate a transition from perceived barbarism to civilisation? As we shall see, Moffat and the LMS did their work at a time when a Kamesian analysis of society was widely accepted. Accordingly, they believed that, alongside preaching, the practice of agriculture would create the types of communities necessary for civilisation and the reign of the coming King.

Comparisons and Contrasts

In a modern and multi-cultural worldview, the idea of bringing civilisation to another place or people is judged inappropriate since civilisation is deemed to be relative. Moreover, since civilisation is closely related to culture, then, just as diversity in culture is to be celebrated, so should diversity in civilisation. Schoeman, when discussing the early Griqua Town missionaries, argued that the missionaries judged native African culture by the standards of contemporary northern Europe and hence, in their estimation, found them sadly wanting, and reported home accordingly, with damning verdicts on traditional culture.[8] This was the line taken by most white observers of the time, and the portrait of native African life which emerged from the earliest accounts was invariably negative.[9] The European home-population assumed that any sensible person would prefer a European style way of life.

This assumption was questioned when Moffat brought Peclu and Teysho to Cape Town in 1824. Peclu was heir apparent to Mothibi of the BaThlaping,

---

8 Schoeman, *The Mission at Griquatown*, 13.

9 The confusion of European culture with Christianity is analysed by Kwame Bediako, 'Christianity as Civilisation', *Theology and Identity,* 225-266.

and Teysho was one of the BaThlaping under-chiefs. Moffat took them to the Cape to impress them with the European way of life in the Colony, and make them more open to the progress he wanted to institute at Kuruman.[10] Whilst Moffat, Peclu and Teysho were in Cape Town, the newly formed *South African Journal* interviewed Teysho about his impression of life there. As reported by the *Journal*, Teysho replied, 'each was best for those who were used to it', and though he saw that 'we were a wiser and more knowing people than the Bechuanas, from long habit he preferred the customs and manner of life of his own country to ours'.[11] Teysho pointed to choice and preference, rather than to one culture being superior to another. His reply was a modern one, and raised important questions.

For example, what is the vital factor, or combination of factors, which makes a society regard itself as more civilised than another? Is it humane behaviour instead of barbarism? Is it technological advance instead of primitive methods? Is it reading and writing, with an accompanying educational system? Is it urbanisation? Does civilisation begin to exist when society makes room for the fine arts? Is it refinement of habits and manners? Is it a more 'sophisticated' religion? Is it the democratisation of society, and the establishment of an impartial legal system? Is it the adoption of a liberal world-view in which freedom is a valued and assured principle? Is it complexity rather than simplicity? Yet, why should a society which has progressed technologically be considered more civilised? Should we identify civilisation with simple village lifestyle? What are the parameters which decide which society has enabled the human spirit to rise farthest? On all these points, vigorous dispute can and does take place. The nineteenth century assumption, that European civilisation had vastly more plus marks than African society, no longer has consensus support.

During the nineteenth century, cruelty, distress, oppression and unfairness existed on the home front in Britain as much as in regions being evangelised by missionaries elsewhere in the world. In the same century as Moffat worked in so-called 'darkest Africa', General Booth, founder of the Salvation Army, wrote his book, *In Darkest England and the Way Out.*[12] At the same time as Mary Moffat taught the refinements of sewing to Tswana ladies,[13] the cotton mills in her native Lancashire were employing men,

---

[10] Moffat took Africaner to Cape Town in 1819 with the same intention.

[11] *The South African Journal, No. 1, 1824,* (Reprint: CT: NLSA, 1974), 79. Teysho's phrase 'wiser and more knowing' was probably directed towards European technology, such as the huge ships floating in Cape Town harbour, which astonished him and Peclu.

[12] William Booth, *In Darkest England and the Way out,* (1890).

[13] Cf. Dickson, *Beloved Partner.*

women and children in appalling conditions, tantamount to slave labour in all but name. As Kuruman was publishing Christian literature in SeTswana, Charles Dickens was publishing novels laying bare the social and economic misery of the working under-classes in a metropolis widely regarded as the world centre of civilisation. In Highland Scotland, whole villages were being ruthlessly cleared through forced eviction and emigration by callous landlords. Given these realities, why should the simplicity of community in an African village be regarded as less civilised than the complexity of an urbanised and industrialised society? But Moffat came from a culture which had confidence in its own ideals, and he was convinced he was taking civilisation to Africa. Yet there is evidence that, when he compared African society with British society, he did not always give a positive verdict on his own culture. He knew the barbaric recent history of his own nation.[14] In 1857 he read Ferguson's *History of England,* and came to some uncomfortable conclusions:

> Surely no nation on the face of the earth was ever saddled with such a low, despicable, sensual, furious, cruel, faithless, lawless, beastly and bloody set of kings. In reading of their dreadful lives, one cannot help adopting the language of the historian, 'Oh that time had woven so thick a veil as for ever to hide these things from human vision!'[15]

When Moffat wrote these words, he was only a few days away from again meeting Moselekatse, whose tyrannical rule he elsewhere described in unsparing terms. Depicting monarchs of England—belonging to supposedly civilised Christendom—in similar fashion was revealing. Also, Moffat did not hesitate to put England's infamous female suicide rate in the same league as that of the Ndebele.[16] And, in a letter to his son-in-law James Vavasseur, he wrote: 'We need not go very far back into the history of our own country to see what a rough set our forefathers were.'[17] Moffat knew of evils and sins in European life. Yet, the opinion of many within the Cape colony was that Britain was the apex of civilisation.[18] Whatever had happened in the past, things were now different.

---

14 Moffat was Scottish, but occasionally used the term 'English' to describe his nationality.

15 RM, *Journal*, 16.9.1857, (*MJ2*, 68). Robert Ferguson, *New and Popular History of England,* (Ldn: Cassell, 1850).

16 RM, *Journal*, 5.10.1857, (*MJ2,* 84).

17 RM, *To James Vavasseur,* 4.10.1863, (SOAS/CWM/Africa/Moffat/Pers/4).

18 E.g. *The South African Journal,* No. 1, 1824, 7*:* 'The name of Britain we need only mention when it is desired to confirm the courage and enlarge the hopes of philanthropy ... [Then praise of British literature, education, constitution, and love of humanity (!)] ... *Britain stands at the head of the history, - of the reality,- almost of the hopes of Man'* (our italics). A similar sentiment was expressed in *The South African Commercial Advertiser,* No. 1, 7.1.1824: 'How

The philosophy of progress and improvement, which Moffat had imbibed from infancy, contributed to a positive view of contemporary society. Thus, though willing to admit that previous generations had no claim to be morally or socially better than 'uncivilised' regions, there was an underlying conviction that current British society and civilisation did represent an apogee of human achievement which was worth reproducing elsewhere. Contrasting it with Moselekatse's brutal regime, Moffat saw his country as an 'enlightened, free and happy land':

> I heard this evening that a man who had been suspected of witchcraft and had been seen joking with the king's [Moselekatse's] wives, was impaled this morning. These are the 'dark places of the earth'. To those conversant with history these things are only what has been acted a thousand times over and [are] still going on in 'kingdoms wide that sit in darkness'[19] and were acted not long ago in our own enlightened, free and happy land.[20]

And yet, around the time Moffat was writing his *Journals* in the 1850s, Elizabeth Gaskell was writing her novel *Mary Barton,*[21] which focused on the misery of life in industrial Manchester. The Moffats had visited Manchester during their leave from 1839 to 1842, which were desperate years for the Manchester working-classes. Were the Moffats blind to the situation at home? Or did they view Moselekatse's barbarism as of a different order? Moffat was aware that misery existed in contemporary England, and knew of contemporary evils which existed in Europe.[22] In Europe, as much as in Africa, he saw war waged with attendant robbery, dominion and oppression. And when he spoke of 'civilised' Europe, he did not mean that European life was absolutely good and worthy of imitation in every respect. Nevertheless, despite caveats, Moffat did believe that life in Europe was less barbaric, more peaceful, and more in accordance with the Word of God than that which existed so far in Africa. However, though Moffat did not overlook the evils

---

stands our native land? Happy, thrice happy ... protected by the invaluable ramparts of her unrivalled Constitution, and guided by Councils of justice and moderation, Great Britain has added another year of peace and gradual prosperity to that long period of tranquility which we hope the Almighty Ruler of Events will crown the efforts she had made for the protection of the Rights and Liberties of herself and her confederates.' This was the standard view of the British colonial exile. Similarly, William Henderson, following the 1857 Indian Mutiny, argued that the way to advance civilisation was for more British people to live in India to pass on their influence! See: Henderson, *The Evangelisation and Civilisation of India: A Sermon delivered on the National Fast Day, October 7th, 1857,* (Edin: Grant & Son, 1857), 17, 20, 23.

19 A line taken from the hymn 'O'er those gloomy hills of darkness' by the revivalist Welsh preacher and hymn-writer William Williams, possibly based on Isaiah 42:7.

20 RM, *Journal*, 12.8.1854, (*MJ1*, 259).

21 Elizabeth Gaskell, *Mary Barton,* (1848).

22 RM, *Journal*, 9.6.1854, (*MJ1*, 168), (our italics).

existing in European society, what he seemed to miss, or at least did not record, were some of the positive advantages in African society, though he did refer to one African merit, a lack of immodest dancing! When Moffat described Ndebele dancing in honour of Moselekatse, he noted: 'Heathenish and savage as these people are, there is no mingling of sexes in the dance, as in the *barbarous* Polkas of Europe'.[23]

The Scottish Model

We cannot examine the whole concept of civilisation. Our task is to explore Moffat's understanding of it, and his convictions concerning the importance of introducing it to southern Africa. When Moffat referred to civilisation, or civilised society, there were two ways in which he could understand the concept. It could refer to the socio-economic basis of society; or it could refer to the manners and customs of society.

The first of these interpretations was to the fore in the transformation of Scotland, especially through the agricultural revolution. We previously noted that John Cockburn of Ormiston, Moffat's family village, was a innovationist in agricultural methods. Cockburn was not unique. He was but one of several wealthy landlords with progressive ideas, who changed rural Scotland from poor, bare, tree-less inefficient farmland—barely able to feed its inhabitants—to a more prosperous country. Whatever other factors laid the basis for enlightenment Scotland, the transformation of its rural economy, creating a radically new environment, was crucial. Rural transformation provided the basis of a society in which other 'higher' notions could be put into practice. Moffat's conviction that agriculturalisation would solve many problems in southern Africa needs to be interpreted in the light of the eighteenth-century transformation of his homeland.

Symon, in his work, *Scottish Farming: Past and Present,* has pointed out that Scotland, in the late-seventeenth and early-eighteenth centuries, had several years of blight and famine, when oats sometimes rose to ten times their former price, with dire consequences.[24] During the 'seven ill years', at the close of the seventeenth century, thirteen out of sixteen resident farm families perished in Monquitter parish, Aberdeenshire. The times were

---

23 RM, *Journal*, 21.9.1854, (*MJ1*, 310). This was the only aspect of African dancing which Moffat commended. The strong connection between African dancing, religious beliefs, sexual practices, and warlike activities made it barbarous in his eyes. Both Robert and John Smith Moffat were repulsed by the sight of Moselekatse's warriors dancing and striking the point of the shield on the ground to signify the number of men they had killed.

24 J.A. Symon: *Scottish Farming: Past and Present,* (Edin: Oliver & Boyd, 1959), 103ff.

desperate. The landscapes were treeless. The land was poor. There were tracks instead of roads. There were pathetic crops. Men such as Cockburn realised that the run-rig system in Scotland, in which the same small parcels of land were sown and cropped year after year, was not the way ahead.[25] But Cockburn saw that there were alternatives, including a crop rotational system and the granting of long-leases, which could benefit both landowner and tenant.[26] And so the area east of Edinburgh, including Haddingtonshire and Ormiston, was in the vanguard of agricultural progress. Fletcher of Saltoun, a doughty opponent of union with England, had been aware of the need for change even earlier. There was also the Countess of Haddington, who persuaded her husband, the sixth Earl, to abandon his beloved field sports to further agriculture and forestry. As early as 8 June 1723 *The Honourable the Society of Improvers* was founded in Edinburgh. Other land-owners, ranging from Aberdeenshire in the north, to Galloway in the south, pursued similar policies. Some, like Craik of Arbigland, were influenced by Jethro Tull.[27] A reported 50 million trees were planted by Archibald Grant of Monymusk, alongside other changes.[28] Others could be named.

Landowners were the only group with resources to invest in the rural economy. There was no assistance from the national Parliament. Help had been negligible when the Parliament sat in Edinburgh, and when it removed to London in 1707 there was none whatever. It is to the credit of many eighteenth-century Scottish landowners that they invested as they did—with ideas and not simply money. The enthusiasm of King George III, known as 'Farmer George', was also a factor, since 'high society' frequently imitated the monarch. The first Corn Laws initially assisted the process by protecting farmers against cheap foreign imports. These gave farmers 'breathing-space' whilst going through transition. However, after the Napoleonic Wars ended

---

[25] Scottish Law Lords were at the forefront of enlightened thought. Lord Jeffery, Lord Cockburn, Lord Kames, and Lord Monboddo, made immense contributions. Of the three traditional 'professions' in Scotland (Law, Medicine, and Divinity), it was the wealthy Law Lords who had the time to indulge in their outside interests.

[26] In 1718, Adam Cockburn gave a 38-year lease to Robert Wight, with 19-year options thereafter, and his leases were arranged for three generations. Cockburn built the village of Ormiston with trees, wide streets, and neat stone houses. After John Cockburn succeeded to the estate in 1734, he offered advantageous feu conditions if householders held to his principles. The long leases benefited the likes of Wight but, during a period of severe inflation, they impoverished Cockburn. This led to him selling Ormiston Hall in the 1740s (Anon, 'John Cockburn of Ormiston', *The Farmer's Magazine,* Vol 5, 1804, 129-147).

[27] Jethro Tull was an English agriculturist, known for his innovations in farming techniques and equipment. His ideas were incorporated in a book, *The New Horse Houghing [Hoeing] Husbandry* (1731), greatly expanded in 1733.

[28] Symon, *Scottish Farming: Past and Present,* 110.

in 1815, the Corn Laws resulted in a capitalist form of protectionism which resulted in the price of corn being kept so high that many could not afford bread. The hardship was not felt on the farms, where workers were paid in kind as well as cash, but was intense in the towns whose inhabitants had to pay the market rate.

Issues of poverty, health, security and education were all linked to the central problem of the land being unable to feed the people. Therefore, as agriculture changed for the better, so did other aspects of life. This bred a conviction that civilised society depended on the state of agriculture. This principle, proven by experience, was expounded philosophically by Lord Kames. A revolution took place. Scotland's energies, 'for centuries held fast in the grip of feudalism, superstition, internal and external strife, religious discord, misrule, and fanatical adherence to outmoded customs and practices, had been released.'[29] In industry, trade, art, literature, science, medicine, and architecture, striking advances took place. Scottish thinkers, artists, and political economists achieved international fame. Critically, the mood of 'improvement' which swept over Scotland during the eighteenth century was built on a reappraisal of the agricultural base of society.[30]

Moffat came from a nation which had gone through fundamental change. There was radical improvement in society as a whole, with the agricultural revolution the driving-force for much of what had gone right. Food security controls the health of any nation, determining the potential for advance in the economic, political, and cultural life of society. No society which struggles to exist can develop at higher levels. This was what Scotland had experienced. Given this background, it is not surprising that, for Moffat, the term 'civilisation' was frequently placed alongside comments on progress in horticulture and agriculture. Though the term was occasionally associated with other factors, such as 'polite manners', the predominant concern for Moffat was changing the socio-economic basis of society through the advancement of horticulture and agriculture.

When Moffat came across the 'Kuruman Eye', a permanent natural spring of water in the sub-Kalahari, disgorging hundreds of thousands of gallons of water every day of the year, he must have thought that his every dream and

---

29 Ibid, 141.

30 In 1754, the poet Allan Ramsay established *The Select Society* which was concerned with cultural advancement. A philosophy of improvement also lay behind Sinclair's mammoth project, *A Statistical Account of Scotland,* which covered every parish in the land.

prayer were fulfilled.[31] This made the Kuruman site far superior to anything he had come across in Africaner's Namaqua country.[32] The 'Eye' supplied the water, and Moffat's canal took it where it was needed. The mission station was three miles from the Eye, but Moffat dug a trench which proved useable for the next ninety years. Its course is still traceable today. Moffat now had the necessary ingredients of water and land, with which he could initiate a sociological revolution built on the development of agriculture. Moffat himself observed that, if he had continued at the previous station, 'a complete barrier was ever in our way of being useful in point of civilisation, *which must originate and depend on the culture of the ground*.'[33]

For Moffat, civilisation originated and depended on the culture of the ground. Civilisation was linked with tilling the soil. Yet much more lay behind that link than Moffat's personal interest in gardening. His linking of 'civilisation' and horticulture was expressed in an even earlier letter, written to Kitchingham, concerning the mission station at Pella: 'Much has been done as it regards civilisation under Mr. Bartlett; there is an abundance of water, about 30 gardens.'[34] Moffat equated civilising with Bartlett's efforts in the direction of agriculture. To take another example, in 1835 Moffat reported that at Kuruman, the number of houses was 236, that the people possessed 11 wagons and 3 ploughs; that the cultivation of ground was extending; and that the settlement was prospering in regard to the circumstances of the people, as well as in their spiritual improvement.[35] This was a typical Moffat way of reporting progress in terms of civilising. And as early as 1805, the Cape Governor had specified that any permitted missions were to be involved in the task of 'teaching and promoting *religion* and *cultivation* among the heathen nations.'[36]

It is no surprise that annual LMS forms, issued to all stations, and not just to Kuruman, laid stress on the state of agriculture. The following extract from the 1835 Kuruman return demonstrates this. This large form had sections for

---

31 Kuruman was not Eden. There were limits to the amount of ground able to be irrigated. 'The irrigable gardens at Kuruman are, however, comparatively few in number and limited in extent, and the country being unfavourable to cattle, great distress frequently prevails' (Mackenzie, *Ten Years North,* 70).

32 Cf. Du Plessis, *A History of Christian Missions in South Africa*, 156: 'It was soon apparent to Moffat that the spot where Africaner's kraal stood was no place in which to gather a community or establish a mission. The country was barren in the extreme. Water was scarce and poor in quality. No garden could be planted, no wheat grown, no vegetables raised.'

33 RM, *Journal,* 30.5.1825, (*AAK,* 188) (our italics).

34 RM, *To Kitchingham*, 13.1.1818, (Le Cordeur, *Kitchingham Papers*, 53).

35 LMS, *Annual Reports* 1835, 96.

36 Governor J.W. Janssens, *Proclamation for the Work of Missionaries*, 20.2.1805.

population statistics, church statistics, and educational statistics; but the major part, with the most detailed questions, related to the state of agriculture. We again emphasise that this was not a form drafted specifically for Moffat's Kuruman. It was for each and every LMS station.[37]

Cattle & Implements						
Horses	Oxen	Cows and Calves	Sheep	Goats	Waggons	Ploughs
16	750	687	630	780	6	2

Land & Houses					
Morgens of:					No. of Houses
Premises	Garden Ground	Corn Fields	Meadow	Common	
					279

State Of Cultivation							
Sown or planted							Tobacco[38] grown, lbs.
Bushels of						No. of Trees[39]	
Wheat	Oats[40]	Barley	Rye	Peas & Beans	Potatoes		
171	180	6	74	7	16	1660	680

David Livingstone shared this belief in the importance of agriculture. In a letter to his sister, he wrote of how pleased he was that ploughs were so cheap at Uddingston, a Scottish village near his own hometown of Blantyre.

---

37 LMS, *Schedule to be made annually by Missionaries in SA*, (SOAS/CWM /SA/Box15).

38 Livingstone favoured cotton. On Moffat recommending tobacco, see: RM, *Journal*, 30.5.1825, (*AAK*: 187).

39 The section for trees is important. It parallelled a policy of reforestation which took place in England and Scotland during the eighteenth century.

40 Moffat erased 'Oats' and wrote 'Mays' (maize). He also erased 'Rye' and wrote 'Millet'.

He added that Moffat had urged him to order one from Uddingston; if they are good we shall have learned something.'[41]

The LMS was not the only mission organisation with a strong emphasis on agriculture. Moffat's friend, the Wesleyan missionary Barnabas Shaw, also underscored its importance.[42] What the missionaries sought to accomplish in southern Africa was to introduce knowledge which had benefited their own countries.[43] Their intention was to give what they believed was the best, even if sometimes they were naïve in their interpretation of the situation. In Scotland, the Moffat family had experienced nothing but benefit from the Agricultural Revolution, and from the emerging Industrial Revolution which had brought the Carron Iron Works to Bothkennar Parish, providing employment, security and relative wealth.[44] These were seen as the way ahead, and the missionaries wanted Africa to know the same benefits.

THE KAMESIAN THEORY OF CIVILISATION

A focus on agriculture suited Moffat, with his personal interest in gardening. But a deeper philosophical theory, connecting agriculture and civilisation, existed within Scottish thinking, feeding into Moffat's understanding. An overarching theory of societal development was promoted by the Scottish Law-Lord, Lord Kames (Henry Home).[45] Kames put forward an intellectual analysis which sought to explain why agriculturalisation produced a higher civilisation. In Kames' thinking, 'becoming civilised' was a process involving a fundamental movement of society from a 'lower' socio-economic state to a 'higher' one. It was his socio-economic understanding of civilisation, adopted

---

41 Livingstone, *To Janet Livingstone,* 20.2.1849, (*DLFL,* Vol. 2, 36). Cf. Livingstone, *To Mr and Mrs Livingstone,* 9.2.1851, (*DLFL,* Vol. 2, 119).

42 Cf. Shaw, *Memorials of South Africa,* 192.

43 When *The South African Commercial Advertiser* was founded as a weekly newspaper in Cape Town in 1824, its prospectus of 20.12.1823 made a direct link between civilisation and agriculture: 'As we are desirous of obtaining the earliest information tending to improvements in Agriculture, we shall be happy to receive communications from persons acquainted with the Branch of Science'. See; *SACA,* (Reprint: CT, NLSA, 1978).

44 Adam Smith had pointed out that any national economic strategy should look beyond agriculture to commerce. Smith did recognise that different countries might have different bases: some would have commerce based on agriculture, others would have commerce based on manufacture (Smith, *An Inquiry into the Nature and Causes of the Wealth of Nations,* IV/9).

45 Alongside Cockburn, Kames was one of the foremost agricultural innovators. He had two farms: one in Berwickshire, and the other, through his wife, at Blair Drummond in the Forth Valley. At Blair Drummond, he raised part of the waters of the River Teith by 17 feet through means of a water wheel, storing the water in reservoirs and releasing it when necessary. He also advocated the teaching of agricultural science by Edinburgh University. This was a new concept in a University traditionally devoted to the classics.

by such figures as Adam Smith,[46] which lay behind Moffat's approach. Though the LMS did not consciously borrow from Kames, it adopted the Kamesian model through it being contemporary wisdom.

As a legal man, the underlying motive for Kames' studies was his desire to answer questions such as 'Why do laws exist?' and 'What makes it possible for human beings not only to institute rules and regulations for their conduct, but also to agree to abide by them?'[47] His initial answer was a well-known one: laws were instituted to protect property since a sense of property marked the starting line for all social relationships.[48] He wrote that the 'sense of property' was an inherent sense in humanity; that without private property there would be no industry;[49] and that without industry men would remain savages forever.[50] He argued that it was the desire to protect property which made human beings willing to surrender personal freedoms and become a community governed by law, hence becoming a *civilised* society.[51] Being civilised was equivalent to being law-abiding. Another Enlightenment Scot, Francis Hutcheson, taught an idealist theory, proposing that humans formed governments in order to pursue the common good from an instinctive altruism.[52] Kames had a more sceptical view of human nature, viewing self-interest as the basis for law, not altruism.[53] Kames' theory about the basis of law was not original. What was new was his theory about human

---

46 Martin Cohen, *Smith's 'Wealth of Nations',* (Ldn: Hodder & Stoughton, 2001), 19, wrote: 'In the *Wealth of Nations* Adam Smith invariably, even monotonously, writes of four stages of society: an age of hunters; an age of shepherds; an agrarian age; and, an age of commerce.' Like Kames, Smith argued that society only begins to need laws and government in the second stage. Broadie, *The Scottish Enlightenment: An Anthology,* 476f, has an account of Smith's version of the four-stage theory, almost identical to Kames'.

47 Herman, *The Scottish Enlightenment*, 81. Cf. Kames, *Essays Upon the Principles of Morality and Natural Religion* (Edin: 1751). See also: Kames, *Historical Law Tracts* (Edin: 1758).

48 Herman, *The Scottish Enlightenment*, 81.

49 By 'industry' Kames meant 'productive work'. This applied to agriculture as much as to 'industry' in the narrower sense.

50 Kames, *Sketches of the History of Man, Vol. 1*, 63, 67.

51 Kames' emphasis on law was a typically Calvinist way of thinking. Though Calvin did not use the word civilisation, his remarks on what constituted a decent society focused on good law and order being applied by a Christian civil magistrate (Cf. Calvin's *Commentaries* on Psalm 82:5, Romans 13:3, 1 Timothy 2:2). In Calvin's thought, peace and security were essential for a good society to flourish. Wallace, *Calvin's Doctrine of the Christian Life,* (Edin: Oliver &Boyd, 1959), pointed out that, for Calvin, it was when the Christian Civil Magistrate was making good laws for society that the *Imago Dei* was being established (161, referring to *Institutes* IV, xx, 4). Good law and order were fundamental for good society (civilisation).

52 Hutcheson taught that humanity was, or could be, motivated by benevolence as much as by selfishness. This contrasted traditional Calvinism.

53 Cf. Herman, *The Scottish Enlightenment*, 82, & Daiches, Jones, & Jones, (eds): *The Scottish Enlightenment 1730-1790,* (Edin: Saltire Society, 1996), 23.

societies which he built on that foundation. It led him to develop his four-stage theory of civilisation, with the third stage particularly important.[54]

1. *Hunting and Fishing Communities.* In Kames' analysis, hunting and fishing were the original occupations of humanity.[55] But the hunter or fisher tended to avoid other humans apart from family. Kames saw the San of South Africa and the Eskimo as examples of such communities. Moffat described the San in a way corresponding to Kames' analysis: 'They exist a wandering people without homes, or cattle, or even nationality of character.'[56]

2. *Pastoral Nomadic Communities.* Kames noted that successful hunter-gathering necessitated a development of society. Food-surplus promoted population. But, as consumption of food increased with population, then wild animals became rarer and shyer. Pressed for food, men tried other means for supplying their wants.[57] They learned to follow the animal herds and how to domesticate them. This created larger societies of clans and tribes, though as yet with only a loose connection between them.[58] Growth of population, with competing land needs, inevitably demanded a new stage in societal evolution since, 'neighbouring tribes, straitened in their pasture, go to war for extension of territory, or to migrate to land not yet occupied.'[59]

3. *Agricultural Communities.* For Kames, the dilemma created by expanding pastoral nomadic communities was solved by agriculture. Thus for Kames the true spirit of society, in which the work of the individual profited others as well as himself, came with this third stage, the Agricultural Community. Cultivating fields was, by necessity, a communal experience, in contrast to hunting and shepherding which, in Kames' view, were more individualistic. In the Agricultural Community, new occupations arose: ploughman, craftsman, blacksmith, stonemason etc. New relationships developed: landlord and tenant, master and servant, user and supplier. New

---

[54] Sometimes called the *Stadialist Concept,* and summarised by Herman, *The Scottish Enlightenment*, 84. For Kames' mature presentation, see: Kames, *Sketches of the History of Man: A New Edition in 3 Vols, Vol. 1,* (Edin: Ogle, Alliance & Thomson, 1819), 48-60.

[55] Kames, *Sketches of the History of Man, I,* 48f. Cf. Herman, *The Scottish Enlightenment,* 88.

[56] RM, *MLSSA*, 7. Cf. Moffat's additional remarks: 'They have neither house nor shed, neither flocks nor herds. ... Accustomed to a migratory life, and entirely dependent on the chase for a precarious subsistence, they have contracted habits which could scarcely be credited of human beings' (53). He made similar comments in his 1840 LMS *Sermon,* emphasising that the San had not yet even progressed to the pastoral/nomadic stage, (RM, *Africa,* 54: n. C).

[57] Kames, *Sketches of the History of Man, I,* 50.

[58] Moffat mistakenly thought that the San had been Khoikhoi, but who decided to live free of village life. This meant that San were stage-one people, who had been stage-two people (Khoikhoi). Within a Kamesian analysis, they had 'regressed' (RM, *MLSSA*, 5ff).

[59] Kames, *Sketches of the History of Man, I,* 51.

forms of cooperation were required. Concomitantly, competing interests were more frequent. It was therefore in the Agricultural Community that extensive law and government became essential. The first two stages only needed a rudimentary form of law which could be exercised by the 'heads of families over children and domestics.' But agricultural communities created a complex mix of rights and obligations which earlier custom was inadequate to control.[60] Kames's view was that in every society, the advance of government toward perfection *was strictly proportioned to the advance of the society toward intimacy of inter-dependence*.[61] Only in stage-three did society, by necessity, produce true law which was the basis of true civilisation. Agriculturalisation was essential for a movement into civilised society built upon law. This was the crucial link in Kames' thought.

4. *Commercial Communities.*[62] Agricultural communities were not the end of the process. They initiated sophisticated forms of trade, which became the springboard for Kames' fourth and final stage of society: the Commercial Community. This brought even more benefits, but required even more cooperation. Being a complex society, it required even more complex laws, and it created new attitudes and new ways of living. In Kames' view a Commercial Community was disposed to peace.[63] This desire did not come from heightened moral values, but from commercial self-interest.[64] The trader and the businessman were bound by self-interest to be guardians of public tranquility. Such a society would not welcome war, but would embrace peace. Hence civilisation, in terms of law and order, peace, and humane behaviour, occurred when the higher stages were reached.

---

60 Ibid, 51f: 'First there was common land, common crop, common distribution, [then] a lasting division of the land among the members of the state, securing to each man the product of his own skill and labour, was a great spur to industry, and multiplied food exceedingly. Population made a rapid progress, and government became an art; for agriculture and commerce cannot flourish without salutary laws.'

61 Herman, *The Scottish Enlightenment*, 84 (our italics).

62 If Kames had lived a century later he may have incorporated another stage: 'The Industrial Society', placing it between the Agricultural Society and the Commercial Society.

63 James Steuart, a Scottish philosopher of the same period, argued differently. He insisted that war, not peace, created trade. See: Sir James Steuart, *Political Economy*, (Broadie, *The Scottish Enlightenment: An Anthology,* 422): 'Trade and industry owe their establishment to war and to ambition; and perhaps mankind may hope to see the day when this establishment will put an end to the first, by exposing the expensive folly of the latter.'

64 Moffat wanted to move the Tswana from stage-two to stage-three of Kames' model. David Livingstone, with his concept of 'Commerce and Christianity' concentrated on establishing stage-four. He believed that if Central Africa could profit by establishing healthy trade with Europe, then the reasons behind the triple evils of tribal wars, connivance with the slave-trade, and some direct selling of fellow Africans into slavery, would be abolished.

Kames' theory was deterministic. Social evolution was inevitable and also virtuous. It led to community and law, it regularised social relationships, and it created an environment which promoted peace and the higher qualities of humanity. His four-stage theory defined human history as a paradigm of progress. His view was that, under harsh living conditions, such as those experienced by hunter-gatherer San, the laws executed by tribal elders were also harsh. In contrast, under prosperous conditions, such as found in mercantile London or Edinburgh, the laws of society were more humane. Correspondingly the manners of society changed from barbarism to reasonableness.[65]

Kames published in the mid-eighteenth century, and in the following decades his ideas diffused into British intellectual thinking. Kames, Adam Smith, David Hume, William Robertson and Edward Gibbon, all shared a similar outlook.[66] Becoming civilised—in the sense of creating a society in which good law, reasonable behaviour, and humane customs prevailed—required becoming the sophisticated society produced by the latter stages in Kames' model. Movement toward civilisation would not occur through making people simply copy European manners. It would occur through societies experiencing fundamental transformation in moving from hunter-gatherer, to pastoral-nomadic, to agricultural, and to commercial societies. This was seen as essential in creating an environment conducive to the enjoyment of all the benefits of peace, good law, and humanity.[67] The crucial stage was stage-three: the Agricultural Community.

It can now be seen why mission organisations encouraged a settled agricultural lifestyle. It was not to keep people in one place so that they could be more easily evangelised. More was involved. It was a strategy which aimed at creating a better standard of life, law, liberty and community. Formal education was vital in the process, but If society were locked in stages one or two, then it was difficult to get formal education off the ground. When society entered the third stage, there were conditions in which formal education, and even the adoption of 'refined manners' became possible. Agriculturalisation was fundamental to the whole movement. It was crucial

---

65 Herman, *The Scottish Enlightenment*, 86f.

66 David Hume followed a similar interpretation of social progress in his *History of England* (1754-1762). Also: William Robertson, *The History of the Reign of Emperor Charles V* (1759). Cf. Herman, *The Scottish Enlightenment*, 85.

67 Bruno Gutmann, with his Romanticist roots, would disagree with almost all of this theory. However, in Kames' time, the towns and cities of Scotland were still relatively small and retained a 'community identity'. By Gutmann's day, the great towns and cities of industrial Germany personified anonymity and lack of community.

in the formation of stable societies. In Kames' analysis, the progress of civilisation through the four stages was what prompted an increase in justice and liberty. For Kames, societies in the latter stages moved away from the terrors of despotism, which the earlier stages fostered. Progression brought not only economic benefit, but social advantage. The 'power of the despot' was more easily broken in stages three and four.

Moffat and the Kamesian Model

Moffat was the ideal facilitator. He was a gardener, hence an agriculturalist. He saw himself as introducing the Tswana to a new form of society, dependent upon a settled, non-nomadic lifestyle which agriculture both demanded and made possible. As Kames had written: 'Agriculture, which fixes people to a spot, is an invincible obstacle to migration'.[68] Permanence of community led toward a positive evolution of society. The LMS believed that agricultural communities tended to bring peace—an essential ingredient of civilisation and the coming reign of Christ—whilst hunting communities tended to bring violence. This was why Moffat compared the Ndebele unfavourably with the MaShona, whom the Ndebele displaced in southern Zimbabwe: 'The MaShona are evidently a *civilised* and *industrious* people, while the Matabele are emphatically men of war, a tribe of warriors.'[69]

In Moffat's writings, the connection between civilisation and agriculture was consistently strong. This was echoed by Andrew Geddes Bain, who visited Kuruman in 1834. Bain remarked that what pleased him much, at Kuruman and at Motito, was to see large fields of yellow wheat belonging to the indigenous peoples vying with the crops of the missionaries, through them having been well cultivated and irrigated. Bain commented: 'This is a grand step towards civilisation and, would my time permit, I could tell you of many more.'[70] Bain also believed that civilisation was marked by settled life and agriculturalisation.

The tribes which Moffat encountered mostly had societies corresponding to the first and second stage of the Kamesian analysis, with an occasional step into the third.[71] Moffat felt that if they had contact with the Cape, then,

---

68 Kames, *Sketches of the History of Man, I,* 53.

69 RM, *Journal*, 2.8.1854, (*MJ1*, 250).

70 Andrew Geddes Bain, *To J.C. Chase,* 18.12.1834: Lister (ed.), *Journals of Andrew Geddes Bain,* (Cape Town: Van Riebeck Society, 1949), 154. Bain was a Scotsman, who settled in Graaff-Reinet, South Africa. In 1835, he accompanied Dr Andrew Smith's scientific journey. He then set off on his own, looking for natural history specimens and curios.

71 The Tswana and the Ndebele had agricultural skills before Moffat came. The Tswana grew a few crops, as did the Ndebele. Moselekatse, through his slaves, had developed agriculture

by imitation, they would be helped to advance in civilisation. That was why he recommended to Africaner that he should visit the Cape in 1819, and why he suggested the same to Peclu and Teysho in 1824.[72] But did Moffat simply want Africaner to see society existing at the next stage of socio-economic progress? Or did he want him to see better 'manners' and 'habits of living' which he might copy? Moffat was primarily thinking about factors which moulded the type of society which Africaner's people had, and about the stage of socio-economic development which they had reached. The evidence lies in Moffat referring to barriers which, in his view, hindered Africaner's people from advancing in civilisation. These were: the state of the country, the climate, and want of intercourse with the Colony. In citing the 'state of the country' and 'the climate' as barriers to civilisation, what Moffat had in mind was sluggishness in agricultural progress. These factors revealed his Kamesian roots. The tenor of Moffat's remarks points to him wanting Africaner to be made aware of a new way of doing things, with the hope that this would create a desire to implement these at home, taking his people to the next stage. He wanted Africaner to be exposed to new and better ways, in the same way as Scottish landlords during the eighteenth century had been influenced by seeing new agrarian methods in England. That resulted in the transformation of Scotland. Perhaps the same could happen in Africa.

Kamesian thinking can also be detected in Moffat's earlier writings on difficulties encountered in founding missions in remote Namaqualand. He pointed out that, if the *civilising* of the Namaqua presupposed a change from a wandering, nomadic life to a settled style of living, then, in order to effect a change, it would be necessary to bring the means of sustaining such a style of living to the Namaqua.[73] These included agricultural implements and the ability to bore for water. Yet, even if boring for water were introduced, far more rain would be required in Namaqualand. Consequently, he urged Africaner to find a more fertile spot for his people. A clear link between 'civilisation' and moving from a nomadic to a settled lifestyle, was also alluded to when Moffat considered the effect of the Gospel on the Coranna

---

to the extent of growing vast acres of grain. In 1854 Moffat expressed admiration of Moselekatse's agriculture, see: RM, *Journal,* 10.7.1854, (*MJ1,* 214). But it was a fringe activity. Moffat wanted to make it a core one. This was also how Livingstone saw the situation, see: Livingstone, *To Livingston Family,* 29.9.1841, (*DLFL,* 42).

[72] RM, *MLSSA*, 173. Africaner's reputation as a murderous bandit was well-known. His appearance in Cape Town caused consternation. It created a new interest in mission work, since it showed that missionaries were true pioneers of Christian civilisation. Importantly, it left a profound impression in the mind of the Governor, Lord Charles Somerset, giving the LMS a standing it had never before enjoyed (Du Plessis, *The Evangel in South Africa,* 27).

[73] RM, *MLSSA*, 189f.

and the Griqua, mentioning the capacity for creating a 'true' nation which a settled lifestyle brought:

> We have also seen the civilising effects of the Gospel, of whom it may be affirmed, that though they were without a country or a name, they are now numbered amongst the tribes; and that though they were not a people, they have become a people.[74]

Moffat took the phrase, 'Though they were not a people, they have become a people' from the New Testament (1 Peter 2:10). The context in *Missionary Labours* indicates that they became 'a people' for Moffat, not simply because they became a people believing in his God, but because, in becoming a settled people, they became a proper nation with a stable society.[75]

*

In 1870 Moffat summarised his life's work in his Port Elizabeth farewell speech. In that address he emphasised that missions had led to the progress of peace, law and order in the remote interior, not through subjugation of the indigenous population, but through change by means of the Gospel itself.[76] And for Moffat, the Gospel brought civilisation, not only through the spiritual power of the message, but through the socio-economic transformation of society which accompanied it.

---

74 RM, *MLSSA*, 213f.

75 For Moffat, nationhood, or 'becoming a people with a country', involved a settled, non-nomadic existence. But was this a European view of national identity, rather than an African one? Yet, even if Moffat's notion of 'nationhood' was a limited one, he wanted the peoples he worked with to have a respected status, and not viewed as less than true nations.

76 RM, *Port Elizabeth Speech, 1870*, (Deane, *Robert Moffat,* 141ff.).

Chapter 36
The Critique of Civilisation

THE MISSIONARY ENCOURAGEMENT for indigenous peoples to become settled communities tilling a specific area of land, provided a substantial bulwark against land-grabbing colonists. Clinton pointed out that, within the Colony during the 1820s, when John Philip was campaigning for equal rights for the Khoikhoi, the missionaries were aware that freedom and protection would avail the Khoikhoi very little unless they had an alternative to working for farmers. It was a cardinal point in missionary strategy that Government should provide the Khoikhoi with land of their own, so that they might cultivate it and become useful citizens on an equal footing with the Colonists.[1] At Kuruman, which was outside the Colony, Moffat pre-emptively established the principle of *indigenous* use of land as agricultural land. This indicated that such land was not 'empty' land or 'unused' land—the argument used by settlers as they grabbed huge tracts of it. The missionary vision of indigenous land use was radically different from that of J.M. Bowker, which he set out in his 1841 'Springbok' speech. Bowker, a leader of the 1820 Boer Settlers, enthused over the beauty of the springbok, but added:

> My feelings toward the Kafir are not of that stamp. I know him to be the great bar to all improvement among us. I know that rapine and murder are in all his thoughts, and I see them in his looks and hate him accordingly ... *Is it just that a few thousands of restless, worthless savages are to sit like a nightmare upon a land that would support millions of civilised people happily*?[2]

Bowker had no thought that the indigenous people might themselves farm the land. The LMS missionaries had a diametrically opposite outlook. They believed in progress for all people and not just some. They wanted the indigenous population to enjoy the full fruits available from the land. Most of all, they wanted the indigenous population to experience the benefits of law, order, security, education, and general advancement which a transformation from a Kamesian stage-two to stage-three would, in their judgment, inevitably bring. Whereas Bowker dismissed the indigenous population as a dead-weight, and as an obstacle to 'civilisation', LMS workers

---

1 Clinton, *The South African Melting Pot,* 46.

2 J.M. Bowker, Speeches, *Letters and Selections from Important Papers of the late John Mitford Bowker,* facsimile reprint (CT: 1962), 116-25, cited by Ross: *David Livingstone: Mission and Empire,* 37f, (our italics).

saw the indigenous population as part of a civilising process involving the whole of humanity, for the betterment of all.

Having emphasised one of the important positive aspects of the missionary philosophy of civilisation, we need also to acknowledge some of its negative qualities. Cultural norms would be challenged in implementing Moffat's policy, not the least of which was that in traditional Tswana society it was considered below the dignity of a man to dig or cultivate the ground.[3] Another factor which Moffat may not have fully appreciated was that a total shift from a nomadic culture to an agricultural culture would bring difficulties in such a dry area as southern Africa, which was quite different from Scotland with its abundant rainfall.[4] Apart from these, there were many other questions around the notion of 'civilisation'.

Did Moffat underestimate the extent to which a pastoral or semi-nomadic group—even hunter-gatherers—was a community? What Moffat thought he came across were isolated family units in separation from their fellows. He saw the Gospel, in its role as a civilising force, creating community over against individualism. This view differed from missiologists such as Gutmann, who saw missions as contributing to the fragmentation of traditional community life. Given that Kames' model was closely related to Adam Smith's *The Wealth of Nations,* in which self-interest was seen as the driving force behind economic progress,[5] it is not surprising that movement through the Kamesian stages can be linked to selfish individualism as opposed to cooperative communalism, though that was not Moffat's understanding.[6]

Agriculturalisation meant a primary focus on tilling the land for crops, but for many tribes the traditional focus was on cattle and grazing. Prah, in his work, *Aspects of Tswana Feudalism in the Pre-Colonial Period,* has pointed out that, unlike some parts of Africa where land had greater commodity value, in Tswana society cattle was by far the article of trade with greatest significance in the feudal political economy.[7] Prah argued that what elsewhere in Africa were traditional types of tenancy relations in terms of

---

3 RM, *Bechuana Customs,* (SOAS/CWM/SA/Moffat/Personal/Box 4).

4 Lye and Murray, *Transformations,* 25: 'Overgrazing by cattle, sheep and goats, destruction by the natural fauna, burning of the natural grasses, increasing densities of human population and cultivation have all reduced the natural ground cover and led to severe erosion.' The Eye of Kuruman water enabled Moffat to work in an untypical environment.

5 Adam Smith was not the arch-apostle of selfish self-interested capitalism which he is often portrayed as being. His emphasis on mutual benefits is not unexpected, since he had been a pupil of Francis Hutcheson, who saw benevolence as a primary human instinct.

6 E.g. Shillington, *The Colonisation of the Southern Tswana: 1870-1900.*

7 Prah: *Notes and Comments on Aspects of Tswana Feudalism in the Pre-Colonial Period*, 11.

land, among the Tswana these were tenancy relations in terms of cattle-loaning. A man rented cattle rather than land, with a tribute or 'livestock feu duty' (*dikgafela*[8]) paid to the chief in kind, labour and regimental service. This meant that the missionary emphasis on land rather than cattle cut across traditional ways in which tribal life was organised. As such, Moffat's emphasis on land could be critiqued as having the *potential* to weaken traditional feudal ties between chief and people, as the role of cattle diminished. This point was also raised by Jacobs, who argued that Moffat—in putting into practice his theology of civilisation through agriculture—devalued the traditional appreciation of cattle and undermined traditional Tswana social structure by raising tilling of the soil to the apex of environmental management.[9] Land was not unimportant in traditional Tswana tribal life. But Moffat brought a radical difference of emphasis.

Class, Capitalism and Commercialisation

Jacobs conceded that any critique of Moffat's emphasis on agriculturalisation should not miss the obvious truth that part of his drive towards agriculturalisation was his position as a father with a hungry family in an unfamiliar environment.[10] Nevertheless, some have viewed his emphasis as a symbol of something more, and have interpreted his agriculturalisation as a statement from a European concerning power and redemption. John Mackenzie, not the nineteenth-century Kuruman missionary, but a twentieth-century scholar of the same name, has written:

> The Scots missionary Robert Moffat perceived environmental control as the distinctive characteristic of the Christian, contrasted with the heathen African's alleged helplessness. An engraving of his mission in his book *Missionary Labours and Scenes in Southern Africa,* published in 1842, reveals ordered hedges, paths, plantings and buildings contrasting with the

8 Prah used the term *'dikgafela'* to describe the 'feu duty' tribute given to a Chief. Matumo, in his *Setswana-English-Setswana Dictionary,* defines *'dikgafela'* as: 'Remnants of corn at the bottom of sack or bin; tribute, in the form of corn given to a ruler of a community for the entertainment of strangers; a form of thanksgiving in which the first fruits of corn are given to the ruler in his position as priest representative of God: same as *'naka'* even though the ceremonies differ; some Christian denominations have borrowed and adopted the practice as it is similar to the biblical title'.

9 Jacobs, *Environment, Power and Injustice,* 253.

10 Ibid, 259. Jacobs states this point, but only in a footnote: 'In the light of the Moffats' food shortages the practical incentive to irrigate must not be underestimated.' (253: fn. 15).

> wilderness beyond. Such polarities appeared in the illustrations of countless works on settlers and their power.[11]

Was neat gardening a statement about control and power? As a young man, training as a gardener at mansions in Scotland and England, putting plants and vegetables in neat rows was how Moffat was taught to garden! That was how any professional gardener did his work. The neat rows and paths at Kuruman were not created in order to emphasise power through order, but to get the best yields. That they contrasted the scraggy bush country beyond the mission station was a visual reality, not a metaphor!

As discussed earlier, Grove argued that Moffat read the barren landscape as an exposition on the story of the Fall, motivating him to irrigate and cultivate as an attempt to redeem the landscape.[12] Yet, whilst Moffat would see certainly 'improvement' of the land as a sign of the redemption of creation, his primary motivation came from practical necessity. The need for food. Jacobs followed a similar argument to that of Grove, and which was also put forward by the Comaroffs, seeing Moffat holding a metaphysical vision in which agriculture was a metaphor for civilisation and Christianity, and in which he saw irrigation, like preaching, bringing the water of life to a wasteland.[13] Without concluding that such an analysis is wholly fanciful, we would again stress Moffat's functional motivations. Agriculture was not a metaphor but a solution. Moffat did not deal in symbols but in practical entities. Agriculture as *metaphor* is the view of a scholar and philosopher; agriculture as *functional* is the language of a practical man who wanted his family to eat, and the community around him to progress.

1. *The Question of Class.* The Comaroffs deplored the missionary fixation with agriculture. In their essay 'Cultivation, Christianity and Colonialism',[14] they analysed the enterprise from a Marxist perspective, though at some points conflating LMS intentions with later Boer policies.[15] In a revealing passage they stated:

> While the agrarian revolution [brought by the LMS] gave rise to an assertive class of commercial farmers, for many it brought a harvest of hunger. Having come to recreate the lost British yeomanry, the missions had contributed to

---

[11] John Mackenzie, 'Empire and the Apocalypse', *Ecology and Empire: Environmental History of Settler Societies,* (Edin: Keele University Press, 1997), 216.

[12] Grove, 'Scottish Missionaries in Southern Africa: 1820-1900', *JSAS,* 1989: 15.

[13] Jacobs, *Environment, Power and Injustice,* 253, with ref. to: Comaroff, *Revelation and Revolution, Vol 2:* 1997, 174-5, 206-14.

[14] Comaroff, 'Cultivation, Christianity and Colonialism': De Gruchy (ed.), *The LMS in Southern Africa,* 55-81.

[15] The Marxist aspect is strong on page 75 of, 'Cultivation, Christianity and Colonialism'.

> making not an independent peasantry, but an army of wage-workers; or rather, a population of peasant-proletarians caught up in a cycle of economic dependency.[16]

The Comaroffs asserted that agriculturalisation meant that the upper classes of the indigenous population profited, to the detriment of the lower, servant classes. But whatever may have been the case elsewhere, this was the opposite of what happened at Kuruman. Yet, regardless of the evidence, the Comaroffs argued that the 'upper-class' natives were most attracted to, influenced by, and benefited from, attachment to the missions and Christianity,[17] with the result that, 'just as the upper peasantry became a bourgeoisie, so the poorest segment of the populace became a class of peasant-proletarians.'[18] The Comaroffs were so keen to link together capitalist oppression, colonialism and apartheid that they read it back into the early missionary period.[19] However, as shown in our chapter on the Kuruman Awakening, the indigenous people at Kuruman were the poor, the refugees, and those with little power. The same had been true at Bethelsdorp. The Comaroffs repeated a common but erroneous view, that the LMS concentrated on the tribal aristocracy, and that they implemented changes, such as agriculturalisation, through the 'ruling classes', with concomitant benefits to the 'ruling classes' at the expense of the 'ordinary working class'. But that was not how things happened. Moffat, like other missionaries, had to develop good relationships with the chief and tribal elders, but when change occurred at Kuruman, whether spiritual or agricultural, the tribal aristocracy were not the people most immediately involved. The main beneficiaries were those who had virtually nothing.

In some cases, Moffat's methods meant that those who had previously been almost destitute now become the *nouveau riche.* Moffat himself was aware that poverty led people to seek employment with him, and as those working the land became richer they also began to employ their poorer neighbours. Settling on the mission became a means for recovery in the ecological cycle.[20] But there is little evidence that the changes instituted by Moffat led to a new ruling-class or to a new under-class.

It is undeniable that agriculturalisation had consequences. There was the intended one of regular food supply, new social relationships, and an

---

16 Comaroff, 'Cultivation, Christianity, and Colonialism', 81.

17 Ibid, 80.

18 Ibid, 77.

19 De Gruchy, 'Alleged Political Conservatism of Robert Moffat', 17-36, reckoned that the Comaroffs applied principles from one historical situation to others which were very different.

20 Jacobs, *Environment, Power and Injustice,* 64.

improvement in law, order and education. But there were other cultural impacts. In an early study, Schapera pointed out that the political conquest of South Africa by the Europeans, accompanied by missionary effort, education, administrative action, and above all by the introduction of a new economic system, had 'differentiated the natives to such an extent that it is no longer possible to generalise about their habits and characteristics as a whole.'[21]

2. *The Question of Capitalism.* Agriculturalisation eventually gave rise to Kames' Commercial Society, and, with it, to the economic system to which Schapera referred, and which changed everything permanently, including the nature of indigenous society. But was the corruption of the new type of society, by unwise colonial administration and by Afrikaner Boers, a perversion imposed upon the process, or an inevitable consequence? Kevin Shillington has argued that LMS missionaries brought with them a Christianity which was indivisibly bound up with an ethic of individualism born of a new and growing materialism. This capitalist culture had emerged from the British agricultural and industrial revolutions.[22] Whereas Kames saw progression from stages one and two to stages three and four as a good thing, forging communities with proper law and regulated relationships, Shillington saw the missionary introduction of agriculturalism and commercialism as doing the opposite. He held that the kind of work with which Moffat was engaged made the later process of exploitative colonisation easier, even inevitable. Shillington did not argue that the missionaries deliberately introduced individualistic capitalism, or that they intended to take advantage of the indigenous population. But he did suggest that an emphasis on tribes changing to agriculture was sparked, if unknowingly, by a European individualistic capitalist philosophy:

> From the start nearly everything about the Southern Tswana's primarily pastoral, social, and economic organisation was anathema to the missionaries' view of a Christian society. Inspired by Robert Moffat of Kuruman, the LMS missionaries believed that the first prerequisite for conversion to Christianity was to develop among the men the industrious habit of agricultural cultivation, through the important innovations of the plough and irrigation. Basically, they hoped to change the Southern Tswana pastoral society into communities of small-scale individual farmers, independent of 'heathen' chiefly control. ... In order to be assured of candidates for conversion, therefore, they had to persuade their 'flocks' to

---

21 Schapera, 'Present-day Life in the Native Reserves', *Western Civilisation and the Native of South Africa: Studies in Culture Contact,* (Ldn: Routledge, 1934), 39.

22 Shillington, *The Colonisation of the Southern Tswana: 1870-1900*, 17.

> adopt this settled, agricultural way of life.[23] ... [Also], the increasing scale of the traffic in firearms [game hunting] upset the delicate ecological balance of the Southern Tswana economy and necessitated a greater reliance upon agriculture.'[24]

There is some justification in this, and we have already noted links between Kames, Adam Smith and capitalism. Yet, some of Shillington's statements were loaded. When he wrote, 'In order to be assured of candidates for conversion, therefore, they had to persuade their 'flocks' to adopt this settled, agricultural way of life', Shillington implied that the reason why missionaries promoted agriculture was not philanthropic, but spiritually exploitative. Agriculture was an insincere device to aid proselytisation. But sincerity depends on intention, and intention is governed by a person's self-understanding, even if that self-understanding is deemed by later generations to have been misplaced. In our view, Moffat's intention, in bringing a new stage of civilisation to African tribes, had the aim of 'improving' the living conditions and lifestyle of the native peoples. Of course, it was also true that if a more settled lifestyle were adopted by the Tswana then evangelism would be easier. Moffat himself recognised this.[25] But the twin concerns of civilisation and evangelism each existed in their own right. They were inter-related, but a positive value was placed on each. Both sprang from a desire to establish the reign of God upon the earth: a reign of peace, contentment, benevolence, and fullness of life.

Does progression into stages three and four of the Kamesian model necessarily introduce exploitative capitalism?[26] A problem for scholars who work in a southern African context is reading all history in the shadow of colonialism and apartheid. But were colonialism and apartheid additional forces, which distorted the concept of civilisation through agriculture? The

---

23 Kames was aware that adoption of agriculture meant the cessation of migration (*Sketches of the History of Man, Vol. 1,* 53).

24 Shillington, *The Colonisation of the Southern Tswana: 1870-1900*, 17f.

25 Barnabas Shaw, *Memorials of South Africa,* 100f: 'He who goes to convert a wandering tribe to Christianity must either collect them together for this purpose or himself become a wanderer. If he collect them together, he must show them some method of obtaining subsistence, that they may remain with him; otherwise, the few cattle they possess will soon be slaughtered for immediate use, after which they must either die of hunger or again repair to the chase in search of food. ... [I chose] teaching them to live by agriculture.'

26 Moving societies from stage-two to stage-three of the Kamesian model implies the eventual adoption of stage-four, the commercial society. It was this which Shillington pin-pointed as exploitative. Yet, trying to create equitable trading relationships between weak partners (native African communities) on the one hand, and strong partners (European colonial communities) on the other hand, is difficult. Shillington was correct insofar that, in such an unequal situation with inherent profound economic imbalances, exploitation was virtually unavoidable, even though contrary to the missionaries' plans.

concept which Moffat was concerned with did not, by itself, produce the unwelcome results which Shillington described. In fact, it can be argued that agriculturalisation aided resistance to exploitation. This was an argument used by Mackenzie of Kuruman. He warned of a coming wave of white men, but assured local chiefs that permanent settlement and intensive production would protect Africans' hold on the land.[27] Dispossession of agriculturalists was more difficult than dispossession of pastoral or nomadic tribes.

3. *The Question of Commercialism.* Moffat aimed at giving indigenous Africans the opportunity to own their own land in a way compatible with a new socio-economic system. A century later, it took the brutal power of the deliberately divisive Group Areas Act of 1950, backed by all the machinery of the apartheid state, to break Moffat's model. The Group Areas Act declared Kuruman to be a white area, undoing co-existence stretching back 130 years. For example, the LMS policy had been integrated worship as one body of Christ, quite different from the policy within the Colony of the Dutch *Nederduits Gereformeerde Kerk* which, in 1857, decided to allow separate services for white and non-white members. In Moffat's model, all people, regardless of racial origin, tilled the land, benefited from it, and worshipped together.

It was a process which involved more than agriculturalisation. Kames taught that the Agricultural Community led to the Commercial Community, and Moffat, in letters to the LMS, was keen to highlight the increase of commerce between Kuruman and the Colony, often stating the annual cash amount. Economic intercourse involved trade, and trade involved transport. In 1844 for example, when he wrote for the children's *Juvenile Missionary Magazine*, one of the positive indicators of civilisation which he described among the Christian Tswana was their purchase of wagons:

> Formerly the Bechuanas were pedestrians to a man, never riding on a horse, or ox, or in a wagon; and although it is only about ten years since they began to purchase wagons, a very dear article, from 50 pounds to 100 pound it is quite astonishing to see the number they now possess. This is one grand step in civilisation, especially in a country like this.[28]

It was not wagon ownership as such that was important, as if possession of advanced technological products was itself civilisation. Rather, the wagons symbolised the new stage of society which the Tswana had reached. Commercial trading with the outside world had started. But this brought long-term effects. These included problems faced by a people, in socio-

---

27 Jacobs, *Environment, Power and Injustice,* 82.

28 RM, 'Returning to Kuruman', *The Juvenile Missionary Magazine,* October 1844, 99ff.

economic transition, in withstanding the impact of stronger economies. Moffat thought in simple terms: development brought benefits. But socio-economic transitions initiated many factors, not all of which were beneficial. Becoming a commercial community opened up a society with a weak economy to the pitfalls of a trading deficit. John Smith Moffat was aware of this. In an 1868 letter to the LMS, in which he described the poor land outside of Kuruman and the poor prospects for real economic advancement through trade, he wrote that he despaired, 'of much advance in civilisation, when their resources are so small, and then the European trade is on the principle of enormous profit and losses.'[29] Like his father, John Smith Moffat still linked civilisation with socio-economic progress, but he saw the difficulties of a weak trading partner (the Tswana) being overwhelmed by a strong trading partner (the Cape Colony.

John Philip had also had an inkling of this problem. In relation to the Khoikhoi, he realised that the Colony—and the industrial strength of Britain which lay behind it—was a massive producer, dwarfing what the indigenous population could create; and if the indigenous population were to be involved in trade with an economic giant then there could be no economic balance unless the economic status of the Khoikhoi was raised.[30] Some kind of protectionism was needed, lest the indigenous population became victims of an economic slavery. Moffat came from Scotland, whose rural economy had only been able to make a successful transition because it had been protected by the early Corn Laws (though the same laws would eventually bring increasing hardship to working-class families). But no equivalent protection existed within the Colony for Africans who were struggling to compete. Yet, being outside the Colony, Kuruman had a form of inbuilt accidental protectionism through its isolation. Though Kuruman folk struck up trade with the Colony, their remoteness meant that they only touched the fringes of the Colony's powerful economy. But John Smith Moffat was aware of problems increasing in the future.[31]

---

29 JSM, *To the LMS Directors,* 12.10.1868: Deane, *Robert Moffat,* 166.

30 Briggs & Wing, *The Harvest and the Hope,* 34.

31 Should Moffat have been more aware of these issues? In his defence, trade was on a very small scale during most of his life at Kuruman. Yet the effects, both positive and negative, of a protected economy were well-known in Ormiston from the perspective of both farmer and consumer. The *British Library* has important letters written on this subject by (i) an Ormiston farmer and (ii) a Haddington town resident. See: William Mackie of Ormiston, *To Lt. Col. Dirom, Edinburgh,* 10.12.1795, & 13.1.1796, in: Alexander Dirom, *An Inquiry into the Corn Laws and Corn Trade of Great Britain and their Influence on the Prosperity of the Kingdom,* (Edin: Creech, 1796: British Library copy), 177ff, and 257f. Also see: A Hammerman', *To the Hon. Mr. Baron*

One further point may be made. The Comaroffs pointed out that some religious non-conformists accepted the 'necessary' inequality of human-kind, expressed in terms of class, position and wealth.[32] That this was sometimes true is undeniable. In Britain some non-conformist mill-owners and factory-owners had a vested interest in maintaining the social *status quo*—and if a far-fetched theological backing for the status quo were available then they welcomed it. However, the Comaroffs implied that *most* non-conformists followed this line, including missionaries. But the evidence is thin. From a Marxist perspective, the Comaroffs focussed on the coming of bourgeois values and capitalism into southern Africa and were keen to link the activities of non-conformist missionaries with the introduction of these values. It is undeniable that Moffat delighted in the Tswana becoming prosperous, owning wagons and oxen. Was he thereby introducing systems conducive to capitalism which ultimately led to inequalities and poverty? The verdict depends on the political philosophy of the commentator.

Manners and Polite Society

Did Moffat use the word 'civilisation' in relation to the customs and manners of 'refined' European society? Very rarely. In his writings he nearly always used the term in the context of socio-economic process, though there are some passages in which he did use it to refer to 'polite' society.[33] For LMS missionaries, evangelism was always more than the adoption of habits, values, and customs which prevailed in European society, and 'civilising' involved the transformation of social and economic structures, enabling people to fulfill their potential. That was the vision. It was that deeper work which Moffat sought to accomplish. However, there were a few instances in which Moffat stressed 'manners' which included good conduct plus appropriate behaviour, dress and language.

Hepburn, in Answer to his Speech delivered at a Meeting of the Free-Holders of the County of Haddington, March 3rd, 1814, on the Corn-Laws, (Edin: Orphoot, 1814).

32 Comaroff, *Revelation and Revolution,* Vol. 1, 273.

33 Moffat, *MLSSA*, 42, deplored Van der Kemp's habit of not dressing in proper European fashion: 'Frequently at home and abroad, he would dispense with hat, shirt, and shoes, while the patron and advocate of civilisation.' In a passage quoted by Moffat (*MLSSA*, 194) the LMS missionary Anderson used the term 'civilisation' in conjunction with having proper clothing: 'When I went among the Griquas, and for some time after, they were without the smallest marks of civilisation. If I except one woman (who had by some means got a trifling amount of colonial raiment) they had not one thread of European clothing among them: and their wretched appearance and habits were such as might have excited in our minds aversion to them.' Anderson's connection between civilisation and European manners is revealing.

On the mission-field, one of the main issues involving 'manners' was the question of clothing. For example, in 1825 Moffat commented on Mahura, brother to Mothibi, of the BaThlaping:

> We might just add at this place that the way in which Mahura has behaved, and his strong predilection for civilisation, gives us some hope. He with his attendants are always seen in European dress as far as is practicable. They have also commenced planting maize and tobacco, a thing unknown among those western tribes.[34]

In this extract, Moffat referred to both aspects of civilisation. He referred to horticulture, and he also mentioned clothing and dress. When Moffat saw some beginning to wear even rudimentary clothing he commented that Dr Chalmers, one of the fathers of the Free Church of Scotland, 'would have called this the upheavings of civilisation'.[35] In another passage, Moffat described Sechele and his family as being, 'wonderfully advanced in civilisation'. This was after he had seen Sechele and his wife Ma-Sebele, 'sitting, as man and wife ought to sit, each in a chair over the fire'.[36] Whilst more contributed to Moffat's happy judgment than simply a scene of domestic bliss, in which man and wife were contentedly seated by the fire, his comments show that symptoms of good 'manners' were important to him in evaluating Gospel progress. Three general points may be made before we discuss particular issues.

Firstly, in nineteenth-century evangelical society, in Britain as well as overseas, tidiness and cleanliness were regarded as 'next to godliness'. Bebbington cited a striking example of a home being moralised under Christian influence, in which a little girl had carried home a text from church which said, 'Let all things be done decently and in order'.[37] Her 'godly tidiness' had a spiritual effect on the family. Tidiness and cleanliness were seen as signs of godliness in a person's life.

Secondly, Steve de Gruchy pointed out that if the missionaries simply identified civilisation with 'polite manners' and if the goal of the missionaries was simply 'to create civilised Englishmen out of the heathen', then creating a class of people who used English would have gone a long way towards that goal.[38] Moffat, and other LMS missionaries, used the vernacular. Civilisation was not identified with linguistic imperialism. This was in stark contrast to

---

34 RM, *Journal*, 30.5.1825, (*AAK*, 187).

35 RM, *Journal*, 19.9.1857, (*MJ2*, 67).

36 RM, *Journal*, 9.6.1854, (*MJ1*, 168).

37 Bebbington, *Holiness in Nineteenth Century England*, 43f. The fact that the girl had her own room pointed to her coming from the relatively wealthy middle-class.

38 De Gruchy, 'Alleged Political Conservatism of Robert Moffat', 27.

attitudes at the Cape, where it was assumed that civilisation depended upon indigenous languages being subordinated to English or even eliminated.[39]

Thirdly, whereas Moffat's references to civilisation were most often connected with horticulture and agriculture, in the next generation of the Moffat family (his daughter Elizabeth and daughter-in-law Emily), the word 'civilisation' was nearly always associated with 'manners.'[40] This may reflect different areas of interest between the gardener and his family, or it may reflect the difference between first-generation missionaries and second-generation ones who took the new state of society for granted.

Clothing: The Issue of Nakedness

Kwame Bediako made a comparison between Christian mission in the first two centuries and Christian mission in the eighteenth and nineteenth centuries.[41] He pointed out that the apostolic mission was sometimes bogged down by Judaising attitudes in which customs appropriate for one culture were confused with the core of the Christian message and imposed unnecessarily upon other cultures. So also, he argued, many missionaries of the eighteenth and nineteenth centuries confused European customs with Christianity and created unnecessary difficulties by imposing these on new converts. The question of clothing highlights this issue. For Moffat, decent clothing was a mark of a civilised Christian, and involved two issues. One was the question of nakedness. The other was the question of European-style dress. In Moffat's eyes, the issue of nakedness related to *shame,* and the issue of European-style dress related to *dignity*. Intriguingly, though many Europeans associated nakedness with lust, Moffat admitted that the nakedness of Moselekatse's people was not necessarily accompanied by lust. Moffat admitted that lack of lust among the Ndebele was in strong contrast to what would have been the case in European society. In 1854, as excited

---

[39] E.g. an entry in the *Journal* of George Champion, an *ABCFM* missionary to southern Africa in 1835: 'There is an opinion prevalent here (Cape Town) among those interested in missions, that those entering new missionary fields should sit down immediately and in the infant school teach the children the English language, in order that in the course of two or three generations the native language may be extirpated. The English introduced, and all that the stores of literature, science and religion that there are in the English tongue may be laid at their feet. Thus, you save translations, and you have a language adapted to civilised and Christian men. The language then will not cramp their minds as those minds expand under the influence of Christianity.' See: Champion, *Journal,* 18.2.1835, in: Booth (ed.), *The Journal of an American Missionary in the Cape Colony 1835,* (CT: NLSA, 1968), 5.

[40] Cf. Una Long (ed.), *The Journals of Elizabeth Lees Price: Written in Bechuanaland, Southern Africa 1854-1883,* (Ldn: Edward Arnold, 1956) for the views of Elizabeth Lees Price (Moffat).

[41] Kwame Bediako, 'Christianity as Civilisation', *Theology and Identity,* 225-266.

crowds accompanied his wagon on the last few miles to Moselekatse's headquarters, Moffat noted:

> There they were, scampering, [naked] men, women, boys and girls. In their eyes there was nothing indecent. They have been born and brought up to it. Either from habit or law (and I have had opportunities of close observation) I never saw anything like the sensual looks I have witnessed in civilised society. Mary, this is for your information only![42]

Years earlier, in 1823, Moffat had written to his brother Alexander reassuring him that the sight of naked women did nothing to inflame his passions:

> I feel grateful for the sympathy you all manifest as it regards my critical situation among a kind of naked people with licentious habits. From the numerous examples of fallen missionaries, nor is our Society alone, you have abundant reason to infer that the path is slippery; but let me assure you, that custom renders these sights familiar, so that they have no more influence on the corrupt affections of the heart than a group of nuns, etc.[43]

Despite conceding that nakedness did not necessarily result in lustfulness, Moffat still had objections, believing that nakedness was not fitting before God. In 1829, he spoke firmly to Moselekatse on the issue:

> I strongly recommended him to change the costume of his nation, and told him that naked men and women were a sight which grieved us; that God intended man to be covered, and that those like the Matabele were a mere nothing compared to all the other nations of the earth. At these remarks he laughed most heartily, but listened with more sedateness when I told him that all those nations whom he would esteem wise and great covered their bodies. Alas the idea of shame never was in all his thoughts. He remarked at the close of the conversation that when once his country was like the Kuruman he and his people would wear clothes.[44]

For Moffat, nakedness was considered to be shameful, and the Reformed understanding of Genesis moulded his view.[45] This was the theological foundation behind his comments on the dress code of the Ndebele, and

---

42 RM, *Journal*, 22.7.1854, (*MJ1*, 228f), (our italics).

43 RM, *To Alexander Moffat,* Jan. 1823, (*AAK*, 70).

44 RM, *To the LMS Directors,* 20.11.1836, (*MJ1,* 27).

45 There was also occasional reference to the story in the Gospels of the demoniac who, after being healed, was 'clothed and in his right mind', suggesting that not being properly clothed indicated a deranged mind. Cf. Moffat's comments in his 1840 LMS *Sermon:* 'It was only when the Gospel was made the power of God unto salvation, and their hearts became regenerated by the Spirit of God, that they began to cast aside their heathenish garb, with the degrading habits of their former state, and became clothed not only in their right mind, but also in becoming attire.' (RM, *Africa,* 43).

which Moselekatse found so amusing.[46] It is true that Moffat also brought with him the cultural habits of his European background, but for Moffat the 'nakedness question' was essentially a biblical issue. Nakedness might give rise to lust, so no real Christian would wish to encourage lustful feelings. Yet, as we have seen, he conceded that the nakedness of Moselekatse's people was not always accompanied by lustfulness. Despite his 1854 observations, when Moffat revisited the Ndebele in 1857 he stuck to his view that 'nakedness' brought 'shame', and was surprised that the notions of 'nakedness' and 'shame' did not seem to go together for the Ndebele:

> With few exceptions the females were *lintompees* [virgins] of all ages, many of them without a shred on their tail ends, with precious little anywhere else. Much as I have been among the Matabele, I do feel disgusted with both male and female attire. I must enquire if they have got 'shame' in their language.[47]

Moffat linked lack of shame with lack of a sense of sin. This confirmed to him the seriousness of how far the Ndebele had fallen away from God.

CLOTHING: THE ISSUE OF EUROPEAN DRESS

The Tswana traditionally had a rudimentary form of clothing.[48] In Moffat's mind this was sufficient to deal with the issue of 'shame'. However, being clothed in roughly shaped animal skins was, for Moffat, insufficient to symbolise the new dignity which a person should have when they became

---

46 Moselekatse's amusement at Moffat's fastidiousness is recorded in: RM, *Journal,* 14.10.1857, (*MJ2,* 96). Moffat explained to Moselekatse that, in Moffat's culture, a sign of respect when in the presence of a king was the wearing of clean, tidy clothes.

47 RM, *Journal,* 25.9.1857, (*MJ2,* 73). For the Ndebele, shame occurred when a family member dishonoured the community, tribe, or Chief. Moffat could not understand why Ndebele women were unconcerned about their nakedness. Cf. RM, *To Mary Moffat,* 21.12.1859, (*MJ2,* 251): 'Many more, in full womanhood, may be seen, with a light exception, from top to toe in pristine unadorned beauty; but who is there who likes to see one of such, and especially gross. Nothing less than seeing would convince most people of the entire absence of the feeling of shame in women of almost all ages going about with bare *marago* [buttocks]. I might say much more of a descriptive character on this subject, but *you* [Mary] need no such information'.

48 Schapera, *The Tswana,* 25: 'Formerly, clothing was made chiefly from the skins of wild and domestic animals. Babies went naked; small boys wore a flap barely covering the genitals, youths and men a loin-skin passing between the legs and tied round the waist; small girls wore a tiny apron of fringes made of bast or skin, older girls and women a large apron in front and a skirt at the back. A kaross and sandals were often added, and men and boys sometimes wore skin caps or grass hats. Everybody, including babies, also had ornaments of some kind such as necklaces, bangles, and anklets, made of beads, copper wire, or woven grass. Distinctive and more elaborate costumes were worn on occasions by initiands and warriors, but, on the whole, everybody of the same sex and age usually dressed alike. ... [Nowadays] 'respectable' dress is obligatory for Church members.'

Christian. He viewed a willingness to be 'properly' clothed, and not simply covered, as a sign of spiritual progress. Writing in the 1840s about the situation in 1831, he stated:

> Among the treasures brought with us from the Colony, was a box of materials for clothing, for the encouragement of such as were making efforts to clothe themselves. This was the first supply of the kind, and nothing could be more seasonable to a people just beginning to emerge from barbarism, the impoverished remains of scattered tribes, but the first-fruits of the Gospel among the Bechuanas.[49]

The 'first-fruits of the Gospel among the Bechuanas', meant the people, not their willingness to be 'properly' clothed. But for Moffat, such willingness was an additional indicator of Christian growth.[50] Progress from rudimentary coverings of roughly fashioned skins to 'proper' clothing was referred to with satisfaction in an 1861 letter to a Miss Kent in Colchester:

> It requires a long time to implant habits of cleanliness and tidiness and order. The grown-up folks can now help themselves to make their own dresses. The day is gone when Mrs. Moffat used to cut out skins for both men and women. When individuals in native costume and naked shanks enter our congregation they look queer, and they feel it too, though they know well that they are welcomed. We sometimes cannot help from smiling to see those who are pretty well dressed giving such as wide berth as they can.[51]

Moffat was amused that Tswana, who had adopted European dress, were disdainful toward those who were still clad in traditional attire. This was a widespread missionary attitude, and can be criticised as fostering a shame of traditional culture. Moffat's intentions were philanthropic, but the charge remains. He did not think in terms of parallel cultural values. His vision was a linear one, a single line, with barbarism at one end and civilisation at the other. Everything he did was geared towards moving people further along this single line towards the fullness of civilisation, involving a new type of society with enjoyment of the refinements of life.

*

---

[49] RM, *MLSSA*, 564f. The phrase: 'impoverished remains of scattered tribes', underlines that the initial fruit at Kuruman was among former refugees. In 1829, Moffat, *To Miles,* 12.8.1829, (SOAS/CWM/SA/Box11/3/D) wrote of how, immediately on conversion, two women changed the way they dressed.

[50] Setiloane, *The Image of God,* 98, commented: 'As soon as one accepted [the missionary] teaching and became 'Christian' they made him put on clothes. It is important to notice that the way a man was clothed became an identifying factor as to whether he still lived and accepted [the ways of the fathers] ... or had taken to [the way of the white man]' For Setiloane, true Tswana identity was in the 'ways of the fathers', not the new mission identity.

[51] RM, *To Miss Kent,* 28.8.1861, (Grey/MSB/349/1/4).

On rare occasions Moffat displayed an awareness that what was considered civilised in one culture may not be so regarded in another. He admitted that Moselekatse might consider him as 'uncivilised' since he did not always respect the Ndebele culture of flattering, as a code of polite behaviour.[52] On another occasion, he admitted that some BaKwena ladies were offended when he insensitively enlarged on the advantages of European civilisation in contrast to their own.[53] But such admissions were rare exceptions. Missionaries such as Moffat can easily, and often rightly, be accused of confusing European lifestyle, habits and culture with a Christian way of life. Yet this was because they had a holistic view of mission, in which the whole of life should be transformed by Gospel values. The fact that Moffat occasionally confused Gospel values with European culture does not detract from his enterprise, nor does it diminish the large vision he had of the Gospel affecting all of society to the glory of God: 'Though our great work is to evangelise, yet we can never feel satisfied without seeing corresponding progress in civilisation.'[54] The Gospel brought the Kingdom of God. It brought a new way of life for the community as well as for the individual. This was a greater vision than a one-dimensional call to salvation.

In mission studies, it is common to highlight how missionaries imported European culture into Africa, crudely assuming that all missionaries believed that Christian values could be identified with European culture. We have tried to avoid that assumption. We have tried to understand Moffat's way of thinking, why he believed such-and-such, how his background affected him, how he applied his faith within an African context, and how he might have defended his ways. We are rightly hesitant to claim that the 'manners' of nineteenth-century 'Christian' Europe, scarred by war, revolution, and social deprivation, were higher than the 'manners' of the indigenous societies which Moffat encountered. But Moffat was not so hesitant, and like most of his contemporaries he was convinced of European pre-eminence. If pressed, he may have had three defences against accusations of 'cultural arrogance'.

Firstly, he had to deal with actualities rather than with theories. In Africa he saw with his own eyes terrible examples of brutality, torture, and inhumanity. European society also had brutality, torture and inhumanity, but Moffat was not aware of these from personal experience. He simply

---

52 RM, *Journal*, 4.8.1854, (*MJ1*, 252).

53 RM, *Journal*, 8.6.1854, (*MJ1*, 163): 'The dames pitied my bad taste.'

54 RM, *To Thomas Barnes*, 25.6.1849, (SOAS/CWM/Africa/Moffat/Pers/Box 4).

contrasted the manner of life he had grown up with in the villages of Scotland with the manner of life he saw in tribal society.[55]

Secondly, Moffat did not see himself as arguing for 'European' manners. He saw himself as introducing 'advanced' manners. He would have had the view that any 'advanced' culture (such as China) developed similar refinements of living. It was not Europeanisation, but advancement. He believed that Christianity had enabled Europe to progress, and he wanted others to experience a transformation of their own society. He wanted to bring that society to fulfillment. If he erred, it was through naivety, and because he was born in 1795, and not in the socially analytic early twenty-first century.

Thirdly, Kames' theory made it inevitable that the manners of a hunter-gatherer or nomadic-pastoral society would be considered inferior to those of a mercantile society. The four-stage theory presumed social evolution, in which the manners of a society at a more 'progressive' stage of that evolution *had to* be 'higher' and 'better' than those of a society at an earlier stage.

As the time approached for the millennial reign of Christ, then, in the missionary mind, enlightened progress throughout the world was part of the coming kingdom. For Moffat the *method* which would enable advance toward true civilisation was through societies becoming settled agricultural or commercial communities. The core criteria of civilisation involved law and order, peace and security, humane behaviour, education and true religion. Moffat believed that a new basis of society would foster these qualities. If intention is to be commended, then Moffat was outstanding. If being blind to the value of differing cultures is to be criticised, then he was guilty.

---

55 In Scotland he did not see aged mothers and fathers left to die in the fields because they were of no more use to their families (RM, *MLSSA*, 132ff). Nor did he see cruel executions such as happened when the offender was pierced by a stake from anus to breast-bone and then left in the bush, bound, and still alive, for the hyena to feed on; nor did he see practices such as burying living infant children with their dead mothers (*MLSSA*, 57). What appalled him was that these things were accepted with indifference. There was infanticide, torture, cruelty, in Britain also, but these were hidden to Moffat.

Chapter 37
Positioning Moffat's Theology

What was the faith burning in Moffat's heart? His faith was that God is the Creator, Provider and Sustainer of all things; that God is the Lord whom all should honour and to whom all must answer; that men and women of every race, are created with immortal souls and cannot avoid the eternal consequences of sin; that there is an urgent necessity to repent and acknowledge God as the Lord; and that redemption accomplished in Jesus Christ makes salvation possible. The goal of mission was to glorify God, and to spread his Word over the entire globe so that nations and individuals may be transformed in every aspect of life into holiness and peace. In that way the reign of God would be established in all the nations, and the world would be prepared for the millennial reign of Christ. Moffat envisaged men and women coming to faith one by one, and had a vision of the transformation of society, in accord with God's Word.

The missionary theology of Robert Moffat was a moderate Calvinism, which had been profoundly influenced by the values of early nineteenth-century Scottish culture, enriched by the Evangelical Revival, and occasionally modified by the situation he encountered in southern Africa. Woven deeply into his message was a concern about the crisis of judgment, His solemn belief was that every man and woman will give an account of themselves to God, and that the only escape from this crisis is in Jesus Christ.

A Moderate Calvinism

Two aspects of Calvinism drove Moffat's theology. The first was that God is Sovereign. Moffat did not discuss election, but he had a clear doctrine of God's sovereignty. This was expressed in his understanding of providence, and of God as the Lord of creation. The believer's task was to trust and obey, and to leave all to the sovereign will of God. All response to God was rooted in obedience. On some doctrines, such as the 'perseverance of the saints', Moffat was uncommitted. But on the core essence of Calvinism—the majesty of God, and humanity's response in terms of obedience—Moffat was solid. It was this which, on the one hand, gave him his sense of duty, and, on the other hand, gave him confidence to do his work. God was the Lord. God was sovereign. God would work his purposes out.

The second aspect was that God is Holy. There could be no compromise with moral holiness in the life of missionary, individual believer, or the church as a body. Quantity of converts was secondary to the quality of converts. And the holiness of God had implications for all humanity, not just for converts. Moffat was Calvinist in terms of the expansive vision he had of the Christian message affecting society. The ultimate goal was to produce a holy people and a holy society for the glory of God. Yet, though he had a theology which envisaged the whole of society coming to obedience of faith, he differed from traditional Scottish Presbyterianism in that he wanted Church to be free from the State. Here his Secessionist and Independency connections triumphed.

The Evangelical Revival

Moffat was a child of the Evangelical Revival. The hymns he loved, the expressions he used, the sentiments he expressed, all bear witness to that. In his preaching and teaching, these influences were set within a decidedly Calvinist framework. The glory, honour and sovereignty of God, the awesome wonder of the Creator and his works, the invariable ordinances of the divine law, were of first importance in presenting his message. Accordingly, his evangelistic preaching concentrated on the nature of God, and presented human response to the Gospel as a requirement of obedience. Calvary was important—without the Redeemer's blood there would be no salvation—but above all else humanity had a *duty* to believe, a *duty* to repent, a *duty* to worship, and a *duty* to live in a godly way. These things were owed by humanity to the Creator, Governor and Provider of all things. Life was to be God-centred, not human-centred.

When Moffat assessed the genuineness of converts, he turned to the piety of the Evangelical Revival. He looked for the affections of the heart being moved. He was not satisfied with a faith which simply assented to certain beliefs. Nor was he satisfied with a faith which even resulted in regular church going. Nor was he fully satisfied with a change of life, though that may be an indication of a deeper change in the soul. What he wanted to see were tears shed for sin, and tears shed for love of the Saviour. This pietism governed the way he ran Kuruman, both in terms of who were accepted as church members, and in terms of his expectation concerning the spirituality of converts. At the same time, he was uncomfortable with some of the emotions which revival produced. Decency, order, and sobriety of religious behaviour were important. Unpredictable enthusiasm was suspect.

Moffat was a cessationist as far as extraordinary spiritual gifts were concerned, viewing these as restricted to the apostolic age. Dreams, visions, and new prophecies were also suspect. What was required was the solid ground of the Word of God. Holiness and sanctification were vital for a person to be used of God, though Moffat did not adopt the notion of a special power of the Spirit being released through a holiness experience. Moffat's was a simpler, old-fashioned, theology: a holy God only uses a holy life.

The Reign of God

The Psalms taught that 'God would be exalted among the heathen', and that the 'reign of God would be established over all the earth'. This resonated with Moffat's Calvinism and missionary zeal. Though Moffat was prepared to alter his initial theory of a general knowledge of God in the light of what he thought he encountered in Africa, no actual beliefs inherent in African Traditional Religion were absorbed into his theology. He saw himself as coming to a land in which all traditional religious expressions were degraded and to be discarded by converts. He saw darkness, inhumanity and barbarity. He saw a struggle between Satan and God. The only solution was for the Gospel of Christ to conquer the influence of Satan. Later missionaries would be more open to the notion of a preparation for the Gospel existing in traditional religions. For them, the Gospel *fulfilled* traditional religion, it did not *conquer* it. That was not Moffat's approach.

The southern African situation, in which indigenous peoples were heavily discriminated against, made Moffat develop deep convictions of the equality of all races under the Gospel. He was strong on this, though this important feature is often missed by scholars. As Steve de Gruchy emphasised, Moffat's positive impact in terms of social and political awareness needs to be looked at afresh. In the past, Moffat was compared unfavourably to Philip and Livingstone. His slower but long-term impact has been overlooked.

Moffat came from an age of confident faith, with a secure Christian world view. He had no doubt he was bringing the word of life to a 'sick and dying world'. For Moffat, the Gospel brought liberation. Liberation from superstition, from ungodly practices, from fear of witchcraft, from the despotism of chiefs, from war and murder, from oppression of women, and from darkness and ignorance. In Moffat's eyes, the Gospel was the herald of the soon to be realised reign of Christ on earth, which would be a halcyon period of peace, security, and fraternity. Moffat saw himself as a messenger of the Prince of Peace, with a Gospel which transformed men and women's prospects both for the present and for eternity. Moffat's worldview was an all-embracing schema covering the whole of life, involving both soul and body. No part of life was exempt from the benefits of the Gospel.

*

Moffat had clear blind-spots in relation to people, issues, and culture. We have acknowledged these. We have also shown why he thought the way he did. Our aim has been to understand matters from within Moffat's mind. Any person should first be assessed from within that person's self-understanding, only then can there be true appreciation of what they did well and what they did poorly. In considering Moffat's missionary theology one concept which stands out is 'hopefulness'. He had the confident expectation that the glorious reign of God was about to break in, bringing a transformed era of peace and joy to all nations. That drove him on. The great motivating force for Moffat was his eschatology. Things would soon become new and better. Hope fed his irrepressible determination. He saw himself as part of an advance guard, commissioned to help (humanly speaking) inaugurate the reign of Christ. When peoples set aside warfare for peace, or when roaming groups began to till the land (with the prospect of each man sitting under his own 'fig tree'), or when 'heathen darkness' was replaced by education and new ways of living, then, for Moffat these were undeniable signs that success was attending the work, and that the glorious day was approaching.

Optimism is more energising than pessimism. For Moffat, the kingdom of Christ would change every part of life for the better. This all-embracing, society-transforming attitude, shot through by hope, was uplifting. To take Moffat seriously, is to listen to the prophetic voice of the Gospel in relationship to religion, culture, and society. It is to challenge society and its way of life. It is to address the nature of the church as a holy people of God. It is to do all these things within the context of a conviction that Christ's kingdom of righteousness and truth will come to pass.

Bibliography

Section 1: Robert Moffat's Works

1.1 Published Work: English

This includes: (a) Writings which Moffat authorised for publication: (b) Writings, such as speeches, which have been published in books about Moffat; (c) compilations of Moffat's writings which were published by Schapera and Wallis; and (d) other Moffatiana which have been included in compilations published by Baxter & Burke, Le Cordeur, and Wallis. The abreviation UD indicates 'undated'.

1838: *Letter from the Rev. Robert Moffat, Missionary of the London Missionary Society in Africa, to the Rev. G. Browne, 3rd July 1838,* (Extract published in: *35th British and Foreign Bible Society Report, 1839*).

1840: *'Africa: or Gospel Light shining in the midst of heathen darkness. A Sermon on Isaiah 9:2 preached before the Directors of the London Missionary Society,* (Anniversary Sermon for the LMS, 13.5.1840: London: Snow, 1940).

1840: *Speech at LMS 46th Annual Meeting, 14 May 1840,* in: *The Evangelical Magazine and Missionary Chronicle, 1840,* (Ldn: Thomas Ward, 1840).

1842: *Missionary Labours and Scenes in Southern Africa,* (Ldn: John Snow, 1842).

1842: *Edinburgh Address,* (3.11.1842), in: Campbell (ed.), *Farewell Services of Robert Moffat in Edinburgh, Manchester and London,* (Ldn: Snow, 1843), 12-25.

1842: *Walworth Address,* (21.11.1842), in: Campbell (ed.), *Farewell Services,* 60-89.

1843: *Barbican Chapel Address,* (22.1.1843), in: Campbell (ed.), *Farewell Services,* 97-129.

1843: *Valedictory Sermon at the LMS Mission House, London,* (23.1.1843), in: Campbell (ed.), *Farewell Services,* pp. 145-150.

1843: *Parting Words before boarding Ship,* in: Campbell (ed.), *Farewell Services,* 162.

1844: *'Returning to Kuruman'*, in: *The Juvenile Missionary Magazine,* October 1844, (Ldn: 1844).

1845: *'An African Scholar'*, in: *The Juvenile Missionary Magazine:* October 1845, (Ldn: 1845).

1863: *Adventures of a Missionary; or Rivers of Water in Dry Places; an Account of the Introduction of Christianity into South Africa and of Mr. Moffat's Missionary Travels and Labours,* (1863, New York edition 1869, Carlton & Porter, 1869: reprint. Miami: Mnemosyne, 1969).

1870: *Speech at Port Elizabeth, May 1870,* in: Deane, *Robert Moffat of Kuruman* (Ldn: Pickering & Inglis), 141f.

1870: *Speech to the Directors of the LMS,* 1 August 1870, in: Walters, *Life and Labours of Robert Moffat: Missionary in South Africa,* pp. 209-213.

1872: *Remarks on Visit to Ormiston,* 23rd August 1872, in: *Haddingtonshire Chronicle,* (August 1872), [Haddington Public Library Archives/Moffat Box].

1878: *Speech to the General Conference on Foreign Missions,* October 1878, in: Walters, *Life and Labours of Robert Moffat: Missionary in South Africa,* pp. 220-224.

UD: *'Account of his leaving his parents to go to England'* (Bible Society, 'Gleanings for the Young' Magazine: in: Deane, 23).

Baxter, T.W. & Burke, E.E. (ed.): *Guide to the Historical Manuscripts in the National Archives of Rhodesia,* (Salisbury: National Archives of Rhodesia, 1970).

Kirby, Percival R: *Robert Moffat's Visit to Mzilikazi in 1835,* (Bantu Studies, Monograph Series, No. 1: Witwatersrand University Press, 1940).

Le Cordeur, Basil, & Saunders, Christopher: *The Kitchingham Papers: Missionary Letters and Journals, 1817-1848, from the Brenthurst Collection Johannesburg,* (Johannesburg: Brenthurst, 1976).

Schapera, Isaac (ed.): *Apprenticeship at Kuruman: Being the Journal and Letters of Robert and Mary Moffat, 1820-1828,* (Ldn: Chatto & Windus, 1951).

Wallis, J.P.R. (ed.): *The Matabele Journals of Robert Moffat, 1829-1860. Volumes 1 & 2,* (Ldn: Chatto & Windus, 1945).

Wallis, J.P.R. (ed.): *The Matabele Mission: A Selection from the Correspondence of John and Emily Moffat, David Livingstone, and others, 1858-1878,* (Ldn: Chatto & Windus, 1945).

1.2 Published Work: SeTswana

The following list only includes translations into SeTswana which were available to me in my research. A fuller list of Moffat's SeTswana writings can be found in: F.R. Bradlow, *Printing for Africa: The Story of Robert Moffat and the Kuruman Press,* (Kuruman: Kuruman Moffat Mission Trust, 1987). We may also note that, starting in October 1857, another Kuruman missionary, William Ashton, tried to establish a regular local language newspaper.

1830: *Evangelia Kotsa Mahuku A Molemo A Kuariloeng Ki Luka,* (Cape Town: Government Printing Office, 1830): [Translation of the Gospel of St. Luke into SeTswana: British Library copy].

1831: *Buka ea Pocho ea Tuto le Poluko tsa Yesu Kereste,* (1831), (Translation of *Brown's Catechism* into SeTswana: Grey Collection copy, NLSA, Cape Town, ref: Grey/9/c/3/8).

1838: *A Book of Hymns in Sechwana, Schlapi Dialect* (Kuruman: Mission Press, 1838): [National Library of Scotland copy].

1840: *Kholagano Enca Ea Yesus Keresete, Eo E Len Morena Oa Rona Le Morebuluki: E E Hetolecoen Mo Puon Ea Secuana,* (Ldn: McDowall, 1840). [British Library copy].

1843: *Lihela tsa Tihelo ea Morimo: Tse ri Kuarileon mo puon ea Secuana,* (Ldn: Unwin, 1843): [SeTswana hymn book, 1843 edn: NLS copy].

1843: *Hymns in the Sechwana Language,* (Ldn: Religious Tract Society, 1843), (NLS copy).

1857: *Bibela Ea Boitsepho E E Cutsen Kholagano E Kholugolu Mo Puon Ea Secuana: Kabo Ea Botu,* (Kuruman: For the BFBS, 1857).

1857f: William Ashton (ed.), *Mokaeri oa Becuana, le Muleri oa Mahuki,* (Kuruman: 1857, and running to 20 copies until 1859). All editions may be found in the South African National Library, CT, (Grey/10/c/22/4). They were printed by William Ashton, Kuruman.

1.3 Unpublished Work: General

This list does not include Moffat's letters. All Moffat's letters which I personally read as part of the research for this book may be found listed in the next section. The abreviation UD indicates 'undated'.

1816: *Sermon on Matthew 24:44,* December 1816 (Probably written on board ship as Moffat travelled to Africa), [Ms.] SOAS/CWM/SA/Moffat/Personal/Box 4.

1844: *Contract between the Burgh of Inverkeithing and Robert Moffat Senior and Robert Moffat Junior,* undated and incomplete, NAS/B34/15/53 [Concerning the alteration of a water channel: Two stamps on the document: 19/9/43 and 9/4/44]

1860: *Occasional Journal: 1860-1862, 1868,* [Ms.] SOAS/CWM/SA/Moffat /Personal/Box 4.

1866: *Reflections on his 71st Birthday, 1866,* [Ms.] SOAS/CWM/SA/Moffat /Personal/Box 4.

1870: *Notes written at Grosvenor Street Chapel, Manchester,* 23 September 1870, [Ms.] SOAS/CWM/Africa/Moffat/Pers/4

UD: *Incidents worth Remembering, (c. 1870),* [Ms.] SOAS/CWM/SA/ Moffat/Personal/Box 4.

UD: *Occasional Remarks, (c. 1870s),* [Ms.] SOAS/CWM/SA/Moffat/Personal/Box4.

UD: *Charms,* [Ms.] SOAS/CWM/SA/Moffat/Personal/Box 4.

UD: *Notes on travelling in South Africa, (c. mid 1870s),* [Ms.] NLS/20317/181.

UD: *Autobiographical Memoir,* (Extracts included in JSM, *Lives*).

UD: *Bechuana Customs,* [Ms.] SOAS/CWM/SA/Moffat/Personal/Box 4.

Section 2: Biographies

Anon: *Missionary Stories: Mr. Moffat's Visit to the Children of Manchester, 1842,* (Ldn: John Snow, 1843).

Anon: *Moffat the Missionary and other Stories,* (Ldn: Groombridge & Sons, 1872).

Cherry, E.F: *Pleasant Evenings with Reading and Song: Book no. 2: Incidents in the Life of Robert Moffat, the Apostle of Africa,* (Ldn: Sunday School Union, Weekes & Co., c. 1882).

Deane, David J: *Robert Moffat of Kuruman,* (Ldn: Pickering & Inglis, undated).

Ellis, J.J: *Robert Moffat: The Gardener Boy who became a Great South African Pioneer,* (Ldn: Pickering & Inglis, undated).

Dickson, Mora: *Beloved Partner: Mary Moffat of Kuruman,* (Ldn: Gollancz, 1974).

Marrat, Jabez: *Robert Moffat: African Missionary,* (Ldn: Woolmer, 1884).

Manning, Anne: *Heroes of the Desert: The Story of the Lives and Labours of Moffat and Livingstone,* (Ldn: Nelson, 1880; new edn 1885), (An abridgement of *MLSSA*).

Moffat, John Smith: *The Lives of Robert and Mary Moffat by their son John Smith Moffat,* (New Edition: New York: Armstrong & Son, 1888).

Northcott, Cecil: *Robert Moffat: Pioneer in Africa,* (Ldn: Lutterworth, 1961).

Smith, Edwin William: *Robert Moffat, One of God's Gardeners,* (Ldn: SCM, 1925).

Walters, William: *Life and Labours of Robert Moffat, D.D,* (Ldn: Walter Scott, 1882).

Western-Holt, J.C: *Robert Moffat,* (Ldn: Oliphants, 1954), [A children's book].

Section 3: Newspapers, Journals and Periodicals

References to academic journals such as *Missionalia* and *The Scottish Bulletin of Evangelical Theology* will appear in the main body of the bibliography, in relation to specific articles.

Haddingtonshire Chronicle, 23.8.1872; 28.3.1873; 24.4.1885; 26.3.1915 [Haddington Public Library Archives/Moffat Box].

Scotsman (Newspaper), 2.11.1842, [NLS/mf.N.3]. Other editions of the *Scotsman* were consulted on its public access internet archive, opened in December 2005.

South African Commercial Advertiser: No. 1, 7.1.1824 to No. 18 May 5, 1824, (Reprint: CT: NLSA, 1978).

South African Journal: No. 1, 1824, (Reprint: CT: NLSA, 1974).

Section 4: The Scottish Context

Anon: *Baptismal Records of Bothkennar Parish Church, Scotland,* (Microfilm Copy, Box 546, Section 473-Bothkennar), (Callendar House History Research Centre, Falkirk, FK1 1YR).

Anon: *Nursery Songs,* (Glasgow: David Robertson, 1844).

Anon: *History of Congregationalism in Scotland from 1798-1848,* (Unpublished Ms., National Library of Scotland, ABS.8.88.8).

Anon: *Witch-Hunting in East Lothian,* (Haddington: East Lothian District Library, 1976).

Anderson, James: *An Enquiry into the Nature of the Corn-Laws with a view to the New Corn-Bill proposed for Scotland,* (Edin: Mundell, 1757).

Andrews, William: *Bygone Church Life in Scotland,* (Ldn: Andrews, 1899)

Arthur, Alexander: *The Millennial Church: or, the End of the World not yet Come, but the Millennium already Begun: A Sermon preached in Milton Church on Wednesday 21st March [1855], The National Fast,* (Glasgow: Stark, 1855).

Bain, Andrew: *Education in Stirlingshire from the Reformation to the Act of 1872,* (Ldn: University of London Press, 1964).

Baptie, Diane: *Registers of the Secession Churches in Scotland,* (Aberdeen: Scottish Association of Family History Societies, 2000).

Barclay, P: *A Survey of Foreign Missions,* (Edin: Blackwood, 1897).

Broadie, Alexander (ed.): *The Scottish Enlightenment: An Anthology,* (Edin: Canongate, 1997).

Broadie, Alexander: *The Scottish Enlightenment,* (Edin: Birlinn, 2001).

Broadie, Alexander: *The Cambridge Companion to the Scottish Enlightenment,* (Cambridge: CUP, 2003).

Brough, Robin: *Two Links in a Chain: Wishart St Andrews Parish Church Tranent,* (Tranent: Wishart St Andrews Parish Church, 1977).

Brown, Callum: *The Social History of Religion in Scotland since 1730,* (Ldn: Methuen, 1987).

Brown, John: *The ABC with the Assembly's Shorter Catechism: to which are added some Short and Easy Questions for Children,* (Paisley: Neilson, 1791).

Brown, John: *Two Short Catechisms, Mutually Connected,* (edited by Ebenezer Brown, Paisley: S&A Young, 1811: NLS Microfilm copy Mf.13/4[8]).

Brown, John: *An Historical Account of the Rise and Progress of the Secession,* (Edin: Guthrie & Tait, 1819).

Brown, T: *Annals of the Disruption; with Extracts from the Narratives of Ministers who left the Scottish Establishment in 1843,* (Edin: MacNiven & Wallace, 1884).

Brown, William: *Christian Instructions for Children from Three to Seven years of age, Containing: a Catechism; Passages of Scripture; Hymns,* (2nd Ed. Edinburgh: James Robertson, 1820).

Brown, William: *Memoir and Select Remains of the Rev. John Brown, Minister of the Gospel, Haddington,* (Philadelphia: Presbyterian Board of Publication, 1856).

Brown, William: *History of the Propagation of Christianity among the Heathen since the Reformation: Vols. I, II, III,* (Edin: Blackwood, 1854).

Bruce, John: *The Moral Discipline of Divine Providence, or: An Humble Attempt towards the Practical Improvement of Jehovah's Dealings with the Nations, and *particularly with Great Britain, in the Awful and Elevating Events of the Last Twenty Years,* (Dundee: Rintoul, 1814)

Buchan, James: *Capital of the Mind: How Edinburgh Changed the World,* (Ldn: John Murray, 2003).

Burleigh, J.H.S: *A Church History of Scotland,* (Ldn: OUP, 1960).

Burnet, James (Lord Monboddo): *Of the Origin and Progress of Language: In Six Volumes, Vol. 1,* (Edin: Kincaid & Creech, 1773. Facsimile edn: R.C. Alston (ed.), *English linguistics 1500-1800: A Collection of Facsimile Reprints, No. 48,* Menston: The Scholar Press, 1967).

Calder, James M: *Scotland's March Past: The Share of Scottish Churches in the London Missionary Society,* (Ldn: Livingstone Press, 1945).

Calderwood, David: *History of the Kirk of Scotland,* (Edin: Woodrow Society edn, 1843).

Cameron, Nigel de. S. (ed.): *Dictionary of Scottish Church History and Theology,* (Downers Grove: IVP, 1993).

Campbell, John: *The Progress of the Kingdom of Christ, the Great End of Divine Providence: A Sermon Preached in George Street Chapel, Glasgow, on Thursday April 4th, 1833, on Occasion of the Twenty-First Annual Meeting of the Congregational Union of Scotland,* (Glasgow: Gallie, 1833).

Chalmers, Thomas: *The Evidence and Authority of the Christian Revelation, (1817),* (Reprint: Bristol: Thoemmes, 2002).

Chalmers, Thomas: *On Natural Theology*, vol. 1, (Glasgow: Collins, 1835).

Church of Scotland: *The Form of Process in the Judicatories of the Church of Scotland,* (Glasgow: Bryce, 1780).

Clark, I.M: *A History of Church Discipline in Scotland,* (Aberdeen: Lindsay, 1929).

Cockburn, John: *Letters of John Cockburn of Ormistoun to his Gardener: 1727-1744,* (Edin: Scottish History Society, imprint 1904).

Cockburn, Henry, *Memorials of his Time:1779-1830,* (Edin: Foulis, 1910 edn).

Cohen, Martin: *Smith's 'Wealth of Nations',* (Ldn: Hodder & Stoughton, 2001)

Combe, George: *A System of Phrenology,* (Edin: John Anderson, 2nd edn, 1825)

Combe, George: *On the Relation between Religion and Science,* (Edin: Maclachlan, Stewart & Co., 1847).

Combe, George: *Answer by George Combe to the Attack on 'The Constitution of Man' contained in 'Nature and Revelation Harmonious: A Defence of Scripture Truths assailed in Mr. George Combe's work on the Constitution of Man etc., by the Rev. C.J. Kennedy, Paisley.'* (Edin: Maclachlan, Stewart & Co., 1848).

Combe, George: *The Constitution of Man considered in Relation to External Objects,* (New York: Fowlers and Wells, 1856).

Combe, George: *Elements of Phrenology,* (Edin: Maclachlan & Stewart, 10th edn, 1873).

Cumming, John: *Apocalyptic Sketches, Vols. I, II, III,* (Ldn: Hall, 1858).

Cunninghame, William: *Review of Rev. Dr Wardlaw's Sermon on the Millennium: with an answer to His arguments against the millennial resurrection and reign of the Saints and Martyrs of Jesus Christ,* (Glasgow: Smith, 1830).

Daiches, David & Jones, Peter & Jones, Jean (eds): *The Scottish Enlightenment 1730-1790: A Hotbed of Genius,* (Edin: The Saltire Society, 1996).

Dallimore, Arnold: *The Life of Edward Irving: Fore-runner of the Charismatic Movement,* (Edin: BOT, 1983).

Davidson, F. (ed.): *History and Doctrine of the United Original Secession Church of Scotland,* (Edin: Henderson, 1924).

Dunn, Henry (Delta): *The Revelation of St. John, simply analyzed and briefly expounded,* (Ldn: Nisbet, 1850).

Dunn, Henry (Delta): *The Destiny of the Human Race: A Scriptural Enquiry, Vols. 1 & 2,* (Ldn: Simpkin, Marshall & Co., 1863).

Dick, Thomas: *The Christian Philosopher: or, the Connection of Science with Religion,* (Edin: Black, 1823).

Dick, Thomas: *The Philosophy of a Future State,* (Glasgow: Collins, 1828).

Dick, Thomas: *The Discoveries of Modern Geology not Inconsistent with Revelation,* (Edin: Dalrymple, 1842).

Dick, Thomas: *Harmony of the Discoveries of Modern Science with Revealed Religion,* (Edin: Dalrymple, 1842).

Dirom, Alexander: *An Inquiry into the Corn Laws and Corn Trade of Great Britain and their Influence on the Prosperity of the Kingdom,* (Edin: Creech, 1796).

Escott, H: *A History of Scottish Congregationalism,* (Glasgow: Congregational Union of Scotland, 1960).

Ewing, Greville: *A Defence of Missions from Christian Societies to the Heathen World: An Address to the Edinburgh Missionary Society,* 2.2.1797, (Edin: Ritchie, 1797).

Ewing, Greville: *A Memorial on Education for the Ministry of the Gospel,* (Glasgow: Lang, 1808).

Forrester & Murray: *Studies in the History of Worship in Scotland,* (Edin: T&T Clark, 1984).

Gibb, John: 'The Millennial Reign of Christ and His Saints: Revelation 20:4-6' in: Aikman, Ewing & Wardlaw (ed.): *Sermons by Ministers of the Congregational Union of Scotland,* (Glasgow: Curil, 1823).

Gillespie, W.H: *Exposure of the unchristian and unphilosophical principles set forth in Mr. Combe's 'Constitution of Man',* (Edin: pamphlet, 1837: NLS, ABS.2.97.33/19).

Gillies, J: *Historical Collections relating to Remarkable Periods of the Success of the Gospel,* (1754, revised 1845: BOT edn, Edinburgh, 1981).

Giustino, David de: *Conquest of Mind: Phrenology and Victorian Social Thought,* (Ldn: Croom Helm, 1975).

Graham, Henry G: *The Social Life of Scotland in the Eighteenth Century,* (Ldn: A&C Black, 1906).

Haldane, Alexander: *The Lives of Robert and James Haldane,* (3rd edn, 1853, reprinted: Edin: BOT, 1990).

Haldane, James: *Journal of a Tour through the Northern Counties of Scotland and the Orkney Islands in autumn 1797: undertaken with a view to promote the knowledge of the Gospel of Jesus Christ,* (Edin: Ritchie on behalf of SPGH, 1798).

Haldane, James: *The Doctrine of the Atonement: with strictures on the recent publications of Drs. Wardlaw and Jenkyn on the subject,* (Edin: 1845).

Henderson, G.D: *The Church of Scotland: A Short History,* (Edin: Church of Scotland, 1939).

Henderson, William: *The Evangelisation and Civilisation of India: A Sermon delivered on the National Fast Day,* 7.10.1857, (Edin: Grant & Son, 1857).

Herman, Arthur: *The Scottish Enlightenment: The Scot's Invention of the Modern World,* (Ldn: Fourth Estate, Harper Collins, 2001).

Hewat, E.G.K: *Vision and Achievement 1796-1956: A History of the Foreign Missions of The Churches united in the Church of Scotland,* (Edin: Nelson, 1960).

Hodge, Archibald Alexander: *The Confession of Faith,* (1869, reprint: Edin: BOT, 1958).

Home, Henry (Lord Kames): *Essays on the Principles of Morality and Natural Religion, in Two Parts,* (Edin: Kincaid & Donaldson, 1751. Facsimile edition, London: Garland Publishing, 1976, for the series 'British Philosophers and Theologians of the 17th and 18th centuries: A collection of 101 volumes', edited by René Welleck).

Home, Henry (Lord Kames): *Sketches of the History of Man: A New Edition in 3 Volumes,* (Edin: 1774. Consulted edn, Edin: Ogle, Alliance & Thomson, 1819).

Hopkins, Bob: Article: 'In the Shadow of Livingstone', *Scottish Memories June 2000,* (Glasgow: Lang Syne Publishers, 2000).

Hutton, James: *Abstract of a Dissertation read in the Royal Society of Edinburgh concerning the System of the Earth, its Duration and Stability,* (Edin: 1795. Facsimile edn: Edin: Scottish Academic Press, 1987).

Innes, William: *Instruction for Young Inquirers,* (Edin: Waugh & Innes, 1828).

Keay & Keay (eds): *Collins Encyclopaedia of Scotland,* (Ldn: HarperCollins, 1994).

Kinniburgh, R: *Fathers of Independency in Scotland: or, Biographical Sketches of Early Scottish Congregational Ministers, 1798-1851,* (Edin: Fullarton, 1851).

Kirk, E.H.F: *Annals of Erskine: Erskine Church Falkirk, 1737-1987,* (Falkirk: Erskine Church, 1987).

Leckie, J.H: *Fergus Ferguson: His Theology and Heresy Trial,* (Edin: T&T Clark, 1923).

Love, James: *The Schools and Schoolmasters of Falkirk,* (Falkirk: Falkirk Herald Office, 1898).

Love, James: *Local Antiquarian Notes and Queries, Vol. I,* (Falkirk: Johnstone, 1908).

Love, James: *Local Antiquarian Notes and Queries, Vol. IV,* (Falkirk: Johnstone 1928).

Lyell, Annie: *Ye see it a': the Ormiston Story,* (Haddington: East Lothian Council, 2001).

MacFarlan, Patrick: *The Influence of the Holy Spirit essential to the Success of the Gospel: A Sermon preached before the Society in Scotland for Propagating Christian Knowledge,* (Edin: SSPCK, Waugh & Innes, 1826).

MacKelvie, W: *Annals and Statistics of the United Presbyterian Church,* (Edin: Oliphant, 1873).

MacKie, J.D: *A History of Scotland,* (Ldn: Penguin, 2nd edn, 1978).

Mackintosh, John: *History of Civilisation in Scotland, Vols. 1-4,* (Ldn: Gardner, 1895).

MacLaren, William B: *Annals of a Country Parish: A Fascinating Picture of Old Days and Ways in Bothkennar Parish,* (Falkirk: Falkirk District Council, 1988).

MacLeod, John: *Scottish Theology in Relation to Church History since the Reformation,* (Edin: The Free Church of Scotland, 1943).

MacRae, Alexander: *Revivals in the Highlands and Islands in the 19th Century,* (Stirling: Mackay, undated).

McGuinness, Arthur E: *Henry Home, Lord Kames,* (New York: Twayne, 1970).

McKerrow, J: *History of the Secession Church, Vols. I & II,* (Edin: Oliphant, 1839).

McKerrow, J: *History of the Foreign Missions of the Secession and United Presbyterian Church,* (Edin: Elliot, 1867).

McNaughton, W.D: *The Scottish Congregational Ministry: 1794-1993,* (Glasgow: Congregational Union of Scotland, 1993).

McNaughton, W.D: *Early Congregational Independency in the Highlands and Islands and the North-East of Scotland,* (Tiree: Trustees of Ruaig Congregational Church, 2003).

M'Crie, C.G: *The Confessions of the Church of Scotland: their evolution in History,* (Edin: MacNiven & Wallace, 1907).

Mechie, Stewart: *The Church and Scottish Social Development: 1780-1870,* (Ldn: OUP, 1960).

Meek, Donald E: 'Falling Down as If Dead: Attitudes to Unusual Phenomena in the Skye Revival of 1841-1842' in *Scottish Bulletin of Evangelical Theology: Volume 13, Number 2,* (Edin: Rutherford House, 1995)

Miller, Hugh: *The Testimony of the Rocks: or, Geology in its bearings on the two theologies Natural and Revealed,* (Edin: Constable, 1857).

Phillipson & Mitchison: *Scotland in the Age of Improvement,* (Edinburgh University Press, paperback edn, 1996).

Polland, R: *'I will build my Church': A History of Falkirk Baptist Church,* (Edin: Polland, 1999).

Scott, D: *Annals and Statistics of the Original Secession Church,* (Edin: Elliot, 1886).

Scott, H: *Fasti Ecclesiae Scoticanae: The Succession of Ministers in the Church of Scotland from the Reformation,* (Various Volumes), (New Ed: Edin: Oliver & Boyd, 1920).

Simpson, Eric: *Dalgety Bay: Heritage and Hidden History,* (Dunfermline: Dalgety Bay & Hillend Community Council, 1999).

Small, R: *History of the Congregations of the United Presbyterian Church: 1733-1900,* (Edin: DM Small, 1904).

Smith, Adam: *An Inquiry into the Nature and Causes of the Wealth of Nations,* (1776), (Consulted ed: Hutchins (ed.), *Great Books of the Western World, No. 39,* [Chicago: Benton, 1952]).

Smith, Gavin D: *The Scottish Smuggler,* (Edin: Birlinn, 2003).

Sinclair, John: *The First Statistical Account of Scotland, (various volumes,)* (1791-1799).

Strachan, Gordon: *The Pentecostal Theology of Edward Irving,* (Ldn: Darton, Longman & Todd, 1973).

Symon, J.A: *Scottish Farming: Past and Present,* (Edin: Oliver & Boyd, 1959).

Thain, G. M: *The New Parish Church of Polmont, 1845,* (Polmont: Thain, 1995).

Thomson, J.E.H: *The Present Heresy Case in the United Presbyterian Church with Statement by Rev. Fergus Ferguson,* (Edin: Andrew Elliot, 1878).

Torrance, Thomas F: *The School of Faith,* (Ldn: James Clarke, 1959).

Wardlaw, Ralph: *The Doctrine of a Particular Providence. A Sermon preached in Albion Street Chapel, Glasgow, on Lord's Day, 23.8.1812, on Occasion of the Death of the Author's Brother, Captain John Wardlaw, who fell in the Battle of Salamanca on the 22nd of the Preceding Month,* (Glasgow: Duncan, 1812).

Wardlaw, Ralph: *Systematic Theology: Vols. 1, 2, 3,* (Edin: A&C Black, 1857).

Whyte, Iain: 'Scotland's Anti-Slavery Battle', in: Church of Scotland, *Life and Work,* (Edin: June 2005), pp. 6-9.

Willison, John: *The Mother's Catechism for the Young Child: Or, A Preparatory Help for the Young and Ignorant, in order to the more easy Understanding the Assembly's Shorter Catechism,* (Glasgow: Napier, 1800)

Whitehead, W.Y: *History of Ormiston,* (Haddington: Croal, 1937).

Wyk, Jurgens Johannes Van: *The Historical Development of the Offices according to the Presbyterian Tradition of Scotland,* (Zomba: Kachere, 2004).

Section 5: General

Anderson, David & Grove, Richard (eds): *Conservation in Africa: People, Politics, and Practice,* (CUP, 1987).

Anderson-Morshead, A.E.M: *The History of the Universities' Mission to Central Africa, Vol. 1, 1859-1909,* (Ldn: UMCA, 6th edn, 1956).

Anon: *Elements of Natural History; being an Introduction to the Systema Naturae of Linnaeus, Vols. 1 & 2,* (Edin: Creech, 1801).

Anon: 'Bethelsdorp', *Report of LMS 22nd Annual Meeting, 9th May 1816.*

Anon: 'Progress of Civilisation in Africa', *Report of LMS 22nd Annual Meeting, 9th May 1816.*

Anon: 'Review of Moffat's 1840 LMS Sermon', *The Evangelical Magazine and Missionary Chronicle, 1840,* (Ldn: Thomas Ward, 1840).

Anon: 'The Missionary Museum', *The Juvenile Missionary Magazine, October 1847,* (Ldn: 1847).

Anon: *The History of the Setswana Bible: Ka Ga Baebela Ya Setswana,* (Gaborone: Bible Society of Botswana, 1989).

Archbell, James: *A Grammar of the Bechuana Language,* (Grahamstown: Meurant & Godlonton, 1837).

Arnot, F.S: *Missionary Travels in Central Africa,* (Ldn: Holness, 1914).

Baëta, CG (ed.): *Christianity in Tropical Africa,* (Ldn: OUP, 1968).

Bagster, (Pubs.): *The Bible of Every Land: A History of The Sacred Scriptures in every Language and Dialect into which Translations have been made,* (Ldn: Samuel Bagster & Sons, 2nd edn, 1860).

Barrow, J.W: *A Brief History of the Bloemfontein Mission, South Africa, from its Commencement to 1876, Parts 1 and 2,* (Ldn: Hayes, 1876).

Barth, Karl: *A Shorter Commentary on Romans,* (Ldn: SCM, 1959).

Baumgartner, F.J: *Longing for the End: A History of Millennialism in Western Civilisation,* (New York: Palgrave, 1999).

Beaumont (Jnr), Joseph: *The Life of the Rev. Joseph Beaumont, M.D.,* (Ldn: Hamilton, Adams & Co., 1856).

Beaumont, Joseph: *Choice and Select Sermons by the Rev. Dr Beaumont,* (Published posthumously: Ldn: Partridge, 1859).

Bebbington, David: *Holiness in Nineteenth Century England,* (Carlisle: Paternoster, 2000).

Bediako, Kwame: *Theology and Identity: The Impact of Culture upon Christian Thought in the Second Century and in Modern Africa,* (Oxford: Regnum Books, 1999).

Beeching, Jack: *An Open Path: Christian Missionaries 1515-1914,* (Ldn: Hutchison, 1979).

Bhebe, Ngwabe: *Christianity and Traditional Religion in Western Zimbabwe, 1859-1923,* (Ldn: Longman, 1979).

Bonnke, Reinhard: *Evangelism by Fire,* (Eastbourne: Kingsway, 1994).

Bogue, David: *On Universal Peace: 1813, Tract VI of the Society for the Promotion of Permanent and Universal Peace,* (Ldn: Ward, reprinted 1839).

Bogue, David: *Missionary Lectures by David Bogue: Tutor, Missionary Seminary Gosport,* (Ms. Transcribed by Robert Moffat, SOAS/CWM/Home Odds Box 25).

Bogue, David: *Theological Lectures,* (Posthumously edited by Joseph Samuel C.F. Frey in 2 Volumes. New York: Lewis Colby, 1849).

Booth, Alan R. (ed.): *The Journal of an American Missionary in the Cape Colony, 1835 (George Champion),* (CT: NLSA, 1968).

Bosch, David: *Transforming Mission: Paradigm Shifts in Theology of Mission,* (New York: Orbis Books, 1991).

Boswell, James: *The Life of Samuel Johnson,* (Ldn: Penguin, 1979: 1st publ. 1791).

Bradlow, Frank R: *Printing for Africa: The Story of Robert Moffat and the Kuruman Press,* (Kuruman: Kuruman Moffat Mission Trust, 1987).

Briggs & Wing: *The Harvest and the Hope: The Story of Congregationalism in Southern Africa,* (Johannesburg: UCCSA, 1970).

British Government: *The Sand River Convention, 17th of January 1852,* (Copy in British Library, London: Shelf No. J 8155 h 24).

Brock, Peter: *Pacifism in Europe to 1914,* (Princeton University Press, 1972)

Bromiley, G.W: *Historical Theology: An Introduction,* (Edin: T&T Clark, 1978).

Brown, John: 'Sermon: Missionary Exertions Crowned with Success, preached before the London Missionary Society, 8.5.1816', *Report of LMS 22nd Annual Meeting, 9th May 1816.*

Brown, J.T: *Among the Bantu Nomads,* (New York: Negro Universities Press, 1926 [reprint 1969]).

Brownlee, Margaret: *The Lives and Work of South African Missionaries: Bibliography,* (Cape Town: University of Cape Town Libraries, 1952).

Bulpin, T.V: *Lost Trails of the Transvaal,* (Somerset West: Stephan Phillips, 2002 edn; 1st edn, 1956).

Calvert, George H: (ed.): *Illustrations of Phrenology,* (Baltimore: Neal, 1832).

Campbell, Iain D: 'Jonathan Edwards' *Religious Affections* as a Paradigm for Evangelical Spirituality', *Scottish Bulletin of Evangelical Theology,* Vol. 21, No. 2, Autumn 2003.

Campbell, John: *Travels in South Africa, undertaken at the request of the Missionary Society,* (Ldn: LMS, 1815).

Campbell, John: *The Life of Africaner: A Namaqua Chief of South Africa,* (Ldn: Religious Tract Society, c. 1830).

Capp, Philip L: 'Eschatology: It's relevance to mission from an Evangelical perspective', *Missionalia,* Vol. 15, No.3, November 1987, pp.110-117.

Carey, William: *An Enquiry into the Obligations of Christians to use Means for the Conversion of the Heathens,* (1792), (Didcot, Oxfordshire: Baptist Missionary Society, Facsimile edn, 1961).

Chaplin, William: *The Example and Success of Primitive Missionaries: A Sermon Preached before the London Missionary Society,* 14th May 1823, (Ldn: Holdsworth, 1823).

Chingota, Felix: *The Role of the Church in Peace-building,* (A paper presented at Church Leaders' Workshop held at Boadzulu, from 6th to 11th December 2004).

Clegg, A: 'Some Aspects of Tswana Cosmology', *Botswana Notes and Records, Vol. 18,* pp. 33-37, (Gaborone: 1986).

Clinton, Desmond K: *The South African Melting Pot: A Vindication of Missionary Policy, 1799-1836,* (Ldn: Longmans, 1937).

Comaroff, Jean & John: *Of Revelation and Revolution: Christianity, Colonialism, and Consciousness in South Africa, Vol. 1,* (Chicago: University of Chicago Press, 1991).

Conradie, Ben: *Andrew Murray na Honderd Jaar,* (Stellenbosch: Christen Studenten Verenigingmaatskappij, 1951).

Cooper, Bill: *Paley's Watchmaker: Abridged edition of Wm. Paley's Natural Theology,* (Chichester: New Wine Press, 1997).

Cormack, David & New, George: *Why Did I Do That: Understanding and Mastering Your Motives,* (Ldn: Hodder & Stoughton, 1997).

Cuncliffe-Jones, H: *Christian Theology since 1600,* (Ldn: Duckworth, 1970).

Cuthbertson, Gordon: 'Van der Kemp and Philip: The missionary debate revisited', *Missionalia,* Vol. 17, No. 2, August 1989, pp.77-94.

Davies, Horton & Shepherd, R.H.W: *South African Missions 1800-1950: An Anthology,* (Ldn: Nelson, 1954).

Dolan, J.A: *The Northwood Story: The History of High Leigh Independent Methodist Church, 1783-1983,* (Manchester: Dolan, 1983).

Douglas, J.D. (ed.): *The New International Dictionary of the Christian Church,* (Exeter: Paternoster Press, 1978).

Du Plessis, J: *A History of Christian Missions in South Africa,* (Ldn: Longmans, Green & Co., 1911).

Du Plessis, J: *The Evangel in South Africa,* (Cape Town: Cape Times Ltd., 1912).

Du Plessis, J: *The Life of Andrew Murray of South Africa,* (Ldn: Marshall Brothers, 1919).

Edwards, Jonathan: *A Jonathan Edwards Reader: Edited by Smith, Stout & Minkema,* (Yale University Press, 2003).

Edwards, Jonathan: *Treatise on the Religious Affections,* (Boston: 1746).

Eliade, M, (ed.): *The Encyclopedia of Religion,* (New York: Macmillan Publishing Company, 1987).

Ellis, John: *The Knowledge of Divine Things from Revelation not from Reason or Nature,* (3rd ed., London: William Baynes, 1811).

Ellis, William: *The History of the London Missionary Society, Vol. 1,* (Ldn: John Snow, 1844).

Elphick & Davenport: *Christianity in South Africa: A Political, Social and Cultural History,* (Cape Town: David Philip, 1997).

Enklaar, I.H: *Life and Work of Dr J. Th. Van Der Kemp, 1847-1811,* (Cape Town: Balkema, 1988).

Enklaar, I.H: *De Levensgeschiedenis van Johannes Theodorus Van der Kemp,* (Wageningen: Veenman en Zonen, 1972).

Fiedler, Klaus: *The Story of Faith Missions: From Hudson Taylor to Present Day Africa,* (Oxford: Regnum Books, 1994).

Fiedler, Klaus: 'Shifts in Eschatology – Shifts in Missiology', in: Jochen Ebner (ed.), *Hope does not Disappoint,* (Bonn: VKW, Bangalore, 2001).

Fiedler, Klaus: *Christianity and African Culture: Conservative German Protestant Missionaries in Tanzania 1900-1940,* (Blantyre: CLAIM, 1999).

Fiedler, Klaus: *A Revival Disregarded and Disliked: or, What do Seventh-Day Adventists, Churches of Christ, Jehovah's Witnesses, and the New Apostolic Church have in Common?,* (A paper presented at Chancellor College, University of Malawi, Department of Theology and Religious Studies, 18 March 2004).

Frere, James Hatley: *A Combined View of the Prophecies of Daniel, Esdras, and St. John,* (2nd edn, London: Hatchard, 1815).

Gann, L.H: *A History of Southern Rhodesia: Early Days to 1934,* (Ldn: Chatto & Windus, 1965).

Gay, Peter: *The Enlightenment, An Interpretation, Vol. 1, The Rise of Modern Paganism,* (Ldn: Weidenfeld & Nicolson, 1967).

Gay, Peter: *The Enlightenment, An Interpretation: Vol. 2, The Science of Freedom,* (Ldn: Weidenfeld & Nicolson, 1970).

Goodall, Norman: *History of the London Missionary Society: 1895-1945,* (Ldn: 1954).

Goodall, N. & Orchard, R.K.: *Church and Mission: A Discussion of the relation of the London Missionary Society to the Congregational Union,* (Ldn: LMS, 1949).

Grant, Sandy: 'The revival of Bogwera in the Kgatleng - Tswana Culture or Rampant Tribalism? A description of the 1982 Bogwera', in: *Botswana Notes and Records, Vol. 16,* pp. 7-17, (Gaborone: 1984).

Griffiths, Tom & Robin, Libby: *Ecology and Empire: Environmental History of Settler Societies,* (Edin: Keele University Press, 1997).

Grove, Richard H: *Ecology, Climate and Empire: Colonialism, and Global Environmental History, 1400-1940,* (Cambridge: The White Horse Press, 1997).

Gruchy, John de, (ed.): *The London Missionary Society in Southern Africa: Historical Essays in Celebration of the Bicentenary of the LMS in Southern Africa, 1799-1999,* (Cape Town: David Philip, 1999).

Hammond-Tooke, David: *The Roots of Black South Africa: An Introduction to the Traditional Culture of the Black People of South Africa,* (Johannesburg: Jonathan Ball, 1993).

Hendricks, H. Jurgen: *Studying Congregations in Africa,* (Wellington: NETACT, 2004).

Hofmeyr, Millard: & Froneman: *History of the Church in South Africa: A Document and Source Book,* (Pretoria: UNISA, 1991).

Horne, Silvester C: *The Story of the London Missionary Society, 1795-1895,* (Ldn: John Snow, 1895).

Höschele, Stefan: *From the End of the World to the Ends of the Earth: The Development of Seventh-Day Adventist Missiology,* (Zomba: Kachere, 2004).

Hylson-Smith, Kenneth: *Evangelicals in the Church of England: 1734-1984,* (Edin: T&T Clark, 1988).

Irving, Edward: *For Missionaries after the Apostolical School: A Series of Orations in Four Parts,* (Ldn: Hamilton, Adams & Co., 1825).

Irvine, Mark: 'Tiger Kloof', *Optima,* (February 1996).

Jacobs, Nancy J: *Environment, Power and Injustice: A South African History,* (Cambridge: CUP, 2003).

Janson, Tore & Tsonope, Joseph: *Birth of a National Language: The History of Setswana,* (Gaborone: Heinemann Botswana, 1991).

Jardine, Alexander Johnstone: *A Fragment of Church History at the Cape of Good Hope,* (CT: Bridekirk, 1827), [Reprint: Bradlow (ed.), *NLSA Reprint Series, No. 8;* (CT: NLSA, 1979)].

Kalu, Ogbu U (ed.): *African Christianity: An African Story,* (Pretoria: University of Pretoria, 2005).

Kilby, Stella E: *No Cross Marks the Spot,* (Southend on Sea: Galamena, 2001).

Kittel, G. (ed.): *Theological Dictionary of the New Testament, Vols. 1, 6,* (Grand Rapids: Eerdmans, 1964).

Koester, C.R: *Revelation and the End of all Things,* (Grand Rapids: Eerdmans, 2001).

Kotze, D.J: (ed.), *Letters of the American Missionaries: 1835-1838,* (Cape Town: The Van Riebeck Society, 1950).

Kuruman Moffat Mission: *Welcome to Moffat Mission,* (Kuruman: undated leaflet).

Landau, Paul Stuart: *The Realm of the Word: Language, Gender and Christianity in a Southern African Kingdom,* (Cape Town: David Philip, 1995).

Landau, Paul Stuart & Kaspin, Deborah D: *Images and Empires: Visuality in Colonial and Postcolonial Africa,* (Berkeley: University of California Press, 2002).

Legassick, M.C: *The Griqua, the Sotho-Tswana, and the Missionaries, 1780-1840: the Politics of a Frontier Zone, Parts 1 & 2,* (PhD dissertation, University of California, 1969).

Liechtenstein, W.H.C: *Foundation of the Cape & About the Bechuanas: 1807,* (Translated and edited by Dr OH Spohr: CT: A.A. Balkema, 1973, translation of *Ueber die Beetjuanas*).

Lister, M.H: (ed.), *Journals of Andrew Geddes Bain,* (CT: The Van Riebeck Society, 1949).

Livingstone, David: *Missionary Travels and Researches in South Africa,* (Ldn: 1857).

Livingstone, David & Charles: *Narrative of an Expedition to the Zambezi and its Tributaries: and of the discovery of the Lakes Shirwa and Nyassa, 1858-1864,* (1st publ. 1865 by John Murray, London. Consulted edn: Ldn: Duckworth, 2001).

LMS: *Transactions of the Missionary Society: Vol. 1, 1795-1802,* (2nd edn, Ldn: LMS, 1804).

LMS: *Transactions of the London Missionary Society: Vol. IV, 1813-1818,* (Ldn: LMS, 1818).

LMS: *Report to the 29th Annual Meeting, 1823,* (Ldn: LMS, Westley, 1823). See also the LMS *Reports* for the years 1824 to 1870.

LMS: *Annotated Register of LMS Missionaries: 1796-1923,* (LMS: Ldn).

Loetscher, Lefferts A: *Facing the Enlightenment and Pietism: Archibald Alexander and the founding of Princeton Theological Seminary,* (Ldn: Greenwood, 1983)

Long, Una (ed.): *The Journals of Elizabeth Lees Price: Written in Bechuanaland, Southern Africa 1854-1883,* (Ldn: Edward Arnold, 1956).

Lovett, Richard: *History of the London Missionary Society: 1795-1895,* (Ldn: Henry Froude, 1899).

Lye, W.F. & Murray, C.: *Transformations on the Highveld: The Tswana and Southern Soto,* (Totowa NJ: Barnes & Noble, 1980).

Mackenzie, John: *Ten Years North of the Orange River: A Story of Everyday Life and Work among the South African Tribes from 1859-1869,* (Edin: Edmonston & Douglas, 1871).

Macmillan, W.M: *Bantu, Boer and Briton: The Making of the South African Native Problem,* (Oxford: Clarendon, 1963).

Magubane, Peter: *African Heritage: Ceremonies,* (Cape Town: Struik, 2001).

Makwenda, Charles: *The Custom at Baptism of replacing African Names by so-called Christian Names, especially in relation to the Anglican Churches of Malawi,* (BD, Zomba Theological College, 2005).

Matumo, Z.I: *Setswana English Setswana Dictionary,* (Gaborone: Macmillan Botswana, 4th edn, 1993).

Mbiti, John S: *African Religions and Philosophy,* (Oxford: Heinemann, 2nd edn, 1990).

Moffat, Robert Unwin: *John Smith Moffat: Missionary, a Memoir,* (Ldn: John Murray, 1921: repr. 1969, Negro Universities Press, Greenwood Publishing, New York).

Monk, (ed.): *Livingstone's Cambridge Lectures,* (Cambridge: Bell, 1858).

Moody, D.L: *The Second Coming of Christ,* (Ldn: Morgan & Scott, undated).

Moorhouse, G: *The Missionaries,* (Ldn: Eyre Methuen, 1973).

Moravians: *A Brief Account of the Mission established among the Esquimaux Indians on the coast of Labrador by the Church of the Brethren or Unitas Fratrum,* (Ldn: The Brethren's Society for the Furtherance of the Gospel, 1774, printed by Lewis, 1 Paternoster Row: NLS, microfilm, 3(39.728; filmed from the holdings of the Huntingdon Library).

Moreau, A. Scott (ed.): *Evangelical Dictionary of World Missions,* (Grand Rapids: Baker Books, 2000).

Mortimer, Favell Lee: *Line upon Line,* (Ldn: Hatchard & Co, 1866, 2nd Series, part 1).

Orme, William: *An Expostulatory Letter to the Rev. Edward Irving occasioned by his Orations for Missionaries after the Apostolical School,* (Ldn: Holdsworth, 1825).

Paley, Morton D: *Apocalypse and Millennium in English Romantic Poetry,* (Oxford: Clarendon Press, 1999).

Parsons, Janet S: *Kolobeng: Home of the Livingstones and the BaKwena, 1847-1852,* (Gaborone: Botswana Society, 1985).

Parsons, Janet Wagner: *The Livingstones at Kolobeng: 1847-1852,* (Gaborone, The Botswana Society and Pula Press, 1997).

Pauw, B.A: *Religion in a Tswana Chiefdom,* (Ldn: OUP, 1960).

Peters, Marguerite Andrée & Tabane, Matthew Mathêthê: *Bibliography of the Tswana Language: A bibliography of books, periodicals, pamphlets and manuscripts to the year 1980, (Bibiliokerafi ya Puo ya Setswana),* (Pretoria: The State Library, 1982).

Philip, John: *Researches in South Africa (1828),* (Reprint: New York, Negro Universities Press, 1969).

Phiri, Desmond Dudwa: *From Nguni to Ngoni: A History of the Ngoni Exodus from Zululand and Swaziland to Malawi, Tanzania and Zambia,* (Limbe: Popular Publications, 1982).

Piggin, Stuart: *Making Evangelical Missionaries: 1789-1858,* (Sutton: Courtnay, 1984).

Prah, K.K: *Notes and Comments on Aspects of Tswana Feudalism in the Pre-Colonial Period,* (National Institute for Research in Development and African Studies Documentation Unit, Working Paper 15. Gaborone: 1977).

Preston-Whyte, Eleanor M: 'Zulu Religion', in: Mircea Eliade (ed.), *The Encyclopedia of Religion,* (New York: Macmillan, 1987), Vol. 15, pp. 591-595.

Prichard, James Cowles: *The Natural History of Man: comprising Inquiries into the Modifying Influence of Physical and Moral Agencies on the Different Tribes of the Human Family,* (Ldn: Bailliere, 1843).

Pringle, Thomas: *African Sketches: Narrative of a residence in South Africa,* (Ldn: Moxon, 1834).

Rheenen, Gailyn Van: *Biblical Foundations and Contemporary Strategies: Missions,* (Grand Rapids: Zondervan, 1996).

Roberts, Samuel: *The Negro's Friend: the Sheffield anti-slavery album (in prose and verse),* (Sheffield: Blackwell, 1826).

Robinson, Gordon: *William Roby (1766-1830) and the Revival of Independency in the North,* (Ldn: Independent Press, 1954).

Roby, William: *Theological Lectures,* (Transcribed by RM, 1817: Ms. in SOAS/CWM, Home Odds Box 25).

Roby, William: *A Defence of Calvinism: or, Strictures on a recent publication entitled 'St. Paul against Calvin',* (Ldn: Williams & Smith, 1810).

Roby, William: *The Glory of the Latter Days: A Discourse delivered in the Independent Chapel, Mosley-Street, Manchester, 12th January 1814,* (2nd edn, Ldn: Condor, 1814).

Roby, William: *Protestantism: An Address particularly to the Labouring Classes in defence Of the Protestant Principle 'that the Scriptures, not Tradition, are the Rule of Faith',* (Ldn: Westley, 3rd edn, 1822).

Ross, Andrew C: *John Philip 1775-1851: Missions, Race and Politics in South Africa,* (Aberdeen University Press, 1986).

Ross, Andrew C: *David Livingstone: Mission and Empire,* (Ldn: Hambledon & London, 2002).

Sabine, James: *The Relation the Present State of Religion bears to the Millennium: A Sermon delivered in the Old South Church Boston, before the Foreign Mission Society of Boston and the Vicinity, January 8th, 1823,* (Boston: Crocker & Brewster, 1823).

Sandilands, Alistair: 'Historical Background of the Tswana 'Centenary' New Testament', *Botswana Notes and Records, Vol. 3,* pp. 1-5, (Gaborone: 1971)

Sandilands, Alistair: 'The Ancestor of Tswana Grammars', *Botswana Notes and Records, Vol. 4,* pp. 101-106, (Gaborone: 1972).

Schapera, Isaac (ed.): *Western Civilisation and the Native of South Africa: Studies in Culture Contact,* (Ldn: Routledge, 1934).

Schapera, Isaac (ed.): *The Bantu Speaking Tribes of South Africa,* (Cape Town: Maskew Miller, 1937).

Schapera, Isaac: *Ethnographical Survey of Africa, Southern Africa, Part III: The Tswana,* (Ldn: International African Institute, 1953).

Schapera, Isaac: *A Handbook of Tswana Law and Custom,* (Ldn: OUP, 2nd ed. 1955).

Schapera, Isaac (ed.): *David Livingstone, Family Letters: 1841-1856, Vols. 1,2,* (Ldn: Chatto & Windus, 1959).

Schapera, Isaac (ed.): *Livingstone's Missionary Correspondence, 1841-1856,* (Ldn: Chatto & Windus, 1961).

Schapera, Isaac (ed.): *Praise Poems of Tswana chiefs,* (Oxford: Oxford, 1965).

Schapera, Isaac: *Tribal Innovators: Tswana Chiefs and Social Change, 1795-1940,* (Ldn: University of London Press, Revised version 1970).

Schapera, Isaac (ed.): *David Livingstone South African Papers: 1849-1853,* (Cape Town: Van Riebeeck Society, Second Series No. 5, 1974).

Schapera, Isaac: 'Notes on the early history of the Kwena (Bakwena-bagaSechele)', *Botswana Notes and Records, Vol. 12,* pp. 83-87, (Gaborone: 1980).

Schoeman, Karel: *A Thorn Bush that Grows in the Path: The Missionary Career of Ann Hamilton, 1815-1823,* (Cape Town: NLSA, 1995).

Schoeman, Karel: *The Mission at Griquatown, 1801-1821,* (Griquatown: GTV, 1997).

Shaw, Barnabas: *Memorials of South Africa,* (Ldn: Mason, 1840).

Shaw, Mark: *The Kingdom of God in Africa,* (Grand Rapids: Baker Books, 1996).

Shillington, Kevin: *The Colonisation of the Southern Tswana: 1870-1900,* (Braamfontein: Ravan Press, 1985).

Setiloane, Gabriel M: *The Image of God among the Sotho-Tswana,* (Rotterdam: Balkema, 1976).

Sillery, Anthony: *Sechele,* (Ldn: OUP, 1954)

Slater, Maud Isabella: *Isabella Price: Pioneer,* (Ldn: Livingstone Press, 1931).

Smith, A etc. (ed.): *The Bushmen of Southern Africa: A Foraging Society in Transition,* (Claremont: David Philip, 2000).

Smith, Edwin William (ed.): *African Ideas of God,* (Ldn: Edinburgh House Press, 2nd edn, 1961).

Smith, Edwin William: *Great Lion of Bechuanaland: The Life and Times of Roger Price, Missionary,* (Ldn: LMS & Independent Press, 1957).

Southall, Aidan: 'Tswana Religion', in: Mircea Eliade (ed.), *The Encyclopedia of Religion,* (New York: Macmillan, 1987), Vol. 15, pp. 75-77.

Stanley, Brian (ed.): *Christian Missions and the Enlightenment,* (Grand Rapids: Eerdmans, 2001).

Stein, S.J: *Jonathan Edwards: Apocalyptic Writings,* (New Haven & London: Yale University Press, 1977).

Sundkler, Bengt & Steed, Christopher: *A History of the Church in Africa,* (Cambridge: CUP, 2000).

Tabler, E.C. (ed.): *The Zambezi Papers of Richard Thornton: Geologist to Livingstone's Zambezi Expedition. Vol. 1, 1858-1860,* (Ldn: Chatto & Windus, 1963).

Tanner, Ralph E.S: *Transition in African Beliefs,* (New York: Mary Knoll, 1967).

Thema, B.C: 'The Church and Education in Botswana during the 19th Century', *Botswana Notes and Records, Vol.1 1968,* pp. 1-4, (Gaborone: 1968).

Thom, George: *Memoir of Mrs. Christiana Louisa Thom,* (Ldn: Nisbet, 1822).

Thom, George: *Minutes of a Missionary 'Synod', Cape Town, August 1817,* (SOAS/CWM/Box 7/2/C).

Thomas, Thomas Morgan: *Eleven Years in Central South Africa, (1872),* (2nd edn, Cass Library of African Studies, No. 23: Ldn: Cass & Co., 1971).

Thompson, H.C: *The Kuruman Mission,* (Kuruman: 1967).

Thorogood, Bernard (ed.): *Gales of Change, Responding to a Shifting Missionary Context: The Story of the London Missionary Society 1945-1977,* (Geneva: WCC, 1994).

Tippett, Alan: 'Conversion as a Dynamic Process in Christian Mission', *Missiology, Vol. 5/2,* (Pasadena: American Society of Missiology, 1977).

Trail, A: 'Linguistic Research among the !xo Bushmen', *Botswana Notes and Records, Vol. 2, 1970,* 127, (Gaborone: 1970).

Tucker, Ruth: *From Jerusalem to Irian Java,* (Grand Rapids: Zondervan, 1983).

Vail, Leroy & White, Landeg: *Power and the Praise Poem: Southern African Voices in History,* (Charlottesville: University Press of Virginia, 1991).

Vargish, Thomas: *The Providential Aesthetic in Victorian Fiction,* (Charlottesville: University Press of Virginia, 1985).

Volz, Stephen: *Chief of a Heathen Town: Kgosi Sechele and the Arrival of Christianity among the Tswana,* (African Studies Program, University of Wisconsin-Madison, 2001).

Wallace, Ronald S: *Calvin's Doctrine of the Christian Life,* (Edin: Oliver & Boyd, 1959).

Walsh, M: *Dictionary of Christian Biography,* (Ldn: Continuum, 2001).

Watson, Thomas: *A Body of Divinity: Sermons upon the Westminster Assembly's Catechism,* (Ldn: BOT, 1958).

Watson, Thomas: *The Lord's Prayer*, (Edin: BOT, reprint 1965).

Werner, Alice: *Myths and Legends of the Bantu,* (Ldn: Harrap, 1933).

Whitehouse, John Owen: *London Missionary Society: A Register of Missionaries and Deputations from 1796 to 1877,* (Ldn: Yates & Alexander, 1877).

Willoughby, W.C: *Tiger Kloof: The London Missionary Society's Native Institution in South Africa,* (Ldn: LMS, 1912).

Willoughby, W.C: *Race Relations in the New Africa,* (Oxford: Clarendon Press, 1923).

Willoughby, W.C: *The Soul of the Bantu,* (Ldn: SCM, 1928).

Worden, Nigel & Crais, Clifton (ed.): *Breaking the Chains: Slavery and its Legacy in the Nineteenth-Century Cape Colony,* (Johannesburg: Witwatersrand University Press, 1994).

Appendix 1
Brown's Catechism

Q1. Who made the sun, the moon, and the stars?

R1. It was God.

Q2. Who made the sea, the trees, and the beasts?

R2. It was God.

Q3. Who made you?

R3. It was God.

Q4. Was it God who made all things?

R4. Yes.

Q5. How many Gods are there?

R5. There is but one God.

Q6. Where does He dwell?

R6. In heaven.

Q7. Where is heaven?

R7. Far away, beyond the sun, the moon, and the stars.

Q8. Had God ever a beginning?

R8. No.

Q9. Will He ever die?

R9. No.

Q10. Is God present in every place?

R10. Yes.

Q11. Can you see God?

R11. No: nobody ever saw God.

Q12. Does God always see you?

R12. Yes: he sees me wherever I am, both by night and by day.

Q13. Does God know all things?

R13. Yes: he knows everything that is past, everything that is present, and everything that is to come.

Q14. Is God very powerful?

R14. Yes: he is able to do all things.

Q15. Does he ever do anything that is wrong?

R15. No: he is perfectly holy.

Q16. Is God very good?

R16. Yes: he is kind to all his creatures.

Q17. Is he far greater and more excellent than you are able to conceive?

R17. Yes.

Q18. How long did God take to make all things?
R18. Six days.
Q19. Of what did he make all things?
R19. Of nothing.
Q20. By what means did he make all things?
R20. By commanding them to be.
Q21. In what condition did he make all things?
R21. He made all things very good.
Q22. Who was the first man that God made?
R22. Adam.
Q23. Who was the first woman?
R23. Eve.
Q24. Where did God put the first man and woman?
R24. In the garden of Eden.
Q25. Did God permit them to eat of all the trees in the garden?
R25. Yes, except the tree in the midst of the garden.
Q26. Did they keep that command?
R26. No: they ate of the tree which God had forbidden them.
Q27. Was it very sinful of them to eat of that tree?
R27. Yes.
Q28. Did their eating of that tree hurt any besides themselves?
R28. Yes: it hurts all children as soon as they are born.
Q29. How does it hurt us?
R29. It makes us all come into the world sinful and miserable creatures.
Q30. Do even little children shew that they are bad?
R30. Yes: they quarrel, they strike one another, they do other ill things.
Q31. Is there any body in the world who is without sin?
R31. No, all have done what is evil.
Q32. Have you done many bad things?
R32. Yes: I have broken the commands of God hundreds and thousands of times.
Q33. In what way do you break the commands of God?
R33. I think many evil thoughts; I speak many foolish words; I do many wicked actions.
Q34. Do you ever do anything perfectly good?
R34. No; there is sin in everything I do.
Q35. Is God angry with you when you do what is evil?
R35. Yes; very angry.
Q36. What does God do to children who are bad?
R36. He sends them to hell when they die.
Q37. What kind of place is hell?

R37. It is a place that burns with fire and brimstone

Q38. Do you deserve to be sent to hell?

R38. Yes: for I am often very bad.

Q39. Where do good children go when they die?

R39. To heaven.

Q40. What kind of place is heaven?

R40. A very happy place.

Q41. Is it as a reward for being good children that they go to heaven when they die?

R41. No: we can never deserve heaven for any good things we do; if we ever go there it must be through the love [fn: merits] of Jesus Christ.

Q42. Will you ever get to heaven if you continue a wicked child?

R42. No: though it is not as a reward for being good children that any are taken to heaven, yet unless we are holy, we shall never go to that happy place.

Q43. Who is Jesus Christ?

R43. He is the Son of God.

Q44. What did Jesus Christ become?

R44. He became a man.

Q45. Was it very wonderful in the son of God to become a man?

Q45. Yes: very wonderful.

Q46. Who was his mother?

R46. The Virgin Mary, a poor woman.

Q47. Where was he born?

R47. In a stable.

Q48. Where did he sleep?

R48. In the manger.

Q49. What did Jesus Christ do when on earth?

R49. He went about doing good.

Q50. What were some of the good things he did?

R50. He healed the sick; made the lame to walk; the blind to see; the deaf to hear; and the dead to live again.

Q51. Was Jesus Christ very kind to little children?

R51. Yes: He said 'suffer little children to come unto me, and forbid them not, for of such is the kingdom of heaven.'

Q52. Did Jesus ever do anything that was bad?

R52. No: he was without sin.

Q53. What kind of a life had Jesus Christ on earth?

R53. A very sorrowful life.

Q54. Did Jesus Christ ever die?

R54. Yes.

Q55. What kind of a death did he die?

R55. The shameful and painful death of the cross.

Q56. How was Jesus Christ treated before and when he was on the cross?

R56. His head was crowned with thorns; his back was scourged with stripes; his hands and feet were pierced with nails; and his side was wounded with a spear.

Q57. Was there anything wonderful happened when Jesus Christ was on the cross?

R57. Yes: the sun was darkened, the earth quaked, the rocks rent, and many of the dead rose from the grave.

Q58. What did Jesus Christ say on the cross?

R58. He cried with a loud voice, 'My God, my God, why hast thou forsaken me!'

Q59. Was God angry with Jesus Christ, when he left him to die on the cross?

R59. No: he still loved him with the greatest affection.

Q60. Why then did God make him suffer all these things?

R60. It was for our sins.

Q61. Why did Jesus Christ suffer the punishment of our sins?

R61. It was to save us from being punished on account of them.

Q62. Is Jesus Christ still dead?

R62. No: he became alive again.

Q63. When did he become alive again?

R63. On the third day after his death.

Q64. What became of him after he rose from the grave?

R64. He went up into heaven.

Q65. What does he do in heaven?

R65. He bestows [gives] on us the blessings [good things] he has purchased [bought] by his sufferings and death.

Q66. Can he pardon the bad things you have done?

R66. Yes: though my sins are great and many, he can pardon them all.

Q67. Can he make you holy? [good]

R67. Yes: though I am strongly inclined to break his commands, he can enable me to obey them.

Q68. Can he keep you from hell?

R68. Yes: though I deserve to go to hell, he can deliver me from it.

Q69. Can he take you to heaven?

R69. Yes: though I am unworthy to go to heaven, he can bring me to it.

Q70. Will Jesus Christ take everybody to heaven?

R70. No: there are still many who go to hell.

Q71. What must you do, that Jesus Christ may take you to heaven?

R71. I must believe in him.

Q72. What is it to believe in Jesus Christ?

R72. It is to credit what the Bible says about Christ as a Saviour, and to trust in him to save me.

Q73. Will you ever believe in Jesus Christ of yourself?

R73. No: never.

Q74. Why will you never believe in Jesus Christ of yourself?

R74. Because I am so bad.

Q75. Who then can make you believe in Jesus Christ?

R75. God only.

Q76. Should you ask God to make you believe in Jesus Christ, and to give you the other good things you need?

R76. Yes.

Q77. For whose sake are you to ask these blessings from God?

R77. For the sake of Jesus Christ.

Q78. Why may you not ask them for your own sake?

R78. Because I am unworthy of the smallest favour from him.

Q79. How often should you pray to God?

R79. At least every morning when I rise, and every night when I go to bed.

Q80. Are those very bad children who neglect to pray to God?

R80. Yes.

Q81. Will God answer your prayers if you do not care for the things you ask?

R81. No: for then I should only mock him.

Q82. Are you able to pray in a right manner?

R82. No: but I must ask God to help me.

Q83. Should you love God more than all the other things in the world?

R83. Yes: it would be shameful to prefer [love more] anything to God.

Q84. Why should you love God above all things?

R84. Because he is so excellent, and he is so kind to me.

Q85. How has God been kind to you?

R85. It was he who made me, and who sent his Son to save me, and he gives me food and clothes, and all the other good things I have.

Q86. Are there many children who are not so well provided for?

R86. Yes: there are many who have no house in which to dwell, no clothes but rags to wear, no food to eat when they are hungry, and no fire to warm them when they are cold.

Q87. Do you then love God in the manner you ought?

R87. Alas! no; I do not love him at all.

Q88. Why do you think you do not love God at all?

R88. Because I am not careful to do these things that please him, nor to avoid these things which offend him.

Q89. Should you love your father and mother?

R89. Yes.

Q90. Should you love your brothers and sisters?

R90. Yes: I should be very kind to them; if they were to die, I would be very sorry if I had used them ill.

Q91. Should you love everybody?

R91. Yes, I should love every body as much as I love myself.

Q92. May you hurt those that hurt you?

R92. No: I should do good to them who do ill to me.

Q93. Should you do whatever your father or mother bid you?

R93. Yes: I should do all I can to please them and to make them happy, for they have done much for me.

Q94. Is it sinful for children to quarrel or fight with one another?

R94. Yes.

Q95. Is it sinful to tell lies?

R95. Yes: if I tell lies, nobody will believe me, even when I speak truth.

Q96. Is it sinful to curse and swear and say other ill words?

R96. Yes.

Q97. Is it sinful to steal anything?

R97. Yes.

Q98. Is it sinful to play, or to work, or to walk for pleasure on the Sabbath day?

Q98. Yes.

Q99. Is it sinful to keep company with wicked boys or girls?

R99. Yes: if I keep company with wicked children, they will make me as bad as themselves.

Q100. Is it sinful to cheat your companions at play?

R100. Yes.

Q101. Is it sinful to despise others because they are poorer than yourself?

R101. Yes: I might have been a beggar myself, had it not been for the kindness of God.

Q102. Is it sinful to be peevish or angry about every little thing?

R102. Yes: if I am peevish or angry about every little thing, I shall make myself very unhappy, and every body will dislike me.

Q103. Is it sinful to hurt the birds and beasts?

R103. Yes.

Q104. Should you be sorry for the many bad things you have done?

R104. Yes.

Q105. Does God behold you when you do what is bad?

R105. Yes.

Q106. Does he know whatever you think?

R106. Yes.

Q107. Does he hear whatever you speak?

R107. Yes.

Q108. Does he see whatever you do?

R108. Yes.

Q109. Will God ever call you to an account for what you have done when you were in the world?

R109. Yes.

Q110. When will he call you to an account?

R110. When I die.

Q111. Do little children die as well as old people?

R111. Yes: many are dead who are younger than I.

Q112. Do you know when you will die?

R112. No.

Q113. May you die very soon?

R113. Yes: though I am well today, I may be dead before tomorrow.

Q114. Should you be preparing [making ready] every day to die?

R114. Yes: I should try to spend every day as if it were to be my last.

Q115. May you delay [put off] preparing for death until you are dying?

R115. No: for I may then have no opportunity: I may be killed by some accident without any warning; or I may be so sick, that I may not be able to think about any thing.

Q116. Will your soul die as well as your body?

R116. No: my body only will die; my soul will never die.

Q117. Will your body ever come alive again after it is dead?

R117. Yes.

Q118. Who will raise your body to life again?

R118. Jesus Christ.

Q119. When will Jesus Christ raise your body to life again?

R119. When he comes again to the world.

Q120. When will he come again into the world?

R120. At the last day.

Q121. Will Jesus Christ appear at the last day, in the same condition as he did long ago?

R121. No: when he was formerly in the world, he was poor and despised; now he will be very great and glorious.

Q122. Who will attend Jesus Christ at the last day?

R122. Ten thousands of holy angels.

Q123. What will Jesus Christ do at the last day?

R123. He will bring all mankind before him, and make them give an account of everything they have done when they were in the world.

Q124. Will any be able to avoid appearing before Jesus Christ at the last day?

R124. No: it is impossible to escape his notice, to flee from his presence, or to resist his power.

Q125. Will Jesus Christ, at the last day, separate the righteous from the wicked?

R125. Yes.

Q126. Where will he place the righteous?

R126. On his right hand.

Q127. Where will he place the wicked?

R127. On his left hand.

Q128. What shall he say to the righteous?

R128. 'Come ye blessed of my father, inherit the kingdom prepared for you from the foundation of the world.'

Q129. What shall he say to the wicked?

R129. 'Depart from me, ye cursed, into everlasting fire, prepared for the devil and his angels.'

Q130. Where shall the righteous go after receiving this sentence?

R130. They shall go with Jesus Christ into heaven.

Q131. Shall the righteous ever feel any sorrow in heaven?

R131. No; they shall be perfectly happy.

Q132. Shall they ever do anything that is sinful in heaven?

R132. No; they shall be completely holy.

Q133. Shall they ever die in heaven?

R133. No; they shall live for ever and ever.

Q134. What shall become of the wicked after receiving their sentence?

R134. They shall all go to hell.

Q135. What shall they do in hell?

R135. They shall weep, and wail, and gnash their teeth.

Q136. Shall you have any rest from torment?

R136. No; not for one moment, neither day nor night.

Q137. Shall they ever come out of hell again?

R137. No; they shall be tormented with fire and brimstone for ever and ever.

Q138. Should you then be very earnest to escape from hell and go to heaven?

R138. Yes.

Q139. Should you seek this above all things?

R139. Oh yes; above all things; for if I do not get to heaven at last, it would have been better for me that I had never been born.

Appendix 2
The Sand River Convention (1852)

THE FOLLOWING COMPRISES part of the text of the *Sand River Convention,* signed on 17 January 1852. The copy which I consulted was in the British Library, London. [Ref: J/8155/h/24)].

> [Article 1] The Assistant Commissioners guarantee in the fullest manner, on the part of the British Government, to the Emigrant Farmers beyond the Vaal River, the right to manage their own affairs and to govern themselves according to their own laws, without any interference on the part of the British Government; ….
>
> [Article 3] Her Majesty's Assistant Commissioners hereby disclaim all alliances whatever and with whomsoever of the coloured nations to the north of the Vaal River. …
>
> [Article 4] It is agreed that no slavery is or shall be permitted or practised in the country to the north of the Vaal River by the Emigrant Farmers. …
>
> [Article 6] It is agreed that no objection shall be made by any British Authority against the Emigrant Boers purchasing their supplies of ammunition in any of the British Colonies and possessions of South Africa; it being mutually understood that all trade in ammunition with the native tribes is prohibited both by the British Government and the Emigrant Farmers, on both sides of the Vaal River.
>
> [Signed: Pretorius, Lombard, Owen, Hogge, etc. (18 names in all)]

Appendix 3
Letters from the Missionary Meeting (1853)

1. Rev. Holloway Helmore (Sec.), *Letter to Rev. Dr Arthur Tidman (LMS),*12th July 1853.

THIS COMPRISES PART OF the Rev. Holloway Helmore's, Letter to Rev. Dr Arthur Tidman (LMS), 12th July 1853, (SOAS/CWM/SA/Box28/1/B). This is a record of the missionary meeting held on the 12th July 1853 at Likhatlong, the Rev. Helmore's station, to discuss Boer misrule of the indigenous population following the Sand River Convention. The meeting was prompted by William Thompson, the LMS agent in Cape Town. Holloway had been appointed secretary of the meeting, with Moffat in the chair. Those present were: Moffat, Hughes, Ross, Solomon, Inglis and Helmore (all LMS); Jousse (Paris Evangelical Missionary Society); and Mayforth (Berlin Missionary Society). Moffat's seniority in the missionary community, plus his role as chairman of the meeting, plus being appointed as a messenger for the concerns of the meeting, means that there is little doubt that the views expressed were totally in line with Moffat's own stand, and that the decision to formally lobby the official Government representative, was something he was happy with.

> A meeting of the Brethren was held yesterday the 11th of July to deliberate on the present circumstances and the threatening dangers of our Griqua and Bechuana Missions. There were present: Messrs. Moffat, Hughes, Ross, Solomon, Inglis and Helmore of the LMS; Rev. W. Jousse of the Paris Society and Rev. Mayforth of the Berlin Society. After reading the Scriptures and prayer Mr. Moffat was called to the chair. From information collected from the Brethren it appeared that no immediate danger threatened our stations – the storm had lulled for a time. This impression was produced by the reception of certain letters written by Mr. Pretorius, Commandant General of the Boer Republic in which he disclaimed all intentions of depriving the Batlapi tribes of their lands and guns. At the same time none of the Brethren present felt the slightest confidence in the said letter for the Boer have declared their intention to possess themselves of the whole country north of the Vaal River down to the Atlantic Ocean and Pretorius showed to Mr. Inglis a document written by Mr. Owen one of her Majesty's Assistant Commissioners sanctioning the claim. Divisions among themselves, inability to occupy the country they have already laid waste, and fear of the various tribes which have combined in these quarters have obliged Pretorius to adopt the present course. The Brethren therefore resolved that a Memorial should be drawn up and presented by Messrs Moffat, Solomon and Inglis to Sir George Russel Clerk, Her Majesty's Commissioner to the Sovereignty, a copy of which I enclose. ....

2. Rev. Holloway Helmore (Sec.), *Memorial to George Russel Clerk, Her Majesty's Special Commissioner for the Orange River Sovereignty,* 13th July 1853.

This comprises the bulk of an official letter, agreed on by the missionary meeting of the 13th July 1853, at Likhatlong, and addressed to: *George Russel Clerk, Her Majesty's Special Commissioner for the Orange River Sovereignty,* 13th July 1853 (Signed, Robert Moffat, Chairman; Holloway Helmore, Secretary). The copy I consulted was the copy sent to the LMS, and now lodged in the LMS archives in: [Ms.] SOAS/CWM/SA/Box28/1/B. The main plea of the letter is that George Russel Clerk will properly carry out his duties of fair oversight of the Orange River Sovereignty, call the Boers into line, and that the British would not abandon the Sovereignty. Moffat, Solomon and Inglis were entrusted to deliver the letter and argue for its contents.

> Honourable Sir: As forming a portion of the Missionaries of various Evangelical Societies, labouring in South Africa, and occupying stations among natives residing in the Trans-[?], we desire to express our satisfaction at the appointment of a Special Commissioner to investigate matters connected with the Orange River Sovereignty – to congratulate you on having been selected to sustain this important though difficult office – and to give utterance to our eternal hope that by your adopting wise and judicious measures much permanent good may result to all the inhabitants of this part of Africa. We trust that we shall not be deemed intruding upon your time and attention in bringing before you some statement which we feel it our duty to make with regard to the native inhabitants of the Trans-Vaal country.
>
> You have arrived in this country at a most eventful period of its history: a great extent of country north of the Vaal River is in a very disorganised state, and a tone of feeling has been given to the native mind, both within and beyond the Sovereignty, which we cannot look upon without the deepest regret and the greatest apprehension. A very general impression has been made upon the native mind that the white man is combining for the destruction of the black. The cause of this feeling is principally the events which have recently transpired in the Trans-Vaal country. It cannot be unknown to you that there have lately been much commotion and bloodshed in that quarter. The immigrant farmers have always entertained very low views of the rights and privileges of the aborigines – have ever seized upon every opportunity of showing their superior might and of bringing the natives into subjection; but since the Convention made between Her Majesty's Assistant Commissioners and the immigrant farmers in 1852, their demands and [?] have passed all bounds.
>
> Since that Convention several native chiefs have been attacked and five mission stations, four belonging to the London and one to the Wesleyan Society, have been destroyed by the Boers. We have no hesitation in stating it to be our firm conviction that these attacks have been unprovoked on the part of the natives, and can be traced to no other source than the love of plunder, the lust of power, and the aim of obtaining constrained and unpaid labour on the part of the Boers. Nothing will satisfy them but the entire

destruction of native [?], the complete subjection of all the native tribes to the arbitrary authority of the republic.

In addition to the breaking up of five mission stations, on which occasion much valuable property belonging to the missionaries and the society was either taken away or wantonly destroyed, we have to inform you that two missionaries of the London Society, Messrs Edwards and Inglis, were summoned before the Republic Tribunals and on the most flimsy pretext have been banished from the Trans-Vaal Country and much of their property either confiscated or sacrificed. We have also to lament that notwithstanding the insertion of an article in the Convention between Her Majesty's Assistant Commissioners and the Trans-Vaal Boers, whereby slavery was expressly prohibited, many hundreds if not thousands of the natives are, under various disguises, held in slavery by the Boers. In fact the whole system pursued by them towards the natives under their control is reducing them all to a state of servitude which cannot be distinguished from slavery.

The result of these movements is that a general combination is being formed among the natives in order to resist the encroachment of the Boers, and we have the dark gloomy prospect of a long and bloody war between the black and white races in the Trans-Vaal country. We are sure that the native will never submit to the demands of the Boers and unless something be done to prevent it, a collision must take place, not merely between the Boers and some individual tribes of Bechuanas, but between the Trans-Vaal Republic and all the native tribes in that region, including Bechuana, Corannas, and Griquas. This contest will be long and bloody, and however it may terminate must involve great misery to all parties and throw the country many years back, besides putting an entire stop to the progress of commerce and discovery in the interior regions of Africa. It is true that some notices have lately been issued by the Commandant General of the Republic, disclaiming all intention of depossessing the natives in the lower parts of the Trans-Vaal country of their lands and arms, but we have every reason to believe that these notices have been forced from the Commandant General by the present emergencies of the Republic, and though they yield us the prospect of a short lull, give us no ground to hope for permanent peace and tranquility.

It is of course natural that the natives under such circumstances should regard the Boer with apprehension and hatred; but it grieves us to be compelled to state that these feelings of the natives extend beyond the Boers, and the British Government is beginning to be regarded by them with distrust and suspicion, since they look upon it as combined with the Boer in depriving them of their rights and liberties. Many reasons concur to produce this feeling among the natives, some of which we would briefly state.

They reason that the most outrageous acts of the Boers have immediately followed their Convention with Her Majesty's Assistant Commissioner; hence they argue that that convention is the cause of those outrages. They complain that in that convention no sympathy is expressed for, and no protection extended, to the aborigines; that protection hitherto extended to them by the British Parliament has been withdrawn – that while weapons and ammunition are freely and to an unlimited extent supplied to the Boers, not a single gun nor a pound of powder, nor even a single gun flint can be obtained by the natives to defend their lives and property – connected with this they are acquainted with various acts of injustice perpetrated by the British Government upon native tribes residing within the Sovereignty – they see the very evident desire of the Government to divest itself of obligations resulting from treaties freely entered into with native tribes and solemnly confirmed by the Home Authorities, and all these things combine to produce the impression we so sincerely deplore, but for which we blush to say so much cause has been given.

We cannot conclude without expressing our deep-rooted conviction that all the evils at present existing, as much as those we apprehend in this country, will be greatly increased should Her Majesty's Government be induced to abandon the control of the Orange River Sovereignty, a step which we cannot too earnestly deprecate. We look upon the present state of the country with such apprehension; we feel a deep interest in the prosperity of this land. Some of us have been many years in it, labouring to evangelise the native tribes, and not-withstanding the various difficulties in our way, our labours have been attended with very considerable success. We long for permanent peace whereby the interests of all classes in this country may be served, and we therefore bring the case before you as Her Majesty's Special Commissioner, trusting and praying that you may be enabled in your wisdom to devise some plan by which the horrors of an exterminating war may be avoided – the evils of slavery terminated – the stigma of tolerating or encouraging that slavery removed from the British name – the aborigines protected in the enjoyment of their rights – confidence in British integrity and affection for British influence re-established in the native mind, so that we may have the prospect before us of devoting in peace and security the remainder of our lives to the great work in which we are engaged, of enlightening – civilising – elevating and evangelising the aborigines of South Africa.

Appendix 4
Reflections on his 71st Birthday

21st December 1866

Those who wish to retain the venerable custom of keeping birth days devised a plan by which my 71st birth day might be kept. All the old people on the station and beyond it were invited to a tea meeting in the chapel. Men and women were provided with tickets. About .... attended. After an abundant repast which was prefaced by a few remarks from John S. Moffat, and a hymn being sung, I addressed them on thoughts to which the present ... gave rise. I began with my leaving England as a youth, residence in Namaqualand, appointment to Kuruman, opposition to the work, and difficulties and trials – our only encouragement, the promises of God – the longed-for blessing sent.

What we now see, churches gathered – the Bible translated – more than 30 places where there are missionaries, teachers and schools and thousands who can now read in their own language – the wonderful works of God. He has done great things for the Bechuana tribes. I have much to gladden besides having my own children in the work – but there is much to sadden ... have not seen all nor the half of what I expected to see of the influence of the Gospel.

Compared to the multitudes to whom the word of God has been spoken, the number of believers are few. I had been now 50 years in the service of the heathen; of these 47 the servant of the Bechuanas. I had lived 71 years and could not be expected to do much more for the situation of those who were still in unbelief.

I looked on grey headed sinners before me with sorrow. They had heard my voice for many long years prating them in Christ's stead to be reconciled to God. I should now cease to warn and exhort and leave some worse than I had found them but there were those whom I hoped to be my joy and crown of rejoicing in the day of Christ.

I told them that they were my witnesses and the witnesses of MaMary that we had laboured all these years, often by night as well as by day, to administer to their temporal as well as to their spiritual wants; that I could say with truth that these hearts had innumerable times ministered to their necessities. Concluded with entreating all to prepare to meet God; which, prepared or unprepared, we must soon all do. The season was one of no common interest.

Index